Lecture Notes in Computer Science   7465

Commenced Publication in 1973
Founding and Former Series Editors:
Gerhard Goos, Juris Hartmanis, and Jan van Leeuwen

T0189831

Gerald Quirchmayr   Josef Basl
Ilsun You   Lida Xu   Edgar Weippl (Eds.)

Multidisciplinary Research and Practice for Information Systems

IFIP WG 8.4, 8.9/TC 5
International Cross-Domain Conference and Workshop
on Availability, Reliability, and Security, CD-ARES 2012
Prague, Czech Republic, August 20-24, 2012
Proceedings

 Springer

Volume Editors

Gerald Quirchmayr
University of South Australia, Adelaide, Australia
E-mail: gerald.quirchmayr@unisa.edu.au

Josef Basl
University of Economics, Prague, Czech Republic
E-mail: basljo@rek.zcu.cz

Ilsun You
Korean Bible University, Seoul, South Korea
E-mail: isyou@bible.ac.kr

Lida Xu
Old Dominion University, Norfolk, VA, USA
E-mail: lxu@odu.edu

Edgar Weippl
Vienna University of Technology and SBA Research, Austria
E-mail: edgar.weippl@tuwien.ac.at

ISSN 0302-9743   e-ISSN 1611-3349
ISBN 978-3-642-32497-0   e-ISBN 978-3-642-32498-7
DOI 10.1007/978-3-642-32498-7
Springer Heidelberg Dordrecht London New York

Library of Congress Control Number: 2012943607

CR Subject Classification (1998): H.4, K.6.5, H.3.1, H.3.3-5, E.3, K.4.4, H.2.3, H.2.8, H.5.3, D.2, J.1

LNCS Sublibrary: SL 3 – Information Systems and Application, incl. Internet/Web and HCI

Typesetting: Camera-ready by author, data conversion by Scientific Publishing Services, Chennai, India

Printed on acid-free paper

Springer is part of Springer Science+Business Media (www.springer.com)

Preface

The Cross-Domain Conference and CD-ARES Workshop are focused on a holistic and scientific view of applications in the domain of information systems.

The idea of organizing cross-domain scientific events originated from a concept presented by the IFIP President Leon Strous at the IFIP 2010 World Computer Congress in Brisbane, which was seconded by many IFIP delegates in further discussions. Therefore, CD-ARES concentrates on the many aspects of information systems in bridging the gap between the research results in computer science and the diverse application fields.

This effort has been concentrated on the consideration of various important issues of massive information sharing and data integration that will (in our opinion) dominate scientific work and discussions in the area of information systems in the second decade of this century.

The organizers of this event who are engaged within IFIP in the area of Enterprise Information Systems (WG 8.9), Business Information Systems (WG 8.4) and Information Technology Applications (TC 5) very much welcome the typical cross-domain aspect of this event. The collocation with the SeCIHD 2012 Workshop was another possibility to discuss the most essential application factors.

The papers presented at this conference were selected after extensive reviews by the Program Committee with the essential help of associated reviewers.

We would like to thank all the PC members and the reviewers for their valuable advice, and foremost the authors for their contributions.

June 2012

Gerald Quirchmayr
Josef Basl
Ilsun You
Lida Xu
Edgar Weippl

Organization

Cross-Domain Conference and Workshop on Multidisciplinary Research
and Practice for Information Systems (CD-ARES)

General Chair

Josef Basl   University of Economics, Prague,
                              Czech Republic
Erich J. Neuhold   Vienna University of Technology, Austria
                              (IFIP TC5 Chair)

Program Committee Chair

Gerald Quirchmayr   University of South Australia, Australia
Edgar Weippl   Vienna University of Technology, Austria
                              (IFIP WG 8.4 Chair)

Program Committee

Amin Anjomshoaa   Vienna University of Technology, Austria
Silvia Avasilcai   Technical University "Gheorghe Asachi" of Iasi,
                              Romania
Wichian Chutimaskul   King Mongkut University KMUTT, Thailand
Andrzej Gospodarowicz   Wroclaw University of Economics, Poland
Abdelkader Hameurlain   Paul Sabatier University Toulouse, France
Hoang Huu Hanh   Hue University, Vietnam
Ismael Khalil   Johannes Kepler University Linz, Austria
Elmar Kiesling   Software Business Austria
Josef Küng   Research Institute for Applied Knowledge
                              Processing, Austria
Vladimir Marik   Czech University of Technology Prague,
                              Czech Republic
Günter Müller   University of Freiburg, Germany
Nguyen Thanh Binh   International Institute for Advanced Systems
                              Analysis, Laxenburg, Austria
Günther Pernul   University of Regensburg, Germany
Josef Schiefer   UC4 Software, Washington, USA
Stefanie Teufel   University of Fribourg, Switzerland
Janusz Wielki   University of Business, Wroclaw, Poland

A Min Tjoa	Vienna University of Technology, Austria
Simon Tjoa	St. Poelten University of Applied Sciences, Austria
Lida Xu	Old Dominion University, USA
Ilsun You	Korean Bible University, Republic of Korea

Second International Workshop on Security and Cognitive Informatics for Homeland Defense (SeCIHD)

General Chair

| Ilsun You | Korean Bible University, Republic of Korea |

General Vice Chair

| Hyun Sook Cho | ETRI, Republic of Korea |

Program Co-chairs

| Aniello Castiglione | University of Salerno, Italy |
| Kangbin Yim | Soonchunhyang University, Republic of Korea |

Publicity Chair

| Sang-Woong Lee | Chosun University, Republic of Korea |

Program Committee

Francesca Bosco	United Nations Interregional Crime and Justice Research Institute, Italy
Pascal Bouvry	Luxembourg University, Luxembourg
Jörg Cassens	Norwegian University of Science and Technology, Norway
Antonio Colella	Italian Army, Italy
Christian Czosseck	NATO Cooperative Cyber Defense Centre of Excellence, Tallinn, Estonia
Stefania Ducci	Research Institute for European and American Studies, Greece
Joseph Fitsanakis	Security and Intelligence Studies Program, King College, USA
Alessandro Gigante	European Space Agency, ESRIN Health, Safety, and Security Officer, Italy

Table of Contents

Conference

Cross-Domain Applications: Aspects of Modeling and Validation

Trust, Security, Privacy and Safety

Mobile Applications

Data Processing and Management

Retrieval and Complex Query Processing

E-Commerce

Workshop

International Workshop on Security and Cognitive Informatics for Homeland Defense (SeCIHD)

Ontology-Based Identification
of Research Gaps and Immature Research Areas[*]

Kristian Beckers[1], Stefan Eicker[1], Stephan Faßbender[1],
Maritta Heisel[1], Holger Schmidt[2], and Widura Schwittek[1]

[1] University of Duisburg-Essen, paluno - The Ruhr Institute for Software Technology
{firstname.lastname}@paluno.uni-due.de
[2] ITESYS - Institut für technische Systeme GmbH, Germany
h.schmidt@itesys.de

Abstract. Researchers often have to understand new knowledge areas, and identify research gaps and immature areas in them. They have to understand and
link numerous publications to achieve this goal. This is difficult, because natural
language has to be analyzed in the publications, and implicit relations between
them have to be discovered. We propose to utilize the structuring possibilities of
ontologies to make the relations between publications, knowledge objects (e.g.,
methods, tools, notations), and knowledge areas explicit. Furthermore, we use
Kitchenham's work on structured literature reviews and apply it to the ontology.
We formalize relations between objects in the ontology using Codd's relational
algebra to support different kinds of literature research. These formal expressions
are implemented as ontology queries. Thus, we implement an immature research
area analysis and research gap identification mechanism. The ontology and its
relations are implemented based on the Semantic MediaWiki+ platform.

Keywords: ontologies, research gaps, knowledge management, facetted search.

1 Introduction

Getting an overview of existing engineering methods, tools and notations (referred to as
Knowledge Objects – KOs) for specific fields (referred to as Knowledge Areas – KAs)
is of major importance for software engineering researchers. This knowledge is the
basis for finding research gaps and problems in this field, which require their attention.
Our objective is to develop a technique for finding missing methods, notations and tools
in specific knowledge areas.

Researchers usually have to rely on their experience during a research area analysis,
which includes the activities of finding research gaps and identifying research areas.
This can lead to a biased outcome of a research area analysis. Hence, research gaps or
immature research areas might be overlooked repeatedly. In addition, researchers have
to find relations between publications, which are sometimes implicit.

---

[*] This research was partially supported by the EU project Network of Excellence on Engineering
Secure Future Internet Software Services and Systems (NESSoS, ICT-2009.1.4 Trustworthy
ICT, Grant No. 256980).

G. Quirchmayr et al. (Eds.): CD-ARES 2012, LNCS 7465, pp. 1–16, 2012.

In order to ameliorate this situation, we propose a structured approach for research area analysis. This approach utilizes the extensive research of Kitchenham et al. [1–8] for structured literature reviews. We apply Kitchenham's methods to a special *ontology*, the Common Body of Knowledge (CBK) of the EU project *Network of Excellence (NoE) on Engineering Secure Future Internet Software Services and Systems (NESSoS)*[1]. One of the major goals of this NoE is the integration of the disciplines of software, service, and security engineering. Hence, the CBK ontology contains information about these areas in numerous KOs that refer to KAs.

Our approach is threefold: We carry over Kitchenham's research for structured literature reviews to informal queries for the CBK, and we also extend the CBK to support these informal queries. In the next step we refine these informal queries into formal CBK relations using Codd's relational algebra [9]. For this purpose, we apply the *DOOR* method by Allocca et al. [10] for capturing the semantics of relations in ontologies and to formally specify these relations. The technical realization of the CBK is a *Semantic MediaWiki+* platform, and we implemented the relational algebra expressions as CBK queries.[2]

The queries result in tables that show the relations between KAs and KOs. The tables also contain the information of *how many* KOs are in a KA and *what kind of* KOs exist in it, e.g., methods, tools, techniques, and notations. These compact results of a query are more effective than analyzing the natural language in publications. Moreover, the creation and execution of a query in the CBK is less time consuming than finding relevant literature for a KA and analyzing it.

The paper is organized as follows: we explain background about structured literature surveys and the NESSoS CBK in Sect. 2. We present in Sect. 3 a structured research area analysis method, which contains research gap analysis and immature research area identification. We show in Sect. 4 our realization of the approach for the field of engineering secure software and services using the NESSoS CBK. Section 5 presents related work. Finally, we conclude and raise ideas for future work in Sect. 6.

2   Background

We explain Kitchenham's structured approach to structured literature reviews in Sect. 2.1 and the basic structure of the NESSoS Common Body of Knowledge in Sect. 2.2.

2.1   Literature Research According to Kitchenham

To gain a structured overview of the state of the art and existing literature before starting new research is one fundamental element of scientific work. For the area of software engineering, Kitchenham was one of the first, who described a structured literature review process [1]. Over the years this inital process was extended and improved by Kitchenham herself and others [1–8].

There are several reasons and goals why researchers might want to perform a literature review. And there are also different types of literature reviews, which can serve

---

[1] http://www.nessos-project.eu/
[2] http://www.nessos-cbk.org

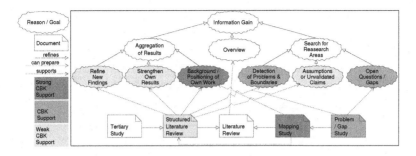

Fig. 1. Types of literature researches and reasons and goals to perform them [1–8]

the different goals. Fig. 1 shows a condensed view of findings and statements from different publications in the field of systematic literature reviews in software engineering [1–8]. The overall reason to do any kind of literature research is Information Gain. This top-level goal can be refined into the goal to get a mere Overview without a specific motivation [1]. In contrast, the goals of Aggregation of Results and Search for Research Areas have a well-founded motivation.

When aggregating results, one might want to Refine New Findings based an the aggregated data [1, 2]. Or the findings and data of other publications are used to Strengthen Own Results [1, 2]. A last reason for aggregation is to give a Background / Positioning of Own Work [4, 5, 7, 8]

When searching for research areas, a Detection of Problems & Boundaries [1, 2, 5, 6] of a certain method or set of methods can be the goal. Another option is to search for Assumptions or Unvalidated claims [1, 2, 5, 6]. These two sub-goals aim at finding immature research areas and improve them with further research. In contrast, finding Open Questions and Gaps aims at research fields, where no publications about solutions exist [2, 5, 8].

All types of Literature Reviews support the goal of obtaining an overview. The quality of the overview differs in how structured and planned the literature review was performed. A special type is the Structured Literature Review (SLR) [1–3, 6]. A SLR is a comprehensive literature review considering a specific research question. Kitchenham's method to perform a SLR was developed to find empirical primary studies considering a specific question and to aggregate the data in the first place. Additionally it turned out later that SLRs also make it possible for researchers to find immature research areas [5, 6]. A special kind of the SLR is the Tertiary Study [2, 4]. Such a study aggregates the results of other SLRs, hence it relies on secondary studies. Another type of literature review is the Mapping Study [2, 5, 7, 8]. Here it is not the aim to extract any data, but to map studies to research fields or problems. When also the problems and gaps discussed in the studies are obtained while doing the mapping, a Problem / Gap Study as a special kind of mapping study is the result [2, 8, 7]. This kind of study serves to find real gaps or to find immature methods. For assessing immaturity, a gap study should be combined with a SLR.

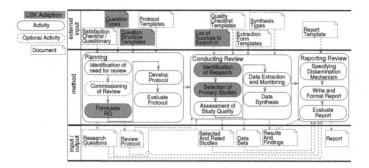

Fig. 2. Process proposed by Kitchenham for undertaking a SLR [1, 2, 6, 3]

Kitchenham et al also propose a process to conduct SLRs [1–3, 6]. It is shown in Fig. 2. This process can be also used for mapping studies with some slight adaptions [2, 5, 8]. The process is split up in three major phases. First the Planning phase takes place, followed by the Conducting Review phase, and finally the Reporting Review phase ends the review process.

The Planning starts with an Identification of need for review step The next step is optional as in Commissioning of Review the SLR is tendered to other research groups. The first real step towards a SLR is to Formulate RQ (Research Questions). The research questions are the core of an SLR. All later decisions and results are checked against the RQ later on. In Develop Protocol the review itself is planned. The step Evaluate Protocol is performed to detect misunderstandings, ambiguities, and insufficient definitions. To ease the planning there are predefined Satisfaction Checklists / Questionaries, Question Types, Question Structure Templates, and Protocol Templates. For Question Structure Templates, Kitchenham and Chaters proposes to use the PICOC criteria framework to structure research questions [2]. PICOC stands for the criteria *population*, e.g. application area or specific groups of people, *intervention*, e.g. the method which is of interest, *comparison*, e.g. the benchmark, *outcomes*, what is the improvement to be shown, and *context*, a description of the setting in which the comparison takes place. All these documents serve as an input and guide for certain planning steps. The result of the planning phase are the Research Questions and the Review Protocol. They serve as input to the Conducting Review phase.

The review starts with the Identification of Research, which results in a set of studies which might be relevant. According to defined inclusion and exclusion criteria the step Selection of Primary Studies is performed. The selected studies are then rated in the step Assessment of Study Quality. For those studies with a satisfying quality level the data contained in the studies is extracted in the step Data Extraction and Monitoring. Afterwards the Data Synthesis is performed. The input to this phase are a List of Sources to Search In, Quality Checklist Templates, Extraction Form Templates, and Synthesis Types. Outputs produced in the conducting review phase are the Selected And Rated Studies, the Data Sets extracted form these studies, and the Results and Findings of the data synthesis.

All previously generated outputs serve as an input for the last phase Reporting Review. As external input, Report Templates are given. Based on the inputs, the step Specifying Dissemination Mechanism is executed Then the report is actually written in the step Write and Format Report. As last activity a Evaluate Report step is performed The Report is the output of the entire SLR process.

2.2 NESSoS Common Body of Knowledge

Ontologies are used to capture knowledge about some domain of interest. In our case, that domain is the field of engineering secure software and services. An ontology provides a catalogue of the classes of objects that exist in the domain. Moreover, an ontology consists of relations between these classes, and of the objects contained in the classes. We present the ontology we use in this paper in Fig. 3 as a Unified Modeling Language (UML) class diagram.[3], this ontology presents the subset of the CBK, which is relevant for this work. The classes in light grey represent the most relevant classes in our ontology for this work, and the classes in dark grey are classes that inherit from the most relevant classes.

The class KnowledgeArea divides the field of secure software and services into knowledge areas (KA). The central class in our ontology is the class KnowledgeObject, which represents all types of knowledge objects (KO) we want to capture. As examples, we consider the KOs of the types Tool, Method, and Notation. The equally named classes inherit general properties from the class KnowledgeObject. In general, the properties that are inside of a class box are simple properties, e.g., of type String or Boolean, while there also exist structured properties connected to class boxes via associations. Simple properties are, for instance, contextDescription, problemDescription, and solutionDescription, which represent textual descriptions of the context, the tackled problem, and the solution for tools, methods, and notations. These properties are part of the class KnowledgeObject. An example for a structured property is the association publications, which connects the class KnowledgeObject and the class Publication. This property is structured, because every publication consists of a BibTeX entry or links to DBLP[4] (bibtexEntriesOrLinksToDBLP), and a flag indicating the importance of a publication (isPrimaryLiterature).

The class CommonTerm has several defined terms, and these can be related to terms of KOs. Moreover, some structured properties refer to enumeration types labeled with the UML ≪enumeration≫ stereotype, e.g., the association maturityLevel that connects the class KnowledgeObject and the class MaturityLevel. This enumeration type allows us to rate every tool, method, and notation according to its maturity.[6]

Multiplicities at the association ends specify constraints on the number of elements contained in an association end. For instance, the 1 at the association end of the association maturityLevel describes that each KO has exactly one maturity level. KOs have

---

[3] http://www.uml.org/

[4] http://www.informatik.uni-trier.de/~ley/db/

[5] The UML stereotype ≪enumeration≫ is used for classes that have a fixed set of attributes, which are referred to by other classes. This use differs from the specification in the UML standard.

[6] In general, enumeration types allow us to pre-define values a property might have.

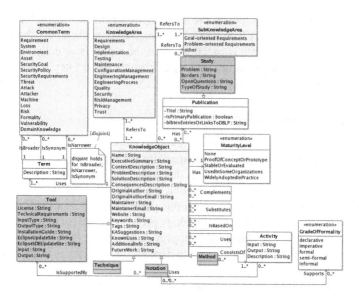

Fig. 3. An Ontology for the Common Body of Knowledge for Secure Software and Services[5]

several relations between each other, e.g., that one KO Uses another. However, these were extended for the contribution of this work and, hence, we explain them in Sect. 3.2.

Specific types of KOs are Notations, which can be supported by Tools (IsSupportedBy). A Notation supports a grade of formality (GradeOfFormality). Methods can be divided into Activities. Activities (Activity) help to structure Methods and to describe workflows based on Inputs, Outputs, and a Description. This means that an activity can use the output of another activity as input. Techniques have just one action, which makes them less complex than Methods.

Using the presented ontology structure, we can adequately capture and process knowledge in the field of engineering secure software and services. In addition, we evolved the ontology for this work with the elements Term, Study, and SubknowledgeArea and we also extended the attributes of KnowledgeObject. We explain these new elements in Sect. 3.2.

3   Structured Research Area Analysis

This section describes the main scientific contribution of this paper. We present in Sect. 3.1 how our work integrates into the approach of Kitchenham described in Sect. 2.1. We show the preparation of our ontology in order to support research area analysis in Sect. 3.2. We describe how to support research area analysis in Sect. 3.3. In Sect. 3.4, we specify the relations between the different ontology parts in detail. These relations enable us to substantiate the envisaged research area analysis by the semantics of the knowledge stored in the ontology.

3.1   Extension/Integration of Kitchenham and CBK

There are several points of integration for the CBK and the literature review process introduced in Sec. 2.1. These points are the inputs Question Types, Question Structure Templates, and the List of Sources to Search In, and the process steps Formulate RQ, Identification of Research, and Selection of Primary Studies (see Fig. 2). To improve the integration for some of these points, the CBK and / or the literature review process have to be adapted.

Question Types. The original question types defined by Kitchenham at al are formulated for SLRs [1, 2]. For mapping studies, a selection of questions and their generalization can be found in the works of Kitcheham et al [5], and Petersen et al. [8].These insights combined with the structure of the CBK (see Fig. 3) result in some new question types:

- How many different KOs exist for the KA in question?
- Which KA(s) are covered by a certain KO?
- Which are the problems and future work mentioned for (a) given KA(s)?
- What is the maturity of KOs for (a) given KA(s)?
- What are the main publications for a given KO or KA?

Question types help to formulate research questions. They give evidence which questions can be of interest and how to formulate them. Moreover, whenever a research question within an actual review maps to one of the questions types given above, this question can be answered by the CBK directly.

Question Structure Templates. For the question structure template, Kitchenham and Chaters proposes to use the PICOC criteria framework to structure research questions [2] as we already described in Sect. 2.1. But when investigating the CBK meta-model (see Fig. 3) it seems to be reasonable to add some criteria.

The main addition is to define the knowledge area(s) explicitly, unlike having them implicit in the context. In most cases of conducting a SLR or mapping study, there is a very specific focus on a special part of software engineering. An overview given by Kitchenham et al. shows that evidence [4]. This focus should be captured within the criteria, because some electronic sources support to select knowledge areas [6, 2]. Moreover, for mapping studies these knowledge areas are often used for structuring the report [5, 7, 8]. In the case of the CBK the knowledge areas are one of the core concepts, and searching the CBK utilizes the knowledge areas.

A minor addition is to distinguish between general terms of the population and special terms of the knowledge area(s). The special terms have a great weight when searching and can help to structure the results [6, 5].

Using this new question structure makes important parts of the questions more explicit. And they ease the use of the CBK, because the separation between general search terms,common terms and knowledge areas are directly reflected in the formulation of the search queries (We will see in Sect. 3.4).

List of Sources to Search In. The CBK and its searching capabilities has to be added to the list of sources to search in [2, 6]. Adding the CBK itself is trivial, but for the capabilities it has also to be checked which new capabilities the CBK introduces. For example, the missing relations between KOs and between publications, which has been found as issue for all existing search sources [6], is explicitly addressed in the CBK. A detailed discussion is skipped at this point due to the lack of space.

Having the CBK in the source list with an explanation of its capabilities helps to plan the research and clarifies in which cases the CBK is of superior use in comparison to other sources.

Formulate RQ. Besides the two inputs, the Question Types and the Question Structure Templates, the CBK can directly support the formulation of research questions. The CBK already defines an ontology of knowledge areas. With an extension, it will support sub-knowledge areas (see Sec. 3.2). Those areas can help to focus the research questions, because it gives an orientation how to refine knowledge areas and how knowledge areas are related. To find the focus for the own research is considered challenging without such a support [3, 4, 7]. Additionally the adapted CBK presented in Sec. 3.2 provides the common terms used in these knowledge areas. These terms help to sharpen the questions and to avoid ambiguities.

The integration of the CBK and Formulate RQ improves the outcome of the whole literature review process, because it helps to avoid the formulation of imprecise search questions with respect to missing / wrong focus and wrong / ambiguous wording.

Identification of Research. The ontology of common terms and related synonyms contained in the CBK also helps to formulate the search queries, not only for the CBK, but also for other search sources.

This formulation of search terms is a crucial step and the knowledge about relations between terms and the existence of a synonym list improves this step of finding research a lot [1–8].

Selection of Primary Studies. For the selection of primary studies the CBK provides information for some comprehensive and sophisticated selection criteria. The CBK already contains information, which is very specific and useful to rate KOs, like the maturity level. And this information is available for all results obtained from the CBK. These criteria are hard to evaluate for results from other search sources [2, 3, 6]. Examples for inclusion criteria:

– Only include KOs and related publications with a certain maturity level
– Only include KOs, which are a core concept of a KA and therefore many other KOs are based on these KOs
– Only include publications, which are considered as most significant by the editors of KOs

Having a set of precise selection criteria, which can be evaluated for all results, improves the outcome of the whole review process. The probability of excluding relevant studies and the bias caused by including literature of low quality can be reduced. And the whole review process speeds up when using the CBK, because the information for evaluating the criteria is available explicitly.

3.2 Preparing the Ontology

We prepared the NESSoS CBK ontology (see Sect. 2.2) in order to support the concepts of the structured literature reviews from Kitchenham explained in Sects. 2.1 and 3.1. Hence, we extended the CBK ontology (see Fig. 3) with the classes SubKnowledgeArea, Publication, and Study.

We consider keywords and tags in knowledge objects. Keywords are given according to the guidelines of a specific system, e.g., the ACM-keyword-system [11]. Tags are chosen without any restriction and provide the possibility to choose any possible word.

We want to use the CBK ontology for finding research gaps. This requires KnowledgeObjects that do not have a solution description yet, but only problem descriptions. We also included the MaturityLevel None for these KnowledgeObjects. In addition, KnowledgeObjects now have a FutureWork attribute that states research not yet carried out. The difference between these two is that KnowledgeObjects that only have a problem description represent a research area that needs a significant amount of research for providing a solution. The FutureWork attribute in KnowledgeObjects represents possible research that can build upon an existing solution. Researchers that use our approach might look for one or the other.

KnowledgeObjects have relations between each other. These relations are relevant for the investigation of research areas. KOs can be based on other KOs (IsBasedOn), and they can use each other (Uses). In addition, KOs can be used in combination. In this case, one KO Complements another. If KOs can be exchanged, these have a Substitutes relation.

We include the class Term that holds the terms a specific KnowledgeObject uses. The class CommonTerm contains a set of well-defined terms. A Term of a KnowledgeObject is either broader, synonymous, or narrower than a CommonTerm. This allows a comparison of KnowledgeObjects using the CommonTerms. Without these any comparison would lack precision, because terms and notions differ in KnowledgeObjects.

3.3 Identifing Research Gaps Using the CBK

While a Mapping Study and a Problem/Gap Study is supported best by the CBK, it at least partially supports a Structured Literature Review and a Tertiary Study (see Fig. 1). In the following, the CBK support for all different kinds of studies, as defined by Kitchenham, is described in more detail. The support, as described in this section, sketches only a first idea, which will be refined in Sect. 3.4, where we only consider the well supported Mapping Study and Problem/Gap Study.

Mapping Study. For a Mapping Study researchers have to specify one or more KAs, one or more sub-KAs or one or more common terms . Additionally, they can constrain the search by providing further search terms. The CBK returns KOs grouped by KAs. Depending on the scope of the search, 20 results,for example , for one KA can be interpreted as a sign for maturity of a field or immaturity of a field. For example, 20 results for the KA Requirements has a different meaning than 20 results for the sub-KA Goal-oriented Requirements including the search terms *Cloud* and *Law*.

Problem/Gap Study. Conducting a Problem/Gap Study is also well supported by the CBK. The researcher specifies one or more KAs, one or more sub-KAs or one or more common terms and provides search terms. In this case, the CBK not only groups KOs along the specified KAs, sub-KAs or common terms as described for the Mapping Study, but extends the search to the following classes and fields of the CBK ontology: ProblemDescription and FutureWork of the class KnowledgeObject,

Problem and Border in the class Study. These results support the creation of a Problem/Gap Study because all relevant information is presented to the researcher in a structured way.

Structured Literature Review. While the researcher is able to retrieve KOs for the selected KAs, sub-KAs or common terms and, thus, all relevant literature references, can only be regarded as a starting point to conduct a full-fledged Structured Literature Review. A SLR involves an in-depth analysis of the actual literature, which is out of the CBK's scope.

Tertiary Study. Conducting a Tertiary Study is only supported in theory, because it requires all relevant secondary studies to be part of the CBK. If this is not the case, there is no support for this kind of study using the CBK.

3.4   Formalizing Research Area Analysis

We now identify and specify relevant relations for the identification of research gaps, making use of the ontology and the knowledge it stores and structures. For the analysis, the relations between different tools, methods, and notations, i.e., different KO types, and KAs are of particular relevance.

Allocca et al. [10] present the *DOOR* method to capture the semantics of relations between different ontologies and to formally specify these relations. While we partly adopt the DOOR steps to support our approach to identify and specify relations between different KOs, we abstain from building an ontology of these relations. We use the ontology structure presented in Sects. 2.2 and 3.2 on the one hand for typing the relations and, more importantly, on the other hand to refine the semantics of the relations. We divide our approach into the following three steps:

1. Identify and specify top-level relations
2. Identify and specify variants and sub-relations, and characterize their algebraic properties
3. Compose relations

We will use the following abbreviations in the formalization: KA = Knowledge Area, SKA = SubKnowledgeArea KO = Knowledge Object P = Publication, ST = Study, CT = CommonTerm, T = Term, and ML = MaturityLevel.

Top-Level Relations: The following relations are abstracted top-level relations that support the kinds of queries sketched in Sect. 3.3.

MappingStudy_KAxKO. Describes a mapping study as a relation between knowledge areas and knowledge objects.

MappingStudy_SKAxKO. Describes a more fine granular mapping study as a relation between sub-knowledge areas and knowledge objects.

MappingStudy_CTxKO. Describes a mapping study as a relation between common terms and knowledge objects.

ProblemGapStudy_KAxKOxST. Describes a problem or gap study as a relation between knowledge areas, knowledge objects, and studies.

ProblemGapStudy_SKAxKOxST. Describes a more fine granular problem or gap study as a relation between sub-knowledge areas, knowledge objects, and studies.

ProblemGapStudy_CTxKOxST. Describes a problem or gap study as a relation between common terms and knowledge objects and studies.

Variants, Sub-relations, and Algebraic Properties: Variants and sub-relations shed light on various facets of the top-level relations with regard to the structured design of the ontology. We express the relations using relational algebra based upon the work of Codd [9]. We use an extention of the relational algebra [12, 13] that offers aggregation and grouping functionalites. The symbol ξ groups the output according to specifed atribute(s). π projects only specified columns of a table. σ selects rows in a table for which specified boolean expression(s) hold. $\bowtie$ joins tables according to common attributes. All rows that do not have these attributes are left out. $\bowtie$ joins tables, but also displays rows of the left table that do not have all the common attributes. We use relational algebra, because the algebra expressions can be translated to SMW+ queries in a straightforward way, see Sect. 4.

For the specifications of the relations, we assume that the structural design of the ontology presented in Sect. 2.2 and 3.2 is given as tables. Classes that have 1..* cardinalities on both ends of the relation in our ontology require connection tables. Otherwise we would require multiple relations between tables, which is to be avoided during database design. For example, we want to create a table for knowledge objects. One row in the table is allowed to have multiple relations to rows in the knowledge area table. Instead, we would have to create numerous columns for these relations in the knowledge area, because we do not know how many relations we need. Hence, we create a further table for these relations. We denote these tables, which we add in the formalization, with "Connect" and append the names of the classes this table connects. For example, the connection table for the tables KnowledgeObject and KnowledgeArea is stated as: ConnectKAtoKO. These connection tables have two columns, which contain the the primary keys of each of the tables they connect.

Inheritance in the ontology is translated into one main table for the superclass and one table for each class that inherits from this class. These classes have a relation to the table that represents the superclass and have only the additional attributes of the inherited class. For example, the superclass KnowledgeObject has the class Tool that inherits from it, and one of the additional attributes is Input. Hence, we create a table KnowledgeObject and a table Tool, which has the attribute Input.

Searchterm: We define an algebraic expression ST, which represents a boolean expression for one or more searchterms.

$$ST ::= ST \diamond ST \mid \kappa = String \mid (ST) \mid \neg ST$$
$$\diamond ::= \wedge \mid \vee$$
$$\kappa ::= Tag \mid Keywords \mid ExecutiveSummary \mid Name$$

For example, the expression " Tags='cloud' $\vee$ Tags='law' " can be used with σ for the table KnowledgeObject. This results in a table with all KOs that have 'cloud' or 'law' as tags.

KnowledgeArea: We define KAB to be a boolean expression for the selection of one or more knowledge areas.

$$KAB ::= KAB \vee KAB \mid KnowledgeArea = KAS$$
$$KAS ::= Requirements \mid Design \mid Implementation \mid Maintenance \mid$$
$$ConfigurationManagemen \mid EngineeringManagement \mid EngineeringProcess \mid$$
$$Quality \mid Security \mid RiskManagement \mid Privacy \mid Trust$$

We defined Maturity Level (MLB), Sub-KnowledgeArea (SKAB), and Common Terms (CTB) in a similar manner.

MappingStudy_KAxKO: We specify queries for mapping studies as database relations. We explain the query in detail starting with the σ_{ST}, where we join the tables KA, ConntectKAtoKA, and KO and select rows accordng to ST. The query filters the resulting table for rows that have the required MLB and KAB. The result is projected onto the columns KnowledgeArea, MaturityLevel, Name, ExecutiveSummary, Tags, and Keywords. The query groups the results according to KnowledgeArea, MaturityLevel, Name, ExecutiveSummary, Tags, and Keywords.

$$MappingStudy\_KAxKO =$$
$$\xi_{KnowledgeArea,MaturityLevel,Name,ExecutiveSummary,Tags,Keywords}\big($$
$$\pi_{KnowledgeArea,MaturityLevel,Name,ExecutiveSummary,Tags,Keywords}\big($$
$$\sigma_{KAB}\big(\sigma_{MLB}\big($$
$$\sigma_{ST}(KA \bowtie ConnectKAtoKO \bowtie KO)\big)\big)\big)\big)$$

We define MappingStudy_SKAxKO, and MappingStudy_CTxKO in a similar manner.

Extending Searchterm: For a problem gap study we extend the fields of the CBK that can be searched as follows.

$$\cdots$$

$$\kappa ::= Tag \mid Keywords \mid ExecutiveSummary \mid Name \mid FutureWork \mid$$
$$Title \mid Problems \mid Borders \mid OpenQuestions$$

ProblemGapStudy_KAxKOxST: To perform problem gap studies, we include existing studies in the search relation and enriches the output with problem and future work descriptions. We formalize this relation as an variant of the relation MappingStudy_KAxKO. The symbol $\bowtie$ between KO and $(ConnectKOtoP \bowtie P \bowtie ST)$ causes that also KOs are selected that do not have a publication or study.

$$ProblemGapStudy\_KAxKOxST =$$
$$\xi_{KnowledgeArea,Name,ExecutiveSummary,FutureWork,Tags,Title,Problem,Borders,OpenQuestions}\big($$
$$\pi_{KnowledgeArea,Name,ExecutiveSummary,FutureWork,Tags,Title,Problem,Borders,}$$
$$_{OpenQuestions}\big($$
$$MappingStudy\_KAxKO \bowtie KO \bowtie (ConnectKOtoP \bowtie P \bowtie ST)\big)\big)$$

We define ProblemGapStudy_SKAxKOxST, ProblemGapStudy_CTxKOxST in a similar manner.

Compose Relations. Complex relations can be composed from simple ones, as shown in the following example.

MappingStudy_KAxSKAxKOxCT: We merge the different mappings for knowledge area, sub-knowledge area, and the common term and define the following relation that returns the name of the knowledge object, maturity level, the executive summary, the tags, and the keywords, grouped by knowledge area, sub-knowledge area and common terms.

$$MappingStudy\_KAxSKAxKOxCT =$$

$\xi_{KnowledgeArea,Sub-KnowledgeArea,CommonTerm,MaturityLevel,Name,ExecutiveSummary,Tags,}$
$_{Keywords}($

$\quad \pi_{KnowledgeArea,Sub-KnowledgeArea,CommonTerm,Name,MaturityLevel,ExecutiveSummary,}$
$_{Tags,Keywords}(MappingStudy\_KAxKO \bowtie MappingStudy\_SKAxKO$
$\bowtie MappingStudy\_CTxKO))$

ProblemGapStudy_KAxSKAxKOxCTxST: Finally we merge the different problem or gap study relations for knowledge area, sub knowledge area, and the common terms and define the following relation that returns the name of the knowledge object, common term, the executive summary, future work, the tags the keywords, title of the study, problem, borders and open questions grouped by knowledge area, sub-knowledge area and common terms. We specified this relation in the following.

$$ProblemGapStudy\_KAxSKAxKOxCTxST =$$

$\xi_{KnowledgeArea,Sub-KnowledgeArea,CommonTerm,Name,ExecutiveSummary,FutureWork,Tags,}$
$_{Keywords,Title,Problem,Borders,OpenQuestions}($

$\quad \pi_{KnowledgeArea,Sub-KnowledgeArea,CommonTerm,Name,ExecutiveSummary,FutureWork,}$
$_{Tags,Keywords,Title,Problem,Borders,OpenQuestions}($
$\quad ProblemGapStudy\_KAxKOxST \bowtie ProblemGapStudy\_SKAxKOxST$
$\bowtie ProblemGapStudy\_CTxKOxST))$

To sum up, we applied the DOOR method for the structured creation of ontology relations to the CBK ontology for implementing the Kitchenham structured research area analysis. First, we defined the top-level relations for mapping studies and problem/gap studies. We formalized these relations, using relational algebra, and we derived further relations from these. In addition, we have shown an example for a composed relation of the previously defined relations. We checked all the relational algebra expressions using the *relational* tool.[7] For future semi-automatic use of the relations and in the light of the technical realization (see Sect. 4), the composition of relations can be left to the users. For example, the Semantic MediaWiki+ allows its users to easily switch the predicates of the relations on and off to generate a result set as required.

4 Realization

Our ontology behind the CBK allows us to specify various queries realizing the relations presented in Sect. 3.4 using the SMW query language (SMW-QL). SMW-QL was introduced as a comfortable means to query the SMW [14, 15]. The SMW+ platform provides an inline syntax to integrate queries into a wiki page and a graphical query builder to support the creation of such queries (see Fig. 4). In the following, some of the queries specified previously in relational algebra will be translated into SMW-QL. We start with a simple query referring to the relation MappingStudy_KAxKO, followed by a complex query referring to the relation ProblemGapStudy_KAxKOxST. The query given in Listing 1.1 is read like this: retrieve all KOs that belong to the

---

[7] http://galileo.dmi.unict.it/wiki/relational/doku.php

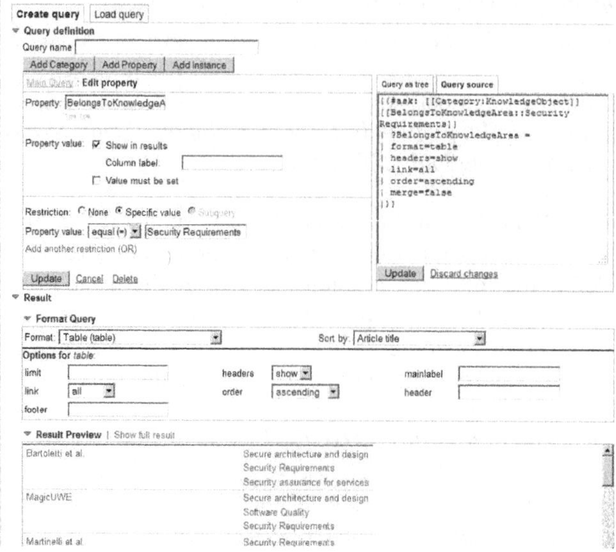

Fig. 4. Mapping study support realized as SMW-QL query

KA Security Requirements and which contain the search term **attacker** and/or **invader** in the executive summary. The search term can be further specified using comparator operators and wildcards. The result is returned as a table. Each row represents one knowledge object, whereas each column represents an attribute specified in the query indicated by the question mark. In our case, the table contains the columns **RefersTo-KnowledgeArea, HasMaturityLevel, ExecutiveSummary, Tags** and **Keywords**. The table is sorted along the KAs and MaturityLevel. The user is able to customize sorting by clicking on the table's header. The SMW-QL query given in Listing 1.2 refers to the relation **ProblemGapStudy_KAxKOxST**, thus supporting a Problem/Gap Study. Therefore it is necessary to additionally output the attributes **ProblemDescription** and **FutureWork** from the **KO** class and the attributes **Problem** and **Border** from the Study class.

In contrast to definition of **ProblemGapStudy_KAxKOxST** in Sect. 3.4, the first SMW-QL query is not reused in this query. While subqueries are in principal possible with SMW-QL, it is recommended to express sub-queries as queries where possible. In this case, it is realized as a flat query, not only because of performance advantages, but also for the sake of simplicity.

```
1  {#ask: [[Category:KnowledgeObject]]
2  [[RefersToKnowledgeArea::Security Requirements]]
3  [[ExecutiveSummary::~*attacker*]] OR [[ExecutiveSummary::~*invader*]]
4  | ?RefersToKnowledgeArea | ?HasMaturityLevel | ?ExecutiveSummary | ?Tags
5  | ?Keywords | sort=RefersToKnowledgeArea,HasMaturityLevel |}
```

Listing 1.1. Query for supporting a Mapping Study

```
1  {#ask: [[Category:KnowledgeObject]] [[Category:Study]]
2  [[RefersToKnowledgeArea:: Security Requirements]]
3  [[ExecutiveSummary::~*attacker*]] OR [[ExecutiveSummary::~*invader*]]
4  | ?RefersToKnowledgeArea | ?HasMaturityLevel | ?ExecutiveSummary | ?FutureWork
5  | ?Problem | ?Title | ?Borders | ?OpenQuestions | ?Tags | ?Keywords
6  | sort=RefersToKnowledgeArea,HasMaturityLevel |)
```

Listing 1.2. Query for supporting a Problem/Gap Study

5   Related Work

Tools for structured literature reviews that are regularly used by the software engineering research community are major search engines and digital libraries such as ACM, CiteSeer, IEEE Xplore, Google Scholar, Science Direct and Web of Science [11]. All of these work similarly by specifying boolean search expressions. While they differ in evaluating search expressions and ranking the results, it can be stated that none of these search engines and digital libraries was created to support structured literature reviews [6], as our dedicated approach does.

6   Conclusion and Outlook

We have formalized the Kitchenham approach for structured literature reviews in relational algebra. Furthermore, we implemented these queries in an SMW+ ontology. Thus, we provide a semi-automatic support for the Kitchenham approach that eases the burden of manual literature reviews.

Our approach offers the following main benefits:

- Systematic execution of mapping and problem/gap studies according to Kitchenham based upon ontologies for specific domains (here: secure software and service engineering)
- A structured approach to analyze a research area
- Improving the outcome of literature studies via structured processing of knowledge using ontologies
- Further analysis of research domains can be executed with little effort

Our approach has the limitation that it cannot detect research gaps that are not part of the content of the CKB. Hence, the quality of the outcome of our work is dependent on the quality and quantity of CBK content. However, the possibility also exists that publications might be overlooked when manually executing a literature review according to Kitchenham. Moreover, research gaps, ideas for future work, etc. that only exist in the heads of researchers also cannot be found by any of these approaches.

The work presented here will be extended to support further, more extensive research questions in the future. Examples are the refinement of new findings or the strengthening of own results. We will also work on further automating our approach. We envision an extension of the approach towards other existing ontologies.

References

1. Kitchenham, B.: Procedures for performing systematic reviews. Technical report, Keele University and NICTA (2004)
2. Kitchenham, B., Charters, S.: Guidelines for performing Systematic Literature Reviews in Software Engineering. Technical Report EBSE 2007-001, Keele University and Durham University Joint Report (2007)
3. Kitchenham, B.A., Brereton, P., Turner, M., Niazi, M., Linkman, S.G., Pretorius, R., Budgen, D.: Refining the systematic literature review process - two participant-observer case studies. Empirical Software Engineering 15(6), 618–653 (2010)
4. Kitchenham, B., Pretorius, R., Budgen, D., Brereton, P., Turner, M., Niazi, M., Linkman, S.G.: Systematic literature reviews in software engineering - a tertiary study. Information & Software Technology 52(8), 792–805 (2010)
5. Kitchenham, B.A., Budgen, D., Brereton, O.P.: Using mapping studies as the basis for further research - a participant-observer case study. Information & Software Technology 53(6), 638–651 (2011)
6. Brereton, P., Kitchenham, B.A., Budgen, D., Turner, M., Khalil, M.: Lessons from applying the systematic literature review process within the software engineering domain. Journal of Systems and Software 80(4), 571–583 (2007)
7. Budgen, D., Turner, M., Brereton, P., Kitchenham, B.: Using Mapping Studies in Software Engineering. In: Proceedings of PPIG 2008, pp. 195–204. Lancaster University (2008)
8. Petersen, K., Feldt, R., Mujtaba, S., Mattsson, M.: Systematic Mapping Studies in Software engineering. In: EASE 2008: Proceedings of the 12th International Conference on Evaluation and Assessment in Software Engineering (2008)
9. Codd, E.F.: A relational model of data for large shared data banks. Commun. ACM 13(6), 377–387 (1970)
10. Allocca, C., d'Aquin, M., Motta, E.: DOOR - towards a formalization of ontology relations. In: Proceedings of the International Conference on Knowledge Engineering and Ontology Development (KEOD), pp. 13–20. INSTICC Press (2009)
11. Turner, M.: Digital libraries and search engines for software engineering research: An overview. Technical report, Keele University (2010)
12. Klug, A.: Equivalence of relational algebra and relational calculus query languages having aggregate functions. J. ACM 29(3), 699–717 (1982)
13. Agrawal, R.: Alpha: an extension of relational algebra to express a class of recursive queries. IEEE Transactions on Software Engineering 14(7), 879–885 (1988)
14. Krötzsch, M., Vrandecic, D., Völkel, M., Haller, H., Studer, R.: Semantic wikipedia. J. Web Sem. 5(4), 251–261 (2007)
15. Bao, J., Li Ding, J.A.H.: Knowledge representation and query in semantic mediawiki: A formal study. Technical report, Computer Science Department at RPI (2008)

A Context-Aware Mashup Integration Guideline
for Enterprise 2.0

Gerald Bader, Amin Anjomshoaa, and A Min Tjoa

Institute of Software Technology and Interactive Systems
Vienna University of Technology,
Favoritenstraße 9-11/188, A-1040, Vienna, Austria
gbader@gmx.at, {anjomshoaa,amin}@ifs.tuwien.ac.at

Abstract. Recent advances in Internet Computing have changed the outlook of business and enterprise cooperation models. Many companies have started to leverage their services in order to move toward Enterprise 2.0. In this regard enabling technologies such as Mashups play a significant role to shift away from traditional information management environments towards dynamic and collaborative systems.

In this paper, different business aspects of Mashup architecture in enterprise use-cases will be explored and the SWISHGUIDE-framework for capturing the needs and readiness factors of target organization will be introduced. The proposed SWISHGUIDE framework provides a decision-making guideline for transition from traditional information management systems to a successful Enterprise Mashup architecture.

Keywords: Enterprise 2.0, Mashup, SOA, Migration, Business Services, Crowd Sourcing, Social Networks, Web 2.0.

1   Introduction

The business today needs fast, accurate and reliable information resources in order to make real-time and effective decisions; however the existing business solutions are not flexible enough to fulfill the requirements of future business and get adapted to dynamic business changes. In today's highly competitive marketplace, businesses need to differentiate themselves from the competitors, connect and engage customers and potential customers, get their brand recognized, and sell their products and services [1].

In this context, the Enterprise 2.0 is introduced as a system of web-based technologies that provide rapid and agile collaboration, information sharing, emergence, and integration capabilities in the extended enterprise [2]. The need for Enterprise 2.0 is forced by technology trends such as Web 2.0 [3], crowd computing, and cloud computing combined with the business trends such as consolidation and knowledge management [4].

Enterprise 2.0 describes how organizations can benefit from such new technologies, how they can implement it, and what organizational changes and impacts need to be

G. Quirchmayr et al. (Eds.): CD-ARES 2012, LNCS 7465, pp. 17–30, 2012.
© IFIP International Federation for Information Processing 2012

considered. Enterprise 2.0 is also considered to benefit from Web 2.0 paradigm and its relevant technologies for sake of business purposes [5]. From another perspective, the Enterprise 2.0 can be at its simplest level defined as the extension of traditional organizations by social platforms to fulfill the effective collaboration and information sharing requirements. In order to have an all-embracing Enterprise 2.0 landscape, technology added-values such as blogs, RSS feeds, wikis, enterprise search and Mashup solutions need to be considered [6,7].

On the other hand, companies have to realize that Enterprise 2.0 will come anyway [8] and the change from a traditionally working and acting company to Enterprise 2.0 is a time consuming process which cannot be done in course of a few months. Especially changing the mindset and cultural issues is a long lengthy process [9]. In short the practice of management is changing from strict rules and fixed processes to a more liberate and open information space in modern cooperation models [10].

It is also important to note that the Enterprise 2.0 can only be a success story by involving and training the employees and information workers to understand how to use such tools and products and how to create the most and best outcome from it.

In this paper we exploit Enterprise Mashups as an enabling technology to get a step closer to Enterprise 2.0 goals. We will also explore the shift from traditional IT architectures to Enterprise 2.0 from different perspectives. The main contribution of this paper is the introduction of a context-aware Mashup integration guideline -called SWISHGUIDE- for assessing the readiness of a generic organization for undertaking Enterprise Mashups. In this context the corresponding opportunities and risks of the proposed solution will be discussed in details.

2   Enterprise Mashups

The organizations of today are confronted by business pressures to decrease costs, reduce workforce and transform their business from an internally focused organization into a service oriented and customer centric organization, which target the need of their customers. Therefore organizations have to deal with different knowledge domains and bring them together, which in turn means also dealing with many common business process concepts and architectures [11].

SOA (Service Oriented Architecture) and RIA (Rich Internet Applications) are leading the standardized access to business functionality and data with desktop-like interaction over the Web. But for information workers it is difficult to use these new technologies to improve their daily tasks. Furthermore SOA-enabled companies are now facing difficulties to manage and to provide information on how the services interact and whether they are used in the right way [12]. Mashups enable users to get access to data sources through SOA by a user-driven process with short development cycles.

Enterprise Mashups (also known as Business Mashups) can be defined as user-created applications that combine internal and external resources and publish the results in appropriate way on enterprise portals [13]. Enterprise Mashups have a strong focus on data and service integration, merging, and distribution of content. Unlike the Data-Mashups and Consumer-Mashups, Enterprise Mashups are used in business use-cases for more fundamental, complex and sometimes business-critical tasks. Therefore topics such as trust & security, governance and stability play an important role for this group of Mashups and need a closer examination [14,15].

In order to provide a Mashup transition guideline for organizations, an in-depth understanding of the Mashup patterns is required. Some of these patterns can be summarized as follows [16]:

- **Self-service Pattern:** Business users create Mashups on their own to handle business needs. Unlike traditional organizations where the solutions are solely created and managed by the IT department, business users with average IT skills can also take the lead in creating the required solutions.
- **Source Integration Pattern:** Companies can integrate both internal and external resources for certain business processes or decision-making. In its simplest form, the organizations can present their backend information as services. These can be used to generate additional business value via information transparency and reaching more end-users.
- **Share & Reuse Pattern:** The Mashup solutions provide good potential for solution sharing and solution reuse. This aspect of Mashup solutions can save lots of time for creating new solutions provided that the proper documentation and service governance is in place. Many companies are now thinking about the benefits of public and private clouds that host the shared services and data resources.
- **Democratization of Data:** The Mashup solution can also be used for encapsulating the business logic and making the data accessible via data feeds and APIs. In other words, the data which was previously limited to one department can now be freely used by other authorized people to make useful ad-hoc solutions.

3   Need-Readiness Matrix for Enterprise Mashups

In order to guaranty a smooth and reliable transition from traditional architecture to Enterprise Mashup landscape, the technical, organizational and social aspects should be studied carefully and considered in all transition phases. Such analysis can be conducted in two directions, namely: Readiness of target organization for integrating Mashup and Organizational Need for Mashups.

The Mashup Readiness aims to estimate the acceptance level of Enterprise Mashup solutions in the target company and covers both technical-readiness and people-readiness aspects. On the other hand, the "Need for Mashups" studies the business needs and requirements that can be addressed by Enterprise Mashups. After an appropriate analysis of these two dimensions the decision makers will have a clearer outlook of business opportunities and can evaluate the balance between benefits and the required transition efforts according to the readiness factors.

The correlation between Mashup Readiness and Need for Mashup, can be summarized in a Readiness-Need estimation matrix as shown in Table 1.

Table 1. Readiness-Need estimation Matrix for Enterprise Mashups implementation

	Low Need	High Need
Ready	Target organization is fulfilling the technical, organizational and social prerequisites of Mashup undertaking but the use-cases of target organization cannot benefit from Mashup features to a big extent.	The organization has the required IT infrastructure and a broad spectrum of support from the stakeholders. The high readiness coupled with the high business need offer the best condition for a successful and valuable enterprise Mashup migration.
Not Ready	The company does not fulfill the prerequisites sufficiently neither there seems to be a need for it. Therefore an implementation is not recommendable.	The organization is not owning the required IT infrastructure or do not have a broad spectrum of support from the stakeholders. Through the high need for Mashups solutions it is recommendable to increase the readiness by certain initiatives before starting a Mashup undertaking.

Obviously the implementation of an Enterprise Mashup solution is very relevant for the top right quarter of this matrix, where on one hand the company is ready to realize the new architecture, and on the other hand the business use-cases demand a Mashup-based approach.

Although the areas of the Readiness-Need matrix have a simple and straightforward definition, but the main challenge remains, to find the proper location of a given organization in this matrix.

In the next chapters we will introduce some indicators in order to position the target organization in the Readiness-Need matrix during the transition phases. For this purpose we will first introduce SWISHGUIDE which facilitates study of target organization based on a unique approach and then define the required methods to assess the readiness and business need indicators.

4   SWISHGUIDE

SWISHGUIDE is the abbreviation for the main advantages that a business can gain from utilization of Mashup-based solutions. The SWISHGUIDE factors will be used to assess the Mashup-readiness and business needs of target organizations. These items are grouped in three main categories: business aspects, facility aspects and social aspects. The business category contains some required factors in order to increase the efficiency and generate business added-value for target organization.

The facility aspects focus on more effective management and sharing of information resources and finally the social category describes the benefits of Mashup solutions for end-users and how they can be used to promote social solutions.

Figure 1 demonstrates the SWISHGUIDE categories and the relevant factors of each category. In the rest of this section, the SWISHGUDE factors will be introduced in more detail.

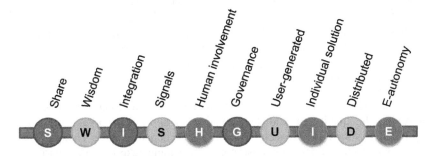

Fig. 1. SWISHGUIDE

4.1   Business Aspects

Enterprise Mashups have a strong focus on data and service integration, merging and distribution of content. One of the major problems in modern business is that many vital processes between stakeholders are to a large extent managed manually and require human intervention for tasks such as recognition, extraction, and reformatting. These manual processes may hamper the effective and timely interoperation between stakeholders. Enterprise Mashups can change the situation by automating parts of such processes by liberating the business users from uninteresting and monotonous tasks and letting them focus on their business solutions.

In this context the major benefits of Mashups for business can be described as shared wisdom, user-generated resources, information alerts (signals) and finally information distribution. These factors will be explained in more details below.

- **Wisdom:** The plethora of business user interactions in the business field and the domain knowledge of experts is a precious resource that can be shared with community in order to facilitate more effective decision making processes. Knowledge, as the most important asset of companies, needs to be captured and transferred to the right employees at the right time, via appropriate channel, and in an understandable format. The Mashups may support the process of creating collective wisdom and sharing the expert solutions by capturing and documenting reusable components and information resources.
- **User-Generated:** The business users, who are not necessarily IT experts, usually need to access the information resources and adopt them according to their specific requirements in their daily tasks [17]. Most of such micro-solutions fall under the long tail of user requirements and are not covered by standard business solutions.

- **Signals:** The business users and especially managers need to make decisions based on actual and accurate data. Companies often struggle to keep their decision makers up to date regarding data resources and processes. Mashups have big potential for more efficient and simpler signaling methods among systems and users to keep the business users automatically and instantly updated about data resources and processes.
- **Distributed:** Through the heterogeneous IT landscape and complex business processes the interaction of IT systems is a challenging issue. Many business processes rely on an intensive interaction between IT systems in order to fulfill their business requirements and have to interact with partners, suppliers or customers in a technically sophisticated, timely and competitive manner.

4.2   Facility Aspects

Besides the business aspects, companies can also benefit from IT services of Mashups for improving the quality of knowledge management in their organization. In a Mashup-based business environment the role of IT departments is changing from software providers to services administrators who should take care of security and governance aspects of available services. Such services range from complex proprietary services to simple directories for existing and user-generated services.

As such, business users have the freedom to assemble their applications for their daily challenges from exposed services in a productive way. By applying the appropriate governance policies such as security, versioning, and legislation the user-generated solutions will be readily available for reuse in other business solutions.

In this section three main aspects of Enterprise Mashups namely sharing, integration, and governance for supporting the IT facilities will be introduced.

- **Share:** Neglecting the effective sharing of the business information in a modern business may cost extra time and money. In order to address this issue, companies should establish instant and trustable communication channels. Today knowledge sharing is done via traditional methods such as email, phone, etc and rarely through a central knowledge management system. Therefore only a small group of people have access to certain knowledge. Mashups may provide enhanced sharing and reusing of business knowledge and information via:

  − organization-wide business taxonomies
  − uniform information query and retrieval and
  − addressable data resources and information feeds

- **Integration:** The fast changing market, demands continuous change in the companies' business relationships such as changing partners, new suppliers, new customers, etc. The dynamic of relationships should be also reflected in the underlying systems and processes, which is one of the most challenging issues that companies are facing today. In order to adjust their business to follow impulse market changes, companies need to adopt existing solutions and processes instantly by integration of new resources. Mashup solutions can facilitate the integration of internal and external resources via APIs, web-services, feeds, etc.

- **Governance:** Without governance a project will fail, company processes end up in chaos and the IT landscape will get out of control. Governance is the management- and structural backbone in organizations to define clear roles and responsibilities and to ensure a stable and trustworthy environment [18]. Mashup solutions can bring more effective governance of services, solutions and data via
  - a centralized pool of annotated data resources and services
  - a uniform security schema and roles

4.3   Social Aspects

Finally the social aspects of SWISHGUIDE, focus on the inherited features from Web 2.0, namely Human involvement, Individual solutions, and E-autonomy. In the rest of this section, the social aspects are presented with more details.

- **Human Involvement:** "Mastery over life skills, curiosity and learning, social support, and shared goals were keys to the survival and prosperity of early humans. If you think of humans as a social species then it makes sense to think of us as tuned to do things to help the group" [19].As the world changes more and more towards knowledge-based societies, companies and their employees need to change into knowledge workers. But knowledge which is not shared is lost. For example, if an employee leaves the company also his knowledge will leave the company. The key for better knowledge management is the exchange of knowledge between users. Mashups empower users to capture the knowledge of employees and share their expertise which leads to better team-working.
- **Individual Solutions:** In order to undertake daily tasks, users usually invent their own personalized solutions parallel to company's standard solutions which are usually led to manual and duplicated work. Since these solutions are a matter of taste, IT departments cannot support users with individual solutions. With Mashups business users can easily create individual solutions based on personal preferences and specific needs. Such solution can be also filtered and ranked based on some quality indicators (assessed by IT department, or user community) and reused in other business use-cases.
- **E-autonomy:** It is already a known fact that generally software solutions cannot cover the long tail of requirements [20] and the standard solutions of IT departments only address around 20% of the user requirements. Since IT departments are usually overloaded with user requirements, the business departments often start their own initiatives to solve their specific issues via ordering added-value solutions which may lead to data silos, and heterogeneous IT landscapes. With the self-service and easy-to-use approach of Mashups everybody can create their own solutions and IT departments are then responsible to provide holistic advanced services such as security, versioning, legislation, etc.

5   Organization Readiness for Mashup Migration

In order to start with a Mashup undertaking, the first step is to identify the readiness of the candidate organization by taking the current IT state and people-support into consideration. From technical perspective we need to assess the infrastructure profile of the target company, which includes different aspects such as existing software, hardware, and frameworks. This result should be combined with People Readiness to obtain the overall readiness of the target company. The following sections provide more details on assessing the readiness factors.

5.1   Infrastructure Readiness

The existence of a proper infrastructure and supporting framework in an organization can guarantee the success of Mashup implementation to a large extent. Before starting a Mashup transition, the relevant tools, services and infrastructure should be captured and documented. Without any doubt, the SOA framework and the SOA-enabled tools play an important role in Mashup transition and companies who have already employed SOA in their software landscape will have a better initial position for a Mashup undertaking. Likewise, a Mashup implementation can benefit greatly from well-established trust, security and knowledge management models.

In order to capture and analyze the infrastructure readiness of an organization, a survey of the current state, needs to be done in order to answer questions such as:

- Is there a broadband internet connection available?
- Are processes web-accessible and addressable?
- Are services web-accessible and addressable?
- Are data resources web-accessible and addressable?
- Are your applications accessible via dedicated APIs?
- Is your business logic accessible via dedicated APIs?
- Are there any search mechanisms in place for finding resources?
- Is there a SOA architecture in place?
- Are there security guidelines and rules for new technologies like Web 2.0 and Cloud Computing?

The designed survey, based on the above questions, will be answered by IT experts of the target organization. The result is summarized as a total score, which indicates the infrastructure readiness and will be later on used in combination with people-readiness to assess the organization readiness for a Mashup undertaking.

The infrastructure readiness is just one side of the coin for a successful Mashup transition; the people readiness plays also a significant role. The reason for this, lies on the fact that in a Mashup-based environment some traditional responsibilities of IT-departments will be carried out by the end-users. As a result the end-user's acknowledgment and effective use of new frameworks is of great importance. In the next section, the people readiness is explained in more details and a method for quantifying its state will be presented.

5.2   People Readiness

Most of the time, IT undertakings are seen and planned only as technical projects. In such projects, architecture definition, tool evaluation or data integration are the center of attention and the social aspects do not receive appropriate emphasis. However, the success of a project is strongly dependent upon the involved people and the stakeholders. Therefore the mindset of the people adaptability to change, their expectations and fears, and also their needs and requirements have to be considered [21].

This issue gets even more important in case of a Mashup undertaking, because the Mashup solution by definition is taking benefit from user-generated solutions and collaboration. So if the end-users are already using Enterprise 2.0 technologies and are working and living in a collaborating and self-servicing environment the possibility of success is much greater, compared to traditional organizations.

In order to assess the people readiness in context of Mashup solutions, we will define the mapping between people readiness factors and the main Mashup benefits which were defined previously in the SWISHGUIDE. This mapping, which is shown in Table 2, provides the basis for measuring the people readiness of a target organization. As an example the "Web 2.0 literacy" factor which demonstrates the familiarity level of end-users with Web 2.0 platforms such as Twitter or Facebook can promote the Mashup environment via collective wisdom. Also the end-users, who are already used to notification mechanisms and modern communication channels of Web 2.0, can benefit more effectively from instant interactions in a Mashup environment.

Table 2. People readiness indicators

People Readiness	S	W	I	S	H	G	U	I	D	E
P1 - Web 2.0 literacy		✓		✓						
P2 - Micro-solution					✓		✓	✓		✓
P3 - Finding, Reformatting & Recreating			✓	✓	✓		✓	✓		✓
P4 - Interoperability			✓	✓					✓	
P5 : Broadcasting	✓				✓		✓			
P6 - Digital information organization	✓	✓			✓					

This mapping concept will be extended to a questionnaire which will be answered by everybody in the target organization. It is important to note that the questionnaires can be customized according to organization requirements by expanding each factor and making appropriate questions that correspond to the given factor. Finally the results should be summarized and grouped according to introduced factors.

6   Enterprise Need for Mashups

As the company processes get more complex, business users need to accomplish more elaborated tasks. At the same time companies have to compete with other companies all over the world and adapt themselves to market changes. To stay competitive, they need flexible and agile IT solutions that can support dynamic business models. In this context, Mashup vendors promise improved collaboration, easier knowledge integration with lower costs and shorter development cycles. On the other hand the gain of various businesses from Mashup solution is different and determining the level of need is a challenging issue.

In this section, we will first define the need factors and then a method for evaluation the business needs, based on SWISHGUIDE, will be presented. The business need together with readiness factor of previous section, provides a solid basis for the decision about Mashup undertaking in a given organization.

Table 3. Business need indicators

Business need	S	W	I	S	H	G	U	I	D	E
B1- Customizations					✔		✔	✔		
B2- Collaboration and reuse	✔	✔			✔		✔			
B3 - Managed Interdependency	✔		✔						✔	
B4- Reformatting and recreating information	✔						✔	✔		✔
B5- Service pool						✔	✔			
B6- Service taxonomy	✔		✔	✔		✔				
B7- Security, trust and privacy policies						✔				
B8- Business Adoption		✔		✔			✔	✔		✔
B9- Interoperability	✔		✔	✔					✔	
B10- E-community interaction	✔	✔	✔	✔					✔	

Table 3 demonstrates the mapping between business need factors and the different Mashup benefits which are denoted as SWISHGUIDE. Similar to the readiness survey, a questionnaire will be designed according to the business need factors. Unlike the readiness questionnaire, the business need questionnaire is targeting only the business users.

During the questionnaire design, each business need item (items in Table 3) will correspond to one or more survey questions and finally the summarized result for each business need factor is calculated.

It is important to note that the Mashup need and successful Mashup implementation are two completely different points. The discussed approach should be considered as an input for decision makers and stakeholders regarding business needs.

A simple questionnaire based on the defined indicators in Table 3 which should be answered by business users, looks as follows:

- B1: How extensive are the requests for customizations, new features, new reports or other temporal solutions?
- B2: How important is it for your organization to support collaborative use-cases by sharing and reuse of user-generated solutions?
- B3: In what extent are different departments of your organization dependent to each other (level of data exchange and process dependency)?
- B4: How heavily are manual tasks and self-programmed applications used in your organization?
- B5: How strong is the central governance of department services and user-generated applications in your organization?
- B6: How well are your data resources documented and shared?
- B7: How good are the security, trust and privacy policies implemented in your organization?
- B8: How effectively is your business solution reacting to market changes?
- B9: How often do you run collaborative scenarios with internal and external actors?
- B10: Are you a member of a business online community?

7   Discussion

The proposed method will result in two values: those for "Mashup need" and "Mashup readiness". In addition we need also to define the borderlines of the need-readiness matrix that shape the final decision about the Mashup undertaking process. These borderlines should be decided by domain experts who are also familiar with Mashup solutions. Basically the "need borderline" is depending on the business branch of target organization and the "readiness borderline" should be set based on both branch and organization size. Generally a big enterprise with complex processes should have a higher readiness borderline. It means that such companies should deal with Mashup undertaking more conservatively and consider all aspects very carefully. On the other hand, in a small company (such as a reseller company) the readiness borderline can be set lower compared to the previous case. This is due to the fact that the risk and the business impact are usually lower compared to the case of a big enterprise.

After setting the borderlines, the Mashup undertaking decision can be made according to assessed values for need and readiness in the target organization. For instance, Figure 2 demonstrates the case where the target organization meets the readiness requirements but the business use-cases cannot fully benefit from Mashup solutions. So in this case, the recommendation of Mashup expert could be to keep an eye on business use-cases, and wait till the business needs are big enough for Mashup-based solutions.

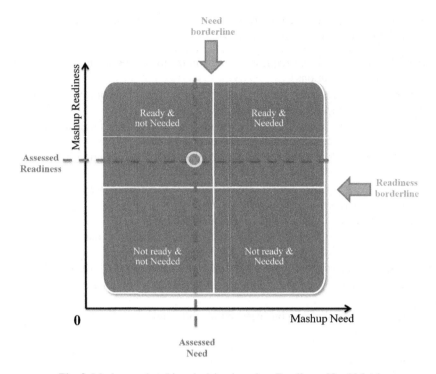

Fig. 2. Mashup undertaking decision based on Readiness-Need Matrix

8   Evaluation

For the evaluation and showing the usefulness of proposed guideline, an international industry and IT service-provider company was selected. This industry company has a strong international adjustment with an increasing need for collaboration and data sharing. Employees from all over the world work together in a project based environment. There are many different applications and systems for project-management, time sheeting, CRM etc used, which gives a good impression on the heterogeneity of the IT landscape.

The evaluation was accomplished following the implementation roadmap of the SWISHGUIDE Framework. The main input for the evaluation was received by interviews according the defined surveys. Based on the survey data the discussed implementation approach was verified.

The evaluation pointed out that the understanding for Mashup solutions and in general for Web 2.0 is still missing in companies. Companies are aware of Web 2.0 technologies like wikis, blogs or social networks, but they often do not know how to benefit from these technologies. Especially for the need survey it was clear that the people could not answer all the questions without additional clarification.

For this specific company, the need for enterprise Mashups was ascertainable; however, the missing fulfillment of the prerequisites and the insufficient readiness factors lead to a no-go decision based on the need-readiness matrix.

9   Conclusion

Enterprise Mashups have gained momentum in modern business and in fulfilling the requirements of Enterprise 2.0; however, the decision about undertaking a Mashup solution in bigger organizations is a major strategic step that involves both objective and subjective decision making processes. Many technical and social factors should be considered before starting with a Mashup solution.

In this paper, the interrelationship between Mashup success factors and business needs are presented and the result is summarized as SWISHGUIDE framework. It is also important to note that the presented methodology is vendor-neutral and discusses an integration guideline to an ideal Mashup-based environment. The results of this study is also shedding a light on business requirements and highlighting the big expectations from a perfect Mashup solution which can be useful for Mashup vendors. This may help them to get a better outlook of Enterprise 2.0 requirements and to get a step closer to perfect Mashup solutions.

References

1. Sweeney, S., Craig, R.: Social Media for Business, p. XV (2011) ISBN: 978-1931644914
2. Newman, A., Thomas, J.: Enterprise 2.0 Implementation: Integrate Web 2.0 Services into Your Enterprise. McGraw-Hill, Osborne (2009)
3. O'Reilly, T.: What Is Web 2.0: Design Patterns and Business Models for the Next Generation of Software (2005), http://oreilly.com/web2/archive/what-is-web-20.html (retrieved June 2012)
4. Jeon, S., Kim, S.T., Lee, D.H.: Web 2.0 business models and value creation. International Journal of Information and Decision Sciences 3(1), 70–84 (2011)
5. Vossen, G.: Web 2.0: From a Buzzword to Mainstream Web Reality. In: Obaidat, M.S., Filipe, J. (eds.) ICETE 2009. CCIS, vol. 130, pp. 53–67. Springer, Heidelberg (2011)
6. Büchner, T., Matthes, F., Neubert, C.: Functional Analysis of Enterprise 2.0 Tools: A Services Catalog. In: Fred, A., Dietz, J.L.G., Liu, K., Filipe, J. (eds.) IC3K 2009. CCIS, vol. 128, pp. 351–363. Springer, Heidelberg (2011)
7. McAfee, A.: Enterprise 2.0: New Collaborative Tools for Your Organization's Toughest Challenges. Harvard Business School Press (2009)
8. Hinchcliffe, D.: The state of Enterprise 2.0 (2007), http://www.zdnet.com/blog/hinchcliffe/the-state-of-enterprise-20/143 (retrieved April 18, 2011)
9. Schein, E.H.: The corporate culture survival guide. John Wiley & Sons (2009)
10. Thomas, D.B., Barlow, M.: The Executive's Guide to Enterprise Social Media Strategy: How Social Networks Are Radically Transforming Your Business. Wiley and SAS Business Series, p. 43 (2011)
11. Andjomshoaa, A., Bader, G., Tjoa, A.: Exploiting Mashup Architecture in Business Use Cases. In: International Conference on Network-Based Information Systems, Indianapolis, USA, pp. xx–xxvii. IEEE (2009)
12. Becker, A., Widjaja, T., Buxmann, P.: Nutzenpotenziale und Herausforderungen des Einsatzes von Serviceorientierten Architekturen. Ergebnisse Einer Empirischen Untersuchung aus Anwender- und Herstellersicht. Wirtschaftsinformatik (2011), doi: 10.1007/s11576-011-0280-4

13. JackBe Corporation, A Business Guide to Enterprise Mashups (2009),
    `http://www.jackbe.com/downloads/jackbe_business_guide_to_ent`
    `erprise_mashups.pdf` (retreived June 2012)
14. Bader, G., Anjomshoaa, A., Tjoa, A.: Privacy Aspects of Mashup Architecture. In: The Second IEEE International Conference on Information Privacy, Security, Risk and Trust (PASSAT 2010), Minneapolis, Minnesota, USA, pp. 1141–1146 (2010)
15. Lawton, G.: Web 2.0 Creates Security Challenges. Computer 40(10), 13–16 (2007), doi:10.1109/MC.2007.367 (retrieved)
16. Ogrinz, M.: Mashup Patterns, Design and Examples for the Modern Enterprise. Addison-Wesley (2009)
17. Tapp, A.: Principles of Direct and Database Marketing: A Digital Orientation, p. 302. Financial Times Prentice Hall (2008)
18. Müller, R.: Project Governance (Fundamentals of Project Management), p. 2. Gower Publishing Ltd. (2009)
19. Pentland, A.S.: Of kith and contentment (2010),
    `http://www.psychologytoday.com/blog/`
    `reality-mining/201004/kith-and-contentment` (retrieved June 2012)
20. Spolsky, J.: Strategy Letter IV: Bloatware and the 80/20 Myth - Joel on Software (2001),
    `http://www.joelonsoftware.com/articles/fog0000000020.html`
    (retrieved June 2012)
21. Lussier, R.N.: Management Fundamentals: Concepts Applications Skill Development, pp. 203–207. South Western Education Publisher (2008)

Artificial Neural Networks Approach
for the Prediction of Thermal Balance
of SI Engine Using Ethanol-Gasoline Blends

Mostafa Kiani Deh Kiani[1], Barat Ghobadian[1,*],
Fathollah Ommi[1], Gholamhassan Najafi[1], and Talal Yusaf[2]

[1] Tarbiat Modares University, Tehran - Iran P.O. Box 14115-111
ghobadib@modares.ac.ir
[2] University of Southern Queensland (USQ) Australia, Toowoomba Campus,
Faculty of Engineering and Surveying Mechanical and Mechatronic Engineering,
talal.yusaf@usq.edu.au

Abstract. This study deals with artificial neural network (ANN) modeling of a spark ignition engine to predict engine thermal balance. To acquire data for training and testing of ANN, a four-cylinder, four-stroke test engine was fuelled with ethanol-gasoline blended fuels with various percentages of ethanol and operated at different engine speeds and loads. The performance of the ANN was validated by comparing the prediction data set with the experimental results. Results showed that the ANN provided the best accuracy in modeling the thermal balance with correlation coefficient equal to 0.997, 0.998, 0.996 and 0.992 for useful work, heat lost through exhaust, heat lost to the cooling water and unaccounted losses respectively. The experimental results showed as the percentage of ethanol in the ethanol-gasoline blends is increased, the percentage of useful work is increased, while the heat lost to cooling water and exhaust are decreased compared to neat gasoline fuel operation.

Keywords: SI engine, thermal balance, ethanol-gasoline blends, artificial neural network.

1 Introduction

Artificial neural networks (ANN) are used to solve a wide variety of problems in science and engineering, particularly for some areas where the conventional modeling methods fail. A well-trained ANN can be used as a predictive model for a specific application, which is a data-processing system inspired by biological neural system. The predictive ability of an ANN results from the training on experimental data and then validation by independent data. An ANN has the ability to re-learn to improve its performance if new data are available [1]. An ANN model can accommodate multiple input variables to predict multiple output variables. It differs from conventional

---

* Corresponding author.

G. Quirchmayr et al. (Eds.): CD-ARES 2012, LNCS 7465, pp. 31–43, 2012.
© IFIP International Federation for Information Processing 2012

modeling approaches in its ability to learn the system that can be modeled without prior knowledge of the process relationships. The prediction by a well-trained ANN is normally much faster than the conventional simulation programs or mathematical models as no lengthy iterative calculations are needed to solve differential equations using numerical methods but the selection of an appropriate neural network topology is important in terms of model accuracy and model simplicity. In addition, it is possible to add or remove input and output variables in the ANN if it is needed. Some researchers studied this method to predict internal combustion engine characteristics. Najafi and his co-worker [2] used ANNs to predict Performance and exhaust emissions of a gasoline engine. Authors in reference [3] have investigated the effect of cetane number on exhaust emissions from engine with the neural network. Canakci and his co-worker [4] analyzed performance and exhaust emissions of a diesel engine fuelled with biodiesel produced from waste frying palm oil using ANN. The effects of valve-timing in a spark ignition engine on the engine performance and fuel economy was investigated by Golcu et al. [5]. Kalogirou [6] reviewed Artificial intelligence for the modeling and control of combustion processes. A number of AI techniques have been described in this paper. Czarnigowski [7] used neural network model-based observer for idle speed control of ignition in SI engine. References [8–15] investigated the performance of various thermal systems with the aid of ANN. The ANN approach was used to predict the performance and exhaust emissions of internal combustion engines [16-22]. In the existing literatures, it was shown that the use of ANN is a powerful modeling tool that has the ability to identify complex relationships from input–output data. Therefore, the objective of this study is to develop a neural network model for predicting the thermal balance of the engine in relation to input variables including engine speed, engine load and fuel blends. The thermal balance was respect of useful work, heat lost through exhaust, heat lost to the cooling water and unaccounted losses (i.e. heat lost by lubricating oil, radiation). This model is of a great significance due to its ability to predict thermal balance of engine under varying conditions.

2   Data Gathering Method

In this study, the experiments were performed on a KIA 1.3 SOHC, four-cylinders, four-stroke, and spark ignition (SI) gasoline engine. Specifications of the engine are presented in Table 1. A 190 kW SCHENCK-WT190 eddy-current dynamometer was used in the experiments in order to measure engine brake power. Fuel consumption rate was measured by using laminar type flow meter, Pierburg model. Air consumption was measured using an air flow meter. The temperatures for the various points were recorded using thermocouples. All of the thermocouples were type-K (Cr–Al). Temperature measuring points are presented in Table 2. Five separate fuel tanks were fitted to the gasoline engine and these contained gasoline and the ethanol-gasoline blends. The experimental setup for gathering data is shown in Fig. 1. The thermal balance from the engine running on ethanol- gasoline blends (E0, E5, E10, E15 and E20) were evaluated. All the blends were tested under varying engine speed (1000-5000 rpm with 500 rpm interval) and at constant engine loads of 25, 50, 70% and full load conditions. Properties of fuels used in this research have been indicated in Table 3.

Table 1. Technical specifications of the test engine

Engine type	SOHC, fuel injected
Number of cylinder	4
Compression ratio	9.7
Bore (mm)	71
Stroke (mm)	83.6
Displacement volume (cc)	1323
Max. power (kW)	64 at 5200 rpm
Cooling system	Water-cooled

Table 2. Points of thermocouples

T1	Inlet water to engine
T2	Outlet water from engine
T3	Inlet air
T4	exhaust gases

Table 3. Properties of ethanol and gasoline

Fuel property	Ethanol	Gasoline
Formula	C2H5OH	C4 to C12
Molecular weight	46.07	100-105
Density, g/cm^3 at 20 ºC	0.79	0.74
Lower heating value, MJ/kg	25.12	45.26
Stochiometric air- fuel ratio, Wight	9	14.7
Specific heat, kJ/kg K	2.38	1.99
Heat of vaporize, kJ/kg	839	305

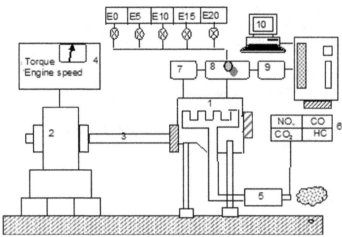

1. Engine; 2.Dynamometer; 3.Drive shaft; 4.Dynamometer control unit, load & speed indicator; 5.Exhaust; 6.Gas analyzer; 7. Air flow meter; 8.Fuel measurement system; 9.Measuring boom; 10.Computer

Fig. 1. Schematic diagram of experimental setup

The thermal losses through the various points were calculated as follows.
The total heat supplied by the fuel (Q_t) was calculated by the following formula:

$$Q_t = \dot{m}_f \cdot CV \tag{1}$$

Where, $\dot{m}_f$ is the fuel consumption rate (kg/s) and CV is the lower calorific value of the fuel, (kJ/kg). The useful work (P_b) was measured by the dynamometer. The heat rejected to the coolant water (Q_w) was determined by:

$$Q_w = \dot{m}_w \cdot C_w \cdot (T_2 - T_1) \tag{2}$$

Where, $\dot{m}_w$ is the water flow rate (kg/s), C_w is the specific heat of water (kJ/kg °C), T_1 is the inlet water temperature (°C) and T_2 is the outlet water temperature (°C). The sensible enthalpy loss is considered for the exhaust flow in this study. The heat lost through the exhaust gases (Q_e) was calculated considering the heat necessary to increase the temperature of the total mass (fuel + air), $\dot{m}_e$ (kg/s), from the outside conditions T_3 (°C) to the temperature of the exhaust T_4 (°C). This heat loss is also known as sensible heat, and to calculate it, it is necessary to calculate the mean specific heat of the exhaust gases (C_e), which, in this case, is assumed to be the value for air with a mean temperature of the exhaust [23].

$$Q_e = \dot{m}_e \cdot C_e \cdot (T_4 - T_3) \tag{3}$$

The unaccounted heat losses are the heat rejected to the oil plus convection and radiation heat losses from the engine external surfaces. The unaccounted heat losses (Q_u) are given as:

$$Q_u = Q_t - (Qw + Qe + Pb) \tag{4}$$

3   Neural Network Design

To get the best prediction by the network, several structures were evaluated and trained using the experimental data. Back-propagation is a network created by generalizing the Widrow-Hoff learning rule to multiple-layer networks and nonlinear differentiable transfer functions. Input vectors and the corresponding target vectors are used to train a network until it can approximate a function.

Networks with biases, a sigmoid layer, and a linear output layer are capable of approximating any function with a finite number of discontinuities. Standard back-propagation is a gradient descent algorithm, as is the Widrow-Hoff learning rule, in which the network weights are moved along the negative of the gradient of the performance function. Each neuron computes a weighted sum of its n input signals, x_j, for j=1, 2... n, and then applies a nonlinear activation function to produce an output signal y:

$$y = \varphi\left(\sum_{j=1}^{n} w_i x_j\right) \tag{5}$$

The performance of the network can be evaluated by comparing the error obtained from converged neural network runs and the measured data. Error was calculated at the end of training and testing processes based on the differences between targeted and calculated outputs. The back-propagation algorithm minimizes an error function defined by the average of the sum square difference between the output of each neuron in the output layer and the desired output. The error function can be expressed as:

$$E = \frac{1}{P}\sum_P \sum_K (d_{PK} - O_{PK})^2 \tag{6}$$

Where p is the index of the p training pairs of vectors, k is the index of elements in the output vector, d_{pk} is the kth element of the pth desired pattern vector, and o_{pk} is the kth element of the output vector when pattern p is presented as input to the network. Minimizing the cost function represented in equation (6) results in an updating rule to adjust the weights of the connections between neurons.

In this research study, the back-propagation neural networks (BPNN) were trained using the training sets formed by including 80 percent of data. After training, the BPNNs were tested using the testing datasets including 38 samples. There were three input and four output parameters in the experimental tests. The input variables are engine speed in rpm and the percentage of ethanol blending with the conventional gasoline fuel and engine load as percentage. The four outputs for evaluating thermal balance include useful work, heat lost through exhaust, heat lost to the cooling water and unaccounted losses as shown in Fig. 2. Therefore the input layer consisted of 3 neurons while the output layer had 4 neurons (Fig. 2).

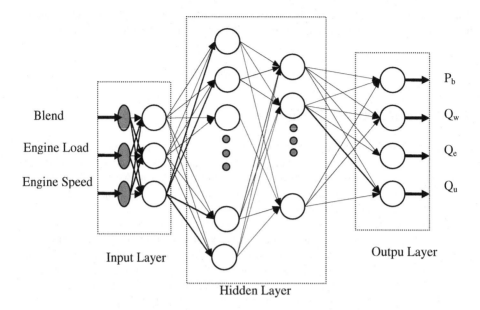

Fig. 2. Configuration of multilayer neural network for predicting engine parameters

The number of hidden layers and neurons within each layer is determined by the complexity of the problem and dataset. In this study, the number of hidden layers varied from one to two. To ensure that each input variable provides an equal contribution in the ANN, the inputs of the model were preprocessed and scaled into a common numeric range (-1,1). The activation function for hidden layer was selected to be the tangent-sigmoid transfer function which is shown in Table 4 as "tan". The output of this function will fall into (-1,1) range. Furthermore, the "sig" symbol in Table 4 represents log-sigmoid transfer function which squashes inputs into (0, 1) range. Linear function suited best for the output layer which is shown as "lin" in Table 4. Therefore, by sig/lin as an example it is meant log-sigmoid transfer function for hidden layer and linear transfer function for the output layer. This arrangement of functions in function approximation problems or modeling is common and yields better results. However many other networks with several functions and topologies were examined which is briefly shown in Table 4. The network topography comprises the number of neurons in the hidden layer and output layer. As depicted in Table 4, several topographies were examined but the 1 hidden layer networks e.g. [25, 4], which implies 25 neurons for the hidden layer and 4 neurons for the output layer, were preferred to 2 hidden layer ones e.g. (15,10,4), 15 neurons for the first hidden layer and 10 neurons for the second hidden layer, since the smaller size of networks is highly preferred. The training algorithms used in this paper were reported as the fastest and the most profitable for the back-propagation algorithm [22]. These fast algorithms fall into two main categories. The first category uses heuristic techniques, which were developed from an analysis of the performance of the standard steepest descent algorithm [22]. Variable learning rate (traingdx) and resilient back-propagation (trainrp) are algorithms of this category. The second category uses standard numerical optimization techniques, which include algorithms like Levenberg- Marquardt (trainlm) and Scaled Conjugate Gradient (trainscg). The function traingdx combines adaptive learning rate with momentum training. Trainrp algorithm has about the same storage requirements as traingdx but is a bit faster. The trainlm algorithm appears to be the fastest method for training moderate-sized feedforward neural networks (up to several hundred weights). Moreover, the basic idea of trainscg is to combine the model-trust region approach (used in the Levenberg-Marquardt algorithm), with the conjugate gradient approach [22].

Three criteria were selected to evaluate the networks and as a result to find the optimum one among them. The training and testing performance (MSE) was chosen to be the error criterion. The complexity and size of network is very important since the selection of hidden layers as well as neurons in the hidden layers should be well adjusted to the network inputs. A reasonably complex model will be able to handle (recognize/classify) new patterns and consequently to generalize. A very simple model will have a low performance and many patterns misclassified. Otherwise, a very complex model may well handle the exceptions present in the training set but may have poor generalization capabilities and hence over-fit the problem. So the smaller ANNs had the priority to be selected. Finally, a regression analysis between the network response (predicted values) and the corresponding targets (measured values) was performed to investigate the network response in more detail. Different training algorithms were tested and Levenberg-Marquardt (trainlm) and trainscg was selected. The computer program MATLAB (R2010a), neural network toolbox was used for ANN design.

Table 4. Summary of different networks evaluated to yield the criteria of network performance

Activation function	Training rule	Net Topography	Testing error	r
sig/lin	trainscg	[10,4]	8.01×10^{-1}	0.99983
tan/lin	trainscg	[15,4]	7.06×10^{-1}	0.99986
tan/lin	traingdx	[20,4]	0.96	0.99875
tan/lin	trainrp	[15,4]	2.33×10^{-1}	0.99928
tan/lin	trainrp	[20,4]	1.23×10^{-1}	0.99921
sig/lin	trainlm	[10,4]	1.06×10^{-1}	o.99933
tan/lin	trainlm	[10,4]	4.56×10^{-2}	o.99963
tan/lin	trainlm	[15,4]	4.06×10^{-2}	o.99976
tan/lin	trainlm	[20,4]	6.09×10^{-2}	0.99986
tan/lin	trainlm	[10,10,4]	1.78×10^{-1}	0.99983
tan/lin	trainlm	[15,15,4]	7.26×10^{-2}	0.99981
tan/lin	trainlm	[15,10,4]	2.11×10^{-1}	0.99985
tan/lin	trainlm	[20,15,4]	3.86×10^{-2}	0.99997
tan/lin	trainlm	[20,20,4]	3.12×10^{-2}	0.99998
tan/lin	trainlm	[25,25,4]	6.17×10^{-2}	0.99995

4   Results

4.1   Results of ANN

The number of hidden layers and neurons within each layer can be determined by the complexity of the problem and data set. In this study, the network was decided to consist of two hidden layers with 20 neurons. The criterion r was selected to evaluate the networks to find the optimum solution. The complexity and size of the network was also an important consideration, and therefore smaller ANNs had to be selected. A regression analysis between the network response and the corresponding targets was performed to investigate the network response in more detail. Different training algorithms were tested and Levenberg-Marquardt (trainlm) was selected. The r-values in Table 4 represent the correlation coefficient between the outputs and targets. The r-value didn't increase beyond 20 neurons in the hidden layers. Consequently the network with 20 neurons in the hidden layers would be considered satisfactory.

From all the networks trained, few ones could provide the low error condition, from which the simplest network was chosen. The results showed that the training algorithm of Back-Propagation was sufficient for predicting useful work, heat lost through exhaust, heat lost to the cooling water and unaccounted losses for different engine speeds, loads and different fuel blends ratios. The predicted versus experimental values for the experimental parameters are indicated in Fig. 3. There is a high correlation between the predicted values by the ANN model and the measured values resulted from experimental tests, which imply that the model succeeded in prediction of the engine thermal balance. It is observed in this figure that the ANN provided the best accuracy in modeling thermal balance with correlation coefficient of 0.997, 0.998, .0.996 and 0.992 for useful work, heat lost through exhaust, heat lost to the cooling water and unaccounted losses respectively. Generally, the artificial neural network offers the advantage of being fast, accurate and reliable in the prediction or approximation affairs, especially when numerical and mathematical methods fail. There is also a significant simplicity in using ANN due to its power to deal with multivariate and complicated problems. The experimental results of this study indicate that as the percentage of ethanol in the ethanol-gasoline blends increased, the percentage of useful work increased, while the other losses decreased as compared to neat gasoline fuel. This is due to the heat of vaporize of ethanol is higher than that of gasoline which makes the temperature of intake manifold lower, and decrease the peak temperature inside the cylinder, so both the exhaust gas temperature as well as the cooling water temperatures, were lower in the case of ethanol-gasoline blend operations, there was less heat loss through these channels, and as such, more useful work was available at the engine crankshaft.

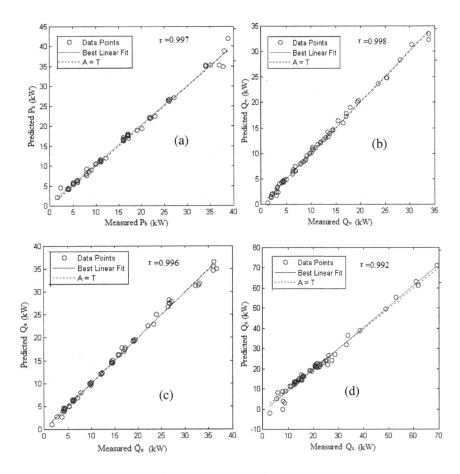

Fig. 3. The predicted outputs vs. the measured values, (a) useful work; (b) heat lost to the cooling water; (c) heat lost through exhaust; (d) unaccounted losses

4.2   Experimental Results

The thermal balance of the test engine operating on gasoline and ethanol-gasoline blends was established at different engine speed and load conditions. The thermal balance analysis and evaluation was carried out regarding useful work, heat lost to cooling water, heat lost through the exhaust and unaccounted losses. The engine thermal balance for the gasoline alone and ethanol-gasoline blends at various speeds and full load are presented in Tables 5-9. It can be seen from these tables that as the percentage of ethanol in the ethanol-gasoline blends is increased, the percentage of useful work is increased, while the heat lost to cooling water and exhaust are decreased compared to neat gasoline fuel operation. At E0, the average of the useful work was 16.76%, whereas it increased to 17.44, 18.11, 18.91 and 19.14% for E5, E10, E15 and E20 ethanol- gasoline blends respectively. Moreover, average of heat lost to cooling water was observed as 16.16, 16.30, 15.77, 15.42 and 14.71% for E0, E5, E10, E15 and E20 respectively. The average of heat lost was 23.07, 22.44, 21.91, 21.36 and 20.71% for the exhaust, and 43.51, 43.82, 44.21, 44.50 and 45.75% for unaccounted losses at E0, E5, E10, E15 and E20 ethanol- gasoline blends respectively. This is due to ethanol contains an oxygen atom in its basic form; it therefore can be treated as a partially oxidized hydrocarbon. When ethanol is added to the blended fuel, it can provide more oxygen for the combustion process and leads to more efficient combustion as compared to gasoline. The heat of vaporize of ethanol (839 kJ/kg) is higher than that of gasoline (305 kJ/kg) which makes the temperature of intake manifold lower, and decrease the peak temperature inside the cylinder, so both the exhaust gas temperature as well as the cooling water temperatures, were lower in the case of ethanol-gasoline blend operations, there was less heat loss through these channels, and as such, more useful work was available at the engine crankshaft.

Table 5. Data of the thermal balance for E0

Speed (rpm)	Q_t (kW)	P_b (kW)	Q_w (kW)	Q_e (kW)	Q_u (kW)
1000	31.31	7.44	3.95	5.18	14.75
1500	48.85	12.13	6.35	7.76	22.61
2000	66.38	17.06	8.96	11.78	28.58
2500	83.92	22.00	11.89	16.88	33.15
3000	101.45	27.16	14.62	22.57	37.10
3500	120.24	32.00	18.54	26.15	43.55
4000	141.54	33.89	23.35	32.15	52.14
4500	162.83	37.00	27.94	36.10	61.78
5000	176.61	37.86	30.43	35.50	72.82

Table 6. Data of the thermal balance for E5

Speed (rpm)	Qt (kW)	Pb (kW)	Qw (kW)	Qe (kW)	Qu (kW)
1000	32.79	8.08	4.47	5.34	14.90
1500	47.80	12.00	6.69	7.90	21.21
2000	64.95	16.78	9.46	12.06	26.65
2500	83.34	21.84	12.50	16.77	32.23
3000	99.27	26.90	15.53	22.90	33.95
3500	117.65	32.00	19.46	26.35	39.85
4000	138.49	34.00	23.54	32.23	48.72
4500	159.32	36.79	28.12	35.90	58.52
5000	174.03	38.13	31.59	35.06	69.25

Table 7. Data of the thermal balance for E10

Spee (rpm) d	Q_t (kW)	P_b (kW)	Q_w (kW)	Q_e (kW)	Q_u (kW)
1000	29.75	7.47	4.32	5.34	12.63
1500	46.41	12.12	7.01	7.74	19.55
2000	63.08	17.00	10.09	11.81	24.18
2500	80.93	21.79	13.42	17.19	28.53
3000	96.40	27.00	16.70	23.06	29.65
3500	113.06	32.02	20.35	26.33	34.36
4000	134.48	34.79	24.93	31.77	42.99
4500	154.72	37.06	29.61	35.66	52.39
5000	169.00	38.89	33.16	36.01	60.94

Table 8. Data of the thermal balance for E15

speed (rpm)	Q_t (kW)	P_b (kW)	Q_w (kW)	Q_e (kW)	Q_u (kW)
1000	28.88	7.55	4.40	5.52	11.41
1500	45.05	11.93	7.21	8.02	17.89
2000	61.22	17.12	10.25	12.32	21.52
2500	77.39	21.84	13.32	16.57	25.66
3000	94.71	27.07	17.05	23.32	27.27
3500	109.73	31.92	20.37	27.08	30.36
4000	130.52	34.06	25.26	32.77	38.43
4500	151.31	36.07	30.26	36.51	48.47
5000	165.17	38.96	33.78	35.70	56.73

Table 9. Data of the thermal balance for E20

speed (rpm)	Q_t (kW)	P_b (kW)	Q_w (kW)	Q_e (kW)	Q_u (kW)
1000	28.11	7.62	4.5	5.54	10.45
1500	43.85	11.96	7.35	8.17	16.37
2000	59.60	16.69	10.39	12.62	19.90
2500	76.46	22.97	13.76	17.27	22.46
3000	92.20	26.98	17.39	23.59	24.24
3500	107.95	32.06	20.74	27.01	28.14
4000	127.06	35.08	25.21	33.10	33.67
4500	147.30	37.00	29.70	36.72	43.89
5000	160.80	38.10	33.77	36.11	52.82

5   Conclusion

An artificial neural network (ANN) was developed and trained with the collected data of this research work. The results showed that the three layer feed-forward neural network with two hidden layers ([20,20,4]) was sufficient enough in predicting thermal balance for different engine speeds, loads and different fuel blends ratios. It can be concluded that high values of regression coefficients yielded when setting a regression line for predicted and measured datasets.

The experimental results showed as the percentage of ethanol in the ethanol-gasoline blends is increased, the percentage of useful work is increased, while the heat lost to cooling water and exhaust are decreased compared to neat gasoline fuel operation.

References

1. Graupe, D.: Principles of artificial neural networks. In: Circuits and Systems, 2nd edn. Advanced Series, p. 303. World Scientific, USA (2007)
2. Najafi, G., Ghobadian, B., Tavakoli, T., Buttsworth, D., Yusaf, T., Faizollahnejad, M.: Performance and exhaust emissions of a gasoline engine with ethanol blended gasoline fuels using artificial neural network. Applied Energy 86, 630–639 (2009)
3. Yuanwang, D., Meilin, Z., Dong, X., Xiaobei, C.: An analysis for effect of cetane number on exhaust emissions from engine with the neural network. Fuel 81, 1963–1970 (2003)
4. Canakci, M., Ozsezen, A.N., Arcaklioglu, E., Erdil, A.: Prediction of performance and exhaust emissions of a diesel engine fueled with biodiesel produced from waste frying palm oil. Expert Systems with Applications 36, 9268–9280 (2009)
5. Golcu, M., Sekmen, Y., Erduranli, P., Salman, S.: Artificial neural network based modeling of variable valve-timing in a spark ignition engine. Applied Energy 81, 187–197 (2005)
6. Kalogirou, S.A.: Artificial intelligence for the modeling and control of combustion processes: a review. Progress in Energy and Combustion Science 29, 515–566 (2003)
7. Czarnigowski, J.: A neural network model-based observer for idle speed control of ignition in SI engine. Engineering Applications of Artificial Intelligence 23, 1–7 (2010)
8. Kalogirou, S.A.: Application of artificial neural-networks for energy systems. Applied Energy 7, 17–35 (2006)
9. Prieto, M.M., Montanes, E., Menendez, O.: Power plant condenser performance forecasting using a non-fully connected ANN. Energy 26, 65–79 (2001)
10. Chouai, A., Laugeier, S., Richon, D.: Modelling of thermodynamic properties using neural networks – application to refrigerants. Fluid Phase Equilibria 199, 53–62 (2002)
11. Sozen, A., Arcaklioglu, E., Ozalp, M.: A new approach to thermodynamic analysis of ejector-absorption cycle: artificial neural networks. Applied Thermal Engineering 23, 937–952 (2003)
12. Arcaklioglu, E.: Performance comparison of CFCs with their substitutes using artificial neural network. Energy Research 28, 1113–1125 (2004)
13. Ertunc, H.M., Hosoz, M.: Artificial neural network analysis of a refrigeration system with an evaporative condenser. Applied Thermal Engineering 26, 627–635 (2006)

14. De Kaiadi, M., Fast, M., Assadi, M.: Development of an artificial neural network model for the steam process of a coal biomass cofired combined heat and power (CHP) plant in Sweden. Energy 32, 2099–2109 (2007)

15. Hannani, S.K., Hessari, E., Fardadi, M., Jeddi, M.K.: Mathematical modeling of cooking pots' thermal efficiency using a combined experimental and neural network method. Energy 31, 2969–2985 (2007)

16. Canakci, M., Erdil, A., Arcaklioglu, E.: Performance and exhaust emissions of a biodiesel engine. Applied Energy 83, 594–605 (2006)

17. Arcaklioglu, E., Celikten, I.: A diesel engine's performance and exhaust emissions. Applied Energy 80, 11–22 (2005)

18. Celik, V., Arcaklioglu, E.: Performance maps of a diesel engine. Applied Energy 81, 247–259 (2005)

19. Parlak, A., Islamoglu, Y., Yasar, H., Egrisogut, A.: Application of artificial neural network to predict specific fuel consumption and exhaust temperature for a diesel engine. Applied Thermal Engineering 26, 824–828 (2006)

20. Ghobadian, B., Rahimi, H., Nikbakht, A.M., Najafi, G., Yusaf, T.: Diesel engine performance and exhaust emission analysis using waste cooking biodiesel fuel with an artificial neural network. Renewable Energy 34(4), 976–982 (2009)

21. Sayin, C., Ertunc, H., Hosoz, M., Kilicaslan, I., Canakci, M.: Performance and exhaust emissions of a gasoline engine using artificial neural network. Applied Thermal Engineering 27, 46–54 (2007)

22. Kiani Deh Kiani, M., Ghobadian, B., Nikbakht, A.M., Najafi, G.: Application of artificial neural networks for the prediction of performance and exhaust emissions in SI engine using ethanol-gasoline blends. Energy 35(1), 65–69 (2010)

23. Hakan, O., Soylemez, M.S.: Thermal balance of a LPG fuelled, four stroke SI engine with water addition. Energy Conversion and Management 47, 570–581 (2006)

Validation of XML Documents with SWRL[*]

Jesús M. Almendros-Jiménez

Dpto. de Lenguajes y Computación,
Universidad de Almería, Spain
jalmen@ual.es

Abstract. In this paper we describe how XML documents are mapped into an OWL ontology and how SWRL rules are used to validate the semantic content of XML documents. XML completion and data constraints are specified with SWRL. The semantic completion of the XML document can be mapped into a semantic completion of the corresponding ontology. Besides, SWRL serves for specifying and reasoning with data constraints. We will illustrate our approach with an example that shows that user intervention is vital to XML mapping and completion and SWRL helps to detect relevant data constraints. The approach has been tested with the well-known Protégé tool.

1 Introduction

In the database scientific community many efforts have been achieved to give semantic content to data sources. The entity-relationship (ER) model, functional dependences and integrity constraints are key elements of database design. ER model gives semantics to data relations and restrict cardinality of relations. Functional dependences establish data dependences and key values. Integrity constraints impose restrictions over data values in a certain domain.

The *eXtensible Markup Language (XML)* [W3C07] is equipped with data definition languages (*DTD* [W3C99] and *XML Schema* [W3C09c]) whose aim is to describe the syntactic structure of XML documents. Well-formed XML documents conform to the corresponding DTD and XML Schema. However, even when XML documents can be well-formed, the content can be redundant which can lead to inconsistency, as well as the content can violate imposed restrictions over data.

Most available XML resources lack in the description of semantic content. But it also happens for syntactic content: DTD and XML schemas might not available in Web resources. It makes that data exchange fails due to bad understanding of XML content. Nevertheless, XML records can follow the same pattern and the user could help to discover and recover the semantic content of XML resources. This task is not easy and should be supported by tools. Such tools should be able

---

[*] This work has been supported by the Spanish Ministry MICINN under grant TIN2008-06622-C03-03, Ingenieros Alborada IDI under grant TRA2009-0309, and the JUNTA de ANDALUCÍA (proyecto de excelencia) ref. TIC-6114.

G. Quirchmayr et al. (Eds.): CD-ARES 2012, LNCS 7465, pp. 44–57, 2012.

to analyze the semantic content of XML data revealing fails on interpretation. In order to help tools in the interpretation, the user could provide the intended meaning of resources.

RDF(S) [KC04] and OWL [MPSP+08] emerge as solutions for equipping Web data with semantic content. Unfortunately, most of database management systems do not offer exporting facilities to RDF(S) and OWL, although some efforts have been carried out (see [KSM08] for a survey). XML has been usually adopted as database exchange format. For this reason, some authors have described how to map XML into RDF(S)/OWL and add semantic content to XML documents.

On one hand, most proposals focus on the mapping of the XML schema into RDF(S)/OWL. In some cases, the mapping is exploited for reasoning (conformance and completion, among others). On the other hand, in many cases, the mapping, when the XML schema is present, can be automatically accomplished. Nevertheless, some of them work when the XML schema is missing, requiring the user intervention, who specifies a set of mapping rules. Finally, most of cases tools have been developed with this end, based on XML transformation and query languages like XSLT and XPath.

In this paper we describe how XML documents are mapped into an OWL ontology and how SWRL rules are used to validate the semantic content of XML documents. SWRL rules enable to express constraints on XML data, and they can be triggered in order to validate the constraints. The approach has been tested with the well-known Protégé tool.

We can summarize the main contributions of our proposal as follows:

- XML into OWL mapping is carried out by specifying mappings from tags and attributes into concepts, roles and individuals of the ontology. Such mappings are defined with XPath. The ontology is created from the mapping, firstly, at instance level and, secondly, by adding ontology axioms with SWRL.
- SWRL is used for two main tasks:
  (a) to add new semantic information to the ontology instance generated from the XML document. Such information can be considered as a completion of the XML model. In particular, such rules can create additional classes and roles, and therefore extending the ontology initially created from the mapping with new axioms and instance relations. In other words, SWRL serves as ontology definition language in the phase of completion; and
  (b) to express data constraints on the XML document. SWRL can be used for expressing relations that the ontology instance has to satisfy. Therefore SWRL is a vehicle for reasoning with the semantic content and therefore for analyzing XML resources.

Our approach aims to provide a method for specifying a transformation rather than to consider automatic mapping from the XML Schema. XML completion and data constraints are specified with SWRL. The semantic completion of the XML document can be mapped into a semantic completion of the corresponding ontology. Besides, SWRL serves for specifying and reasoning with data constraints. We will illustrate our approach with an example that shows that user intervention is vital to XML mapping and completion and SWRL helps to detect relevant data constraints.

The drawbacks of our approach are the following. The kind of ontology we can handle is limited to SWRL expressivity. Since we create the target ontology with SWRL, OWL meta-data axioms are defined with SWRL rules. In other words, SWRL is taken as ontology definition language in the line of [KMH11, KRH08]. However, therefore there are some completions/data constraints that cannot be specified. In particular, those involving universally quantified constraints cannot be specified.

One feasible extension of our work is to move to SQWRL [OD09], which extends SWRL to a more powerful query language. It is considered as future work. With regard to the choice of SWRL as ontology definition language, we could express completions/data constraints with a suitable OWL 2 fragment (for instance, EL, RL and QL) [W3C09a, W3C09b]. However, in such a case, we would also have a limited expressivity.

1.1   Related Work

XML Schema mapping into RDF(S)/OWL has been extensively studied.

In an early work [FZT04] XML Schema is mapped into RDF(S) meta-data and individuals. In [BA05], they propose an small set of mapping rules from XML Schema into OWL and define a transformation with XSLT. In [TC07], they also propose an XSLT based transformation from XML Schema to OWL that allows the inverse transformation, i.e. convert individuals from OWL to XML. The inverse transformation is usually called *lowering*, and the direct one is called *lifting*. Besides, in [XC06], XML schemas are mapped into RDF(S) and they make use of the mapping for query processing in the context of data integration and interoperation. This is also the case of [BMPS+11], in which the authors propose a set of patterns to automatically transform an XML schema to OWL. Such patterns are obtained from pattern recognition. Manual mapping has been considered in [TLLJ08], in which the authors translate XML schemas and data to RDF(S) with user intervention.

In some cases the target ontology has to be present, that is, the mapping from XML into OWL aims to populate the ontology with individuals. For instance, in the proposals [RRC08, AKKP08, RRC06, VDPM+08], the authors transform XML resources to RDF(S) and OWL format, in the presence of an existing ontology and with user intervention. The mapping rules can be specified with Java (for instance, in [RRC08]), and with domain specific languages (for instance, with XSPARQL [AKKP08]).

Manual mappings are in many cases based on XPath expressions. In [GC09], they describe how to map XML documents into an ontology, using XPath for expressing the location in the XML document of OWL concepts and roles. In [OD11] they employs XPath to map XML documents into OWL, extending the set of OWL constructors to represent XML resources. Besides XPath is used to describe mappings in the XSPARQL framework [AKKP08].

Finally, some authors have explored how to exploit the mapping for XML validation. For instance, in [WRC08], they describe how to map the XML Schema into Description Logic (DL) and they make use of DL for model validation and completion and as query language. Besides, in [ZYMC11], they map XML into OWL (and DL) and they study how to reason about the XML schema, in the sense of that, to check conformance of XML documents, and to prove inclusion, equivalence and disjointness of XML schemas. SWRL has been employed in [LSD$^+$09] for data normalization, encoding schemas and functional dependences with DL.

Comparing our work with existent proposals we find some similarities with the work described in [OD11] in which they employ XPath for manual mapping and a rich OWL fragment for describing concept and role relations.

1.2   Structure of the Paper

The structure of the paper is as follows. Section 2 will present a running example. Section 3 will describe how to map XML documents into OWL. Section 4 will focus on how to complete the semantic content of XML documents. Section 5 will show how to validate XML constraints and, finally, Section 6 will conclude and present future work.

2   Running Example

Let us suppose that we have the XML resource of Figure 1. The document lists *papers* and *researchers* involved in a *conference*. Each *paper* and *researcher* has an identifier (represented by the attribute *id*), and has an associated set of labels: *title* and *wordCount* for *papers* and *name* for *researchers*. Furthermore, they have attributes: *studentPaper* for *papers* and *isStudent, manuscript* and *referee* for *researchers*. The meaning of the attributes *manuscript* and *referee* is that the given researcher has submitted the paper of number described by *manuscript* as well as (s)he has participated as reviewer of the paper of number given by *referee*.

It is worth observing that the document uses identifiers for cross references between papers and researches. It is just for simplifying the example, and it is not real restriction of our approach. It does not mean that interesting examples come from resources where cross references are given.

Now, let us suppose that we would like to analyze the semantic content of the XML document. We would like to know whether some paper violates the restriction on the number of words of submissions. In order to do this we could execute the following XPath query:

```
/conference/papers/paper[wordCount>10000]
```

and it gives us the papers whose attribute *wordCount* is greater than 10000. This is a typical restriction that can be analyzed with XPath.

```
<?xml version='1.0'?>
<conference>
<papers>
<paper id="1" studentPaper="true">
<title> XML Schemas </title>
<wordCount> 1200 </wordCount>
</paper>
<paper id="2" studentPaper="false">
<title> XML and OWL </title>
<wordCount> 2800 </wordCount>
</paper>
<paper id="3" studentPaper="true">
<title> OWL and RDF </title>
<wordCount> 12000 </wordCount>
</paper>
</papers>
<researchers>
<researcher id="a" isStudent="false" manuscript="1"
         referee="1">
<name>Smith </name>
</researcher>
<researcher id="b" isStudent="true" manuscript="1"
         referee="2">
<name>Douglas </name>
</researcher>
<researcher id="c" isStudent="false" manuscript="2"
         referee="3">
<name>King </name>
</researcher>
<researcher id="d" isStudent="true" manuscript="2"
         referee="1">
<name>Ben</name>
</researcher>
<researcher id="e" isStudent="false" manuscript="3"
         referee="3">
<name>William </name>
</researcher>
</researchers>
</conference>
```

Fig. 1. Running Example

However, we can complicate the situation when papers are classified as student and senior papers which have different restrictions of length. Fortunately, each paper has been labeled with this information, that is, with the attribute *studentPaper*. However, it is redundant in the document. That is, we have information about submitters and whether they are student or not. In the case papers are not labeled with the attribute *studentPaper*, the XPath query becomes more complex. In general, missing and redundant information in XML resources makes XPath based analysis more complex to make.

The goal of our approach is to be able to extract from the XML document the semantic content and validate the content. In particular, it involves to analyze cross references. Besides, the process of extraction is guided by the user who knows (or at least (s)he can suspect) the meaning of the given labels and attributes.

In XML Schema based translations, such semantic information could not be specified in the document therefore the user intervention is also required. Semantic validation of XML documents ranges from restrictions imposed over data such as "the attribute *wordCount* has to be smaller than 10000" to properly integrity constraints as "the reviewer of a paper cannot be the submitter". Assuming that senior papers cannot have students as authors, inconsistent information comes from senior papers having an student as author.

Validation can be improved by completing the XML model. Completion means to add new information that can be deduced from the original resource.

For instance, in the running example, we can add the *author* for each *paper*, which can be obtained as the inverse of the value of the *manuscript* attribute of each *researcher*. In the case the attribute *studentPaper* was not included, we can add this information from the information about *researcher*s using the *isStudent* attribute. Besides, the semantic extraction can be more accurate. For instance, we can define the classes *Student, Senior* as subclasses of *Researcher*, and *PaperofSenior* and *PaperofStudent* as subclasses of *Paper*. *PaperofSenior* class is defined as the subclass of papers whose value *studentPaper* is false and *Student* can be defined as the subclass of researchers whose value *isStudent* is true. We can also define the *Reviewed* class as the subclass of papers which have at least one *referee*.

The definition of such ontology based completion facilitates the description of data constraints. For instance, *authors* of *PaperofSenior* cannot be *Student*s. In order to express data constraints we have adopted a simple solution in our approach. We will define new ontology classes that represent data constraints. For instance, the class *BadPaperCategory* can be defined as the class of senior papers having an student as author, while the class *NoSelfReview* can be defined as the class of papers having a referee which is also the author of the paper. When the classes *BadPaperCategory* and *NoSelfReview* are not empty, the XML document violates the required constraints.

Our approach has in the spirit to provide a methodology for XML validation. Our proposal distinguishes three steps: mapping, completion and validation. The following sections will describe each one of these steps using the running example.

3   Mapping XML into OWL

The first step consists in the XML into OWL mapping with rules. Mapping rules establish a correspondence from XPath expressions to ontology concepts:

$$xp_1 \mapsto C_1, \ldots, xp_n \mapsto C_n$$

and from pairs of XPath expressions to ontology roles:

$$(xp'_1, xp''_1) \mapsto r_1 \ldots, (xp'_m, xp''_m) \mapsto r_m$$

Mapping works at the instance level, creating instances of concepts and roles from XML items. Concepts and roles belong to the target ontology.

For instance, let us suppose that the programmer wants to transform the running example. The programmer, firstly, has to define paths to access to individuals and property values:

```
(a)  doc('papers.xml')//papers/researcher/@id
(b)  doc('papers.xml')//papers/researcher/name
(c)  doc('papers.xml')//papers/researcher/isStudent
(d)  doc('papers.xml')//papers/researcher/@manuscript
(e)  doc('papers.xml')//papers/researcher/@referee
```

and, secondly, has to map them into ontology concepts and roles as follows: $a \mapsto$ Researcher, $(a, b) \mapsto$ name, $(a, c) \mapsto$ isStudent, $(a, d) \mapsto$ manuscript and $(a, e) \mapsto$ referee. The same can be done from papers:

```
(f)  doc('papers.xml')//papers/paper/@id
(g)  doc('papers.xml')//papers/paper/title
(h)  doc('papers.xml')//papers/paper/wordCount
(i)  doc('papers.xml')//papers/paper/@StudentPaper
```

in which the mapping is as follows: $f \mapsto$ Paper, $(f, g) \mapsto$ title, $(f, h) \mapsto$ wordCount and $(f, i) \mapsto$ StudentPaper.

The mapping obtains and ontology for researchers (see Figure 2) and an ontology for papers (see Figure 3).

4 Semantic Completion

The second step consists in the XML completion using SWRL rules. The completion is defined in terms of the target OWL ontology.

SWRL rules are used to define new concepts and roles $C'_1, \ldots, C'_s, r'_1, \ldots, r'_l$ from $C_1, \ldots, C_n$ and $r_1, \ldots, r_m$. Completion aims to structure the semantic information and to infer new information.

SWRL allows to express "and" conditions by means of "$\wedge$", and OWL classes and properties can be used as atoms in the antecedent and the consequent: $C(?x)$ means that $?x$ is an individual of the class C, and $P(?x, ?y)$ means that the property P holds for $?x$ and $?y$, where $?x$ and $?y$ are variables that in SWRL starts with "?". Moreover, SWRL admits the use of the built-ins "greaterThanOrEqual" and "lessThan" whose role is to restrict the numeric value of the variables.

For instance, let us suppose that the programmer wants to specify the completion of the running example by defining the concepts *PaperofSenior*, *PaperofStudent* and *Reviewed* as subclasses of the concept *Paper*:

```
<rdf:RDF>
<owl:Class  rdf:about="#Researcher"/>
<rdf:Property  rdf:about="#manuscript"/>
<rdf:Property  rdf:about="#referee"/>
<owl:DatatypeProperty  rdf:about="#name"/>
<owl:DatatypeProperty  rdf:about="#isStudent"/>
 <owl:Thing  rdf:about="#a">
    <rdf:type  rdf:resource="#Researcher"/>
    <name>Smith</name>
    <isStudent>false</isStudent>
    <manuscript  rdf:resource="#1"/>
    <referee  rdf:resource="#1"/>
 </owl:Thing>
<owl:Thing  rdf:about="#b">
    <rdf:type  rdf:resource="#Researcher"/>
    <name>Douglas</name>
    <isStudent>true</isStudent>
    <manuscript  rdf:resource="#1"/>
    <referee  rdf:resource="#2"/>
 </owl:Thing>
<owl:Thing  rdf:about="#c">
    <rdf:type  rdf:resource="#Researcher"/>
    <name>King</name>
    <isStudent>false</isStudent>
    <manuscript  rdf:resource="#2"/>
    <referee  rdf:resource="#3"/>
 </owl:Thing>
 </rdf:RDF>
```

Fig. 2. Ontology for researchers

```
PaperofSenior(?x) -> Paper(?x)
Reviewed(?x) -> Paper(?x)
studentPaper(?x,false) -> PaperofSenior(?x)
studentPaper(?x,true) -> PaperofStudent(?x)
referee(?x,?y) -> Reviewed(?x)
```

Moreover, (s)he defines the inverse relations of *manuscript* and *referee* (defined as *author* and *submission*), and the classes *Student* and *Senior* as subclasses of *Researcher* as follows:

```
manuscript(?x,?y) -> author(?y,?x)
referee(?x,?y) -> submission(?y,?x)
isStudent(?x,true) -> Student(?x)
isStudent(?x,false) -> Senior(?x)
Student(?x) -> Researcher(?x)
Senior(?x) -> Researcher(?x)
```

```
<rdf:RDF>
<owl:Class rdf:about="#Paper"/>
<owl:DatatypeProperty rdf:about="#studentPaper"/>
<owl:DatatypeProperty rdf:about="#title"/>
<owl:DatatypeProperty rdf:about="#wordCount"/>
 <owl:Thing rdf:about="#1">
    <rdf:type rdf:resource="#Paper"/>
    <studentPaper>true</studentPaper>
    <title>XML Schemas</title>
    <wordCount>1200</wordCount>
 </owl:Thing>
 <owl:Thing rdf:about="#2">
    <rdf:type rdf:resource="#Paper"/>
    <studentPaper>false</studentPaper>
    <title>XML and OWL</title>
    <wordCount>2800</wordCount>
 </owl:Thing>
 <owl:Thing rdf:about="#3">
    <rdf:type rdf:resource="#Paper"/>
    <studentPaper>true</studentPaper>
    <title>OWL and RDF</title>
    <wordCount>12000</wordCount>
 </owl:Thing>
</rdf:RDF>
```

Fig. 3. Ontology for papers

Let us remark that SWRL is used for describing meta-data relationships, and some of them correspond to OWL 2 relationships. For instance, they can be expressed as

$$\text{PaperofSenior} \sqsubseteq \text{Paper}$$

$$\exists \text{studentPaper}.\{\text{false}\} \sqsubseteq \text{PaperofSenior}$$

$$\exists \text{referee}.\top \sqsubseteq \text{Reviewed}$$

However, we make use of SWRL as ontology definition language for expressing ontology relationships.

The semantic completion will obtain the ontologies of Figures 4 and 5. We have classified researchers and papers as seniors and students, and papers as papers of students and seniors, and reviewed.

5   Validation

The last step consists in the definition of data constraints with SWRL. New concepts are defined from $C_1, \ldots, C_n, C'_1, \ldots, C'_s, r_1, \ldots, r_m$ and $r'_1, \ldots, r'_l$, and individuals of such concepts violate data constraints.

```
<rdf:RDF>
    <owl:Thing rdf:about="#a">
      <submission rdf:resource="#1"/>
      <rdf:type rdf:resource="#Senior"/>
    </owl:Thing>
    <owl:Thing rdf:about="#b">
      <submission rdf:resource="#2"/>
      <rdf:type rdf:resource="#Student"/>
    </owl:Thing>
    <owl:Thing rdf:about="#c">
      <submission rdf:resource="#3"/>
      <rdf:type rdf:resource="#Senior"/>
    </owl:Thing>
    <owl:Thing rdf:about="#d">
      <submission rdf:resource="#1"/>
      <rdf:type rdf:resource="#Student"/>
    </owl:Thing>
    <owl:Thing rdf:about="#e">
      <submission rdf:resource="#3"/>
      <rdf:type rdf:resource="#Senior"/>
    </owl:Thing>
</rdf:RDF>
```

Fig. 4. Completion of researchers

```
<rdf:RDF>
<owl:Thing   rdf:about="#1">
      <rdf:type rdf:resource="#PaperofStudent"/>
      <rdf:type rdf:resource="#Reviewed"/>
      <author rdf:resource="#a"/>
      <author rdf:resource="#b"/>
    </owl:Thing>
    <owl:Thing rdf:about="#2">
      <rdf:type rdf:resource="#PaperofSenior"/>
      <rdf:type rdf:resource="#Reviewed"/>
      <author rdf:resource="#c"/>
      <author rdf:resource="#d"/>
    </owl:Thing>
    <owl:Thing rdf:about="#3">
      <rdf:type rdf:resource="#PaperofStudent"/>
      <rdf:type rdf:resource="#Reviewed"/>
      <author rdf:resource="#e"/>
    </owl:Thing>
</rdf:RDF>
```

Fig. 5. Completion of papers

For instance, in the running example, the programmer can define the concepts *PaperLength, NoSelfReview, NoStudentReview* and *BadPaperCategory* with the following rules:

```
wordCount(?x,?y) ^ greaterThanOrEqual(?y,10000)
                        -> PaperLength(?x)
manuscript(?x,?y) ^ submission(?x,?y)
                        -> NoSelfReview(?x)
Student(?x) ^ submission(?x,?y)
                        -> NoStudentReviewer(?x)
manuscript(?x,?y) ^ Student(?x)
    ^ PaperofSenior(?y)    -> BadPaperCategory(?x)
```

Finally, they can be triggered, obtaining the following results:

```
<result>
    <owl:Thing    rdf:about="#3">
      <rdf:type  rdf:resource="#PaperLength"/>
    </owl:Thing>
    <owl:Thing    rdf:about="#a">
      <rdf:type  rdf:resource="#NoSelfReview"/>
    </owl:Thing>
    <owl:Thing    rdf:about="#e">
      <rdf:type  rdf:resource="#NoSelfReview"/>
    </owl:Thing>
    <owl:Thing    rdf:about="#b">
      <rdf:type  rdf:resource="#NoStudentReviewer"/>
    </owl:Thing>
    <owl:Thing    rdf:about="#d">
      <rdf:type  rdf:resource="#NoStudentReviewer"/>
    </owl:Thing>
    <owl:Thing    rdf:about="#d">
      <rdf:type  rdf:resource="#BadPaperCategory"/>
    </owl:Thing>
    <owl:Thing    rdf:about="#2">
      <rdf:type  rdf:resource="#BadPaperCategory"/>
    </owl:Thing>
</result>
```

The result shows that the paper length is exceeded by paper #3, the authors of #a and #e have reviewed their own paper, #b and #d are students that review a paper, and finally the researcher #d is an student with a senior paper and #2 is a senior paper with an student as author.

We have tested our approach with the Protégé tool (version 4.1) using the Hermit reasoner (version 1.3.4). The Hermit reasoner has been used for triggering the completion rules and data constraints from the mapping of XML into OWL. Figure 6 shows an snapshot of the validation results obtained from Hermit and Protégé.

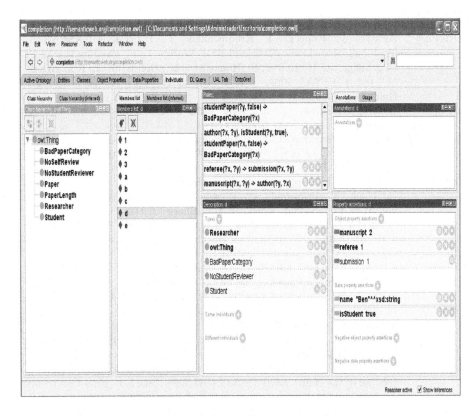

Fig. 6. Visualization of Validation in Protegé

6   Conclusions and Future Work

In this paper we have studied how to validate XML documents from a mapping into OWL and the use of SWRL. We have described how to complete XML/OWL models and how to specify data constraints with SWRL.

As future work, we would like to extend our work in the following directions. Firstly, we could move to a more expressive language, SQWRL, in order to be able to express more complex data constraints. Secondly, we would like to study how to map XML into OWL by using the XML Schema. Finally, we would like to fully integrate our proposal with the Protégé tool. We have in mind the development of a Protégé plugin for the edition and execution of transformations in Protégé. The plugin would allow to validate XML documents in Protégé, and the use of OWL constructors/SWRL to specify completions/data constraints.

References

[AKKP08]   Akhtar, W., Kopecký, J., Krennwallner, T., Polleres, A.: XSPARQL: Traveling between the XML and RDF Worlds – and Avoiding the XSLT Pilgrimage. In: Bechhofer, S., Hauswirth, M., Hoffmann, J., Koubarakis, M. (eds.) ESWC 2008. LNCS, vol. 5021, pp. 432–447. Springer, Heidelberg (2008)

[BA05]   Bohring, H., Auer, S.: Mapping XML to OWL ontologies. Leipziger Informatik-Tage 72, 147–156 (2005)

[BMPS⁺11] Bedini, I., Matheus, C.J., Patel-Schneider, P.F., Boran, A., Nguyen, B.: Transforming XML Schema to OWL Using Patterns. In: ICSC, pp. 102–109. IEEE (2011)

[FZT04]   Ferdinand, M., Zirpins, C., Trastour, D.: Lifting XML Schema to OWL. In: Koch, N., Fraternali, P., Wirsing, M. (eds.) ICWE 2004. LNCS, vol. 3140, pp. 354–358. Springer, Heidelberg (2004)

[GC09]   Ghawi, R., Cullot, N.: Building Ontologies from XML Data Sources. In: 20th International Workshop on Database and Expert Systems Application, DEXA 2009, pp. 480–484. IEEE (2009)

[KC04]   Klyne, G., Carroll, J.J.: Resource Description Framework (RDF): Concepts and Abstract Syntax. Technical report (2004), http://www.w3.org/TR/2004/REC-rdf-concepts-20040210/

[KMH11]   Krisnadhi, A., Maier, F., Hitzler, P.: OWL and Rules. In: Polleres, A., d'Amato, C., Arenas, M., Handschuh, S., Kroner, P., Ossowski, S., Patel-Schneider, P. (eds.) Reasoning Web 2011. LNCS, vol. 6848, pp. 382–415. Springer, Heidelberg (2011)

[KRH08]   Krötzsch, M., Rudolph, S., Hitzler, P.: Description Logic Rules. In: Proceeding of the 2008 conference on ECAI 2008: 18th European Conference on Artificial Intelligence, pp. 80–84. IOS Press (2008)

[KSM08]   Konstantinou, N., Spanos, D.E., Mitrou, N.: Ontology and database mapping: A survey of current implementations and future directions. Journal of Web Engineering 7(1), 1–24 (2008)

[LSD⁺09]   Li, Y.F., Sun, J., Dobbie, G., Lee, S., Wang, H.H.: Verifying semistructured data normalization using SWRL. In: Third IEEE International Symposium on Theoretical Aspects of Software Engineering, TASE 2009, pp. 193–200. IEEE (2009)

[MPSP⁺08] Motik, B., Patel-Schneider, P.F., Parsia, B., Bock, C., Fokoue, A., Haase, P., Hoekstra, R., Horrocks, I., Ruttenberg, A., Sattler, U., et al.: OWL 2 web ontology language: Structural specification and functional-style syntax (2008), http://www.w3.org/TR/owl2-syntax/, Technical report, www.w3.org

[OD09]   O'Connor, M.J., Das, A.K.: SQWRL: a query language for OWL. In: Fifth International Workshop on OWL: Experiences and Directions, OWLED (2009)

[OD11]   O'Connor, M.J., Das, A.K.: Acquiring OWL ontologies from XML documents. In: Proceedings of the Sixth International Conference on Knowledge Capture, New York (2011)

[RRC06]   Rodrigues, T., Rosa, P., Cardoso, J.: Mapping XML to Exiting OWL ontologies. In: International Conference WWW/Internet, pp. 72–77 (2006)

[RRC08]   Rodrigues, T., Rosa, P., Cardoso, J.: Moving from syntactic to semantic organizations using JXML2OWL. Computers in Industry 59(8), 808–819 (2008)

[TC07]   Tsinaraki, C., Christodoulakis, S.: XS2OWL: A Formal Model and a
              System for Enabling XML Schema Applications to Interoperate with
              OWL-DL Domain Knowledge and Semantic Web Tools. In: Thanos, C.,
              Borri, F., Candela, L. (eds.) Digital Libraries: R&D. LNCS, vol. 4877,
              pp. 124–136. Springer, Heidelberg (2007)
[TLLJ08]   Thuy, P., Lee, Y.K., Lee, S., Jeong, B.S.: Exploiting XML Schema for In-
              terpreting XML Documents as RDF. In: IEEE International Conference
              on Services Computing, SCC 2008, vol. 2, pp. 555–558. IEEE (2008)
[VDPM⁺08]   Van Deursen, D., Poppe, C., Martens, G., Mannens, E., Walle, R.: XML
              to RDF conversion: a Generic Approach. In: International Conference
              on Automated Solutions for Cross Media Content and Multi-channel
              Distribution, AXMEDIS 2008, pp. 138–144. IEEE (2008)
[W3C99]   W3C. Document Type Definition. Technical report (1999),
              http://www.w3.org/TR/html4/sgml/dtd.html
[W3C07]   W3C. Extensible Markup Language (XML) (2007),
              http://www.w3.org/XML/, Technical report, www.w3c.org
[W3C09a]   W3C. OWL 2 Web Ontology Language Direct Semantics (2009),
              http://www.w3.org/TR/owl2-direct-semantics/, Technical report,
              www.w3.org
[W3C09b]   W3C. OWL 2 Web Ontology Language RDF-Based Semantics (2009),
              http://www.w3.org/TR/owl2-rdf-based-semantics/,
              Technical report, www.w3.org
[W3C09c]   W3C. W3C XML Schema Definition Language (XSD) (2009),
              http://www.w3.org/XML/Schema, Technical report, www.w3.org
[WRC08]   Wu, X., Ratcliffe, D., Cameron, M.A.: XML Schema Representation and
              Reasoning: A Description Logic Method. In: IEEE Congress on Services-
              Part I, pp. 487–494. IEEE (2008)
[XC06]   Xiao, H., Cruz, I.: Integrating and Exchanging XML Data Using Ontolo-
              gies. In: Spaccapietra, S., Aberer, K., Cudré-Mauroux, P. (eds.) Journal
              on Data Semantics VI. LNCS, vol. 4090, pp. 67–89. Springer, Heidelberg
              (2006)
[ZYMC11]   Zhang, F., Yan, L., Ma, Z.M., Cheng, J.: Knowledge representation and
              reasoning of XML with ontology. In: Proceedings of the 2011 ACM Sym-
              posium on Applied Computing, pp. 1705–1710. ACM (2011)

A Taxonomy of Dirty Time-Oriented Data

Theresia Gschwandtner[1], Johannes Gärtner[2],
Wolfgang Aigner[1], and Silvia Miksch[1]

[1] Institute of Software Technology and Interactive Systems (ISIS)
Vienna University of Technology
Favoritenstrasse 9-11/188, A-1040 Vienna, Austria
{gschwandtner,aigner,miksch}@cvast.tuwien.ac.at
http://www.cvast.tuwien.ac.at/
[2] XIMES GmbH
Hollandstraße 12/12, A-1020 Vienna, Austria
gaertner@ximes.com
http://www.ximes.com/en/

Abstract. Data quality is a vital topic for business analytics in order to gain accurate insight and make correct decisions in many data-intensive industries. Albeit systematic approaches to categorize, detect, and avoid data quality problems exist, the special characteristics of time-oriented data are hardly considered. However, time is an important data dimension with distinct characteristics which affords special consideration in the context of dirty data. Building upon existing taxonomies of general data quality problems, we address 'dirty' time-oriented data, i.e., time-oriented data with potential quality problems. In particular, we investigated empirically derived problems that emerge with different types of time-oriented data (e.g., time points, time intervals) and provide various examples of quality problems of time-oriented data. By providing categorized information related to existing taxonomies, we establish a basis for further research in the field of dirty time-oriented data, and for the formulation of essential quality checks when preprocessing time-oriented data.

Keywords: dirty data, time-oriented data, data cleansing, data quality, taxonomy.

1 Introduction

Dirty data leads to wrong results and misleading statistics [1]. This is why data cleansing – also called data cleaning, data scrubbing, or data wrangling – is a prerequisite of any data processing task. Roughly speaking, data cleansing is the process of detecting and correcting dirty data (e.g., duplicate data, missing data, inconsistent data, and simply erroneous data including data that do not violate any constraints but still are wrong or unusable) [2]. Dirty data include errors and inconsistencies in individual data sources as well as errors and inconsistencies

G. Quirchmayr et al. (Eds.): CD-ARES 2012, LNCS 7465, pp. 58–72, 2012.
© IFIP International Federation for Information Processing 2012

when integrating multiple sources. Data quality problems may stem from different sources such as federated database systems, web-based information systems, or simply from erroneous data entry [1].

The process of data cleansing, as described in [1], involves several steps:

- Data analysis
- Definition of transformation workflow and mapping rules
- Verification of the transformation workflow and the transformation definitions
- Transformation
- Replacement of the dirty data with the cleaned data in the original sources

Others describe the different steps as data auditing, workflow specification, workflow execution, and post-processing/control [3]. In any case, it is mandatory to analyze the given data before any actual cleansing can be performed. To this end, a classification of dirty data is of great value, serving as a reference to identify the errors and inconsistencies at hand. There are several different general approaches to create a taxonomy of dirty data, such as [1–5].

Other interesting studies on data quality include Sadiq et al. [6] who present a list of themes and keywords derived from papers of the last 20 years of data quality research, Madnick and Wang [7] who give an overview of different topics and methods of quality research projects, and Neely and Cook [8] who combine principles of product and service quality with key elements (i.e., management responsibilities, operation and assurance cost, research and development, production, distribution, personnel management, and legal function) of data quality across the life cycle of the data. However, none of these approaches systematically builds a taxonomy of data quality problems.

When dealing with the detection of errors in time-oriented data there are special aspects to be considered. Time and time-oriented data have distinct characteristics that make it worthwhile to treat it as a separate data type [9–11]. Examples for such characteristics are: Time-oriented data can be given either for a time point or a time interval. While intervals can easily be modeled by two time points, they add complexity if the relationship of such intervals are considered. For example, Allen [12] describes 13 different qualitative time-oriented relationships of intervals. Also, intervals of validity may be relevant for domain experts but might not be explicitly specified in the data. When dealing with time, we commonly interpret it with a calendar and its time units are essential for reasoning about time. However, these calendars have complex structures. For instance, in the Gregorian calendar the duration of a month varies between 28 and 31 days and weeks do not align with months and years. Furthermore, available data may be measured at different levels of temporal precision. Given this complex structure of time, additional errors are possible and correspondingly a specific taxonomy is helpful in addressing these issues.

To start with, we give an outline and summarization of taxonomies of general data quality problems in Section 2. In Section 3 we take a closer look at the different types time-oriented data that demand special consideration.

We introduce some terms on different types of time-oriented data in Section 3.1 before we continue with a detailed description of our main contribution–the categorization of dirty time-oriented data in Section 3.2. In Section 4 we provide a short outlook on further work we have planned to carry out in this area, and we sum up the main results of our work in Section 5.

2   Related Work

In preparing our taxonomy of dirty time-oriented data and data quality problems we start with a review of some general taxonomies. More specifically, we look at the general partitions used in this research (e.g., single-source problems versus multi-source problems), but are especially interested in the 'leafs of the taxonomies', i.e. those types of possible errors that are specific enough to be covered by a specific test (e.g., duplicates, missing values, contradictory values). The leafs mentioned in those general taxonomies are summarized in an overview table (see Tab. 1).

Rahm and Do [1] provide a classification of the problems to be addressed by data cleansing. They distinguish between single-source and multi-source problems as well as between schema- and instance-related problems (see Fig. 1). Multi-source problems occur when there are multiple data sources that have to be integrated such as different data representations, overlapping or contradicting data. Schema-related data problems are quality problems that can be prevented by appropriate integrity constraints or an improved schema design, while instance-related problems cannot be prevented at the schema level (e.g., misspellings).

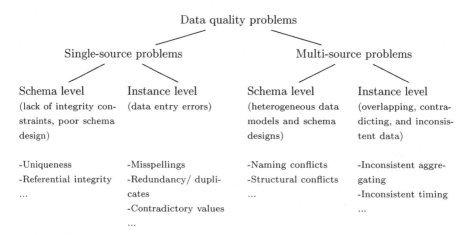

Fig. 1. Classification of data quality problems by Rahm and Do [1]

Later, Kim et al. [2] published a comprehensive classification of dirty data. They aimed at providing a framework for understanding how dirty data arise and which aspects have to be considered when cleansing the data to be able to provide reliable input data for further processing steps. To this end, they present a taxonomy consisting of 33 primitive dirty data types. However, in practice dirty data may be a combination of more than one type of dirty data. Kim et al. start with a root node with only two child nodes – missing data and not-missing data – and continue to further refine these categories adopting the standard 'successive hierarchical refinement' approach (see Fig. 2). Thus, they keep the fan-out factor at each non-leaf node small in order to make intuitively obvious that all meaningful child-nodes are listed. Furthermore, they distinguish wrong data in terms of whether they could have been prevented by techniques supported in today's relational database systems (i.e., automatic enforcement of integrity constraints). When Kim et al. talk about their category of 'outdated temporal data' they refer to the time instant or time interval during which a data is valid (e.g., an employee's occupation may no longer be valid when the employee gets promoted).

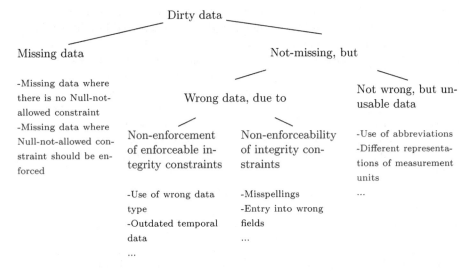

Fig. 2. Classification of dirty data by Kim et al. [2]

Müller and Freytag describe a rougher classification of data anomalies [3]. They start with the differentiation of syntactical anomalies, semantical anomalies, and coverage anomalies (missing values). Syntactical anomalies include lexical errors, domain format errors, and irregularities concerning the non-uniform use of values (e.g., the use of different currencies). Semantic anomalies include integrity constraint violations, contradictions (e.g., a discrepancy between age and date of birth), duplicated entries, and invalid tuples. In this context, invalid tuples do not represent valid entities from the mini-world but still do not violate any integrity constraints. Coverage anomalies can be divided into missing values and missing tuples (see Fig. 3).

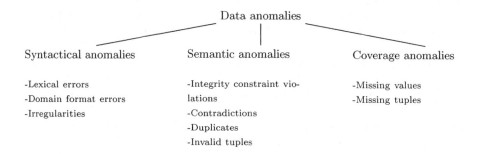

Fig. 3. Classification of data anomalies by Müller and Freytag [3]

Oliveira et al. organize their taxonomy of dirty data by the granularity levels of occurrences [4]. They act on the assumption that data is stored in multiple data sources each of which is composed of several relations with relationships among them. Moreover, a relation contains several tuples and each tuple is composed of a number of attributes. Consequently, they distinguish problems at the level of attributes/tuples (e.g., missing values, misspellings, existence of synonyms in multiple tuples), problems at the level of a single relation (e.g., duplicate tuples, violation of business domain constraints), problems at the level of multiple relations (e.g., referential integrity violations, heterogeneity of syntaxes, incorrect references), and problems at the level of multiple data sources (e.g., heterogeneity of syntaxes, existence of synonyms/homonyms, duplicate tuples) (see Fig. 4).

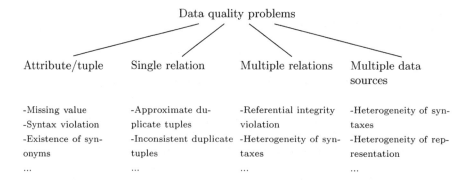

Fig. 4. Classification of data quality problems by Oliveira et al. [4]

Barateiro and Galhardas published a paper [5] about data quality tools including a classification of dirty data which contains problems that are very similar to those of Kim et al. [2]. The clustering of these problems, however, differs from the clustering in [2]. Instead it shows some similarities to the clustering of Rahm and Do [1]: They divide data quality problems into schema level problems (i.e., problems that can be avoided by existing relational database management systems (RDBMS) or an improved schema design) and instance level problems (i.e., problems that cannot be avoided by a better schema definition because they are concerned with the data content). Moreover, schema level data problems are divided into problems that can be avoided by RDBMS and those that cannot. Instance level data problems are further grouped into problems concerning single data records and problems concerning multiple data records (see Fig. 5).

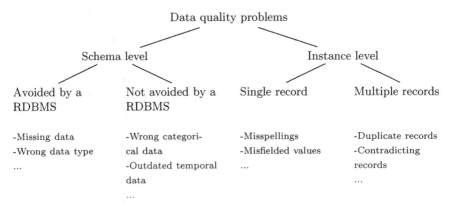

Fig. 5. Classification of data quality problems by Barateiro and Galhardas [5]

These approaches construct and sub-divide their taxonomies of dirty data quite differently. However, when it comes to the actual leaf problems of dirty data, they arrive at very similar findings (see Tab. 1). We omitted the category 'Integrity guaranteed through transaction management' from Kim et al. [2] which contains the problems 'Lost update', 'Dirty read', 'Unrepeatable read', and 'Lost transaction', since we do not consider these kinds of technical problems in the context of this paper. Moreover, we did not include the distinction between schema level problems and instance level problems because we wanted to investigate data quality problems on a more general level and not limit our research to the database-domain. In the following we introduce some definitions and explain our derived taxonomy of dirty time-oriented data using examples to ease understanding.

Table 1. Comparison of taxonomies of general data quality problems. (•...included in taxonomy; ○...further refinement, included in parent problem)

	Rahm & Do, 2000 [1]	Kim et al., 2003 [2]	Müller & Freytag, 2003 [3]	Oliveira et al., 2005 [4]	Barateiro et al. 2005 [5]
Single source					
Missing data	•	•	•	•	•
Missing value	•	•	•	•	•
Missing tuple	○	○	•	○	○
Semi-empty tuple	○	○	○	•	○
Dummy entry (e.g., -999)					•
Syntax violation / wrong data type	•	•	•	•	•
Duplicates	•	•	•	•	•
Inconsistent duplicates / Contradicting records	•	•	•	•	•
Approximate duplicates	•	○	•	•	•
Unique value violation	•	•		•	•
Incorrect values	•	•	•	•	•
Misspellings	•	•	•	•	•
Domain violation (outside domain range)	•	•	•	•	•
Violation of functional dependency (e.g., age-birth)	•	•	•	•	•
Circularity in a self-relationship	○	○	○	•	○
Incorrect derived values (error in computing data)	○	•	○	○	○
Unexpected low/high values			•		
Misfielded values	•	•	•		•
Invalid substring / Embedded values	•	•		•	•
Ambiguous data; imprecise, cryptic values, abbreviations	•	•		•	•
Outdated temporal data		•			•
Inconsistent spatial data (e.g., incomplete shape)		•			•
Multiple sources					
References	•	•		•	•
Referential integrity violation / dangling data	•	•		•	•
Incorrect references	•			•	
Heterogeneity of representations	•	•	•	•	•
Naming conflicts	•	•	•	•	•
Synonyms	•	•	•	•	•
Homonyms	•	•		•	•
Heterogeneity of syntaxes	•	•		•	•
Different word orderings	•	•		•	•
Uses of special characters	○	•		○	○
Heterogeneity of semantics	•	•	•	•	•
Heterogeneity of measure units (EUR vs. $)	•	•	•	•	•
Heterogeneity of aggregation/abstraction	•	•	•		•
Information refers to different points in time	•	•			•
Heterogeneity of encoding formats (ASCII, EBCDIC, etc.)		•			•

3   Dirty Time-Oriented Data

When extending the taxonomies of dirty data to dirty time-oriented data, we focus our research on types of dirty time-oriented data that are distinct to general errors listed in the overview of existing taxonomies above. I.e., we try to add leafs that help to think about possible errors, to build tests to detect these errors, and possibly to correct them.

One of the authors is CEO of a time intelligence solution provider and has extensive business experiences in dealing with real life problems of dirty time-oriented data. In his projects, numerous time-oriented datasets provided by customers are used to support addressing questions of work organization (e.g., working time, staffing levels, service levels) with software solutions specifically developed for these purposes [13, 14]. A typical project may consist of 5 to 20 different types of data files, some of them in more or less structured Excel [15] formats and others exported from databases. Some of these data files may be very small (e.g., a list of active employees), others may be mid-size (e.g., working times of 1000's of employees over many years), and sometimes they are rather large (> 10mio records). Overall more than 50 such projects were pursued in the course of the last years and problems with the quality of data were always a substantial and painful part of the overall projects.

Before we actually present the taxonomy of quality problems, we introduce some terms on different types of time-oriented data. The categorization originates from the observation that checking the data for given problems turns out to be different for these distinct types of time-oriented data.

3.1   Definitions: Types of Time-Oriented Data

An *interval* is a portion of time that can be represented by two points in time that denote the beginning and end of the interval. Alternatively, intervals can be modeled as start time (i.e., a point in time) in combination with its duration (i.e., a given number of seconds, minutes, hours, etc.), or as duration in combination with end time [9]. For instance, 08:00–09:00; 08:17–17:13; 8:17+50'.

A *raster* can be defined as a fragmentation of time without gaps consisting of raster intervals (usually with same lengths). For example, a 30' raster interval that is typically aligned with coarser time units: 00:00–00:30; 00:30–01:00; ...

A *raster interval* is a unit of time that constitutes a raster: 'hour', 'day', 'week', or 30'. In exceptional cases raster intervals may also be of uneven length, such as for the temporal unit 'month'.

Moreover, raster intervals may have *attributes* attached such as 'weekday', 'holiday', 'opening hour', 'working hour', 'school day', or 'Christmas season'. Consequently, there are attributes that can be calculated (e.g., the attribute 'weekday') and attributes that require further information (e.g., the attribute 'holiday').

A given *rastered data set*, however, may contain gaps between the raster intervals, for instance sales data with gaps on weekends and holidays.

Overall we propose to distinguish the following types of time as they may cover errors in different ways:

1. Non-rastered points in time
2. Non-rastered intervals (i.e., start+end, start+duration, or duration+end):
   (a) Start/End of non-rastered intervals (non-rastered points in time)
   (b) Duration of non-rastered intervals
3. Rastered points in time
4. Rastered intervals (i.e., start+end, start+duration, or duration+end):
   (a) Start/End of rastered intervals (rastered points in time)
   (b) Duration of rastered intervals

For instance, rastered time-oriented data may have distinct errors. On the one hand, the raster itself may be violated (e.g., a data set rastered on an hourly basis which contains an interval of minutes). On the other hand, the attributes of rastered intervals may indicate incorrect data values (e.g., sales values outside opening hours), or the values within the rastered intervals may violate some constraint such as 'each rastered interval must contain a value greater than 0 for a given data attribute'. In addition, a further type of data has to be considered when dealing with quality problems of time-oriented data, namely time-dependent values such as 'sales per day'.

3.2   Categorization of Time-Oriented Data Problems

From a methodological perspective, we applied an iterative mixed-initiative approach combining a bottom-up grounded theory procedure [16] with a top-down theory-centric view. On the one hand, our work gathered, modeled, and coded iteratively a number of time-oriented data quality problems that appeared in our real-life data analysis projects. These projects led to a large collection of examples of time-oriented data quality problems in diverse industry sectors and diverse kinds of data. On the other hand, we analyzed, compared, and merged the existing taxonomies discussed above that aim to model dirty data aspects (see Sec. 2 and Tab. 2–4).

In the course of integrating the time-oriented data quality problems with the categorizations of general data quality problems, we re-arranged, refined, extended, and omitted some categories according to our needs and practical experiences. We kept the concept of categorizing data quality problems into problems that occur when the data set stems from a single source and those that occur when two or more data sets need to be merged from multiple sources. Single source problems may of course occur in multiple source data sets too but the provided list of multiple source problems focuses on problems that specifically emerge when dealing with data sets from multiple sources (as mentioned by Rahm and Do [1]). Moreover, we excluded some categories of quality problems which do not relate to any time-oriented aspect such as 'inconsistent spatial data'.

We categorized the considered data types into non-rastered and rastered data. Each category contains the temporal units 'point in time' and 'interval' – the

Table 2. Time-oriented data quality problems within a **single source** (•...has to be checked for this data type)

		Description / *Example*	non-rastered Point in time	non-rastered Start/End of interval	non-rastered Duration	rastered Point in time	rastered Start/End of interval	rastered Duration	Time-dependent values
Single source									
Missing data	Missing value	Missing time/interval and/or missing value *(Date: NULL, items-sold: 20)*	•	•	•	•	•	•	•
		Dummy entry *(Date: 1970-01-01); (duration: -999)*	•	•	•	•	•	•	
	Missing tuple	Missing time/interval + values *(The whole tuple is missing)*				•	•	•	•
Duplicates	Unique value violation	Same time/interval (exact same time/interval though time/interval is defined as unique value) *(Holidays: 2012-04-09; 2012-04-09)*	•	•	•	•	•	•	
	Exact duplicates	Same time/interval and same values *(Date: 2012-03-29, items-sold: 20 is in table twice*	•	•	•	•	•	•	•
	Inconsistent duplicates	Same real entity with different times/intervals or values *(patient: A, admission: 2012-03-29 8:00)* vs. *(patient: A, admission: 2012-03-29 8:30)*	•	•	•	•	•	•	•
		Same real entity of time/interval (values) with different granularities (rounding) *(Time: 11:00 vs. 11:03); (Weight: 34,67 vs 35)*	•	•	•				•
Implausible values	Implausible range	Very early date / time in the future *(Date: 1899-03-22); (date: 2099-03-22); (date: 1999-03-22, duration: 100y)*	•	•	•	•	•	•	
	Unexpected low/high values	Deviations from daily/weekly... profile or implausible values *(Average sales on Monday: 50) vs. (this Monday: 500)*							•
		Changes of subsequent values implausible *(Last month: 4000 income) vs. (this month: 80000 income)*							•
		Too long/short intervals between start–start/end–end *Below one second at the cash desk*		•	•				
		Too long/short intervals between start–end/end–start *Off-time between two shifts less than 8h*		•	•				
		Too long/short overall timespan (first to last entry) *Continuous working for more than 12 hours*	•	•	•	•	•	•	
		Same value for too many succeeding records *17 customers in every intervall of the day*							•
Outdated	Outdated temporal data	Only old versions available *Sales values from last year*	•	•	•	•	•	•	
		New version replaced by old version *Project plan tasks overwritten by prior version*	•	•	•	•	•	•	

Table 3. Time-oriented data quality problems within a **single source** (continued) (•...has to be checked for this data type)

		Description / *Example*	non-rastered			rastered			Time-dependent values
			Point in time	Start/End of interval	Duration	Point in time	Start/End of interval	Duration	
Single source (continued)									
Wrong data	Wrong data type	No time/interval *Date: AAA; duration: ***	•	•	•	•	•	•	
	Wrong data format	Wrong date/time/datetime/ duration format *(Date: YYYY-MM-DD) vs. (date: YY-MM-DD); (duration: 7.7h) vs. (duration: 7h42')*	•	•	•	•	•	•	
		Times outside raster (e.g., for denoting end of day) *1-hour-raster but time is 23:59:00 for the end of the last interval*				•	•	•	
	Misfielded values	Time in datefield, date in time field/duration field *(Time in datefield: 14-03, date in timefield: 12:03:08)*	•	•	•	•	•	•	
		Values attached to the wrong/adjacent time/interval *GPS data shows sprints followed by slow runs although the velocity was constant*	•	•	•	•	•	•	•
	Embedded values	Date+time in date field, timezone in time field/duration field *(Time: 22:30) vs. (time: 22:30 CET)*	•	•	•	•	•	•	
	Coded wrongly or not conform to real entity	Wrong time zone *UTC data in stead of local time*	•	•		•	•		
		Valid time/interval but not conform to the real entity *(Admission: 2012-03-04) vs. (real admission: 2012-03-05)*	•	•	•	•	•	•	
	Domain violation (outside domain range)	Outliers in % of concurrent values (attention with small values) for a given point in time/interval *On average (median) 30 customers in a shop in a given hour – in a 10' interval within that hour, a value of 200 is present*							•
		Uneven or overlapping intervals *Turnover data for 8:00–9:00, 9:00–11:00, 11:00–12:00*					•	•	
		Minimum/Maximum violation for given time/interval/type of day *Sales at night even though no employees were present*							•
		Sum of sub-intervals impossible *Seeing the doctor + working hours longer than regular working hours*		•	•		•	•	
		Start, end, or duration do not form a valid interval *(End ≤ start); (duration ≤ 0)*		•					
		Circularity in a self-relationship *Interval A ⊂ interval B, interval B ⊂ interval A, A ≠ B*		•	•		•	•	
	Incorrect derived values	Error in computing duration *Error computing sum of employees present within two intervals: (interval: 8:00–8:30, employees: 3), (interval: 8:30–9:00, employees: 3) → (interval: 8:00–9:00, employees: 6); no proper dealing with summer time-change; computing the number of work hours per day without deducting the breaks*	•	•	•	•	•	•	•
Ambiguous data	Abbreviations or imprecise/unusual coding	Ambiguous time/interval/duration due to short format *(Date: 06-03-05) vs. (date: 06-05-03); 5' interval encoded as '9:00': (interval: 8:55–9:00) vs. (interval: 9:00–09:05); average handling time per given interval: 3' – not clear: (average of completed interactions) vs. (average of started interactions) within this interval*	•	•	•	•	•	•	
		Extra symbols for time properties *+ or * or 28:00 for next day*	•	•	•	•	•	•	

Table 4. Time-oriented data quality problems between **multiple sources** (•...has to be checked for this data type)

			non-rastered			rastered			
		Description *Example*	Point in time	Start/End of interval	Duration	Point in time	Start/End of interval	Duration	Time-dependent values
Multiple Sources									
Heterog. syntaxes	Different data formats/ synonyms	Different date/duration formats *(Date: YYYY-MM-DD) vs. (date: DD-MM-YYYY); (Date: 03-05 (March 5)) vs. (date: 03-05 (May 3))*	•	•	•	•	•	•	•
	Different table structure	Time separated from date vs. date+time or start+duration in one column *(Table A: start-date, start-time) vs. (table B: start-timestamp)*	•	•	•	•	•	•	•
Heterog. semantics	Heterogeneity of scales (measure units / aggregation)	Different granularities; different interval length *(Table A: whole hours only) vs. (table B: minutes)*	•	•	•	•	•	•	•
	Information refer to different times/intervals	Different times/intervals *(Table A: current sales as of yesterday) vs. (table B: sales as of last week)*	•	•	•	•	•	•	•
References	Referential integrity violation/ dangling data	No reference to a given time/interval in another source *(Table A: sales per day), (table B: sales assistants per day), problem: table B does not contain a valid reference to a given day from table A or table A does not contain any referencing time*	•	•	•	•	•	•	•
	Incorrect reference	Reference exists in other sources but not conform to real entity *Sales of one day (table A) are assigned to certain sales assistants (from table B) because they reference the same day, however, in reality a different crew was working on that day*	•	•	•	•	•	•	•

latter being defined by either two points in time (i.e., start and end of the interval), by its start (i.e., one point in time) and its duration, or its end and its duration (as defined in Sec. 3.1). Besides the temporal units, we especially consider time-dependent values (e.g., all events at a given point in time, all events within a given interval). With respect to these categories we outline which data quality problems arise for which data type (indicated by bullets in Tab. 2–4). The first two columns of the tables reflect the general categories derived from existing taxonomies. The third column gives descriptions and examples of specific time-dependent quality problems for each category.

In the course of investigating data quality problems from real-life projects, we realized that the kinds of problems that are subject of this paper (i.e., wrong, duplicated, missing, inconsistent data, etc.) are not the only ones that need to be identified and resolved. Tasks, like checking the credibility of data entries that cannot easily be categorized as 'wrong', or transforming the data table into a specific format that is suitable for further processing steps are strongly linked to the process of data cleansing and need special consideration. Also, a relevant number of problems occur as a consequence of cleansing/transforming the data set, thus such dirtiness might be created by the process itself.

4   Further Work

The generated taxonomy serves as important basis for further planned initiatives to support time-oriented data quality issues. Specifically, we plan to develop a prototype that

1. checks time-oriented data for these kinds of quality problems,
2. generates a report about the problems found,
3. visualizes the 'dirtiness' of the data set and its progress,
4. provides tools for data cleansing:
   - means to specify automatic transformations, and
   - Information Visualization [17] methods for interactive manipulation of the whole dataset as well as of selected entries.
5. supports the management of various versions and corrections/partial updates of the dataset.

The majority of types of dirty data require intervention by a domain expert to be cleansed [2]. Thus, a combination of means for transforming the whole dataset at once with means for interactively investigating the data problems and manipulate single table entries or groups of table entries seems to be a promising solution. Since the sight is the sense with the highest bandwidth we believe that visualization is a good way to communicate a compact overview of the 'dirtiness' of the data as well as to point the user to those cases of data quality problems where manual interaction is needed. Moreover, we plan to realize an interactive Information Visualization [17] prototype that allows for direct manipulation of the data set. This would not only facilitate the task of cleaning the data but it would also provide immediate visual feedback to user actions.

Another important issue of data cleansing is the transformation of the given data table into a table structure that is suited for subsequent processing steps, such as splitting/merging of columns, removing additional rows (e.g., summary rows and comments), or the aggregation of temporal tuples into rastered intervals. A couple of software tools exist to aid this transformation [13, 18–20]. However, further research is needed on which kinds of transformations should be supported and how to support them most efficiently as well as how to organize the management of the various versions and updates.

5   Conclusion

A catalog of general data quality problems which integrates different taxonomies draws a comprehensive picture of problems that have to be considered when dealing with data quality in general. It serves as a reference when formulating integrity constraints or data quality checks.

In this paper we have investigated different approaches of categorizing data quality problems. We have examined a number of relevant taxonomies of dirty data and carved out their similarities and differences. Furthermore, we have focused on the data quality problems that occur when dealing with time-oriented data, in particular. We have derived a number of time-oriented data quality problems from our experience in numerous projects in different industry sectors and we merged the results of the literature review of existing taxonomies with our practical knowledge in dealing with time-oriented data.

Specifically, we presented an integrated and consistent view of general data quality problems and taxonomies. Thus, we provided a useful catalog of data quality problems that need to be considered in general data cleansing tasks. In particular, we provide categorized information about quality problems of time-oriented data. Thus, we established an information basis necessary for further research on the field of dirty time-oriented data, and for the formulation of essential quality checks when preprocessing time-oriented data.

The dimension of time implicates special characteristics which cause specific data quality problems. Thus, a catalog of data quality problems focusing specifically on time-induced problems yields benefits. In spite of its length, we do not claim our categorization of time-oriented data problems to be complete. However, we provide a collection of numerous problems from real life projects which constitutes an important basis for further research. Moreover, we integrated this collection with existing taxonomies of general data quality problems to provide a categorized and unified work of reference. This reference comprises several important aspects that need to be considered when dealing with the quality of time-oriented data.

Acknowledgments. The research leading to these results has received funding from the Centre for Visual Analytics Science and Technology CVAST (funded by the Austrian Federal Ministry of Economy, Family and Youth in the exceptional Laura Bassi Centres of Excellence initiative).

References

1. Rahm, E., Do, H.H.: Data Cleaning: Problems and Current Approaches. IEEE Techn. Bulletin on Data Engineering 31 (2000)
2. Kim, W., Choi, B.-J., Hong, E.-K., Kim, S.-K., Lee, D.: A Taxonomy of Dirty Data. Data Mining and Knowledge Discovery 7, 81–99 (2003)
3. Müller, H., Freytag, J.-C.: Problems, Methods, and Challenges in Comprehensive Data Cleansing. Technical report HUB-IB-164, Humboldt University Berlin (2003)
4. Oliveira, P., Rodrigues, F., Henriques, P.: A Formal Definition of Data Quality Problems. In: International Conference on Information Quality (MIT IQ Conference) (2005)
5. Barateiro, J., Galhardas, H.: A Survey of Data Quality Tools. Datenbankspektrum 14, 15–21 (2005)
6. Sadiq, S., Yeganeh, N., Indulska, M.: 20 Years of Data Quality Research: Themes, Trends and Synergies. In: 22nd Australasian Database Conference (ADC 2011), pp. 1–10. Australian Computer Society, Sydney (2011)
7. Madnick, S., Wang, R., Lee, Y., Zhu, H.: Overview and Framework for Data and Information Quality Research. Journal of Data and Information Quality (JDIQ) 1(1), 1–22 (2009)
8. Neely, M., Cook, J.: A Framework for Classification of the Data and Information Quality Literature and Preliminary Results (1996-2007). In: 14th Americas Conference on Information Systems 2008 (AMICS 2008), pp. 1–14 (2008)
9. Aigner, W., Miksch, S., Schumann, H., Tominski, C.: Visualization of Time-Oriented Data. Springer, London (2011)
10. Andrienko, N., Andrienko, G.: Exploratory Analysis of Spatial and Temporal Data: A Systematic Approach. Springer, Berlin (2006)
11. Shneiderman, B.: The Eyes Have It: A Task by Data Type Taxonomy for Information Visualizations. In: IEEE Symposium on Visual Languages, pp. 336–343. IEEE Computer Society Press (1996)
12. Allen, J.: Towards a General Model of Action and Time. Artificial Intelligence 23(2), 123–154 (1984)
13. XIMES GmbH: Time Intelligence Solutions – [TIS], http://www.ximes.com/en/software/products/tis (accessed March 30, 2012)
14. XIMES GmbH: Qmetrix, http://www.ximes.com/en/ximes/qmetrix/background.php (accessed March 30, 2012)
15. Microsoft: Excel, http://office.microsoft.com/en-us/excel/ (accessed March 30, 2012)
16. Corbin, J., Strauss, A.: Basics of Qualitative Research: Techniques and Procedures for Developing Grounded Theory, 3rd edn. Sage Publications, Los Angeles (2008)
17. Card, S., Mackinlay, J., Shneiderman, B.: Readings in Information Visualization: Using Vision to Think. Morgan Kaufmann, San Francisco (1999)
18. Raman, V., Hellerstein, J.: Potter's Wheel: An Interactive Data Cleaning System. In: 27th International Conference on Very Large Data Bases (VLDB 2001), pp. 381–390. Morgan Kaufmann, San Francisco (2001)
19. Kandel, S., Paepcke, A., Hellerstein, J., Heer, J.: Wrangler: Interactive Visual Specification of Data Transformation Scripts. In: ACM Human Factors in Computing Systems (CHI 2011), pp. 3363–3372. ACM, New York (2011)
20. Huynh, D., Mazzocchi, S.: Google Refine, http://code.google.com/p/google-refine (accessed March 30, 2012)

Combining Relational and Semi-structured Databases for an Inquiry Application

Marius Ebel and Martin Hulin

University of Applied Sciences Ravensburg-Weingarten, 88250 Weingarten, Germany
{ebelma,hulin}@hs-weingarten.de

Abstract. The popularity of NoSQL databases keeps growing and more companies have been moving away from relational databases to non-relational NoSQL databases. In this paper, the partitioning of a relational data model of an inquiry system into semi-structured and relational data for storage in both SQL and NoSQL databases is shown. Furthermore, the CAP theorem will be applied to categorize the storing of the correct parts of the model into their corresponding databases. As a result of these reorganizations and the introduction of additional histogram data, overall performance improvements of about 93% to 98% are achieved.

Keywords: NoSQL, Document Stores, MongoDB, semi-structured data, inquiry system.

1   Introduction

Not Only SQL (NoSQL) – reintroduced by Evans in 2009 [7] – stands for a variety of new data stores which now are gaining population on the market [10]. Long time fully relational data stores have been sufficient for most purposes. But since companies and organizations have started to collect huge amounts of data, such as customer, sales and other data for further analysis, several types of non-relational data stores are preferred over the relational ones [10]. Traditional SQL databases come with the need of a fixed schema organized in tables, columns and rows, which cannot handle the changed needs for today's database applications.

NoSQL does not necessarily mean schema-free. There are also NoSQL databases for structured data like Google's Bigtable [4]. Among the schema-free NoSQL databases there are numerous data stores like the key-value-stores Redis [11] and the document stores like Amazon SimpleDB [15], Apache CouchDB and MongoDB. NoSQL data stores themselves provide a variety of sophisticated techniques like MapReduce [6] and better mechanisms for horizontal scalability [3] among others.

NoSQL document stores form only one group of this large variety of NoSQL data stores. *These databases store and organize data as collections of documents, rather than as structured tables with uniformsized fields for each record. With these databases, users can add any number of fields of any length to a document* [10, p. 13]. They organize data in—as the name indicates—documents. Documents are treated as objects with dynamic properties, which means that a

G. Quirchmayr et al. (Eds.): CD-ARES 2012, LNCS 7465, pp. 73–84, 2012.

document can be interpreted as a dynamic list of key-value pairs. The approach described in this paper makes use of the absence of schemas in document-oriented NoSQL databases to store dynamic, semi-structured data.

SQL databases mostly use proprietary connection drivers to handle communication with the server, where data transfer is just a "black box". NoSQL databases are different in this case. Many of them use *Representational State Transfer* (REST) [8,14] where often a community-developed connection driver has to be used (Redis, Apache CouchDB), but some also come with a proprietary connection driver (MongoDB). In most projects there is either no time for developing a connection driver or it is unsafe to rely on community projects. Therefore, the presence of a proprietary connection driver can be a very important factor for choosing the appropriate NoSQL database.

The approach to use semi-structured data structures is basically not new. For instance, the database system CDS/ISIS is a type of semi-structured NoSQL database, which is used since the 1980's by a vast amount of academic libraries [13]. But the way of using semi-structured data described in the following section focuses on reorganizing previously relational data into semi-structured record sets and on the optimization of computational effort of statistical data.

Furthermore, we will show an approach to affect data organization through dynamic semi-structured data and the subsequent querying, which is also applied in the inquiry system INKIDU[1].

2   Methodology

The use case of the methods described in the sequel is the online inquiry platform INKIDU. INKIDU provides the user with the ability to design questionnaires, which can be statistically evaluated after completing the inquiry. Questionnaires in INKIDU are user-defined sequences of questions. Each question can be of a different type such as rating questions, single and multiple choice questions, free text questions, etc. After submitting a questionnaire, the submitted data has to be stored for further result analysis. A questionnaire therefore has two factors affecting the possible amount of data, which can be produced by each user: The number of questions and for each question its subsequent type. The effective structure and amount of answers of an answer set is finally determined by the questions, which the user decided to give an answer for. Hence, there is no way to predict the exact amount and structure of data, which will be produced by each user. Conclusively only a rough estimate of the structure is known: A list of key-value-pairs, i.e. the key is the question identifier and the value is the user-given answer. Considering the variable length of such a list and not knowing the data type of each value, only semi-structured data is given. In a system meant for strictly structured relational data, the presence of just semi-structured data leads to a conflicting situation of storing a set of semi-structured data with an unpredictable number of fields and data types.

---

[1] http://www.inkidu.de/

2.1   Current Data Organization

The current way of organizing answer sets is shown in Figure 1, where answer sets are organized vertically. An answer set containing all of an user's answers belonging to a questionnaire is split into tuples consisting of the mandatory primary key, the inquiry this answer belongs to, the answered question, and a field referencing the first primary key value of all answers belonging to the same answer set. The last field is created by the need of making the assignment of answers reconstructable, e.g. for data export and for allowing further statistical cross-analysis. As the data model shows, the redundant reference to the inquiry is not necessary, but is held to eliminate the need of a table join and therefore to keep query times at a reasonable level, when e.g. retrieving all answer sets belonging to a certain inquiry. These bottlenecks such as redundant foreign keys, complex queries and huge index data, arise from the RDBMS' need of a fixed table schema, which requires a predefined and therefore predictable structure of the data.

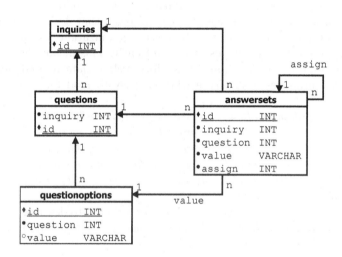

Fig. 1. Excerpt from the current fully relational data model of INKIDU being reorganized

In order to demonstrate the current data organization and the approaches described in the following, a questionnaire with one rating question and one multiple choice question with three options is taken as a reference example. There are two answer sets to be shown in different manners of data organization:

```
(rating=1, multiple choice=[option 1, option 2])
(rating=4, multiple choice=[option 1, option 2, option 3])
```

Applying the fully relational approach on the reference example data, answer sets, shown in Table 1, are produced.

Table 1. Answer sets which result from storing the above described example data in the fully relational data model. The values of the column *answers* for *option 1 – 3* are foreign keys referencing record sets of the the table *questionoptions*.

id	inquiry	question	answers	assign	*remarks*
3042397	18722	366519	1	3042397	rating value 1
3042400	18722	366519	4	3042400	rating value 4
3042398	18722	366520	203648	3042397	option 1
3042399	18722	366520	203649	3042397	option 2
3042401	18722	366520	203648	3042400	option 1
3042402	18722	366520	203649	3042400	option 2
3042403	18722	366520	203650	3042400	option 3

2.2 Organizing Answer Sets

In the following, the approach of reorganizing the above data structure is described. With the emergence of schema-free databases that do not depend on a predefined structure of data records, the data reorganization can be done not only much more intuitively, but also more efficiently. This means that the construction of the data records requires less effort such as data redundancies and index data and produces a structure which is easy to read for machines and humans as well.

Semi-structured data is often explained as "schemaless" or "self-describing", terms that indicate that there is no separate description of the type or structure of data. Typically, when we store or program with a piece of data, we first describe the structure (type, schema) of that data and then create instances of that type (or populate) the schema. In semi-structured data we directly describe the data using a simple syntax [1, p. 11].

In this case we use *JavaScript Object Notation* (JSON) to describe an answer data set, e.g. in terms of NoSQL a document such as the following record sets, which result from the reference example data.

```
{ // first answer set:
  // (rating=1, multiple choice=[option 1, option 2])
  inquiry: 18722,
  data : {
    366519 : 1
    366520 : [ 203648, 203649 ]
  }
}

{ // second answer set:
  // (rating=4, multiple choice=[option 1, option 2, option 3])
  inquiry: 18722,
  data : {
```

```
      366519 : 4
      366520 : [ 203648, 203649, 203650 ]
  }
}
```

The use of JSON notation is proposed by MongoDB, which is used for this project. Binary JSON (BSON) is the format used by MongoDB to store documents and to transfer them via network [12,3]. As shown above an answer set, formerly to be divided into several records, can now be grouped into one single, semi-structured record, which uses a key-value list mapping question ids to the user-given answers. Hence, a convention of a basic loose structure of an answer set can be decribed as the following: a reference to the inquiry the user participated and n key-value pairs of the data mapping as described before.

The advantage of a non-structured NoSQL-Database is now clearly visible: All the data belonging to the same answer set can be kept in one single record that can be easily queried by the inquiry field and still does not need to fulfill the requirement of a predefined number of fields or data types. This way of storing data simplifies data management and is easier to understand.

2.3 Data Condensation

The approach described above can be refined to group all answer sets into a single record, i.e. to condense data from multiple record sets into a single one. The reference example data would result in a record set shown below.

```
{
  inquiry: 18722,
  data : [
    { // first answer set:
      // (rating=1, multiple choice=[option 1, option 2])
      366519 : 1
      366520 : [ 203648, 203649 ]
    },
    { // second answer set:
      // (rating=4, multiple choice=[option 1, option 2, option 3])
      366519 : 4
      366520 : [ 203648, 203649, 203650 ]
    }
  ]
}
```

Such a condensed record set can grow very large, which is a disadvantage especially for real-world applications. It increases the memory consumption of answer processing outside the database resulting in severe scalability problems for the whole application. But with smaller amounts of data or less strict scalability requirements, such approach is still a better way of data modeling with comfortable handling.

Databases use B-Trees for indexing data [5]. The previously fully relational data model required three fields per answer record set (i.e. for every answer to every question) to be indexed in order to keep query times at a reasonable level. The B-Trees indexing only the answer sets of INKIDU consume more storage space than the data itself. Using the semi-structured approach the index data is minimized, because only one field per collection (*inquiry*) and less record sets have to be indexed. This is true whether the answer sets are stored in multiple records or are condensed to one record.

2.4   Histograms

The price to pay for less index data and easier queries is that some functions formerly used in SQL queries aren't available anymore. Examples for some of these functions are minimum/maximum, average, standard deviation, etc. Keeping in mind that an inquiry application also includes the statistical analysis of the retrieved answers, the absence of these functions is fatal. These functions have to be regained and unfortunately have to be implemented outside the database. Using the situation to our benefit, the computation of statistical data can be done more efficiently by introducing another semi-structured dynamic data structure, which is described in the following. For better understanding the formula of the arithmetic mean has to be considered first:

$$\bar{x}_{\text{naive}} = \frac{1}{n} \sum_{i=1}^{n} x_i = \frac{x_1 + x_2 + x_3 + \ldots + x_i}{n} \tag{1}$$

This naive formula implies that every element $x \in X$ has to be processed for calculating $\bar{x}_{\text{naive}}$. This means that the computations of the arithmetic mean and the standard deviation result in severe scalability problems for larger or growing amounts of answers. The computational effort for e.g. the average grows linearly by $\mathcal{O}(n)$ with n as the number of record sets. Therefore these calculations have to be optimized, which is now done by storing additional data. The linear growth of computational effort by the number of record sets is—especially in the described scenario—a bottleneck. To tackle the challenge of reducing the computational effort, data is reorganized to histograms.

Per definition, a histogram is a graphical representation of the distribution of data. In the above described scenario, a histogram represents the distribution of answers to a single question holding the absolute frequency of every option. An option can be either a foreign key referencing a question option of a multiple/single choice question or a rating value of a rating question. Hence, the histogram can be represented as a set of option-frequency pairs, which can be used to do a much more efficient calculation of the arithmetic mean and the standard deviation. The following schema shows a representation of a histogram, which can be easily projected onto a semi-structured NoSQL document. In this schema

o stands for *option* and f stands for *frequency*, where a list of these option-frequency mappings is the actual data part of a histogram, $H_{\text{inquiry, question}}$, without the inquiry and question information.

$$\text{data}(H_{\text{inquiry, question}}) = \begin{bmatrix} o_1 \, , \, f_1 \\ o_2 \, , \, f_2 \\ o_3 \, , \, f_3 \\ \vdots \, , \, \vdots \\ o_k \, , \, f_k \end{bmatrix} \stackrel{\text{e.g.}}{=} \begin{bmatrix} 1 \, , \, 594 \\ 2 \, , \, 453 \\ 3 \, , \, 203 \\ 4 \, , \, 134 \\ 5 \, , \, 43 \end{bmatrix} \tag{2}$$

As shown in Eqns. 2+3, every option is "weighted" by its absolute frequency, which means that the set of data is not iterated over every record set, but over every question option instead. This makes the computational effort still grow linearly by $\mathcal{O}(k)$ where k is the number of available question options (revise following sentence), but rather by the number of available question answers than by the number of given record sets.

$$\bar{x}_{\text{hist}} = \frac{1}{n} \sum_{i=1}^{k} (o_i \cdot f_i) = \frac{o_1 f_1 + o_2 f_2 + o_3 f_3 + \ldots o_k f_k}{n} \tag{3}$$

The correctness of Eqn. 3 is given by the fact that the sum of all frequencies is equal to the number of given answers: $\sum_{i=1}^{k} f_i = n$. Now the number of different question options is a predefined number, which is independent from the growing number of incoming answers and therefore makes the computational effort predictable and as small as possible: It is independent of the number of users taking part in a questionnaire. Of course, the complete computation time for calculating the mean remains the same. However it is moved from a time critical part of the application (statistical analysis) to an uncritical part (storing new answer sets). Additionally the computational effort is distributed over every user submitting answers to the system, which results in shorter processing times for visualizing and displaying statistical analysis reports (see Section 3.3).

The disadvantage of storing redundant frequency values is justified by the performance gain of the statistical analysis, a core feature of inquiry applications. As mentioned above a document in terms of a document-oriented NoSQL database is a list of nestable key-value pairs. The semi-structure of a histogram data set now can be modeled as follows; consisting of a fixed and a dynamic part. The fixed part is the identifying header, which includes the inquiry id and the associated question id. The dynamic part is the actual mapping from question option onto absolute frequency.

3 Software Architecture

In this section the realization of the above concepts is described. The application is, as already mentioned, the online inquiry platform INKIDU, which allows the user to create and evaluate user-defined questionnaires.

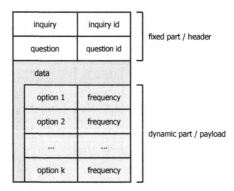

Fig. 2. Structure of a semi-structured histogram record. The upper part ("header") is the fixed part, which can be found in every histogram record. The lower part ("payload") is the dynamic part, which is variable in its number of key-value-pairs.

3.1 System Overview

The concept of integration in case of INKIDU includes the parallel usage of a traditional SQL database and a NoSQL document store. The NoSQL document store is provided by MongoDB[2] while MySQL[3] is used as the data store of the relational data model.

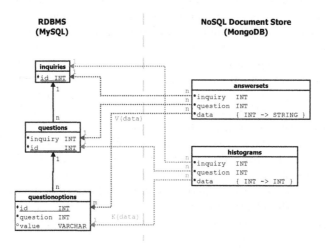

Fig. 3. Excerpt of the data model of INKIDU showing which parts belong to the relational and non-relational data model

---

[2] http://www.mongodb.org/

[3] http://www.mysql.de/

Consistency and referential integrity are important features in relational data models. With the features of mass data storage, database scalability and high availability NoSQL databases often do not provide native support for ACID transactions. NoSQL databases are able to offer performance and scalability and keep strong consistency out of their functionalities, which is a problem for several types of applications [10]. For instance, in case of INKIDU there are parts of the data model which do require ACID transactions and strong consistency as well as parts which do not require this functionality. Therefore, as Figure 3 shows, the data model is distributed over the two different databases. So the decision to make it a hybrid system consisting of relational and non-relational databases is explained by two different factors. The first factor is, that the approach of increasing system performance by reorganizing data works also on single server setups. Other mechanisms increasing performance by scaling a system horizontally (e.g. load balancing) need a multiple server setup to work. The second factor is defined by the different requirements towards consistency and referential integrity. However, there are approaches to ensure consistency within a non-relational data model [16], which for now exceeds the resources of this project.

The hierarchy consisting of inquiries, questions, questionoptions, etc. has to be consistent at any time. This includes on one hand ACID transactions and on the other hand referential integrity, such that e.g. no orphaned records can exist. This means that the absence of foreign key checking and the presence of eventual consistency as achieved by MongoDB is not sufficient. Therefore MySQL is still used to store these structured data. NoSQL database management systems can store data, which change dynamically in size much better than relational ones; for instance nodes can be added dynamically to increase horizontal scalability. Considering the three guarantees *consistency, availability and partition-tolerance* of the CAP theorem [2,9], consistency and availability are most important for the relational part. Availability and partition-tolerance are most important for the non-relational of INKIDU due to the fact that it is not tolerable that data is not accessible or gets lost in case of a database server node crashing.

3.2   Implementation

There exist a variety of different NoSQL database concepts and implementations: key-value stores, document stores and extensible record stores [3]. To choose the appropriate NoSQL database management system for INKIDU three key requirements were considered:

- **Extensibility:** The possibility to migrate the full data model into the NoSQL database has to be preserved. This means the database has to be capable of storing objects of higher complexity than histograms and answer sets.
- **Indexing:** Besides the unique ID of every record set a second additional field has to be indexed.
- **Reliability:** The database itself and the driver have to work well with PHP. Especially the driver has to be well-engineered for simple and reliable use.

The requirements to store more complex objects and indexing more than one field led to the decision to use document stores. In order to find the right document store fulfilling all of the above key requirements Apache CouchDB and MongoDB were investigated. CouchDB offers some drivers developed by community projects, but without support. MongoDB offers one well developed proprietary driver, which is known to work well with PHP. Therefore MongoDB was chosen for this project.

A point not linked to the key requirements but still notable is the presence of atomic operations in MongoDB. Atomic operations allow changes to individual values. For instance to increment a value the modifier $inc can be used in an update command, $push adds a value at the end of an array and $pull removes it. These updates occur *in place* and therefore do not need the overhead of a server return trip [3]. This is especially of advantage for the updating of histograms, where often only one single value has to be increased.

3.3   Performance Results

In order to measure the performance of the reconstructed system the fully relational and the hybrid implementation were compared against each other in two different scenarios: Firstly, the generation of the visualized histograms. This includes the querying of the histogram, the calculation of the average and the standard deviation and the rendering of a histogram image displayed to the user. Secondly, the export of all answer sets of an inquiry, which includes the querying of all answer data belonging to an inquiry and formatting it into a CSV file. These scenarios were chosen, because they are the most affected parts of the reconstruction. The test procedures were supplied with 100 different anonymized real-life inquiries with one to 200 questions. The inquiries itself had participants within the range from 10 to 1000. During the test scenarios the following two values were measured:

- **Query Timings:** The time needed to query the database itself.
- **Processing Timings:** The time the whole process needed to complete including the query time.

The reason to distinguish between querying and processing timings is that we also have to take into account the time consideration for the optimization of the computation processes outside the database. Table 2 shows the query timings and Table 3 shows the processing timings. The measurements show that the average querying time was reduced by about 30% to 95% and the average processing time by about 93% to 98%.

Histograms could have also been realized using a relational database. However all reasons of Section 2.2 to store answer sets in a NoSQL database are true for histogram data as well. These data are also semi-structured and change in size dynamically. Therefore the overall performance improvements are the result of the combination of the relational database with a NoSQL database. Another possible approach - using an object database - was not investigated in this project.

Table 2. Query timings for histogram and data export querying

	Histogram Querying (μs)		
	Min	*Avg*	*Max*
Relational	12	36	279
Hybrid	2	24 (**−30%**)	167
	Data Export Querying (μs)		
	Min	*Avg*	*Max*
Relational	14	4423	83699
Hybrid	3	200 (**−95%**)	8791

Table 3. Processing timings for histogram generation and data export

	Histogram Generation (μs)		
	Min	*Avg*	*Max*
Relational	179	166695	2355661
Hybrid	113	3983 (**−98%**)	116779
	Data Export (μs)		
	Min	*Avg*	*Max*
Relational	155	114837	2617227
Hybrid	141	8380 (**−93%**)	193134

4 Conclusion

This paper illustrates an approach to distribute a fully relational data model into a relational and a non-relational part in order to deal with different requirements concerning consistency, availability and partition-tolerance. Before partitioning a relational data model into multiple parts, the choice of the database(s) has to be made carefully. Especially with regard to NoSQL databases, there is a large variety of different types of data stores available. In this project, the decision to select MongoDB as NoSQL database management system has been strongly influenced by the presence of a reliable driver for database connection and atomic operations, which provide the ability to make simple update operations as fast as possible.

The data model of the INKIDU inquiry application is separated in two parts: The structured part is still stored using the relational DBMS MySQL, which guarantees ACID transaction control. The semi-structured part, the answer sets of a questionnaire, is stored in the document store MongoDB. This reduces the amount of stored data by more than 50% because three of the four indexes can be omitted.

In a second step histograms are stored to increase the performance of a questionnaire's statistical analysis - a core feature of an inquiry application. MongoDB is used to store histogram data because they are semi-structured, too. The time the queries take to retrieve the histogram and export data has been reduced by about 30% and 95%. The overall performance for the processes of generating histograms and exporting data has increased by 98% and 93% respectively.

Acknowledgements. We gratefully acknowledge Wolfgang Ertel for collaboration and Michel Tokic for his valuable feedback on this paper.

References

1. Abiteboul, S., Buneman, P., Suciu, D.: Data on the Web: From relations to semistructured data and XML. Morgan Kaufmann Publishers Inc., San Francisco (2000)
2. Brewer, E.A.: Towards robust distributed systems (abstract). In: Proceedings of the Nineteenth Annual ACM Symposium on Principles of Distributed Computing, PODC 2000, p. 7. ACM, New York (2000)
3. Cattell, R.: Scalable SQL and NoSQL data stores. SIGMOD Record 39(4), 12–27 (2010)
4. Chang, F., Dean, J., Ghemawat, S., Hsieh, W.C., Wallach, D.A., Burrows, M., Chandra, T., Fikes, A., Gruber, R.E.: Bigtable: A distributed storage system for structured data. In: Proceedings of the 7th Conference on USENIX Symposium on Operating Systems Design and Implementation, vol. 7, pp. 205–218 (2006)
5. Comer, D.: The Ubiquitous B-Tree. ACM Computing Surveys 11, 121–137 (1979)
6. Dean, J., Ghemawat, S.: MapReduce: Simplified data processing on large clusters. In: Proceedings of the 6th Symposium on Opearting Systems Design & Implementation. USENIX Association (2004)
7. Evans, E.: Eric Evans' Weblog (May 2009), http://blog.sym-link.com/2009/05/12/nosql_2009.html (retrieved March 03, 2012)
8. Fielding, R.T.: Architectural styles and the design of network-based software architectures. Ph.D. thesis, University of California (2000)
9. Gilbert, S., Lynch, N.: Brewer's conjecture and the feasibility of consistent, available, partition-tolerant web services. SIGACT News 33, 51–59 (2002)
10. Leavitt, N.: Will NoSQL Databases Live Up to Their promise? Computer 43, 12–14 (2010)
11. Lerner, R.M.: At the Forge - Redis. Linux Journal 2010 (197) (September 2010), http://www.linuxjournal.com/article/10836 (retrieved February 27, 2012)
12. MongoDB: BSON, http://www.mongodb.org/display/DOCS/BSON (retrieved February 26, 2012)
13. Ramalho, L.: Implementing a Modern API for CDS/ISIS, a classic semistructured NoSQL Database. In: Todt, E. (ed.) Forum Internacional Do Software Livre, XI Workshop Sobre Software Livre, Porto Alegre, vol. 11, pp. 42–47 (2010)
14. Riva, C., Laitkorpi, M.: Designing Web-Based Mobile Services with REST. In: Di Nitto, E., Ripeanu, M. (eds.) ICSOC 2007. LNCS, vol. 4907, pp. 439–450. Springer, Heidelberg (2009)
15. Robinson, D.: Amazon Web Services Made Simple: Learn how Amazon EC2, S3, SimpleDB and SQS Web Services enables you to reach business goals faster. Emereo Pvt. Ltd., London (2008)
16. Xiang, P., Hou, R., Zhou, Z.: Cache and consistency in NOSQL, vol. 6, pp. 117–120. IEEE (2010)

Hunting for Aardvarks:
Can Software Security Be Measured?

Martin Gilje Jaatun

Department of Software Engineering, Safety and Security
SINTEF ICT
NO-7465 Trondheim, Norway
martin.g.jaatun@sintef.no
http://www.sintef.no/ses

Abstract. When you are in charge of building software from the ground up, software security can be encouraged through the use of secure software development methodologies. However, how can you measure the security of a given piece of software that you didn't write yourself? In other words, when looking at two executables, what does "a is more secure than b" mean? This paper examines some approaches to measuring software security, and reccommends that more organisations should employ the Building Security In Maturity Model (BSIMM).

1 Introduction

When discussing secure software engineering, the main argument for employing a secure software development lifecycle is that it makes the software "more secure" - but exactly what that means isn't entirely clear.

One way of measuring security could be to count the number of security bugs/flaws/attacks against a given software product over time, which is generally the service offered by the Common Vulnerability and Exposures (CVE) [1] and the National Vulnerability Database (NVD) [2]. You could argue that this gives an after-the-fact comparison between different products, with the products with the least number of vulnerabilities claiming the "most secure" title. However, these kind of statistics can easily degenerate into the "damn lies" category [3], since they do not take into account the following factors:

- What is the distribution of the software product?
- What is the attacker's incentive for breaking the product?

For instance, an obscure piece of software could easily go for decades without making it into any vulnerability databases even if it were riddled with security flaws, whereas one reason for the high number of discovered security flaws in Microsoft products can be that due to its large user base, Microsoft remains the target of choice among the hacker population. Also, to quote Fred Brooks: "More users find more bugs." [4].

G. Quirchmayr et al. (Eds.): CD-ARES 2012, LNCS 7465, pp. 85–92, 2012.

The remainder of this paper is organized as follows: In section 2 we[1] present some other approaches toward measuring software security. In section 3 we discuss how different development methodologies might affect software security, and in section 4 we briefly consider what role testing might play in measuring software security. In section 5 we outline the Building Security In Maturity Model (BSIMM), and argue why it could be a good approach to software security metrics. We discuss our contribution in section 6, and offer conclusions in section 7.

2   Background

We will in the following present some previous work on measuring software security, all of which has been presented at the MetriCon series of workshops.

2.1   A Retrospective

Ozment and Schechter [5] studied the rate of discovered security flaws in OpenBSD over a span of 7 years and 6 months. Unsurprisingly, they found that the rate of new bugs discovered in unchanged code dropped toward the end of the period (i.e., the number of latent security flaws are presumably constant, and as time goes by, more and more of the flaws will be found). However, new code is continually added to the code base, and this means that also new vulnerabilities are introduced - Ozment and Schechter found that comparatively fewer vulnerabilities were introduced through added code, but attributed this to the fact that the new code represented a comparatively small proportion of the total code base (39%). In fact, that 39% of code had 38% of the total security flaws, which is within the statistical margin of error.

This contrasts with Brooks' contention that "Sooner or later the fixing ceases to gain any new ground. Each forward step is matched by a backward one. Although in principle usable forever, the system has worn out as a base for progress." [4] It is possible that different rules apply to operating systems than application programs – or that we still haven't reached the "trough of bugginess" in OpenBSD.

2.2   The MetriCon Approach to Security Metrics

The MetriCon workshop was held for the first time in August 2006, in conjunction with the USENIX Security Symposium. Since this workshop doesn't publish regular proceedings, details are a bit hard to come by for those that did not attend, but luckily the workshop publishes a digest[2] of the presentations and ensuing discussions, reported by Dan Geer [6–8] and Daniel Conway [9].

MetriCon covers a wide swath of what can be called security metrics, but is a reasonable place to look for contribtutions to measuring software security.

---

[1] The reader is free to interpret this as the "royal we".

[2] At least for the first four events.

A discussion at the first MetriCon [6] touched upon *code complexity* as a measure of security. This is an approximate measure, at best, since complex code is more difficult to analyze (and may thus help to hide security flaws); but correctly written complex code will not in itself be less secure than simple code. However, if proof of secure code is needed, complexity is likely to be your downfall – it is no coincidence that the highest security evaluation levels typically are awarded to very simple systems.

3   Comparing Software Development Methodologies

Traditional approaches to developing secure software have been oriented toward a waterfall development style and "Big Requirements Up Front" – see e.g. the documentation requirements of a Common Criteria evaluation [10].

However, the jury is still out in the matter of the security of code produced using e.g. agile methods vs. waterfall. There are proponents who claim that XP works just dandy in safety-critical environments (and, presumably, by extension with great security), while other examples demonstrate that an agile mindset purely focused on "let's get this thing working, and let's worry about security later" does not present the best starting point for achieving secure code.

Eberlein and Leite [11] state that the main reason agile methods result in poor security requirements is that the agile methods do not provide verification (are we building the product right), only validation (are we building the right product). Beznosov [12] thinks XP can be good enough, while Wäyrynen et al. [13] claim that the solution to achieving security in an XP development is simply to add a security engineer to the team.

Beznosov and Kruchten [14] compare typical security assurance methods with generic agile methods, and identify a large number of the former that are at odds with the latter (in their words: mis-match). Unsurprisingly, this indicates that it is not possible to apply current security assurance methods to an agile software development project. The authors offer no definite solution to this problem, but indicate two possible courses of action:

1. Develop new agile-friendly security assurance methods. The authors concede that this will be very difficult to achieve, but are not able to offer any insights yet on what exactly such methods could be.
2. Apply the existing security assurance methods at least twice in every agile development project; once early in the lifecycle, and once towards the end.

Siponen et al. [15] believe that all will be well if think about security in every phase. While Poppendieck [16] argues that agile methods (specifically: XP) are just as suitable as traditional development methods for developing safety-critical applications. Kongsli [17] opines that agile methods provide an opportunity for early intervention in connection with securing deployment, and argues for collective ownership of security challenges. However, a security specialist is still required as part of the team.

4 Testing for Security

There exist various static analysis tools that can analyze source code and point out unfortunate content, but just like signature-based antivirus products, these tools can only tell you about a set of pre-defined errors [18].

The ultimate challenge is to be presented with an executable and trying to figure out "how secure is this?". Jensen [19] discusses several approaches to evaluate an executable for unwanted side-effects, but this only covers software with hostile intent, not software that is poorly written.

Fuzzing [20] is a testing technique based on providing random input to software programs, and observing the results. This is an automated version of what used to be referred to as the "kindergarten test"; typing random gibberish on the keyboard. Unfortunately, while it may be possible to enumerate all intended combinations of input to a program, it is not possible to do exhaustive fuzz testing – even if you leave the fuzzer running for weeks, it will still not have exhausted all possible combinations. Thus, fuzzing is not a suitable candidate for a software security metric – if you find flaws, you know the software has flaws; if you don't find flaws, you know ... that you didn't *find* any flaws – but there may be flaws hiding around the next corner.

5 BSIMM and vBSIMM

The Building Security In Maturity Model (BSIMM) [21] and its simpler "younger brother"[3] BSIMM for Vendors (vBSIMM) were introduced by McGraw as an attempt to bypass the problem of measuring software security; arguing that if you cannot measure the security of a given piece of software, you can try to measure second-order effects, i.e. count various practices that companies that are producing good software security are doing.

5.1 The BSIMM Software Security Framework

BSIMM defines a Software Security Framework (SSF) divided into four domains each covering three practices (see Table 1). Each practice in turn covers a number of activities grouped in three levels (see below).

- The **Governance** domain includes practices *Strategy and Metrics, Compliance and Policy*, and *Training.*
- The **Intelligence** domain includes practices *Attack Models, Security Features and Design*, and *Standards and Requirements.*
- The **SSDL Touchpoints** domain refers to McGraw's approach to a Secure Software development Lifecycle [23], and includes practices *Architecture Analysis, Code Review*, and *Security Testing.* There are more touchpoints listed in McGraw's book, but these three have been identified by McGraw as the most important.

---

[3] In a way the opposite of Sherlock Holmes' smarter older brother Mycroft - "When I say, therefore, that Mycroft has better powers of observation than I, you may take it that I am speaking the exact and literal truth." [22]

– The **Deployment** domain includes practices *Penetration Testing, Software Environment,* and *Configuration Management and Vulnerability Management.*

Table 1. The BSIMM Software Security Framework

Governance	Intelligence	SSDL Touchpoints	Deployment
Strategy and Metrics	Attack Models	Architecture Analysis	Penetration Testing
Compliance and Policy	Security Features and Design	Code Review	Software Environment
Training	Standards and Requirements	Security Testing	Configuration Management and Vulnerability Management

5.2 Maturity Is One of the M-s in BSIMM

Each BSIMM practice contains a number of *activities* grouped in three maturity levels. Each maturity level is given a textual description, but it's not entirely clear if *all* the activities in a lower level need to be in place to progress to the next level – it may be assumed that the BSIMM "auditors" employ some discretion here when collecting the interview data.

To take a random example, we can look at the *Security Testing* (ST) practice within the **SSDL Touchpoints** domain. ST level 1 is labeled "Enhance QA beyond functional perspective", and comprises the activities:

– ST1.1: Ensure QA supports edge/boundary value condition testing.
– ST1.2: Share security results with QA.
– ST1.3: Allow declarative security/security features to drive tests.

ST level 2 is labeled "Integrate the attacker perspective into test plans", and currently has only two activities:

– ST2.1: Integrate black box security tools into the QA process (including protocol fuzzing).
– ST2.3: Begin to build/apply adversarial security tests (abuse cases).

The third ST level is labeled "Deliver risk-based security testing", and has four activities:

– ST3.1: Include security tests in QA automation.
– ST3.2: Perform fuzz testing customized to application APIs.
– ST3.3: Drive tests with risk analysis results.
– ST3.3: Leverage coverage analysis.

The BSIMM authors reccommend that if using BSIMM as a cookbook, an organization should not try to jump to the third level all at once, but rather implement the first-level activities first, and then move on only once the first level is truly embedded. This is partly because some higher-level activities build on the lower-level ones (e.g., ST2.1 and ST1.1), but also because the higher-level activities typically are more difficult and require more resources.

5.3   BSIMM in Practice

The BSIMM documentation is freely available under a Creative Commons license, and in theory there is nothing to stop anyone from using it to compare new organizations to the ones already covered. However, it is clear that the raw data used in creating the BSIMM reports is kept confidential, and BSIMM is no interview cookbook – it is safe to assume that participants are not asked directly "do you use attack models?", but exactly how the BSIMM team goes about cross-examining their victims is not general knowledge, and is thus difficult to reproduce.

Using the BSIMM as a research tool may therefore be more challenging than using it as a self-assessment tool, and the latter is certainly more in line with the creators' intentions.

6   Discussion

It is unlikely that we'll see any "fire and forget" solution for software security in the near future, but we may aspire to a situation of "forget and get fired", i.e. where software security becomes an explicit part of development managers area of responsibility.

Recently, we have seen in job postings for generic software developers that "knowledge of software security" has been listed as a desired skill – this may be a hint that the software security community's preaching has reached beyond the choir.

If you want a job done right, you have to do it yourself – but if you can't do it yourself, you need other evidence. It seems that for lack of anything better, the BSIMM approach of enumerating which of the "right" things a software company is doing is currently the best approach to achieve good software security. It is true that past successes cannot guarantee future happiness; but on the other hand, a company that has demonstrated that it cares enough to identify good software security practices is more likely to follow these in the future than a company that does not appear to be aware of such practices in the first place.

7   Conclusion and Further Work

There is currently no good metric which can easily decide which one of two executable is better from a software security point of view. It seems that currently, the best we can do is is to measure second-order effects to identify which software companies are trying hardest. If we are concerned about software security, those are the companies we should be buying our software from.

More empirical work is needed on comparing software produced by different methodologies, e.g. agile vs. waterfall. Intuitively, the former may seem less formal and thus less security-conscious, but an interesting starting point may be to compare the number of secure software engineering practices employed in the different organizations. Retrospective studies may also compare the track record of various methodologies over time, but the main challenge here may be to identify software that is sufficiently similar in distribution and scope to make the comparison meaningful.

Acknowledgment. The title of this paper is inspired by an InformIT article by Gary McGraw and John Stevens [18]. Thanks to Jostein Jensen for fruitful discussions on software security for the rest of us.

References

1. CVE: Common Vulnerabilities and Exposures (CVE), http://cve.mitre.org/
2. NVD: National Vulnerability Database Home, http://nvd.nist.gov
3. Clemens, S.L.: Notes on 'innocents abroad': Paragraph 20 (2010) (There are three kinds of lies: lies, damned lies, and statistics - Attributed to Disraeli), http://marktwainproject.org
4. Brooks, F.P.: The Mythical Man-Month. Addison-Wesley (1995)
5. Ozment, A., Schechter, S.E.: Milk or wine: does software security improve with age? In: Proceedings of the 15th Conference on USENIX Security Symposium, USENIX-SS 2006, vol. 15. USENIX Association, Berkeley (2006)
6. Geer, D.: MetriCon 1.0 Digest (2006), http://www.securitymetrics.org/content/Wiki.jsp?page=Metricon1.0
7. Geer, D.: MetriCon 2.0 Digest (2007), http://www.securitymetrics.org/content/Wiki.jsp?page=Metricon2.0
8. Geer, D.: MetriCon 4.0 Digest (2009), http://www.securitymetrics.org/content/Wiki.jsp?page=Metricon4.0
9. Conway, D.: MetriCon 3.0 Digest (2008), http://www.securitymetrics.org/content/Wiki.jsp?page=Metricon3.0
10. ISO/IEC 15408-1: Evaluation criteria for it security part 1: Introduction and general model (2005)
11. Eberlein, A., do Prado Leite, J.C.S.: Agile requirements definition: A view from requirements engineering. In: Proceedings of the International Workshop on Time-Constrained Requirements Engineering (TCRE 2002) (2002)
12. Beznosov, K.: eXtreme Security Engineering: On Employing XP Practices to Achieve "Good Enough Security" without Defining It. In: Proceedings of the First ACM Workshop on Business Driven Security Engineering, BizSec (2003)
13. Wäyrynen, J., Bodén, M., Boström, G.: Security Engineering and eXtreme Programming: An Impossible Marriage? In: Zannier, C., Erdogmus, H., Lindstrom, L. (eds.) XP/Agile Universe 2004. LNCS, vol. 3134, pp. 117–128. Springer, Heidelberg (2004)
14. Beznosov, K., Kruchten, P.: Towards agile security assurance. In: Proceedings of New Security Paradigms Workshop, Nova Scotia, Canada (2004)
15. Siponen, M., Baskerville, R., Kuivalainen, T.: Integrating security into agile development methods. In: Proceedings of Hawaii International Conference on System Sciences (2005)

16. Poppendieck, M., Morsicato, R.: XP in a Safety-Critical Environment. Cutter IT Journal 15, 12–16 (2002)
17. Kongsli, V.: Towards agile security in web applications. In: Companion to the 21st ACM SIGPLAN Symposium on Object-Oriented Programming Systems, Languages, and Applications, OOPSLA 2006, pp. 805–808. ACM, New York (2006)
18. McGraw, G., Steven, J.: Software [In]security: Comparing Apples, Oranges, and Aardvarks (or, All Static Analysis Tools Are Not Created Equal) (2011)
19. Jensen, J.: A Novel Testbed for Detection of Malicious Software Functionality. In: Proceedings of Third International Conference on Availability, Security, and Reliability (ARES 2008), pp. 292–301 (2008)
20. Miller, B., Fredriksen, L., So, B.: An empirical study of the reliability of unix utilities. Communications of the ACM 33(12) (1990)
21. McGraw, G., Chess, B., Migues, S.: Building Security In Maturity Model (BSIMM 3) (2011)
22. Doyle, A.C.: Memoirs of Sherlock Holmes, http://www.gutenberg.org/files/834/834-h/834-h.htm
23. McGraw, G.: Software Security: Building Security. Addison-Wesley (2006)

A Foundation for Requirements Analysis of Privacy Preserving Software*

Kristian Beckers and Maritta Heisel

paluno, The Ruhr Institute for Software Technology, University of Duisburg, Essen
firstname.lastname@paluno.uni-due.de

Abstract. Privacy requirements are difficult to elicit for any given software engineering project that processes personal information. The problem is that these systems require personal data in order to achieve their functional requirements and privacy mechanisms that constrain the processing of personal information in such a way that the requirement still states a useful functionality.

We present privacy patterns that support the expression and analysis of different privacy goals: anonymity, pseudonymity, unlinkability and unobservability. These patterns have a textual representation that can be instantiated. In addition, for each pattern, a logical predicate exists that can be used to validate the instantiation. We also present a structured method for instantiating and validating the privacy patterns, and for choosing privacy mechanisms. Our patterns can also be used to identify incomplete privacy requirements. The approach is illustrated by the case study of a patient monitoring system.

Keywords: privacy, common criteria, compliance, requirements engineering.

1 Introduction

Westin defines privacy as "the claim of individuals, groups, or institutions to determine for themselves when, how, and to what extent information about them is communicated to others" [1]. A number of guidelines for privacy are available. *The Fair Information Practice Principles* – or short FIPs) [2] – are widely accepted, which state that a person's informed consent is required for the data that is collected, collection should be limited for the task it is required for and erased as soon as this is not the case anymore. The collector of the data shall keep the data secure and shall be held accountable for any violation of these principles. The FIPs were also adapted into the Personal Information Protection and Electronic Documents Act in Canada's private-sector privacy law. In the European Union the *EU Data Protection Directive*, *Directive 95/46/EC*, does not permit processing personal data at all, except when a specific legal basis explicitly allows it or when the individuals concerned consented prior to the data processing [3]. The U.S. have no central data protection law, but separate privacy laws, e.g., the Gramm-Leach-Bliley Act for financial information, the Health Insurance Portability and Accountability Act for medical information, and the Children's Online Privacy Protection Act for

---

* This research was partially supported by the EU project Network of Excellence on Engineering Secure Future Internet Software Services and Systems (NESSoS, ICT-2009.1.4 Trustworthy ICT, Grant No. 256980).

G. Quirchmayr et al. (Eds.): CD-ARES 2012, LNCS 7465, pp. 93–107, 2012.

data related to children [4]. These legal guidelines must be implemented by any given software system for which the guidelines apply.

However, in order to comply with these guidelines the privacy requirements for a given software system have to be elicited. In order to do this we have to formulate specific privacy goals. We use two distinct approaches that specify privacy terms that can used for this purpose, namely the terminology by Pfitzmann and Hansen [5] and the privacy specification in the ISO 15408 standard - Common Criteria for Information Technology Security Evaluation (or short CC) [6]. Pfitzmann and Hansen [5] introduced a terminology for privacy via data minimization. They define central terms of privacy using items of interest (IOIs) , e.g., subjects, messages and actions. *Anonymity* means that a subject is not identifiable within a set of subjects, the anonymity set. *Unlinkability* of two or more IOIs means that within a system the attacker cannot sufficiently distinguish whether these IOIs are related or not. *Undetectability* of an IOI means that the attacker cannot sufficiently distinguish whether it exists or not. *Unobservability* of an IOI means undetectability of the IOI against all subjects uninvolved in it and anonymity of the subject(s) involved in the IOI even against the other subject(s) involved in that IOI. A pseudonym is an identifier of a subject other than one of the subject's real names. Using pseudonyms means *pseudonymity*. The CC contains the privacy requirements anonymity, pseudonymity, unlinkability, and unobservability [6, pp. 118-125].

In this paper, we provide patterns for these privacy requirements, building on the problem frame terminology, and we explain the difference between the privacy notions in the CC and the Pfitzmann and Hansen terminology.

The rest of the paper is organized as follows. Section 2 presents the problem frame approach, and Sect. 3 explains how to work with privacy patterns. We introduce our patterns in Sect. 4 and illustrate them using a case study. Section 5 contains related work, and Sect. 6 concludes.

2   Problem Frames

We use a problem frames approach to build our privacy patterns on, because problem frames are an appropriate means to analyze not only functional, but also dependability and other quality requirements [7,8].

Problem frames are a means to describe software development problems. They were proposed by Jackson [9], who describes them as follows: *"A problem frame is a kind of pattern. It defines an intuitively identifiable problem class in terms of its context and the characteristics of its domains, interfaces and requirement."*. It is described by a *frame diagram*, which consists of domains, interfaces between them, and a requirement. We describe problem frames using class diagrams extended by stereotypes as proposed by Hatebur and Heisel at Safecomp 2010 [10](see Fig. 1). All elements of a problem frame diagram act as placeholders, which must be instantiated to represent concrete problems. Doing so, one obtains a problem description that belongs to a specific kind of problem.

The class with the stereotype machine represents the thing to be developed (e.g., the software). The other classes with some domain stereotypes, e.g., *CausalDomain* or *BiddableDomain* represent *problem domains* that already exist in the application environment. Domains are connected by interfaces consisting of shared phenomena.

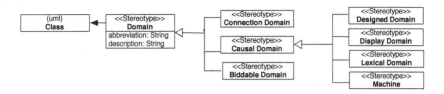

Fig. 1. Inheritance Structure of different Domain Types

Shared phenomena may be events, operation calls, messages, and the like. They are observable by at least two domains, but controlled by only one domain, as indicated by an exclamation mark. These interfaces are represented as associations, and the name of the associations contain the phenomena and the domains controlling the phenomena.

Jackson distinguishes the domain types **CausalDomain**s that comply with some physical laws, **LexicalDomain**s that are data representations, and **BiddableDomain**s that are usually people. According to Jackson, domains are either **designed**, **given**, or **machine** domains. The domain types are modeled by the subclasses *BiddableDomain*, *CausalDomain*, and *LexicalDomain* of the class *Domain*. A lexical domain is a special case of a causal domain. This kind of modeling allows one to add further domain types, such as *DisplayDomain*s as introduced in [11] (see Fig. 1).

Problem frames support developers in analyzing problems to be solved. They show what domains have to be considered, and what knowledge must be described and reasoned about when analyzing the problem in depth.

Software development with problem frames proceeds as follows: first, the environment in which the machine will operate is represented by a *context diagram*. Like a frame diagram, a context diagram consists of domains and interfaces. However, a context diagram contains no requirements. Then, the problem is decomposed into subproblems. If ever possible, the decomposition is done in such a way that the subproblems fit to given problem frames. To fit a subproblem to a problem frame, one must instantiate its frame diagram, i.e., provide instances for its domains, phenomena, and interfaces. The instantiated frame diagram is called a *problem diagram*.

Since the requirements refer to the *environment* in which the machine must operate, the next step consists in deriving a *specification* for the machine (see [12] for details). The specification describes the machine and is the starting point for its construction.

3 Working with Privacy Patterns

We developed a set of patterns for expressing and analyzing privacy requirements, which are presented in more detail in Sect. 4. An important advantage of these patterns is that they allow privacy requirements to be expressed without anticipating solutions. For example, we may require data to be anonymized before these are transmitted without being obliged to mention k-Anonymity [13], which is a means to achieve anonymity.

The benefit of considering privacy requirements without reference to potential solutions is the clear separation of problems from their solutions, which leads to a better understanding of the problems and enhances the re-usability of the problem descriptions, since they are completely independent of solution technologies.

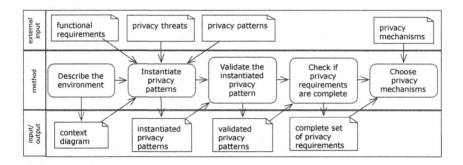

Fig. 2. A Method for Using Privacy Patterns

We provide a method for privacy requirements elicitation using our privacy patterns. The entire method is depict in Fig. 2. This approach helps to elicit and complete privacy requirements within a given software engineering process. We use the resulting set of requirements to choose privacy-enhancing mechanisms.

The first step in our method is to *describe the environment*, because privacy requirements can only be guaranteed for a specific intended environment. For example, a software may preserve privacy of its users in a social media setting, where it is only exchanging information about concert tickets, but not for a medical setting exchanging more sensible information about the health status of its stakeholders. This step results in a context diagram (see Sect. 2) of the intended software system.

We apply our patterns after a privacy threat analysis has been conducted, e.g., according to the PIA method of the Australian Government [14], and functional requirements of the system have been elicited. The requirements describe how the environment should behave when the machine is in action. The description of the requirements must consist of domains and phenomena of the environment description. The functional requirements and privacy threats, as well as our privacy patterns are used to *instantiate privacy patterns*. For each privacy threat, a textual representation of a privacy pattern is instantiated using the context diagram. This results in an initial set of privacy requirements. These are linked to the previously described functional requirements.

The next step is to *validate the instantiated privacy patterns* using the corresponding privacy predicates. Our privacy requirements patterns are expressed in natural language and logical predicates. The natural text has parts written in **bold**, which have to be instantiated with ***domains*** of a context diagram for the system. These present a structured analysis of the required elements in order to specify the requirement. In addition, the logical predicates refer to **domain types** in a context diagram that have a kind-of relationship to the domains in the natural language pattern. This allows us to check if the instantiated domains have the correct domain types.

Privacy requirements are separated from functional requirements. On the one hand, this limits the number of patterns; on the other hand, it allows one to apply these patterns to a wide range of problems. For example, the functional requirements for data transmission or automated control can be expressed using a problem diagram. Privacy requirements for anonymity, unlinkability, unobservability, and pseudonymity can be added to that description of the functional requirement, as shown in Sect.4.

The predicate patterns are expressed using the domain types of the meta-model described in Figure 1, i.e., **Domain**, **BiddableDomain**, **CausalDomain**, and **LexicalDomain**. From these classes in the meta-model, subclasses with special properties are derived. We explain the domain types that are relevant for this step in the method:

- A **Stakeholder** is a **BiddableDomain** (and in some special cases also a **CausalDomain**) with some relation to stored or transmitted personal information. It is not necessary that a stakeholder has an interface to the machine.
- A **CounterStakeholder** is a **BiddableDomain** that describes all subjects (with their equipment) who can compromise the privacy of a **Stakeholder** at the machine. We do not use the term attacker here, because the word attacker indicates a malicious intent. Privacy of stakeholders can also be violated by accident.
- **PersonalInformation** is a **CausalDomain** or **LexicalDomain** that represents personal information about a **Stakeholder**. The difference between these domains is that a **LexicalDomain** describes just the stored information, while a **CausalDomain** also includes the physical medium the data is stored upon, e.g., a hard drive.
- **StoredPersonalInformation** is **PersonalInformation**, which is stored in a fixed physical location, e.g., a hard drive in the U.S.
- **TransmittedPersonalInformation** is **PersonalInformation**, which is transmitted in-between physical locations, e.g., data in a network that spans from Germany to the U.S.
- **InformationAboutPersonalInformation** is is a **CausalDomain** or **LexicalDomain** that represents information about **PersonalInformation**, e.g., the physical location of the name and address of a stakeholder.

The *check if privacy requirements are complete* is a check that all the textual gaps are instantiated. For example, a requirement that has to be instantiated with a **Stakeholder** has to name an instance of a biddable domain from the context diagram, e.g., **Patient**s. Several privacy patterns require instantiation with sets of biddable domains. For example, a privacy pattern might not only be directed towards **Patient**s, but also towards **Visitor**s of patients. In this case we can reason for all biddable domains in the context diagram if they are a **Stakeholder** or not.

In addition, a requirement might be missing, e.g. because of an incomplete threat analysis. In order to execute this check all personal information in the system has to be elicited. For each **CausalDomain** or **LexicalDomain**, we have to check if these are **StoredPersonalInformation**, **TransmittedPersonalInformation** or **InformationAboutPersonalInformation**. If this is the case, we check if these were considered in the privacy threat analysis. If this is not the case, we have to re-do the privacy threat analysis and start our process again.

The last step of our approach is to *choose a privacy mechanism* that solves the problem. For example, to achieve pseudonymity, a privacy-enhancing identity management systems [15] can be chosen.

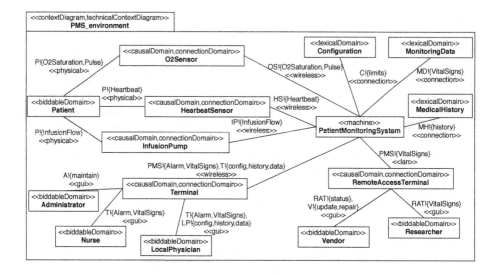

Fig. 3. Patient Monitoring System Context Diagramm

4 Privacy Patterns

We illustrate our method with the development of a *patient monitoring system (PMS)*, which monitors the vital signs of patients, reports these to physicians and nurses, and controls an infusion flow according to specified rules. The context diagram of the system is shown in Fig. 3. The configuration is stored in a database of the system, as well as the monitoring data of each patient over time and the medical history of each patient. This history shall help physicians to determine the correct settings for the PMS. Nurses and physician have access to alarm messages of the system and the information about the vital signs of patients. An administrator has access to the system for maintenance purposes. The system also allows a remote access for the vendor in order to receive status messages and send updates or repair the system. In addition, the system provides information of monitored data to researchers. The **privacy threat** to be avoided is that a counterstakeholder reveals personal information of the patient to one or more unauthorized persons.[1] Examples for the **described environment** are the properties of the infusion pump and the heartbeat and O2 flow sensors. Further examples are the assumed opportunities of a counterstakeholder to gather personal information about patients and to distribute it. A possible counterstakeholder can be a stakeholder of the system. In addition, we assume here that a counterstakeholder, who is not also a stakeholder of the system, can only access the WAVE/WLAN interface. Stakeholders and counterstakeholders are biddable domains in the context diagram shown in Fig. 3. The elicitation of stakeholders and counterstakeholders from biddable domains is part of the instantiation process. Hence, the reasoning of which biddable domain is either a stakeholder or counterstakeholder or both is essential. The information from the privacy threat serves as a

---

[1] The privacy threat analysis is left out here.

support in this task. The **functional requirement** of the PMS is to keep the infusion flow controlled according to the configuration.

R1 The PMS shall control the infusion flow of a *Patient* using the *InfusionPump* according to the *Configuration* given by a *Physician* based upon the vital signs of the *Patient*, which are transmitted using a wireless network (WAVE/WLAN interface).

R2 The PMS should raise an alarm for *Physicians* and *Nurses* using the *Terminal*, if the vital signs of a *Patient* exceed the limits defined in the *Configuration*.

R3 *Physicians* can change the *Configuration*, according to the *MonitoringData* of the vital signs and the *MedicalHistory* of a *Patient* in the PMS using the *Terminal*, which sends the *Configuration* to the PMS using a wireless network (WAVE/WLAN interface).

R4 *Researchers* can use the collected data about *Patients*' vital signs for a long term medical study using the *RemoteAccessTerminal* that sends the data over a wired network (LAN interface) from the PMS. The *Vendor* can query the status of the PMS and send patches to the PMS using the *RemoteAccessTerminal*.

R5 *Administrators* can use the *Terminal* to maintain the PMS.

We **instantiate privacy requirements** as a next step. We describe privacy patterns as textual patterns. The parts of the pattern's textual description printed in *bold and italics* should be instantiated according to the concrete problem. Hence, the instantiation should use only domains from the context diagram. We complement the textual description of the patterns with predicates. They must be described in such a way that it is possible to demonstrate that the privacy predicate holds for all objects of this class. The instantiated predicates are helpful to analyze conflicting requirements and the interaction of different privacy requirements, as well as for finding missing privacy requirements.

4.1 Anonymity

For the functional requirement **R4**, we formulate a privacy requirement for anonymity. The textual pattern for anonymity requirements is:

> Preserve anonymity of *Stakeholders* and prevent disclosure of their identity by *CounterStakeholders*.

The privacy requirement pattern can be expressed by the anonymity predicate:

$$anon_{cs} : BiddableDomain \times \mathbb{P}\, BiddableDomain \rightarrow Bool$$

The suffix "cs" indicates that this predicate describes a requirement considering a certain CounterStakeholder. The definition of anonymity by Pfitzmann and Hansen [5] states that a stakeholder shall not be identifiable from a set of stakeholders. This is the so-called *anonymity set*, which is represented in our pattern by a biddable domain and in turn a specific type of biddable domain called *Stakeholder*. We interpret a domain according to Jackson [9] also as a set. Hence, all the persons that are *Stakeholders* used to instantiate the anonymity pattern form the anonymity set. The second argument of the predicate $anon_{cs}$ must be instantiated with a *set* of biddable domains, because we might have more than one kind of counterstakeholder. We analyze the context diagram (see Fig. 3) for counterstakeholders that might gain personal information using the *RemoteAccessTerminal*. This leads to the *Researcher*.

> Preserve anonymity of *Patients* and prevent disclosure of their identity by *Researchers*.

In this case all instances of *Patients* are elements of the anonymity set.

We **validate the instantiated privacy pattern** by checking if predicate is instantiated with domains belonging to the required domain types: The *Patient* is a biddable domain and the *Researcher* is also a biddable domain, which forms the only member of the set of counterstakeholder. Hence, the anonymity predicate is instatiated in a type-correct way. As a next step we **check if the privacy requirement is complete**.

The counterstakeholders are a set of biddable domains. This demands that we inspect the context diagram (see Fig. 3) again for further possible counterstakeholders. Another biddable domain has access to the *RemoteAccessTerminal*, the *Vendor*. Therefore, we add the *Vendor* to the list of counterstakeholders. We **choose a privacy mechanism** as a final step for anoymity, e.g., based upon the work in [16].

$$anon_{cs} : Patients \times \{Researcher, Vendor\} \to Bool$$

Common Criteria. The common criteria divides requirements for anonymity into two categories. The first one is just called anonymity and the second one is a refinement of the first and called anonymity without soliciting information. The first demands from a privacy mechanism that it shall ensure that a set of "users" or "subjects" are unable to determine the "real name" related to a set of "subjects or operations or objects" [6, p. 119]. This demand is similar to the requirement above. The set of users is translated into *CounterStakeholders* and subjects are *Stakeholders*. The second kind of anonymity the CC considers is the so-called "anonymity without soliciting information" about the real user name for a set of services and subjects [6, p. 119]. This requirement needs the first requirements as a prerequisite.

We formulate an anonymity without soliciting personal information requirement :

> Preserve anonymity of *Stakeholders* via not soliciting *personal information* via *ConstrainedDomains* and, thus, prevent disclosure to certain *CounterStakeholders*.

where a *ConstrainedDomain* is a *CausalDomain* or a *ConnectionDomain* that is constrained by a functional or privacy requirement.

The privacy requirement pattern can be expressed by the anonymity without soliciting personal information predicate:

$$anonCC_{cs} : BiddableDomain \times \mathbb{P} \, LexicalDomain \times \mathbb{P} \, ConstrainedDomain \to Bool$$

The first kind anonymity requirement of the CC is instantiated with the requirement stated above. We instantiate also the textual pattern for the second kind of requirement using the context diagram. We instantiate the *ConstrainedDomain* with the *RemoteAccessTerminal* and the *personal information* with *MedicalHistory*:

> Preserve anonymity of *Patient*s via not soliciting *MedicalHistory* via *RemoteAccessTerminal* and, thus, prevent disclosure to *Researcher*s and *Vendor*s.

4.2   Unlinkability

The textual pattern for unlinkability requirements is:

> Preserve unlinkability of two or more *ConstrainedDomain*s for *Stakeholder*s and prevent *CounterStakeholder*s of disclosing that the *ConstrainedDomain*s have a relation to the *Stakeholder*.

The privacy requirement pattern can be expressed by the unlinkability predicate:

$$unlink_{cs} : \mathbb{P} \ CausalDomain \times BiddableDomain \times \mathbb{P} \ BiddableDomain \\ \rightarrow Bool$$

We also **instantiate privacy requirements** for the functional requirement **R3**. The following privacy requirement for unlinkability can be stated using the textual pattern:

> Preserve unlinkability of *Configuration*s, *MonitoringData*, and *MedicalHistory* for a *Patient* and prevent *Nurse*s and *Administrator*s of disclosing that the *Configuration*s, *MonitoringData*, and *MedicalHistory* have a relation to the *Patient*.

We again **validate the instantiated privacy pattern** by checking if predicate is instantiated with domains belonging to the required domain types: The domains *Configuration*s, *MonitoringData*, and *MedicalHistory* are lexical domains according to the context diagram (see Fig. 3) and these are refined causal domains (see Fig. 1). The *Patient* is a biddable domain and *Nurse*s and *Administrator*s are also biddable domains. Hence, the unlinkability predicate is instatiated in a type-correct way.

   We **check if the privacy requirement is complete**. The *LocalPhysician* also has access *Terminal*, but **R3** states that the *LocalPhysician* requires access to these data. Thus, *LocalPhysician*s are excluded from the unlinkability requirement. We **choose a privacy mechanism** for unlinkability, e.g., based upon the work in [17].

Common Criteria. The common criteria lists requirements for unlinkability of just one category. This demands from a privacy mechanism that it shall ensure that a set of "users" or "subjects" are unable to determine if "operations" are used by the same users or have other recurring relations [6, p. 122].

4.3 Unobservability

The textual pattern for unobservability requirements is:

> Preserve unobservability of **ConstrainedDomain**s that are used by **Stakeholder**s and prevent **CounterStakeholder**s from recognizing that the **ConstrainedDomain**s exist.

The privacy requirement pattern can be expressed by the unobservability predicate:

$$unobserv_{cs} : \mathbb{P} \ CausalDomain \ \times \ BiddableDomain \ \times \ \mathbb{P} \ BiddableDomain \\ \rightarrow Bool$$

An example of an instantiated unobservability requirement is:

> Preserve unobservability of a **MedicalHistory** that is used by **LocalPhysician**s and prevent **Administrator(s),Nurse(s)** from recognizing that the **MedicalHistory** exists.

Common Criteria. The common criteria divides requirements for unobservability into four categories. The first demands from a privacy mechanism that it shall ensure that a set of "users" or "subjects" are unable to observe certain "operations" on "objects" [6, p. 123-125]. This first requirements is equivalent to the requirement stated previously.

The second kind of unobservability the CC considers is the so-called "allocation of information impact unobservability". The CC demands a privacy mechanism that ensures that "unobservability related information" is distributed to different parts of the machine, such that specific conditions hold, which ensure allocation of information impact unobservability [6, p. 123-125]. The standard does not specify these conditions. This kind of unobservability needs the first kind of unobservability requirement as a prerequisite.

We formulate an allocation of information impact unobservability requirement:

> Distribute **InformationAboutPersonalInformation** of **Stakeholder**s on the machine, such that a **CounterStakeholder** cannot recognize its existence.

Specific conditions have to be derived in order to be able to check whether the requirement is fulfilled. The privacy requirement pattern can be expressed by the unobservability related information predicate:

$$unobservRelInf_{cs} : CausalDomain \ \times \ BiddableDomain \ \times \ \mathbb{P} \ BiddableDomain \\ \rightarrow Bool$$

The third kind of unobservability the CC considers is the so-called "unobservability without soliciting information". This demands unobservability without soliciting information about personal information [6, p. 123-125].

We formulate an unobservability without soliciting personal information requirement:

Preserve unobservability without soliciting personal information of **Stakeholder**s via not soliciting **PersonalInformation** and, thus, prevent disclosure to a certain **CounterStakeholder**.

The privacy requirement pattern can be expressed by the unobservability without soliciting personal information predicate:

$$unobservWoSol_{cs} : BiddableDomain \times LexicalDomain \times \mathbb{P}\,BiddableDomain \\ \rightarrow Bool$$

The fourth kind of unobservability the CC considers is the so-called "authorized user observability". The standard demands a solution that offers a list of "authorized users" that can observe the usage of "resources and services" [6, p. 123-125].

We formulate an authorized user observability unobservability requirement :

Provide access of authorized **Stakeholder**s to **InformationAboutPersonalInformation**.

We also **instantiate privacy requirements** for the functional requirement **R3**. The privacy requirement pattern can be expressed by the unobservability related information predicate:

$$unobservRelInf_{cs} : \mathbb{P}\,BiddableDomain \times LexicalDomain \rightarrow Bool$$

4.4   Pseudonymity

A **Pseudonym** is a **LexicalDomain** used as an identifier of a **Stakeholder** without revealing **PersonalInformation**. An **Authorized User** is a **Stakeholder** who is allowed to know the identity of the **Stakeholder** the **Pseudonym** belongs to.

The textual pattern for pseudonymity requirements is:

Preserve pseudonymity of **Stakeholder**s via preventing **CounterStakeholder**s from relating **Pseudonym**s to **Stakeholder**s.

The privacy requirement pattern can be expressed by the pseudonymity predicate:

$$pseudo_{cs} : LexicalDomain \times BiddableDomain \times \mathbb{P}\,BiddableDomain \\ \rightarrow Bool$$

For the functional requirement **R5**, we formulate a privacy requirement for pseudonymity:

Preserve pseudonymity of **Patient**s via preventing **Administrator**s from relating **Pseudonym**s to **Patient**s.

Common Criteria. The common criteria divides requirements for pseudonymity into three categories [6, p. 120-121]. The first demands from a privacy mechanism that it shall ensure that a set of "users" or "subjects" are unable to determine the real user name of "subjects or operations or objects" or "operations" or "objects". In addition, the privacy mechanism shall use "aliases" of the real user name for "subjects". Moreover, the privacy mechanism shall decide which "alias" the user gets assigned. The "alias" has to conform to an "alias metric". The following kinds of pseudonymity requirements have the first kind of pseudonymity requirements as a prerequisite.

The second kind of pseudonymity the CC considers is the so-called "reversible pseudonymity". This demands that authorized users can determine the user identity under a list of conditions [6, p. 120-121]. The standard does not specify these conditions further.

We formulate an reversible pseudonymity requirement:

Preserve pseudonymity of **Stakeholder**s via preventing that a certain **CounterStakeholder** from relating a **Pseudonym** to its **Stakeholder**. An **Authorized User** shall be able to relate a **Pseudonym** to its **Stakeholder**.

The privacy requirement pattern can be expressed by the reversible pseudonymity predicate:

$$pseudoRe_{cs} : LexicalDomain \times BiddableDomain \times \mathbb{P}\ BiddableDomain \\ \times BiddableDomain \to Bool$$

The third kind of pseudonymity the CC considers is the so-called "alias pseudonymity". This demands if a **Stakeholder** gets a **Pseudonym** assigned it shall either be always the same or the two **Pseudonym**s shall not be related at all [6, p. 120-121].

We formulate an alias pseudonymity requirement:

Provide the same **Stakeholder** with the same or completely unrelated **Pseudonym**s.

The privacy requirement pattern can be expressed by the alias pseudonymity predicate:

$$pseudoAl_{cs} : LexicalDomain \times BiddableDomain \to Bool$$

5   Related Work

The authors Deng et al. [18] generate a threat tree for privacy based upon the threat categories: linkability, identifiablitiy, non-repudiation, detectability, information disclosure, content unawareness, and policy/consent noncompliance. These threats are modeled for the elements of an information flow model, which has data flow, data store, processes and entities as components. Privacy threats are described for each of these components. This method can complement our own. The results of the privacy threat analysis from Deng et al. can be used as an input for our method.

The PriS method elicits privacy requirements in the software design phase. Privacy requirements are modeled as organizational goals. Further privacy process patterns are used to identify system architectures, which support the privacy requirements [19]. The PriS method starts with a conceptual model, which also considers enterprise goals, stakeholders, privacy goals, and processes [19]. In addition, the Pris method is based upon a goal oriented requirements engineering approach, while our work uses a problem based approach as a foundation. The difference is that our work focuses on a description of the environment as a foundation for the privacy analysis, while the Pris method uses organizational goals as a starting point.

Hafiz described four privacy design patterns for the network level of software systems. These patterns solely focus on anonymity and unlinkability of senders and receivers of network messages from protocols e.g. http [20]. The patterns are specified with several categories. Among them are intent, motivation, context, problem and solution, as well as forces, design issues and consequences. Forces are relevant factors for the applicability of the pattern e.g. number of users or performance. Design issues describe how the forces have to be considered during software design. For example, the number of stakeholders have to have a relevant size for the pattern to work. Consequences are the benefits and liabilities the pattern provides. For example, an anonymity pattern can disguise the origin of a message, but the pattern will cause a significant performance decrease [20]. This work focuses on privacy issues on the network layer and can complement our work in this area.

Hatebur and Heisel proposed similar patterns for expressing and analyzing dependability requirements [7].

6   Conclusions

In this paper, we have presented a set of patterns for eliciting and analyzing privacy requirements. These patterns are separated from the functional requirements and expressed without anticipating solutions. They can be used to create re-usable privacy requirements descriptions for a wide range of problems.

Our work also includes a structured method for instantiating privacy patterns and validates the correctness and completeness of the instantiated patterns in a systematic way. The patterns are based upon natural language privacy goals: anonymity, unlinkability, unobservability, and pseudonymity. The instantiated parameters of the patterns refer to domains of the environment descriptions and are used to describe the privacy requirements precisely. Predicates exist for each of the patterns, which can be used to validate that the instantiated parameters from the environment description have the correct domain types. In addition, several values of the privacy patterns can be instantiated with a set of subclasses of a specific domain type. Hence, we can reason about all domains of that type in the environment description, if they are part of this set or not.

In summary, our pattern system has the following advantages:

- The privacy patterns are re-usable for different projects.
- A manageable number of patterns can be applied on a wide range of problems, because they are separated from the functional requirements.
- Requirements expressed by instantiated patterns only refer to the environment description and are independent from solutions. Hence, they can be easily re-used for new product versions.

- The patterns closely relate textual descriptions and predicates. The textual description helps to instantiate the privacy requirements, while the predicates are used for validation of the instantiation.
- The patterns help to structure and classify the privacy requirements. For example, requirements considering anonymity can be easily distinguished from unlinkability requirements. It is also possible to trace all privacy requirements that refer to one domain.
- The patterns also have variations to satisfy the privacy requirements stated in the common criteria.

In the future, we plan to elaborate more on the later phases of software development. For example, we want to apply our patterns to software components to show that a certain architecture enforces privacy for its intended usage. Additionally, we plan to systematically search for privacy requirements using existing specifications (e.g., public privacy statements). Moreover, we want to evaluate a chosen privacy mechanism against the capabilities of the known counterstakeholders in order to evaluate its usefulness.

Acknowledgements. We thank Stephan Faßbender and Denis Hatebur for their extensive and valuable feedback on our work.

References

1. Westin, A.F.: Privacy and Freedom. Atheneum, New York (1967)
2. OECD: OECD Guidelines on the Protection of Privacy and Transborder Flows of Personal Data. Technical report, Organisation for Economic Co-operation and Development, OECD (1980)
3. EU: Directive 95/46/EC of the European Parliament and of the Council of 24 October 1995 on the protection of individuals with regard to the processing of personal data and on the free movement of such data. Technical report, European Community (EU) (1995)
4. Hansen, M., Schwartz, A., Cooper, A.: Privacy and Identity Management. IEEE Security & Privacy 6(2), 38–45 (2008)
5. Pfitzmann, A., Hansen, M.: A terminology for talking about privacy by data minimization: Anonymity, unlinkability, unobservability, pseudonymity, and identity management - version v0.34. Technical report, TU Dresden and ULD Kiel (2011)
6. ISO and IEC: Common Criteria for Information Technology Security Evaluation – Part 2 Security functional components. ISO/IEC 15408, International Organization for Standardization (ISO) and International Electrotechnical Commission (IEC) (2009)
7. Hatebur, D., Heisel, M.: A Foundation for Requirements Analysis of Dependable Software. In: Buth, B., Rabe, G., Seyfarth, T. (eds.) SAFECOMP 2009. LNCS, vol. 5775, pp. 311–325. Springer, Heidelberg (2009)
8. Alebrahim, A., Hatebur, D., Heisel, M.: A method to derive software architectures from quality requirements. In: Thu, T.D., Leung, K. (eds.) Proceedings of the 18th Asia-Pacific Software Engineering Conference (APSEC), pp. 322–330. IEEE Computer Society (2011)
9. Jackson, M.: Problem Frames. Analyzing and structuring software development problems. Addison-Wesley (2001)
10. Hatebur, D., Heisel, M.: A UML Profile for Requirements Analysis of Dependable Software. In: Schoitsch, E. (ed.) SAFECOMP 2010. LNCS, vol. 6351, pp. 317–331. Springer, Heidelberg (2010)

11. Côté, I., Hatebur, D., Heisel, M., Schmidt, H., Wentzlaff, I.: A systematic account of problem frames. In: Proceedings of the European Conference on Pattern Languages of Programs (EuroPLoP 2007), Universitätsverlag Konstanz (2008)
12. Jackson, M., Zave, P.: Deriving specifications from requirements: an example. In: Proceedings 17th Int. Conf. on Software Engineering, Seattle, USA, pp. 15–24. ACM Press (1995)
13. Sweeney, L.: Achieving k-anonymity privacy protection using generalization and suppression. Int. J. Uncertain. Fuzziness Knowl.-Based Syst. 10, 571–588 (2002)
14. Australian Government - Office of the Privacy Commissioner: Privacy Impact Assessment Guide. Australian Government (2010),
    http://www.privacy.gov.au/materials/types/download/9509/6590
15. Clauß, S., Kesdogan, D., Kölsch, T.: Privacy enhancing identity management: protection against re-identification and profiling. In: Proceedings of the 2005 Workshop on Digital Identity Management, DIM 2005, pp. 84–93. ACM (2005)
16. Cormode, G., Srivastava, D.: Anonymized data: generation, models, usage. In: Proceedings of the 35th SIGMOD International Conference on Management of Data, SIGMOD 2009, pp. 1015–1018. ACM (2009)
17. Kapadia, A., Naldurg, P., Campbell, R.H.: Distributed enforcement of unlinkability policies: Looking beyond the chinese wall. In: Proceedings of the POLICY Workshop, pp. 141–150. IEEE Computer Society (2007)
18. Deng, M., Wuyts, K., Scandariato, R., Preneel, B., Joosen, W.: A privacy threat analysis framework: supporting the elicitation and fulfillment of privacy requirements. Requir. Eng. 16, 3–32 (2011)
19. Kalloniatis, C., Kavakli, E., Gritzalis, S.: Addressing privacy requirements in system design: the pris method. Requir. Eng. 13, 241–255 (2008)
20. Hafiz, M.: A collection of privacy design patterns. In: Proceedings of the 2006 Conference on Pattern Languages of Programs, PLoP 2006, pp. 7:1–7:13. ACM (2006)

On Complexity Reduction of User Interfaces
for Safety-Critical Systems

Andreas Holzinger[1], Evgenia Popova[1], Bernhard Peischl[2], and Martina Ziefle[3]

[1] Medical University Graz, A-8036 Graz, Austria
Institute for Medical Informatics, Statistics & Documentation,
Research Unit Human-Computer Interaction
{a.holzinger,e.popova}@hci4all.at
[2] Softnet Austria, A-8010 Graz, Austria
bernhard.peischl@soft-net.at
[3] RWTH Aachen University, D-52062, Germany
Communication Science, Human Technology Centre (Humtec)
ziefle@humtec.rwth-aachen.de

Abstract. Control and communication systems used at power plants or incineration facilities offer various graphical visualizations of the physical parts of the site; however, they rarely provide sufficient visualization of the signal data. There is the problem, that such facilities contain 10,000 or more data acquisition points; each of them continuously sending data updates to the control system (once in 20 ms or less). This huge load of data can be analyzed by a human expert only if appropriately visualized. Such a visualization tool is AutoDyn, developed by the company Technikgruppe, which allows processing and visualizing complex data and supports decision making. In order to configure this tool, a user interface is necessary, called TGtool. It was originally developed by following a system-centered approach, consequently it is difficult to use. Wrong configuration can lead to incorrect signal data visualization, which may lead to wrong decisions of the power plant personnel. An unintentional mistake could have dramatic consequences. The challenge was to re-design this tool, applying a user-centered approach. In this paper we describe the re-design of the configuration tool, following the hypothesis that a user-centered cognitive map structure helps to deal with the complexity without excessive training. The results of the evaluation support this hypothesis.

Keywords: Complexity reduction, data visualization, process visualization, usability engineering, safety-critical systems, industrial design.

1 Introduction and Motivation for Research

Simplicity and complexity seem to be opposites. However, there is an interesting asymmetry in their opposition. It is as though absolute simplicity is the center point of an n-dimensional sphere, where absolute complexity is the surface. In other words, there are many ways of moving away from simplicity toward complexity. In the

G. Quirchmayr et al. (Eds.): CD-ARES 2012, LNCS 7465, pp. 108–122, 2012.

iterative process of design and behavioral observation, it is relatively difficult to move inward toward greater simplicity, while it is relatively easy to move along the surface of a sphere, resolving some types of complexity while simultaneously introducing others, and therefore increasing neither overall simplicity nor ease of use [1].

Similarly, many dimensions are involved in Human-Computer Interaction (HCI). Each of them influences the overall complexity, consequently the usability of the graphical user interface (GUI).

System complexity should be hidden from end-users, so that they can concentrate on their tasks. Task complexity can also vary, e.g. mobile phone prototypes sending a message belongs to simple task and saving a schedule to complex tasks [2]. A GUI is supposed to support a user through the tasks; however, a useful GUI is not necessarily usable. A GUI is representing the system in front of a user, thus visual complexity should be adjusted.

System complexity, task complexity and visual complexity, contribute to the overall graphical user interface complexity. The elements of the GUI are perceived by the users, who immediately create a mental model (cognitive map) of the system; such mental models help users to interpret perceptions from the environment, in order to work out appropriate actions. Simplified, we can say that external visualizations are internalized as mental models [3]. The complexity of such a model is referred to as cognitive complexity.

In this paper we are dealing with intelligent user-centred data visualization, in a safety-relevant area, including decision support within a control system of a power plant. Advantages of user-centred approaches will be demonstrated at the example of a configuration tool called TGtool developed by the company Technikgruppe Mess-, Steuer- und Regeltechnik GmbH. In order to describe what this tool is capable of and what it is responsible for, two other systems are described briefly:

Control System: Technikgruppe is working in the power plant branch. Each power plant has its own control system produced by various corporations including Siemens, ABB or OPC Foundation. A control system can be seen as an information system (IS) for the whole facility. The system keeps track of all the measuring points, their settings and the data. Each measuring point (sensor) sends regularly its measurement (signal value) to the control system. All this data is saved; however, there is no sufficient way to visualize signal data in a longitudinal way on the time axis.

Decision-Support System AutoDyn: For the purpose of signal visualization Technikgruppe has developed a tool called AutoDyn (see Figure 1) which supports the decision-making process. AutoDyn allows visualization of signal values over time in order to analyse correlations and other dependencies between signals. It supports the expert end user in their decision-making processes, offering correct visualization of different situations. Inappropriate or incorrect visualisation may have severe consequences as the visualisation has a major impact of the decision-making process in operating the whole power plant.

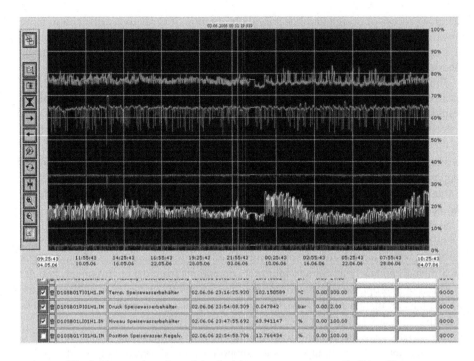

Fig. 1. The user interface of the decision support system, called AutoDyn

2   Related Work

In the paper *"How to measure cognitive complexity in HCI"* Rauterberg (1996) transferred the broad definition of cognitive complexity into the context of HCI. Accordingly, "the complexity of the user's mental model of the dialog system is given by the number of known dialog contexts ("constructs") on one hand and by the number of known dialog operations ("relationships") on the other hand" [4].

A GUI with a defined level of complexity will be perceived differently by expert and novice users. There is interesting research on this topic by Coskun & Grabowski (2004) [5]: They compared complexity of original and improved versions of Navigation and Piloting Expert Systems (NPES). These are operational decision support systems (DSS) which provide intelligent decision support to Chevron oil tanker ship's masters, mates and pilots navigating the restricted waters of San Francisco Bay. Three users took part in the evaluation process. Two of them were experts in navigation and piloting with both theoretical and practical knowledge. The third participant was a senior student with theoretical knowledge but less practical experience. Users had to complete the same task scenarios in both NPES-1 and NPES-2 and afterwards to fill out a questionnaire and to take part in an interview.

The result showed that the users preferred the original version of NPES-1, which used a raster image digital chart, even though it provided less detailed information and was visually more complex. NPES-2 used a fully vectorized electronic chart, reduced visual complexity and offered more functionality. However, in order to get information in NPES-2 a user had to click several times and this was a disturbing factor for the participants. They preferred to have all available data short and concise at one glance without clicking around. The officers also felt annoyed using NPES-2, as its intelligent implementation analyzed the data and offered a ready solution (users only had to push the "Accept" button) without requiring users to think. Expert users would like NPES to play the role of helper and not a director telling them, what to do. The senior student was more loyal to NPES-2, as the lack of practical experience made him use programs suggestions more often.

This study demonstrated that user interface complexity can be perceived differently by users of different experience and knowledge levels. While novice or less experienced users need to be lead through the tasks, get recommendations and ready made decisions to accept, experts prefer to have the program under their control and be free to analyze and decide what to do themselves.

Afacan & Erbug (2009) [6] demonstrated how heuristic evaluation as a usability evaluation method (see [7] for an overview) can contribute to building design practice to conform to universal design principles [8]. They took seven universal design principles as a set of heuristics and applied an iterative sequence of heuristic evaluation in a shopping mall, aiming to achieve an efficient evaluation process. The evaluation was composed of three consecutive sessions: Five evaluators from different professions were interviewed regarding the construction drawings in terms of universal design principles; each evaluator was asked to perform predefined task scenarios; finally, the evaluators were asked to reanalyse the construction drawings. The results showed that heuristic evaluation can integrate universal usability into building design practice.

The most valuable result of the work of Afacan & Erbug is, that out of 53 usability problems identified by all five evaluators, 28 were identified as major problems and had already been identified during pre-interview on construction drawings.

This research has demonstrated that usability pre-evaluation of safety-critical systems allows detection and a significant decrease in the amount of serious usability problems, which might generate further major and minor problems.

Safety-critical systems are not always effectively testable in artificial conditions [9]. An everyday example is the usability of driver information systems used in cars [10]: a new, previously unknown road ahead is unpredictable and demands full attention for safe driving. Funk & Hamacher (2008) [11] demonstrated the successful application of automatic usability evaluation instruments in such car driver IS: They introduced a two-step approach; where an observation component is embedded into the driver IS and collects data during habitual use. This component is a D'PUIS framework (www.softreliability.org/dpuis): The collected data is put into a rule-based expert system REVISER (www.hamacher.eu/reviser), which reasons over the aggregated data and evaluates it according to integrated guidelines.

During automated testing of the driver information systems AUDI MMI and BMW iDrive (refer also to the work of [12]). REVISER identified numerous faults in both of them. The tool has also provided proposals and hints for improvement. Empirical evaluation confirmed almost all automatically identified faults. This experiment demonstrated that the use of automatic usability evaluation methods can speed up usability testing and make this process more valuable.

3   Methods and Materials

The branch of this research is quite specific and so is the configuration tool. It is fairly hard to use, evaluate or test without special background knowledge and training. This narrows the choice of possible test users and evaluators. Consequently, for this project only three persons could be involved as domain experts. Only they are able to carry out complex task, for example the process of go-live configurations.

Applied usability engineering and evaluation methods should take this limitation into account. For routine configurations (simple tasks) theoretically there is no limitation on possible attendances. As a policy, Technikgruppe allows participation by its own employees only.

In order to retrieve as much valuable information as possible from the three domain experts, the interviewing was chosen as a main inspection method, which was applied for the first phase of analysis and design as well as during iterative refinement of the new GUI. The general methodology for the research looks as follows:

- Define core and complementary functionality
- Define requirements
- Define problems of the TGtool
- Produce interface ideas and create their low-fidelity prototypes
- Pick the best idea and iteratively refine it
- Implement the refined idea into a high-fidelity prototype
- Process thinking aloud tests and improve the prototype
- Evaluate the high-fidelity prototype performance compared to TGtool performance

The first three points were cleared during interview sessions with the domain experts. Afterwards, based on the results of the interviews several GUI ideas were produced, low-fidelity prototypes were sketched for promising ideas. The prototypes were discussed and evaluated during the second interview session and the best one was chosen and iteratively developed into the high-fidelity prototype. The development process had an iterative character, whereas domain experts provided their feedback, after completion of each development iteration.

Finally, several simple tasks (in our context "simple" means routine configurations) were created and a thinking aloud test was performed by the end users of the tool. Thus, usability problems, which were not detected during the interviews and the development process, were found. The thinking aloud test results enabled a final optimization of the tool.

Finally, in order to evaluate the result most adequately both an objective and a subjective method were applied.

Given routine tasks, the amount of mouse clicks necessary for completion of each of the tasks in both configuration tools was calculated.

Heuristic evaluation was completed for both the old and the new GUIs, following some guidelines from the medical domain – which is a similar safety-critical application area [13], [14], [15], [16].

Thinking Aloud Test

Out of the broad spectrum of Usability Engineering Methods one particular method is very beneficial: Thinking-aloud (aka TA). This „think out loud" originally derived from problem solving research [17] and allows to get insight into mental processes of people [18], [19].

For our TA tests we prepared six tasks (see Table 1) as well as a test environment. The videos were recorded with a Canon Exilim 12.1 mega pixels camera and Debut Video Capture Software (http://debut-video-capture-software.softonic.de) was used for registering user's activity on the screen.

Table 1. Tasks for TA

Task #	Task description
Task 1	Look around.
Task 2	Create a new signal.
Task 3	Edit signal's properties.
Task 4	Create a new signal group.
Task 5	Add this signal to the group.
Task 6	Delete both the group and the signal.

Table 2. Hard- and software environment

Environment	Details
Room	Standard work place (individual for each test)
Hardware	Intel(R) Core(TM) Duo CPU T2450, 2 GB RAM
OS	Windows 7 Professional.
Monitor Colours	32 bit
Monitor Resolution	1280 x 800
Monitor Size	13" TFT

In order to achieve more objectivity in TA results "fresh" test users were required, who had not seen the prototype before. Also due to the Technikgruppe's policy, only real end users of the tool could take part in the testing process, in particular the Technikgruppe employees, who are working as:

- PLS (in German: ProcessLeitSystem) technicians,
- commissioning (in German: Inbetriebnahme) technicians,
- measurement (in German: Mess- und Regel-) technicians,
- plant operators (in German: Anlagenbediener).

These requirements decreased the amount of possible test users to three persons. Although for any usability test it is important to have a higher amount of test users, we were limited to these three persons. In order to get more out of this limitation, we decided to apply an *iterative TA,* so that after each TA session all critical issues were first analyzed and implemented, and only then the next TA session took place. This approach allowed us to concentrate on the finding of more usability problems instead of discovering the same problems again and again in each TA session.

The average profile of a test user according to a background questionnaire was a 39 years old male with education in electrical engineering, working as a commissioning technician with 26 years of PC experience, working around 40 hours per week with PC, predominantly on the Windows operating system.

This average user needs to process different routine configurations in order to update decision supporting AutoDyn quite often in his professional life, however, in most cases he delegates this to the developers of the tool as he does not feel confident working with it and is afraid to make a mistake.

In the context of our research these three test users (one pilot and two test users) had to accomplish prepared tasks using the configuration tool prototype.

Process Description

At the beginning of the test the user went through the orientation script, filled out a background questionnaire and signed the non-disclosure and consent form. Afterwards he trained to think aloud painting a house in Paint (Windows application). On completion the test person opened the prototype and performed six prepared tasks. Finally the user was interviewed and in the end he filled out the feedback questionnaire.

The test was performed iteratively. It means that the feedback of each user had been analyzed, GUI "debugging" was done and then the next user tested the prototype in a thinking aloud session. This approach (eliminating small and easy-to-fix problems after each TA session) was chosen in order to reduce the amount of already known minor problems and concentrate the users' attention on discovering more severe ones.

After the TA completion all the minor and major findings were analyzed and implemented during final optimization of the configuration tool.

4   Experimental Results and Lessons Learned

During the interviews, the participants ran into problems and had difficulties with obvious tasks of the tool. The request to demonstrate the whole functionality was too complexfor two out of three. Many problems of the current GUI were revealed very fast. The disadvantages of the TGtool were formulated by the interviewees as follows:

Table 3. Pros and Contras of TGtool

No.	Disadvantages	Details
1	No distinction between two configuration types	GUI does not distinct between two types of configuration
2	Inconsistent titles	Different terms used for the same object, some titles do not correspond with their functions
3	Inconsistent links	Different categories offer the same web pages, different pages have the same functionality, some pages are broken
4	Minimalistic functionality	Often at one page users can perform only one action
5	Status of the system is not visible	Users do not see if an operation has been completed and whether it has been completed successfully
6	No progress status on time-consuming operations	The text "This operation may take about several minutes" is usually provided
7	Tool does nothing when it should	Users have to press some 'secret' button, obvious for the developer, but not for the users. Documentation does not point it out
8	Unnatural to add elements from right to left	Users are used to adding elements into the list from left to right
9	Absence of warning messages	Users would not be aware of a mistake until it affects the system
10	Absence of error messages	If users get one, they would not be able to diagnose it
11	No user management	No information on who has done changes. No opportunity to manage users, passwords and rights
12	No language support	Only German is supported
13	Poor documentation	The available documentation is not adequate

Outcome of the Thinking Aloud Test

In the first session with the pilot user (TP1) the highest amount of minor problems has been discovered. Already during the first look-around task five minor problems have been detected. For instance:

- no last access data was displayed,
- current language has been set to Russian, while the interface was in English
- the maintenance user has been allowed to create users and associate access rights

Other usability "bugs" have been discovered during the test, e.g. buttons not working, absence of a sandglass, when processing needs over one second, no explicit description of a filter field etc.

All these issues have been fixed before the next session. Interestingly, the second test user found more consistency problems in the titles and dock widget's usage. As well as the pilot user he also complained about the tool's speed and discovered more operations where the sand clock was missing. The absence of a sand clock seemed to be an important issue as some tasks took over five seconds for processing and the user was confused since no feedback was given.

In the third session some more usability problems were discovered, like the password field at the login page was to the right of the user field and not under it, as is commonly done. Several minor usability 'bugs" were detected as well.

In general users have successfully accomplished all the tasks without any training or help, relying only on their cognition and domain knowledge. The diagram below shows time curves, minutes per task for each test person TP; the task number 1 has not been taken in account as a looking around task cannot have a concrete definition of success. Thus some users took a long time (about 3 min) to explore the tool, others clicked over two menu options rapidly (30 sec) and said they are done;on the horizontal axis the task number and its complexity grade and on the vertical axis the time in minutes is shown.

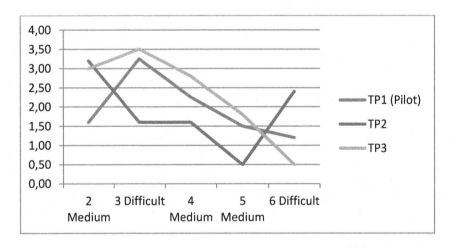

Fig. 2. Minutes per task

Though there is some deviation due to the users' individual cognition, the general trend is clear – after the completion of the first two tasks the time required for the tasks with the same complexity level (medium and difficult) decreases. The fact that the third TP required more time than first and second, can be hardly evaluated due to the individuality of users' cognition process and too few TPs. A higher amount of test users would provide more representative results.

In TA sessions after the completion of all the tasks the users have had to fill out a feedback questionnaire. Figure 3 outlines the results.

The graph demonstrates the result of the iterative approach, whereas the TP1 has graded the prototype with the lowest points (average grade 3.1). The TP2's average grade is notably higher (4.5). And the last user TP3 demonstrates the highest satisfaction with the average of 4.8, however, only a small growth of 0.3 point can be observed as most problems have already been fixed after the first session.

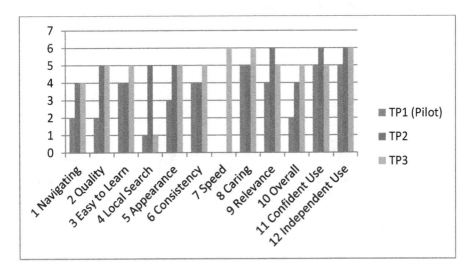

Fig. 3. Feedback questionnaire result

During the TA sessions the TP1 discovered a usability problem and TP3 a computational problem at a signal filter, whereas the TP2 did not. This explains their evaluation of the fourth feedback aspect "Local Search".

In order to eliminate the speed problem another hardware test environment with 4 GB RAM (see Table 4) was used for the last test. A monitor size of a test computer became bigger, which influenced slightly the test results, as the TP3 required more time for each task due to smaller items.

Table 4. Hardware environment for the last TA

Environment	Details
Hardware	Intel(R) Core(TM) Duo CPU T9600, 4 GB RAM
Monitor Colours	64 bit
Monitor Resolution	1900 x 1200
Monitor Size	15,6" TFT

This explains why TP1 and TP2 have graded the seventh feedback aspect "Speed" with 0 points while TP3 has given almost the maximum - 6 points.

In general, the results of the feedback questionnaire follow a positive trend, as in evaluation of 9 aspects out of 12 every following TP gave it equal or more points.

Result of the Mouse Click Measurement

In order to see if users really require less clicks in order to successfully complete their task a mouse click measurement has been performed. The same tasks have been used in this experiment as in the TA. In Figure 4 it can be seen that at any task processing less clicks have to be done in prototype.

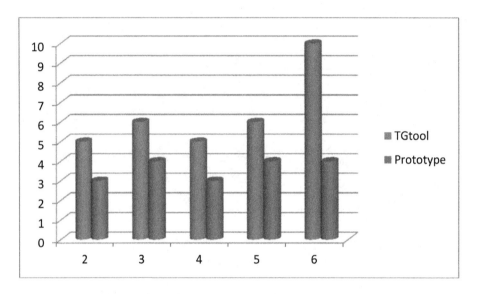

Fig. 4. Minimal amount of clicks per task

It is remarkable that in the tasks 2 to 5 the prototype needs exactly 2 clicks less than the TGtool.

The reason is found in the nested menus of TGtool. As it has been demonstrated in the introduction of this work, the TGtool offers 6 menus to choose at the access point. Selecting one menu the user gets to the next page where again from 4 to 7 menus can be chosen. This is an inefficient clicking process where the user does not perform the actual task but navigates to the page, where the task can be performed. And this makes, according to this research, two more clicks than is actually necessary.

The final task where the user deletes both the signal group and the signal shows a difference of 6 clicks. As TGtool provides an individual page for signal configuration and another individual page for signal group configuration, each of them has to be navigated to in order to complete the task. Thus the amount of "navigation" clicks doubles and only 6 out of 10 clicks are efficient.

Outcome of the Heuristic Evaluation

Heuristic evaluation has been performed by two heuristic experts with domain knowledge. They have evaluated the TGtool and the prototype on the basis of ten heuristics from Nielsen (1993) [20]. The five-point rating scale from Pierotti [21], has been applied. In this scale, 1 point refers to cosmetic problems, and 5 to catastrophic ones. In the net-diagram (Figure 5) the results can be seen.

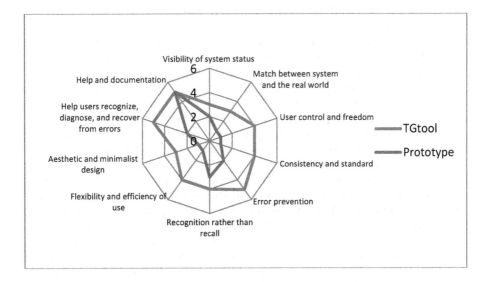

Fig. 5. Heuristic evaluation results

The user-centered prototype is not yet perfect; however, its heuristic evaluation has demonstrated a strong improvement in comparison to TGtool. It can be seen clearly on the network diagram, that there is no aspect where the prototype would be evaluated worse than the TGtool.

5   Conclusion and Future Research

In this work a usability engineering approach was applied to the development of configuration tool prototype, in order to reduce complexity, or more specifically, to adapt visualization of a complex system to the end user's cognitive map. To achieve this, end users were actively integrated into the whole development process from the very beginning to the very end. A big amount of usability problems was detected during the TA session, even though all the decisions upon GUI design were made by the end users during the interview sessions.

The research came up with interesting findings as TA was performed. In the TA test "fresh" end users participated, who did not see a prototype before and did not take part in interview sessions during development. These test persons detected 20 usability problems. However, all of the problems were classified as minor problems which were easy to fix.

This finding confirms that the iterative user-centered GUI design and development minimizes the amount of major problems, because it iteratively adapts the GUI to the end users' cognitive map. All of the TA tasks were successfully completed by all of the users with the average trend of time required for a task decreasing. Therefore, the users succeeded to learn the tool on their own within a short time and all of them stated that they felt confident using the tool. Furthermore, they all shared the opinion that the prototype was hard to use only at the beginning but, as soon as the users got the hang of it, it became easy.

Finally, objective and subjective inspections of the TGtool and the prototype confirmed the effectiveness of usability engineering and clearly pointed out the faults of the prototype to be improved, like the absence of help and documentation and weak recognition support. Mouse click measurement demonstrated the efficiency and minimalistic design of the prototype. The HE fully confirmed that result and TA participants were satisfied with a clear and consistent layout design.

Although TA was performed during the last phase of development and HE afterwards, their results correlate to a great extent. Almost all the heuristics from Nielsen (1993) were commented by the test users in a positive or a negative way. The heuristics like *visibility of system status*, *match between system and the real world*, *consistency* and *recognition* were heavily criticized in the TA sessions and thus have been improved in the last development phase before HE. The *error prevention* aspect as well as the *aesthetic and minimalist design* and *help users recognize, diagnose, and recover from errors* were evaluated positively. The other heuristics for *user control*, *flexibility* and *help and documentation* were not mentioned by the TPs. This basically implies that despite a significant intersection, HE uses a wider range of aspects which allows evaluating a GUI more thoroughly and objectively, whereas TA concentrates on the issues which have caught the users' attention, which is subjective. In this work the knowledge of visual complexity and its influence on the users' perception and cognition has been applied in development of safety-critical software. The aim was to reduce complexity of the configuration tool, more specifically, to design complexity of a tool in accordance to the users' cognitive map. For this purpose iterative usability engineering method was used, so that decisions on GUI design were made by the end users of the GUI. This approach ensured that structure and complexity of the prototype would match users' cognitive map structure. As the main development process was completed, thinking aloud test was applied for the refinement of the configuration tool prototype. Usability evaluation of both TGtool and the developed prototype was performed by means of mouse click measurement test and heuristics evaluation.

Neither heuristics evaluation test nor mouse click measurement could refute the hypothesis that an end user-centered cognitive map structure helps to deal with complexity without excessive training. On the contrary, the result of heuristics evaluation demonstrated clearly that there was no usability aspect where the user-centered prototype would be inferior to system-oriented TGtool. The mouse click measurement determined the prototype as more efficient than TGtool. Moreover, the thinking aloud test showed that the users could successfully deal with the complexity of the prototype without excessive training. This evidence supports the hypothesis of this works.

There are some limitations of this research.

The TA and the mouse click measurement were performed on the basis of the same six tasks. Thus the space of these tasks restricts the validity of their test results.

The participants of TA were the Technikgruppe employees, who had at least some minimal knowledge of the system behind the software. Thus application of new configuration tool might require more training for the technicians from customers' side.

The other limitation is the absence of the stress factor. In real conditions of a safety-critical system users (commissioning technicians, plant operators) are stressed while working with the configuration tool, because they are aware of consequences which can be caused by wrong action. This stress factor influences users' emotional state, thus their perception and cognition.

Acknowledgements. We are grateful for the industrial cooperation with the Technikgruppe, especially to Matthias Lukic. The work presented herein has been partially carried out within the competence network Softnet Austria II (www.soft-net.at, COMET K-Projekt) and funded by the Austrian Federal Ministry of Economy, Family and Youth (bmwfj), the province of Styria, the Steirische Wirtschaftsförderungsgesellschaft mbH (SFG), and the City of Vienna, in support of the Center for Innovation &Technology (ZIT).

References

1. Thomas, J.C., Richards, J.T.: Achieving psychological simplicity: Measures and methods to reduce cognitive complexity. In: Sears, A., Jacko, J.A. (eds.) The Human-Computer Interaction Handbook: Fundamentals, Evolving Technologies and Emerging Applications, 2nd edn., pp. 489–508 (2008)
2. Ziefle, M.: The influence of user expertise and phone complexity on performance, ease of use and learnability of different mobile phones. Behaviour & Information Technology 21(5), 303–311 (2002)
3. Liu, Z., Stasko, J.T.: Mental Models, Visual Reasoning and Interaction in Information Visualization: A Top-down Perspective. IEEE Transactions on Visualization and Computer Graphics 16(6), 999–1008 (2010)
4. Rauterberg, M.: How to measure cognitive complexity in human-computer interaction. Cybernetics and Systems Research, 815–820 (1996)
5. Coskun, E., Grabowski, M.: Impacts of User Interface Complexity on User Acceptance in Safety-Critical Systems. In: Proceedings of the 10th American Conference on Information Systems, AMCIS 2004, pp. 3433–3443 (2004)
6. Afacan, Y., Erbug, C.: An interdisciplinary heuristic evaluation method for universal building design. Applied Ergonomics 40(4), 731–744 (2009)
7. Holzinger, A.: Usability engineering methods for software developers. Communications of the ACM 48(1), 71–74 (2005)
8. Shneiderman, B.: Universal usability. Communications of the ACM 43(5), 84–91 (2000)
9. Bastide, R., Navarre, D., Palanque, P.: A tool-supported design framework for safety critical interactive systems. Interacting with Computers 15(3), 309–328 (2003)

10. Heimgärtner, R., Holzinger, A.: Towards Cross-Cultural Adaptive Driver Navigation Systems. In: Holzinger, A., Weidmann, K.-H. (eds.) Empowering Software Quality: How Can Usability Engineering Reach These Goals?, pp. 53–67. Austrian Computer Society (2005)

11. Funk, M., Hamacher, N.: Concept of Automatic Usability Evaluation of Safety-Critical Interactive Systems in the Field (Konzept der automatischen Bewertung der Gebrauchstauglichkeit sicherheitskritischer Systeme). i-com 7(1), 18–23 (2008)

12. Holzinger, A., Waclick, O., Kappe, F., Lenhart, S., Orasche, G., Peischl, B.: Rapid Prototyping on the example of Software Development in the automotive industry: The Importance of their Provision for Software Projects at the Correct Time ICE-B 2011, pp. 57–61. SciTePress, INSTICC, Setubal (2011)

13. Holzinger, A.: Application of Rapid Prototyping to the User Interface Development for a Virtual Medical Campus. IEEE Software 21(1), 92–99 (2004)

14. Holzinger, A., Errath, M.: Mobile computer Web-application design in medicine: some research based guidelines. Universal Access in the Information Society International Journal 6(1), 31–41 (2007)

15. Holzinger, A., Stickel, C., Fassold, M., Ebner, M.: Seeing the System through the End Users' Eyes: Shadow Expert Technique for Evaluating the Consistency of a Learning Management System. In: Holzinger, A., Miesenberger, K. (eds.) USAB 2009. LNCS, vol. 5889, pp. 178–192. Springer, Heidelberg (2009)

16. Holzinger, A., Kosec, P., Schwantzer, G., Debevc, M., Hofmann-Wellenhof, R., Frühauf, J.: Design and Development of a Mobile Computer Application to Reengineer Workflows in the Hospital and the Methodology to evaluate its Effectiveness. Journal of Biomedical Informatics 44(6), 968–977 (2011)

17. Duncker, K.: On problem-solving. In: Dashiell, J.F. (ed.) Psychological Monographs of the American Psychologoical Association, APA, vol. 58, pp. 1–114 (1945)

18. Nisbett, R.E., Wilson, T.D.: Telling More Than We Can Know: Verbal Reports on Mental Processes. Psychological Review 84(3), 231–259 (1977)

19. Holzinger, A., Leitner, H.: Lessons from Real-Life Usability Engineering in Hospital: From Software Usability to Total Workplace Usability. In: Holzinger, A., Weidmann, K.-H. (eds.) Empowering Software Quality: How Can Usability Engineering Reach these Goals?, pp. 153–160. Austrian Computer Society (2005)

20. Nielsen, J.: Usability Engineering. Morgan Kaufmann, San Francisco (1993)

21. Pierotti, D.: Usability Techniques: Heuristic Evaluation Activities, http://www.stcsig.org/usability/topics/articles/he-activities.html (last access June 01, 2012)

Security SLAs – An Idea Whose Time Has Come?

Martin Gilje Jaatun[1], Karin Bernsmed[1], and Astrid Undheim[2]

[1] Department of Software Engineering, Safety and Security
SINTEF ICT
NO-7465 Trondheim, Norway
http://www.sintef.no/ses
[2] Telenor Research and Future Studies
Trondheim, Norway

Abstract. Service Level Agreements (SLAs) have been used for decades to regulate aspects such as throughput, delay and response times of services in various outsourcing scenarios. However, security aspects have typically been neglected in SLAs. In this paper we argue that security SLAs will be necessary for future Internet services, and provide examples of how this will work in practice.

1 Introduction

The future Internet will provide an open ecosystem of services that can be mixed and matched according to customers' individual requirements. Service oriented architectures will form the basis for future applications and software products where complex service compositions and dynamic changes and replacement of individual service components will be common practice. New components will be picked not only based on functionality, but also based on their availability, performance, security, quality and price. In order to differentiate themselves in a highly competitive market, service providers will have to front the differentiating advantages of their services in order to attract potential customers.

The obvious downside of complex applications involving multiple providers is that they introduce the specter of uncertainty; it will be difficult for the customers to ensure that the final service compositions, i.e., the products they are paying for, behave as expected and that the individual service components can be trusted. From the customer's point of view, security and trustworthiness through the whole chain of service components may very well be the key issue that differentiates one potential service provider from another.

To illustrate the complexities of a composite service, we will employ the example depicted in Figure 1 [1]. Here, the service provider is a telecom operator with its own voice telephony service who wants to offer a Unified Communications (UC) service to its customers. To do this, it needs to combine its own voice service with conferencing, messaging and presence services from subcontractors. The telecom operator will hence act as a service provider towards the final UC

G. Quirchmayr et al. (Eds.): CD-ARES 2012, LNCS 7465, pp. 123–130, 2012.
© IFIP International Federation for Information Processing 2012

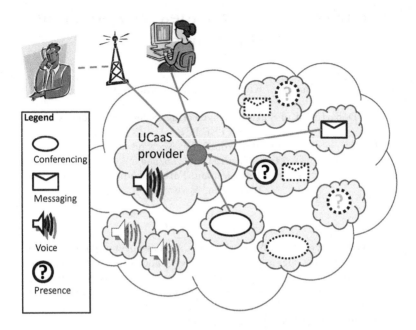

Fig. 1. Example of Unified Communication as a Composite Service[1]

users and as a service customer towards its subcontractors. In the following we will see how the UC provider can offer a defined security level to its customers through the use of Security Level Agreements with its subcontractors.

2   Service Level Agreements

A Service Level Agreement (SLA) is a common way to specify the conditions under which a service is delivered. An SLA addresses three fundamental questions: what is delivered; where is it delivered; when is it delivered? The purpose of an SLA is to serve as a binding agreement between the service customer and the service provider. The SLA will help ensure that the service keeps the right level of quality and that customers are credited accordingly in terms of contract violations. SLAs have been used for many years to specify the quality of service delivered to corporate customers by for example telecom operators, as well as for regulating outsourcing contracts in the IT domain. However, SLAs have until recently not received much interest from the public at large.

Service Level Agreements come in a variety of forms. Today, a typical SLA states the obligations of the provider, the circumstances under which it is valid, and the penalties if the SLA is broken. An SLA often has both business and technical parts, but here we will focus on the technical part. To verify that the provider delivers service in accordance with the agreement, an SLA usually contains Quality of Service (QoS) parameters. QoS refers to the (measurable) ability of a system to provide the network and computation services such that the customer's expectations are met.

QoS has traditionally covered the dependability and performance characteristics of a service. Service dependability is usually defined as a combination of the service availability (the proportion of time a system delivers service in accordance with the requirements) and service reliability (the system's ability to provide uninterrupted service). Service performance is usually characterized by throughput (the number of bits of data transmitted or processed per second) and delay (the number of seconds used for transmission or processing) [2]. The term QoS usually does not include security, even though several initiatives have tried to extend the term in this respect [1]. Today many service providers offer QoS guarantees as a part of their SLAs, however the focus in most cases is on availability. For example, the SLA for Amazon's Elastic Compute Cloud is in principle limited to the following statement: "AWS will use commercially reasonable efforts to make Amazon EC2 available with an Annual Uptime Percentage (defined below) of at least 99.95% during the Service Year." From the customers' point of view, the lack of guarantees of other non-functional attributes is a major drawback; e.g., a service with very low performance will be perceived as being unavailable.

3   The Need for Security SLAs

Even though service availability and performance are critical issues, security is often stated as the main barrier against outsourcing critical data and applications to actors where no previous trust relations exist. To mitigate the security risks associated with service oriented architectures, and to increase the trust in the providers, existing security mechanisms and their effectiveness should be formalized in contracts. Since the SLA is used to explicitly state the obligations of the provider, the implemented security mechanisms, their effectiveness and the implications of possible mismanagements should be a part of the SLA. This concept is also known as Quality of Protection (QoP); the ability of a service provider to deliver service according to a set of specific security requirements. In the following we will call such a contract a "security SLA". A security SLA should (at least) include:

- A description of the service that is to be provided
- The security requirements that the provider will commit to
- The process of monitoring security, including what evidence to collect and present, how the evidence will be collected and who will be responsible for it.
- The process of reporting problems, threats or security related incidents. This also includes information on what person to contact when a problem occurs and the acceptable time for resolving the problem.
- Consequences for cases when the provider (or customer) breaks the terms stated in the SLA, in terms of service credits or financial compensation. The service provider may also want to include constraints on the customer

behavior and escape clauses defining when statements in the agreement do not apply.
- Legal and regulatory issues, including references to existing legislations and directives that may affect the service as well as the terms under which the SLA will not be valid.

To return to our UC example (Figure 1), the UC provider intends to offer a service to end-users that can satisfy a set of security requirements, and in order to accomplish this, it must establish a security SLA with each of the subcontractors. For the messaging service, assume that we have the following security requirements [1]:

1. User profile information must be stored in an encrypted state
2. Only a hashed value of the user password will be stored.
3. A user profile will only require a valid email address and username; age, gender, name, picture and phone number will be optional fields.
4. Information exchanged among the participants must be kept confidential
5. All text messages must be digitally signed
6. Authentication shall be based on symmetric encryption using a trusted third party as authenticator
7. The endpoints of all connections must be mutually authenticated
8. Only one instance of an authenticated user can participate in a communication session
9. Only the service provider will have access to statistical information
10. Asymmetric communication must be stored in an encrypted state and not for more than 48 hours
11. All location data must be logged for a minimum of 48 hours and maximum of 168 hours.

The security SLA also states that problems shall be reported to the messaging provider's contact email address, and that any security breaches and other security notifications shall be reported from the messaging provider to the UC provider's email contact point. General security monitoring shall be performed by an Intrusion Detection System (IDS), with specific filters to verify that no clear text user information, passwords or messages are transmitted. The IDS will detect unauthorized attempts to extract statistical information, and also verify that only one instance of an authenticated user will participate in a session, and check that all messages are signed. Spot-check audits are required to verify that user profile information and passwords are not stored in clear text, and that the logging requirements are fulfilled. In addition to the security requirements, the messaging service is subject to the European Data Retention Directive, requiring logging of communication endpoint IDs for six months.

4   Managing the SLA

Today's SLAs are usually in textual format; however, in the near future we envision an SLA as a dynamic construct, which will need to be renegotiated as the context changes [1]. There are several possible events that may trigger a change in the security terms; e.g., the user's needs may change during the validity period of an SLA, but more importantly, the provider's ability to provide a given level of security may change, e.g. due to recently discovered flaws in specific components.

We envision an SLA lifecycle as illustrated in Figure 2, which consists of six phases: Providers first publish their SLA templates, and users then initiate negotiation based on these. Once the negotiation is successful, providers and users formally have to commit to the resulting SLA, and the provider effectuates the provisioning. While the service is running, monitoring should ensure that the SLA terms are met, and when the relationship between user and provider comes to an end, the SLA must be terminated. Feedback loops are used when it is necessary to return to the negotiation phase from any of the active phases; e.g., if either of the parties cannot commit to a negotiated SLA, if the provider is unable to provision the service (due to overbooking), or if monitoring reveals that SLA terms are broken. In practice, the contracting period may vary from very short periods like a minute (e.g. the temporary lease of a fiber optic communication channel) to months and years for more stable services (e.g. a backup service for corporate data).

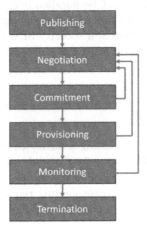

Fig. 2. The SLA lifecycle [1]

For composite services, security SLAs will need to be established between all actors that participate in the final service composition. The SLAs will therefore be negotiated and managed on several layers before a final service can be delivered to the customer; in fact, the customer need not even be aware that different service providers deliver these services.

Returning to the UC example, we assume a service delivery and security SLA has been established between the customer and the UC provider, providing voice, instant messaging, presence and conferencing services, with associated security service levels. For the UC provider, the risk of violating the security SLA towards the customer must be handled by ensuring satisfactory security SLAs towards its subcontractors. These agreements may be the results of a traditional Request for Quotation (RFQ) process, in which case the various service providers have a static business relationship and security SLA with the UC provider, or it can be a more dynamic process where the UC provider queries potential service providers on demand. This is related to the publishing phase above.

The necessary negotiation phase is the same irrespective of the publishing scenario chosen. In this specific example, the UC provider has its own voice service, and as long as this can satisfy all voice-related requirements, the UC provider will not query or start negotiations with additional external providers. For the messaging service, provider B is the only one that fulfills all the security requirements listed, and is chosen over providers A and C. The same selection procedure is followed for the remaining services.

After the negotiation phase is completed, the UC provider initiates the commitment phase where the service providers commit to deliver the previously offered service and all parties digitally sign the security SLA. The necessary resources for service provisioning were reserved during the negotiation phase, and the service can easily be provisioned. The UC provider will then monitor the service fulfillment from the service providers, possibly using an external independent auditor, and breaches must be handled accordingly. This may result in renegotiation of the contract or eventually termination of the contract.

For the UC provider, establishing a security SLA towards its subcontractors minimizes the risk of violating the SLA they have committed to with their customers.

5   Technical Challenges

To facilitate the process of negotiating security SLAs with different potential service providers, to make the comparison of different service offerings simpler, and to simplify the commitment phase of the service lifecycle, there is a need for common industry standards and corresponding templates for machine-readable agreements [1]. However, there are no such templates for security SLAs available today.

Establishing a security SLA is not sufficient in itself; the agreed terms need to be monitored and controlled as well. However, monitoring and controlling security terms are inherently difficult. While other QoS aspects, such as the service availability, can easily be measured and controlled by the users themselves, security tends to be more difficult to monitor. One reason is the nature of service oriented architectures, which are designed to hide the inner workings of the services from the user, exposing only their APIs to the developers. Another reason is that the security requirements are often stated in terms of what should not happen, making it difficult to verify that the preventive mechanisms works as intended, until a breach has already occurred. In addition, the really clever attacks often go unnoticed.

6   Past, Present and Vision

The interest in and demand for security SLAs has varied throughout the years. Researchers began investigating security SLAs as much as twenty years ago [3]. Early work on security agreements was performed by Henning [4], who already then raised the question whether security can be adequately expressed in an SLA. The interest in security SLAs received a new boost in the late nineties when QoS agreements in IP-based network was a hot topic in the research community, especially in the telecommunication sector [5]. Researchers pointed out the need for security as a QoS attribute but did not manage to define service levels that were useful to users and service providers [6]. A second wave of interest was raised when the increased adoption of Service Oriented Architectures (SOA) drew attention to non-functional attributes, such as security and performance of web services [7–10]. More recently, the advent of the Cloud concept, which is characterized by elastic and on-demand measurable services, has given rise to a new demand for such agreements [1, 11–13].

To facilitate dynamic and automatic SLA negotiation between the service consumers and service customers, including renegotiation of SLAs, a machine-readable contract language will be necessary. The WS-Agreement specification [14] is a protocol for establishing SLAs between two parties, such as service providers and consumers. It is an open standard and it has been widely adopted for QoS support for service oriented architectures in web and grid contexts. WS-Agreement allows the use of any service term, and is therefore suitable for security agreements as well. The specification provides a template for the agreement, which consists of the name of the agreement (this is optional), the context (the participants and the lifetime of the agreement), and the agreement terms. The agreement terms are used to specify the obligations of the parties and the associated guarantee terms are used to provide assurance to the service consumer on the service quality and/or resource availability offered by the service provider. The current version of WS-Agreement does not include any ontology for incorporating security requirements in the SLAs, but the specification can relatively easily be extended with this feature [13].

7   Conclusion

We believe that the time of security SLAs has finally arrived. A security SLAs will not only ensure that the service consumer receives the required level of security, but may also put restrictions on the consumer, for example in terms of acceptable usage of the outsourced service. Effective security SLAs will also make sure that the service providers and consumers have a common understanding of the service terms. To achieve an open federated ecosystem of independent actors where services can be easily purchased, replaced and terminated whenever necessary, we need to see widespread use of machine-readable security SLAs. This will increase the uptake of service oriented architectures in new domains and foster innovation amongst developers, service providers, service customers, as well as end users.

References

1. Bernsmed, K., Jaatun, M.G., Meland, P.H., Undheim, A.: Security SLAs for Federated Cloud Services. In: Proceedings of the Sixth International Conference on Availability, Reliability and Security, AReS 2011 (2011)
2. International Telecommunication Union: Terms and Definitions Related to Quality of Service and Network Performance Including Dependability, ITUT E.800 (2008)
3. Irvine, C.: Quality of security service. In: Proc. ACM New Security Paradigms Workshop, pp. 91–99 (2000)
4. Henning, R.R.: Security service level agreements: quantifiable security for the enterprise? In: Proceedings of the 1999 Workshop on New Security Paradigms. NSPW 1999, pp. 54–60. ACM, New York (2000)
5. Grgic, I., Røhne, M.: Agreements in IP-based Networks. Telektronikk 2(3), 186–212 (2001)
6. Lindskog, S., Jonsson, E.: Adding Security to Quality of Service Architectures. In: Proceedings of the SS-GRR Conference (2002),
   http://www.cs.kau.se/~stefan/publications/SSGRR02s/paper.pdf
7. SLA@SOI Consortium: SLA@SOI (2011), http://sla-at-soi.eu/
8. Righi, R.R., Kreutz, D.L., Westphall, C.B.: Sec-mon: An architecture for monitoring and controlling security service level agreements. In: XI Workshop on Managing and Operating Networks and Services (2006)
9. Casola, V., Mazzeo, A., Mazzocca, N., Rak, M.: A SLA evaluation methodology in Service Oriented Architectures. In: Gollmann, D., Massacci, F., Yautsiukhin, A. (eds.) Quality of Protection. Advances in Information Security, vol. 23, pp. 119–130. Springer, US (2006)
10. Frankova, G., Yautsiukhin, A.: Service and protection level agreements for business processes. In: Young Researchers Workshop on Service (2007)
11. de Chaves, S.A., Westphall, C.B., Lamin, F.R.: SLA Perspective in Security Management for Cloud Computing. In: Proceeding of the 2010 Sixth International Conference on Networking and Services, pp. 212–217. IEEE (March 2010)
12. mOSAIC Consortium: mOSAIC (Open source API and platform for multiple clouds) (2011), http://www.mosaic-cloud.eu/
13. Meland, P.H., Bernsmed, K., Jaatun, M.G., Undheim, A., Castejon, H.: Expressing Cloud Security Requirements in Deontic Contract Languages. In: Proceedings of the 2nd International Conference on Cloud Computing and Services Science, CLOSER (2012)
14. Open Grid Forum: Web Services Agreement Specification, WS-Agreement (2007)

UML Representation
of Extended Role-Based Access Control Model
with the Use of Usage Control Concept

Aneta Poniszewska-Maranda

Institute of Information Technology, Technical University of Lodz, Poland
anetap@ics.p.lodz.pl

Abstract. This paper presents an extension of role-based access control model with the use of usage control concept together with its representation using the Unified Modeling Language (UML). The presented model is developed for role engineering in the security of information system. The presented implementation of URBAC (Usage Role-Based Access Control) model consists in creation of security profiles for the users of information system.

1 Introduction

Recently, rapid development in different technologies of information systems have caused the computerizing of many applications in various business areas. Data has become very important and critical resource in many organizations and therefore efficient access to data, sharing the data, extracting information from the data and making use of the information has become an important and urgent necessity.

Access control is a significant part of each information system. It is concerned with determining the allowed activities of system users and mediating every attempt by a user to access a resource in the system. The evident objective of access control is to protect the system resources from any undesired user accesses. Nowadays, the access control is connected with the great development of information technologies and methodologies that allow to create more complex, dynamic information systems.

Data protection against improper disclosure or modification in the information system is the important issue of each security policy realized in the institution. Access control policies, strategies or models should also be changed to manage the security requirements of modern information systems (e.g. to manage the dynamic aspects of access control), such as dispersion of data and resources, dynamic changes both in data proprieties and users' proprieties, responsibilities and abilities from the point of view of access control rules, dispersion of users, complex system organization with different users, rules and security principles that are sometimes mutually exclusive. On the other hand, distributed information systems or federation of information systems provide the access of many different users to huge amount of data, sometimes stored in different locations

G. Quirchmayr et al. (Eds.): CD-ARES 2012, LNCS 7465, pp. 131–145, 2012.

and secured by different strategies, security policies and models or inner enterprise rules. These users have different rights to the data according to their business or security profiles that depend on their organization positions, actual locations and many other conditions. The system data is transferred between the particular nodes of distributed system.

It is also important to protect the information against non-controlled utilization and control the usage and diffusion of the information. It gives the possibility to specify how it can be used and specify the utilization constraints. It seems, the new mechanisms of access control security should be defined to apply for distributed information systems.

Compared to the traditional models, URBAC approach assures the usage control in data accessing that is very important, especially in distributed information systems, and the organization of the access control strategies well-described in RBAC (Role-Based Access Control) model or its extensions. In the paper we propose the new access control approach for dynamic, complex information systems that additionally provides the common coherence of information system components on the global level of access control strategy.

This paper presents an extension of the role-based access control model with the use of usage control concept together with its representation using the Unified Modeling Language (UML). The presented model is developed for role engineering in the security of information system. The presented implementation of RBAC model consists in creation of security profiles for the users of information system. The entire procedure is performed in two stages: defining the permissions assigned to a function and providing the definitions of functions assigned to a particular role.

The paper is structured as follows: section 2 presents the related works on access control concepts, section 3 deals with security requirements of dynamic information systems and describes the extension of access control model for dynamic information systems. Section 4 shows the representation of URBAC approach using the UML concepts while section 5 describes the rules for production of roles based on URBAC approach.

2 Role Concept and Usage Concept in Access Control

The development of access control policies and models has a long history. It is difficult to mention all the access control models that were specified in literature and this is not the objective of this paper. It is possibly to distinguish two main approaches. The first one represents the group of traditional access control models. Discretionary Access Control (DAC) model [15, 17], the first model in these group, manages the users access to information based on user identification and on the rules defined for each user (i.e. subject) and each object in the system using the access control matrix. However, the DAC model has the inherit weakness that information can be copied from one object to another and it is difficult for DAC to enforce the safety policy and protect the data against some security attacks.

In order to prevent the shortcomings of DAC model, the Mandatory Access Control (MAC) model was created to enforce the lattice-based policies [15]. In this model each subject has their own authorization level that permits them the access to objects starting from the classification level, which has lower or equal range. MAC does not consider the covert channels but they are expensive to eliminate. Next, Sandhu et al. proposed the Role-Based Access Control (RBAC) model [1, 2] that has been considered as an alternative to DAC and MAC models. This model requires the identification of roles in a system. The RBAC model was a progress in access control but it is still centered around the access control matrix and has static character, particularly from the point of view of distributed information systems [1].

The second approach of access control models corresponds to the temporal models that introduce the temporal features into traditional access control. The temporal authorization model was proposed by Bertino and al. in [18] that is based on the temporal intervals of validity for authorization and temporal dependencies among authorizations. Next, the Temporal-RBAC (TRBAC) model was proposed in [19]. This model introduces the temporal dependencies among roles. Other model - Temporal Data Authorization model (TDAM) was presented in [20] and extends the basic authorization model by temporal attributes associated to the data such as transition time or valid time. Recently, the TRBAC model was extended to Generalized Temporal RBAC (GTRBAC) model in [21] to express the wider range of temporal constraints.

Currently, traditional access control models are not sufficient and adequate in many cases for information systems, especially modern, dynamic, distributed information systems, which connect different environments by the network. Some disadvantages of these models in security domain were found [12]:

- traditional access control models provide only the mechanisms for definition of authorizations but do not give the possibility to define the obligations or conditions in the access control,
- access rights can be only pre-defined by the developers or security administrators and granted to the subjects,
- decision about the access can be only made before the required access, not during the access,
- it is not possibly to define the mutable attributes for subjects and for objects.

These disadvantages and the needs of present information systems caused the creation of unified model that can encompass the use of traditional access control models and allow to define the rules for dynamic access control. Two access control concepts are chosen in our studies to develop the new approach for dynamic information systems: role concept and usage concept. The first one allows to represent the whole system organization in complete, precise way while the second one allows to describe the usage control with authorizations, obligations, conditions, continuity (ongoing control) and mutability attributes.

Role-Based Access Control (RBAC) [1, 2] requires the identification of roles in a system. The role is properly viewed as a semantic structure around which the access control policy is formulated. In *extended RBAC (eRBAC)* model [10, 11] each role realizes a specific task in the enterprise process and it contains many functions that the user can take. For each role it is possible to choose the necessary system functions. Thus, a role can be presented as a set of functions that this role can take and realize.

The *Usage Control (UCON)* [7–9] is based on three sets of decision factors: authorizations, obligations and conditions that have to be evaluated for the usage decision. The obligations and conditions are added in the approach to resolve certain shortcomings characteristic for the traditional access control strategies.

3   Access Control Approach for Dynamic Information Systems

Actual information systems can contain many different components, applications, located in different places in a city, in a country or on the globe. Each of such components can store the information, can make this information available to other components or to different users. The authorized users accessing the information can change this information, its status, role or other attributes at any time. These changes can cause the necessity of modifications in security properties of accessed data on access control level. Such modifications are dynamic and often should be realized ad hoc because other users from other locations can request the access to the information almost at the same time. Many different users from different locations can access information system. Sometimes, they need to have the direct and rapid access to actual information. However, the conditions of such access are very often dynamic, they can change for example because of actions of other users. It is necessary to ensure the ad hoc checking of current rights of an user basing on their current conditions that can change dynamically.

An example can be a health-care system that contains the sensitive information and should provide secure access to highly sensitive patient information over Internet. Patient records can be modified by a primary physician or by a specialist and almost at the same time can be used by the receptionist to schedule the consultation or special treatment. Some patient records, new or modified, can be sensitive and closed to other users. Decision to allow the access to these records or not should be taken ad hoc basing on new attributes or modified attributes related with information that can change dynamically depending on the accesses of authorized users and its operations and transaction of these data.

Therefore, there is the need to have the access control approach that will describe the organization that should be secured, their structure in proper and complete way, like RBAC model does, and on the other hand it will be appropriate and sufficient for dynamic information system, like usage control concept.

Usage Role-Based Access Control Approach. The proposed access control approach is based on two access control concepts: role concepts and usage concepts. It was named Usage Role-based Access Control (URBAC).

The core part of URBAC approach essentially represents the extended RBAC model (Fig. 1). We distinguished two types of users in URBAC: single user (*User*) and group of users (*Group*). These two elements are represented by the element **Subject** that is the superclass of User and Group. *Subjects* can be regarded as individual human beings. They hold and execute indirectly certain rights on the objects [22].

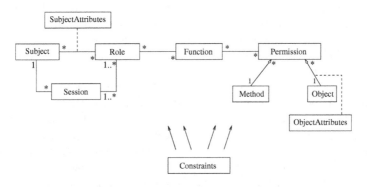

Fig. 1. Elements of Usage Role-based Access Control

Subject permits to formalize the assignment of users and groups to the roles. Subject can be viewed as the base type of all users and groups in a system. It can be presented as an abstract type, so it can not have direct instances - each subject is either a user or a group. A **User** is a human being, a person or a process in a system, so it represents the system entity, that can obtain some access rights in a system. **Group** represents a group of users that have the same rights. Subjects can be assigned to the groups by the aggregation relation *SubjectGroup* that represents an ordering relation in the set of all system subjects. Groups of users are often created in enterprise management information systems as PLM systems or ERP systems to provide the possibility to assemble a set of people in a group with the same obligations, responsibilities or privileges (e.g. persons that realize the same business project in an enterprise).

The **Session** element represents the period of time during which the user is logged in a system and can execute its access rights. In our model the *Session* is assigned directly to the *Subject*, i.e. an individual user or a user from a group is login into information system during a single session. On the other hand a session is connected with the *roles* and this association represents the roles that can be activated during one session.

A **Role** is a job function or a job title within the organization with some associated semantics regarding the authority and responsibility conferred on a member of the role. The role can represent a competency to do a specific task, and it can embody the authority and responsibility. The roles are created for various job functions in an organization.The users are assigned to the roles, based on their responsibilities and qualifications. The direct relation is established between roles and subjects that represent the users or groups of users. The user can take different roles on different occasions and also several users (*Group* element) can play the same role. It is also possible to define the hierarchy of roles, represented by aggregation relation *RoleHierarchy*, which presents the inheritance relations between the roles. Hierarchy of roles represents also the inheritance relations between the roles. The role of the part end of the relation inherits all privileges of parent role. The association relation between the roles and subjects is described by the association class **SubjectAttributes** that represents the additional subject attributes (i.e. subject properties) as in usage control. *Subject attributes* provide additional properties, describing the subjects, that can be used for the usage decision process, for example an identity, enterprise role, credit, membership, security level.

Each role allows the realization of a specific task associated with an enterprise process. A role can contain many functions **Function** that a user can apply. Consequently, a role can be viewed as a set of functions that this role can take to realize a specific job. It is also possible to define the hierarchy of functions, represented by relation named *FunctionHierarchy*, which provides the hierarchical order of system functions. Hierarchy of functions, just like hierarchy of roles, represents also the inheritance relations between the functions. The function of the part end of the relation inherits all privileges of the parent function.

Each function can perform one or more operations, a function needs to be associated with a set of related permissions **Permission**. A function can be defined as a set or a sequence (depending on particular situation) of permissions. To perform an operation one has the access to required object, so necessary permissions should be assigned to corresponding function. Therefore, all the tasks and required permissions are identified and they can be assigned to the users to give them the possibility to perform the responsibilities involved when they play a particular role. Due to the cardinality constraints, each permission must be assigned to at least one function to ensure the coherence of the whole access control schema [8].

The permission determines the execution right for a particular method on the particular object. In order to access the data, stored in an object, a message has to be sent to this object. This message causes an execution of particular method **Method** on this object **Object**. Very often the constraints have to be defined in assignment process of permissions to the objects. Such constraints are represented by the authorizations and also by the obligations and/or conditions.

Authorization (A) is a logical predicate attached to a permission that determines the permission validity depending on the access rules, object attributes and subject attributes. **Obligation (B)** is a functional predicate that verifies the mandatory requirements, i.e. a function that a user has to perform before or during an access. They are defined for the permissions but concerning also the subjects - *Subject* can be associated with the obligations which represent different access control predicates that describe the mandatory requirements performed by a subject before (*pre*) or during (*ongoing*) an access. **Conditions (C)** evaluate the current environmental or system status for the usage decision concerning the permission constraint. They are defined also for the permissions but they concern the session - *Session* can be connected with the set of conditions that represent the features of a system or application.

A constraint determines that some permission is valid only for a part of the object instances. Therefore, the *permission* can be presented as a function $p(o, m, Cst)$ where o is an object, m is a method which can be executed on this object and *Cst* is a set of constraints which determine this permission. Taking into consideration a concept of authorization, obligation and condition, the set of constraints can take the following form $Cst = \{A, B, C\}$ and the permission can be presented as a function $p(o, m, \{A, B, C\})$. According to this, the permission is given to all instances of the object class except the contrary specification.

The **objects** are the entities that can be accessed or used by the users. The objects can be either privacy sensitive or privacy non-sensitive. The relation between objects and their permissions are additionally described by association class **ObjectAttributes** that represents the additional object attributes (i.e. object properties) that can not be specified in the object's class and they can be used for usage decision process. The examples of object attributes are security labels, ownerships or security classes. They can be also mutable or immutable as subject attributes do.

The **constraints** can be defined for each main element of the model presented above (i.e user, group, subject, session, role, function, permission, object and method), and also for the relationships among the elements. The concept of constraints was described widely in the literature [5, 6, 13, 14, 16]. It is possible to distinguish different types of constraints, static and dynamic, that can be attached to different model elements.

The URBAC distinguishes the following general types of constraints:

- *Authorizations* - constraints defined for the permissions, basing on access rules defined by enterprise security policy but also basing on objects' attributes and subjects' attributes. The authorizations evaluate the subject attributes, object attributes and the requested permissions together with a set of authorization rules for the usage decision. Authorizations can be either *pre-authorizations* (decision is made before the access) or *ongoing-authorizations* (decision is made during the access).
- *Obligations* - constraints defined for the permissions but concerning also the subjects - *Subject* can be associated with the obligations which represent different access control predicates that describe the mandatory requirements performed by a subject before (*pre*) or during (*ongoing*) an access. These requirements should be verified before or during an access realized by a user. They can represent the security constraints that are defined on the subjects (i.e. users or groups) and they can be static or dynamic. The obligations can be *pre-obligations* (utilize a history function to check if the certain activities have been fulfilled or not) or *ongoing-obligations* (have to be satisfied continuously or periodically while the allowed rights are during a usage).

– *Conditions* - constraints defined also for the permissions but they concern
the session - *Session* can be connected with the set of conditions that represent the features of a system or application. They can describe the current
environmental or system status and states during the user session that are
used for the usage decision. There are two types of *conditions*: *pre-condition*
(checked before a usage and *on-condition* (has to be satisfied while a usage).
The example of conditions can include current time for accessible time period
(e.g. business hours), current location of a user for accessible location data
(e.g. enterprise area) or system security status (e.g. normal, alert, attack).
The conditions mainly focus on evaluations of environmental, system-related
restrictions that have no direct relationships with subjects, users and accessible data for the usage decision. The subject or object attributes can be
used to select which condition requirements have to be used for a request.
The evaluation of conditions cannot update any subject or object attributes.
– Constraints on roles and on functions. The most popular type in this group
of constraints are *Separation of Duty (SoD)* constraints [5, 11].
– Constraints on relationships between the model elements [5, 11, 12].

The detailed view of usage role-based access control approach with the set of all
elements and relationships presented above is given on figure 2.

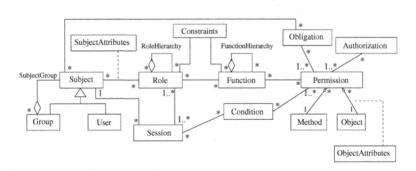

Fig. 2. Meta-model of URBAC model

4   Representation of URBAC with the Use of UML Concepts

Currently, Unified Modeling Language (UML) is a standard language for analysis and design of information systems [3, 4]. It is widely known and used in
software engineering field to support the object oriented approach. UML gives
the possibility to present the system using different models or points of view. It
has a set of diagrams to represent the elements of whole information systems or
one of its components. Some chosen features of UML can be used to implement
URBAC approach, especially during the design of information system and its
associated security schema based on URBAC.

Therefore, UML can be used in role engineering process to implement and realize URBAC approach. To accomplish this, the concepts of UML and URBAC should firstly be joined. Two types of UML diagrams have been chosen to provide the URBAC: use case diagram and interaction diagram. The use case diagram presents the system's functions from the user point of view. It define the system's behavior without functioning details. According to UML meta-model, each use case from use case diagram should be described by a scenario and in consequence by at least one interaction diagram (i.e. sequence diagram or communication diagram). The interaction diagram describes the behavior of one use case [3, 4]. It represents the objects and messages exchanged during the use case processing.

The relationships between UML concepts and concepts of usage role-based access control are presented below (Fig. 3).

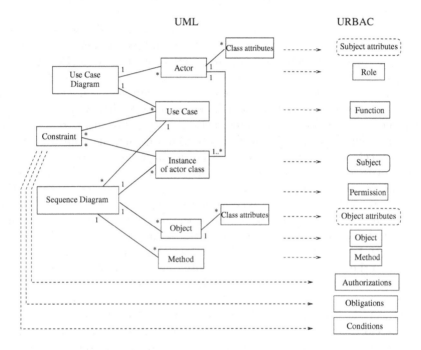

Fig. 3. Relationships between concepts of URBAC and UML concepts

4.1   Elements of URBAC and Corresponding UML Concepts

UML describes the processes that occur in a system or application and such processes are use case oriented. Use case is the main concept of UML used in analysis and design of software. It is used for specifying required usages of a system, to capture the requirements of a system, describes what a system is supposed to do.

This approach is realized with the use of use case diagram that is one of two the most important diagrams in the design process. Use case diagram contains the concept of an actor that is very close to the role concept of RBAC model. UML defines an actor as a coherent set of roles playing by the users of an use case during the interaction with this use case or in general with a system. Therefore, a role from access control can be presented as an UML actor.

Each actor cooperates with one or more use cases representing the system's functions. Each use case specifies some behavior, possibly including variants, that the system can perform in collaboration with one or more actors. These behaviors, involving interactions between the actors and the system, may result in changes to the state of the system and communications with its environment. Thus, a function from URBAC can be represented by an UML use case. As it was presented in the previous section, a set of functions can be determined for each role. Similar situation exist in UML design - each actor can be in interaction with a set of use cases and these relations specify the relations of R-F type (between roles and functions).

In UML approach each use case from use case diagram should be described by scenario and in consequence by at least one interaction diagram (sequence diagram or communication diagram). Although, both the interaction diagrams return the similar results, the sequence diagrams gives more possibilities from version 2.0 of UML. The concept of sequence diagram has been chosen for this reason (it allows to represent the remaining elements of URBAC).

Sequence diagram represents an interaction of objects by means of a sequence of messages sent between these objects. In each sequence diagram there is one or more objects representing the actors who can in this way participate directly in the process of sending the messages between the objects. It is possible to distinguish different types of messages sent to objects in sequence diagram. One of them represents a method call. The methods executed in sequence diagram and also in other UML diagrams can represent the methods of URBAC. Similarly, the objects that occur in UML diagrams, e.g. sequence diagram, collaboration diagram, can be attached to the object concept of access control model.

Access to the object, that is the possibility of execution of method on an object, is controlled with respect to the right of the method execution possessed by a message sender (i.e. subject) over an object. The access model allows for each subject the specification of a list of methods that the subject can execute. Therefore, for each use case it is necessary to specify the permissions for method's execution and as it is shown above these permissions can be found examining the sequence diagram describing the particular use case (that represents the URBAC function). These permissions are assigned to the functions by the function-permission (F-P) relation.

The relations between the elements of URBAC can be found also by the examination of use case diagram and interaction diagram (in particular sequence diagram). A use case diagram offers four types of relations between its elements:

- communication relation between an actor and a use case that represents the relation between a role and a function, i.e. R-F relation,
- generalization relation between actors, representing the inheritance relation between roles (R-R relation),

– two types of relations between use cases represent the inheritance relations between functions of URBAC, i.e. F-F relations: including relation (with stereotype *include*) corresponds to standard inheritance relation and extending relation (with stereotype *extends*) corresponds to inheritance relations with additional constraints that specify the conditions of these extensions.

The second important diagram of UML, besides the use case diagram, is class diagram. This type of UML diagrams is used to describe the types of objects in a system and their relationships. Set of attributes and set of operations can be defined for each class in class diagram.

Each actor specified in the use case diagram can be also defined in details in form of UML class on the class diagram. The system user (i.e. person) is one of actor's types, thus a user is an instance of actor class. The set of class attributes forms the attributes characteristic for this actor. Therefore, the subject attributes (e.g. user attributes) from URBAC can be represented by the set of attributes defined for an instance of actor class of UML.

According to UML meta-model, each system's object has to be of particular type, thus new objects in a systems can be created only for classes defined in class diagram. Each class has among other the set of attributes. Therefore, the concept of object attributes from URBAC can be attached to set of attributes defined for this object in its class specification.

4.2 Constraints of URBAC and Corresponding UML Concepts

The concept of constraints in URBAC approach corresponds directly to the constraint concept existing in UML. The security constraints of URBAC can be defined for different elements and for relations between these elements. These constraints can be presented on UML diagrams corresponding to types and locations of elements for which these constraints will be defined with the use of OCL (object Constraint Language) that is the part of UML approach.

Five types of security constraints were identified for URBAC approach (Section 3). The authorization is a constraint attached to a permission that determines the permission validity depending on defined access rules. It can be represented by the UML constraint defined for the method's execution in sequence diagram.

The obligation is a constraint defined on a permission but it concerns also the subject (e.g. a user) - subject should fulfill the obligation executing a function before or during an access. This type of constraints can be presented as UML constraint in sequence diagram (as pre-condition or an invariant), especially from version 2.0 of UML that provide the combined fragments in sequence diagrams (e.g. "alt" or "opt") allowing the definition of constraint conditions.

The UML constraints representing the authorizations or obligations can be also supported by relations between the elements concerning these constraints.

The condition is a constraint also defined on a permission but it concerns the session element. It defines current environmental or system status and states during the user session that can be used for the usage decision. The conditions can be also represented by UML constraints defined in sequence diagrams (mainly as an invariants).

Remaining types of constraints represent the constraints defined for the roles, functions and their relations. Such constraints are represented by the UML constraints defined for actors, use cases and their relations on use case diagrams or sometimes on sequence diagrams.

5   Production of Roles Based on URBAC Approach

Security policies of a system generally express the fundamental choices taken by an organization to protect the data. They define the principles on which access is granted or denied. Role-based access control models are highly effective models, especially in large companies that have high turnover rates due to the fact of allowance for the administrator to simply place the new employees into the roles instead of creating the new permissions for each new person who joins the company and needs to be included in the system.

However, on the other hand, access control mechanisms still demand clear definition of set of activities and operations for each system's user that he will be allowed to execute. Consequently, a set of permissions should be defined for the user. As it was shown above, a set of permissions composes indirectly the system's roles. Therefore, the production of roles using the URBAC approach consists in determination of permissions for the functions and next functions for the application/system role with the consideration of defined security constraints (e.g. authorizations, obligations, etc.).

The process of role production can be automatic or partially automatic and is based on the connections between UML and URBAC, described in section 4. This process is realized with the use of use case diagrams, where system roles and functions are defined and with the use of sequence diagrams, where permissions are assigned to the rights of execution of methods realized in each use case. These two types of diagrams should be examined to identify the roles of URBAC, the functions that are used by these roles to interact with the information system and the permissions needed to realize these functions. First of all the rules for creation of set of roles were defined.

5.1   Rules for Creation of Roles

Each subject (i.e. user or group of users) in an information system is assigned to a security profile (i.e. user profile) which is defined by the set of roles that can be played by him. A security profile is defined by a pair *(s, listRoles(s))*: *s* is a subject, *listRoles(s)* is a set of roles assigned to this subject. Taking into consideration the concept of user, such profile can be defined as follows: *(u, listRoles(u))*, where *u* is a user, *listRoles(u)*.

It is possibly to give the rules of role creation and the assignments of these roles to users or groups of users:

1. A access control profile should be defined for each subject (i.e. user) who interact with the system

$$s_i \vdash securityProfile_{s_i}$$

or in particular for an user:

$$u_i \vdash securityProfile_{u_i}$$

2. This profile is defined by a set of roles which can be assigned to the subject (i.e. user) with the respect of subject attributes defined mainly on level of security administrator

$$securityProfile_{s_i} \vdash setRoles_{s_i}, subjectAtt_{s_i}$$

in particular for an user:

$$securityProfile_{u_i} \vdash setRoles_{u_i}, subjectAtt_{u_i}$$

To receive a significant profile, each subject (i.e. user) should be assigned at least to one role.

3. A role is defined by a set of functions assigned to this role with respect of potential security constraints defined for them

$$r_j \vdash setFunctions_{r_j}, cst_{r_j}$$

To receive a significant role, each role should have at least one function assigned.

In UML meta-model, each actor should be assigned at least to one use case in the use case diagram

$$a_j \vdash setUseCases_{a_j}, setConstraints_{a_j}$$

4. A function is defined by a set of permissions necessary to perform such function in accordance with potential security constraints defined for such functions or security constraints defined on the permissions (i.e. authorizations, obligations, conditions)

$$f_k \vdash setPermissions_{f_k}, cst_{f_k}, setPermissionCst_p$$

where

$$setPermissionCst_{p_l} \vdash A_{p_l}, B_{p_l}, C_{p_l}$$

To receive a significant function, each function should have at least one permission assigned. In UML description, using the interaction diagram (in our case sequence diagram) each use case should be defined by detail description, i.e. represented by a set of methods executed on the objects

$$uc_k \vdash setPrivileges_{uc_k}, setConstrains_{uc_k}$$

5.2   Creation of User Profiles

The creation process of user profiles, i.e. production of set of roles, in an information system with the use of UML diagrams contains two stages [12]:

- determination of a *set of privileges* (i.e. permissions) for a *use case* in order to define a function and
- determination of a *set of use cases* (i.e. functions) for an *actor* in order to define a role.

In order to define the security profiles for the system's users or groups of users, the set of roles should be assigned to the subject profiles (i.e. user profiles). This task is realized by the security administrator during the exploitation stage. Administrator has to take into consideration the security constraints defined on the global level and subject attributes defined for subjects (i.e. users or groups of users) that determine the access control rights of particular system's users.

6   Conclusion

The extended RBAC is used for managing secure organizations and their functions in information systems. On the other hand, usage control enables dynamic access control during the user access to the information systems by introducing obligations and conditions in access control model. Both role management and usage control are important aspects of access control for modern information systems governed by a certain organization.

Usage Role-based Access Control approach presented above allows to define the access control policy based on access request, as traditional access control models, and the access decision can be evaluated during the access to information to which we want to control the usage. The model takes into consideration the provisional aspects in access security. The components of URBAC can create the framework based on three criteria: functional decision predicates (i.e. authorizations, obligations and conditions), continuity feature (control decision can be taken before or during the access) and mutability feature (updates of subject or object attributes can be done at different time).

The aspects of presented approach are implemented on the software platform that provides to manage the logical security of company information system from the point of view of application developer and from the point of view of security administrator. The platform allows the realization of role engineering process based on URBAC and to allow the management of information system security on access control level.

References

1. Sandhu, R.S., Coyne, E.J., Feinstein, H.L., Youman, C.E.: Role-Based Access Control Models. IEEE Computer 29(2), 38–47 (1996)
2. Ferraiolo, D., Sandhu, R.S., Gavrila, S., Kuhn, D.R., Chandramouli, R.: Proposed NIST Role-Based Access control. ACM TISSEC (2001)

3. Booch, G., Rumbaugh, J., Jacobson, I.: The Unified Modeling Language User Guide. Addison-Wesley (2004)
4. OMG Unified Modeling Language (OMG UML): Superstructure, Version 2.2, The Object Management Group (February 2009), http://www.omg.org/technology/documents/formal/uml.htm
5. Ahn, G.-J., Sandhu, R.S.: Role-based Authorization Constraints Specification. ACM Transactions on Information and Systems Security (2000)
6. Park, J., Zhang, X., Sandhu, R.: Attribute Mutability in Usage Control. In: 18th IFIP WG 11.3 Working Conference on Data and Applications Security (2004)
7. Lazouski, A., Martinelli, F., Mori, P.: Usage control in computer security: A survey. Computer Science Review 4(2), 81–99 (2010)
8. Pretschner, A., Hilty, M., Basin, D.: Distributed usage control. Communications of the ACM 49(9) (September 2006)
9. Zhang, X., Parisi-Presicce, F., Sandhu, R., Park, J.: Formal Model and Policy Specification of Usage Control. ACM TISSEC 8(4), 351–387 (2005)
10. Poniszewska-Maranda, A., Goncalves, G., Hemery, F.: Representation of Extended RBAC Model Using UML Language. In: Vojtáš, P., Bieliková, M., Charron-Bost, B., Sýkora, O. (eds.) SOFSEM 2005. LNCS, vol. 3381, pp. 413–417. Springer, Heidelberg (2005)
11. Poniszewska-Marańda, A.: Access Control Coherence of Information Systems Based on Security Constraints. In: Górski, J. (ed.) SAFECOMP 2006. LNCS, vol. 4166, pp. 412–425. Springer, Heidelberg (2006)
12. Goncalves, G., Poniszewska-Maranda, A.: Role engineering: from design to evaluation of security schemas. Journal of Systems and Software 81(8), 1306–1326 (2008)
13. Poniszewska-Maranda, A.: Conception Approach of Access Control in Heterogeneous Information Systems using UML. Journal of Telecommunication Systems 45(2-3), 177–190 (2010)
14. Strembeck, M., Neumann, G.: An Integrated Approach to Engineer and Enforce Context Constraints in RBAC Environments. ACM Trans. Information and System Security 7(3), 392–427 (2004)
15. Castaro, S., Fugini, M., Martella, G., Samarati, P.: Database Security. Addison-Wesley (1994)
16. Bertino, E., Ferrari, E., Atluri, V.: The Specification and Enforcement of Authorization Constraints in Workflow Management Systems. ACM Transactions on Information and System Security (TISSEC) 2(1) (February 1999)
17. Dows, D., Rub, J., Kung, K., Jordan, C.: Issues in discretionary access control. In: Proc. of IEEE Symposium on Research in Security and Privacy, pp. 208–218 (1985)
18. Bertino, E., Bettini, C., Samarati, P.: Temporal Access Control Mechanism for Database Systems. IEEE Trans. on Knowledge and Data Engineering (8) (1996)
19. Bertino, E., Bonatti, P., Ferrari, E.: A Temporal Role-based Access Control Model. ACM Trans. on Information and System Security 4(3), 191–233 (2001)
20. Gal, A., Atluri, V.: An Authorization Model for Temporal Data. ACM Transaction on Information and System Security 5(1) (2002)
21. James, B., Joshi, E., Bertino, U., Latif, A., Ghafoo, A.: A Generalized Temporal Role-Based Access Control Model. IEEE Transitions on Knowledge and Data Engineerin 17(1), 4–23 (2005)
22. Poniszewska-Maranda, A.: Implementation of Access Control Model for Distributed Information Systems Using Usage Control. In: Bouvry, P., Kłopotek, M.A., Leprévost, F., Marciniak, M., Mykowiecka, A., Rybiński, H. (eds.) SIIS 2011. LNCS, vol. 7053, pp. 54–67. Springer, Heidelberg (2012)

A Formal Equivalence Classes Based Method for Security Policy Conformance Checking

Eckehard Hermann, Udo Litschauer, and Jürgen Fuß

Department of Secure Information Systems
University of Applied Sciences Upper Austria, Austria
{eckehard.hermann,udo.litschauer,juergen.fuss}@fh-hagenberg.at

Abstract. Different security policy models have been developed and published in the past. Proven security policy models, if correctly implemented, guarantee the protection of data objects from unauthorized access or usage or prevent an illegal information flow. To verify that a security policy model has been correctly implemented, it is important to define and execute an exhaustive list of test cases, which verify that the formal security policy neither has been over-constrained nor under-constrained. In this paper we present a method for defining an exhaustive list of test cases, based on formally described equivalence classes that are derived from the formal security policy description.

Keywords: security models, test generation, access control, conformance testing.

1 Introduction

Different security policy models have been developed and published in the past. In 1989 Brewer and Nash presented their Chinese Wall Security Policy model that is based on conflict of interest classes [2]. Other security policy models are a formalization of a military security model like the one from Bell and LaPadula [4], they address the integrity of data objects in commercial transactions, as stated by Clark and Wilson [5], control the information flow like the Limes Security Model from Hermann [6] or they are a model of access control like the access matrix defined by Lampson [1]. Each of these models defines the security requirements that have to be correctly implemented by a system for achieving a given security objective. If the security model has not been correctly implemented, the resulting system will be over-constrained or under-constrained. After the correctness of the formal specification of the security model has been verified, the system implementation has to be validated against the security model. As discussed by Hu and Ahn in [7] a system is under-constrained if, based on the security model, undesired system states are granted and over-constrained if desired system states are denied, which probably causes availability problems. Murnane and Reed argument in [8].

> testing software after it is completed remains an important aspect of software quality assurance despite the recent emphasis on the use of formal methods and 'defect-free' software development processes.

G. Quirchmayr et al. (Eds.): CD-ARES 2012, LNCS 7465, pp. 146–160, 2012.

Our approach, presented in this paper, is a method for defining an exhaustive list of test cases based on formally described equivalence classes that are derived from the formal security policy description. The paper is organized as follows. Section 2 introduces some background on security models and testing, in particular equivalence class testing and section 3 gives an overview of related work. Our approach is presented in section 4. We start with a formal definition of equivalence classes. For explaining the application of our approch, we define the equivalence classes of the Bell and LaPadula model. Section 5 outlines opportunities for future work and draws conclusions.

2   State of the Art

2.1   Security Models

A security model defines rules and demonstrates, that if security requirements are correctly and completely educed from the rules and these requirements are correctly and completely implemented by a system, the system achieves a given security objective. Different security policy models like the one from Bell and LaPadula, are a formalization of a military security model in [4] or they address the integrity of data objects in commercial transactions, as stated by Clark and Wilson [5]. Grimm defined in [9] that all security models contain five elements of description:

1. the definition of a superior security objective (informal),
2. the specification of secure system states (formal),
3. rules for allowed state transitions (formal),
4. a security theorem that proves that an allowed state transition will transfer a secure state always into a secure state (formal),
5. a trust model that describes requirements for the system implementation and for the application environment in order to enable secure system states to achieve the superior security objective (semi-formal or informal).

The Bell and LaPadula Model. In 1973 the first complete formal defined security model has been described by David Elliott Bell and Leonard J. LaPadula in [4]. Bell and LaPadula define a partial ordered set of security levels. The security levels are assigned to subjects - the active entities - and to objects - the passive and data containing entities - in the model. The security level of a subject is called clearance level and the security level of an object is called classification. The superior security objective of the model is the prevention of a vertical information flow from top to bottom according to the partially ordered clearance and classification levels. The model defines two properties. The ss-property defines that in order for a subject to read an object's data, the subject's clearance level must dominate the object's classification. The *-property authorizes a subject, only if the objects classification is more recent than the most sensitive object that it is currently allowed to read. Additionally, Bell and LaPadula define the usage of a Lampson-matrix. In preparation of later usage Table 1 introduces the elements of the Bell and LaPadula model.

Table 1. Elements of the Bell-LaPadula-Model [4]

Set	Element	Semantic
$\mathcal{S}$	$\{S_1, S_2, \ldots, S_n\}$	*subjects*; processes, programs in execution, …
$\mathcal{O}$	$\{O_1, O_2, \ldots, O_m\}$	*objects*; data, files, programs, subjects, …
$\mathcal{C}$	$\{C_1, C_2, \ldots, C_q\}$, where $C_1 > C_2 > \cdots > C_q$	*classifications*; clearance level of a subject, classification of an object
K	$\{K_1, K_2, \ldots, K_r\}$	*needs-to-know categories*; project numbers, access privileges, …
A	$\{A_1, A_2, \ldots, A_p\}$	*access attributes*; read, write, copy, append, owner, control, …
R	$\{R_1, R_2, \ldots, R_u\}$	*requests*; inputs, commands, requests for access to objects by subjects, …
D	$\{D_1, D_2, \ldots, D_v\}$	*decisions*; outputs, answers, "yes", "no", "error"
T	$\{1, 2, \ldots, t, \ldots\}$	*indices*; elements of the time set; identification of discrete moments; an element t is an index to request and decision sequences
$\mathcal{P}(\alpha)$	all subsets of α	power set of α
α^{β}	all functions from the set β to the set α	–
$\alpha \times \beta$	$\{(a, b) : a \in \alpha, b \in \beta\}$	cartesian product of the sets α and β
F	$C^{\mathcal{S}} \times C^{\mathcal{O}} \times K^{\mathcal{S}} \times K^{\mathcal{O}}$ an arbitrary element of F is written $f = (f_1, f_2, f_3, f_4)$	*classification/need-to-know vectors*; f_1: subject *classification* fct. f_2: object *classification* fct. f_3: subject *need-to-know* fct. f_4: object *need-to-know* fct.
X	R^T; an arbitrary element of X is written x	*request sequences*
Y	D^T; an arbitrary element of Y is written y	*decision sequences*
$\mathcal{M}$	$\{M_1, M_2, \ldots, M_c\}$, $c = nm2^p$; an element M_K of $\mathcal{M}$ is an $n \times m$-Lampson-matrix with entries from $\mathcal{P}(A)$; the (i, j)-entry of M_k shows S_i access attributes relative to O_j	*access matrices*
V	$P(S \times O) \times M \times F$	*states*
Z	V^T; an arbitrary element of Z is written z; $z_t = z(t)$ is the t-th state in the state sequence z	*state sequences*

Additionally the following definitions of system states and state-transition relations are done in [4]: A state $v \in V$ is a triple (b, M, f) where

$b \in \mathcal{P}(\mathcal{S} \times \mathcal{O})$,   indicating which subjects have access to which objects in the state v,

$M \in \mathcal{M}$,   indicating the entries of the Lampson-matrix in the state v and

$f \in F$,   indicating the clearance level of all subjects, the classification level of all objects, and the needs-to-know associated with all subjects and objects in the state v.[4]

Definition 1 (Access-Matrix-Function)
Let $S_i \in \mathcal{S}$, $O_j \in \mathcal{O}$ and $M \in \mathcal{M}$. The function

$$m : \mathcal{S} \times \mathcal{O} \to \mathcal{P}(A)$$

is called Access-Matrix-Function in relation to M if $m(S_i, O_j)$ returns the (i, j)-entry of M.

Let $W \subseteq R \times D \times V \times V$. The system $\Sigma(R, D, W, z_0) \subseteq X \times Y \times Z$ is defined by $(x, y, z) \in \Sigma(R, D, W, z_0)$, if and only if $(x_t, y_t, z_t, z_{t-1}) \in W$ for each $t \in T$ where z_0 is a specified initial state usually of the form $(\emptyset, M, f)$ where $\emptyset$ denotes the empty set [4].

The state $v = (b, M, f) \in V$ is a compromise state (compromise) if there is an ordered pair $(S, O) \in b$, such that

1. $f_1(S) < f_2(O)$ or
2. $f_3(S) \not\supseteq f_4(O)$.

The pair$(S, O) \in \mathcal{S} \times \mathcal{O}$ satisfies the security condition relative to f *(SC rel f)* if

3. $f_1(S) \geq f_2(O)$ and
4. $f_3(S) \supseteq f_4(O)$.

A state $v = (b, M, f) \in V$ is a secure state if each $(S, O) \in b$ satisfies SC rel f.[4].

2.2   Testing

Testing a system is an important aspect of quality assurance. But it does not prove the absence of errors; it can only prove the presence of features. Testing can be divided into functional and non-functional testing. By performing functional tests it is verified whether a system fulfils its functional requirements or not. When non-functional testing aspects are tested, they may not be related to a specific functional requirement, such as performance testing. In the past different test techniques have been developed, which can be split into black box and white box techniques. Black box techniques are testing techniques, where the test cases are primarily derived from the system specifications and without knowledge of the inspected system implementations. These kind of testing techniques are testing the systems input and output behavior. Different types of black box testing techniques are equivalence class testing, boundary testing or fuzz testing [10]. White box techniques are testing techniques, which use knowledge about the internal composition of a system for the test case definition.[8]

Equivalence Class Testing. The equivalence class testing technique implies, that the input domain of a system is partitioned into a finte number of sets, called equivalence classes, such that the systems behavior to a test of a representative value, called test case, of one equivalence class is equal to the systems behavior to a test of any other value of the same equivalence class. If one test case of an equivalence class detects an error, any other test case of the same equivalence class will be expected to detect the same error. If one test case of an equivalence class does not detect an error, it is expected that not any of the test case of the same equivalence class will detect an error.[11]

3   Related Work

In [12] Hu et al. propose an approach for conducting conformance checking of access control policies, specified in XACML and they also propose an implementation of conformance checking based on previous XACML policy verification and testing tools. The work is based on a fault model [13], a structural coverage measurement tool for defining policy coverage metrics [15] and a test generator [14], developed by two of the authors in their former work. In [16] De Angelis et al. discuss access policy testing as a vital function of the trust network, in which users and service providers interact. User-centric security management is enabled by using automated compliance testing using an audit bus, sharing audit trails and governance information, to monitor service state and provide users with privacy protection in networks of services and a conceptual framework supporting on-line testing of deployed systems. The authors explain that for each service under test the component continuously verifies that it does not violate any of the declared access control policies running for a set of test cases. Hu and Ahn developed in [7] a methodological attempt to verify formal specifications of a role-based access control model and corresponding policies. They also derived test cases from formal specifications and validate conformance to the system design and implementation using those test cases. In [17] Mouelhi et al. propose a test selection criteria to produce tests from a security policy. They propose several test criteria to select test cases from a security policy specified in OrBaC (a specification language to define the access control rules). Criterion 1 is satisfied if and only if a test case is generated for each primary access control rule of the security model and criterion 2 is satisfied if and only if a test case is generated for each primary and secondary rule of the security model, except the generic rules. Security test cases obtained with one of the two criteria should test aspects, which are not the explicit objective of functional tests. Mutation analysis, which is used by Mouelhi et al. during security test case generation, is a technique for evaluating the quality of test cases at which a mutant is a copy of the original policy that contains one simple flaw.

4   An Equivalence Classes Based Approach for Security Test Case Definition

To verify if a security policy model has been correctly implemented, we propose the definition of an equivalence class for valid as well as for invalid system input values for each rule of a security policy. We distinguish between two principal categories of equivalence class: equivalence class for valid and for invalid system input values. We present our approach by defining the equivalence classes of the Bell and LaPadula model. In relation to the Bell and LaPadula model an equivalence class is defined as:

Definition 2 (equivalence class). *Let $a \in A$ and $b \in \mathcal{P}(\mathcal{S} \times \mathcal{O})$. The equivalence class of (a, b) is the set $\mathrm{ec}_{ab} \subseteq A \times \mathcal{P}(\mathcal{S} \times \mathcal{O})$ with the property:*

$$\mathrm{ec}_{ab} := \{(x, y) \mid (x, y) \text{ is equivalent to } (a, b)\}$$

Let $EC := \{\mathrm{ec}_1, \mathrm{ec}_2, \ldots, \mathrm{ec}_n\}$ be the set of all equivalence classes of a system.

In principal we distinguish between equivalence classes that satisfy the above defined security conditions and equivalence classes that violate these security conditions.

A proof concerning completeness is trivial and can easy be done by performing a logical AND-conjunction of the satisfying equivalence class, that has to be equal to the policy definition and a logical OR-conjunction of the violating equivalence classes, that has to be equal to the negation of the security policy definition.

In a first preparative step the following security conditions SC are defined: The elements of an equivalence class containing *Subject* × *Object* tuples where the Subject is allowed to read access the Object, have to satisfy the f_{read} security condition.

Definition 3 (security condition f_{read})
$(S, O) \in \mathcal{S} \times \mathcal{O}$ satisfies the security condition relative f_{read}, if

1. *$f_1(S) \geq f_2(O)$ and*
2. *$f_4(O) \subseteq f_3(S)$.*

The elements of an equivalence class containing *Subject* × *Object* tuples where the Subject is allowed to write access the Object, have to satisfy the f_{write} security condition.

Definition 4 (security condition f_{write})
$(S, O) \in \mathcal{S} \times \mathcal{O}$ satisfies the security condition relative f_{write}, if

    1. $f_1(S) \leq f_2(O)$ and
    2. $f_4(O) \subseteq f_3(S)$.

The elements of an equivalence class containing $Subject \times Object$ tuples, where the Subject is allowed to read-write access the Object have to satisfy the $f_{\text{read-write}}$ security condition.

Definition 5 (security condition $f_{\text{read-write}}$)
$(S, O) \in \mathcal{S} \times \mathcal{O}$ satisfies the security condition relative $f_{\text{read-write}}$, if

    1. $f_1(S) = f_2(O)$ and
    2. $f_4(O) \subseteq f_3(S)$.

The elements of an equivalence class containing $Subject \times Object$ tuples, where the Subject is allowed to append access the Object have to satisfy the f_{append} security condition.

Definition 6 (security condition f_{append})
$(S, O) \in \mathcal{S} \times \mathcal{O}$ satisfies the security condition relative f_{append}, if

    1. $f_1(S) \leq f_2(O)$ and
    2. $f_4(O) \subseteq f_3(S)$.

The elements of an equivalence class containing $Subject \times Object$ tuples, where the Subject is allowed to execute the Object, have to satisfy the f_{execute} security condition.

Definition 7 (security condition f_{execute})
$(S, O) \in \mathcal{S} \times \mathcal{O}$ satisfies the security condition relative f_{execute}, if

    1. $f_1(S) \geq f_2(O)$ and
    2. $f_4(O) \subseteq f_3(S)$.

4.1   Equivalence Classes Definition

Based on the security conditions defined above, equivalence classes of the Bell and LaPadula model are defined now. As discussed above we distinguish between equivalence classes that satisfy the defined security conditions and equivalence classes that violate these security conditions.

Satisfying Equivalence Classes. The test cases contained by the satisfying equivalence classes can be used to verify if the system is over-constrained.

Definition 8 (equivalence classes $ec_1, \ldots, ec_5$)
Let $b \in \mathcal{P}(\mathcal{S} \times \mathcal{O})$, be $a \in A$ an access attribute, $M \in \mathcal{M}$ the current Lampson-matrix and m the Access-Matrix-Function in relation to M. Then

$$ec_1 := \{(b, a) \mid a = \text{read} \wedge a \in m(b) \wedge$$
$$b \text{ satisfies the security condition relative } f_{\text{read}}\}$$
$$ec_2 := \{(b, a) \mid a = \text{write} \wedge a \in m(b) \wedge$$
$$b \text{ satisfies the security condition relative } f_{\text{write}}\}$$
$$ec_3 := \{(b, a) \mid a = \text{read-write} \wedge a \in m(b) \wedge$$
$$b \text{ satisfies the security condition relative } f_{\text{read-write}}\}$$
$$ec_4 := \{(b, a) \mid a = \text{execute} \wedge a \in m(b) \wedge$$
$$b \text{ satisfies the security condition relative } f_{\text{execute}}\}$$
$$ec_5 := \{(b, a) \mid a = \text{append} \wedge a \in m(b) \wedge$$
$$b \text{ satisfies the security condition relative } f_{\text{append}}\}$$

Violating Equivalence Classes. The test cases contained by the violating equivalence classes show if the system is under-constrained.

Definition 9 (equivalence classes $ec_6, \ldots, ec_{10}$)
Let $b \in \mathcal{P}(\mathcal{S} \times \mathcal{O})$, be $a \in A$ an access attribute, $M \in \mathcal{M}$ the current Lampson-matrix and m the Access-Matrix-Function in relation to M. Then

$$ec_6 := \{(b, a) \mid a = \text{read} \wedge (a \notin m(b) \vee$$
$$b \text{ violates the security condition relative } f_{read})\}$$
$$ec_7 := \{(b, a) \mid a = \text{write} \wedge (a \notin m(b) \vee$$
$$b \text{ violates the security condition relative } f_{\text{write}})\}$$
$$ec_8 := \{(b, a) \mid a = \text{read-write} \wedge (a \notin m(b) \vee$$
$$b \text{ violates the security condition relative } f_{\text{read-write}})\}$$
$$ec_9 := \{(b, a) \mid a = \text{execute} \wedge (a \notin m(b) \vee$$
$$b \text{ violates the security condition relative } f_{\text{execute}})\}$$
$$ec_{10} := \{(b, a) \mid a = \text{append} \wedge (a \notin m(b) \vee$$
$$b \text{ violates the security condition relative } f_{\text{append}})\}$$

4.2 Test Cases Definition

After the equivalence classes have been defined, a functional test can be performed. In the following section we define a sample system. We start by defining the subjects, objects, classification, access attributes and Need-to-Know-categories as well as the Lampson-matrix of the sample system.

Definition of the Sample System. Let $\mathcal{S}$ be the set of all subject in the sample system

$$\mathcal{S} = \{S_1, S_2, S_3, S_4, S_5, S_6, S_7, S_8\},$$

Let $\mathcal{O}$ be the set of all objects in the sample system

$$\mathcal{O} = \{O_1, O_2, O_3, O_4, O_5, O_6, O_7, O_8\},$$

Let $\mathcal{C}$ be a partial ordered set of classification

$$\mathcal{C} = \{\text{top secret}, \text{secret}, \text{classified}, \text{unclassified}\}, \text{where}$$
$$\text{top secret} > \text{secret} > \text{classified} > \text{unclassified}.$$

Let A be the set of allowed access attributes in the sample system

$$A = \{\text{read}, \text{write}, \text{read-write}, \text{execute}, \text{append}\}$$

Let K be the *Need-to-Know*-categories in the sample system

$$K = \{\text{Cat}_1, \text{Cat}_2, \text{Cat}_3, \text{Cat}_4, \text{Cat}_5, \text{Cat}_6, \text{Cat}_7, \text{Cat}_8\}$$

$C_{S_1} = \text{top secret}$	$C_{O_1} = \text{top secret}$
$C_{S_2} = \text{secret}$	$C_{O_2} = \text{secret}$
$C_{S_3} = \text{classified}$	$C_{O_3} = \text{classified}$
$C_{S_4} = \text{unclassified}$	$C_{O_4} = \text{unclassified}$
$C_{S_5} = \text{top secret}$	$C_{O_5} = \text{top secret}$
$C_{S_6} = \text{secret}$	$C_{O_6} = \text{secret}$
$C_{S_7} = \text{classified}$	$C_{O_7} = \text{classified}$
$C_{S_8} = \text{unclassified}$	$C_{O_8} = \text{unclassified}$

Figure 1 shows all the subjects and objects and their classifiction level.

The *Need-to-Know*-categories are as follows:

$$K_{S_1} = \{\text{Cat}_1, \text{Cat}_4, \text{Cat}_5, \text{Cat}_7, \text{Cat}_8\}$$
$$K_{S_2} = \{\text{Cat}_2, \text{Cat}_4, \text{Cat}_5, \text{Cat}_6, \text{Cat}_7, \text{Cat}_8\}$$
$$K_{S_3} = \{\text{Cat}_3, \text{Cat}_4, \text{Cat}_5, \text{Cat}_7, \text{Cat}_8\}$$
$$K_{S_4} = \{\text{Cat}_4, \text{Cat}_5, \text{Cat}_8\}$$
$$K_{S_5} = \{\text{Cat}_1, \text{Cat}_2, \text{Cat}_4, \text{Cat}_5, \text{Cat}_7, \text{Cat}_8\}$$
$$K_{S_6} = \{\text{Cat}_2, \text{Cat}_4, \text{Cat}_5, \text{Cat}_6, \text{Cat}_7, \text{Cat}_8\}$$
$$K_{S_7} = \{\text{Cat}_3, \text{Cat}_4, \text{Cat}_5, \text{Cat}_7, \text{Cat}_8\}$$
$$K_{S_8} = \{\text{Cat}_4, \text{Cat}_5, \text{Cat}_8\}$$

$$K_{O_1} = \{\text{Cat}_1\}$$
$$K_{O_2} = \{\text{Cat}_2\}$$
$$K_{O_3} = \{\text{Cat}_3\}$$
$$K_{O_4} = \{\text{Cat}_4\}$$
$$K_{O_5} = \{\text{Cat}_5\}$$

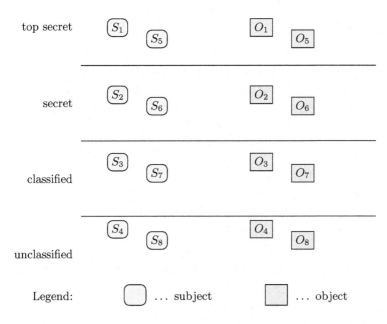

top secret

secret

classified

unclassified

Legend: ⬜ ... subject   ⬛ ... object

Fig. 1. Subjects, objects and classification levels of the sample system

$$K_{O_6} = \{\text{Cat}_6\}$$
$$K_{O_7} = \{\text{Cat}_7\}$$
$$K_{O_8} = \{\text{Cat}_8\}$$

For testing of the equivalence classes, the following Lampson-matrix is defined.

Table 2. Sample Access Matrix

	O_1	O_2	O_3	O_4	O_5	O_6	O_7	O_8
S_1	{r}	{}	{}	{r}	{r}	{}	{r}	{r,w}
S_2	{}	{r,e}	{}	{r}	{a}	{r,w,e}	{r}	{r,w}
S_3	{}	{}	{rw,e}	{r}	{a}	{}	{r,w}	{r,w}
S_4	{}	{}	{}	{r,w,a}	{a}	{}	{}	{r,w}
S_5	{rw,a}	{r}	{}	{r}	{r}	{}	{r}	{r,w}
S_6	{}	{r,w}	{}	{r}	{a}	{r,w,e}	{r}	{r,w}
S_7	{}	{}	{rw,e}	{r}	{a}	{}	{r,w}	{r,w}
S_8	{}	{}	{}	{r,w,a}	{a}	{}	{}	{r,w}

r... read, w... write, rw... read-write, e... execute, a... append

After defining the entities and Lampson-matrix, all entities are assigned to the equivalence classes:

$ec_1 = \{((S_1, O_1), \text{read}), ((S_1, O_4), \text{read}), ((S_1, O_5), \text{read}), ((S_1, O_7), \text{read}),$
$\quad ((S_1, O_8), \text{read}), ((S_2, O_2), \text{read}), ((S_2, O_4), \text{read}), ((S_2, O_6), \text{read}),$
$\quad ((S_2, O_7), \text{read}), ((S_2, O_8), \text{read}), ((S_3, O_4), \text{read}), ((S_3, O_7), \text{read}),$
$\quad ((S_3, O_8), \text{read}), ((S_4, O_4), \text{read}), ((S_4, O_8), \text{read}), ((S_5, O_2), \text{read}),$
$\quad ((S_5, O_4), \text{read}), ((S_5, O_5), \text{read}), ((S_5, O_7), \text{read}), ((S_5, O_8), \text{read}),$
$\quad ((S_6, O_2), \text{read}), ((S_6, O_4), \text{read}), ((S_6, O_6), \text{read}), ((S_6, O_7), \text{read}),$
$\quad ((S_6, O_8), \text{read}), ((S_7, O_4), \text{read}), ((S_7, O_7), \text{read}), ((S_7, O_8), \text{read}),$
$\quad ((S_8, O_4), \text{read}), ((S_8, O_8), \text{read})\}$

$ec_2 = \{((S_2, O_6), \text{write}), ((S_3, O_7), \text{write}), ((S_4, O_4), \text{write}),$
$\quad ((S_4, O_8), \text{write}), ((S_6, O_2), \text{write}), ((S_6, O_6), \text{write}),$
$\quad ((S_7, O_7), \text{write}), ((S_8, O_4), \text{write}), ((S_8, O_8), \text{write})\}$

$ec_3 = \{((S_3, O_3), \text{read-write}), ((S_5, O_1), \text{read-write}), ((S_7, O_3), \text{read-write})\}$

$ec_4 = \{((S_2, O_2), \text{execute}), ((S_2, O_7), \text{execute}), ((S_3, O_3), \text{execute}),$
$\quad ((S_6, O_6), \text{execute}), ((S_7, O_3), \text{execute})\}$

$ec_5 = \{((S_2, O_5), \text{append}), ((S_3, O_5), \text{append}), ((S_4, O_4), \text{append}),$
$\quad ((S_4, O_5), \text{append}), ((S_5, O_1), \text{append}), ((S_6, O_5), \text{append}),$
$\quad ((S_7, O_5), \text{append}), ((S_8, O_4), \text{append}), ((S_8, O_5), \text{append})\}$

$ec_6 = \{((S_1, O_2), \text{read}), ((S_1, O_3), \text{read}), ((S_1, O_6), \text{read}), ((S_2, O_1), \text{read}),$
$\quad ((S_2, O_3), \text{read}), ((S_2, O_5), \text{read}), ((S_3, O_1), \text{read}), ((S_3, O_2), \text{read}),$
$\quad ((S_3, O_3), \text{read}), ((S_3, O_5), \text{read}), ((S_3, O_6), \text{read}), ((S_4, O_1), \text{read}),$
$\quad ((S_4, O_2), \text{read}), ((S_4, O_3), \text{read}), ((S_4, O_5), \text{read}), ((S_4, O_6), \text{read}),$
$\quad ((S_4, O_7), \text{read}), ((S_5, O_1), \text{read}), ((S_5, O_3), \text{read}), ((S_5, O_6), \text{read}),$
$\quad ((S_6, O_1), \text{read}), ((S_6, O_3), \text{read}), ((S_6, O_5), \text{read}), ((S_7, O_1), \text{read}),$
$\quad ((S_7, O_2), \text{read}), ((S_7, O_3), \text{read}), ((S_7, O_5), \text{read}), ((S_7, O_6), \text{read}),$
$\quad ((S_8, O_1), \text{read}), ((S_8, O_2), \text{read}), ((S_8, O_3), \text{read}), ((S_8, O_5), \text{read}),$
$\quad ((S_8, O_6), \text{read}), ((S_8, O_7), \text{read})$

$ec_7 = \{((S_1, O_1), \text{write}), ((S_1, O_2), \text{write}), ((S_1, O_3), \text{write}),$
$\quad ((S_1, O_4), \text{write}), ((S_1, O_5), \text{write}), ((S_1, O_6), \text{write}), ((S_1, O_7), \text{write}),$
$\quad ((S_1, O_8), \text{write}), ((S_2, O_1), \text{write}), ((S_2, O_2), \text{write}), ((S_2, O_3), \text{write}),$
$\quad ((S_2, O_4), \text{write}), ((S_2, O_5), \text{write}), ((S_2, O_7), \text{write}), ((S_2, O_8), \text{write}),$
$\quad ((S_3, O_1), \text{write}), ((S_3, O_2), \text{write}), ((S_3, O_3), \text{write}), ((S_3, O_4), \text{write}),$
$\quad ((S_3, O_5), \text{write}), ((S_3, O_6), \text{write}), ((S_3, O_8), \text{write}), ((S_4, O_1), \text{write}),$
$\quad ((S_4, O_2), \text{write}), ((S_4, O_3), \text{write}), ((S_4, O_5), \text{write}), ((S_4, O_6), \text{write}),$
$\quad ((S_4, O_7), \text{write}), ((S_5, O_1), \text{write}), ((S_5, O_2), \text{write}), ((S_5, O_3), \text{write}),$
$\quad ((S_5, O_4), \text{write}), ((S_5, O_5), \text{write}), ((S_5, O_6), \text{write}), ((S_5, O_7), \text{write}),$

$((S_5, O_8), \text{write}), ((S_6, O_1), \text{write}), ((S_6, O_3), \text{write}), ((S_6, O_4), \text{write}),$

$((S_6, O_5), \text{write}), ((S_6, O_7), \text{write}), ((S_6, O_8), \text{write}), ((S_7, O_1), \text{write}),$

$((S_7, O_2), \text{write}), ((S_7, O_3), \text{write}), ((S_7, O_4), \text{write}), ((S_7, O_5), \text{write}),$

$((S_7, O_6), \text{write}), ((S_7, O_8), \text{write}), ((S_8, O_1), \text{write}), ((S_8, O_2), \text{write}),$

$((S_8, O_3), \text{write}), ((S_8, O_5), \text{write}), ((S_8, O_6), \text{write}), ((S_8, O_7), \text{write})\}$

$ec_8 = \{((S_1, O_1), \text{read-write}), ((S_1, O_2), \text{read-write}), ((S_1, O_3), \text{read-write}),$

$((S_1, O_4), \text{read-write}), ((S_1, O_5), \text{read-write}), ((S_1, O_6), \text{read-write}),$

$((S_1, O_7), \text{read-write}), ((S_1, O_8), \text{read-write}), ((S_2, O_1), \text{read-write}),$

$((S_2, O_2), \text{read-write}), ((S_2, O_3), \text{read-write}), ((S_2, O_4), \text{read-write}),$

$((S_2, O_5), \text{read-write}), ((S_2, O_6), \text{read-write}), ((S_2, O_7), \text{read-write}),$

$((S_2, O_8), \text{read-write}), ((S_3, O_1), \text{read-write}), ((S_3, O_2), \text{read-write}),$

$((S_3, O_4), \text{read-write}), ((S_3, O_5), \text{read-write}), ((S_3, O_6), \text{read-write}),$

$((S_3, O_7), \text{read-write}), ((S_3, O_8), \text{read-write}), ((S_4, O_1), \text{read-write}),$

$((S_4, O_2), \text{read-write}), ((S_4, O_3), \text{read-write}), ((S_4, O_4), \text{read-write}),$

$((S_4, O_5), \text{read-write}), ((S_4, O_6), \text{read-write}), ((S_4, O_7), \text{read-write}),$

$((S_4, O_8), \text{read-write}), ((S_5, O_2), \text{read-write}), ((S_5, O_3), \text{read-write}),$

$((S_5, O_4), \text{read-write}), ((S_5, O_5), \text{read-write}), ((S_5, O_6), \text{read-write}),$

$((S_5, O_7), \text{read-write}), ((S_5, O_8), \text{read-write}), ((S_6, O_1), \text{read-write}),$

$((S_6, O_2), \text{read-write}), ((S_6, O_3), \text{read-write}), ((S_6, O_4), \text{read-write}),$

$((S_6, O_5), \text{read-write}), ((S_6, O_6), \text{read-write}), ((S_6, O_7), \text{read-write}),$

$((S_6, O_8), \text{read-write}), ((S_7, O_1), \text{read-write}), ((S_7, O_2), \text{read-write}),$

$((S_7, O_4), \text{read-write}), ((S_7, O_5), \text{read-write}), ((S_7, O_6), \text{read-write}),$

$((S_7, O_7), \text{read-write}), ((S_7, O_8), \text{read-write}), ((S_8, O_1), \text{read-write}),$

$((S_8, O_2), \text{read-write}), ((S_8, O_3), \text{read-write}), ((S_8, O_4), \text{read-write}),$

$((S_8, O_5), \text{read-write}), ((S_8, O_6), \text{read-write}), ((S_8, O_7), \text{read-write}),$

$((S_8, O_8), \text{read-write})\}$

$ec_9 = \{((S_1, O_1), \text{execute}), ((S_1, O_2), \text{execute}), ((S_1, O_3), \text{execute}),$

$((S_1, O_4), \text{execute}), ((S_1, O_5), \text{execute}), ((S_1, O_6), \text{execute}),$

$((S_1, O_7), \text{execute}), ((S_1, O_8), \text{execute}), ((S_2, O_1), \text{execute}),$

$((S_2, O_3), \text{execute}), ((S_2, O_4), \text{execute}), ((S_2, O_5), \text{execute}),$

$((S_2, O_6), \text{execute}), ((S_2, O_8), \text{execute}), ((S_3, O_1), \text{execute}),$

$((S_3, O_2), \text{execute}), ((S_3, O_4), \text{execute}), ((S_3, O_5), \text{execute}),$

$((S_3, O_6), \text{execute}), ((S_3, O_7), \text{execute}), ((S_3, O_8), \text{execute}),$

$((S_4, O_1), \text{execute}), ((S_4, O_2), \text{execute}), ((S_4, O_3), \text{execute}),$

$((S_4, O_4), \text{execute}), ((S_4, O_5), \text{execute}), ((S_4, O_6), \text{execute}),$

$((S_4, O_7), \text{execute}), ((S_4, O_8), \text{execute}), ((S_5, O_1), \text{execute}),$

$((S_5, O_2), \text{execute}), ((S_5, O_3), \text{execute}), ((S_5, O_4), \text{execute}),$
$((S_5, O_5), \text{execute}), ((S_5, O_6), \text{execute}), ((S_5, O_7), \text{execute}),$
$((S_5, O_8), \text{execute}), ((S_6, O_1), \text{execute}), ((S_6, O_2), \text{execute}),$
$((S_6, O_3), \text{execute}), ((S_6, O_4), \text{execute}), ((S_6, O_5), \text{execute}),$
$((S_6, O_7), \text{execute}), ((S_6, O_8), \text{execute}), ((S_7, O_1), \text{execute}),$
$((S_7, O_2), \text{execute}), ((S_7, O_4), \text{execute}), ((S_7, O_5), \text{execute}),$
$((S_7, O_6), \text{execute}), ((S_7, O_7), \text{execute}), ((S_7, O_8), \text{execute}),$
$((S_8, O_1), \text{execute}), ((S_8, O_2), \text{execute}), ((S_8, O_3), \text{execute}),$
$((S_8, O_4), \text{execute}), ((S_8, O_5), \text{execute}), ((S_8, O_6), \text{execute}),$
$((S_8, O_7), \text{execute}), ((S_8, O_8), \text{execute})\}$

$\text{ec}_{10} = \{((S_1, O_1), \text{append}), ((S_1, O_2), \text{append}), ((S_1, O_3), \text{append}),$
$((S_1, O_4), \text{append}), ((S_1, O_5), \text{append}), ((S_1, O_6), \text{append}),$
$((S_1, O_7), \text{append}), ((S_1, O_8), \text{append}), ((S_2, O_1), \text{append}),$
$((S_2, O_2), \text{append}), ((S_2, O_3), \text{append}), ((S_2, O_4), \text{append}),$
$((S_2, O_6), \text{append}), ((S_2, O_7), \text{append}), ((S_2, O_8), \text{append}),$
$((S_3, O_1), \text{append}), ((S_3, O_2), \text{append}), ((S_3, O_3), \text{append}),$
$((S_3, O_4), \text{append}), ((S_3, O_6), \text{append}), ((S_3, O_7), \text{append}),$
$((S_3, O_8), \text{append}), ((S_4, O_1), \text{append}), ((S_4, O_2), \text{append}),$
$((S_4, O_3), \text{append}), ((S_4, O_6), \text{append}), ((S_4, O_7), \text{append}),$
$((S_4, O_8), \text{append}), ((S_5, O_2), \text{append}), ((S_5, O_3), \text{append}),$
$((S_5, O_4), \text{append}), ((S_5, O_6), \text{append}), ((S_5, O_7), \text{append}),$
$((S_5, O_8), \text{append}), ((S_6, O_1), \text{append}), ((S_6, O_2), \text{append}),$
$((S_6, O_3), \text{append}), ((S_6, O_4), \text{append}), ((S_6, O_6), \text{append}),$
$((S_6, O_7), \text{append}), ((S_6, O_8), \text{append}), ((S_7, O_1), \text{append}),$
$((S_7, O_2), \text{append}), ((S_7, O_3), \text{append}), ((S_7, O_4), \text{append}),$
$((S_7, O_6), \text{append}), ((S_7, O_7), \text{append}), ((S_7, O_8), \text{append}),$
$((S_8, O_1), \text{append}), ((S_8, O_2), \text{append}), ((S_8, O_3), \text{append}),$
$((S_8, O_6), \text{append}), ((S_8, O_7), \text{append}), ((S_8, O_8), \text{append})\}$

Because all subjects, objects and access attributes are assigned to equivalence classes, only one subject, object and access attribute combination of each equivalence class has to be tested.

Table 3. Result of the equivalence classes test

Test	subject	object	attribute	tested ec	result
1	S_1	O_5	read	ec_1	valid
2	S_7	O_7	write	ec_2	valid
3	S_5	O_1	read-write	ec_3	valid
4	S_6	O_6	execute	ec_4	valid
5	S_8	O_5	append	ec_5	valid
6	S_2	O_3	read	ec_6	invalid
7	S_5	O_4	write	ec_7	invalid
8	S_3	O_8	read-write	ec_8	invalid
9	S_4	O_7	execute	ec_9	invalid
10	S_8	O_2	append	ec_{10}	invalid

5 Conclusion

In our paper we presented a method for defining an exhaustive list of test cases based on formally described equivalence classes that are derived from the formal security policy description. We distinguished between satisfying equivalence classes that are used to verify if the system is over-constrained and violating equivalence classes, showing if the system is under-constrained. Additionally we defined the equivalence classes for the Bell and LaPadula model and defined test cases, based on the Bell and LaPadula equivalence classes for a sample system. Our current and further investigations will be in the field of testing formally history based security models like the Limes Security model [6] and the Chinese Wall Security Policy model [2].

Acknowledgement. The authors thank Dipl-Inf. Dieter Kessler for his support in the preparation of this paper.

References

1. Lampson, B.W.: Protection. In: Proceedings of the 5th Princeton Conference on Information Sciences and Systems, Princeton, p. 437 (1971)
2. Brewer, D.F.C., Nash, M.J.: The Chinese Wall Security Policy. In: IEEE Symposium on Security and Privacy, Oakland, pp. 206–214 (1989)
3. Lin, T.Y.: Chinese Wall Security Policy-An Aggressive Model. In: Proceedings of the Fifth Aerospace Computer Security Application Conference, December 4-8, pp. 286–293 (1989)
4. Bell, D., LaPadula, L.: Secure Computer Systems: Mathematical Foundations. Technical Report MTR-2547, Vol. I. MITRE Corporation, Bedford (1973)
5. Clark, D., Wilson, D.: A Comparison of Commercial and Military Security Policies. In: IEEE Symposium on Security and Privacy, pp. 184–194 (1987)
6. Hermann, E.: The Limes Security Model for Information Flow Control. In: FARES Workshop of the Sixth International Conference on Availability, Reliability and Security (ARES 2011), Vienna, Austria, August 22-26 (2011)

7. Hu, H., Ahn, G.-J.: Enabling Verification and Conformance Testing for Access Control Model. In: SACMAT 2008, Estes Park, Colorado, USA, June 11-13 (2008)

8. Murnane, T., Reed, K.: On the Effectiveness of Mutation Analysis as a Black Box Testing Technique. In: 13th Australian Software Engineering Conference (ASWEC 2001), Canberra, Australia, August 27-28 (2001)

9. Grimm, R.: A Formal IT-Security Model for a Weak Fair-Exchange Cooperation with Non-Repudiation Proofs. In: International Conference on Emerging Security Information, Systems and Technologies, Athens, June 18-23 (2009)

10. Godefroid, P., Levin, M.Y., Molnar, D.: Automated Whitebox Fuzz Testing. In: Network and IT Security Conference, San Diego, CA, February 8-11 (2008)

11. Myers, G.: The Art of Software Testing. Wiley-Interscience Publication (1979)

12. Hu, V.C., Martin, E., Hwang, J., Xie, T.: Conformance Checking of Access Control Policies Specified in XACML. In: 31st Annual International Computer Software and Applications Conference, Beijing (2007)

13. Martin, E., Xie, T.: A fault model and mutation testing of access control policies. In: 16th International Conference on World Wide Web (May 2007)

14. Martin, E., Xie, T.: Automated test generation for access control policies. In: 17th IEEE International Conference on Software Reliability Engineering (November 2006)

15. Martin, E., Xie, T., Yu, T.: Defining and Measuring Policy Coverage in Testing Access Control Policies. In: Ning, P., Qing, S., Li, N. (eds.) ICICS 2006. LNCS, vol. 4307, pp. 139–158. Springer, Heidelberg (2006)

16. De Angelis, G., Kirkham, T., Winfield, S.: Access Policy Compliance Testing in a User Centric Trust Service Infrastructure. In: QASBA 2011, Lugano, Switzerland, September 14 (2011)

17. Traon, Y.L., Mouelhi, T., Baudry, B.: Testing security policies: going beyond functional testing. In: 18th IEEE International Symposium on Software Reliability (ISSRE 2007), Sweden, November 5-9 (2007)

Trust as an Organismic Trait of E-Commerce Systems

Tanja Ažderska and Borka Jerman Blažič

Laboratory for Open Systems and Networks, Jozef Stefan Institute, Jamova 39,
1000 Ljubljana, Slovenia
{atanja,borka}@e5.ijs.si

Abstract. The behavior patterns resulting from the interactions of many trusting entities in e-commerce systems are often more complex than the performance of each of the individuals separately; thus, simple rules of trusting behavior give rise to complex, emergent patterns. A major reason these emergent properties were neither successfully captured nor adequately treated by the current formal models is the global trend of addressing technical issues in a mechanistic manner – considering the system merely as a sum of its components and neglecting the interactions between those components. This work introduces the concept of an organismic property of human-centric e-commerce systems and reveals new areas of applicability of trust as an organismic system-trait. We find that the current schemes of modeling trust in e-commerce systems disregard the role of diversity, complexity, and a service provider's responsibility, concentrating mainly on the relationship among the service consumers. The higher purpose, however, is to provide a novel view of analyzing trust-related design-issues, and to give notice of the possible consequences from a systemic ignorance of these issues in e-commerce systems.

Keywords: trust, e-commerce, organismic, complex, responsibility, context.

1 Introduction

An inherent "misfortune" related to social trust-phenomena in e-commerce and marketing systems is that:

- Trust is generally too complex to be even intuitively grasped, let alone formally analyzed; and
- When it comes to representing its properties through various technicalities and formalities, they are often greatly simplified for the sake of practical feasibility.

Marketing phenomena represent the collective result of many individual entities (consumers, sellers, distributors) whose motivations and actions, although combined by simple behavioral rules, manifest in a manner that produces surprising patterns of global and group behavior [1], [2]. Moreover, these aggregate patterns feed back to affect the individuals' choices. Thus, consumers can make buying decisions based on their acquaintances' advice or their social network's recommendations, which affects the diffusion of products and ideas, and in turn influences the dominance of a brand in

G. Quirchmayr et al. (Eds.): CD-ARES 2012, LNCS 7465, pp. 161–175, 2012.

a market. However, the predominant brands also affect an individual's decisions as to which product to purchase or which idea to adopt. The diffusion patterns that result from the interactions of many entities may be, and in fact ARE more often than not, much more complex than the behavior rules of the individuals. There are many reasons why such emergent properties are not captured and adequately treated by the current computational and formal models. Among those with highest relevance, but also greatest subtlety, is the trend of addressing technical design issues in a mechanistic manner, considering the properties of a system as a whole to be traceable to the properties of its parts. On the other hand, there is another, even more pronounced trend of merging together aspects of systems of different nature into a single operational whole. The purpose is to produce human-centric systems that would integrate the functionality of the emerging technologies with the self-organizing nature of human societies. In its most obvious manifestation, this trend can be viewed in the advent of social networks, electronic services, e-commerce systems, and smart cities, all coming under the umbrella of the Internet of Services and Things. The earlier, mechanistic, view on computational systems is rooted in the engineering contexts in which a system's behavior could be predicted by knowing the behavior of the system's components and their operational ranges. Such systems are, for e.g., the factory plants, or wireless sensor networks, consisting of many devices with known physical characteristics and specifications, and predetermined communication protocols. However, for the later trend, this approach is rendered useless, and moreover, points to a possibility of a serious systemic ignorance if the mechanistic view was to continue. An example for this would be: providing a platform for user to interact, contribute content, and even create new products, but not accounting for how the collaborative, competitive, and monetary elements implemented by the providers affect the users' actions and their interaction with the system.

What constitutes an emergent property; what are the conditions in e-commerce systems that give rise to such properties; how their manifestation affects the system; and what trust has to do with all this; are some of the questions that this work tries to answer. Hence, one of our contributions to the current research on e-commerce trust systems is the detection and analysis of the factors that bear responsibility for the emergence of some unintuitive patterns in those systems. More importantly, our work reveals trust as a core aspect of the solutions for the issues of increased complexity, non-accountable authorities, and user bias.

To meet the stated goals, the paper is organized as follows: we first define some basic terms and give a multi-disciplinary overview of the efforts to tackle trust-related issues in an online, particularly e-commerce setting. As we fit our work into the state of the art, we outline the major issues that dictate the need for an organismic view on trust and point out the significance and benefits of such a view. We then detect new key-roles that trust can play in dealing with the identified issues. Section 4 concludes with constructive summary, pointing towards some future directions.

2   Basic Concepts and Related Work

For the sake of clarity, we now briefly define the basic terms that will be employed throughout the remainder of the paper.

2.1   Basic Concepts

Large body of work have shown and analyzed the intricacies of understanding and making trusting choices [3–5]. Complementing this with what we elaborated above explains the hard time researchers have to incorporate trust into online settings analogous to those from the traditional networks. However, following Gambetta [6], we give:

Definition 1a. Trust is the subjective probability that an entity will perform in an expected and beneficial manner, restraining from doing unexpected harm.

Considering trust only as a subjective probability leaves out risk as an important concept related to trust. This fact has catalyzed a vigorous debate between economists and social psychologists [5]. When one entity relies on another, trust choices are inevitably coupled with risk. Thus, borrowing from Josang [7]:

Definition 1b. Trust is the extent of willingness to depend on others' decisions and actions, accepting the risk of undesired outcome.

Despite the generally interchangeable use of trust and reputation, we differ between the two and recognize the role of reputation mechanisms as technical facilitators for managing trust.

Definition 2a. Reputation is the general standing of the community about an entity's trustworthiness, based on entities' past behavior, performance, or quality of service, in a specific context.

Definition 2b. A system that facilitates the reputation foresight and the trust management is called a reputation mechanism.

Next, we provide an interdisciplinary overview of the approaches for tackling trust issues in e-commerce context, and identify the major issues that will be tackled by our work.

2.2   Related Work

Trust and the Need for Accountable Providers. Significant amount of the efforts for formalizing trust-based interactions employed to design and analyze e-commerce systems is rooted in Game Theory, where concepts like risk, cost, and utility are formally defined [8]. There, the fundamental trust-related problems are captured by the Prisoner's Dilemma; it is a principle that demonstrates the tradeoffs in people's decisions to behave either in their own interest, or in a manner that contributes to the overall community welfare [9]. Prisoners' Dilemma has been extensively used to analyze the incentives for accumulating social capital, as well as the importance of repeated interactions in inducing cooperation. However, Prisoner's Dilemma *per se* is not able to account for the eventual presence of an 'authority figure' that might impose its controls or affect the decisions of the system entities, regardless of the given payoffs for their actions. Therefore, additional insights are required into how the presence of an *authority* and the actions made by that authority affect the decisions and interactions of the individuals that are part of the same system hierarchy. In the case of e-commerce, it implies a need to account for the strategic games between different service providers, as well as the policies they establish within their platforms, in addition to analyzing the actions of and the interactions between the users. In the effort to account for these issues, we bring to the front another type of Game Theory problem known as the Colonel Blotto game [10]. The Colonel Blotto captures strategic situations in which players attempt to mismatch the actions of their opponents by allocating limited resources across domains in competitive environments. The game consists of the following: two players allocate resources to a finite number of contests (fronts); each front is won by the player who allocates the greater number of resources to it, and a player's payoff equals the number of fronts won. Thus, a player's goal is to strategically mismatch the actions of its opponent. In short, if lower amount of resources are available compared to the opponent, it pays off to increase the numbers of fronts. Despite the desirable characteristics of altruism and cooperativeness in the interactions between two parties, it is reasonable, especially in an e-commerce context, for competition to be analyzed by different means than those used for studying altruistic cooperation. In this work, we attempt to connect such games of strategic mismatch to the current trends of development of e-commerce systems in order to reveal a new role trust can take in e-commerce systems.

Moving the scale from an individual's to a societal perspective, Ba argues that it is often the actions driven by the people's sense of community that contribute to outcomes that improve the community welfare [11]. Moreover, if members are held responsible for their actions, there is a much greater pressure to adhere to the rules. Fehr and Gächter have shown that, if given the opportunity, individuals vigorously punish selfishness, even if inducing punishment is costly [12]. This reveals the potential of trust mechanisms for sanctioning undesired behavior, especially when the possibility of post-contractual opportunism creates a context of moral hazard. On the other hand, distributing the control only among the community members and entrusting them the role of a regulation mechanism of the system evolution forces the system to rely on their subjective view-points, interpretations and actions. Exposing the community welfare to the subjective views of the entrusted members is not a negative thing in and of itself. However, without the means for monitoring and accountability, such an ideology is often considered as the ultimate cause of degradation of the system's work and hierarchy. Makridakis and Taleb have already elaborated on the limited predictability and the high level of uncertainty in various areas of science, and life in general [13]. There is a remarkable body of empirical evidence speaking about the disastrous consequences of inaccurate forecasts that are distinguished by three types of predictions: those relying on patterns for forecasting, those utilizing relationships as their basis, and those for which human judgment is the major determinant of the forecast. Online trust systems are designed to rely on all the three.

Trust and Complexity Reduction. When it comes to traditional societies, one of the crucial roles of trust is reducing the complexity that may arise in social interactions [14]. In that regard, the potential of employing trust mechanisms for dealing with information asymmetry was recognized long ago. As argued above, in the context of moral hazard, trust mechanisms are employed for sanctioning undesired behavior. However, there is another type of information asymmetry, which arises when an entity is required to choose a transaction partner whose behavioral type (for e.g., good or bad) is unknown in advance, i.e., adverse selection. In his seminal work, Akerlof analyzed the effect of social and trading reputation on transaction outcome and market maintenance [15]. He demonstrated that goods with low quality can squeeze out those of high quality because of the information asymmetry present in the buyers' and sellers' knowledge about the products – the problem of the so called "lemon markets". Trust mechanisms would balance this asymmetry, helping buyers make better-informed decisions by signaling the behavior-type of sellers, but at the same time they would provide an incentive for sellers to exchange high-quality goods. Thus, Akerlof makes an instructive distinction between the signaling and the sanctioning role of trust systems, which was only recently considered in computer science [16]. However, all the models that deal with information asymmetry in an online environment rely on probabilistic signals, but also output uncertain values of the variables representing the entities behavioral characteristics. This reveals that it is absolutely non-trivial to determine and appropriately aggregate the different types of signaling information that can be obtained from trust systems. Furthermore, it points to the need to account for the signals from online trust systems through various mechanisms, depending on the nature of those signals. In this paper, we set the ground for how such analyses could be carried out, although we leave the formal justification as future work.

Trust and Collective Wisdom. Despite the significant work done on signaling in economics and contract theory, the online environment poses additional requirements if the same ideas are to be employed. The operation of online market places depends highly on the collective actions of the individual entities (agents, consumers, sellers, distributors, etc.). Incorporating human elements into the technical workings of e-commerce systems leads to the emergence of complex patterns of group behavior that are not necessarily a product of the rules governing the individuals' behaviors. The high discrepancy between the users' expectations and the e-commerce system performance still sustains and is resembled by different forms of bias manifested in the results obtained from the trust systems [17–20]. However, biased results may not come from biased inputs by the individual entities. The whole chain of dependencies in the e-commerce system has to be considered to determine the causal loops that appear between the system inputs and outputs and to prevent reinforcement of this bias in a cascade manner. Our work will establish the bond between computational trust and the exploitation of "the wisdom of crowds" in e-commerce systems [21]. Moreover, it will detect the detrimental role of dependent and non-diverse opinions in exploiting the benefits of "the wisdom of crowds" and the emergence of user bias.

Despite the early work on trust relations and conflict resolution in Game theory, the notion of computational trust appears significantly later, when Marsh established its formal basis in distributed artificial intelligence [22]. Although distinguished by its simplicity, Marsh brings the substantial finding about the agents' tendency to group into robust clusters with similar trustworthiness and interests. However, he makes no distinction between groups and individuals and the different properties they exhibit, considering groups as entities that equally encounter and resolve trust choices as the individuals comprising them. Thus, the micro-behavior of the system entities are considered to resemble the macro-effects of the overall behavior.

The following section introduces the notion of an *organismic property* of trust systems, analyzing its importance for the design of human-centric e-commerce systems dependent on the trusting choices of their entities.

3   The Organismic Nature of Trust

In a previous work of ours [23], we analyzed trust systems through the General Systems Theory [24]. Based on the Jordan's System Taxonomy [25], we categorized trust systems as *functional*, *organismic*, and *non-purposive* (Table 1), and showed the implications of such a categorization on the overall system's functionality.

Table 1. Organizing principles of Jordan's Systems Taxonomy (bolded and italicized are the categories to which trust systems are ascribed)

Rate-of-change	Purpose	Connectivity
Structural (static)	Purposive (system-directed)	Mechanistic (non-densely connected)
Functional (dynamic)	*non-purposive (environment-directed)*	*Organismic (densely connected)*

Here, we concentrate on the organismic property of trust systems, as we consider that the trend of neglecting it endangers the sustainability of any human-centric system, of which e-commerce systems are a major representative.

A main characteristic of *organismic* (or densely-connected) systems is that they change even when a single connection between their components changes. In contrast, *mechanistic* systems are not affected by the removal of parts or connections in the remaining components. Remarkable proofs of the organismic nature of social systems can be found in Granovetter's threshold model of collective behavior [1], and Shelling's models of segregation [26], both of which show the mismatch between the micro-behavior of the individuals and the macro-effects that appear as a result.

E-commerce trust systems depend highly on the entities' choices and interactions. Their complex nature makes it extremely hard, if not impossible, to predict the impact of these interactions on the system performance. The different types of entities and their differing interests require for each design issue to be analyzed from multiple perspectives.

We now proceed with presenting the major scenarios that dictate the need for an organismic approach of designing trust systems for e-commerce purposes, and define the role that trust plays in tackling the encountered issues.

3.1   Reduction of Complexity

Luhmann has long ago recognized trust as a means for reducing complexity in traditional social systems [14]. However, it is not that trivial to generalize this as an implication for online systems, which are much more dynamic and especially more scalable. Although most of the proposed trust models provide some discussion or evaluation of their scalability (among other performance criteria), scalability is mainly considered a technical nuance of a given solution and is analyzed separately from the interactions between the system entities. However, it is clear that no system can grow infinitely. Thus, the life-span of the natural (organismic) systems spreads through two major and subsequent phases: growth and maintenance [27]. The resources systems use in the first phase are mainly intended for growth; in the second phase, on the other hand, the systems' resources are employed for maintaining the state and preserving/improving the quality of operation (a quick recall of the human as a system would suffice to realize this). This transition from quantity to quality-based operation is often seamless, prospectively unpredictable, and only retrospectively realizable, which is why the mechanistic trend of resolving systemic issues continues.

Hence, the question arises: following Luhmann's view of trust as a means for complexity reduction in a society, can we detect ways in which computational trust reduces complexity in e-commerce systems? One thought in that direction is reducing the complexity of negotiating a transaction, as having a trust system in place implies: finding someone (or information about them), looking at the community's standing (as a signaling device) about their reputation, and deciding whether to transact or not without any prior interaction. But in addition to reducing the complexity, it is clear that it is also the **cost** of negotiation that is reduced, as the protocol of starting a transaction is significantly simplified. However, this holds only if the information is accurate enough, and is also considered reliable by those who should act upon it – in other words, if entities are able to trust the trust information. Therefore, it is not sufficient to only decide what type of information should be loaded into the aggregation mechanisms that compute trust, but also to provide mechanisms that show if the information generated from the system is perceived appropriately by the users. In our future work, this concept will be formalized using a framework of *interpreted and generated signals* [28], which will allow matching the adequate types of trust signals with the various contexts of embedding trust-information in e-commerce systems.

3.2   Enrichment and Diversity

The consumer preferences are directly related to the marketing strategies of the service providers. The change in the former often imposes necessary change in the later. However, users are often unaware of their taste, even for experiences from previously felt outcomes [3], [4], [29]. Not only does this mean that taste is much more subtle than preference, but it also shows that preference itself is not a stable property of human reasoning [30]. In online trust systems, experiments on persistency of user preferences about identical items at different instances of time proved significant fluctuation in the repeated preferential choices [31]. To preserve the dynamics of fluctuating preferences, it is important that an e-commerce system maintains diversity in terms of market strategies, choices offered to their users, the users' behavioral types, their opinions, and the actions they undertake. Surowiecki included diversity as one of the key criteria crucial for exploiting the so called "wisdom of crowds", together with independence, decentralization, and aggregation of opinions (Table 2) [21]. Although deceptively different, the same analogy holds for evolutionary phenomena; namely, that fertilization leads to enrichment (of a certain species), but also to the loss of diversity of species [27].

As discussed in the Related Work section, a great deal of research has shown that the following major issues are common to all e-commerce systems:

- The largest percentage of provided resources comes from the minority of users [19], and most of the users act only as "content-consumers", providing negligible amount of resources [32];
- Small number of system entities drive the general population's opinion [17];
- The presence of the so called *herd behavior* or *bandwagon effect* [3] is manifested as a group polarization in the individual's online actions [33];
- The aggregated results from the feedback mechanisms (through trust and reputation metrics) exhibit a high level of positive bias, even in their steady state [18];
- The marketing strategies employed by the companies and media are very often directed towards creating such biased effects in order to gain a large percentage of consumers (be it tangible goods or content as a product) [34], [35].

Table 2. Key criteria that separate wise crowds from irrational ones

Criteria	Description
Diversity of opinions	Each person should have private information even if it is an eccentric interpretation of the known facts
Independence	People's opinions are not determined by the opinions of those around them
Decentralization	People are able to draw on local knowledge
Aggregation	Some mechanism exists for turning private judgments into a collective decision

By mapping the above issues onto Table 2, the following can be observed:

- Current trust systems do allow for obtaining a local view on the entities' knowledge about the behavioral types of their transaction partners, thus ensuring **decentralization** in the process of inferring trust;
- There is a significant body of work on defining a formal apparatus for **aggregating** trust information. Subjective Logic is among the most prominent, and also one that resembles many of our views about what constitutes a suitable way to cope with the subjective nature of trust [36];
- However, the manifestation of group polarization and user bias as a steady-state phenomenon in all the e-commerce systems that are equipped with trust mechanisms implies a clear lack of diversity, and moreover – lack of independence in the entities' actions (including opinions, decisions, etc.).
- Finally, the marketing strategies of the various companies and the media additionally amplify the effects of initial mismatch between the users' expectations and online services, contributing to cascading effects of biased behavior resembled by the bandwagon effect.

All of the above observations are a strong testimony for the organismic nature of e-commerce trust systems, as they all show that a single action or change of the systems entities can have a huge impact on the overall system behavior and performance. They also show that exploiting the wisdom of crowds can be strongly inhibited by the externalities that the human element brings into the trust system. This, together with the causal loops through which user bias is amplified in the system [37], point to the need of more subtle mechanisms for capturing trust as an emergent, and not an inherent entity's property.

In a recent work of ours, we performed experimental studies of the factors that influence the users' actions and decisions in online reputation, rating and recommendation systems [38]. We found that increasing the granularity of the Likert-scales (analogous to increased diversity of offered user-choices) and adding a "positive spin" to the presented choices for user evaluations in e-commerce systems can act as an incentive for providing more diverse, but also more accurate feedback. These findings and the theoretical analysis presented in the current paper provide a framework for the formal modeling and analysis of diversity as a requirement for efficient trust systems. This formal model will have as its foundation the Diversity Prediction Theorem [39], which connects the crowd's prediction error to the individuals' prediction errors and the crowd's diversity.

3.3   Provider's Accountability

In this section, we connect the notion of 'strategic mismatch' represented by the Colonel Blotto game [10] to the current development trends of e-commerce systems and determine the benefits that the accounting for the provider's trustworthiness have for trust elicitation. To do that, we analyze some microeconomic strategies in e-commerce systems, identify the need for a distributed responsibility scheme, and establish trust as a basic accountability measure to respond to this need.

Since the basic setting of Colonel Blotto defines a zero-sum game (one party's benefits equal the other party's losses) in which the winner gets everything, and requires that the opponents have equal amount of resources, using the original model would be misrepresentative of the true nature of market interactions. Therefore, the reasoning employed here follows the generalized analog of Colonel Blotto - "General Blotto game" [40]. General Blotto's trait of realism lays in the fact that it allows that an opponent has advantage in the number of resources available. Furthermore, it accounts for the additional externalities that can affect the game flow, such as changing circumstances and non-independent fronts. Finally, it extends to an arbitrary number of N players, unlike the original game defined for two players. Because of space constraints, but also because the formal approach deserves special attention and more in-depth justification, we leave these analyses for a subsequent work. In what follows, we directly give our analysis based on the insights from the General Blotto game, but we refer the interested reader to [10] and [40] for justification of the reasoning included here.

Amazon[1] and eBay[2] are the two largest e-commerce companies, and according to the Web Information Company Alexa[3], their sites are also the two top-ranked e-commerce sites (with overall rank of 10th and 21st place respectively). Among the 100 top-ranked sites, there are only four to five e-commerce sites (this number varies on a daily basis). With highest rank are the ones that are not constrained to a unique product offer (books only or movies only) and that provide a wide specter of products and services. These statistics of the general standing of e-commerce sites among other site-types shows that only a handful of e-commerce sites are prevailing on the Internet. Intuitively, this resembles the network effect of the economies of scale, and is arguably similar to the same effect in the traditional world: big stores squeeze the little stores out of the market by providing a more stable and a more convenient offer with a wider range of available products [41]. This is also the reason that we connect these providers' strategies to the games of strategic mismatch. Thus, the same products on Amazon and eBay have been put within a different range of contexts (i.e., fronts), which creates an opportunity for them to be valued differently by the consumers. For example: on Amazon, a book is possible to be published by Amazon, reviewed on Amazon, rated, recommended, sold, bought, stored and backed up, made available on Kindle, shipped by Amazon, processed in some desired way through Amazon's Mechanical Turk[4], etc. On eBay, on the other hand, the same book can be sold, maybe bid for, bought, rated, or shipped (by a seller). This shows two different strategies of allocating the same resource over various contexts, and has proved to affect the companies' revenues in a different manner. However, it is not only the revenues that are being affected. To support our reasoning, we extracted the concrete feedback about the user's satisfaction from Amazon and eBay. Figure 1 shows that, despite the high popularity of the two companies, the general estimates of their platforms differ to a great extent.

---

[1] http://www.amazon.com/

[2] http://www.ebay.com/

[3] http://www.alexa.com/topsites (this list is based on one-month average traffic rank).

[4] https://www.mturk.com/mturk/welcome

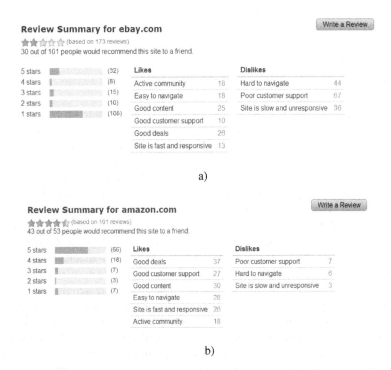

Fig. 1. Alexa review summary for a) Amazon and b) eBay

This is not to illustrate a lower reputation of eBay compared to Amazon; the purpose of the two systems differs sufficiently for them to be incomparable to one another in many aspects. However, the high percentage of positive feedback and the users' reluctance to leave negative feedback within the eBay and Amazon platforms [17] [20], points to a discrepancy between the users' adoption of e-commerce services, their satisfaction of those services, and the feedback they provide within the platforms that offer the services. Considering that trust is an emergent property of a system, and a system designer can only provide the circumstances under which trust can flourish, it is reasonable to state that the basic type of trust required for a functional system is trust in the platform provider. Current trust models do not consider combining this form of *accountability trust* with the trustworthiness traits of the system entities. Yet, there have been important arguments for the benefits that such an approach can have for the reliability of both security systems [42] and socio-technical systems [43]. This intuition was confirmed by simply querying the web for the "top 25 e-commerce sites". The top two results showed that the user preferences are much better inclined for more specialized sites, with respect to both their offer and their design[5]. Hence, considering such accountability trust as an implicit feedback can provide a distribution of responsibility among all the system entities, including accountability for the

---

[5] http://kaleazy.com/top-25-best-e-commerce-sites-of-2011/,
http://www.smashingmagazine.com/2010/01/22/35-beautiful-and-effective-ecommerce-websites/

service providers. This is especially important as e-commerce systems scale up, because in the transition from growth to maintenance, trust will increasingly act as an emergent qualitative signal.

3.4   Discussion

The analyses in this paper contribute to the well-known debate on how people are tuned to think in terms of linearity: to expect growth where there has been a long trend of past growth and to assume double output if there was doubling in system's input. While it is apparent that an organism or a human does not grow infinitely, it is also reasonable to assume that a five-year old (human) is not half a ten-year old one. Also, maintaining a city that has doubled in size requires more than double of the resources spent before its growth, as there is an additional cost of maintaining the interconnections between the system components. The same stands for any human-centric system, regardless of whether it is technical, social, or hybrid. The inclusion of the human element acts as an opening valve of the system towards its environment of deployment, adding complexity in the way the internal structure of the system is maintained. This gives rise to the ascribed non-linearity, expressed as 'the whole not being equal to the sum of its parts'. Thus, an organ exhibits additional properties to those of the cells that comprise it, a human is not a simple sum of organs, a city is more than the sum of its households, and a technical system is neither a mixture of nodes, nor just a union of agents. Among the properties that emerge from the interactions between these entities, trust takes a central place in maintaining quality as the system scales up.

However, it should be stressed that neither of these properties is possessed by an entity in isolation of its environment, or of the rest of the (entity's) world; all of them emerge from the entities' interactions in a particular context, at a particular instance of time, under particular cognitive and affective dispositions of the interacting parties. In the same manner, although we can speak about trust relationships between technical systems entities (humans, agents, items, peers, etc.), we should not ascribe to any externality the role to breath trust into a computational setting, or to any internal force the right to preset an entity's disposition to perceive or act upon trust. Otherwise, we would sacrifice the natural diversity that arises in an organismic system, and inhibit the diffusion of opinions and ideas that the system could cherish. Although we may recognize the external and internal factors as such, it is the entities' awareness of the contextual traits of their environment that will determine their trusting abilities and allow the emergence of trust per se. It would not be an exaggeration to therefore state that a mature e-commerce system is one that accounts for the trusting phenomena emerging from and joining the entities' transactions. Moreover, the efforts to capture these trusting phenomena must also exhibit awareness for the responsibility schema of the actions of all involved entities, regardless of the hierarchical level they have in a system.

Clearly, the interdependency between the human factor and the trust system operation requires additional, more exhaustive and cross-disciplinary research that will confirm and extend the analyses presented here across other types of online systems as well.

4   Conclusion and Future Work

Despite presenting a multidisciplinary overview of the efforts to tackle trust-related issues in e-commerce systems, this work pointed out the significance and benefits of seeing trust as an organismic trait of e-commerce systems. We revealed novel roles that trust can play in dealing with the issues of complexity reduction, diversity of crowd's opinions, and responsibility distribution, and pointed to the providers' trustworthiness as an important property that should be considered as e-commerce systems transit from scaling to maturing. Finally, we again stress the futility of incorporating trust as an inherent property of online system entities; it is only reasonable to think of creating the conditions under which trust can emerge and flourish. Context is, therefore, a major factor that would inevitably gain attention in the design of future computational trust systems.

Although this paper is more a taxonomy of identified factors rather than a modeling effort, it nevertheless bares crucial importance in establishing the borders within which the formal resolution of the problems addressed here is meaningful to be done. All of the identified issues are, therefore, lendable to formal modeling and justification, which will be provided in a consequent and broader study of each of the topics outlined here.

Our future work will also consider an agent-based approach of modeling and resolving trust-related issues in e-commerce systems. Continuing on the same "organismic" note, we will explore the role of redundancy and distribution in the provision of robustness of trust systems, and formalize diversity and conflict as a means for dealing with the issue of user bias. This is especially significant if we recall that a small number of entities drive the public opinion, implying that although current e-commerce systems are robust to failure, they are extremely fragile to targeted attacks.

Acknowledgments. The author wishes to thank Stuart Clayman, Tomaž Klobučar and Dušan Gabrijelčič for their opinions, critiques, and devoted time for discussions regarding the topics of this work.

References

[1] Granovetter, M.: Threshold Models of Collective Behavior. American Journal of Sociology 83(6), 1420–1443 (1978)

[2] Axelrod, R., Hamilton, W.: The evolution of cooperation. Science 211(4489), 1390–1396 (1981)

[3] Kahneman, D.: Maps of Bounded Rationality: Psychology for Behavioral Economics. American Economic Review 93(5), 1449–1475 (2003)

[4] Ariely, D.: Predictably Irrational: The Hidden Forces That Shape Our Decisions, 1st edn. HarperCollins (2008)

[5] Castelfranchi, C., Falcone, R.: Trust Theory: A Socio-Cognitive and Computational Model. John Wiley and Sons (2010)

[6]   Gambetta, D.: Can We Trust Trust? Trust: Making and Breaking Cooperative Relations, 213–237 (1988)

[7]   Josang, A., Ismail, R., Boyd, C.: A survey of trust and reputation systems for online service provision. Decision Support Systems 43(2), 618–644 (2007)

[8]   Chin, S.H.: On application of game theory for understanding trust in networks. In: 2009 International Symposium on Collaborative Technologies and Systems, Baltimore, MD, USA, pp. 106–110 (2009)

[9]   Fudenberg, D., Tirole, J.: Game Theory. MIT Press (1991)

[10] Roberson, B.: The Colonel Blotto game. Economic Theory 29(1), 1–24 (2006)

[11] Ba, S.: Establishing online trust through a community responsibility system. Decision Support Systems 31(3), 323–336 (2001)

[12] Fehr, E., Gächter, S.: Fairness and Retaliation: The Economics of Reciprocity. SSRN eLibrary (March 2000)

[13] Makridakis, S., Taleb, N.: Decision making and planning under low levels of predictability. International Journal of Forecasting 25(4), 716–733 (2009)

[14] Luhmann, N.: Trust and power: two works. Wiley (1979)

[15] Akerlof, G.A.: The Market for 'Lemons': Quality Uncertainty and the Market Mechanism. The Quarterly Journal of Economics 84(3), 488–500 (1970)

[16] Dellarocas, C.: The Digitization of Word of Mouth: Promise and Challenges of Online Feedback Mechanisms. Management Science 49(10), 1407–1424 (2003)

[17] Chevalier, J.A., Mayzlin, D.: The Effect of Word of Mouth on Sales: Online Book Reviews. Journal of Marketing Research 43(3), 345–354 (2006)

[18] Kramer, M.: Self-Selection Bias in Reputation Systems. In: Trust Management. IFIP, vol. 238, pp. 255–268. Springer, Boston (2007)

[19] Dellarocas, C., Wood, C.A.: The Sound of Silence in Online Feedback: Estimating Trading Risks in the Presence of Reporting Bias. Management Science 54(3), 460–476 (2008)

[20] Shen, Z., Sundaresan, N.: eBay: an E-commerce marketplace as a complex network. In: Proceedings of the Fourth ACM International Conference on Web Search and Data Mining, New York, NY, USA, pp. 655–664 (2011)

[21] Surowiecki, J.: The Wisdom Of Crowds. Anchor Books (2005)

[22] Marsh, S.P.: Formalising trust as a computational concept, p. 170 (April 1994)

[23] Ažderska, T., Jerman Blažič, B.: A Novel Systemic Taxonomy of Trust in the Online Environment. In: Abramowicz, W., Llorente, I.M., Surridge, M., Zisman, A., Vayssière, J. (eds.) ServiceWave 2011. LNCS, vol. 6994, pp. 122–133. Springer, Heidelberg (2011)

[24] Bertalanffy, L.V.: General System Theory: Foundations, Development, Applications. George Braziller, Inc. (1969) (revised)

[25] Jordan, N.: Themes in Speculative Psychology. Routledge (2003)

[26] Schelling, T.C.: Micromotives and Macrobehavior. Norton (2006)

[27] Odum, E., Barrett, G.W.: Fundamentals of Ecology, 5th edn. Brooks Cole (2004)

[28] Hong, L., Page, S.: Interpreted and generated signals. Journal of Economic Theory 144(5), 2174–2196 (2009)

[29] Kahneman, D., Tversky, A.: Subjective probability: A judgment of representativeness. Cognitive Psychology 3(3), 430–454 (1972)

[30] Ariely, D., Loewenstein, G., Prelec, D.: Tom Sawyer and the construction of value. Journal of Economic Behavior & Organization 60(1), 1–10 (2006)

[31] Cosley, D., Lam, S.K., Albert, I., Konstan, J.A., Riedl, J.: Is seeing believing?: how recommender system interfaces affect users' opinions. In: Proceedings of the SIGCHI Conference on Human Factors in Computing Systems, New York, NY, USA, pp. 585–592 (2003)

[32] Pouwelse, J.A., Garbacki, P., Epema, D.H.J., Sips, H.J.: A Measurement Study of the BitTorrent Peer-to-Peer File-Sharing System. Science (May 2004)

[33] Yardi, S., Boyd, D.: Dynamic Debates: An Analysis of Group Polarization Over Time on Twitter. Bulletin of Science, Technology & Society 30(5), 316–327 (2010)

[34] Lieberman, M.B., Montgomery, D.B.: First-mover advantages. Strategic Management Journal 9(S1), 41–58 (1988)

[35] An, J., Cha, M., Gummadi, K.P., Crowcroft, J., Quercia, D.: Visualizing Media Bias through Twitter. In: Association for the Advancement of Artificial Intelligence (AAAI), Technical WS-12-11 (2012)

[36] Jøsang, A.: A logic for uncertain probabilities. International Journal of Uncertainty Fuzziness and KnowledgeBased Systems 9(3), 279–311 (2001)

[37] Wolf, J.R., Muhanna, W.A.: Feedback Mechanisms, Judgment Bias, and Trust Formation in Online Auctions. Decision Sciences 42(1), 43–68 (2011)

[38] Ažderska, T.: Co-evolving Trust Mechanisms for Catering User Behavior. In: Dimitrakos, T., Moona, R., Patel, D., Harrison McKnight, D. (eds.) Trust Management VI. IFIP AICT, vol. 374, pp. 1–16. Springer, Heidelberg (2012)

[39] Page, S.E.: The Difference: How the Power of Diversity Creates Better Groups, Firms, Schools, and Societies. Princeton University Press (2007)

[40] Golman, R., Page, S.: General Blotto: games of allocative strategic mismatch. Public Choice 138(3), 279–299 (2009)

[41] Sundararajan, A.: Local Network Effects and Complex Network Structure. The B.E. Journal of Theoretical Economics 7(1) (January 2008)

[42] Schneier, B.: Schneier on Security. John Wiley & Sons (2009)

[43] Taleb, N.N., Martin, G.A.: How to Prevent Other Financial Crises. SSRN eLibrary (2012)

[44] Luhmann, N.: Technology, environment and social risk: a systems perspective. Organization & Environment 4(3), 223–231 (1990)

Making Apps Useable on Multiple Different Mobile Platforms: On Interoperability for Business Application Development on Smartphones

Andreas Holzinger[1], Peter Treitler[1], and Wolfgang Slany[2]

[1] Medical University Graz, A-8036 Graz, Austria
Institute for Medical Informatics, Statistics & Documentation (IMI)
Research Unit Human-Computer Interaction
{a.holzinger,p.treitler}@hci4all.at
[2] Graz University of Technology, A-8010 Graz, Austria
Institute for Software Technology (IST)
wolfgang.slany@tugraz.at

Abstract. The relevance of enabling mobile access to business enterprise information systems for experts working in the field has grown significantly in the last years due to the increasing availability of smartphones; the shipment of smartphones exceeded that of personal computers in 2011. However, the screen sizes and display resolutions of different devices vary to a large degree, along with different aspect ratios and the complexity of mobile tasks. These obstacles are a major challenge for software developers, especially when they try to reach the largest possible audience and develop for multiple mobile platforms or device types. On the other side, the end users' expectations regarding the usability of the applications are increasing. Consequently, for a successful mobile application the user interface needs to be well-designed, thus justifying research to overcome these obstacles. In this paper, we report on experiences during an industrial project on building user interfaces for database access to a business enterprise information system for professionals in the field. We discuss our systematic analysis of standards and conventions for design of user interfaces for various mobile platforms, as well as scaling methods operational on different physical screen sizes. The interoperability of different systems, including HTML5, Java and .NET is also within the focus of this work.

Keywords: Mobile computing, user interfaces, smartphones, mobile platforms, app development, usability engineering, multi-platform, cross-platform.

1 Introduction and Motivation for Research

Mobile devices are gaining more and more importance and smartphones are nowadays a common sight in industrial countries. What started originally as a concept product by IBM in 1992, was a niche product for a long time. This changed rapidly with the release of the Apple iPhone in 2007, bringing smartphones to the mainstream. One year later, Google and the Open Handset Alliance released their Android platform, which gained a lot of popularity in the following years.

G. Quirchmayr et al. (Eds.): CD-ARES 2012, LNCS 7465, pp. 176–189, 2012.
© IFIP International Federation for Information Processing 2012

As of June 2012, there were a total of more than 300,000,000 Android devices shipped worldwide, with more than 900,000 new ones being activated every day. Similarly, the iPhone is very popular with more than 180,000,000 devices shipped in total. The iPad, released in 2010, has been sold more than 55,000,000 times.

Along with this new and big market, new challenges for software developers emerge. Different programming languages, IDEs and platform standards need to be learned rapidly in order to develop native apps for multiple platforms.

HTML5 promises easy multi-platform development, with browsers on most current mobile devices being able to render HTML5 content. Therefore, ideally only a single app would need to be created which then could be executed on multiple target platforms.

However, there are also some disadvantages of HTML5, when compared to native apps, such as limited access to the device hardware or to platform features, look and feel that users are not used to from other apps of the platform, as well as missing market presence. In this paper we try to pinpoint the advantages and disadvantages of HTML5 apps and native apps and try to offer some guidelines as to which to choose for app development.

Besides the number of different platforms, mobile devices come with screens in different sizes, resolutions, and aspect ratios. Additionally, tablets are typically used in landscape mode, whereas smartphones are used in portrait mode, though both can also be used in the other way. This proliferation of interface properties holds especially true for Android, which supports devices with a display diagonal reaching from 2 inches over tablets which typically measure 10 inches up to TV screens with a display diagonal greater than 40 inches.

Many problems arise during the development of mobile applications – especially in industrial, professional and safety-critical environments [1], reaching from security aspects [2] to issues of the user interface [3]. In this paper we concentrate in on the latter and deal with questions including: Are different UI layouts required for different screen sizes? If so, where should designers draw the line between small and large devices? Are there tools which support designers in creating UIs for multiple screen sizes?

2   Background and Related Work

2.1   Business Case: Mobile Access to a Business Information System

During the research for this paper a project was carried out in cooperation with the Austrian business software development company Boom Software AG. The project was concerned with usability evaluation and consulting for the development of a mobile application. We will not discuss the details of the project here, but will illustrate some of the problems and challenges encountered in order to underline the relevance of mobile devices for business applications and the importance of usability of mobile apps. The information on the company and its technologies presented here is based on their marketing documents (January 2012) and personal communication:

Boom Software AG was founded in 1995 and has 50 employees (March 2012). The company primarily develops industrial software for maintenance, management and production control. Boom Software advertises *total customization* [4] of its software in order to meet the specific needs and requirements of individual customers.

The underlying technology which enables the customization of their software is the Business Oriented Rapid Adaption (BORA) Framework. The BORA Framework was created to provide a unified design framework for the developers. According to company representatives, prior to the framework's introduction, their developers spent roughly 80% of their efforts on solving technical issues, whilst only 20% were used to customize the software to optimally meet the end users' needs. The framework provides the base technology for all software products and includes a number of tried and tested user interface elements and concepts, therefore drastically reducing the workload on technical tasks and allowing greater focus on customization.

Boom Software's products manage large amounts of enterprise data. The users, however, are not interested in just having access to the data; they need effective ways to efficiently gain knowledge out of this data [5]. A well-designed, usable interface may help to achieve that goal.

While the main focus of Boom Software's products has historically been on desktop software for Microsoft Windows systems, a platform-independent HTML-based UI layer for BORA applications has also been developed over the last few years. Recently, development on the first mobile app has started. Platforms targeted are Android and Windows 8 (for tablet PCs). Boom Software's goal is to make specific parts of software systems run on smartphones and tablets in order to increase the productivity of outdoor staff like maintenance workers.

2.2   Mobile Work

Many companies today rely heavily on their software systems in their everyday work. At the same time, many jobs require employees to be mobile rather than working in their office. Maintenance workers, for instance, need to be on-site to perform maintenance while they may also need to be able to access information in the company's databases.

This mobile work [6] has often been done on laptop computers where appropriate display resolution supported the necessary visual performance [7]. In the last years, many of these laptop computers were replaced by tablet computers [8]. Mobile work usually includes three dimensions: mobility, location (in-)dependency, and time criticality; and context-related mobile work support functions are: location tracking, navigation, notification, and online job dispatching. According to the task-technology fit (TTF) theory [9], [10] and attitude/behavioral theory [11], it is crucial to find a fit between task characteristics and mobile work support functions; guidelines for development and use of mobile work support systems can be found in [12].

2.3   Variety of Mobile Devices

One major challenge when developing mobile apps (for smartphones, tablets or both) is the wide range of different platforms and device types available.

As detailed in Table 1, there are currently six different mobile platforms, which had a significant market share in 2011: Android, iOS, Symbian, BlackBerry, Bada and Windows Phone.

Table 1. Smartphone shipments (in millions) and shares in the year 2011 by platform [13]

Platform	Full year 2011 shipments	Share	Growth Q4'11 / Q4'10
Total	487.7	100.0%	62.7%
Android	237.8	48.8%	244.1%
iOS	93.1	19.1%	96.0%
Symbian	80.1	16.4%	-29.1%
BackBerry	51.4	10.5%	5.0%
Bada	13.2	2.7%	183.1%
Windows Phone	6.8	1.4%	-43.3%
Others	5.4	1.1%	14.4%

2.4   Multi-platform Development

Developing applications that can be used on all these platforms is often extremely difficult. All platforms have different Software Development Kits (SDKs) along with different libraries and different ways to design user interfaces. The programming languages of these platforms differ as well (see Table 2).

Table 2. Programming languages on mobile platforms

Platform	Programming languages
Android	Java
iOS	Objective-C
Symbian	C++
BlackBerry	Java
bada	C++
Windows Phone	C#

Knowledge of the programming languages required for app development is, however, only a small part of the expertise needed. The SDKs, platform standards and best practices should be known to developers as well. On the legal side, the terms of use of the different markets can also vary to a large degree, e.g. both Apple and Microsoft ban software that contains parts licensed under any GNU license. Gaining all this knowledge for a large number of platforms is a very time-consuming task.

In addition to the platforms themselves, developers need to consider the devices available for these platforms. Android, for instance, has many different devices available, including small smartphones and large smartphones and tablets. IOS, likewise, runs on the iPhone and the iPad.

These devices have different screen sizes and sometimes different aspect ratios as well, which requires effort to make user interfaces well scalable – or sometimes the design of different user interfaces for different screen sizes altogether.

Chae and Kim (2004) [14] have found that the screen size of a device significantly impacts users' behaviors. They have also found different levels of breadth and depth of information structures to be more appealing to users for different screen sizes.

Web technologies, such as HTML5, CSS3 and JavaScript promise an easy solution to the platform segmentation on the mobile market today: Every platform includes a browser which can display web sites and web apps.

The HTML5 standard is still under development. This implies that the browsers used must be up-to-date in order to support all of the most recent features of HTML5.

Web apps have a number of advantages and disadvantages when compared to native apps. These will be addressed in the upcoming sections.

A third approach is the development of so-called hybrid apps. These are native apps which display a web user interface, which can thus be the same across platforms. The platform SDKs offer UI elements which can be used for this purpose.

2.5   Related Work

Work on solving the problem of rendering on multiple user interfaces began a while ago, however, to date very few work is available for mobile devices explicitly. Most of the work was created before the mobile platforms discussed became available and therefore don't consider these platforms and their capabilities specifically. In the following we determine general work versus explicit work on mobile user interfaces:

Farooq Ali et al (2001) [15] discuss the need for a unified language for describing user interfaces in order to facilitate multi-platform UIs. Their approach uses the User Interface Markup Language (UIML) to create a high-level logical model of the UI and then derive models for families of devices from it in a developer-guided process.

Stocq & Vanderdonckt (2004) [16] describe a wizard tool which is able to create UIs for simple and complex tasks based on the domain model of the information system. Their approach also requires input and choices made by the developers. The wizard can create UIs for the Microsoft Windows and PocketPC platforms. The mobile UI needs to be built separately, but some of the information from the creation of the desktop UI can be reused to reduce the workload for the developer.

The work by Mori et al. (2004) [17] focuses on *nomadic applications* which can be accessed by the user on a variety of different devices and platforms as well as the different contexts of use of the applications on these platforms. Their *One Model, Many Interfaces* approach attempts to avoid low-level details by the use of meaningful abstractions. One central task model is created for the nomadic application. System task models, abstract and concrete UIs are then derived incrementally. They also stress that developers need to be aware of the potential target platforms early in the design process in order to create suitable tasks for each one.

Choi et al. (2009) [18] describe an application framework based on the Model-View-Controller pattern to assist the agile development of multi-platform mobile applications. Their approach uses a set of rules for each target platform in order to transform the UI.

3   Methods and Materials

In our research we have closely examined the Android and iOS platforms, along with the tools they offer to design and scale user interfaces and the guidelines they offer on UI design. The issue of web apps versus native apps was also thoroughly surveyed.

3.1   Android

Android is currently available on a wide range of devices. Device manufactures must adhere to Google's Compatibility Definition Document (CDD). According to the current version of the CDD [19], the physical display diagonal of devices must be at least 2.5 inches. The minimum display resolution must be 320 x 240 pixels (QVGA). The aspect ratio must be between 4:3 and 16:9.

The Android framework defines four different classes of screen sizes. These are small, normal, large and extra-large. In addition, there are four density classes: Ldpi (120 dpi), mdpi (160 dpi), hdpi (240 dpi) and xhdpi (320 dpi). Devices should report the next lowest size and density standard, meaning sizes and densities can be anything between and above the standard values.

A detailed breakdown of device shares per size and density can be found in Table 3. This data shows that more than 80% of all Android devices fall into the normal size category.

Table 3. Shares of Android devices per size and density [20]. Data collected by Google and based on devices which accessed the Google Play store in early March 2012.

	ldpi	mdpi	hdpi	xhdpi
small	1.7%		2.4%	
normal	0.7%	18.5%	66.3%	2.5%
large	0.2%	2.8%		
xlarge		4.9%		

3.2   iOS

Unlike Android, iOS only runs on a few devices manufactured by Apple. These include the iPhone, the iPod Touch and the iPad (all in different versions). Furthermore, iOS is the operating system for Apple TV, but this is outside the focus of this paper and will not be discussed in detail.

With regard to screen sizes, this means that developers must support two different sizes, as the iPhone and iPod Touch screens are identical in size. Figure 1 shows the size difference of the devices while Table 4 gives a detailed overview of the screen specifications of mobile iOS devices.

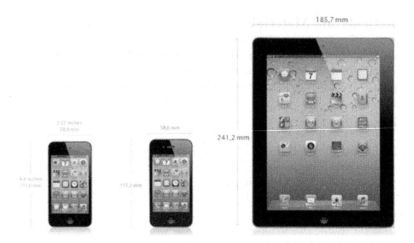

Fig. 1. A side-by-side comparison of the mobile iOS devices. Individual image sources: Technical device specifications as found on www.apple.com.

Table 4. Comparison of the displays of iOS devices. Source: Technical device specifications as found on www.apple.com.

Device	Screen size	Resolution	Aspect ratio
iPhone (up to 3G)	89mm	480 x 320	3:2
iPhone (4 and 4S)	89mm	960 x 640	3:2
iPod Touch (up to 3rd gen.)	89mm	480 x 320	3:2
iPod Touch (4th gen.)	89mm	960 x 640	3:2
iPad (up to 2nd gen.)	250mm	1024 x 768	4:3
iPad (3rd gen.)	250mm	2048 x 1536	4:3

As can be seen in Table 4, all iOS devices had their resolution doubled in a newer generation at some point. In order to make it easy to deal with these differences, Apple has introduced a measurement unit called points. Points, much like Android's density-independent pixels, server to define layouts and measurements independently from display density. One point, for instance, equals one physical pixel on the first iPhone generation while it equals two physical pixels on the iPhone 4S.

Image resources can (and should) also be provided in two different resolutions. The proper image will then be selected and displayed on the device the app is used on.

Beside these simple tools, iOS developers can be sure that the device market will remain manageable in the future with Apple being the only device manufacturer.

3.3   Multi-platform Development

The question whether to develop a native app or a web-based HTML5 app is one which every app developer will inevitably ask herself or himself. The different platforms and environments of mobile devices (see Table 2) make porting an app from one platform to another one a difficult task.

HTML5 is a promising alternative - every one of these platforms has a browser and the capability to run web apps. While HTML5 apps can run on any mobile platform with little to no extra effort, native apps also have advantages (see Table 5). Access to the system's hardware or some hardware-related features such as the camera is often only possible in native apps. Native apps can also integrate themselves seamlessly into the system: They use the native look-and-feel, can offer widgets to be displayed on the home screen, interaction with other apps, running as services in the background, and the use of system notifications. Native apps also tend to have better performance than web apps, though current browsers are getting more and more performance optimizations while at the same time newer devices offer more computational power, making the difference diminish.

Table 5. Advantages of native and HTML5 web apps. Sources: Meier and Mahemoff (2011) and own original research

Native app advantages	Web app advantages
• Broad access to device hardware and platform features • Close integration with platform and other apps • Better performance • Visibility through app store(s) • On-device storage	• Large target audience (mobile platforms + desktop) • Easy multi-platform development • Easy to update across all platforms • No certification required

It is also possible to develop hybrid applications. These are native applications which use views to display HTML5 content, which can be the same across all platforms.

3.4   Multi-platform Frameworks

Since the development of apps for mobile platforms is getting more important with numerous platforms being available on the market, platforms have been developed which should facilitate easy app development on multiple platforms. These multi-platform frameworks come in many variations. Some of them only change the visual appearance of web apps while others offer whole software development kits on their own, which can build the developed apps to multiple target platforms as native apps.

For this paper, we have briefly examined three frameworks: JQuery Mobile, PhoneGap and Titanium Mobile. There are, of course, many more frameworks available. Criteria for the selection of the frameworks were that these were, at the time, some of the most feature-rich and most popular. The aim was also to have frameworks with different key features in order to be able to compare them. Furthermore, the frameworks are also available for free. There are several proprietary frameworks but they could not be tried out thoroughly and were therefore excluded from the selection.

3.4.1 JQuery Mobile

JQuery Mobile [21] is a web app framework which was developed by the developers of the popular JavaScript library jQuery. The main focus of jQuery Mobile lies on the design and presentation of mobile apps.

The technologies used by jQuery mobile are HTML5, CSS3 and JavaScript, which enables it to run on most current mobile devices. JQuery Mobile can be used to both make web apps feel more like native apps and to apply a brand layout to them, giving them a more polished look than a default web app. The layout is scaled to the target device. Small adaptations can be made automatically. For instance, labels can be placed beside input fields on larger devices while being placed above them on smaller devices.

The jQuery mobile website offers a drag-and-drop tool for building simple UI layouts called Codiqa. Components such as buttons, text, images and lists can be dragged into the UI, allowing for rapid prototyping. The resulting source code can then be downloaded and further modified. This makes it much easier for new or inexperienced developers to get started, as the other platforms such as Android have a much steeper learning curve.

The jQuery Mobile framework is free and open source. It can be used under the terms of either the MIT License or the GNU General Public License. The basic version of the Codiqa, which allows the download of the source code created, is free. Advanced versions which offer additional features cost 10$ per month for single users and 30$ per month for teams.

JQuery Mobile offers some more features which are not strictly related to design, most notably the handling of events such as various forms of touch input (e.g., tap, swipe) and orientation change (i.e., the user turning the device from portrait to landscape mode or vice versa).

3.4.2 PhoneGap

PhoneGap [22] is an app platform which can build apps from a single code base for multiple target platforms as native apps. It is based on HTML5, CSS3 and JavaScript and abstracts the hardware of mobile platforms into a JavaScript API. The library provides interfaces for hardware access and certain native features. Hardware access includes the device's accelerometer, the camera and the compass.

Some of the platform features are access to the contact list or to the file system, notifications and geolocation. All of these features are available for Android, iPhone (3GS and above) and Windows Phone 7. Other platforms such as Blackberry or Symbian have a subset of these features available. PhoneGap thus manages to combine many of the advantages of native apps and web apps.

Technically, the resulting apps generated by PhoneGap are not truly native apps but hybrid apps. The apps use web views which display the HTML5 content, but they can be built to the platform's native format and therefore also distributed over several app stores.

Developers need to set up the SDKs for all platforms they want to develop for. This implies some limitations: In order to deploy build PhoneGap apps for iOS the iOS SDK is required, which in turn requires a Mac OS computer. PhoneGap supports the default IDEs for various platform (e.g., Eclipse with the Android Development Tools for Android) and only requires the libraries to be imported.

PhoneGap is an open source project and is available for free. It uses the Apache License (version 2.0).

3.4.3 Titanium Mobile SDK

The Titanium Mobile SDK by Appcelerator Inc. also offers the possibility to create native apps from a single code base. It comes with a complete IDE called Titanium Studio, which is based on the Aptana Studio web development UI. The app logic is written using JavaScript.

Similar to PhoneGap, Titanium offers an extensive API with access to native hardware and software features. It allows the use of additional JavaScript libraries such as jQuery. It currently supports iOS, Android and BlackBerry and also allows the creation of mobile web apps (the latter still being in beta status).

Appcelerator also offers a marketplace for templates, designs and modules for applications.

In contrast to PhoneGap, Titanium Mobile UIs are using real native UI components rather than web views. Like PhoneGap, Titanium Mobile requires the SDKs of the target platforms to be installed and set up within the SDK. It uses the Apache License (version 2.0), but the software is proprietary. The basic version of Titanium Mobile is free. There is also a Professional Edition and an Enterprise Edition. These offer additional support, some additional modules and early access to new features.

The feature of creating native UIs for different platforms is very promising. The SDK was only briefly examined for this paper and further investigation is necessary in order to evaluate how well Titanium handles the rendering of complex native UIs.

While the building of native apps can be an advantage, it also means more overhead as a number of different apps needs to be built and tested with every new update.

3.5   Testing User Interfaces

Testing mobile user interfaces for different screen resolutions in itself is already a major hassle, and testing multi-platform mobile user interfaces can be even much worse [23], [24], [25]. Manual testing is practically feasible only for the most simplistic applications because typical software is usually far too complex to be tested thoroughly, and is continuously developed as it is changed or extended with new functionality.

Automatic testing can be a solution but the test code needs to be continuously kept up-to-date, and the problems arising with different screen sizes and systems are much intensified as then all tests need to be constantly maintained for all systems and display resolutions.

Mesbah & Deursen (2009) [26] propose a method for testing AJAX applications automatically by introducing CRAWLJAX, a crawler for AJAX applications, which can dynamically make a full pass over an AJAX application.

However, the medium term benefits of testing, especially when using test driven development style automatic GUI tests, are huge, e.g., in terms of developer satisfaction due to trustable software documentation (tests can be run and checked – they serve as minimalistic declarative specification/programmer documentation that can be consulted and really correspond to the actual code) and reduced risks associated with evolving code, in particular when refactoring the code of other developers in larger teams (see [27] for more details).

A further problem that is particular to the Android platform is that different hardware providers often add their own UI customization that can introduce subtle changes in the behavior of otherwise identical Android version. E.g., HTC Sense substantially changes the behavior of certain buttons, fields, and the keyboard, thus necessitating either to deal with these differences on an individual basis in automatic GUI tests, or to ignore such hardware dependent differences, in particular as these customizations (which can be quite popular as in the case of HTC or Samsung Android devices) are not available on, e.g., the official Google Android emulator. This of course entails either to write tests for all these differences and to test on actual hardware, which needs a rather complicated setup for automatic tests, or to not test for them, which of course is also far from ideal.

The problem is further complicated for all platforms by the different OS versions. For example, most Android phones currently run Android version 2.x. New models are delivered with Android version 4.x, and older models are increasingly updated to this newer version. However, fundamentally new GUI possibilities have been introduced in the newer versions, e.g., the possibility to have several resizable but non-overlapping "windows" on the screen at the same time (with some limitations), or to have resizable "gadgets" on the home-screen. Testing for different OS versions thus can further complicate the issues for developers, though being able to run automatic GUI tests on an emulator that is able to execute different OS versions can be very helpful. Note however that, e.g., Google's Android emulator does not support OpenGL 2.x and thus is of limited value for game developers. It unfortunately is also very slow.

Additional problems arise when one wants to test hardware features such as sensors (e.g., GPS or gyro-sensors where we would like to simulate sensor input for testing purposes – the OpenIntents sensor simulation framework solves this at least for Android), effectors (e.g., the flash light or the vibration feature), or connectivity like Bluetooth protocol stacks and internet access.

Nevertheless, there exist some very useful tools that allow automatic GUI testing of mobile apps for Android, iOS, Windows Phone devices as well as HTML5/Javascript based applications, including, e.g., Robotium and Roboelectric for Android, or Selenium 2 for mobile HTML5/Javascript (Android and iOS are particularly supported).

4   Results

Our research has shown that different platforms allow different ranges of screen sizes, with the Android platform supporting the highest variability along with a wide collection of tools for designing UIs for multiple screens, such as density independent pixels and size standards.

The iOS platform supports a strictly limited number of screen types. It handles the different resolutions of older and newer devices very well by measuring the resolution in the abstract unit of points rather than physical pixels. The same UI layout can therefore be used for old and new iPhones and iPod Touch devices with little regard to the different physical screen resolutions.

The iPad, however, differs from the other iOS devices in size, resolution and aspect ratio. It is therefore recommended to design separate UIs for iPad and iPhone / iPod Touch.

We have also observed that the platform SDKs offer ways to separate the UI definition from the application logic, therefore supporting the use of the Model-View-Controller (MVC) pattern [28]. We encourage developers to clearly separate the UI definitions from the rest of a code base. This separation makes it much easier to create scalable user interfaces.

Following platform conventions is very important on mobile devices, especially when developing native apps. Standard usability engineering methods [29] are important, but UI designers need to be aware of the platform-specific guidelines for all target platforms in order to successfully apply usability-engineering principles to mobile applications [30].

When comparing native apps to web apps in general, there is no clear recommendation to be given. The choice of whether to develop native apps, web apps, hybrid apps or to use a multi-platform framework depends on a number of things. The requirements of the app and the resources available as well as the target audience should be considered.

The skills of the developers are another important factor, as learning how to develop apps for one or more mobile platforms can be very time consuming. It can be a great asset for app development to have developers who are already skilled in one or more platforms' native programming languages and APIs, or in HTML5, CSS and JavaScript. This advantage should be leveraged.

It is also worth mentioning that multi-platform frameworks are growing very rapidly and both updates to existing frameworks and the introduction of new frameworks occur frequently. We recommend comparing the features of the most recent versions of various frameworks before deciding on one.

Another very important thing is to be aware of the limitations of the frameworks. First and foremost, these frameworks only offer tools for creating UIs for multiple platforms and screen sizes. It is the responsibility of the designers and the developers to ensure that the apps run properly on all the target platforms and devices. None of the frameworks can substitute thorough testing of the app.

5   Conclusion

There are a number of different tools and means to scale user interfaces on the mobile platforms examined. These are, however, only tools and it is up to the designers and the developers to ensure that their user interfaces look good and are well usable on all target devices. While the well thought-out definition of layouts is a good foundation for this, it must be stressed that there is no way around testing the interface. This can be done on actual devices or on various configurations of the emulators provided by the platform IDEs, but there are many hard challenges associated with automatic GUI testing.

With regard to multi-platform development and the choice between developing native apps or HTML5 web apps, no definitive recommendation can be given. The best choice always depends on a number of factors, such as the app's intended features, the target audience or the skills of the development team.

Multi-platform frameworks offer some interesting features, especially for rapid prototyping or the development of very simple apps. These frameworks are growing rapidly and new features are being added frequently, so we recommend inspecting several platforms' features before starting multi-platform development and carefully choosing a well-suited framework.

References

1. Holzinger, A., Hoeller, M., Bloice, M., Urlesberger, B.: Typical Problems with developing mobile applications for health care: Some lessons learned from developing user-centered mobile applications in a hospital environment. In: Filipe, J., Marca, D.A., Shishkov, B., van Sinderen, M. (eds.) International Conference on E-Business (ICE-B 2008), pp. 235–240. IEEE (2008)
2. Weippl, E., Holzinger, A., Tjoa, A.M.: Security aspects of ubiquitous computing in health care. Elektrotechnik & Informationstechnik, E&I 123(4), 156–162 (2006)
3. Alagoez, F., Valdez, A.C., Wilkowska, W., Ziefle, M., Dorner, S., Holzinger, A.: From cloud computing to mobile Internet, from user focus to culture and hedonism: The crucible of mobile health care and Wellness applications. In: 5th International Conference on Pervasive Computing and Applications (ICPCA), pp. 38–45 (2010)
4. Schnedlitz, J.: Total Customizing - Vom Überleben durch Anpassung: The Eagleheaded Chicken Project. Berlin Press, Berlin (2012)
5. Holzinger, A.: On Knowledge Discovery and interactive intelligent visualization of biomedical data. In: Challenges in Human–Computer Interaction & Biomedical Informatics DATA - International Conference on Data Technologies and Applications (in print, 2012)
6. York, J., Pendharkar, P.C.: Human-computer interaction issues for mobile computing in a variable work context. International Journal of Human-Computer Studies 60(5-6), 771–797 (2004)
7. Ziefle, M.: Effects of display resolution on visual performance. Human Factors 40(4), 554–568 (1998)
8. Holzinger, A., Kosec, P., Schwantzer, G., Debevc, M., Hofmann-Wellenhof, R., Frühauf, J.: Design and Development of a Mobile Computer Application to Reengineer Workflows in the Hospital and the Methodology to evaluate its Effectiveness. Journal of Biomedical Informatics 44(6), 968–977 (2011)
9. Zigurs, I., Buckland, B.K.: A theory of task/technology fit and group support systems effectiveness. Mis Quarterly 22(3), 313–334 (1998)
10. Gebauer, J., Ya, T.: Applying the theory of task-technology fit to mobile technology: the role of user mobility. International Journal of Mobile Communications 6(3), 321–344 (2008)
11. Kraft, P., Rise, J., Sutton, S., Roysamb, E.: Perceived difficulty in the theory of planned behaviour: Perceived behavioural control or affective attitude? British Journal of Social Psychology 44, 479–496 (2005)
12. Yuan, Y.F., Archer, N., Connelly, C.E., Zheng, W.P.: Identifying the ideal fit between mobile work and mobile work support. Information & Management 47(3), 125–137 (2010)
13. Canalys: Smart phones overtake client PCs in 2011,
   http://www.canalys.com/newsroom/smart-phones-overtake-client-pcs-2011 (last access: June 01, 2012)

14. Chae, M., Kim, J.: Do size and structure matter to mobile users? An empirical study of the effects of screen size, information structure, and task complexity on user activities with standard web phones. Behaviour & Information Technology 23(3), 165–181 (2004)
15. Farooq Ali, M., Pérez-Quinones, M.A., Abrams, M.: Building Multi-Platform User Interfaces with UIML. In: Seffah, A., Javahery, H. (eds.) Multiple User Interfaces: Cross-Platform Applications and Context-Aware Interfaces, pp. 93–118. Wiley (2001)
16. Stocq, J., Vanderdonckt, J.: A domain model-driven approach for producing user interfaces to multi-platform information systems. In: Advanced Visual Interfaces, AVI 2004, pp. 395–398. ACM (2004)
17. Mori, G., Paterno, F., Santoro, C.: Design and development of multidevice user interfaces through multiple logical descriptions. IEEE Transactions on Software Engineering 30(8), 507–520 (2004)
18. Choi, Y., Yang, J.S., Jeong, J.: Application framework for multi platform mobile application software development. In: 11th International Conference on Advanced Communication Technology, ICACT 2009, pp. 208–213. IEEE (2009)
19. Android: Android 4.0 Compatibility Definition, http://source.android.com/compatibility/4.0/ android-4.0-cdd.pdf (last access: March 03, 2012)
20. Android-developers: Screen Sizes and Densities, http://developer.android.com/resources/dashboard/screens.html (last access: March 15, 2012)
21. JQuerymobile, http://jquerymobile.com (last access: March 15, 2012)
22. Phonegap, http://phonegap.com (last access: June 01, 2012)
23. Holzinger, A., Searle, G., Nischelwitzer, A.K.: On Some Aspects of Improving Mobile Applications for the Elderly. In: Stephanidis, C. (ed.) Universal Access in HCI, Part I, HCII 2007. LNCS, vol. 4554, pp. 923–932. Springer, Heidelberg (2007)
24. Holzinger, A., Trauner, J., Biffl, S.: Work Lists for the Transport of Patients: A case for mobile Applications. In: International Conference on e-Business (ICE-B 2008), pp. 454–459 (2008)
25. Holzinger, A., Mayr, S., Slany, W., Debevc, M.: The influence of AJAX on Web Usability. In: ICE-B 2010 - ICETE The International Joint Conference on e-Business and Telecommunications, pp. 124–127. INSTIC IEEE (2010)
26. Mesbah, A., van Deursen, A.: Invariant-based automatic testing of AJAX user interfaces. In: Proceedings of the 31st International Conference on Software Engineering, pp. 210–220 (2009)
27. Beck, K.: Test Driven Development. By Example. Addison-Wesley Longman, Amsterdam (2002)
28. Holzinger, A., Struggl, K.-H., Debevc, M.: Applying Model-View-Controller (MVC) in Design and Development of Information Systems: An example of smart assistive script breakdown in an e-Business Application. In: ICE-B 2010 - ICETE The International Joint Conference on e-Business and Telecommunications, pp. 63–68. INSTIC IEEE (2010)
29. Holzinger, A.: Usability engineering methods for software developers. Communications of the ACM 48(1), 71–74 (2005)
30. Holzinger, A.: Usability Engineering und Prototyping, Beispiel Mobile Computing. OCG Journal (Forschung und Innovation) 29(2), 4–6 (2004)

Enhancing Business APPification Using SMS Text Messages: Metrics, Strategies and Alternatives

Mersini Paschou, Evangelos Sakkopoulos, Efrosini Sourla, and Athanasios Tsakalidis

Department of Computer Engineering & Informatics
School of Engineering, University of Patras
Rio Campus, 26500 Patras, Greece
{paschou,sakkopul,sourla,tsak}@ceid.upatras.gr

Abstract. Mobile App stores and marketplaces allow sellers and developers to monetize their Apps mainly through the desktop-based download point, or by using the mobile owner's credit card. We would like to turn monetization focus on the fact that there is already another payment channel that should not be overseen, which is fruitfully used through the premium SMSs. In this work, we propose new metrics and strategies to enhance business APPification using SMSs efficiently and effectively, in two ways: a) SMS as a premium text service can be the mean to monetize Apps more easily than using HTTP protocol and credit cards – premium SMSs cost more than regular SMSs and return usage earnings. b) SMSs can be widely used as an additional "web" data transport protocol that may reduce user data access costs in some cases and therefore, allow new margin for monetization of apps. We also show prototype results that the proposed strategies and metrics assist.

Keywords: SMS Mobile App, Premium SMS, Alternative Monetization, Web Appification, Mobile e-Business, Business Apps.

1   Introduction

During the recent years mobile devices have been embraced by everyone, thus creating a huge market that is expected to evolve even more in the years to come. Moreover, many consumers already take advantage of mobile applications to improve and assist their lives. Mobile applications solutions are widely accepted because they are easy to use. This is the reason why already numerous applications are available, which target different groups of people and domains (entertainment, information, health etc).

Frequently, in mobile applications, the need arises for the user to send and receive data, frequently on a regular basis. Many works study the ways mobile applications assist, but they all assume that people involved have access to internet connection and unlimited resources to dispose. However, this is not always the fact, as recent explosion of mobile data traffic indicates that plans that provide unlimited data usage are financially unsustainable. The technical and financial challenges of making such plans available for everyone range from handling outdated network equipment, legacy handsets, and applications. All these issues contribute to additional costs, which need to be minimized. [1]

G. Quirchmayr et al. (Eds.): CD-ARES 2012, LNCS 7465, pp. 190–202, 2012.
© IFIP International Federation for Information Processing 2012

With a 97% delivery and read rate, SMS messaging is increasingly gaining recognition as the perfect customer communication tool [5]. Transactional SMS payment reminders are an extremely popular and cost-effective method of communication used in Europe and Asia [5]. SMSs can also be used in mobile apps to request or refresh content. Moreover, SMS is the only technology with 'push' capability, where the content provider sends SMSs to end users without their prior action. Such content might be advertisements, discounts or offers.

Another clear turn towards the use of premium SMSs is making payments for applications by SMS. Samsung Apps users are provided with this service after selecting an application from the store. They are prompted to select a payment method, one of which is "Phone Bill". In this case the user receives a transaction confirmation via SMS and the subscriber's account is debited the appropriate amount. On the other hand, the KPMG monetizing mobile report [6] shows that SMS text is rapidly losing ground to newer technologies. In part, this is because of the complexity of 'text codes' that act as the doorway to SMS text payments. From the customer perspective, SMS text is also relatively limited in its ability to provide dynamic banking and payments solutions on a mobile device [6].

In this paper, we present a proposal of ways to enhance HTTP Protocol, utilizing the SMS transfer protocol. The latter has been already used for downloading an application, however less has been done for web access and data exchange. We focus on monetization of the application as well as on data transfer issues. We study representative cases and show that it is possible to maximize advantages of both protocols if we combine them wisely. We introduce metrics and apply them in an indicative scenario, without loss of generality. In particular, we point out how different transfer protocols can be used, depending on the volume and type of data to be sent and other environment oriented information. We keep in mind that SMS text protocol can also be utilized as a web services transport protocol.

The rest of the paper is organized as follows: Section 2 discusses related work and Section 3 describes issues related to monetization of applications. Section 4 presents SMS monetization utility metrics and Section 5 discusses three strategies presented through case studies. Section 6 includes the performance evaluation of the proposed metrics through a real-life scenario. Finally, Section 7 concludes the paper and gives ideas for further research.

2   Related Work

There have been several examinations of mobile monetization and the ways it could evolve to attract more customers and to satisfy both advertisers and carriers. The results of such an analysis can be used to provide insight for improvement in available models.

Chang and Huo [2] present the idea of increasing broadband subscribers by providing free or discounted fees through the deployment of mobile advertising framework by the telecommunication system. They describe a framework for delivering appropriate ads of the ideal time at the ideal place to the ideal subscriber.

SMSs may be used normally to provide premium rate services to subscribers of a telephone network, such as to deliver digital content: news, alerts, financial information, logos and ring tones. The first premium-rate media content delivered via the SMS system was the world's first paid downloadable ringing tones in 1998. Premium-rated messages are also used to collect money for charities and foundations, or for televoting services [3].

SMS usage as a marketing and corporate tool is analytically discussed at the 101 guide of [7] where most of the typical SMS based strategies are explained. Note that this typical usage has nothing to do with mobile applications for smartphones, though as we describe below SMS is an excellent way to make a blended tool for Mobile Web monetization. [7]

3   Monetization of Applications

Organizations and enterprises provide, in many cases, a wide variety of e-Services which include internet services and services for mobile devices. These services involve business and financial transactions as well as information services. Proponents of m-Services argue it can help make public information and services available "anytime, anywhere". An example of such beneficial use of mobile technologies would be sending a mass alert to registered citizens via short message service, or SMS, in the event of an emergency.

The arrival of smartphones brought the "application age," a time period in which over the last few years approximately one million of third-party applications have come to market, and revolutionized consumer services in the mobile device industry. The success of third-party applications on mobile platforms has generated significant revenue for mobile carriers and developers. As the App market continues to grow and develop as an industry, monetization of the products and services it provides is becoming increasingly relevant. Monetization of an application can come in many forms, whether it is through charging for the App itself, selling virtual goods, or through in App advertisements.

3.1   Monetization Strategies

For developers who want to monetize mobile applications there are markets that provide endless opportunities for it [4]. There are four common strategies the developers use for this reason [9 - 10].

In-app advertising is a good way to monetize mobile apps for consumer apps which experience a high volume in use, or have a highly targeted audience. This allows developers and marketers to either take advantage of the large number of page views that come with frequent use, or the intrinsic value of a targeted user base to advertisers. Highly targeted mobile apps and some publishers are able to use ads to earn money only from ads. It's possible to make money with mobile apps with individual advertisers; however going through an advertising company is easier and probably more profitable.

Paid Apps charge users a one-time fee for the use of an app. This is one of the longest standing strategies for app monetization, although it is quickly diminishing as a relevant strategy for all but the largest and highest quality offerings. From a publisher's perspective, charging a one-time fee for the use of an app can be a short sighted strategy. This arises from a two part problem: First, the install base of the application is limiting preventing it from reaching critical mass and viral growth. Furthermore, having already paid for the application once, consumers will not readily accept additional charges from within the application. Consumers paying for apps, have expectations of higher quality. If their expectations fail to be met, the app can suffer from bad user reviews or decreased engagement over time.

In-app purchasing and transactions involve developers using virtual stores inside the application that sell everything users might need. This may become the main provider of revenue. For example, 90% of Farmville's revenue (the popular Facebook app) comes from in-app purchases. Virtual goods present an additional avenue of monetization, one which has less of an impact on the user experience than advertisement. Utility (goods which make the users life easier) and Vanity goods (items which allow users to show off) both present an opportunity to monetize user interaction within an app. Developers can create consistent revenue, especially when the consumer spends often small amounts of money instead of paying once for the application.

Subscription models are cases where a customer is granted access to a product or a service after paying subscription. The subscription model helps developers keep their customers, by building loyalty. A common idea is to provide content for free, but restrict access to premium features. Great approaches may prove to be free offers or monthly trials. One of the most important aspects of ensuring success with this strategy is to minimize customer turn-over and acquisition costs.

According to a recent Mobile Developer Report survey [11], conducted by mobile development framework maker Appcelerator and market research firm IDC in July 2011, mobile developers are still divided on how best to monetize mobile apps. Among the 2,000 developers surveyed, a full 50 percent ranked attracting new users who buy software from an app store as a top priority going forward, down from 59 percent earlier that year. Another 50 percent ranked in-app purchasing as a top business model, up from 42 percent earlier that year. IDC suggests the change represents a shift in how mobile developers attract and retain customers. [12]

SMSs consist a competitive alternative that can be applied to any of the monetization strategies presented above, thanks to its adaptability: (a) in places were internet is not available, the mobile app can still refresh content through SMSs and (b) SMSs 'push' capability makes them suitable for transactions, subscriptions, or even in-app advertising.

3.2   SMS Advertising

SMS advertising provides a cost effective method of targeting promotions to specific customer profiles. One might want to remind customers of specific events or promotions, but for whatever reasons, SMS allows passing information directly to the right customer at very affordable prices and fast delivery.

Many companies now utilize this popular communication tool to boost sales and increase profit. Some representative examples follow: (a) an auto dealership's service department could generate substantial add-on revenues by sending customers scheduled SMS notifications for periodical services (e.g. oil changes), (b) the customer of a parking company could be charged for the obtained parking ticket via a mobile application using premium SMS services, (c) a radio station company could profit by publishing daily contests based on SMS premium, (d) a mobile application could inform customer for current prices of nearby gas stations. The last three examples constitute the case studies that are described analytically in following section.

3.3   Premium-Rated SMSs

The premium-rate numbers are typically "short codes" – shorter than usual phone numbers. Each country and carrier regulates short codes different, but usually an oversight body issues the short codes for a fee. In the United States, for example, a dedicated short code may cost $1,500 to set up and then $1,000 per month. A shared short code where the message must be preceded by a keyword can be obtained for $50 per month. When calling or sending an SMS to a short code, the caller is billed a premium rate above the normal cost of an SMS or phone call. The revenue is then shared by the carrier, and the SMS aggregator. Unfortunately, premium-rated SMS services constitute a prosperous ground for attackers to monetize mobile platforms via malware [8].

4   SMS Monetization: Business Opportunities and Metrics

As mentioned before, many works study the ways mobile applications assist, but they all assume that people involved have access to internet connection and unlimited resources to dispose. However, this is not always the fact, as recent explosion of mobile data traffic indicates that plans that provide unlimited data usage are financially unsustainable. Thus, a mobile app provider should take into account all available technologies for mobile communication and data transfer and all possible monetary costs for customers, when developing a mobile app. This would be of great importance to mobile app selling companies, since two of their primary goals are (a) maximizing customer satisfaction by decreasing customer costs and (b) generating additional revenues. Cost minimization for providing basic services through mobile apps, could release space for the advent of special or added value services, where companies could profit using premium SMSs for charging customers.

At first, we take a closer look to the available technologies for mobile communication and data transfer and present the three dominant: SMS, GPRS and Wi-Fi/ADSL Technology. Thereafter, we present a set of metrics to calculate the overall data volume for a 'message' transmission, as well as the corresponding monetary cost for end users, depending on the data transfer method used. Pre-calculating costs is an important step in order to develop the appropriate mobile application that will exchange data using the suitable data transfer method. This potentially leads to minimization of user data access costs and allows new margin for monetization of apps and earnings for the carriers that maintain huge data access infrastructures for peak time coverage.

4.1   Available Architectures for Mobile Communication

One of the main functions of a mobile application is the exchange of data with a web service, and depending on the technology used for the data transfer, three discrete architectures arise, which are briefly described below.

In the 1ˢᵗ architectural approach (Fig. 1), the mobile application sends data to a web service using one or more SMSs. The SMS server receives the SMSs sent through the Mobile Telecommunications Provider and transforms their content to a request to the web service.

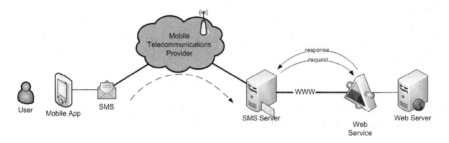

Fig. 1. SMS based Transfer Architecture

In the 2ⁿᵈ architectural approach (Fig. 2), the mobile application is connected to the internet through its Mobile Telecommunications Provider, using GPRS technology. After the connection is established, the application sends data directly to the web service.

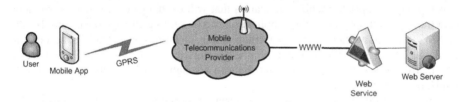

Fig. 2. GPRS based Transfer Architecture

In the 3ʳᵈ architectural approach (Fig. 3), the mobile application exploits the established ADSL internet connection and the existence of a wireless router. Data are sent to the wireless router using Wi-Fi technology and then are forwarded to the web service through the ADSL Internet Provider.

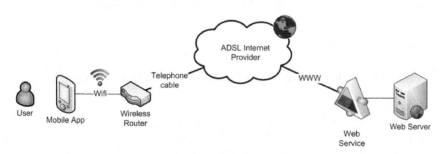

Fig. 3. Wi-Fi / ADSL based Transfer Architecture

4.2   SMS Monetization Utility Metrics

Considering the case a mobile application must exchange data with a web service, the overall data volume for a 'message' transmission, as well as the corresponding monetary cost for customers must be computed. To serve this purpose, a set of metrics is defined below..

Let $V_{MESSAGE}$ be the overall volume of a message and $C_{MESSAGE}$ be the cost of the message sent. Then, depending on the data transfer method used (HTTP or SMS), two metrics can be defined for the computation of $C_{MESSAGE}$. If the SMS method is used:

$$C_{MESSAGE,SMS} = \lceil V_{MESSAGE} / ch_{SMS} \rceil \cdot C_{SMS} \tag{1}$$

where C_{SMS} is the current cost of sending an SMS and ch_{SMS} is the maximum number of characters of the SMS. If the HTTP method is used:

$$C_{MESSAGE,HTTP} = V_{MESSAGE} \cdot C_{BYTE} \tag{2}$$

where C_{BYTE} is the cost of sending a byte using mobile internet. The measurement unit for data volume ($V_{MESSAGE}$) can be bytes or characters, depending on the data transfer method (HTTP or SMS correspondingly).

Depending on the data volume a mobile application exchanges with a remote service, companies can calculate overall monetary costs for their customers for monthly service usage. Pre-calculating costs is an important step for companies, in order to develop the appropriate mobile application that will exchange data using the suitable data transfer method. The mobile application can be set to exchange data using HTTP or SMS transfer method, or even a combination of both, depending on the current needs, having as a further goal to minimize transmission monetary costs for end users. The metrics described above can contribute to a rough cost calculation and cost minimization.

Cost minimization for providing basic services through mobile applications, could release space for the advent of special or added value services, where companies could profit using premium SMSs for charging customers. Profits can be computed using the following metric:

$$C_{MESSAGE,SMS\_premium} = \lceil V_{MESSAGE} / ch_{SMS} \rceil \cdot C_{SMS\_premium} \tag{3}$$

A specific percentage of this amount is received by the mobile telecommunication provider, and the rest of it is received by the mobile application selling company.

5   Case Studies

5.1   Strategy 1: The Case of Minimum Data Monetization - Parking Tickets

Numerous mobile applications have been developed to address the problem of locating a nearby parking place while driving and being charged electronically when occupying it. End-users download and install these applications in their mobile devices and submit once information necessary for charging. Two interesting aspects that arise are (a) the minimization of user input in order to enhance user experience and

(b) the monetization of the mobile application in order to generate substantial add-on revenues for the parking company.

As far as the first issue is concerned, ordinary mobile applications would probably ask the user to provide information (mainly by typing) about the place, duration and phone number in order to be charged for the parking place. Alternative solutions that satisfy the first goal would use GPS technology to locate the vehicle position, minimizing this way user input to a data field for 'parking duration'. The selected parking place could also be determined through QR code technology using the mobile device's camera, in cases GPS is not an option. These solutions simplify the application interface and contribute to the enhancement of user experience.

Coming to the second issue, the mobile parking application could use SMSs to send and receive data with the SMS parking service. In this case study (Fig. 4), SMS is the most suitable solution for data transfer since it is unknown if any other technology would be available in every open space. Data could be sent using premium rated SMS, thus generating add-on revenues for the parking company. Moreover, customers could be charged extra if they enable additional services, such as SMS notification when about 15 minutes have left until the parking session expires.

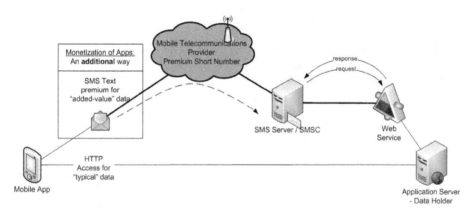

Fig. 4. SMS based Monetization of Apps: Proposed strategy 1

5.2   Strategy 2: Blended Case Premium SMS and Data Intensive HTTP

A notable number of gas station applications for mobile devices are available in the markets and stores. Drivers download and install such applications to their Smartphone and while on road, the application, exploiting drivers' current location through GPS technology, receives and presents a list of nearby gas stations. The list is available to the mobile application on user demand.

This approach requires the use of HTTP transfer protocol and unlimited data usage plans for the user to be able to afford constant update of the available data for the application. With the recent explosion of mobile data traffic, it is obvious that such an allowance is unsustainable. There is need to wean subscribers from these data plans without provoking customer dissatisfaction. This can be achieved with data plans at different price levels, consist with subscribers' needs for data volume, quality of experience, and usage characteristics. [1]

This challenge can be faced effectively by incorporating SMS text delivery as a transport protocol and premium SMS text. (Fig. 5) In order to minimize download costs, a competitive application may include the list of gas stations on initial download, and present only the nearby ones based on driver's location. The application may also already include the location of the gas station as Point of Interest (POI) on a map.

However, as the cost of gas continuously changes, an SMS text based service may inform the user for the current prices of the nearby gas stations. Locating the gas station with the lowest gas prices would be of most convenience for the driver. The application would only need a couple of SMS responses with prices of the requested nearby gas stations. This service could be billable and the user would send a micropayment through SMS, to activate it and receive information.

Similar to our first case study, SMS is the most suitable solution for communication between the mobile application and the corresponding web service and for data transfer, since it is unknown if any other technology would be available in every open space. In fact, such cases show that there is room for completely avoiding the use of HTTP as a transport protocol in mobile applications and transfer all data through SMSs, which means implicit monetization whatsoever!

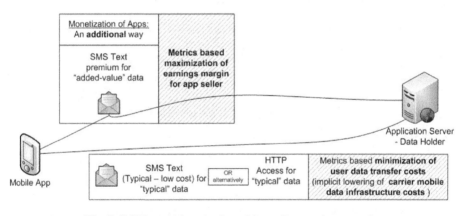

Fig. 5. SMS based Monetization of Apps: Proposed strategy 2

5.3   Strategy 3: In-Bound: HTTP, Out-Bound: SMS

It is not unusual the case where radio station companies offer mobile services to their audience through applications for mobile devices and smartphones. Users are able to receive radio program, announces or even tweets from their mobile application, using HTTP protocol or SMSs to receive content. These services are usually available free of charge. Additional services that the radio station company would offer to users of its mobile application would be the conduction of daily contests with monetary or other kind of prizes. Audience could participate to the contest by sending a premium SMS with the correct answer to the contest question.

6   Experimental Evaluation

The performance evaluation of our proposal is presented in this section through the presentation of an indicative scenario and the application of the proposed metrics. Our scenario concerns a mobile app which presents information for points of touristic and cultural interest (POIs), following user request and data exchange with a web service. This information consist the basic service offered by the mobile app (Fig. 6a).

The two dominant ways of data transmission are the (i) SMS and (ii) HTTP transfer methods. The format of the transmitted data may be one of the following: (a) simple form which consists of comma separated values, (b) parameters that are assigned with values, which is also a relatively simple form and (c) data encoded in XML format, a fully descriptive alternative. In our scenario, the third transmission format was used, due to the fact that it constitutes a machine readable solution and produces messages of larger volume. The corresponding message received by the mobile app would be:

```
<Points>
  <Point>
    <Name>Name</Name>
    <Type>Type</Type>
    <Description>Description of 200 chars</Description>
  </Point>
  <Point>
    ...
  </Point>
  ...
</Points>
```

Our message (3 POIs were considered) consists of approximately 850 characters ($V_{MESSAGE}$). If the SMS transfer method is used, $ch_{SMS} = 160$ (GSM 7-bit) and $C_{SMS} = 0.06€$ (average SMS cost in Greece) and according to Eq. (1) $C_{MESSAGE,SMS} = 0.36€$/request. If information is requested 10 times/month, the overall cost is approximately 3.60€/month. When the HTTP method is used, due to mobile telecommunication providers' policies to offer daily or monthly mobile internet packages, the $C_{MESSAGE,HTTP}$ doesn't exceed 3€ for data traffic up to 60MB/month, while $V_{MESSAGE}$ for our example is 2250 bytes/request (due to HTTP overheads) or 22KB/month.

The application provider, in order to enhance user experience, adds an added value service to the mobile app, which presents information about special discounts or offers in the locations the end users are interested about (Fig. 6b). User explicitly requests this service (by pressing a button) and the mobile app receives the information using premium SMS charge. The information is directly presented through the mobile app and not as a set of SMSs in the mobile device.

Using the procedure presented above and applying Eq. (3), application providers can make an estimation of the profits gained from the extra service.

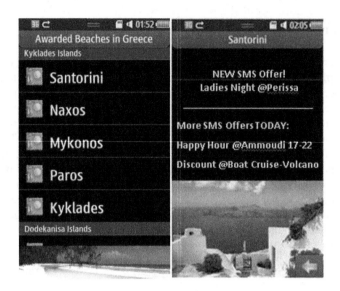

Fig. 6. Prototype of Business APP for touristic industry using SMS networking alternative

Our scenario was tested and evaluated in small scale, from students of the Computer Engineering and Informatics Department, concerning POIs in Patras city. The overall satisfaction grade for the services (on a scale of 5 = very satisfied to 1 = very dissatisfied) ranged from 4.0 to 5.0, with an average value of 4.8. Users evaluated the application as very easy to use and embraced the capability for content availability anywhere and with small costs.

Although this is an indicative scenario, the methodology proposed is general and can be used in any different scenario and with various data plans and different network connections. Taking into account national charges of mobile telecommunication and internet providers, it is clear that for large data volumes (approximately 50,000 chars) the HTTP transfer method is advantageous compared to SMS. On the other hand, SMSs can be a cost effective solution either for small all large data volumes if a suitable economic SMS package is chosen.

SMS text messages usage constitute a communication solution even when internet is not accessible, or when mobile end users prefer not to enable internet access in certain locations due to their limited data plans (packages with few MB available).

7   Conclusions and Future Work

While mobile traffic constantly increases, mobile data plans as provided currently do not allow revenue to grow in proportion. At the same time, the demand for network capacity is defined by busy hour traffic load. The need for exploiting all the available means of data transmission to avoid hardware costs is apparent. The proposed strategies for monetization through SMS are easy and simple solutions to this issue. SMS usage is important to monetization of mobile web also for those who have no easy access to credit cards (developing countries, youngsters) and for those that do not have satisfactory data coverage either in financial or connection terms.

Our proposed strategies and metrics present an efficient alternative to monetization of the Business APPification trend. Business APP Developers, like the ones of the well-known application "Angry Birds", have already figured out some ways to monetize through SMS text messages. In this paper, we discuss "the bigger picture" and present organized strategies and metrics to provide tools for business APP developers to maximize revenue while using SMS text messages.

Future work includes metrics refinement to deal with issues of data fragmentation and SMS bill payments for the carrier side.

Acknowledgements. This research has been co-financed by the European Union (European Social Fund – ESF) and Greek national funds through the Operational Program "Education and Lifelong Learning" of the National Strategic Reference Framework (NSRF) - Research Funding Program: Heracleitus II. Investing in knowledge society through the European Social Fund.

References

1. El-Sayed, M., Mukhopadhyay, A., Urrutia-Valdés, C., Zhao, Z.J.: Mobile data explosion: Monetizing the opportunity through dynamic policies and Qos pipes. Bell Lab. Tech. J. 16(2), 79–99 (2011)
2. Chang, C.-H., Huo, K.-H.: Mobile Advertising: Triple-win for Consumers, Advertisers and Telecom Carriers. In: IA 2011, Workshop on Internet Advertising, China (2011)
3. Goggin, G., Spurgeon, C.: Premium rate culture: the new business of mobile interactivity. New Media & Society, p. 753. SAGE Publications (September 2007)
4. Hargil, P., Noz, A.: Application Enablement: The business cases that drive new revenue opportunities through business, technical and service innovation. In: 15th IEEE International Conference on Intelligence in Next Generation Networks 2011, pp. 11–16 (2011)
5. Lee Sg R.: Monetizing Your Database with Transactional SMS (2008), http://ezinearticles.com/?Monetizing-Your-Database-With-Transactional-SMS (March 29, 2012)
6. Siegel M., Schneidereit F., Houseman D.: Monetizing Mobile. KPMG report (July 2011), http://www.kpmg.at/uploads/media/monetizing-mobile.pdf (March 29, 2012)
7. OpenMarket Inc., Mobile Messaging 201: How to Create Compelling SMS Applications (2011), http://www.openmarket.com/wp-content/uploads/2011/03/How-to-Create-Compelling-SMS-Applications_FINAL.pdf (March 29, 2012)
8. Chien E.: Motivations of Recent Android Malware (2011), http://www.symantec.com/content/en/us/enterprise/media/security_response/whitepapers/motivations_of_recent_android_malware.pdf?securityweek (March 29, 2012)
9. Donnini G.: Marketing Metrics & Monetization Tactics For The Application Age (2012), http://marketingland.com/marketing-metrics-monetization-tactics-for-the-application-age-5885 (March 29, 2012)

10. Anonymous: Mobile App Monetization: 3 Great Ways. (2012),
    `http://smallbizbee.com/index/2011/11/11/`
    `mobile-app-monetization-3-great-ways/` (March 29, 2012)
11. Appcelerator/IDC Mobile Developer Report: Google+ and Apple iCloud Bring Mobile
    Platform Battle to the Cloud (2011),
    `http://www.appcelerator.com/company/survey-results/`
    `mobile-developer-report-july-2011/`
12. Foresman C.: Developers still divided on mobile app monetization, but love the cloud (2011),
    `http://arstechnica.com/apple/news/2011/08/survey-developers-`
    `still-divided-on-mobile-monetization-love-the-cloud.ars`

Near Duplicate Document Detection for Large Information Flows

Daniele Montanari[1] and Piera Laura Puglisi[2]

[1] ICT eni - Semantic Technologies
Via Arcoveggio 74/2, Bologna 40129, Italy
[2] GESP
Via Marconi 71, Bologna 40122, Italy
daniele.montanari@eni.com, pieralaura.puglisi@external.eni.com

Abstract. Near duplicate documents and their detection are studied to identify info items that convey the same (or very similar) content, possibly surrounded by diverse sets of side information like metadata, advertisements, timestamps, web presentations and navigation supports, and so on. Identification of near duplicate information allows the implementation of selection policies aiming to optimize an information corpus and therefore improve its quality.

In this paper, we introduce a new method to find near duplicate documents based on q-grams extracted from the text. The algorithm exploits three major features: a similarity measure comparing document q-gram occurrences to evaluate the syntactic similarity of the compared texts; an indexing method maintaining an inverted index of q-gram; and an efficient allocation of the bitmaps using a window size of 24 hours supporting the documents comparison process.

The proposed algorithm has been tested in a multifeed news content management system to filter out duplicated news items coming from different information channels. The experimental evaluation shows the efficiency and the accuracy of our solution compared with other existing techniques. The results on a real dataset report a F-measure of 9.53 with a similarity threshold of 0.8.

Keywords: duplicate, information flows, q-grams.

1 Introduction

The information explosion due to the development of the web and its technological, organizational, and societal exploits of the last decade, resulted in growing data volumes being transmitted, processed, integrated, interpreted, and used in decision making processes, with a corresponding need for automated and accurate execution. This spurred a large body of research tackling data management from several points of view, including

- **the source**; this viewpoint is studied in fields like viral marketing[13], when issues of coverage and impression are relevant and we are interested in the

G. Quirchmayr et al. (Eds.): CD-ARES 2012, LNCS 7465, pp. 203–217, 2012.
© IFIP International Federation for Information Processing 2012

implicit and explicit diffusion mechanisms which are typical of a networked environment with distributed decision making and local, independent diffusion policies;

- **the receiver**; this is the dual point of view of the previous one, when we want to know whether we receive all and only the items we would like to receive, striving for precision and recall;
- **the structure of the network of infomediaries**; this area concentrates on the effects of network properties on the propagation of information;
- **the content and format of the payload**, namely the impact of channel format, protocols, and content types on the diffusion mechanism;
- **the distribution of affected or interested populations**, namely the positioning of the target population within the network.

This paper takes the receiver point of view and proposes an approach to remove the extra load generated from the spreading and replication mechanisms of the information through the network of intermediaries, which result in several incoming identical or nearly identical copies of the same content. Broadcast news (by news agencies, paper publications, online sites, and other sources of information and analysis) are an example scenario where the replication is quite significant; whenever an article is published by a primary source, many other infomediaries repackage the information for a specific type of readership or for distribution within a geographic area. A receiving system may then acquire the same item from a variety of different channels. The only way to reduce the incoming volume of information (while maintaining a reasonably wide coverage of sources) is to detect duplicate or nearly duplicate items upon arrival to our system, so that the copies may be stopped before entering the costly processing pipeline.

In this paper, we propose a new algorithm to find near duplicate documents based on q-grams extracted from the texts. Duplicate document detection typically consists of finding all document-pairs whose similarity is equal to or greater than a given threshold. Since similarity computation for all document-pairs requires significant resources, these methods usually apply filtering techniques to speed-up the comparison process. Each new item entering the system is normalized and cleaned of all the extra surrounding the core information constituting the payload of the message. Then, a signature of the incoming item is computed. In our case, this signature is the list of occurrences of the q-grams found in the normalized text. This signature is compared with a set of signatures coming from the analysis of other news items received earlier by the system. If a match is found, then the arriving news item is likely to be a duplicate and it is discarded. Otherwise, it is forwarded to the system for acquisition. Our approach introduces two major novelties: first, we maintain an inverted index for each q-gram in order to speed-up the comparison process among different documents and reduce the number of comparisons; second, we provide an efficient memory allocation of the inverted indexes, using a window size of 24 hours. In this paper section 2 introduces the system scenario; after reporting a brief description of the related works, section 3 describes the main algorithm; section 4 discusses the experimental evidence of this method compared to other existing techniques;

section 5 shows the architecture of the solution and section 6 reports conclusions and future work prospects.

2   A Real World Problem and the Corresponding System Scenario

The study reported in this paper stems from a general interest and an actual need to improve a real world system. In this section we provide a description of the relevant features of the latter.

The internet and a new generation of mobile devices have come to offer an unprecedented opportunity for the creation, packaging and distribution of information in real or quasi-real time. This, in turn, has prompted the rise of *infomediaries*, that is intermediaries offering packaged accesses to a huge number of worldwide info sources, the outcome of all this being the potential to collect tens or hundreds of thousands of information items per day, amounting to hundred thousands or even millions of information items per month. Even large organizations have trouble sifting through such vast amounts of information for the items which are relevant at the specific point and time of use.

The standard architecture we are dealing with consists of several concurrent pipelines taking information from the acquisition stage to the final classification and indexing. Figure 1 illustrates the components in this architecture and is briefly described below.

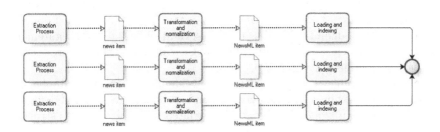

Fig. 1. Flow of news coming from different channels

The Extraction Process includes the mechanisms and the configurations needed to access the remote source of information. In most cases this is a web crawler or a software agent with the necessary functionality for protocol agreement and remote data transfer to a local temporary repository. The outcome of this module is a set of XML or otherwise encoded files carrying structured metadata and raw content.

The Transformation and Normalization Process takes the local material acquired through Extraction and rewrites each item in a final common format suitable for loading into the system. Metadata coming from the acquisition process are usually enhanced or normalized at this stage; normalization includes the removal of all tagging used for the original presentation and later transfer of content.

At last, the Loading and Indexing Process takes the normalized outcome of the previous step into the system, and takes care of the indexing,classifying, and extracting chores.

Due to the open and competitive structure of the info market, the same event or fact may be covered by multiple news agencies, and each article issued by any one of the covering sources may be distributed to several news channels, resulting in multiple acquisitions of the same information. Several estimates concur to suggest that about 10-15% of the acquired information is redundant due to these replication phenomenon.

Both the efficiency of the process and the quality of the resulting corpora of information demand that this redundancy be removed or minimized.

Redundancy reduction at the infomediary level is difficult to achieve, since there are no standards to refer to, resulting in uneven treatment across providers. Also, the providers are unaware of the same information being carried by others (and likely eager to propose their content anyway), hence cross-provider duplication of information cannot be removed at the source. Therefore, the best opportunity for (near) duplicate removal occurs after the acquisition and before injecting the information into the system.

In order to complete the outline of the application scenario we need to discuss what is intended by *near duplicate* information from a user point of view. Ideally, a single fact should appear exactly once in a information corpus. This is however rather exceptional, and occurring in very standardized, controlled domains only. The most common condition is to have several slightly different statements which actually concur a richer description by their presence, time of production, number, and issuing sources.

The policy defining when a pair of documents should be considered duplicate is a very difficult, possibly time- and goal-dependent one. A first level of definition of such a policy is a *similarity threshold* associated with the syntactic structure of the documents, their wording and sentences.

3   The Core Algorithm

3.1   Related Work

Many algorithms have been proposed to solve the duplicate document problem. There are different kinds of approaches in the state of the art: web based tools, methods based on fingerprints or shingling, algorithms that use different similarity measures. Our work is an extension of the method[10] on duplicate records detection in the context of databases that will be described in section 3.3. Some of the existing techniques that address the duplicate detection problem are listed below.

Checksum and Fingerprints. Cryptography checksums like MD5 [1] and SHA1 [14] are sequences of bits used to verify that data transferred have not been altered. The checksum works well to detect any change to a file as a whole, but lacks for small modifications [2].

A fingerprint is a short sequence of bytes used to identify a document. Fingerprints are created by applying a cryptographic hash function to a sequence of tokens. In [4], the author introduced an algorithm to produce approximate fingerprints to detect similar files within a large file system. The algorithm calculates a Rabin fingerprint [5] value with a sliding window of 50 characters.

Andrei Broder's super shingle algorithm[7] converts the document into a set of fingerprints. The algorithm can cluster the near-duplicates within $O(n \log(n))$ time[6] by creating a feature (super fingerprint) using several fingerprints.

I-Match. Another approach is represented by the I-Match algorithm [6] that uses the statistics of the entire document collection to determine which terms to include in the fingerprinting. The words with smaller IDF (Inverse Document Frequency) are filtered out since they often do not add to the semantic content to the document. After filtering, all the terms are sorted (removing duplicates) and only one fingerprint is generated for the document. Two documents would be treated as near duplicates if their fingerprint matches.

Shingles. In [7], the method tokenizes documents into a list of words or *tokens*. A *shingle* is a contiguous subsequence of w tokens contained in a document D. Identical documents contain the same set of shingles whereas near duplicate documents contain overlapping sets of shingles.

SpotSigs. In[11], the proposed algorithm extracts signatures that contribute to filter out noisy portions of Web pages. The method identifies content text of web sites combining stopwords antecedents with sequences of close words. The efficiency of the method is guaranteed by the use of an inverted index that reduces the similarity search space.

LSH. Locality-Sensitive Hashing (LSH)[12] is an algorithm used for solving the near neighbor search in high dimensional spaces. The basic idea is to hash the input items so that similar elements are mapped to the same buckets with high probability. It has also been applied to the domain of near duplicate detection.

3.2 Basic Definitions

This paper represents an extension of [10], an efficient algorithm for computing duplicated records in large databases. The method computes similarity between records using two different q-grams based measures and maintains an inverted index to speed-up comparison process. We start with some basic useful definitions.

Edit Distance and q-Grams. Let Σ be a finite alphabet of size $|\Sigma|$. Let $s_1 \in \Sigma^*$ be a string of length n made up of elements in Σ. The **q-grams** are short character substrings of length q. Given a string s_1, its **positional q-grams**

are obtained by sliding a window of length q over the characters of s_1. See [10] for a general introduction to q-grams. Note that in our work we do not use partial (length less than q) substrings.

For example, the positional q-grams of length $q=2$ for string *tom_smith* are: { (1,to), (2,om), (3,m_), (4,_s), (5,sm), (6,mi), (7,it), (8,th) }. The set of all positional q-grams of a string s_1 is the set of all the $|s_1|$ - q + 1 pairs constructed from all q-grams of s_1. In the example above, the number of all positional q-grams is given by: $|tom\_smith|$ - 2 + 1 = 8.

Inverted Index. Many approaches use filtering techniques in order to reduce storage space and computational time. Some of them use inverted indexes, i.e. data structures storing a mapping from content, such as words or numbers, to its locations in a database file, or in a document or a set of documents. In particular, a *word* level inverted index contains the positions of each word within a document.

Given n documents and w distinct terms, in the worst case (every word occurs in all documents) the index requires $O(nws)$ bytes, where s is the space (number of bytes) needed to save an integer.

In order to reduce space requirements, a binary vector or bitmap is used to handle an inverted index. The bitmap represents the occurrences of a term in the corpus of documents. More precisely, for each document d, the i-th bit of the correspondent bitmap is set if d contains the i-th terms. In the worst case, each term contains all set bits and the space required is $O(nw)$ bits which is an improvement with respect to the above space requirement.

3.3   DDD for Duplicate Document Detection

The work presented here is a variation of a previous work, named DDEBIT [10], for discovering duplicate record pairs in a database. The method is based on the use of two similarity functions together with an efficient indexing technique. Each pair-wise record comparison is performed in two steps: the records are converted into strings and compared using a *lightweight* similarity measure bigram-based. If the similarity is above a *light* threshold, then strings will be compared using a more accurate similarity. We only report the definition of the *lightweight* measure since it will be extended in the present work and used as a similarity function for identifying duplicates in large sets of documents.

Definition 3.31 (Lightweight similarity) *[10]. Let R be a relation and X, Y be strings representing two tuples in R. Let q_X and q_Y be the sets of distinct q-grams of X and Y, respectively. The function $d_{light,q}$ is defined as follows:*

$$d_{light,q}(X,Y) = \frac{|q_X \bigcap q_Y|}{\max(|q_X|, |q_Y|)} \qquad (1)$$

The authors introduce the concept of *bigrams array*, that is a sorted list of all distinct bigrams in the database. For each bigram, the algorithm maintains a bitmap as inverted index: the information stored in the data structure is used to find common bigrams between records.

In our present approach, we address documents in place of records and the new definition of *lightweight similarity for documents* is based on q-grams.

Given a text segment T, we remove white spaces and all the punctuation marks obtaining its *normal form* T_w. For example, if T={A rose is a flower}, then we convert T into the string T_w={Aroseisaflower}. Then, we generate its signature $T_{w,q}$, that is the set of all possible $|T_w| - q + 1$ overlapping q-grams generated from T_w. Suppose q is equal to 3, we obtain: $T_{w,3}$={Aro, ros, ose, sei, eis, isa, saf, afl, flo, low, owe, wer}.

We now state an extended definition of lightweight measure for discovering similarity between documents.

Definition 3.32 (Document similarity measure). *Let C be a corpus of text documents and A and B be two documents in C. Let $A_{w,q}$ and $B_{w,q}$ be the set of all possible overlapping q-grams from A and B, respectively. The function doc_q is defined as follows:*

$$doc_q(A, B) = \frac{|A_{w,q} \cap B_{w,q}|}{\max(|A_{w,q}|, |B_{w,q}|)} \qquad (2)$$

The measure (2) computes the similarity between two documents in terms of common q-grams between texts. This function gives emphasis to collocation of words into sentences, since q-grams are built binding sequential words. For instance, the string "the president" will contain the q-grams 'hep' and 'epr' since the words *the* and *president* are close to each other. Moreover, the denominator contributes to filter out documents similar in minimal area or having different sizes.

The formal definition for duplicated documents is stated next.

Definition 3.33 (Duplicated documents). *Let C be a corpus of text documents and A and B be two documents in C. Let t_d be a threshold (a value between 0 and 1) defined by the user. Then, A and B are considered duplicates if $doc_q(A, B) \geq t_d$.*

3.4   An Efficient Algorithm to Detect Duplicates

This section introduces the proposed solution for the duplicate document detection problem. The pseudo code of the basic version of the algorithm is presented in figure 2.

In line 1, the algorithm allocates the data structure for the bitmap indexes. For each q-gram, it generates a bitmap index (the total number of distinct q-grams $|\Sigma|^q$ depends on the alphabet of characters).

The dimension of the index depends also on the number of total documents in the archive. In real world systems, the number N_t of total documents in the corpus at time t is not constant, due to the asynchronous arrival of new documents and removal of old ones.

Duplicate_document(flowDir: f_dir, sizeOfQgrams: q
dupThreshold dup_t, alphabet Σ)
output: document pairs whose similarity is greater than dup_t

```
1    allocate a list of bitmaps of dimension |Σ|^q
2    for each incoming document d_{n+1} in f_dir
3        allocate a list of integers list_counters of dimension n + 1
4        for each distinct q-gram q_j extracted from d_{n+1}
5            if q_j is new (never met before in the corpus)
6                allocate a bitmap B_{q_j} for q_j of dimension n + 1
7            update B_{q_j} setting the (n + 1) − th bit
8            update list_counters //register common q-grams among d_{n+1} and d_t, 1 ≤ t < n + 1
9        for each element c_{t<n+1} > 0 in list_counters
10           compute doc_q(d_{n+1}, d_t);
11           if doc_q(d_{n+1}, d_t) == 1
12               d_{n+1} is an exact duplicate of d_t
13           if doc_q(d_{n+1}, d_t) >= dup_t
14               d_{n+1} is a near duplicate of d_t;
```

Fig. 2. The duplicate_detection procedure

The algorithm treats the incoming flow of documents by constantly polling the input directory (line 2). After receiving the document $n+1$, where n is the current size of the archive, the algorithm generates its signature $T_{w,q}$. Moreover, for each q-gram $q \in T_{w,q}$, the method updates the correspondent bitmap setting the $(n+1)$-th bit if q occurs in document $n+1$ (lines 4-7). For each new document entering the archive, the measure (2) is computed with respect to the n document of the archive. The computation is straightforward: a temporary list ($list\_counters$ in line 8) stores common q-grams among current document and the others in the repository. If (2) is above the threshold for at least one document in the archive, the document $n+1$ will be considered a near duplicate (lines 9-14).

3.5   Computational Time

Let $Q := |\Sigma|^q$ and denote by N the dimension of the corpus. The algorithm takes $O(Q * N)$ to compare a document with all the elements of the corpus. Since $Q << N$, pairwise comparisons of all the elements of the corpus takes $O(N^2)$, i.e. the algorithm has a quadratic complexity in the dimension of the corpus. The computation of the similarity measure is straightforward since the information are all contained in the temporary structures.

3.6   Temporal Window and Memory Requirement

In this paper, we consider an in-memory version of the algorithm in order to achieve better performance in terms of execution time. A swapping version of the method may also be developed, which stores the index on secondary memory if the main memory is not enough. In this section, we focus on the treatment of the incoming flow of news on an *hourly basis*. This solution speeds up the comparison process and leads to an optimization of the bitmap allocations.

A *temporal window* is a union of time intervals, each spanning *one hour* (see figure 3). Let w be the size of the window, i.e. the number of hours comprising

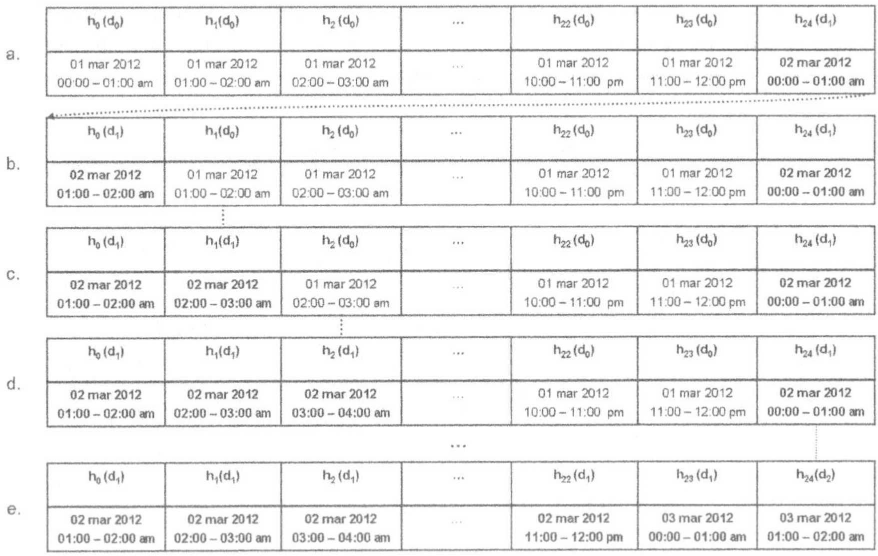

a.

$h_0(d_0)$	$h_1(d_0)$	$h_2(d_0)$	...	$h_{22}(d_0)$	$h_{23}(d_0)$	$h_{24}(d_1)$
01 mar 2012 00:00 – 01:00 am	01 mar 2012 01:00 – 02:00 am	01 mar 2012 02:00 – 03:00 am	...	01 mar 2012 10:00 – 11:00 pm	01 mar 2012 11:00 – 12:00 pm	02 mar 2012 00:00 – 01:00 am

b.

$h_0(d_1)$	$h_1(d_0)$	$h_2(d_0)$	...	$h_{22}(d_0)$	$h_{23}(d_0)$	$h_{24}(d_1)$
02 mar 2012 01:00 – 02:00 am	01 mar 2012 01:00 – 02:00 am	01 mar 2012 02:00 – 03:00 am	...	01 mar 2012 10:00 – 11:00 pm	01 mar 2012 11:00 – 12:00 pm	02 mar 2012 00:00 – 01:00 am

c.

$h_0(d_1)$	$h_1(d_1)$	$h_2(d_0)$	...	$h_{22}(d_0)$	$h_{23}(d_0)$	$h_{24}(d_1)$
02 mar 2012 01:00 – 02:00 am	02 mar 2012 02:00 – 03:00 am	01 mar 2012 02:00 – 03:00 am	...	01 mar 2012 10:00 – 11:00 pm	01 mar 2012 11:00 – 12:00 pm	02 mar 2012 00:00 – 01:00 am

d.

$h_0(d_1)$	$h_1(d_1)$	$h_2(d_1)$	...	$h_{22}(d_0)$	$h_{23}(d_0)$	$h_{24}(d_1)$
02 mar 2012 01:00 – 02:00 am	02 mar 2012 02:00 – 03:00 am	02 mar 2012 03:00 – 04:00 am	...	01 mar 2012 10:00 – 11:00 pm	01 mar 2012 11:00 – 12:00 pm	02 mar 2012 00:00 – 01:00 am

...

e.

$h_0(d_1)$	$h_1(d_1)$	$h_2(d_1)$	...	$h_{22}(d_1)$	$h_{23}(d_1)$	$h_{24}(d_2)$
02 mar 2012 01:00 – 02:00 am	02 mar 2012 02:00 – 03:00 am	02 mar 2012 03:00 – 04:00 am	...	02 mar 2012 11:00 – 12:00 pm	03 mar 2012 00:00 – 01:00 am	03 mar 2012 01:00 – 02:00 am

Fig. 3. Temporal sequence of documents processing using a window size of 24 hours

the window. We set w to 24 since a preliminary analysis of the specific news channels proved that a significant percentage of duplicates usually occurs within *one day* of each other. A higher value of w would cause the creation of more indexes and a huge memory requirement without significant gains in terms of duplicates elimination. Of course, two duplicate documents arriving more than 24 hours apart will not be detected, letting in at most one duplicate every 24 hours.

For each hour h_j, the method creates a local index i_{h_j}, $j = 0..w$. Figure 3a shows the sequence of *local indexes* created by the algorithm for the first $24 + 1$ hours. In the first day of computation (d_0), the documents arrived during hour h_t will be compared with all the documents received during h_j, where $0 <= j <= t$.

Moreover, the first hour of d_1: '00:00 - 01:00 of 02 mar 2012' is compared with all the previous 24 hours starting from time interval: '00:00 - 01:00 am of 01 mar 2012'.

Figures 3b, 3c and 3d show the computation of the hourly indexes after the first 24 hours. In figure 3b, the index i_{h_0} related to d_1 (second day of computation) will overwrite the index i_{h_0} related to d_0, since '00:00 - 01:00 am of 01 mar 2012' and '01:00 - 02:00 am of 02 mar 2012' have a time difference of more than 24 hours and will be not compared anymore.

Finally, figure 3e shows the end of the second day of computation. More precisely, for each hour h_j, the index i_{h_j} will be compared with all the indexes i_{h_y}, where $0 <= y < t$ and $j < y <= w$. The computation continues using always the same window size and overwriting hourly indexes that are older than 24 hours. This implementation uses only the memory required by the actual q-grams occurrences in a specific hour interval.

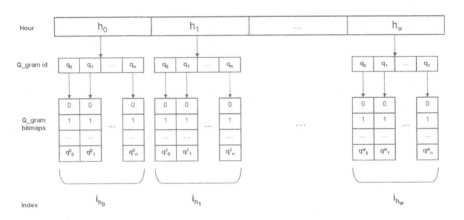

Fig. 4. Inverted index using hourly temporal indexes

Going into more details about the construction of the index, for each hour h_i, the algorithm allocates a static array of q_n entries (see figure 4). For each q-gram q_i, a correspondent bitmap is allocated if and only if q_i is present in a document arrived during hour h_i. Let $N_{h_i}^t$ be the number of documents arrived at instant t since the beginning of hour h_i. Here, the optimization consists in allocating a bitmap of size $N_{h_i}^t$. If a q-gram appears rarely, the re-allocation of the dynamic bitmap will not be frequent; moreover, if a q-gram q_i is not found during hour h_i, the allocation of the bitmap will be not performed at all for h_i.

Let N_{h_i} be the average size of an hourly index. The memory required in the worst case is of $q_n * N_{h_i} * W$ bits.

4   Experimental Analysis of the Core Algorithm

We tested the effectiveness of the algorithm using a corpus of 744 documents. In order to perform this experiment, we extracted this many items from a flow of real news coming from a single channel in a time interval of 24 hours. We inspected each document and found 111 correct matches.

The DDD algorithm is implemented in C++. The current implementation is about 800 lines of code and results in an executable file of about 900 KB. The experiments were performed in a SUSE Linux Enterprise Server, with a Quad-Core AMD Opteron(tm) processor 8356 and 4 GB of RAM. We performed experiments varying the size of q-grams and we found $q = 4$ as the best value. The algorithm introduces many false positives with lower values of q; the performance of DDD decreases with higher values of q since more q-grams require more memory.

We compared the effectiveness of our solution with other existing methods, i.e. SpotSig [11], Lsh [12] and Imatch [15]. We executed these algorithms using the Java implementation provided by the authors of SpotSig [15], setting the default parameters. Figure 5 reports the values of the Recall, Precision and F1-measures for several assigned threshold values. T represents all the matches, whereas $T \cap C$ represents the *correct* matches returned by each method. DDD shows the best value of Recall and F1 in all cases. In particular, it yields the best value of F1 with a threshold of 0.7 since the number of false positives and negatives is greatly reduced (Figure 6). The Imatch algorithm shows an optimal precision, but the recall is very low since it filters out a lot of false negatives. Spotsig registers a good behaviour in terms of both recall and precision (threshold 0.6), but Lsh performs generally better for this dataset.

The effectiveness of the algorithm has been tested by a large set of experiments. Due to space limitations we report the most significant results. Figure 7 reports the average execution time per document for different sizes of the corpus. We performed separated runs for each corpus, starting each run with an empty index. The more the hourly indexes grow, the more comparisons the algorithm performs, and the more the computation time increases, achieving the value of 1.2 seconds with size 8000. In the second experiment (see figure 8), we set the size of the corpus (500 documents) and performed 4 sequential runs of the algorithm starting from hour h_0 and ending the process at hour h_3. As in the previous test, the execution time increases as the the hourly indexes grow. In Figure 9 we show some results varying the size of the document text. We set the dimension of the corpus to 732 and saved the average time per document processing. The computation time depends on the length of the texts. In our system, the average length of the processed texts is about 5K so the execution time per document is less than 0,2 seconds.

Threshold	Method	T	T∩C	Recall	Precision	F1-measure
0,5	DDD	133	110	**0,991**	0,827	**0,902**
	Sigspot	99	84	0,757	0,848	0,800
	Lsh	100	85	0,766	0,850	0,806
	Imatch	64	64	0,577	**1,000**	0,731
0,6	DDD	114	106	**0,955**	0,930	**0,942**
	Sigspot	88	84	0,757	0,955	0,844
	Lsh	89	85	0,766	0,955	0,850
	Imatch	64	64	0,577	**1,000**	0,731
0,7	DDD	101	101	**0,910**	**1,000**	**0,953**
	Sigspot	82	80	0,721	0,976	0,829
	Lsh	83	81	0,730	0,976	0,835
	Imatch	64	64	0,577	**1,000**	0,731
0,8	DDD	101	101	**0,910**	**1,000**	**0,953**
	Sigspot	76	74	0,667	0,974	0,791
	Lsh	77	75	0,676	0,974	0,798
	Imatch	62	61	0,550	0,984	0,705
0,9	DDD	99	99	**0,892**	**1,000**	**0,943**
	Sigspot	76	74	0,667	0,974	0,791
	Lsh	77	75	0,676	0,974	0,798
	Imatch	62	62	0,559	**1,000**	0,717

Fig. 5. Comparisons of DDD with SpotSig, Lsh and Imatch

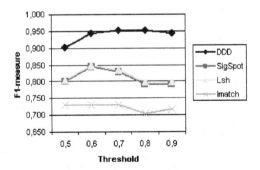

Fig. 6. F1-measure wrt threshold for all methods

5   The Overall Architecture of the Solution

The algorithm has been integrated in the framework of an application for the acquisition, classification, and analysis of news from heterogeneous Internet sources and providers.

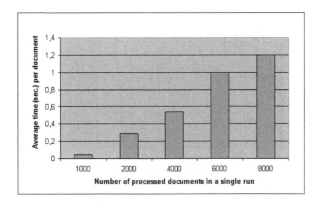

Fig. 7. Processing time versus size of the corpus

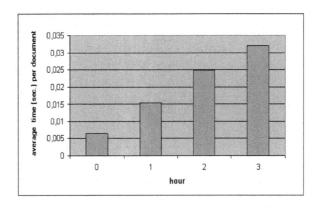

Fig. 8. Execution time with respect to different hours of processing

In this application domain, an effective and efficient extraction of content from heterogeneous transfer and presentation artifacts is required to minimize the impact of overhead information on the similarity evaluation. More specifically, a single document D consists of a *core content* component C (the actual content value) and of an *accompanying content* component A, which includes all the collateral information of the artifact, like navigation and presentation code, as well as extras like advertising that may appear in a web page presenting a news article. We would like to test the similarity on the C component, ignoring the A component. If we can't remove the A component, then it may well happen that the latter outweights the C component (e.g. two news from the same source) and results in a false positive in case our similarity threshold is too low. On the other end, if our similarity threshold is too high, then D_1 and D_2 with $C_1 = C_2$ and $A_1 \neq A_2$ may result in a false negative. However, getting rid of the A component is a difficult exercise, if an automatic system must tackle many different sources of documents, since the encoding of web pages may be complex. We are currently

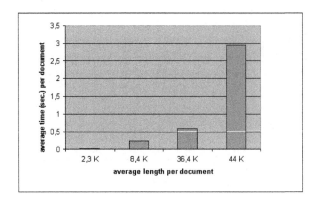

Fig. 9. Processing time varying the size of the document

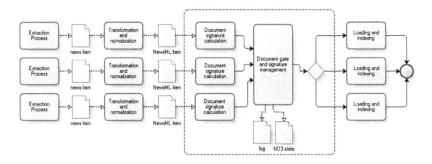

Fig. 10. Flow of the news acquisition system with duplicate document detection

testing our system with a straightforward tag-removal filter, which however will need to be further tested and refined.

The processing of information through the overall system requires an average of approximately $t_p = 10$ seconds/document. We have also pointed out that there are about $P = 10\%$ duplicates in a typical batch of news. Therefore we have an advantage from the adoption of this duplication removal if the time saved Pt_p is more than the time t_3 spent in the extra analysis required. The case study presented here shows that the time to decide whether a single document is a duplicate of something already in the system as seen within our current horizon is less than 5 msec. Hence, we can conclude that the adoption of DDD appears to be definitely convenient.

6   Conclusions and Future Work

This study has offered an early support and validation for the proposed algorithm for near duplicate document detection. It has also helped identify and explore a number of issues which become significant when the system is applied in a real world context with specific complexities. A number of issues have surfaced which will be focus for further studies:

- **clustering** of documents in the system to increase the performance of the comparison function;
- **semantic similarity measures**, to apply semantic analysis to the similarity assessment of a pair of documents;
- high and low **frequencies clipping**, to remove the very frequent and very rare q–grams from the comparison functions;
- **text extraction** to focus the similarity assessment to the core content of each document;
- **memory management** for online uninterrupted analysis of inbound document flows; we would like to study and implement fast memory management routines to adapt the time–sliding window of observation of the documents.

References

1. Berson, T.A.: Differential Cryptanalysis Mod 2 with Applications to MD5. In: Rueppel, R.A. (ed.) EUROCRYPT 1992. LNCS, vol. 658, pp. 71–80. Springer, Heidelberg (1993)
2. Zhe, W., et al.: Clean-living: Eliminating Near-Duplicates in lifetime Personal Storage. Technical Report (September 2005)
3. Kumar, J.P., et al.: Duplicate and Near Duplicate Documents Detection: A Review. European Journal of Scientific Research (2009)
4. Udi, M.: Finding Similar Files in a Large File System. In: USENIX Winter Technical Conference, CA (January 1994)
5. Andrei, Z., et al.: Some applications of Rabin's fingerprinting method. Sequences II: Methods in Communications, Security, and Computer Science. Springer (1993)
6. Chowdhury, A., et al.: Collection statistics for fast duplicate document detection. ACM Transaction on Information Systems 20(2), 171–191 (2002)
7. Broder, A.Z.: Identifying and Filtering Near-Duplicate Documents. In: Proceedings of COM 2000 (2000)
8. Gravano, L., et al.: Approximate string joins in a database (almost) for free. In: VLDB 2001 (2001)
9. Ilinsky, et al.: An efficient method to detect duplicates of Web documents with the use of inverted index
10. Ferro, A., Giugno, R., Puglisi, P.L., Pulvirenti, A.: An Efficient Duplicate Record Detection Using q-Grams Array Inverted Index. In: Pedersen, T.B., Mohania, M.K., Tjoa, A.M. (eds.) DaWaK 2010. LNCS, vol. 6263, pp. 309–323. Springer, Heidelberg (2010)
11. Theobald, et al.: SpotSigs: Robust and Efficient Near Duplicate Detection in Large Web Collections. In: Proceedings of SIGIR (2008)
12. Indyk, P., et al.: Approximate nearest neighbors: towards removing the curse of dimensionality. In: STOC (1998)
13. http://en.wikipedia.org/wiki/Viral_marketing
14. http://en.wikipedia.org/wiki/SHA-1
15. Kolcz, A., et al.: Improved robustness of signature-based near replica detection via lexicon randomization. In: KDD 2004 (2004)

TinyStream Sensors

Pedro Furtado

University of Coimbra,
Polo II, Coimbra
pnf@dei.uc.pt

Abstract. Stream processing engines have been proposed in the past for handling streaming data coming from data sources. But considering sensor networks, there is a need for an approach that allows stream models to reach also
computation-capable constrained embedded devices and to implement storage,
exchange and computation on those. We propose a stream model that implements sensor-device data handling. The stream processing abstraction and interface allows small motes to store and process the data locally and to route
processed data to consumer streams on-demand. This eliminates the need to
code motes operation in lower-level languages, allows easy configuration of
operations of different types and saves communication energy. The approach is
quite useful in diverse contexts, including wireless sensor networks. We
describe the approach and show its advantages experimentally.

Keywords: distributed systems, sensor networks, stream processing.

1   Introduction

Researchers and companies have realized over the years that high-level programming
approaches are necessary for increasing the adoption of technologies in practical settings. Stream and complex event processing engines realize that goal for handling
streaming data from data sources. However, up to now those engines were not available within constrained embedded devices of sensor networks. Devices such as wireless sensors are small nodes with computation, storage and radio power, but they are
programmed in low-level fashion, in spite of being deployed as part of a wider heterogeneous networked system for monitoring and actuating over the physical world.
The use of microcontrollers with some processing and storage capabilities allows in-
sensor processing and retention of data, and the use of flash memory offers gigabytes
of space. Data can be managed inside the embedded node, we can even collect a
whole day or month of data before communicating it to some collector node, saving a
lot of battery.

What is needed is some high-level programming abstraction that models data storage and retrieval using typical operations, data processing, data routing between
producers and consumers, time-ordered operation (e.g. keep a full day of data before
computing some statistics and sending it to a consumer stream in some remote
workstation). Stream models provide all these features, fulfilling the data management needs in the heterogeneous sensor networks context. On the implementation

G. Quirchmayr et al. (Eds.): CD-ARES 2012, LNCS 7465, pp. 218–232, 2012.

perspective, small streams with few samples fit into a few bytes in the small memories of the embedded devices, while larger streams are flash-disk resident. All operations work over both memory and flash streams.

Our TinyStream proposal defines the language, processing engine and efficient implementation of operations in constrained devices. We show how it applies stream processing engine mechanisms to individual sensor nodes as well as the whole distributed system, without the need for application programmers to know low-level programming details of individual devices. This way they concentrate on the application objectives. Our experimental results show that the approach occupies only a conveniently small footprint in constrained embedded devices, which receive simple codified stream commands that are then parsed and executed in the node. Operations are implemented with small memory requirements, in order to run on the constrained devices.

Previous proposals related to this one include complex event processing engines, which are not designed for running in constrained devices and do not fit their limitations, and sensor network middleware such as TinyDB [4] or Cougar [1], which do not manage data inside individual nodes and provide only a system-wide database model, transforming database queries into data collection code forwarding data to the sink. TinyStreams adds the time-ordered stream model – e.g. one can create a stream to collect 10 hours of data, compute a summary and then send it to some remote Smartphone; autonomous node engines and querying – we can create, drop, delete or update streams in memory or flash in individual nodes; as well as easy and powerful stream-based data routing specification as parts of stream commands – we can specify that the stream data should be periodically routed into another remote stream.

The paper is organized as follows: section 2 discusses related work. Section 3 discusses the model and architecture of the approach, then section 4 presents experimental results and section 5 concludes the paper.

2   Related Work

Previous work related to this one includes stream processing engines and high-level programming approaches and middleware for sensor networks.

Stream processing or complex events processing engines have been proposed before in the context of processing high-rate data from data sources. Examples of readily deployable CEP engines include StreamBase and Esper [10,11]. Examples adapted to over the internet integration and processing of data from sensor sources include GSN [12] and Hourglass[13]. However, those engines are not deployable in individual constrained embedded devices (they merely see internet data sources), and there have been no previous works on developing such engines for embedded devices, even though stream models offer extremely useful primitives for time-ordered streams and data routing between streams. There has also been no effort in the past into creating node-wise stream processing engines that allow direct operation in individual embedded device nodes.

Previous works concerning data processing in sensor networks closest to this one include database-like models TinyDB [4] and Cougar [1]. Both TinyDB and Cougar provide a database front-end to a sensor network by running a small database-like query engine at a sink node. They assume that data is forwarded into the sink for processing, without providing means for explicitly commanding how individual nodes should manage their data. They are therefore not node engines, nor do they apply stream processing to manage and route the data inside the sensor network. TinyStreams, on the contrary, creates streams in individual nodes, can place those in memory or flash, provides operations for individual nodes to manage their data and provides stream producer-consumer data routing primitives for intuitive formulation of stream routing between nodes.

While sensor network resident streams are a novelty, databases resident in embedded devices have been mentioned before for instance in [3] and in PicoDBMS [8] (a small database engine developed for smart cards).

From the perspective of sensor network usage in ubiquitous applications, wireless sensor networks are common nowadays and provide means to deploy easily and extensively sensors and actuators in very disparate application settings. Being able to declaratively configure what such a sensor network is to do and how it sends data to some remote logging station is a very important step forward in the wider adoption of the technology.

Many of the use cases involve collecting sensor data. In those applications sensors send data to workstations. Users must specify when to sample, how much time to keep the data, how to transform the data and when and how to transfer data remotely. With TinyStreams this is easily done by non-experts, users may even wish to keep hours or days of data in the sensor devices themselves and issue queries either ad-hoc or pre-planned to retrieve the data when required. In data logging applications the sensed data is stored and the logs are collected later on. The data can be logged in flash and retrieved later with a query. Keeping data in the sensors for longer also reduces energy consumption significantly. This is because data transmission consumes a lot more power than logging data to flash or aggregating it in the sensors and sending it much less often. This capability is crucial in many applications where a wireless sensor network is expected to work autonomously on batteries.

TinyStreams is also a language and operation configuration abstraction for sensor networks. In the rest of this section, we review a classification for sensor network programming abstractions and examples of such approaches.

According to [18], there are two main sub-classes concerning sensor network programming abstractions: one sub-class focuses on providing the programmer with abstractions that simplify the task of specifying the node local behavior of a distributed computation. Consequently, the overall system behavior must be described in terms of pair-wise interactions among nodes within radio range; differently, the second sub-class is characterized by higher-level abstractions used to program the system as a whole (macro-programming), regardless of the single devices. Likewise, in [17] low-level programming abstractions are programming languages that require the programmer to code individual nodes and to specify inter-node communications in detail, while high-level programming abstracts away those details and provides ways to specify the behavior globally. According to [17], some of the relevant characteristics concerning language are: communication and computation perspectives, programming idiom and distribution model.

The communication perspective distinguishes languages that directly offer constructs for physical neighborhoods (e.g. NesC [14] and ATaG [19]), those that allow targeting subsets of nodes depending on application-level information (e.g. Regiment [20] and Pieces [21]) and those offering a global view programming of the system (e.g. TinyDB [4]). The main advantage that some global view programming styles such as TinyDB offer is simplicity, while the drawbacks are related to the lack of flexibility and reach, since the user does not control details. TinyStreams allows users to work at any of those levels, since it is possible to manage and route between neighbors, over groups or over the whole system using individual commands.

The computation perspective distinguishes imperative approaches, which are programming solutions based on sequential or event-driven semantics (e.g. Abstract Regions [22] and Pleiades [23], or platform code such as NesC), and declarative solutions, which are usually very concise in describing the system behavior using, for instance, database-style or rule-oriented semantics (e.g. TinyDB [4] and Cougar [1]). Functional paradigms express application processing by applying one or more functions to data sensed in some part of the system (e.g. Regiment [20] and snBench [24]). Flask [16] is also a functional, domain specific language embedded in Haskell, offering high-level reusable abstractions to the sensor network, and FlaskDB is a macro-programming language over it. Flask uses an intermediate distributed dataflow graph model that is compiled into node-level binaries. If more than a single idiom is associated to address different aspects, those are hybrid approaches, such as the one presented in ATaG [19]. Declarative SQL-like approaches are very intuitive and easy to use and to learn, not so with rule-based systems or functional paradigms. The imperative approaches range from low-level platform languages, which require whole specifications, to more abstract solutions, which are not particularly intuitive or easy to use. TinyStreams is declarative and streamSQL-like, similar to the idioms of stream engines such as Streambase [12].

Distribution models can be classified as database-oriented, where SQL-like queries are used as in a relational database (e.g. TinyDB [4]), data sharing-oriented, where nodes can read or write data in the shared memory space (e.g. Kairos [18] and Abstract Regions [22]); or as message passing, based on exchanging messages between nodes (e.g. NesC [14], DSWare [25] or Contiki [15]). Message passing paradigms are typically much more flexible, since they allow the programmer to specify exactly what is exchanged and how. The advantage of other alternatives such as database-style or data-sharing is to allow the user to specify complex patterns of processing and sharing data with only a few, system-wide commands, hiding the precise details of communications into their code generation logic. Clearly, a good compromise solution would be one that would allow the specification of data exchanges at the level desired by the programmer, which varies with application context. Stream to stream routing, where streams may reside in any node or group of nodes, makes TinyStreams such an approach.

3   TinyStreams

TinyStreams implements a stream model over embedded device nodes and over the heterogeneous system that includes those nodes and other computing devices. Concerning the individual embedded devices, TinyStreams implements a local stream management engine for querying, creating and dropping streams, inserting, deleting and updating tuples, both in memory and on flash. Concerning the distributed system, TinyStreams allows definition of references and stream routing primitives to route data from producers to consumers along the distributed system. Fig. 1 shows the main TinyStreams modules on embedded device nodes. Embedded operating systems such as TinyOS [14] or Contiki [15] offer API primitives concerning memory, file system, radio, sense and actuation. TinyStreams queries are submitted in an sql-like syntax in a client console, parsed locally and forwarded to target nodes preparsed in a compact fixed-offsets bytearray. Embedded nodes have a TinyStreams engine on top of the operating system. The engine receives command byte arrays and stream data messages (through the communication module shown in Fig. 1), parses them and processes the commands and data using data access, sense and act primitives. The 'Stream and Query Processor' module implements tuple-at-a-time processing that requires very little memory and manages streams in memory or flash depending on their size. Memory operation is faster but only serves small streams, while file-based operation is able to handle larger streams. The query processor handles simple select expressions, conditions, alarms, sampling windows and other typical SQL-like primitives.

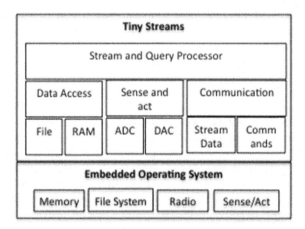

Fig. 1. Node Engine Modules

3.1   Model and Commands

Streams are time-ordered sets of tuples, and a tuple is a sequence of attribute values corresponding to attributes with an attribute data type and domain. Stream metadata is a structure defining the set of attributes and corresponding types and domains. A stream may have a window, which limits the number of tuples that can be in the stream at any time. While flash-resident streams can be created with no window (similar to database tables), memory-resident streams must fit into the constrained memory size, therefore they have window size limitations.

Fig. 2 shows a windowed memory stream and a file-based flash-resident stream.

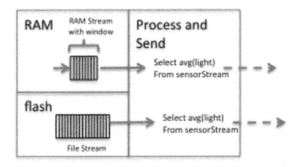

Fig. 2. Memory and Flash Streams

TinyStreams has data access primitives abstracting away from memory versus flash stream residency. Since embedded devices have sensors, there are also prede-fined special "sensor streams" that correspond to each sensor. If the sensor is named "sensorX", the corresponding stream will be called sensorX and will have a single attribute named "value" that corresponds to the sensor readings. A sampling clause allows users to command acquisition with a sampling rate. The syntax for a sensor stream collecting 24 hours' worth of per-minute sensor values is:

```
Create stream sensorXvalues
in DepositsSensorNodes
as select value
from sensorX
window 24 hours
sample every 1 minute;
```

Table 1 shows TinyStreams SQL-like constructs.

Stream data routing is based on consumer streams specifying that they consume data from some producer stream(s). For instance, the following consumer stream seat-ing in a remote control station – SensorXData - gets its data from a producer stream SensorXvalues. The SensorXvalues producer stream can be a stream running in each of a set of sensor nodes.

Table 1. TinyStreams SQL Constructs

Stream creation and dropping (streams with no window and tables are equivalent entities)	``` Create stream a (nodeID numeric, a numeric) Create table a (nodeID numeric, a numeric) Drop stream a; Drop table a; ```
Stream creation from select, with window and sampling rate	``` Create stream sensorXvalues in DepositsSensorNodes as select nodeID, value from sensorX window 24 hours sample every 1 minute; ```
Select command	``` Select nodeID avg(value) from sensorXvalues Group by nodeID ```
Insert command	``` Insert into a values(2); ```

Delete command	```
	Delete from a where
	nodeID=1;
	``

```
Create stream SensorXData
in controlstation as
Select *
From sensorXvalues;
```

If sensorXvalues was created with a 24 hour window, its values will be forwarded into SensorXData in the control station every 24 hours. If, instead of logging every value to the control station, one wants to get only a summary of the values, one way to do that would be to aggregate in the sensors and issue a query for the aggregated values (or registering a control station stream with periodic aggregation query).

Create stream sensorXvalues in DepositsSensorNodes as select nodeID, value from sensorX window 24 hours sample every 1 minute;	Create stream sensorXvaluesAgg in DepositsSensorNodes as select nodeID, avg(value) from sensorXvalues group by nodeID;	Create stream SensorXData in controlstation as Select * From sensorXvaluesAgg;

Fig. 3. Example Collecting Aggregated Stream

3.2   Stream Creation and Querying

Stream creation syntax allows a user to create a stream from a list of attributes or to create a stream as a select command with multiple optional clauses:

```
Create stream streamName
[in [nodeID| nodeSet]] as
Select [select expressions]
From [ sensorID | streamName ]
[Group by clause]
[sample clause]
[window clause]
[storage clause];
```

Commands are submitted through a console in a node with access to the distributed sensor network system. This console has an associated catalog that keeps node addresses information and node referencing identifiers, which are created to ease the task of specifying nodes and node groups in commands. The following example identifies node address suffixes and a set of two nodes as "DepositsSensorNodes".

```
SensorNode1 = "1333:8068";SensorNode2 = "137b:d539";
DepositsSensorNodes = {SensorNode1,SensorNode2};
```

Sensor node identifiers are specified using the "in" clause of stream creation commands. The "from" clause specifies input from streams. The stream with the name in the "from" clause (producer) will be sending its output into the stream that is being created (consumer). The producer and consumer streams may be in different nodes, commanding data forwarding from producer to consumer. Since the producer stream may be in more than one node, we can for instance command stream production in multiple nodes with a single command, by specifying a node set referencing in the "in" clause, and send all the data from those producers to a consumer node by specifying a stream that consumes from that multiple-node stream.

The "sample" clause is useful for sensor streams, indicating how often the sensors should be sampled.

The "window" clause indicates the size of the data that should be kept at any time, in either number of values or time period. This allows data holders to have a constant size, since data enters and leaves in ordered fifo order, while maintaining up to window size of data. When a window fills-up, its data is sent to consumer streams and the window is emptied for another round. A time-based stream window is defined by specifying a time unit (e.g. "window 1 hour"), while a size-based window is specified with a number of tuples (e.g. "window 10 tuples").

A stream may be stored either in memory (if it is sufficiently small to fit there) or on flash disk. The storage clause allows users to specify where to store the data.

A metadata structure describes each stream. The structure contains the stream name, attribute names and domains (NUMERIC, LONG, STRING). The physical representation of tuples is through a compact byte-array record of the attribute values.

Creation of a consumer stream also creates a periodic query to fill the consumer from producer streams. Alternatively, a query can also be posed as a one-time query. Processing a query involves retrieving tuples one-by-one into memory, operating on the tuple, incrementally computing aggregations if specified, then either sending the result tuples through the communication interface to a consumer stream in the form of a stream data message, writing the result in stream storage, or printing the result in the console or in a serial port. The tuple-by-tuple processing saves a lot of memory.

Stream selection projects attributes and may aggregate values along tuples of the stream. The aggregation functions are COUNT, MAX, AVG, MIN, and SUM, each of which is updated for each processed tuple that satisfies the SELECT predicate. The result set of tuples will contain a single tuple for each group of the aggregated values. As an example, the following query retrieves the average and maximum temperature per month:

```
Create stream temperatureSummary
in BuildingNodes
as
SELECT AVG(value),
MAX(value),month(timestamp),year(timestamp)
FROM temperatureSensor
Group by month(timestamp),year(timestamp);
```

The query processor computes aggregations incrementally. For instance, a maximum is computed incrementally as the maximum between the current maximum and the value of the current tuple; likewise, a sum is the current sum plus the new value from the current tuple, and an average is the current sum divided by the current number of tuples. This is done for each aggregation group, groups being addressed as a hashmap with the key being the group attribute values.

Conditions are added through the where clause, selecting a subset of the tuples in a stream. While processing the current tuple, the query processor verifies whether the conditions evaluate to true and only considers the tuple for further processing if the condition is true.

The delete command removes all tuples matching the condition indicated in the command. The delete is implemented by scanning all tuples, selecting those that do not match the delete condition into a new stream that replaces the previous one.

Stream drop commands free the memory occupied by the data and the metadata structure.

Since embedded sensor devices frequently also actuate on some physical system through DAC interfaces, actuation conditions and syntax is added to the approach. Fig. 4 shows an example closing shades if a temperature alarm goes on (temperature > 30) and opening them if it goes off (temperature<25). This is done in the sensor nodes themselves. The example also shows the use of variables and customized functionality (the closeOpenShades code, which is developed in the platform coding language).

```
shades=SensorNodes.Action(code="dev/closeOpenShades",
                  api={closeShades(),openShades()});
shades.openShades();
shadesOpen=true;

create Stream temperatureBasedShadesOpenClose
in SensorNodes as
  select NodeID, value
  From temperatureSensor
  Where temperature>30
  Action {

    If(shadesOpen==true)
      shades.closeShades();
      shadesOpen=false;
  }
  Where temperature<25
  Action {
    If(shadesOpen==false)
      shades.openShades();
      shadesOpen=true;
  }
```

Fig. 4. Specifying an Action

3.3   Query Processor

Fig. 5 shows the command processing path in the networked environment. Users submit a command through a console. A parser interprets the commands and accesses a catalog for addressing references and other details, producing a command bytecode. That bytecode is sent to the target nodes, which receive it through a communications interface, parse it and process against the local streams. The processing of a stream is done by a 'Process & Send' (P&S) functionality.

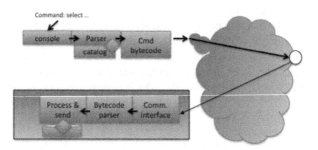

Fig. 5. Command Processing Path

All commands have a command type, and SQL-related bytecoded commands (create, drop, delete, update, insert, select) all have a stream identifier. The drop command only has those elements, but stream creation, selection, delete and update commands have a stream-like structure with fields for expressing query clauses.

The select clause fields may be attributes, constants or aggregation functions, with specific codes for identifying each individual alternative - operands, functions and operators.

The query processor in each node responds to the following timer and network events:

- If a stream creation command arrives through the communication interface, the stream metadata is created and the necessary memory space is created for the stream. If the stream is flash resident, a new file is created for the stream. If the stream has a timed window, a window-related timer is created and armed for periodically waking up and operating on the stream. If the stream is a sensor stream, with sampling rate, then a sensor acquisition-related timer is created and armed for periodically waking up and acquiring the signal through the sensor ADC;
- Stream window timer expiration –> the stream selection query stored in stream metadata is executed against the stored stream using the Process&Send functionality;
- One-time-query (Select command) arriving through the communication interface -> the stream selection query is executed against the stored stream data using the Process&Send functionality;
- Acquisition timer expiration -> the hardware ADC is sampled and a tuple is created with the corresponding values. The tuple is inserted into the stream window, either in memory or in file;
- Stream data arriving through the communication interface -> if stream data arrives in the communication interface, the consumer stream is identified in the message. The data is stored in the data area of that stream, either in memory or in flash.
- Window expiration -> if a stream has a window and a registered select query, and the window size is reached, then the select query stored in the stream metadata is retrieved and applied against the stored stream data using the Process&Send functionality;

- Other commands arriving through the communication interface -> the commands are executed.

Tuple-by-tuple operation is implemented in the "Process & Send" (P&S) functionality in the following manner: the stream data is scanned tuple-by-tuple (either from RAM or flash). For each tuple, the query processor first applies where clause conditions to determine if the tuple is to contribute to further computation and output. If the condition evaluates to true, then P&S looks at each select clause field and:

- If the field is a constant, it outputs the constant into a temporary tuple space;
- If the field is an attribute, it copies the attribute value of the current tuple into the temporary tuple space;
- After a tuple is processed, if the query is not specifying an aggregation, then the result tuple is returned immediately;
- If the field is an aggregation (e.g. sum, count, avg, max, min), the attribute values of the current tuple update a temporary aggregation computation structure for the select aggregation expressions. The aggregation computation structure maintains a set of additive aggregation computations for the select field expression. The additive aggregation computations are: count - n, linear sum -ls, square sum - ss, maximum - max and minimum - min. This structure allows immediate return of (sum, avg, max, min, count) expressions as soon as all the tuples have been processed. If there is a group by clause, then there is a hashmap with the group-by values as keys and an aggregation structure of the type described above for each hashmap entry. Each tuple now updates the aggregation computations for the corresponding aggregation structure.

If the query specifies an aggregation, after all the tuples have been processed, the query processor needs to take the aggregation structures and return the aggregation values that are needed by the query.

4   Evaluation

TinyStreams was implemented as an evolution of a system configuration interface developed for an industrial application in the context of European Project Ginseng - Performance Controlled Wireless Sensor Networks. It was implemented on top of the Contiki operating system using C programming language. It can be ported to other operating systems for resource-constrained devices, by adjusting the storage and communication layers to the new operating system API. The main operating system interface API primitives needed are send/receive and read/write. At the level of Tiny-Streams, the read and write primitives are abstracted, with implementations for both flash and RAM. Flash storage was implemented on the Coffee file system [9] in the prototype.

We measured the code size and query processing performance with simple queries over our experimental testbed.

The total code size of the TinyStreams node component, shown in Fig. 6 (the TinyStreams code running on the embedded device) is less than 8KB, which fits nicely into the ROM available in most typical devices. We also compiled the base Contiki operating system code and then the same code with parts of the TinyStreams functionality, in order to assess the code size of those parts (the difference between the total size and the size of the code with the operating system only). The results show that the simple tuple-by-tuple query processing algorithm with no complex optimizer code and with fixed in-memory stream structures results in a small code size. This is also shown as the number of lines of code.

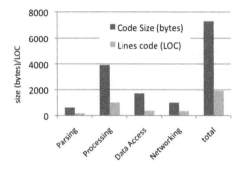

Fig. 6. Code Size for TinyStreams Parts

Fig. 7 shows the time taken for the query 'select value, nodeID from adc0', and the query 'select sum(value) from adc0' to execute, selecting either flash or RAM resident streams with varied sizes. The execution time increaed approaximately linearly with the number of tuples, and the computation of an aggregation expression increases execution time by only a small amount of time. This is as expected, since aggregation is done incrementally over an aggregation structure, with low extra overhead.

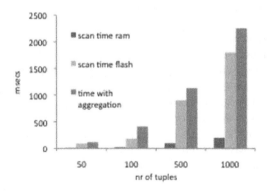

Fig. 7. Query Processing Times (msecs)

Table 2 shows the runtime memory requirements of TinyStreams, not counting the space occupied by each stream metadata and stream data.

Table 2. Runtime Memory Requirements

	Static RAM (bytes)	Heap (bytes)
Query Parser	83	20
Storage	55	60
Communication	110	100
Query Processor	890	102
Total	1138	282

5   Conclusion

We have proposed a TinyStreams model and engine for dealing with data in networked sensor systems with embedded sensing devices. We have shown how the approach allows data storage, retrieval, processing and routing. Memory and file system storage is abstracted into a stream management layer and a producer-consumer stream model allows networked configuration and processing with ease. The major advantage of the approach is that it allows users to specify what each node of a   sensor network with computation-capable devices should do and how the data should be routed in a simple manner.

References

1. Bonnet, P., Gehrke, J., Seshadri, P.: Towards Sensor Database Systems. In: Tan, K.-L., Franklin, M.J., Lui, J.C.-S. (eds.) MDM 2001. LNCS, vol. 1987, pp. 3–14. Springer, Heidelberg (2000)
2. Dai, H., Neufeld, M., Han, R.: Elf: an efficient log-structured flash file system for micro sensor nodes. In: Proceedings of the International Conference on Embedded Networked Sensor Systems (ACM SenSys), Baltimore, MD, USA (November 2004)
3. Diao, Y., Ganesan, D., Mathur, G., Shenoy, P.: Rethinking data management for storage-centric sensor networks. In: Proceedings of the Third Biennial Conference on Innovative Data Systems Research (CIDR), Asilomar, CA, USA (January 2007)
4. Madden, S., Franklin, M., Hellerstein, J., Hong, W.: TinyDB: an acquisitional query processing system for sensor networks. ACM Transactions on Database Systems 30(1), 122–173 (2005)
5. Mathur, G., Desnoyers, P., Ganesan, D., Shenoy, P.: Capsule: an energy-optimized object storage system for memory-constrained sensor devices. In: Proceedings of the International Conference on Embedded Networked Sensor Systems (ACM SenSys), Boulder, Colorado, USA (November 2006)
6. Nath, S., Kansal, A.: FlashDB: Dynamic self-tuning database for NAND flash. In: Proceedings of the International Conference on Information Processing in Sensor Networks (ACM/IEEE IPSN), Cambridge, MA, USA (April 2007)
7. Priyantha, B., Kansal, A., Goraczko, M., Zhao, F.: Tiny web services: Design and implementation of interoperable and evolvable sensor networks. In: Proceedings of the International Conference on Embedded Networked Sensor Systems (ACM SenSys), Raleigh, NC, USA (2008)

8. Pucheral, P., Bouganim, L., Valduriez, P., Bobineau, C.: PicoDBMS: Scaling down database techniques for the smartcard. The VLDB Journal 10(2-3), 120–132 (2001)
9. Tsiftes, N., Dunkels, A., He, Z., Voigt, T.: Enabling Large-Scale Storage in Sensor Networks with the Coffee File System. In: Proceedings of the International Conference on Information Processing in Sensor Networks (ACM/IEEE IPSN), San Francisco, CA, USA (April 2009)
10. Streambase URL (2012), http://www.streambase.com
11. Esper (2012), http://esper.codehaus.org
12. Aberer, K., Hauswirth, M., Salehi, A.: Infrastructure for data processing in large-scale interconnected sensor networks. In: Mobile Data Management (MDM), Germany (2007)
13. Shneidman, J., Pietzuch, P., Ledlie, J., Roussopoulos, M., Seltzer, M., Welsh, M.: Hourglass: An Infrastructure for Connecting Sensor Networks and Applications. Technical Report TR-21-04. Harvard University, EECS (2004)
14. Gay, D., Levis, P., Behren, R.V., Welsh, M., Brewer, E., Culler, D.: The nesC language: A holistic approach to networked embedded systems. In: Proceedings of the ACM SIGPLAN 2003 Conference on Programming Language Design and Implementation, pp. 1–11. ACM, San Diego (2003)
15. Dunkels, Gronvall, B., Voigt, T.: Contiki - A Lightweight and Flexible Operating System for Tiny Networked Sensors. In: Proceedings of the 29th Annual IEEE International Conference on Local Computer Networks, pp. 455–462. IEEE Computer Society (2004)
16. Mainland, G., Welsh, M., Morrisett, G.: Flask: A Language for Data-driven Sensor Network Programs, Harvard University, Tech. Rep. TR-13-06 (2006)
17. Mottola, L.: Programming Wireless Sensor Networks: From Physical to Logical Neighborhoods. PhD Thesis. Politecnico di Milano, Italy (2008)
18. Gummadi, R., Gnawali, O., Govindan, R.: Macro-programming Wireless Sensor Networks Using *Kairos*. In: Prasanna, V.K., Iyengar, S.S., Spirakis, P.G., Welsh, M. (eds.) DCOSS 2005. LNCS, vol. 3560, pp. 126–140. Springer, Heidelberg (2005)
19. Bakshi, Prasanna, V.K., Reich, J., Larner, D.: The Abstract Task Graph: a methodology for architecture-independent programming of networked sensor systems. In: Proceedings of the 2005 Workshop on End-to-end, Sense-and-respond Systems, Applications and Services, pp. 19–24. USENIX Association, Seattle (2005)
20. Newton, R., Morrisett, G., Welsh, M.: The regiment macroprogramming system. In: Proceedings of the 6th International Conference on Information Processing in Sensor Networks, pp. 489–498. ACM, Cambridge (2007)
21. Liu, J., Chu, M., Reich, J., Zhao, F.: State-centric programming for sensor-actuator network systems. IEEE Pervasive Computing 2, 50–62 (2003)
22. Welsh, M., Mainland, G.: Programming sensor networks using abstract regions. In: Proceedings of the 1st Conference on Symposium on Networked Systems Design and Implementation, vol. 1, p. 3. USENIX Association, San Francisco (2004)
23. Kothari, N., Gummadi, R., Millstein, T., Govindan, R.: Reliable and efficient programming abstractions for wireless sensor networks. SIGPLAN Not. 42, 200–210 (2007)
24. Ocean, M.J., Bestavros, A., Kfoury, A.J.: snBench. In: Proceedings of the 2nd International Conference on Virtual Execution Environments - VEE 2006, Ottawa, Ontario, Canada, p. 89 (2006)
25. Li, S., Son, S., Stankovic, J.: Event Detection Services Using Data Service Middleware in Distributed Sensor Networks. Telecommunication Systems 26, 351–368 (2004)

Distributed Sampling Storage
for Statistical Analysis of Massive Sensor Data

Hiroshi Sato[1], Hisashi Kurasawa[1], Takeru Inoue[1],
Motonori Nakamura[1], Hajime Matsumura[1], and Keiichi Koyanagi[2]

[1] NTT Network Innovation Laboratories, NTT Corporation
3-9-11, Midori-cho, Musashino, Tokyo, Japan
[2] Faculty of Science and Engineering, Waseda University
2-7 Hibikino, Wakamatsu-ku, Kitakyushu, Fukuoka, Japan

Abstract. Cyber-physical systems interconnect the cyber world with the physical world in which sensors are massively networked to monitor the physical world. Various services are expected to be able to use sensor data reflecting the physical world with information technology. Given this expectation, it is important to simultaneously provide timely access to massive data and reduce storage costs. We propose a data storage scheme for storing and querying massive sensor data. This scheme is scalable by adopting a distributed architecture, fault-tolerant even without costly data replication, and enables users to efficiently select multi-scale random data samples for statistical analysis. We implemented a prototype system based on our scheme and evaluated its sampling performance. The results show that the prototype system exhibits lower latency than a conventional distributed storage system.

Keywords: data accuracy, random sampling, relaxed durability.

1 Introduction

Thanks to advances in sensor devices and networking technologies, it is becoming possible to retrieve people's behavior, object states, and environmental conditions as sensor data in real-time. These sensor data are massive and continuously increasing since there are an infinite number of targets to sense in the physical world. Applications with significant socio-economic impact will be developed using such physical world data. Systems that interconnect the cyber world with the physical world are referred to as *cyber-physical systems* (CPSs)[1]. Applications of CPSs include, but not limited to, environmental monitoring, transportation management, agriculture management, pandemic prevention, disaster recovery, and electric grid management.

There are many technical challenges with CPSs. One key challenge is providing real-time sensor data to applications. Gathered sensor data are attractive for various applications. CPSs have to simultaneously deal with huge amounts of sensor data for applications. Because the physical world is ever-changing, CPS applications must timely and continuously adapt to these changes, predict what

G. Quirchmayr et al. (Eds.): CD-ARES 2012, LNCS 7465, pp. 233–243, 2012.

will occur, and perform the appropriate actions. Of course, not every CPS application is required to do these in real time. CPS applications can be divided into two types; real-time, as mentioned above, which place a high priority on timely data acquisition, and batch processing, which places a high priority on accurate results and attempts to use data exhaustively. For batch processing applications, software frameworks, such as MapReduce[2], have been proposed and already applied to some domains. They tend to be extremely large; only limited organizations have environments equipped to process such massive data exhaustively. These applications are a minority. Thus, our target applications are real-time ones. We adopt a kind of approximate query processing technique to speed up the data providing; it is a sampling. The sampling reduces the size of data, and reduce the latency of processes.

Another key challenge is reducing storage cost for sensor data. Since sensor data is massive and continuously increasing, storage cost is a serious issue. Although fault-tolerance is generally mandatory, it is not realistic in terms of cost to keep doubling, tripling, etc.. data. We need another scheme for ensuring fault-tolerance. It sounds impossible to ensure fault-tolerance without data replication; however, we realize this by a novel approach that emphasizes statistical properties of the data instead of individual data values. This approach enabled us to translate the data durability into the data accuracy. Therefore, we can relax the data durability unless applications always request the maximum accuracy.

The rest of this paper is organized as follows. Section 2 discusses requirements for storage systems that process massive amounts of sensor data. Section 3 describes our approach and proposes a storage scheme that satisfies these requirements. Section 4 evaluates the performance of a prototype system by comparing it with a conventional storage system. Section 5 describes related work and compares them with ours. Section 6 concludes the paper and describes future work.

2   Requirements

To clarify the requirements for storage systems, we first describe the characteristics of data generated by sensors in a large-scale sensor network. Next, we describe the characteristics of applications using such data. Then, we discuss the requirements for storage systems that store and query the data.

2.1   Characteristics of Sensor Data

Individual sensor data records are tiny but are collectively massive. A single sensor data record generally consists of a sensing value/values and its/their metadata such as sensor, temporal, and spatial attributes. On the other hand, there is a massive amount of sensors in a network, which continuously generate and transmit data. Although each record is small, they collectively become an enormous data stream through a large sensor-network. Consequently, sensor data are massive and continuously increasing.

A sensor data record is just a sample of a physical condition, e.g., temperature. Sensor data records may have a margin of error in their sensing values and are sparse. These are inherently defective data; therefore, analyzers must lump them together at a suitable granularity to enhance the quality of each cluster. Statistical analysis is thus a quite natural method for understanding sensor data.

In summary, sensor data are massive and defective but each record is unimportant; therefore, they need to be lumped together and statistically analyzed.

2.2   Application Characteristics

When processing a massive amount of data, most applications, especially real-time applications, tend to quickly obtain an overview of the data rather than inquire about each piece of data since analyzing all data is too detailed and costly. In this case, "overview" involves statistics such as averages, trends, and histograms. A key factor of statistical analysis is its accuracy.

Generally, latency of analyzing correlates with the size of the data to process, and accuracy also correlates with the size of the data; consequently, there is a trade-off between speed and accuracy. As mentioned above, our target applications place a high priority on quick analysis. On the other hand, each application has its own accuracy requirement. In addition, the level of accuracy depends on the context of the application. The accuracy requirement dynamically changes. Therefore, the most appropriate data set for an application is the minimal set satisfying its dynamic accuracy requirement.

In summary, applications prioritize quick response. They require the minimal set of data that satisfies their dynamic accuracy requirement.

2.3   Storage Requirements

So far, we described the characteristics of sensor data and applications. Now, we discuss the requirements for storage systems.

The first requirement is *scalability* because sensor data are massive and continuously increasing. Although there are other ways of mitigating the increasing amounts of data, such as compression and disposition, they have the following disadvantages. Compression requires encoding and decoding, which increases latency of processing. Disposition is effective if all potential applications using the data can share a common policy to dispose of data; however, this is prohibitively difficult. Thus, storage must be scalable, which requires adopting a distributed architecture.

The second requirement is *fault-tolerance*. Data durability is mandatory for common storage systems. Slight data loss is acceptable in the case of sensor data, provided that the loss is not biased. Since sensor data should be interpreted by a statistical process, non-biased data loss is not critical. It does not detract from the availability of the system; therefore, fault-tolerance is established. In other words, storage must maintain the statistical properties of data even if it loses partial data. We call this statistical stability.

The last requirement is *quick sampling*, which is a real-time requirement of applications. Reducing the data size to process naturally reduces latency. In statistical analysis, the required size of a sample depends on the accuracy requirement. Therefore, storage must arbitrarily provide the size of a sample according to the application's accuracy requirement.

In the next section, we propose a storage scheme satisfying these three requirements: scalability, fault-tolerance, and quick sampling.

3 Distributed Sampling Storage Scheme

Our scheme is designed for efficient statistical processing and inherently offers a sampling function. The main idea is to distribute random samples among servers to achieve high scalability, fault-tolerance, and efficient sampling.

Our scheme consists of one manager, data servers, and clients. The manager monitors the data servers and provides their live list to clients. The data servers receive requests of inserting, reading, and deleting records from clients and manage them. While the architecture is almost the same as other distributed storage scheme, the main point of our scheme is the method of clients inserting records.

We first explain our approach and procedure, then describe quick sampling, load balancing, and fault-tolerance techniques in detail.

3.1 Approach

We believe that the fundamental cost reduction technique for analyzing data is sampling, and a data storage system should natively provide a sampling function. Although many data mining techniques have been proposed, they require huge computational cost when analyzing all original records. We often extract a random sample from the original and apply data mining techniques to the sample for fast analysis. Randomness of sampling is important for preventing information drop. If sampling is executed regularly, some high-frequency data components may be dropped. Therefore, we developed our scheme on the basis of random sampling processing.

The following conditions are necessary to acquire a fair random sample:

- the data records in the sample are extracted randomly from all original records, and
- the data records in the sample are not biased toward the extraction process.

We assumed that a distributed storage scheme enables efficient sampling if it stores a fair random sample on each node. For the fairness, we adopt a simple method, which is to randomly select a data server to insert each record. If every data server stores a fair random sample, the sampled records are not the same among the data servers but have the same statistical feature. In other words, each server has statistical redundancy with the rest of the servers. Our scheme involves random sampling at inserting records by clients. We discuss load balancing and fault-tolerance from the viewpoint of sampling.

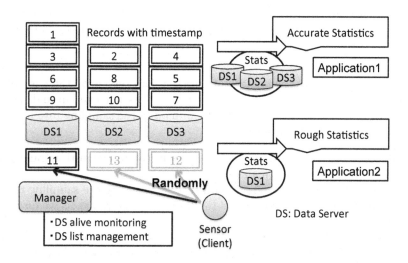

Fig. 1. System overview of distributed sampling storage

3.2   Procedure

We describe the management, insertion, read, and deletion processes as follows. The system overview is shown in Figure 1. The effectiveness of each process is described in Sections 3.3 to 3.5.

Management. The manager maintains live data servers at all times for fault-tolerance and fair sampling. The manager monitors the data servers and maintains a stable scheme. Furthermore, the total number of live data servers determines the sampling rate of the records in a data server. We use the live data server list for not only managing data server status but also for maintaining accurate statistics.

1. The manager accesses the data servers at regular intervals and maintains the live data server list.
2. The manager stores the times when and IDs of data servers join or leave the storage system.

Insertion. A client inserts a record into the randomly selected data server for fair sampling and load balancing. The client randomly selects a data server at each insertion so that data servers store fair random samples. This fair random selection also makes loads of data servers be balanced.

1. A client receives the present data server list from the manager.
2. The client randomly selects one of the data servers in the list for each record.
3. The client directly sends the record insertion request to the data server.

4. If the data server leaves unexpectedly, the client should not reselect another data server. Instead, the client disposes the request to maintain fairness and sampling rate.

Read. A client changes the number of accessed data servers on the basis of the sampling rate. Each sample in the data servers does not overlap and has the same statistical feature. Thus, the client can modify the sampling rate based on the number of accessed data servers.

1. A client sends the read request of records in the insertion time range, and the sampling rate to the manager.
2. The manager calculates enough data servers to satisfy the sampling rate by referring to the data server list in the insertion time range, as we discuss in Section 3.3.
3. The manager notifies the client of the data server list regarding the request.
4. The client sends the record read request of the time range to the data servers in the list.

Deletion. The manager does not manage which data server stores a record. The manager only detects the live data servers for each insertion time. Thus, a client should send the deletion request to all the data servers to which the client may insert records.

1. A client receives the live data server list at the time of inserting the record from the manager.
2. The client sends the record deletion request to all the data servers in the list.

3.3   Quick Sampling Technique

The sampling rate of our scheme can be modified on the basis of the number of accessed data servers.

Each data server has randomly sampled records. If there are N records and n data servers, every data server stores nearly N/n sampled records. If a client needs only the N/n sampled records, the client can quickly obtain it by reading all the records in any one of the data servers. However, clients usually require sampled records with various sampling rates. We should prepare a sampling technique for different sampling rates.

A client can modify the sampling rate by changing the number of accessed data servers because the data servers have non-overlapping and well balanced records. As a result, our scheme returns sampled records quickly regardless of the sampling rate. Let us consider the relation between the number of data servers and the sampling rate α $(0 < \alpha \leq 1)$. We classify this relation into the following three cases.

Case 1. If $\alpha < 1/n$ holds, the request size is smaller than the size of the sampled records in a data server. Then, a client reads all the records in any one of the data servers and randomly extracts its sampled records by setting the sampling rate to $n \cdot \alpha$.

Case 2. If there is a natural number m $(m \leq n)$ such that $\alpha = m/n$ holds, a client may access any m of the data servers and read all the records.

Case 3. Otherwise, it is a combination of cases 1 and 2. A client reads all the records in any $\lceil n \cdot \alpha \rceil$ of the data servers and randomly extracts from one of them at a sampling rate of $n \cdot \alpha - \lfloor n \cdot \alpha \rfloor$.

3.4   Load Balancing Technique

Many data servers are controlled by the manager in our scheme. However, we avoid concentrating heavy loads on the manager and balance the data server loads.

Although the manager monitors data servers and shares their status with clients, the manager does not read or write a record. That is, the manager only updates and provides the data server list. As a result, the traffic of the manager is comparatively small.

The data server loads are due to almost exclusively the requests from clients and are well balanced. There is no synchronization and no status update access among data servers. Since a client randomly selects a data server from the data server list, the insertion requests are not concentrated on a specific data server. Moreover, the reading loads of data servers can be distributed. This is because the manager can determine the load of data servers and select less loaded ones to notify the client.

Our scheme scales out as follows. The new data server does not receive a record until the manager includes it into the data server list. After appearing in the list, a client, who receives the updated list, starts inserting records into the new data server. Over time, the load among the data servers will balance. Note that the data servers in our scheme do not re-allocate records to each other. We cut the record modification process among the data servers to simplify the scheme.

3.5   Fault-Tolerance Technique

Acquiring just a sample is sufficient for most clients. If a client requires a random sample whose sampling rate is α and the records are in n data servers, the client receives the records from $\lceil n \cdot \alpha \rceil$ data servers. Because the data servers have a non-overlapping and well balanced set of records, the client can access any $\lceil n \cdot \alpha \rceil$ data server from the live data servers. That is, the client can obtain the same statistical records if $n - \lceil n \cdot \alpha \rceil$ data servers are left.

The above observation suggests that our scheme does not require costly replication. We believe that statistical stability is important, and our scheme satisfies stability without replication. Our scheme involves fault-tolerance at fair random sampling.

4   Evaluations

In this section, we compare the sampling performances in a prototype distributed sampling storage system based on our proposed scheme with that of a conventional system. We show that the prototype system outperforms the conventional one in sampling and is scalable.

We implemented our simple prototype system using PostgreSQL servers[3] as back-end databases, and conducted two experiments to evaluate its sampling latency and scalability. We selected pgpool-II[4] as a target for comparison, which is an open source middleware working between PostgreSQL servers and a client.

4.1   Experimental Setup

Environments. The experimental environment consists of five PCs (Intel Xeon quad-core X3450 2.55 GHz quad-core, 8-GB memory, 3.5-inch 250-GB 7,200-rpm SATA HDD ×4, CentOS5.6 64 bit) for storage and one PC (Intel Core2 quad-core Q9950 2.83 GHz, 8-GB memory, 3.5-inch 160-GB 7,200-rpm SATA HDD, CentOS5.6 64 bit) for clients. They are connected over Gigabit Ethernet.

Since each storage PC is quad-core and has four physical disks, each one can be regarded as an independent server. Then, on each storage PC, a maximum of four PostgreSQL 8.1 server processes run. Each process links to a database on each disk of the PC. On the client PC, several client processes can run simultaneously.

A record is a fixed length of 56 bytes. Each record consists of fields of record ID, insertion time, sensing time, client ID, client IP address, and value.

Distributed Sampling Storage. To compare the sampling performance derived from the difference in data distribution, we omitted the data server management processes from the prototype system. Therefore, the system only consists of PostgreSQL servers as data servers and clients implemented in C++. The data servers run on four storage PCs, and the clients run on one client PC. Clients detect the live server list from the beginning, randomly select data servers to insert records, and select data servers in turn to read records for load-balancing.

Pgpool-II. We use pgpool-II 3.0 in parallel query mode in which data can be split among multiple data servers, so that a query can be executed on all the servers concurrently. The system consists of PostgreSQL servers as data servers, a pgpool server as a proxy server between a client and data servers, and clients implemented in C++. The data servers run on four storage PCs, the proxy server runs on one storage PC, and the clients run on one client PC. Clients always access the proxy server both to insert and to read. Then the proxy server inserts or reads instead of the clients. In the last read process, clients also extract a sample from the acquired records at the required rate.

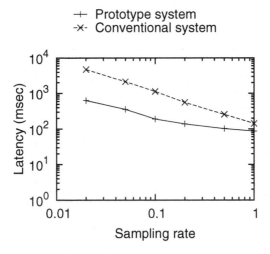

Fig. 2. Latency with respect to sampling rates

4.2   Evaluation 1: Latency of Sampling

We evaluated the sampling response with respect to the sampling rate α, where $0.02 \leq \alpha \leq 1.0$. In preparation, we stored $10,000/\alpha$ records into each storage with 10 data servers. We then simultaneously measured the latency for sampling from the storage at a rate of α by 5 clients. A total of (probably overlapping) approximately $50,000$ sampled records were acquired.

Figure 2 shows the results. The horizontal axis is the sampling rate and the vertical axis is the latency. The prototype system outperformed the conventional system in sampling rate α, and was about ten times faster, where $\alpha \leq 0.1$. This gap is nearly equal to the data size to access. With α smaller than 0.1, the prototype system accessed records in just one data server, whereas the conventional system accessed those in all ten data servers.

4.3   Evaluation 2: Scalability

Next, we evaluated the sampling response with respect to the number of data servers n, where $1 \leq n \leq 10$. In preparation, we stored $100,000$ records into each storage with n data servers. We then simultaneously measured the latency for sampling from the storage at a rate of 0.1 by 5 clients. A total of (probably overlapping) approximately $50,000$ sampled records were acquired.

Figure 3 shows the results. The horizontal axis is the number of data servers and the vertical axis is the latency. The prototype system outperformed the conventional system for any number of data servers n, and became faster as n increased, whereas the conventional system did not. Thus, the prototype system is scalable.

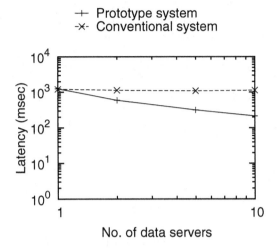

Fig. 3. Latency with respect to number of data servers

5   Related Work

Stream database management systems are being extensively studied. Representative examples are STREAM[5] and Aurora[6]. These systems are mainly aimed at support for continuous query over a data stream and do not support sample extraction from stored data in the repository; thus, they cannot enable efficient sampling.

Sampling-based approximate query processing is also being studied. The aim is quick sampling or answering. As a classical example, Olken et al. studied random sampling on relational databases. They proposed several efficient algorithms[7][8]. Babcock et al.[9] proposed a method of providing fast approximate answers in decision support systems. This method combines samples selected from a family of non-uniform samples to enhance approximation accuracy. Pol et al.[10] proposed online algorithms for maintaining very large on-disk samples of streaming data. These algorithms reduce disk access in updating samples on disk by storing them based on their proposed geometric data model. These studies enable efficient sampling; however, they have to keep a copy of the data in extra storage for fault-tolerance. Therefore, they are costly.

Reeves et al.[11] proposed a framework to archive, sample, and analyze massive time series streams, especially for data center management. This framework is aimed not only for speed but for reducing the size of archives by compression and summarization. This enables simultaneous quick answering and cost reduction; however, it is difficult to share the stored data among various applications since compression parameters and summarization need to be optimized for each application. In addition, the system still needs to duplicate data for fault-tolerance.

6   Conclusion

We proposed a distributed sampling storage scheme to efficiently sample from a massive amount of sensor data. Clients insert a record into the randomly selected data server, then each data server independently stores a fair random sample; consequently, this storage is scalable and fault-tolerant even without costly data replication. Experimental results showed that the prototype system exhibited lower latency of the sampling process than the conventional system, and it is scalable by increasing the number of data servers. We believe that our scheme make a big contribution to the realization of CPSs.

In the future, we plan to add more flexibility to sampling for a wide range of applications.

References

1. Lee, E.A.: Cyber Physical Systems: Design Challenges. In: 2008 11th IEEE International Symposium on Object Oriented Real-Time Distributed Computing (ISORC), pp. 363–369 (2008)
2. Dean, J., Ghemawat, S.: MapReduce: simplified data processing on large clusters. Commun. ACM 51(1), 107–113 (2008)
3. PostgreSQL, http://www.postgresql.org/
4. Pgpool Wiki, http://www.pgpool.net/
5. Arasu, A., Babcock, B., Babu, S., Cieslewicz, J., Datar, M., Ito, K., Motwani, R., Srivastava, U., Widom, J.: STREAM: The Stanford Data Stream Management System. Technical Report, Stanford InfoLab (2004)
6. Abadi, D., Carney, D., Cetintemel, U., Cherniack, M., Convey, C., Erwin, C., Galvez, E., Hatoun, M., Hwang, J.H., Maskey, A., Rasin, A., Singer, A., Stonebraker, M., Tatbul, N., Xing, Y., Yan, R., Zdonik, S.: Aurora: A Data Stream Management System (Demonstration). In: Proceedings of the ACM SIGMOD International Conference on Management of Data, SIGMOD 2003 (2003)
7. Olken, F., Rotem, D., Xu, P.: Random sampling from hash files. In: Proc. SIGMOD 1990, pp. 375–386 (1989)
8. Olken, F., Rotem, D.: Random sampling from B+ trees. In: Proc. VLDB 1989, pp. 269–277 (1989)
9. Babcock, B., Chaudhuri, S., Das, G.: Dynamic sample selection for approximate query processing. In: Proceedings of the 2003 ACM SIGMOD International Conference on Management of Data (SIGMOD 2003), pp. 539–550. ACM (2003)
10. Pol, A., Jermaine, C., Arumugam, S.: Maintaining very large random samples using the geometric file. The VLDB Journal 17(5), 997–1018 (2008)
11. Reeves, G., Nath, J.L.S., Zhao, F.: Managing massive time series streams with multi-scale compressed trickles. Proc. VLDB Endow. 2(1), 97–108 (2009)

Integrating Query Context and User Context in an Information Retrieval Model Based on Expanded Language Modeling

Rachid Aknouche, Ounas Asfari, Fadila Bentayeb, and Omar Boussaid

ERIC Laboratory (Equipe de Recherche en Ingnierie des Connaissances)
5 Avenue Pierre Mends France, 69676 Bron Cedex, France
{Rachid.Aknouche,Ounas.Asfari,Fadila.Bentayeb,
Omar.Boussaid}@univ-lyon2.fr
http://eric.univ-lyon2.fr/

Abstract. Access to relevant information adapted to the needs and the context of the user is a real challenge. The user context can be assimilated to all factors that can describe his intentions and perceptions of his surroundings. It is difficult to find a contextual information retrieval system that takes into account all contextual factors. In this paper, both types of context user context and query context are integrated in an Information Retrieval (IR) model based on language modeling. Here, the query context include the integration of linguistic and semantic knowledge about the user query in order to explore the most exact understanding of user's information needs. In addition, we consider one of the important factors of the user context, the user's domain of interest or the interesting topic. A thematic algorithm is proposed to describe the user context. We assume that each topic can be characterized by a set of documents from the experimented corpus. The documents of each topic are used to build a statistical language model, which is then integrated to expand the original query model and to re-rank the retrieved documents. Our experiments on the 20_Newsgroup corpus show that the proposed contextual approach improves significantly the retrieval effectiveness compared to the basic approach, which does not consider contextual factors.

1 Introduction

Most existing Information retrieval systems depend, in their retrieval decision, only on queries and documents collections; information about actual users and search context is largely ignored, and consequently great numbers of irrelevant results occur. Towards the optimal retrieval system, the system should exploit as much additional contextual information as possible to improve the retrieval accuracy, whenever this is available.

Context is a broad notion in many ways. For instance, [11] define context as any information that can be used to characterize the situation of an entity. An entity is a person, place, or object that is considered relevant to the interaction between a user and an application, including the user and applications themselves. The effective use of contextual information in computing applications still

G. Quirchmayr et al. (Eds.): CD-ARES 2012, LNCS 7465, pp. 244–258, 2012.
© IFIP International Federation for Information Processing 2012

remains an open and challenging problem. Several researchers have tried over the years to apply the context notion in information retrieval area; this will lead to the so-called contextual information retrieval systems which combine a set of technologies and knowledge on the query and the user, in order to deliver the most appropriate answers according to the user's information needs.

As information needs are generally expressed via queries and the query is always formulated in a search context, contextual factors (such as the user's domain of interest, preferences, knowledge level, user task, etc.) have a strong influence on relevance judgments [16]. But it is difficult to find a contextual information retrieval system that takes into account all the available contextual factors at the same time. Thus the context can be defined as the combination of some contextual factors which may be more or less relevant according to the actual performed research. Indeed, in this paper, we try to consider two types of context, user context and query context. We think that these two contextual factors can improve the information retrieval model.

In this paper, the user context is defined by the user's domain of interest or the interesting topic. We propose a thematic algorithm to describe the predefined user's topics which are characterized by a set of documents. Considering the user's interested topics allows providing more relevant results. The second considered contextual factor is the query context, which includes a linguistic and a semantic knowledge about the user query in order to explore the most exact understanding of user's information needs. Thus, we extend the user query by related terms automatically by using the linguistic and semantic knowledge. Also, we propose a framework based on language modeling approach in order to integrate the two contextual factors.

For instance, if a user submits the query "apple" into a Web search engine, knowing that user queries are generally shorts and contain words with several meanings, there are different topics in the top 20 documents selected by the search engine. Some users may be interested in documents dealing with "apple" as "fruit", while other users may want documents related to Apple computers. In order to disambiguate this query, we can assign a set of topics with this query. For example, we can assign the topics "cooking", "fruit" or "computer" with the query "apple". This is the user's domain of interest. In addition, to extend the query "apple" with the so-called query context, we can add concepts to this query like: "Computers", "Systems", "Macintosh", etc.

The language models in information retrieval (IR) are used to compute the probability of generating query q given a document D (i.e. compute: $P(q|D)$); and the documents in the collection C are ranked in descending order of this probability. Several methods have been applied to compute this probability as [19]. In most approaches, the computation is conceptually decomposed into two distinct steps: Estimating the document model and computing the query likelihood using the estimated document model, as in [21].

In this paper, we propose an approach to build a statistical language model that extends the classic language modeling approach for information retrieval in order to integrate the two contextual factors. The extended model has been tested based on one of the common IR test collections; 20_Newsgroup corpus. The results show that our contextual approach improves significantly the retrieval effectiveness compared to the basic approach, which does not consider contextual factors. The rest of this paper is organized as follows: Section 2 introduces the state of the art and some related works; Section 3 introduces our contextual information retrieval model based on language modeling; Section 4 shows the experimental study and the evaluation of our approach. Finally, Section 5 gives the conclusion and future work.

2   Related Works

2.1   Context in Information Retrieval

Several contextual factors can be considered in Information Retrieval (IR) area in order to improve the information retrieval systems. In this section we review some of studies in IR concerning the user context and query context, as long as we take them into consideration to extend the language modeling approach for IR[3].

User Context. The user context can be assimilated to all factors that can describe his/her intentions and perceptions of his/her surroundings [22]. These factors may cover various aspects: physical, social, personal, professional, technical, task etc. Figure 1 shows these factors and examples for each one [18].

However, the problems to be addressed include how to represent the context, how to determine it at runtime, and how to use it to influence the activation of user preferences. It is very difficult to modeling all the contextual factors in one system, so the researchers often take into account some factors, as in [2], they defined the user context as the user's current task together with his/her profile. In the contextual information retrieval, user context has a wide meaning based on the user behavior; we can mention some of them in the following:

- Visited Web pages [26]: Here, the user context is defined as the information extracted by using the full browsing history of the user.
- Recently accessed documents [5]: In this case, the user context is defined as words which indicate a shift in context; these words are identified by information about the sequence of accessed documents. This is carried out by monitoring a user's document access, generating a representation of the user's task context, indexing the consulted resources, and by presenting recommendations for other resources that were consulted in similar prior contexts.
- Past queries and click-through data [25]: Several context-sensitive retrieval algorithms are proposed based on statistical language models to combine the preceding queries and clicked document summaries with the current query for better ranking of documents.
- Recent selected items or purchases on proactive information systems [6].

- Information that is previously processed or accessed by the user via various forms: email, web page, desktop document, etc. Stuff I've Seen SIS, [12].
- Implicit feedback: Implicit feedback techniques often rely on monitoring the user interaction with the retrieval system, and extract the apparently most representative information related to what the user is aiming at [17].

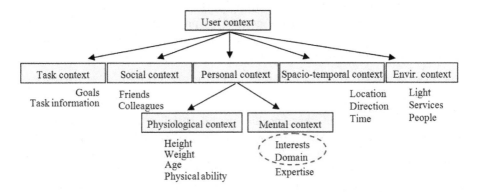

Fig. 1. Context Model

Query Context. The notion of query context has been widely mentioned in many studies of information retrieval like [4][9]. The objective is to use a variety of knowledge involving query to explore the most exact understanding of user's information needs. A query context will minimize the distance between the information need, I, and the query q, [1]. Distance (I to q) is minimized by minimizing:

- The lack of precision in the language used in the query terms. Lexicons which comprise the general vocabulary of a language can minimize this lack of precision in the language by identifying terms with minimal ambiguity.
- The use of the wrong concepts in the query to represent the information needs. Prior research suggests Ontology's for doing that.
- The lack of preferences in the query to constrain the concepts requested. This lack can be minimized by using user profiles.

The query context, in other studies, is defined as the elements that surround the query, such as:

- Text surrounding a query, Text highlighted by a user [13].
- Surrounding elements in an XML retrieval application [15][24].
- Broadcast news text for query-less systems [14].

[10] exploit the query context for predicting the user intent as being informational related to the content retrieval, navigational related to the web site retrieval or transactional related to the online service retrieval. They construct the query context by associating it with ontology concepts from the ODP (Open Directory Project) taxonomy.

2.2   Statistical Language Models

A statistical language model is a probability distribution over word sequences, using language models for information retrieval has been studied extensively, like in [19][21][27], because of its solid theoretical background as well as its good empirical performance. The main idea of language models in IR is to order each document D in the collection C according to their ability to generate the query q. Thus, it is the estimation of the generation probability $P(q|D)$; Probability of a query q given a document D. Several different methods have been applied to compute this conditional probability, such as the works of [21][8].

2.3   Discussion

User query is an element that specifies an information need, but the majorities of these queries are short and ambiguous, and often fail to represent the information need. Many relevant terms can be absent from queries and terms included may be ambiguous, thus, queries must be processed to address more of the user's intended requirements [2]. Typical solution includes expanding the initial user query by adding relevant terms. In this study we will expand the query representation by the query context which is defined above.

As we mentioned previously, it is difficult to consider all the available contextual factors. Thus, in this study, our definition of the user context is the user's interesting topic. Consequently, when we talk about the user context we talk about the user's interesting topics and taking into consideration the query context.

The language models for information retrieval have some limitations to capture the underlying semantics in a document due to their inability to handle the long distance dependencies. Also queries are typically too short to provide enough contexts to precisely translate into a different language. Thus, many irrelevant documents will be returned by using the standard language model approach for IR without integrating contextual factors.

In this paper, we will integrate the above two types of context within one framework based on language modeling. Each component contextual factor will determines a different ranking score, and the final document ranking combines all of them. This will be described in Section 3.

3   Contextual Information Retrieval Model Based on Language Modeling

In this section, we present our approach to construct a statistical language model given user's interested topics, user context, and considering the query expansion by using the linguistic and semantic processing.

3.1 Language Models for IR

Let us consider a query $q = t_1 t_2 ... t_n$, the generation probability is estimated as follows:

$$P(q \mid D) = \prod_{t \in q} P(t \mid \theta_D)^{c(t;q)}$$

$$= P(t_1 \mid \theta_D) P(t_2 \mid \theta_D) ... P(t_n \mid \theta_D) \tag{1}$$

where: $c(t; q)$ Frequency of term t in query q. θ_D is a language model created for a document D. $P(t \mid \theta_D)$: The probability of term t in the document model. In order to avoid zero probability by assigning a low probability to query terms ti which are not observed in the documents of corpus, smoothing on document model is needed. The smoothing in IR is generally done by combining documents with the corpus [27], thus:

$$P(t_i \mid \theta_D) = \lambda P(t_i \mid \theta_D) + (1 - \lambda) P(t_i \mid \theta_C) \tag{2}$$

where: λ is an interpolation parameter and θ_C the collection model. In the language modeling framework the similarity between a document D and a query q (a typical score function) can be also defined by measuring the *Kullback-Leibler* (KL-divergence) [19] as follows:

$$Score(q, D) = -KL(\theta_q \parallel \theta_D) = \sum_{t \in V} P(t \mid \theta_q) \log \frac{P(t \mid \theta_D)}{P(t \mid \theta_q)}$$

$$= \sum_{t \in V} P(t \mid \theta_q) \log P(t \mid \theta_D) - \sum_{t \in V} P(t \mid \theta_q) \log P(t \mid \theta_q)$$

$$\propto \sum_{t \in V} P(t \mid \theta_q) \log P(t \mid \theta_D) \tag{3}$$

Where: θ_q is a language model for the query q, generally estimated by relative frequency of keywords in the query, and V the vocabulary. In the basic language modeling approaches, the query model is estimated by *Maximum Likelihood Estimation* (MLE) without any smoothing [8].

$P(t \mid \theta_q)$: The probability of term t in the query model.

Note that the last simplification is done because $\sum P(t \mid \theta_q) \log P(t \mid \theta_D)$ depends only on the query, and does not affect the documents ranking.

3.2 General IR Model

The classic information retrieval systems (Non-context model) generate query directly based on similarity function or matching between the query and the documents, according to a few terms in the query. In fact, query is always formulated in a search context; contextual factors have a strong influence on relevance judgments. To improve retrieval effectiveness, it is important to create a more complete query model that represents better the information need. In particular, all the related and presumed terms should be included in the query model. In these cases, we construct the initial query model containing only the original terms, and a new contextual model containing the added terms. We generalize this approach and integrate more models for the query.

Let us use θ_q^0 to denote the original query model, θ_q^s to denote the query context model and θ_q^u to denote the user context model. θ_q^0 can be created by MLE (*Maximum Likelihood Estimation*), as in [7]. We will describe the details to construct θ_q^s and θ_q^u in the following sections.

Given these models, we create the following final query model by interpolation:

$$P(t \mid \theta_q) = \sum_{i \in X} a_i P(t \mid \theta_q^i) \qquad (4)$$

where: $X = \{0, u, s\}$ is the set of all component models.
a_i (With $\sum_{i \in X} a_i = 1$) are their mixture weights.
Thus formula (3) becomes:

$$Score(q, D) = \sum_{t \in V} \sum_{i \in X} a_i P(t \mid \theta_q^i) \log P(t \mid \theta_D) = \sum_{i \in X} a_i Score_i(q, D) \qquad (5)$$

Where the score according to each component model is:

$$Score_i(q, D) = \sum_{t \in V} P(t \mid \theta_q^i) \log P(t \mid \theta_D) \qquad (6)$$

Like that, the query model is enhanced by contextual factors. Now we have to construct both query context model and user context model and combine all models. We will describe that in the following sections.

3.3   Constructing Query Context Model

We will use both a linguistic knowledge and a semantic knowledge to parse the user query. Because linguistic knowledge does not capture the semantic relationships between terms and semantic knowledge does not represent linguistic relationships of the terms [1]. We use *WordNet* as the base of a linguistic knowledge. For the semantic knowledge we depend on ODP[1](Open Directory Project) Taxonomy, it is one type of ontology.

The integration of linguistic and semantic knowledge about the user query into one repository will produce the query context which can help to understand the user query more accurately.

Thus the initial query $q = t_1 t_2 ... t_n$ is parsed using *WordNet* in order to identify the synonymous for each query term $\{t_{w1}, t_{w2}, ..., t_{wk}\}$.

The query and its synonyms q_w are queried against the ODP taxonomy in order to extract a set of concepts $\{c_1 c_2 ... c_n\}$ (with $m \geq n$) that reflect the semantic knowledge of the user query. The concepts of the terms set q_w and their sub-concepts produce the query-context $C_q = \{c_1 c_2 ... c_n\}$. Thus the elements of

---

[1] ODP: Open Directory Project: www.dmoz.org

C_q are the concepts extracted from the ODP taxonomy by querying the initial query and its synonyms against it. For each term t, we select the concepts of only first five categories issued from ODP taxonomy.

Among the concepts of query context C_q, We consider only the shared concepts between at least two query terms, that means, a concept $C_i \in C_q$ the context of the query q if one of the following holds:

- C_i and $t \in q$ are the same, *i.e.* a direct relation.
- C_i is a common concept between the concepts of at least two query terms or their synonymous.

For instance, if a user query is "Java Language", the query context C_q, in this case, will be: $< computers, programming, languages, Java, JavaScript >$. Thus, the corresponding query context model θ_q^s is then defined as follows:

$$P(t \mid \theta_q^s) = \sum_{C_i \in C_q} p(t \mid C_i)p(C_i \mid \theta_q^0) \tag{7}$$

Accordingly, the score according to the query context model is defined as follows:

$$Score_s(q, D) = \sum_{t \in V} P(t \mid \theta_q^s) \log P(t \mid \theta_D) \tag{8}$$

3.4   Constructing User Context Model

As we previously mentioned, in this paper, the user context is defined as the user's domain of interest or the interesting topic. We will depend on predefined topics, which are derived from the used corpus. To define these topics, we can use our thematic algorithm, which will be discussed in the following (see Fig.2).

We suppose that the user can select his own topic from these predefined topics by assigning one topic to his query.

We exploit a set of documents already classified in each topic. The documents of each topic can be identified using same thematic algorithm. Thus a language model, for each topic, can be extracted from the documents of this topic. To extract only the specific part of the topic and avoid the general terms in the topic language model, we apply our thematic algorithm as follows (see Fig.2).

A thematic unit refers to a fragment of a document D referring to one topic. The steps are based on a thesaurus that includes all lexical indicators which are considered important for this segmentation process. They are created, in this study, manually but to extend the thematic units coverage in a document, we added synonyms and lexical forms that may have these units in the corpus. The obtained text fragments are then grouped by the thematic unity. Seeking information related to the user context (term context) will be done from these fragments.

Next maximum likelihood estimation is used on the documents of each topic to extract the topic language model.

We suppose that we have the following predefined topics: $TC_1, TC_2, ..., TC_j$, and the user assign the topic TC_j to his query. We can extract the user context

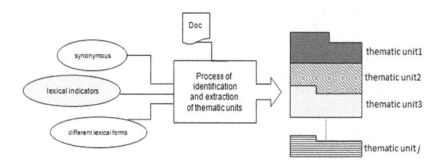

Fig. 2. A thematic algorithm

language model which is extracted from the documents of the topic TC_j, as follows (considering the smoothing):

$$\theta_u = \arg\max \prod_{D \in TC_j} \prod_{t \in D} \left[\mu P\left(t \mid \theta_{TC_j}\right) + (1 - \mu) P\left(t \mid \theta_C\right) \right]^{c(t;D)} \quad (9)$$

Where: $c(t; D)$ is the occurrence of the term t in document D. μ is a smoothing parameter. μ is fixed to 0.5 in the experimentation, because, in our dataset, we have considered the middle point as a smoothing parameter. TC_j is the set of documents in the topic j. In the same method we can compute the set of user context models for all predefined topics. When the user assigns one topic to his query q manually, the related user context model θ_q^s has to be assigned to this query q, and the score depending on this user context model (represented by the related topic) will be:

$$Score_u(q, D) = \sum_{t \in V} P(t \mid \theta_q^u) \log P(t \mid \theta_D) \quad (10)$$

4   Experiments

To validate our approach, we will present an experimental study which is done by using a test collection, 20_Newsgroups[2] corpus. The objective of this experimental study is to compare the results provided by using an information retrieval model on the dataset without considering the contextual factors with those provided by a general information retrieval model considering the contextual factors.

Our approach (including steps) is implemented in Java by using Eclipse environment. The prototype use JWNL[3] (Java WordNet Library), which is an API that allows the access to the thesaurus *WordNet* to find synonyms of query

---

[2] http://people.csail.mit.edu/jrennie/20Newsgroups/
[3] http://jwordnet.sourceforge.net/handbook.html

terms. For the semantic knowledge we depend on ODP Taxonomy which is free and open, everybody can contribute or re-use the dataset, which is available in RDF (structure and content are available separately), i.e., it can be re-used in other directory services. Also we used the Oracle RDBMS database to host: (1) the thesaurus for terms synonyms, (2) the topics which are generated during the process of identification and extraction, and (3) the relevance scores of returned documents. In order to facilitate the evaluation, we developed an interface that helps users to enter their queries, to compute the evaluation criteria, and then to display the results which are ranked according to the degrees of relevance.

4.1   Newsgroup Data Sets

The 20_Newsgroup data set is a common benchmark collection of approximately 20,000 newsgroup documents, partitioned nearly evenly across 20 different newsgroups. This dataset was introduced by [20]. It has become a popular data set for experiments in text applications of machine learning techniques, such as text classification. Over a period of time, 1000 articles were taken from each of the newsgroups, which make this collection. The 20 topics are organized into broader categories: computers, recreation, religion, science, for-sale and politics. Some of the newsgroups are considered to have similar topics, such as the *rec.sport.baseball* and *rec.sport.hockey* which both contain messages about sports, while others are highly unrelated (e.g *misc.forsale/ soc.religion.christian*) newsgroups. Table 1 shows the list of the 20 newsgroups, partitioned (more or less) according to subject matter. This dataset is also used by [23].

Moreover, we preprocessed the data by removing stop words and all documents are stemmed using the *Porter algorithm*. The document-terms matrix is based on language models and each document is represented as a vector of occurrence numbers of the terms within it. The results of this preprocessing phase for the dataset before and after the classification topics are presented in Table2.

The query execution phase, in our approach, returns a ranked list of documents that match the query. The experimentation on the 20_Newsgroups collection doesn't provide the ability to compute the precision and recall metrics. In this way our experiments were conducted with the *Lemur Toolkit*[4] , which is a standard platform to conduct experiments in information retrieval. The toolkit has been used to carry out experiments on several different aspects of language modeling for ad-hoc retrieval. For example, it has been used to compare smoothing strategies for document models, and query expansion methods to estimate query models on standard TREC[5] collections. We used the language models for all our retrieval tasks. All the other parameters were set at their default values. We remove all *UseNet* headers from the Newsgroup articles and we used 20 queries, which are listed in Table 3, to retrieve results from this documents dataset. The queries vary from 1 term to 7 terms.

---

[4] http://www.lemurproject.com
[5] http://trec.nist.gov/

Table 1. A list of the 20 Topics

20 Newsgroups dataset			
comp.graphics	rec.autos	talk.politics.misc	soc.religion.christia
comp.os.ms-windows.misc	rec.motorcycles	talk.politics.guns	sci.crypt
comp.sys.ibm.pc.hardware	rec.sport.baseball	talk.politics.mideast	sci.electronics
comp.sys.mac.hardware	rec.sport.hockey	talk.religion.misc	sci.med
comp.windows.x	misc.forsale	alt.atheism	sci.space

Table 2. Pre-processing phase applied on the dataset

Corpus	docs	stems	Corpus	docs	stems
20 news group	20017	192375	ec.sport.baseball	1001	14000
alt.atheism	1001	15618	rec.sport.hockey	1001	15610
ccomp.graphics	1001	17731	sci.crypt	1001	17436
comp.os.ms-windows.misc	1001	54511	sci.electronics	1001	15622
comp.sys.ibm.pc.hardware	1001	16575	sci.med	1001	19963
comp.sys.mac.hardware	1001	15011	sci.space	1001	18432
comp.windows.x	1001	24915	soc.religion.christian	1001	13915
misc.forsale	1001	17518	talk.politics.guns	1001	20258
rec.autos	1001	15415	talk.politics.mideast	1001	20546
rec.motorcycles	1001	15108	talk.politics.misc	1001	17782

4.2 Baseline

Classic IR Baseline. As a baseline for comparison, for each dataset, we created an index of all the documents using *Lemur's indexer*. Figure 3 shows the indexation interface. Also we used *Lemur's retrieval engine* to return a list of relevant documents using the queries which are described above. This is the standard information retrieval setting. For instance, Figure 4 shows the document's ranking for the query "*athletics play*".

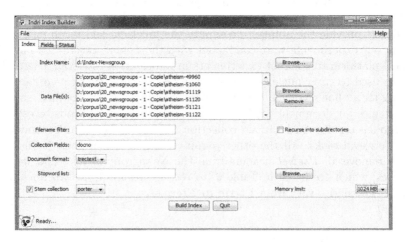

Fig. 3. Lemur's indexer

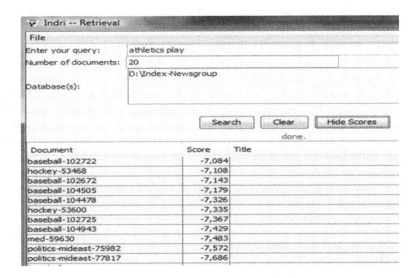

Fig. 4. Lemur's retrieval

Contextual Information Retrieval Baseline. We expanded the query with both user context and query context. In the 20_Newsgroup dataset, the topics names are considered as a user context. The documents are indexed with *Lemur's indexer. Lemur's retrieval* engine was used to perform information retrieval using the expanded query.

Table 3. The experimented queries list

N	Query	N	Query
1	Sport	11	Logitech Bus Mouse adapter
2	athletics play	12	Division Champions
3	Stanley Cup Champion: Vancouver Canucks	13	baseball fan
4	ordinary ISA card	14	HD drive
5	East Timor	15	System requirement
6	High speed analog-digital pc-board	16	memory controller pc
7	Chicago Blackhawks	17	league teams
8	Kevin Dineen play for the Miami Colons	18	macintosh apple hardware
9	National league pitchers	19	science cryptography
10	good defensive catcher	20	society religion

4.3 Results

To evaluate the performance of our approach we use the TREC evaluation software to calculate the metrics. We use *ireval.pl Perl script* which comes with the *Lemur toolkit* distribution for interpreting the results of the program *trec_eval*. Figure 5 illustrates the precision/recall curves of the IR classic and of our contextual retrieval model on the 20_Newsgroup dataset. The results of our approach, presented by the curves, show significantly improvement in measure of Precision/Recall compared to the classical model.

The improvement is precisely in the accuracy rate. It is obtained by using the contextual model which expands the original query model and re-rank the returned documents. Search engines involve query expansion to increase the quality of user search results. It is assumed that users do not always formulate their queries using the best terms. Using the general model which expands the user query with the contextual factors will increase the recall at the expense of the precision. This explains our motivation to consider the contextual factors and topic units in our approach.

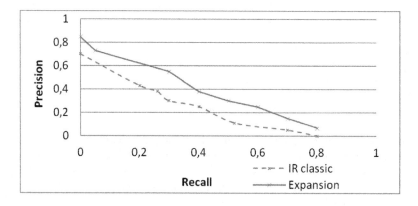

Fig. 5. Precision/recall curves for 20_Newsgroup corpus

5   Conclusion

In order to improve the information retrieval, we considered, in this paper, two types of context, user context and query context. We proposed an approach based on query expansion to provide a more efficient retrieval process. The initial query, the user context and the query context are integrated to create a new query. A thematic algorithm is proposed to describe the user context and both linguistic knowledge (WordNet) and semantic knowledge (ODP taxonomy) are used to represent the query context. The two contextual factors are integrated in one framework based on language modeling. We proposed a new language modeling approach for information retrieval that extends the existing language modeling approach to build a language model in which various terms relationships can be integrated. The integrated model has been tested on the 20_Newsgroup corpus. The results show that our contextual approach improves the retrieval effectiveness compared to the basic approach, which does not consider contextual factors. In the future, we plan to consider more contextual factors. The future objective is to combine our approach with the On-line Analytical Processing (OLAP) systems.

References

1. Asfari, O., Doan, B.-L., Bourda, Y., Sansonnet, J.-P.: A Context-Based Model for Web Query Reformulation. In: Proceedings of the International Conference on Knowledge Discovery and Information Retrieval, KDIR 2010, Spain, Valencia (2010)
2. Asfari, O., Doan, B.-L., Bourda, Y., Sansonnet, J.-P.: Personalized Access to Contextual Information by using an Assistant for Query Reformulation. IARIA Journal, IntSys 2011 4(34) (2011)
3. Asfari, O.: Personnalisation et Adaptation de L'accès à L'information Contextuelle en utilisant un Assistant Intelligent. PhD thesis, Université Paris Sud - Paris XI, tel-00650115 - version 1 (September 19, 2011)
4. Allan, J.: Challenges in information retrieval and language modeling. In: Workshop Held at the Center for Intelligent Information Retrieval, University of Massachusetts, Amherst, SIGIR Forum vol. 37(1), pp. 31–47 (2003)
5. Bauer, T., Leake, D.: Real time user context modeling for information retrieval agents. In: CIKM 2001: Proceedings of the Tenth International Conference on Information and Knowledge Management, pp. 568–570. ACM, Atlante (2001)
6. Billsus, D., Hilbert, D., Maynes-Aminzade, D.: Improving proactive information systems. In: IUI 2005: Proceedings of the 10th International Conference on Intelligent User Interfaces, pp. 159–166. ACM, San Diego (2005)
7. Bai, J., Nie, J., Bouchard, H., Cao, H.: Using Query Contexts in Information Retrieval. In: SIGIR 2007, Amsterdam, Netherlands, July 23-27 (2007)
8. Bouchard, H., Nie, J.: Modèles de langue appliqués à la recherche d'information contextuelle. In: Proceedings of CORIA 2006 Conf. en Recherche d'Information et Applications, Lyon, pp. 213–224 (2006)
9. Conesa, J., Storey, V.C., Sugumaran, V.: Using Semantic Knowledge to Improve Web Query Processing. In: Kop, C., Fliedl, G., Mayr, H.C., Métais, E. (eds.) NLDB 2006. LNCS, vol. 3999, pp. 106–117. Springer, Heidelberg (2006)
10. Daoud, M., Tamine, L., Duy, D., Boughanem, M.: Contextual Query Classification For Personalizing Informational Search. In: Web Information Systems Engineering, Kerkennah Island, Sfax, Tunisia. ACM (Juin 2009)
11. Dey, A.K., Abowd, G.D.: Toward a better understanding of context and context-awareness. In: Workshop on the What, Who, Where, When, and How of Context-Awareness (1999)
12. Dumais, S., Cutrell, E., Cadiz, J.J., Jancke, G., Sarin, R., Robbins, D.C.: (Stuff I've Seen): A system for personal information retrieval and re-use. In: Proceedings of 26th ACM SIGIR 2003, Toronto, pp. 72–79 (July 2003)
13. Finkelstein, L., Gabrilovich, E., Matias, Y., Rivlin, E., Solan, Z., Wolfman, G., Ruppin, E.: Placing search in context: the concept revisited. In: WWW, Hong Kong (2001)
14. Henzinger, M., Chang, B.-W., Milch, B., Brin, S.: Query-free news search. In: The 12th International Conference on World Wide Web, Hungary (2003)
15. Hlaoua, L., Boughanem, M.: Towards Contextual and Structural Relevance Feedback in XML Retrieval. In: Beigbeder, M., Yee, W.G. (eds.) Workshop on Open Source Web Information Retrieval, Compiègne, pp. 35–38 (2005)
16. Ingwersen, P., Jäverlin, K.: Information retrieval in context. IRiX, ACM SIGIR Forum 39(2), 31–39 (2005)
17. Kelly, D., Teevan, J.: Implicit Feedback for Inferring User Preference: A Bibliography. SIGIR Forum 32(2), 18–28 (2003)

18. Kofod-Petersen, A., Cassens, J.: Using Activity Theory to Model Context Awareness. In: American Association for Artificial Intelligence, Berlin (2006)
19. Lafferty, J., Zhai, C.: Language models, query models, and risk minimization for information retrieval. In: SIGIR 2001, The 24th ACM International Conference on Research and Development in Information Retrieval, New York, pp. 111–119 (2001)
20. Lang, K.: NewsWeeder: learning to filter net news. In: The 12th International Conference on Machine Learning, San Mateo, USA, pp. 331–339 (1995)
21. Liu, X., Croft, W.B.: Statistical language modeling for information retrieval. In: Cronin, B. (ed.) Annual Review of Information Science and Technology, ch. 1, vol. 39 (2006)
22. Mylonas, P., Vallet, D., Castells, P., Fernandez, M., Avrithis, Y.: Personalized information retrieval based on context and ontological knowledge. Knowledge Engineering Review 23, 73–100 (2008)
23. Ratinov, L., Roth, D., Srikumar, V.: Conceptual search and text categorization. Technical Report UIUCDCS-R-2008-2932, UIUC, CS Dept. (2008)
24. Sauvagnat, K., Boughanem, M., Chrisment, C.: Answering content and structure-based queries on XML documents using relevance propagation. In: Information Systems, Numéro Spécial Special Issue, SPIRE 2004, vol. 31, pp. 621–635. Elsevier (2006)
25. Shen, X., Tan, B., Zhai, C.: Context-sensitive information retrieval using implicit feedback. In: SIGIR 2005: Proceedings of the 28th Annual International ACM SIGIR Conference on Research and Development in Information Retrieval, pp. 43–50. ACM, Brazil (2005)
26. Sugiyama, K., Hatano, K., Yoshikawa, M.: Adaptive Web Search Based on User Profile Constructed without Any Effort from Users. In: WWW, New York, USA, pp. 17–22 (2004)
27. Zhai, C., Lafferty, J.: Model-based feedback in the language modeling approach to information retrieval. In: Proceedings of the CIKM 2001 Conference, pp. 403–410 (2001)

Indexing and Search for Fast Music Identification[*]

Guang-Ho Cha

Seoul National University of Science and Technology
Seoul 139-743, Republic of Korea
ghcha@snut.ac.kr

Abstract. In this paper, we present a new technique for indexing and search in a database that stores songs. A song is represented by a high dimensional binary vector using the audio fingerprinting technique. Audio fingerprinting extracts from a song a fingerprint which is a content-based compact signature that summarizes an audio recording. A song can be recognized by matching an extracted fingerprint to a database of known audio fingerprints. In this paper, we are given a high dimensional binary fingerprint database of songs and focus our attention on the problem of effective and efficient database search. However, the nature of high dimensionality and binary space makes many modern search algorithms inapplicable. The high dimensionality of fingerprints suffers from the curse of dimensionality, i.e., as the dimension increases, the search performance decreases exponentially. In order to tackle this problem, we propose a new search algorithm based on inverted indexing, the multiple sub-fingerprint match principle, the offset match principle, and the early termination strategy. We evaluate our technique using a database of 2,000 songs containing approximately 4,000,000 sub-fingerprints and the experimental result shows encouraging performance.

1   Introduction

Large digital music libraries are becoming popular on the Internet and consumer computer systems, and with their growth our ability to automatically analyze and interpret their content has become increasingly important. The ability to find acoustically similar, or even duplicate, songs within a large music database is a particularly important task with numerous potential applications. For example, the artist and title of a song could be retrieved given a short clip recorded from a radio broadcast or perhaps even sung into a microphone. Broadcast monitoring is also the most well known application for audio fingerprinting. It refers to the automatic playlist generation of radio, TV or Web broadcasts for, among others, purposes of royalty collection, program verification and advertisement verification.

Due to the rich feature set of digital audio, a central task in this process is that of extracting a representative audio fingerprint that describes the acoustic content of each song. Fingerprints are short summaries of multimedia content. Similar to a human fingerprint that has been used for identifying an individual, an audio fingerprint

---

[*] This study was financially supported by Seoul National University of Science and Technology.

G. Quirchmayr et al. (Eds.): CD-ARES 2012, LNCS 7465, pp. 259–271, 2012.

is used for recognizing an audio clip. We hope to extract from each song a feature vector that is both highly discriminative between different songs and robust to common distortions that may be present in different copies of the same source song.

In this paper, we adopt an audio fingerprinting technique [1] based on the normalized spectral subband moments in which the fingerprint is extracted from the 16 critical bands between 300 and 5300 Hz. The fingerprint matching is performed using the fingerprint from 20-second music clips that are represented by about 200 subsequent 16-bit sub-fingerprints.

Given this fingerprint representation, the focus of our work has been to develop an efficient search method for song retrieval. This problem can be characterized as a nearest neighbor search in a very high dimensional (i.e., 3200 (= 200 × 16)) data space.

High dimensional nearest neighbor search (NNS) is a very well studied problem: given a set P of points in a high dimensional space, construct a data structure which, given any query point q, finds the point p closest to q under a defined distance metric. The NNS problem has been extensively studied for the past two decades. The results, however, are far from satisfactory, especially in high dimensional spaces [2]. Most NNS techniques generally create a tree-style index structure, the leaf nodes represent the known data, and searching becomes a traversal of the tree. Specific algorithms differ in how this index tree is constructed and traversed. However, most tree structures succumb to the curse of dimensionality, that is, while they work reasonably well in a 2 or 3 dimensional space, as the dimensionality of the data increases, the query time and data storage would exhibit an exponential increase, thereby doing no better than the brute-force sequential search [2].

Recent work [3, 4, 5] appears to acknowledge the fact that a perfect search that guarantees to find exact nearest neighbors in a high dimensional space is not feasible. However, this work has not been extended to the fingerprinting system which deals with the binary vectors and the Hamming distance metric. That is, in the fingerprinting system, the bit error rate between two binary vectors is used as a distance metric rather than Euclidean distance. Moreover, the big limitation of their work [3, 4, 5] is that it often needs to search a significant percentage of the database.

In this paper, we adopt the inverted file as the underlying index structure and develop not only the technique to apply the inverted file indexing to high dimensioal binary fingerprint databases but also the efficient search algorithm for fast song retrieval. Though our work focuses on searching songs based on audio fingerprints, the devised technique is generally applicable to other high dimensional binary vector search domains.

2   Related Work

Haitsma and Kalker's fingerprinting [6, 7, 8] is the seminal work on fingerprinting. It extracts 32-bit sub-fingerprints for every interval of 11.6 milliseconds in a song and the concatenation of 32-bit sub-fingerprints extracted constitutes the fingerprint of the song. Each sub-fingerprint is derived by taking the Fourier transform of 5/256 second overlapping intervals from a song, thresholding these values and subsequently computing a 32-bit hash value. They proposed an indexing scheme that constructs a lookup table (LUT) for all possible 32-bit sub-fingerprints and lets the entries in the LUT point to the song(s) and the positions within that song where the respective sub-fingerprint value occurs. Since a sub-fingerprint value can occur at multiple positions in multiple songs, the song pointers are stored in a linked list. Thus one sub-fingerprint value can generate multiple pointers to songs and positions within the songs. By inspecting the LUT for each of the 256 extracted sub-fingerprints a list of candidate songs and positions is generated. Then the query fingerprint block (256 sub-fingerprints) is compared to the positions in the database where the query sub-fingerprint is located.

The first problem of Haitsma-Kalker's method is that the 32-bit LUT containing 2^{32} entries is too large to be resident in memory. Furthermore, LUT is very sparsely filled because only a limited number of songs reside in comparison with the size of LUT. By adopting inverted file indexing we resolve this problem.

In an inverted file index, a list of all *indexing terms* is maintained in the search structure called a *vocabulary*, and the vocabulary is usually implemented by the B-trees. However, in our approach, we employ a hash table instead of the B-trees as the vocabulay in order to accomplish the lookup time of $O(1)$ rather than $O(\log n)$. Contrary to large text databases that widely use the inverted file index where the number of query terms is a few, in fingerprint querying, the number of query terms (i.e, query sub-fingerprints) is several hundreds when we assume the duration of the query song clip is several seconds. Therefor the lookup time of $O(1)$ is crucial.

The second problem of Haitsma-Kalker's method is that it makes the assumption that under *mild* signal degradations at least one of the computed sub-fingerprints is error-free. However, it is acknowledged in the paper that the mild degradation may be a too strong assumption in practice. Heavy signal degradation may be common when we consider transmission over mobile phones or other lossy compressed sources. For example, a user can hear and record a part of a song from the radio in his or her car and then transmit a fingerprint of the song to a music retrieval system using his or her mobile phone to know about the song. Considered those situations, we cannot assume that there exists a subset of the fingerprint that can be matched perfectly.

In order to avoid the above perfect matching problem, if we allow the number of error bits in a sub-fingerprint up to n, then the search time to find matching fingerprints in a database is probably unacceptable. For example, if we cope with the situation that the minimum number of erroneous bits per 32-bit sub-fingerprint is 3, then the number of fingerprint comparisons increases with a factor of 5488 (= $_{32}C_1 + _{32}C_2 + _{32}C_3$) which leads to unacceptable search times. In our approach, we break this dilemma by increasing the number of pointers to a song s by the number of sub-fingerprints with up to the permitted number, say n, of erroneous bits. In other words, in addition to each original 16-bit sub-fingerprint in our system, we generate more $\sum_{i=1}^{n} \binom{16}{i}$ 16-bit sub-fingerprints with up to n toggled bits and use them also as sub-fingerprints for song s. This means that the number of fingerprint comparisons does not increase during the search for song matching even if we cope with the situations that the number of erroneous bits per sub-fingerprint is up to n. By applying this duplication of sub-fingerprints with n toggled bits from original sub-fingerprints to indexing, we are able to resolve the second limitation of Haitsma-Kalker's method.

The third problem of Haitsma-Kalker's method is that their search algorithm is built on the "single match principle", i.e., if two fingerprints are similar, they would have a relatively high chance of having at least one "matching" identical sub-fingerprint, and therefore their method fetches the full song fingerprint from a database and compares it with the query fingerprint as soon as it finds a single sub-fingerprint matched to a certain query sub-fingerprint. They ignore the multiple occurrences of matching. However, in fact, multiple occurrences of sub-fingerprint matching are common and many candidate songs with multiple occurrences of matching are found during the search. Therefore, if the multiple occurrences of matching are not considered in the query evaluation, the search wastes much time to inspect the candidate songs which are eventually judged to be incorrect even though they have several matchings to the query sub-fingerprints. We tackle this problem and improve the search performance by introducing the "multiple sub-fingerprints match principle".

We also introduce the "offset match principle" in the search. It means that if two fingerprints are similar and there are multiple occurrences of sub-fingerprint matching between them, they may share the same relative offsets among the occurrence positions of matching. This offset matching principle improves the search performance greatly by excluding the candidates that do not share the same relative offsets of matching occurrence positions with the query fingerprint. This reduces the number of random database accesses remarkably.

Miller et al. [9, 10] assumed the fingerprint representation of 256 32-bit sub-fingerprints of Haitsma and Kalker [6, 7, 8] and proposed the 256-ary tree to guide the fingerprint search. Each $8192(= 32 \times 256)$-bit fingerprint is represented as 1024 8-bit bytes. The value of each consecutive byte in the fingerprint determines which of the 256 possible children to descend. A path from the root node to a leaf defines a fingerprint. The search begins by comparing the first byte of the query with the children of the root node. For each child node, it calculates the cumulative number of bit errors seen so far. This is simply the sum of the parent errors and the Hamming distance between the 8-bit value represented by the child and the corresponding 8-bit value in the query. Then a test is applied to each child, in order of increasing error, to determine whether to search that child. If the best error rate seen so far is greater than the threshold, then the child is searched. The search continues recursively and when a leaf node is reached, the error rate associated with the retrieved fingerprint is compared to the best error rate seen so far. If it is less, then it updates the best error rate to this new value and assigns this fingerprint as the best candidate nearest neighbor so far.

The first problem of Miller et al.'s method is that the size of the 256-ary tree is too large and the depth of the tree is also too deep to be practical in the disk-based database search. According to their experimental results [9, 10], they search an average of 419,380 nodes, which is 2.53% of the nodes in the index tree that stores about 12,000,000 sub-fingerprints.

Moreover, they assume that each song is also represented by a fingerprint with 8192 bits, i.e., the same number of bits as the query fingerprint. It means that the length of each song in a database is assumed to be the same as that of the query song. It makes the indexing and search problem simpler. But actually an individual song with an average length of 4 minutes has approximately 10,000 sub-fingerprints in Haitsma-Kalker's method. Therefore, it is not practical to model a song with only a 8192-bit fingerprint and thus this mechanism is not feasible to apply to real applications.

The third problem is that Miller et al.'s 256-ary tree uses a probabilistic method based on a binomial distribution to estimate the bit error rate (BER) in each tree node. This BER is used to determine whether to search that node. However, it is difficult to predict the exact BER in advance, and therefore, the correct rate to find the most similar fingerprint is at most 85% in Miller et al.'s method [9, 10]. In order to increase the correct rate, the expected BER in each node should be determined more conservatively, and in that case, the search performance may degenerate to be worse than that of the brute-force sequential search. Therefore, it is difficult to reduce the search space to find the nearest neighbor in a high-dimensional space using the k-ary tree. Furthermore, if the k-ary tree tries to reduce the search space more, the error rate increases inevitably. It means that the k-ary tree approach cannot overcome the curse of dimensionality problem.

Keeping those limitations in mind, in this paper, we propose a new indexing and search algorithm that resolves the limitations of Haitsma-Kalker's method and Miller et al.'s k-ary tree method.

3   Indexing and Search Algorithm

We now describe a new indexing scheme and a new search algorithm for song databases implemented with audio fingerprints. The underlying structure of our indexing is based on the *inverted file* that has been widely used for text query evaluation such as Google [11]. Searching a multimedia database for a multimedia object (video clip or song) is similar to searching a text database for documents. A single multimedia object is represented by multiple atomic units (e.g. subsequent 16-bit sub-fingerprints in our case) and it can be found using the atomic units. Similarly, Documents in a text database are represented by multiple keywords and they are found by keyword matching. This is the reason why we adopt the inverted file as the underlying index structure in our work. However, there are also many differences between them and they make the fingerprint search problem more difficult.

- In the fingerprint search, the query fingerprint may not match any fingerprint in a database because the fingerprint extracted from a query song may have bit errors due to distortions to the query song. In other words, contrary to the text database search where only exact maching is supported, the fingerprint search should identify the correct song in a database even though there is a severe signal degradation of the query song. This means that the fingerprint search must support *imperfect matching* or *similarity search.*

- Individual bits in a fingerprint have their own meaning, and therefore, the Hamming distance between two fingerprints is used as a dissimilarity metric. This means that the search problem is: given a 3200 (= 16×200)-bit vector with errors, how to find the vector most similar to that in the 3200-dimensional binary space. However, the high-dimensional similarity search is known to suffer from the *dimensionality curse.* As aforementioned, the indexing method such as the k-ary tree approach cannot avoid the the dimensionality curse problem.

- The query fingerprint is assumed to be 200 16-bit sub-fingerprints in our work. However, assuming that the duration of the average song is 4 minutes, then the number of sub-fingerprints in a song is approximately 2,000 in our system. This difference of lengths between the query song and songs in a database makes the search problem more difficult.

We resolve the problems explained above by adapting the inverted file index suitably to our high dimensional binary database and creating the search algorithm with several sophisticated strategies.

3.1   Index Struture

An inverted file index works by maintaining a list of all sub-fingerprints in a collection, called a *vocabulary*. For each sub-fingerprint in the vocabulary, the index contains an *inverted list*, which records an identifier for all songs in which that sub-fingerprint exists. Additionally, the index contains further information about the existence of the sub-fingerprint in a song, such as the number of occurrences and the positions of those occurrences within the song.

Specifically, the vocabulary stores the following for each distinct 16-bit sub-fingerprint t,

- a count f_t of the songs containing t,
- the identifiers s of songs containing t, and
- the pointers to the starts of the corresponding *inverted lists*.

Each inverted list stores the following for the corresponding sub-fingerprint t,

- the frequency $f_{s,t}$ of sub-fingerprint t in song s, and
- the positions p_s within song s, where sub-fingerprint t is located.

Then the inverted lists are represented as sequences of $<s, f_{s,t}, p_s>$ triplets. These components provide all information required for query evaluation. A complete inverted file index is shown in Fig. 1.

t	f_t	s	Inverted list for t
1100010010001010	1	<5>	5(2: 24, 45)
0100000111001011	2	<4, 34>	4(1: 8), 34(3:78, 90, 234)
1100110001100001	1	<77>	77(1: 18)
⋮	⋮	⋮	⋮
1010111010101001	3	<102, 981, 1201>	102(1: 62), 981(2: 12, 90), 1201(2: 99, 187)

Fig. 1. Inverted file index. The entry for each sub-fingerprint t is composed of the frequency f_t, song identifiers s, and a list of triplets, each consisting of a song identifier s, a song frequency $f_{s,t}$, and the positions p_s within song s, where sub-fingerprint t is located.

The vocabulary of our indexing scheme is maintained as a hash table instead of the B-trees in order to achieve the lookup time approaching $O(1)$ rather than $O(\log n)$.

Typically, the vocabulary is a fast and compact structure that can be stored entirely in main memory.

For each sub-fingerprint in the vocabulary, the index contains an inverted list. The inverted lists are usually too large to be stored in memory, so a vocabulary lookup returns a pointer to the location of the inverted list on disk. We store each inverted list contiguously in a disk rather than construct it as a sequence of disk blocks that are linked. This contiguity has a range of implications. First, it means that a list can be read or written in a single operation. Accessing a sequence of blocks scattered across a disk would impose significant costs on query evaluation. Second, no additional space is required for next-block pointers. Third, index update procedures must manage variable-length fragments that vary in size, however, the benefits of contiguity greatly outweighs these costs.

3.2   Generating More Sub-fingerprints with Up To n Toggled Bits

Haitsma and Kalker [6, 7, 8] assumed that there exists at least one sub-fingerprint in a query that can be matched perfectly to the correct song in a database. In their experiments, they insisted that about 17 out of the 256 sub-fingerprints in a query were error-free. However, the more noises or errors in a query, the more likely any hits to the correct song are not found.

In order to avoid situations that matching is failed due to some erroneous bits in the query fingerprint, we generate more $\sum_{i=1}^{n} \binom{16}{i}$ 16-bit fingerprints with up to n toggled bits from each original 16-bit sub-fingerprint for a song and index them in the vocabulary together with the original sub-fingerprint. This means that the amount of space requirement in the index increases with a factor of $\sum_{i=1}^{n} \binom{16}{i}$. However, we can achieve $O(1)$ lookup time to find the pointer to its own inverted lists without $\sum_{i=1}^{n} \binom{16}{i}$ times more fingerprint comparisons. Fig. 2 shows this construction in which there exist up to $\sum_{i=1}^{n} \binom{16}{i} + 1$ pointers to the inverted lists for a song.

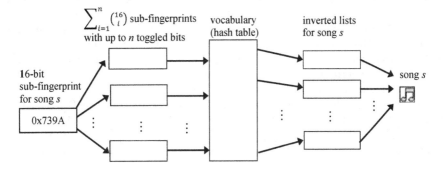

Fig. 2. Inverted file index structure that stores $\sum_{i=1}^{n} \binom{16}{i}$ sub-fingerprints with up to n toggled bits together with the original 16-bit sub-fingerprint for song s in a vocabulary

3.3   Indexed Search

The query evaluation process is completed in two stages. The first stage is a *coarse index search* that uses the inverted file index to identify candidates that are likely to contain song matches. The second stage is a *fine database search* that fetches each candidate's full fingerprint from a song database and then computes the similarity between the query fingerprint and the song's fingerprint fetched. The fine search is more computationally expensive because it requires the random disk access. Therefore, our strategy is to avoid the expensive random disk accesses as possible as we can.

To conduct the coarse index search, we use a ranking structure called *accumulator*. The accumulator records the following:

• the accumulated occurrences of the matched song identifiers (IDs),
• the matching positions both within the query and the matched song IDs, and
• the accumulated number of matchings that have the same relative offset between the matching positions within the query and the retrieved song IDs when there are multiple matchings. We call this *offset-match-count*.

Ultimately, the information what we need is the offset-match-count for every candidate of a search. If a specific song ID has been encountered and its offset-match-count has reached a certain threshold, then we load the full fingerprint from database using the retrieved song ID. The subsequent comparison is based on the Hamming distance between the query fingerprint and the song fingerprint on their matching positions. Computing the Hamming distance involves counting the bits that differ between two binary vectors.

In practical applications, many search candidates that have a single match or even multiple matches with query sub-fingerprints are generated although they are not the correct object what we seek for. Therefore, a significant percentage of the database needs to be searched if the search algorithm loads the full fingerprint of a candidate as soon as it encounters the candidate whose sub-fingerprint matches a certain query sub-fingerprint. In other words, the search strategy such as Haitsma-Kalker's method based on the single match principle is inevitably inefficient in disk-based applications although this problem may be less evident if all data are resident in memory. In fact, the candidate whose offset-match-count has reached a certain threshold (e.g. 3) has the great possibility of being the correct object what we seek for and there are almost no candidates that have their offset-matching-count reaching the threshold while they are not the correct answer. If two fingerprints are similar and there are multiple occurrences of sub-fingerprint matching between them, they may share the same relative offsets among the occurrence positions of matching.

The search algorithm using an inverted file index is illustrated in Fig. 3 and described in Fig. 4. There are six cost components in the fingerprint search, as summarized in Table 1. The first one is to initialize the array *accumulator* that records the accumulated number of matchings that have the same relative offset between the matching positions of the query and the retrieved song IDs. The second one is to compute n sub-fingerprints from a query song clip.These two operations are computed very fast. The third one is to retrieve the index information about songs stored in the inverted file index. This I/O operation is fast because the index information is lightweight and several inverted lists can be read in a single operation since they are

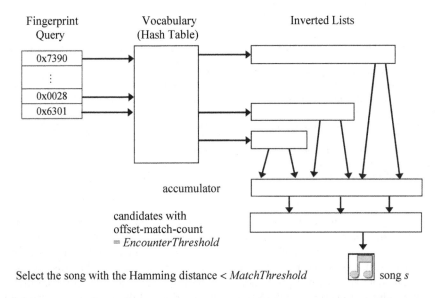

Fig. 3. Using an inverted file index and an accumulator to calculate song's similarity score

[Algorithm] Fingerprint Search

Input: Query song clip Q

Output: Match song P or 'No match'

1: Initialize accumulator $A[j]$, $1 \leq j \leq |DB|$, for each song j in a database (DB).
2: Compute n sub-fingerprints t_1, t_2, ..., t_n (e.g. $n = 200$) from a query Q.
3: **for** $i = 1$ to n **do** {
4:       IDs $\leftarrow$ InvertedFileIndex$[t_i]$ // coarse index search
5:       **for** $j \in$ IDs **do** {
6:             Increment occurrences of j in $A[j]$ by 1.
7:             Compute the offset-matching-count c of j in $A[j]$.
8:             **if** c = EncounterThreshold **then** {
9:                   $P \leftarrow$ DB$[j]$ // fine database search
10:                  **if** HammingDistance(P, Q) < MatchThreshold **then**
11:                        **Return** P;   // early termination
12:            }
13:      }
14: }
15: **Return** 'No match'

Fig. 4. Indexed computation of similarity between a query Q and a fingerprint database

Table 1. Cost Components in Fingerprint Search

No	Components	Computation	Operation	Cost
1	Initialize accumulator	$O(1)$	memory	very fast
2	Compute n sub-fingerprints	$O(1)$	memory	fast
3	Retrieve song IDs	$O(n)$	disk	lightweight
4	Count occurrences	$O(n)$	memory	very fast
5	Load full fingerprint	$O(n)$	disk	heavyweight
6	Compute Hamming Distance	$O(n)$	memory	fast

contiguously stored in a disk. The fourth one is to count the accumulated occurrences of the IDs and their offset-matching-counts. This simply involves read/write accesses to the memory array. The fifth operation is to fetch the full fingerprints of the candidate songs. This is the most expensive I/O operation that includes the random disk accesses to the candidate song's fingerprint database. The final one is to fully compare the retrieved candidate fingerprint with the query fingerprint and this operation is also computed fast. Therefore, our strategy is to make the best use of the fast operations 3 and 4 while avoiding the most expensive operation 5 and the operation 6.

In the search algorithm, the query sub-fingerprints are generated at a time. Initially each song has a similarity of zero to the query, this is represented by creating the array accumulator A initialized by zero and the counts of song occurrences and offset-matching-count of $A[j]$ are increased by matching of song j and its matching of position offset to those of the query, respectively. Contrary to Haitsma-Kalker's method that fetches the full song fingerprint from a database and compares it with query as soon as it finds a song matched to a query, our search algorithm postpones it until the offset-matching-count of the candidate reaches a certain threshold (*EncounterThreshold* in the algorithm of Fig. 4) in order to avoid the expensive operations 5 and 6 in Table 1 as possible as it can. Based on our experimental results, *EncounterThreshold* = 3 shows a suitable trade-off between speed and accuracy. Without considered the offset matching principle and the multiple matching principle, the search algorithm would be similar to Haitsma-Kalker's method.

Besides the "multiple matching principle" and the "offset matching principle", another contribution of our search algortihm to the speedup is the "early termination strategy" shown in steps 10 and 11 in the algorithm of Fig. 4. The fewer errors in a query, the more likely the match is found at an early stage. Even before the full search of n (e.g., $n = 200$) sub-fingerprints is completed, if a song's offset-matching-count meets the condition of *EncounterThreshold*, then the the song is fully compared with query and it can be reported as a match if its Hamming distance to the query is less than a certain threshold (*MatchThreshold* in the algorithm of Fig. 4). This early search termination also contributes to the speedup.

4   Experimental Results

In order to evaluate our indexing scheme and search algorithm, we digitized 2,000 songs and computed about 4,000,000 sub-fingerprints from the songs. 1,000 queries were generated by randomly selecting 20-second portions from the song database and playing them through inexpensive speakers attached to a PC. These song snippets were then digitized to be used as queries using an inexpensive microphone. For each query, we know the answer, i.e. correct song, because we know which song each query is derived from. Therefore, we can compute the error rate that could not identify the correct song. In addition, we generated 100 queries from songs not stored in a database to evaluate the performance when a search returns no match.

We compare our method with Haitsma-Kalker's method to assess the performance of ours. In our experiment, we set *EncounterThreshold* to 3 and *MatchThreshold* to 0.2 in the search algorithm of Fig. 4. In addition, we also generated more 16-bit sub-fingerprints with up to 2 toggled bits from each original 16-bit sub-fingerprint for a song and stored them in the index vocabulary together with the original. Therefore, our index maintains 136 (= $_{16}C_1 + {}_{16}C_2$) times more index entries compared with other indexing methods such as Haitsma-Kalker's method.

We define the *search size* as the percentage of the songs' full fingerprints retrieved for comparison to the whole database size. The search size in our algorithm is in effect only one, in other words, we retrieve the full fingerprint of a song only if it is the correct song. This is due to the "multiple matching principle" and the "offset matching principle". Of between them, the offset matching principle makes the greatest contribution to the very small search size. On the other hand, Haitsma-Kalker's method could not achieve this performance.

First, we study the performance when a search returns no match, hence has no early termination. We conducted the experiment using the songs with no match in the database. In our algorithm, there is no case to load any candidate song's full fingerprint from the database when a match is not found. This is mainly due to the offset match principle because there is almost not the case that the offsets of match positions of sub-fingerprints are also matched although some sub-fingerprints themselves may be matched accidentally when two songs are not actually similar.

However, in Haitsma-Kalker's case, a significant percentage of the database needs to be searched even though there is no match, i.e. its search size approaches the database size. This inefficiency is caused by their method that retrieves the candidate's full fingerprint from the database as soon as it finds a single sub-fingerprint match.

Table 2 reports the proportions of candidate songs in a database that have any matches to the sub-fingerprints in a query even though the songs do not have actual match to the query fingerprint. It means that Haitsma-Kalker's method searches 85% (number of sub-fingerprint matches = 1 in Table 2) of the database when no match is found because it retrieves the candidate song's full fingerprint as soon as it finds the sub-fingerprint matched to a portion of query but does not succeed in finding actual song match.

Second, let us study the performance when a search returns a match, hence it has early termination. Even in this case, Haitsma-Kalker's method searches a significant percentage ($\approx 18\%$) of the database in our experiment. It is particularly inefficient to retrieve sporadically dispersered data from disk. Fingerprints in a database are actuallly

Table 2. Proportions of candidates that have sub-fingerprint matches to a query

number of sub-fingerprint matches	≥ 20	≥ 10	≥ 8	≥ 6	≥ 4	≥ 2	= 1
proportions of candidates	3.8%	22%	32%	45%	54%	77%	85%

Table 3. Comparison between our algorithm and Haitsma-Kalker's algorithm

Algorithm	False dismissal rate	Search size	Average search time
Our algorithm	0.74%	0.05%	30 msec
Haitsma-Kalker's algorithm	0.95%	18%	3120 msec

retrieved randomly and it is very costly contrary to the access of inverted lists of index. On the other hand, our method retrieves only the correct song's full fingerprint. This is also due to the offset match principle of our algorithm.

Third, let us consider the false dismissal rate in the search. In our algorithm, false dismissal is occurred when offset-match-counts of candidates are less than *EncounterThreshold*. Although we adopt the offset match principle to avoid the expensive operation of retrieving full fingerprints, the false dismissal rate of our algorithm is less than 1% (Table 3). In effect, the fewer error bits in a query, the more likely the false dismissal error is reduced.

Finally, in the speed test, our method is far faster than Haitsma-Kalker's method. This speedup is achieved since our search algorithm checks only the correct song, while Haitsma-Kalker's method has to load and compare a significant percentage of the database. This is due to employing the strategy of postponing the access of database to fetch the full fingerprint of a song as well as the early termination strategy without considering all sub-fingerprints. The above experimental results show both of the effectiveness and efficiency of our indexing and search strategy. Table 3 summarizes the experimental results for both our algorithm and Haitsma-Kalker's algorithm.

5   Conclusion

In this paper, we propose a new search algorithm based on inverted indexing for efficiently searching a large high dimensional binary database. The indexing method employs the inverted file as the underlying index structure and adopts the strategy of maintaining duplicated fingerprints with toggled bits, so that it reduces the song recognition error rate and achieves the efficient song retrieval.

The search algorithm adopts the "multiple match principle", the "offset match principle", and the "early termination strategy", so that it postpones the fetch of full fingerprints and therefore it reduces the number of expensive random disk acceses dramatically.

The experimental result shows the performance superiority of our method to Haitsma-Kalker's. This makes our new indexing and search strategy a useful technique for efficient high dimensional binary database searches including the application of song retrieval.

References

1. Seo, J.S., et al.: Audio Fingerprinting Based on Normalized Spectral Subband Moments. IEEE Signal Processing Letters 13(4), 209–212 (2006)
2. Cha, G.-H., Zhu, X., Petkovic, D., Chung, C.-W.: An efficient indexing method for nearest neighbor searches in high-dirnensional image databases. IEEE Tr. on Multimedia 4(1), 76–87 (2002)
3. Gionis, A., Indyk, P., Motwani, R.: Similarity Search in High Dimensions Via Hashing. In: Proc. VLDB Conf., pp. 518–529 (1999)
4. Zezula, P., Amato, G., Dohnal, V., Batko, M.: Similarity Search: The Metric Space Approach. Springer (2006)
5. Aggarwal, C.C., Yu, P.S.: On Indexing High Dimensional Data with Uncertainty. In: Proc. SIAM Data Mining Conference, pp. 621–631 (2008)
6. Haitsma, J., Kalker, T.: A Highly Robust Audio Fingerprinting System With an Efficient Search Strategy. J. New Music Research 32(2), 211–221 (2003)
7. Haitsma, J., Kalker, T.: Highly Robust Audio Fingerprinting System. In: Proc. Int. Symp. on Music Information Retrieval, pp. 107–115 (2002)
8. Oostveen, J., Kalker, T., Haitsma, J.: Feature Extraction and a Database Strategy for Video Fingerprinting. In: Chang, S.-K., Chen, Z., Lee, S.-Y. (eds.) VISUAL 2002. LNCS, vol. 2314, pp. 117–128. Springer, Heidelberg (2002)
9. Miller, M.L., Rodriguez, M.C., Cox, I.J.: Audio Fingerprinting: Nearest Neighbor Search in High Dimensional Binary Spaces. J. VLSI Signal Processing 41, 285–291 (2005)
10. Miller, M.L., Rodriguez, M.C., Cox, I.J.: Audio Fingerprinting: Nearest Neighbor Search in High Dimensional Binary Spaces. In: Proc. IEEE Multimedia Signal Processing Workshop, pp. 182–185 (2002)
11. Brin, S., Page, L.: The anatomy of a large-scale hypertextual Web search engine. Computer Networks and ISDN Systems 30, 107–117 (1998)

Ontology-Based Retrieval of Experts – The Issue of Efficiency and Scalability within the eXtraSpec System

Elżbieta Bukowska, Monika Kaczmarek,
Piotr Stolarski, and Witold Abramowicz

Department of Information Systems,
Faculty of Informatics and Electronic Economy,
Poznan University of Economics
al. Niepodleglosci 10, 61-875 Poznan, Poland
{e.bukowska,m.kaczmarek,p.stolarski,w.abramowicz}@kie.ue.poznan.pl
http://www.kie.ue.poznan.pl

Abstract. In the knowledge-based economy, organizations often use expert finding systems to identify new candidates or manage information about the current employees. In order to ensure the required level of precision of returned results, the expert finding systems often benefit from semantic technologies and use ontologies in order to represent gathered data. Usage of ontologies however, causes additional challenges connected with the efficiency, scalability as well as the ease of use of a semantic-based solution. Within this paper we present a reasoning scenario applied within the eXtraSpec project and discuss the underlying experiments that were conducted in order to identify the best approach to follow, given the required level of expressiveness of the knowledge representation technique, and other requirements towards the system.

Keywords: expert finding system, expert ontology, reasoning approach.

1 Introduction

In the competitive settings of the knowledge-based economy [OECD, 1996], knowing the skills and expertise of employees as well as conducting an appropriate recruitment process, is a crucial element for the success of an organization. Therefore, organizations turn to IT technology for help [OECD, 1996] and very often take advantage of expert retrieval systems. The traditional expert retrieval systems, being a subset of information retrieval (IR) systems [van Rijsbergen, 1995] , face the same problems as the latter ones. These problems are caused by application of different keywords and different levels of abstraction by users when formulating queries on the same subject or using different words and phrases in the description of a phenomenon, based on which indexes are created. In order to address these issues, very often semantics is applied. There are many initiatives aiming at the development of expert retrieval systems supported by semantics. One of such initiatives is the eXtraSpec project [Abramowicz et al., 2010]. Its main goal

G. Quirchmayr et al. (Eds.): CD-ARES 2012, LNCS 7465, pp. 272–286, 2012.

is to combine company's internal electronic documents and information sources available on the Internet in order to provide an effective way of searching experts with competencies in the given field. The eXtraSpec system needs not only to be able to acquire and extract information from various sources, but also requires an appropriate information representation supporting reasoning over person's characteristics. In addition, the reasoning and querying mechanism should, on the one hand, allow to precisely identify required data, and, on the other hand, be efficient and scalable.

The main goal of this paper is to present various reasoning approaches considered within the eXtraSpec project given the required level of expressiveness of the knowledge representation technique, and to discuss the underlying motivation, which led to the development of a semantic-based mechanism to retrieve experts in its current state. The work conducted encompassed both research and practical related aspects. On the one hand, the aim was to contribute to a general understanding of the problem, and on the other hand, the aim was to develop a system that could not only be used as a proof for testing, but also could constitute a fully fledged tool to be used by users. Thus, the System Development Method (SDM) was utilized [Burstein, 2002]. According to Burstein – SDM "allows the exploration of the interplay between theory and practice, advancing the practice, while also offering new insights into theoretical concepts". The approach followed consisted out of three main steps.

First, the concept building phase took place, which resulted in the theoretical concepts presented in the next sections. The next step was system building encompassing development of a system based on the theoretical concepts established. The system development was guided by a number of identified querying strategies that an employer may use in order to discover a potential candidate. The last step was the system evaluation together with the evaluation of three different approaches and the discussion of the obtained results.

In order to meet the defined goal, the paper is structured as follows. First the related work in the relevant research area is shortly discussed. Then, the identified requirements are presented. Next, we focus our attention on the considered reasoning scenarios and the experiments performed in order to select the most appropriate one. The paper concludes with final remarks.

2   Related Work

Following [McDonald and Ackerman, 2000] expert finding systems may aim at expertise identification trying to answer a question: who is an expert on a given topic?, or aim at expertise selection trying to answer a question: what does X know? Within our research, we focus on the first aspect, i.e., on identifying a relevant person given a concrete need.

First systems focusing on expertise identification relied on a database like structure containing a description of experts' skills (e.g., [Yimam-Seid and Kobsa, 2003]). However, such systems faced many problems, e.g., how to ensure precise results given a generic description of expertise and simultaneously fine-grained and specific queries [Kautz et al., 1996], or how to guarantee the accuracy and validity of stored information given the static nature of a database and volatile nature of person's characteristics. To address these problems other systems were proposed focusing on automated discovery of up-to-date information from specific sources such as, e.g., e-mail communication [Campbell et al., 2003], Intranet documents [Hawking, 2004] or social networks [Michalski et al., 2011] [Metze et al., 2007].

When it comes to the algorithms applied to assess whether a given person is suitable to a given task, at first, standard information retrieval techniques were applied [Ackerman et al., 2002] [Krulwich and Burkey, 1996]. Usually, expertise of a person was represented in a form of a term vector and a query result was represented as a list of relevant persons. If matching a query to a document relies on a simple mechanism checking whether a document contains the given keywords then, the well-known IR problems occur: low precision of returned results, low value of recall and a large number of documents returned by the system the processing of which is impossible. Therefore, a few years ago, the Enterprise Track at the Text Retrieval Conference (TREC) was started in order to study the expert-finding topic. It resulted in further advancements of the expert finding techniques and the application of numerous methods, such as probabilistic techniques or language analysis techniques, to improve the quality of finding systems (e.g., [Balog et al., 2006] [Petkova and Croft, 2006] [Fang and Zhai, 2007] [Serdyukov and Hiemstra, 2008]).

As the Semantic Web technology [Berners-Lee et al., 2001] is getting more and more popular [Shadbolt et al., 2006], it has been used to enrich descriptions within experts finding systems. Semantics in the search systems may be used for analysing indexed documents or queries (query expansion [Navigli and Velardi, 2003]) or operating on semantically described resources with the use of reasoners (e.g., operating on contents of RDF (Resource Description Framework [W3C, 2012]) files and ontologies represented in e.g., OWL (Web Ontology language [OWL, 2012])). Within the expert finding systems, both approaches have been applied as well as a number of various ontologies used to represent competencies and skills were developed, e.g., [Gómez-Pérez et al., 2007] [Dorn et al., 2007] [Aleman-Meza et al., 2007].

There are many initiatives that use reasoning over ontologies, e.g., [Goczya et al., 2006] [Haarslev and Mller, 2003]. In [Dentler et al., 2011] authors provide comprehensive comparison of Semantic Web reasoners, considering several characteristics and not limiting it only to reasoning method or computation complexity, but also they analysed supported interfaces or the operating platform. The survey shows that despite significant variety among reasoners, reasoning over complex ontology is still time and resource-consuming.

The problem tackled within this paper is related to the semantic-based expert finding. The eXtraSpec system acquires information from outside and assumes that one can build a profile of a person based on the gathered information. It is important for the users of an expert finding system that the system operates on a large set of experts. More experts imply bigger topic coverage and increased probability of a question being answered. However, it simultaneously causes problems connected to the heterogeneity of information as well as low values of both the precision and recall measures of the system.

In order to address these issues, the eXtraSpec system benefits from the already developed technologies and tools. However, it offers an added value through their further development and creation of new artefacts. For the needs of the system, a distinct set of ontologies (tailored to the needs of the Polish market as well as taking into account additional non-hierarchical relations) together with a distinct normalization and reasoning (with the pre-reasoning stage) approach have been designed, adjusted to the specific needs of a system.

Within next section we discuss the requirements and show various scenarios considered.

3 Requirements

The eXtraSpec system is to support three main scenarios: finding experts with desired characteristic, defining teams of experts and verifying data on a person in question. In order to identify the requirements towards the persons' characteristics, the scope of information needed to be covered by ontologies, as well as the querying and reasoning mechanism developed within the eXtraSpec system, first, exemplary searching scenarios a user looking for experts may be interested in, were considered. The scenarios have been specified based on the conducted studies of the literature and interviews with employers conducting recruitment processes. Six most common searching goals are as follows:

1. To find an expert with some experience at a position/role of interest.
2. To find an expert having some specific language skills on a desired level.
3. To find an expert having some desired competencies.
4. To find students who graduated recently/will graduate soon in a given domain of interest.
5. To find a person having expertise in a specific domain.
6. To find a person with specific education background, competencies, fulfilled roles, etc. Although the enumerated goals (1-5) sometimes are used separately, usually they constitute building blocks of more complex scenarios within which they are freely combined using various logical operators.

The above querying goals imposed some requirements on the information on experts that should be available (e.g., information on the history of employment, certificates), and in consequence, also ontologies that needed to be developed for the project's needs, as well as reasoning and querying mechanism.

3.1 Requirements on Ontology and Its Expressiveness

The creation of ontology for the needs of the eXtraSpec project was preceded by thorough analysis of requirements resulting from the scenarios supported by the system:

1. The ontology MUST represent a *is-a* hierarchy of different positions and jobs allowing for their categorization and reasoning on their hierarchical relations.

2. The ontology MUST represent languages certificates (*is-a* hierarchy) to-gether with information on the language and the proficiency level, mapped to one scale.
3. The ontology MUST represent skills and competencies and their hierarchical dependencies as well as some additional relations as appropriate.
4. The ontology MUST provide a hierarchy of educational organizations allow-ing for their categorization and reasoning on their hierarchical dependencies.
5. The ontology SHOULD provide information on organizations allowing for their categorization (*is-a* relation) as well as provide information on the domains they operate in.
6. Requirements on ontologies are the same as in scenarios 1-5.

Once, the requirements have been identified, the consequences of applying vari-ous formalisms and data models for the ontology modelling and its further appli-cation, were investigated. In consequence, three assumptions were formulated: only few relations will be needed and thus, represented; developed ontologies should be easy to translate into other formalisms; expressiveness of used ontol-ogy language is important, however, the efficiency of the reasoning mechanism is also crucial. As the result of the conducted analysis of different formalisms and data models, the decision was taken to use the OWL language as the un-derlying formalisms and the SKOS model as a data model. The criteria that influenced our choice were as follows (for details see [Abramowicz et al., 2012]): relatively easy translation into other formalisms; simplicity of representation; expressiveness of used ontology language, and finally, efficiency of the reasoning mechanism.

The basic element of the eXtraSpec system is an already mentioned profile of an expert. Each expert is described with series of information, for example: name and family name, history of education, career history, hobby, skills, ob-tained certificates. For the needs of the project, a data structure to hold all that information was designed. To make the reasoning possible, a domain knowl-edge for each of those attributes is needed. The domain knowledge is repre-sented by the ontology. An ontology, according to the definition provided by Gruber [Gruber, 1995], is a formal, explicit specification of a shared conceptu-alization. It provides a data model, i.e., shared vocabulary that may be used for describing objects in the domain (their type, properties and relations). The important part of every ontology are the instances forming a knowledge base. Instances refer to a concrete object being an instantiation of an object type represented by the ontology. While annotating texts, the ontology is populated: each word or text snippet may be assigned a proper type from the ontology. During annotation process an instance of ontology is assigned to a given object.

Ten attributes from the profile of an expert were selected to be a 'dictionary reference', i.e., the attributes, which values are references to instances from an ontology. Those attributes are, e.g., Educational organization (name of organi-zation awarding the particular level of education or educational title), Skill (an ability to do an activity or job well, especially because someone has practiced it) or Scope of education (the domain of education (for example: IT, construction, transportation)) (for the full list see [Abramowicz et al., 2011]). While building the ontology for the needs of the eXtraSpec system, a wide range of taxonomies and classifications has been analyzed in order to identify best practices and solutions. As the eXtraSpec system is a solution designed for the Polish language, so is also the developed ontology.

Performed analysis of the requirements imposed on the ontology for the needs of reasoning, concluded with the definition of a set of relations that should be defined: *hasSuperiorLevel* – to represent hierarchical relations between concepts; *isEquivalent* – to represent substitution between concetps; *isLocatedIn* – to represent geographical dependencies; *isLocatedInCity* – to represent geographical dependencies; *isLocatedInVoivodeship* – to represent geographical dependencies; *provesSkillDegree* – connection between skill and certificate; *worksInLineOfBusiness* – to represent dependencies between organizations and lines of business; *isPartOf* – for representation of composition of elements, for example: ability of using MSWord is a part of ability of using MSOffice (however, knowing MSWord does not imply that a person knows the entire MSOffice suit). Additionally, set of SKOS relations have been used: *broader, hasTopConcept, inScheme, narrower* and *topConceptOf*.

3.2 Requirements towards the Reasoning and Querying Mechanism

One of the most important functionalities of the eXtraSpec system is the identification of persons having the desired expertise. The application of the Semantic Web technologies in order to ensure the appropriate quality of returned results implies application of a reasoning mechanism to answer user queries. The mentioned reasoning mechanism should fulfill the following requirements:

1. The querying and reasoning mechanism MUST be able to integrate experience history (e.g., add the length of duration from different places, but gained on the same or similar position) and then reason on a position's hierarchy (i.e., taking into account narrower or broader concepts).
2. If the information is not explicitly given, the querying and reasoning mechanism SHOULD be able to associate different certificates with languages and proficiency levels.
3. The querying and reasoning mechanism SHOULD be able to operate not only on implicitly given competencies, but also reason on jobs and then on connected competencies. Thus, the querying and reasoning mechanism SHOULD tackle also other relations than *is-a*.
4. The querying and reasoning mechanism MUST be able to reason on the hierarchy of educational organizations, on dates and results.
5. The querying and reasoning mechanism SHOULD be able to associate organizations with domains they operate in.
6. The querying and reasoning mechanism MUST be able to combine results from various querying strategies using different logical operators.

In addition to the requirements mentioned, the following requirements for the querying and reasoning mechanism also need to be considered:

- building queries in a structured way (i.e., feature: desired value);
- supporting definition of desired values of attributes in a way suitable to the type of data stored within the given feature;
- joining a subset of selected criteria within the same category into one complex requirement using different logical operators;
- formulating a set of complex requirements within one category with different logical operators;
- joining complex requirements formulated in various profile categories into one criteria with different logical operators.

The logical operators between different set of criteria and criteria themselves, include such operators as: must, should, must not.

In addition, the developed mechanism is to be used within the settings of large companies or for the needs of the employment market dealing with thousands of people registered and hundreds of queries to be answered. That is why, the reasoning mechanism itself should, on the one hand, support precise identification of required data (it should be ensured by application of the semantic technologies), however, on the other hand, needs to be efficient and scalable.

The next section presents the test-bed and experiments that were conducted in order to identify the best scenario to fulfil the identified requirements (precision and recall on the one hand, and efficiency and scalability on the other), taking into account the identified scenarios and the desired level of expressiveness of the knowledge representation language.

4   Experiment Testbed and Results

The main process in the eXtraSpec system flows as follows. The eXtraSpec system acquires automatically data from dedicated sources, both company external (e.g., LinkedIn portal) and internal ones. As the eXtraSpec system was developed for the needs of Polish market, it operates on the Polish language. The content of an HTML page is parsed and the relevant building blocks are identified. Then, within each block, the relevant information is extracted. The extracted content is saved as an extracted profile (PE), which is an XML file compliant with the defined structure of an expert profile based on the European Curriculum Vitae Standard. Therefore, it consists of a number of attributes, such as, e.g., education level, position, skill, that are assigned to different profile's categories such as, e.g., personal data, educational history, professional experience

Next, data in PE is normalized using the developed ontology (see previous section). As a result of the normalization process, the standardized profile is generated (PN). An important assumption is: one standardized profile describes one person, but one person may be described by a number of standardized profiles (e.g., information on a given person at different points in time or information acquired from different sources). Thus, normalized profiles are analysed and then aggregated, in order to create an aggregated profile (PA) of a person (i.e., one person is described by one and only one PA).

Finally, the reasoning mechanism is fed with the created aggregated profiles and answers user queries on experts. The queries are formulated with the help of specially developed Graphical User Interface (GUI).

4.1 Considered Scenarios

Given the defined requirements from the previous section as well as the already implemented system flow, three possible scenarios of using the reasoning mechanism were considered.

The *first* scenario involves using the *fully-fledged semantics* by expressing all expert profiles as instances of an ontology during normalization phase, formulating queries using the defined ontology, and then, executing a query using the reasoning mechanism. This approach involves the need to load all ontologies into the reasoning engine and representing all individual profiles as ontology instances (see fig. 1).

The *second* scenario relies on the *query expansion* using ontology, i.e., adding keywords to the query by using an ontology to narrow or broaden the meaning of the original query. Thus, each user query needs to be normalized and then expanded using ontology, therefore, application of a reasoner is necessary (see fig. 2).

The *third* scenario called *pre-reasoning* involves two independent processes: (1) creation of enriched profiles (indexes), to which additional information reasoned from the ontology is added and saved within the repository as syntactic data; (2) formulating query with the help of the appropriate GUI using the defined ontology serving as a controlled vocabulary. Then, the query is executed directly on a set of profiles using the traditional mechanisms of IR (e.g., Lucene). There is no need to use the reasoning engine while executing a query (see fig. 3).

In order to make an informed decision, we have run a set of experiments to check the performance and the fulfilment of the identified requirements.

4.2 Experiment Design

The implementations of the experiments were preceded with the conceptualization stage. The effect of the conceptualization is presented on the pseudo-UML flow diagrams. Each diagram represents one experiment and is strictly coupled with the implementation given in details below. Note that classes and methods names are not included into conceptual charts. Instead the conceptual operations are only present.

We decided to build a general-purpose framework that will enable to run all experiments. All experiments encompassed two main phases: data preparation and running live experiments.

In the data preparation phase the XML-based profile (being in fact a set of XML files) is being converted into either SQL or OWL (depending on the scenario). Both conversions are made using the generic *XMLConversionFactory* class. The factory uses the concretizations of *AbstractXMLConverter*, which is either *XMLToOWLConverter* or *XMLToSQLConverter* to perform the actual task.

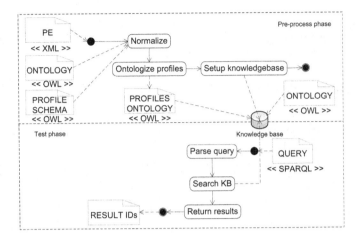

Fig. 1. First scenario – fully-fledged semantics

The OWL conversion employs the XSLT style-sheet prepared with the Java XML2OWL Mapping Tool[1] experimental software by Toni Rodrigues and Pedro Costa. As a consequence, the conversion limits itself to running the style-sheet transform engine targeted at each profile XML file. The OWL schema was prepared manually by an knowledge architect using the Protege OWL editor[2], based on the XML schema definition of an expert profile.

The SQL Lite 3 relational database system[3] has been chosen as an SQL engine. SQL Lite is well known free software, which delivers an out-of-the-box, simple, yet powerful tool. The decision to use SQL Lite was influenced by the fact that other modules of the eXtraSpec project are using this SQL engine. Moreover, it is useful as it works on single files as storage units, which makes management of the databases easy. Similarly to OWL, the SQL schema reflecting the profile information, was prepared manually by a human expert.

We needed to tailor the *XMLToSQLConverter* class in order to produce the proper SQL statements in the SQL Lite flavour. This is normal as almost any SQL engine has some deviations from the standard[4]. In contrast to the OWL conversion, this time the converter class produces JAXB[5] instances of *Profile-Extracted* class - a native eXtraSpec artifact. Then, the content of the instance is serialized into series of INSERT statements.

In the case of OWL life-cycle, before the live experiment phase one more step had to be done in advance. The *OntologiesMerger* instance is being used in order to merge all the generated and required ontologies. This includes: OWL profile schema, OWL-converted profile instances, as well as eXtraSpec thesauri and ontologies; the latter being in fact the SKOS vocabulary.

[1] http://jxml2owl.projects.semwebcentral.org/
[2] http://protege.stanford.edu/
[3] http://www.sqlite.org/
[4] http://www.contrib.andrew.cmu.edu/ shadow/sql/sql1992.txt
[5] http://www.oracle.com/technetwork/articles/javase/index-140168.html

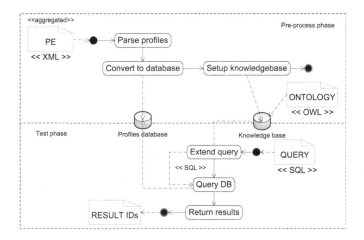

Fig. 2. Second scenario – query expansion

We have chosen the Pellet 2.2 ontology reasoning engine[6] to manage the knowledge bases as well as a SPARQL end-point. The rationale behind the decision is that the engine is provided with moderately good documentation and code examples and it is free to use. Finally, it offers three approaches to internally represent the knowledge base, one being a RDF graph. The representation as RDF is needed when joining SKOS and OWL together.

The *IExperiment* interface contracts only one operation: *runExperiment*. By calling the method on every class which implements *IExperiment* we start the test cycles.

AbstractQuererer class has two concrete subclasses that do the task of firing queries. The *SPARQLQuererer* instance is able to query the Pellet inference engine with the SPARQL language whereas *SQLQuererer* do the same for SQL Lite end-point. The *AbstractQuererer* provides the solution to consume single embedded queries, as well as fire a list of queries taken from the text file. As the result the effects are stored into results file.

The *SQLQuererer* may use the *SQLQueryExpander* instance, if there is registered one. The *SQLQueryExpander* class provides mechanism for parsing SQL SELECT statements and enrich the WHERE clauses in such a way that a larger set of results will be returned. The query expansion so far extracts keywords in the SQL IN conjunction and works on the eXtraSpec SKOS vocabularies in order to find any sub-concepts matching the keyword. If the result set is not empty, then the initial keyword is being replaced with the list of keywords reflecting sub-concepts and the concept itself. The rationale for replacing the IN sets and not parsing the whole WHERE clause with every single condition is the simplicity. On the other hand the IN operator is recognized as of little poorer performance with SELECT queries.

---

[6] http://clarkparsia.com/pellet/

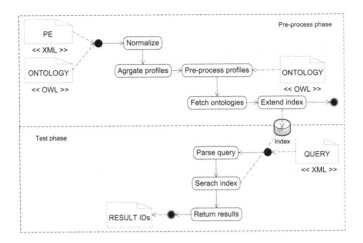

Fig. 3. Third scenario – pre-reasoning

To realize the information retrieval side of the third mechanism, the open-source java library Lucene [Apache, 2012], supported by the Apache Software Foundation, was selected. Instead of searching text documents directly, Lucene searches the previously prepared index. This speeds up the searching process.

Finally, we run all the experiments within the NetBeans 6.9 IDE[7]. The environment is perfect for programming tasks, but above all it provides a ready set of code profilers. The profilers can be thoroughly configured and allow for easy results management together with tools for raw data export into popular data analysis software.

4.3   Results

The test set consisted of nineteen profiles. Test profiles were carefully selected in order to provide sufficient level of reasoning complexity. Profiles were prepared based on real examples extracted from web sources, but enhanced manually in order to cover as many information types as possible. Simultaneously, twelve sample queries have been created. Test queries were prepared to cover as much searching scenarios as possible, including reasoning over different ontologies. We prepared an answer template that combines queries and test profiles that should be returned. This template was used to calculate precision and recall of the examined methods. This step was important especially due to the fact that most searching scenarios required reasoning mechanism in order to achieve high recall and precision. Reasoning mechanism had to not only analyze concepts used in queries and profiles, but also super- and sub-concepts from ontologies.

Since we measured system efficiency based on prototype that contains limited resources (i.e., limited number of profiles and branches in ontologies), test queries were executed 100 times in a row which gave a set of 1200 queries. We have

---

[7] http://netbeans.org/

obtained the results presented in tab 1, while usage of the memory is presented in fig. 4.

Table 1. Experiments results

	SparqlExperiment	QueryExpansion	Pre-reasoning (native)
No. of queries	1200	1200	1200
Execution time (ms)	43937	82173	30597
Precision	0,99	0,86	0,98
Recall	0,96	0,63	0,95

Our experiments showed that applying the fully-fledged semantics is a precise, but neither efficient nor scalable solution – in our settings it was not able to fulfill the expected load of the system.

The query expansion provides an increased precision of the results (in comparison to the traditional IR mechanisms) and has better scalability and efficiency than the fully-fledged semantics, however, does not allow to take full advantage of the developed ontologies and existing relations between concepts.

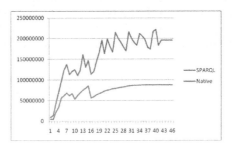

Fig. 4. Memory usage

Only application of the third considered scenario allows taking advantage of the mature IR mechanisms while increasing the accuracy and completeness of the returned results by: introducing a preliminary stage called pre-reasoning in order to create enriched indexes and the minimum use of the reasoning engine during the search.

The slight decrease in the precision and recall values in the comparison to the fully-fledged semantics was caused by the errors that occurred within the normalization phase, and were not caused by the reasoning mechanism itself. The identified errors in the normalizer component were corrected and the precision and recall values obtained within the new run equalled to the ones of the fully-fledged semantics.

Thus, taking into account the formulated requirements and obtained results, we decided to use the third scenario:

- First, creating indexes of profiles – optimized for search, i.e., structured so as to enable a very fast search based on criteria pre-set by a user. The aggregated profile is analysed, divided into relevant sections, and then enriched with additional information using an ontology (pre-reasoning). Any modification of the ontology forces the need to change indexes.
- The second process that needs to be supported is defining the query matching mechanism on the enriched indexes – this process is initiated by the task of a user formulating queries using a graphical interface. An employer, constructing a query, points interesting criteria and values they should meet. In the background of the interface, the desired values of various features from the lists and combo boxes, point to specific elements from the ontology.

5   Conclusions

The main goal of the eXtraSpec project was to develop a system supporting analysis of company documents and selected Internet sources for the needs of searching for experts from a given field or with specific competencies. The provided system focuses on processing texts written in the Polish language. The obtained information is stored in the system in the form of expert's profiles and may be consolidated when needed.

Within this paper, we have discussed the concept and considered scenarios regarding the implementation of the reasoning mechanism for the needs of the eXtraSpec system. We argue that by introducing the pre-reasoning phase, the application of semantics may be used to achieve precise results when searching for experts and at the same time, ensure the proper performance and scalability. The conducted experiments have shown that the selected scenario constitute a compromise between the expressiveness and efficiency of the developed solution.

Applying semantics undoubtedly offers a way to handle precision, recall, and helps to normalize data, however, application of semantics impacts the performance as well as scalability of the system. Therefore, a design decision needs always to be taken regarding the way the semantics should be applied in order to ensure the required quality of the system, given the expected expressiveness level of the knowledge representation. Thus, semantic technology has undoubtedly many to offer, however, its adoption in real-life scenarios will be hampered, until the set of mature tools is delivered.

References

[Abramowicz et al., 2011] Abramowicz, W., Bukowska, E., Kaczmarek, M., Starzecka, M.: Semantic-enabled efficient and scalable retrieval of experts. In: International Conference on Information, Process, and Knowledge Management, eKNOW 2011 (2011)

[Abramowicz et al., 2012] Abramowicz, W., Bukowska, E., Kaczmarek, M., Starzecka, M.: Ontology structure, reasoning approach and querying mechanism in a semantic-enabled efficient and scalable retrieval of experts. International Journal on Advances in Software (accepted for publication, 2012)

[Abramowicz et al., 2010] Abramowicz, W., Kaczmarek, T., Stolarski, P., Wecel, K., Wieloch, K.: Architektura systemu wyszukiwania ekspertów eXtraSpec. In: Technologie Wiedzy w Zarzadzaniu Publicznym (2010)

[Ackerman et al., 2002] Ackerman, M., Wulf, V., Pipek, V.: Sharing Expertise: Beyond Knowledge Management. MIT Press (2002)

[Aleman-Meza et al., 2007] Aleman-Meza, B., Bojārs, U., Boley, H., Breslin, J.G., Mochol, M., Nixon, L.J., Polleres, A., Zhdanova, A.V.: Combining RDF Vocabularies for Expert Finding. In: Franconi, E., Kifer, M., May, W. (eds.) ESWC 2007. LNCS, vol. 4519, pp. 235–250. Springer, Heidelberg (2007)

[Apache, 2012] Apache: (2012), http://lucene.apache.org (last access date: March 22, 2012)

[Balog et al., 2006] Balog, K., Azzopardi, L., De Rijke, M.: Formal models for expert finding in enterprise corpora. In: Proceedings of the ACM SIGIR, pp. 43–50 (2006)

[Berners-Lee et al., 2001] Berners-Lee, T., Hendler, J., Lassila, O.: The semantic web (2001), http:www.scientificamerican.comarticle.cfm?id=the-semantic-web (May 20, 2009)

[Burstein, 2002] Burstein, F.: Systems development in information systems research. In: Research Methods for Students and Professionals: Information Management and Systems, 2nd edn., vol. 2, pp. 147–158. Centre for Information Studies, Charles Sturt University, Wagga Wagga, Australia (2002)

[Campbell et al., 2003] Campbell, C.S., Maglio, P.P., Cozzi, A., Dom, B.: Expertise identification using email communications. In: CIKM 2003: Proceedings of the Twelfth International Conference on Information and Knowledge Management, pp. 528–321. ACM Press (2003)

[Dentler et al., 2011] Dentler, K., Cornet, R., Ten Teije, A., De Keizer, N.: Comparison of reasoners for large ontologies in the owl 2 el profile. Semantic Web Journal 1(2), 1–5 (2011) (to appear), http://www.semantic-web-journal.net

[Dorn et al., 2007] Dorn, J., Naz, T., Pichlmair, M.: Ontology development for human resource management. In: Proceedings of 4th International Conference on Knowledge Management. Series on Information and Knowledge Management, pp. 109–120 (2007)

[Fang and Zhai, 2007] Fang, H., Zhai, C.: Probabilistic Models for Expert Finding. In: Amati, G., Carpineto, C., Romano, G. (eds.) ECiR 2007. LNCS, vol. 4425, pp. 418–430. Springer, Heidelberg (2007)

[Goczya et al., 2006] Goczyła, K., Grabowska, T., Waloszek, W., Zawadzki, M.: The Knowledge Cartography – A New Approach to Reasoning over Description Logics Ontologies. In: Wiedermann, J., Tel, G., Pokorný, J., Bieliková, M., Štuller, J. (eds.) SOFSEM 2006. LNCS, vol. 3831, pp. 293–302. Springer, Heidelberg (2006)

[Gruber, 1995] Gruber, T.: Toward principles for the design of ontologies used for knowledge sharing. International Journal of Human-Computation Studies 43, 907–928 (1995)

[Gómez-Pérez et al., 2007] Gómez-Pérez, A., Ramírez, J., Villazón-Terrazas, B.: An Ontology for Modelling Human Resources Management Based on Standards. In: Apolloni, B., Howlett, R.J., Jain, L. (eds.) KES 2007, Part I. LNCS (LNAI), vol. 4692, pp. 534–541. Springer, Heidelberg (2007)

[Haarslev and Mller, 2003] Haarslev, V., Möller, R.: Racer: An owl reasoning agent for the semantic web. In: Proc. Int'l Wkshp on Applications, Products and Services of Web-based Support Systems (Held at 2003 IEEE/WIC Int'l Conf. on Web Intelligence), pp. 91–95. Society Press (2003)

[Hawking, 2004] Hawking, D.: Challenges in enterprise search. In: Proceedings of the 15th Australasian Database Conference, ADC 2004, vol. 27, pp. 15–24. Australian Computer Society, Inc., Darlinghurst (2004)

[Kautz et al., 1996] Kautz, H., Selman, B., Milewski, A.: Agent amplified communication. In: Proceedings of the Thirteenth National Conference on Artificial Intelligence (AAAI 1996), pp. 3–9 (1996)

[Krulwich and Burkey, 1996] Krulwich, B., Burkey, C.: Contactfinder agent: answering bulletin board questions with referrals. In: Proceedings of the National Conference on Artificial Intelligence, pp. 10–15 (1996)

[McDonald and Ackerman, 2000] McDonald, D.W., Ackerman, M.S.: Expertise recommender: a flexible recommendation system and architecture. In: CSCW 2000: Proceedings of the 2000 ACM Conference on Computer Supported Cooperative Work, pp. 231–240. ACM Press (2000)

[Metze et al., 2007] Metze, F., Bauckhage, C., Alpcan, T.: The "spree" expert finding system. In: Proceedings of the First IEEE International Conference on Semantic Computing (ICSC 2007), pp. 551–558. IEEE Computer Society (2007)

[Michalski et al., 2011] Michalski, R., Palus, S., Kazienko, P.: Matching Organizational Structure and Social Network Extracted from Email Communication. In: Abramowicz, W. (ed.) BIS 2011. LNBIP, vol. 87, pp. 197–206. Springer, Heidelberg (2011)

[Navigli and Velardi, 2003] Navigli, R., Velardi, P.: An analysis of ontology-based query expansion strategies. In: Workshop on Adaptive Text Extraction and Mining, Cavtat Dubrovnik, Croatia, September 23 (2003)

[OECD, 1996] OECD. The knowledge-based economy. General Distribution, OCDE/GD(96)102 (1996) (retrieved),
http://www.oecd.org/dataoecd/51/8/1913021.pdf

[OWL, 2012] OWL (2012),
http://www.w3.org/TR/2004/REC-owl-features-20040210/ (last access date: March 22, 2012)

[Petkova and Croft, 2006] Petkova, D., Croft, W.: Hierarchical language models for expert finding in enterprise corpora. In: Proceedings of the 18th IEEE International Conference on Tools with Artificial Intelligence, pp. 599–608 (2006)

[Serdyukov and Hiemstra, 2008] Serdyukov, P., Hiemstra, D.: Modeling Documents as Mixtures of Persons for Expert Finding. In: Macdonald, C., Ounis, I., Plachouras, V., Ruthven, I., White, R.W. (eds.) ECIR 2008. LNCS, vol. 4956, pp. 309–320. Springer, Heidelberg (2008)

[Shadbolt et al., 2006] Shadbolt, N., Berners-Lee, T., Hall, W.: The semantic web revisited. IEEE Intelligent Systems 21(3), 96–101 (2006)

[van Rijsbergen, 1995] van Rijsbergen, C.J.: Information Retrieval and Information Reasoning. In: van Leeuwen, J. (ed.) Computer Science Today. LNCS, vol. 1000, pp. 549–559. Springer, Heidelberg (1995)

[W3C, 2012] W3C (2012), http://www.w3.org/RDF/ (last access date: March 22, 2012)

[Yimam-Seid and Kobsa, 2003] Yimam-Seid, D., Kobsa, A.: Expert finding systems for organizations: Problem and domain analysis and the demoir approach. Journal of Organizational Computing and Electronic Commerce 13(1), 1–24 (2003)

OrderBased Labeling Scheme
for Dynamic XML Query Processing

Beakal Gizachew Assefa and Belgin Ergenc

Department of Computer Engineering, Izmir Institute of Technology
35430 Urla, Izmir-Turkey
{beakalassefa,belginergenc}@iyte.edu.tr

Abstract. Need for robust and high performance XML database systems increased due to growing XML data produced by today's applications. Like indexes in relational databases, XML labeling is the key to XML querying. Assigning unique labels to nodes of a dynamic XML tree in which the labels encode all structural relationships between the nodes is a challenging problem. Early labeling schemes designed for static XML document generate short labels; however, their performance degrades in update intensive environments due to the need for relabeling. On the other hand, dynamic labeling schemes achieve dynamicity at the cost of large label size or complexity which results in poor query performance. This paper presents OrderBased labeling scheme which is dynamic, simple and compact yet able to identify structural relationships among nodes. A set of performance tests show promising labeling, querying, update performance and optimum label size.

Keywords: XML Query Processing, Dynamic Labeling Scheme, OrderBased Labeling Scheme.

1 Introduction

The fact that XML has become the standard format for structuring, storing, and transmitting information has attracted many researchers in the area of XML query processing. XPath and XQuery are languages for retrieving both structural and full text search queries from XML documents [1 and 2]. XML labeling is the basis for structural query processing where the idea is to assign unique labels to the nodes of an XML document that form a tree structure. Label of each node is formed in a way to convey the position of the node in XML tree and its relationship with neighbor nodes. These relationships are Ancestor-Descendent (AD), Parent-Child (PC), Sibling and Ordering [2].

There are basically two approaches to store XML document. The first one is to shred the XML document to some database model. The XML document is mapped to the destination data model example, relational, object oriented, object relational, and hierarchical. The second approach is to use native XML Database (NXD) [27, 28, 29, 30 and 31]. Native XML database (NXD) is described as a database that has an XML document as its fundamental unit of storage and defines a model for an XML

G. Quirchmayr et al. (Eds.): CD-ARES 2012, LNCS 7465, pp. 287–301, 2012.

document, as opposed to the data in that document (its contents). It represents logical XML document model and stores and manipulates documents according to that model. Although XML labeling is widely used in NXD, it also plays a role in the shredding process.

Labeling schemes can be grouped under four main categories namely; Range based, Prefix based, Multiplication based, and Vector based. Range based labeling schemes label nodes by giving start and end position which indicate the range of labels of nodes in sub trees [3, 4, 5 and 23]. Prefix based labeling schemes concatenate the label of ancestors in each label using a delimiter [6, 7, 8, 9 and 10]. Multiplication based labeling schemes use multiplication of atomic numbers to label the nodes of an XML document [16 and 19]. Vector based labeling schemes are based on a mathematical concept of vector orders [17, 18 and 24]. Recently, it is common to see a hybrid labeling schemes which combine the advantages of two or more approaches [25] and [26].

A good labeling scheme should be concise in terms of size, efficient with regard to labeling and querying time, persistent in assuring unique labels, dynamic in that it should avoid relabeling of nodes in an update intensive environment, and be able to directly identify all structural relationships. Last but not least, a good labeling scheme should be conceptually easy to understand and simple to implement. Finding a labeling scheme fulfilling those properties is a challenging task. Generally speaking, labeling schemes that generate small size labels either do not provide sufficient information to identify all structural relationships among nodes or they are not dynamic [3, 4 and 5]. On the other hand, labeling schemes that are dynamic need more storage which results in decrease of query performance [6, 7, 8, 9, 10 and 20] or are not persistent in assuring unique labels [9 and 10].

This paper presents a novel dynamic labeling scheme based on combination of letters and numbers called OrderBased. Each label contains level, order of the node in the level and the order of its parent. Keeping the label of the existing nodes unaltered in case of updates and guaranteeing optimized label size are the main strengths of this approach. Label size and dynamicity is achieved without sacrificing simplicity in terms of implementation.

In performance evaluation OrderBased labeling scheme is compared with LSDX [9] and Com-D [10]. These labeling schemes are chosen because using combinations of letter and numbers, including the level information of a node in every label, and avoiding relabeling when update occurs are the common features and design goals of the three schemes. Storage requirement, labeling time, querying time, and update performance are measured. Results show that OrderBased labeling scheme is smaller in size and faster in labeling and query processing than LSDX labeling scheme. Although Com-D labeling scheme needs slightly less storage than OrderBased, its labeling, querying, and update performance is the worst due to compression and decompression overhead cost.

The paper is organized as follows: Section 2 presents a brief discussion of related work, section 3 presents OrderBased labeling scheme. Section 4 illustrates storage requirements, labeling time, querying, and update performance of OrderBased labeling scheme in comparison with LSDX and Com-D labeling schemes. Finally, section 5 gives conclusion and a glimpse of future works.

2   Related Work

Labeling schemes can be defined as a systematic way of assigning values or labels to the nodes of an XML tree in order to speed up querying. The problem of finding a labeling scheme that generates concise, persistent labels, supporting updates without the need of relabeling, and ease of understanding and implementation dates back to 1982[3]. In the pursuit of solving the labeling scheme problem, a number of approaches have been proposed. These labeling approaches can be grouped in four major categories: Range based, Prefix based, Multiplication based and Vector based.

Range based labels for a node X has a general form of <start-position, end-position>, where start-position and end-position are numbers such that for all nodes Y in the sub tree of X, start_position(Y)> start-position(X) and end-position (Y) < end-position(X). The variations among range based labeling schemes are due to the definition of start-position and end-position. For instance, [3, 4 and 5] define the start-position as pre-order traversal of a tree. Traversal Order, Dynamic Range Based labeling schemes take the end-position as post traversal order of a tree, Extended Traversal Order [4] consider it as the size of the sub tree which is greater than or equal to the total number of nodes in the sub tree. On the other hand, SL (Sector based Labeling scheme) [27] defines the ranges as angles. The sectors are allocated to nodes in such a way that the angle formed by a parent's sector at the origin completely encloses that of all its children. Range based labeling schemes generally produce concise labels and are fast in determining ancestor descendant relationships; however, except for Sector Based labeling scheme, they do not provide sufficient information to determine parent-child and sibling-previous/following relationships. In addition, even the dynamic labeling schemes do not avoid relabeling completely, they only support updates to some extent.

In Prefix based labeling schemes, node X is an ancestor of node Y if the label of node X is the prefix of node Y. The main advantage of Prefix based labeling approach is that all structural relationships can be determined by just looking at the labels. The main critics about prefix based labeling schemes is its large storage requirement. Simple Prefix labeling scheme [6] and Dewey ID [7] are not efficient for dynamic document since insertion needs relabeling of nodes. ORDPATH [8] supports updates without relabeling by reserving even and negative integer. However, after the reserved spaces are used up, relabeling is unavoidable. LSDX – Labeling Scheme for Dynamic XML documents [9] is a fully dynamic prefix labeling scheme. Nonetheless, it generates huge sized labels and does not guarantee unique labels. Com-D – Compact Labeling Scheme [10] reasonably reduces the size of labels through compression. However, compression while labeling and decompression while querying dramatically degrades its efficiency. Whereas LSDX avoids relabeling after updates at the cost of storage, Com-D achieves reasonably small storage requirement at the cost of labeling and querying time.

Multiplicative labeling schemes use atomic numbers to identify nodes. Relationships between nodes can be computed, based on some arithmetic properties of the node labels. The main limitations of this approach lies in its expensive computation and large size. Hence, it is unsuitable for labeling a large-scale XML document. Prime Number labeling scheme [19] and Unique Identifier labeling scheme [16] are examples of a multiplication based labeling schemes.

The other groups of labeling scheme that are seen in literature are based on vector order. A vector code is a binary tuple of the form (x, y) where $x > 0$. Given two vector codes A: $(x1, y1)$ and B: $(x2, y2)$, vector a precedes vector B in vector order if and only if $\frac{x1}{y1} \leq \frac{x2}{y2}$. If we want to add a new vector C between vector A and B, the vector code of C is computed as $x1+x2$, $y1 +y2$).The vector order of A<B<C because $\frac{x1}{y1} \leq \frac{x1+x2}{y1+y2} \leq \frac{x2}{y2}$ holds true [17]. It is demonstrated that the vector based approach can be applied to both range based and prefix based labeling schemes [18]. DDE and CDDE are application of vector order approach to Dewey ID [24] whereas V-containment its application to range containment labeling scheme [24]. Vector based labeling schemes avoid relabeling in update intensive environment and can be applied to any other labeling schemes, however, there is always a computation overhead to determine relationship among nodes.

Recently it is common to see a hybrid labeling schemes which balances the weakness of one approach with the strength of another approach [25 and 26]. There are also labeling schemes that capitalize on the characteristics of data structures [22], or make use of the type information or DTD [21]. Moreover, Twig pattern matching algorithms has been researched for fast xml query processing [32, 33 and 34].

Generally, labeling schemes that generate small sized labels neither provide sufficient information to determine all structural relationships nor are efficient in a dynamic environment [3, 4 and 5]. On the other hand, labeling schemes that generate labels that provide enough structural relationship information and also support updates without relabeling either are large in size or are inefficient in query processing.

3   OrderBased Labeling Scheme

OrderBased labeling scheme presented in this paper is based on combination of letters and numbers. Each label contains level, order of the node in the level and the order of its parent. First part of the label is numeric and indicates the level information of a given node. The second part gives alphabetical order of the node relative to the left most node of the level. The last part is the order of the parent node. The order and the level information guarantee unique labels. The usage of characters enables it to generate a completely new order before and after the position of a given node, and also between two nodes without affecting existing order in case of insertions. For instance given two orders O1, and O2 where O1="abc" and O2= "bd", we can generate as many strings as we need which are between O1 and O2 in alphabetic order ("abcb", "abcd", "abce"..).

In OrderBased labeling scheme each label is a triple <level, order, parentorder>, where level is an integer that represents the distance of the node from the root node, order is a character that represents the level based horizontal distance of the node from the left most node at each level, parentorder is the parent's order of a given node .The level of the root node is 0, and the level of the children of the root node is 1. Likewise, the levels of other nodes can be computed as the distance of the node from the root node as seen in Fig 1.

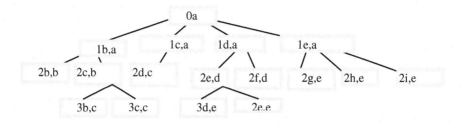

Fig. 1. OrderBased labeling scheme

An OrderBased label provides the information of the parent-child, and siblings-following/previous in a direct way, and ancestor-descendant relationships in recursive manner. For example in Fig 1, the node with label "1e, a" is the parent of the nodes with labels "2g, e", "2h,e", and "2i,e". This parent to child relationship is provided because the parent order of the three nodes is "e", and presumably their level is 1+1=2. Moreover, nodes that have the same level information and with the same parent order are siblings. However, to find the ancestors /descendants of a given node, first there is a need to move to the parent/children, and then the parent of the parent/children recursively till the intended level is reached.

3.1 Optimizing the Size

To address the problem of large storage size, OrderBased labeling scheme has a routine which optimizes the label size of every level. Small label sizes enhance query, update and labeling performances. Before labeling or making any insertions, the OrderBased labeling scheme computes the optimal number of characters needed to label the nodes at every level. To illustrate the need of optimizing the size, we will give a brief description of the size requirement in terms of number of characters.

Assume the total number of nodes at a given level is M. If we start labeling order of the first node in the level by 'b', the labeling continues with 'c', accordingly the orders of the 25th and 26th nodes will be 'z' and 'zb' respectively. Since there is a need of concatenating extra 'b' after reaching the letter 'z' in ever 26th node, the size of the order increases dramatically. If the total number of nodes at a given level M is not greater than 25, we can generate M unique one character length orders using alphabets from b to z. If M is between 26 and 50 inclusive, we use 25 single character alphabets and (M-25) double character length. For example If M= 10, 40, 66, and 90, then size requirement is then 1(10) =10, 1(25) + 2(40-25) =55, 1(25) + 2(25) + 3(66-50) = 123, and 1(25) +2(25) + 3(25) + 4(90-75) = 210 number of characters respectively.

The total size requirement for orders at a given level with a total number of nodes M can be generalized as,

$$25 * \sum_{i=1}^{w} i \ + \text{M mod } 25*(w+1) \tag{1}$$

where w=floor (M/25). In order to have an optimal size of orders, the OrderBased labeling first calculates the number of characters needed to label M number of nodes.

$$25^x = M$$

$$\log 25^x = \log M$$

$$X = Ceil(\frac{\log M}{\log 25})$$

The function Ceil returns the smallest integer that is greater than or equal to the given expression. For example, ceiling (1.45) =2, ceiling (9.8) =10.

By this approach the first child is labeled with X number of b's. For example if M is 625, X computed to be 2 , the order of the 1st ,2nd , 26th, 624th , and 625th is 'bb','bc','cb','zy', and 'zz' respectively. By this approach, the total size of orders for all nodes of a given level is

$$M * Ceil\left(\frac{\log M}{\log 25}\right) \tag{2}$$

Table 1. Analytical storage requirement

M	Optimized	Un- optimized
24	24	24
50	100	75
75	150	75
100	200	250
1000	3000	20500
2000	6000	81000
1000000	5000000	20000500000

Table 1 shows a comparison of the total number of characters needed to label the order of nodes using optimized and un-optimized approaches. For M<=25 both approaches need same storage requirement, while the number of nodes M is from 26 to 99, storage requirement for the un-optimized approaches is slightly smaller. Generally, for the number of nodes M>100, the storage requirement for the optimized approach is always smaller than the storage requirement of the un-optimized approach. The difference of the storage requirements for the two approaches considerably increases as the number of nodes M increases. This makes the optimized approach to be preferred to the un-optimized approach.

In OrderBased labeling scheme, optimizing the size is a prior operation before labeling and inserting a sub tree. The Determine-size routine seen in Fig 2, takes the XML tree to be labeled or inserted as input computes the number of nodes at every level, then returns a string array.

For example , if a given XML document has 500, 3000, 9000 , 1000000, and 2000000 number of nodes at 1st, 2nd ,3rd, 4th and 5th level respectively, the above routine returns Y, where Y[1]='bb', Y[2]='bbb', Y[3]='bbb', Y[4]='bbbbb', and Y[5]=' bbbbb'.

Determine-size (XML tree)
{

        String array Y[height of tree]
        Integer array X[height of tree]
        Determine the total number of nodes per each level
        Put them into an integer array X
        for (i=0 to height of tree)
        {

$$X[i] = Ceil(\frac{\log X[i]}{\log 25})$$

        Y[i]=concatenate X[i] number of 'b'

        }
        Return Y

}

Fig. 2. Determine-size routine

3.2   Generating the Order of a Node

Rule 1

Label the order nodes of a given level starting by the concatenation of b's returned by the Determine-size routine. For the second, third, and forth node, increment the last character to 'c','d', and 'e' respectively. Accordingly for the rest of the nodes, increment the orders alphabetically.

For example if 'bbb' is the string returned for a given level, the order of the 1st, 2nd , 25th , 26th , an 15625th node are labeled as 'bbb', 'bbc',' bbz', 'bcb',and 'zzz' respectively.

3.3   Generating Orders for New Inserted Nodes

Rule 2

To insert a node before the first node of a given level, get the order of the node then count down to the preceding alphabet, if all characters are "b", insert "a" before the last "b".

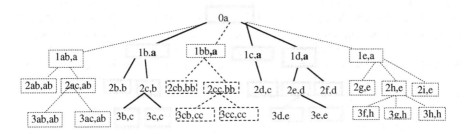

Fig. 3. Sub tree insertion before the first node of a given level, between two nodes and after the last node of a given level

Fig 3 shows how insertion before the first node of a given level is handled by Order-Based labeling scheme. Here Rule 2 is applied to insert a node before "1b,a". Because there is no node before it we add 'a' before 'b' then we will have "1ab,a". At the second level, there are two nodes to be inserted before "2b,b". Thus, applying Rule 2, the labels of the inserted nodes will be "2,ab,ab", and "2aab,ab". Similarly, the labels of the two nodes at level 3 will be "3ab,ab" and "3aab,ab". Insertions before the first node of a given level can be handled by applying Rule 2 without the need of relabeling.

Rule 3
To insert a node between two nodes, keep counting from the code standing before it so that the code for the new node will be greater than the code of its previous sibling and less than the code of its next sibling.

It can be seen from Fig 3 that, insertion between two nodes can be made without affecting the order of the existing nodes. Applying Rule 3 at the first level a unique label "1bb,a" is generated between "1b,a" and "1c,a". Likewise at level 3 and level "2cb,bb" , "2cc,bb", and "3cb,cc", "3cc,cc" respectively are unique labels generated between two nodes without the need or relabeling.

Rule 4
To insert a node after the last node of a level, increment the order of the last order alphabetically.

Fig 3 shows how insertion after the left most node of a tree is handled. Rule 4 states that insertion after the last node of a given node is handled by incrementing the order of the last node alphabetically. That is after "1d,a" is "1e,a", likewise, "2g,e" , "2h,e" and "3f,k","3g,k' are after "2i,h" and "3e,e" respectively.

Fig 3 demonstrates that inserting a sub tree at any arbitrary position does not need any relabeling of nodes. Rules 2, 3 and 4 guarantee unique labels are given to the newly inserted nodes or sub tree with regardless of the point of insertion. OrderBased labeling scheme is persistent in that it insures a uniqueness of labels in a dynamic environment.

4   Performance Evaluation

In this performance evaluation part of the study, OrderBased labeling scheme is compared with the LSDX and Com-D (Compressed LSDX) labeling schemes. These labeling schemes are chosen because they share main feature and design goals. Using combinations of letter and numbers, including the level information of a node in every label, and avoiding relabeling when update occurs are the common feature and design goals of the three schemes. Moreover, because three of them contain the information about the label of the parent node, they can be grouped under prefix based labeling scheme.

There are four sets of tests in this performance evaluation: the first set compares the storage requirement of three schemes. The second set analyzes labeling time. The third set examines the query performance and the last set investigates update performance.

4.1   Experimental Setting

The performance evaluation is conducted on an Intel(R) Core™2Duo CPU E8400 @3GHz.27 GHz and 2.00 GB of RAM Windows 7 Professional computer. All schemes are implemented using Visual Basic .net 2010. So as to avoid discrepancy, each querying and labeling time performance test is run 5 times and the average is taken.

A B+ tree is used to store the labels. In the non-leaf nodes of the B+ tree, only labels are stored. In addition to labels, the leaf nodes contain the name of nodes of the XML tree or attributes with their corresponding values [15 and 22].

4.2   Characteristics of Datasets

The datasets used in this performance evaluation are generated using xmlgen of the XMark: Benchmark Standard for XML Database Management [11]. The xmlgen produces XML documents modeling an auction website, a typical e-commerce application. It generates a well-formed, valid and meaningful XML data. Xmlgen is well known for its efficient and scalable generation of XML documents of several GBs.

Number and type of elements are chosen according to a template and parameterized with certain probability distributions. The words for text paragraphs are taken from Shakespeare's plays. The generator is deliberately designed to have only a single parameter: factor. The factor parameter determines the size of the document generated. It accepts float number from 0 to any number. Zero value for the factor generates the minimum document.

Table 2. Characteristics of datasets

Da-taset	Factor	Size(MB)	No of Nodes	Max Fan-out
D05	0.5	56.2	832911	12750
D06	0.6	68.2	1003441	15300
D07	0.7	79.7	1172640	17850
D08	0.8	90.7	1337383	20400
D09	0.9	102	1504685	22950
D10	1.0	113	1666315	25500

By giving values from 0.5 to 1.0 to the factor parameter of the xmlgen, six datasets with size of 56.2 to 113 MB, with number of nodes ranging from 832,911 to 1666315 and maximum fan-out starting 12750 to 25,500 are generated. The characteristics of the datasets are seen in Table 2.

4.3   Storage Requirement

In this performance evaluation test set, the storage requirement for the three schemes is studied. For the six datasets introduced in the previous section, the sizes of labels in MB are shown in Fig 4.

The storage requirement of LSDX labels is the largest as compared to the rest of the two. This resulted from the fact that LSDX label size depends on fan-outs and the height of the tree. To illustrate: for the first 25 children the size of a LSDX label is 25 characters (letter b to z) plus the label of the all its ancestors. Since after every 25th children we reach at letter z, there is a need to concatenate b. This makes the label size to increase by one character. The storage requirement for LSDX labels depend on the fan-outs and the height of the tree (since each label contains the label of its ancestor nodes). The more the number of fan-outs and the taller the tree, the larger is the label size.

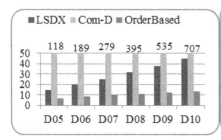   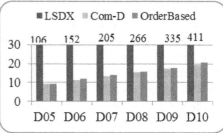

Fig. 4. Storage requirement(MB)   **Fig. 5.** Labeling time(seconds)

Com-D is a compressed version of LSDX. The compression is done by counting the number of times a letter is consecutively repeated. For example if the LSDX label of an XML node is abzzzzzzrr.dd, its equivalent Com-D label is ab6z2r.2d [10].

As it can be seen from Fig 6, for all the datasets used in this performance analysis, Com-D needs the least storage requirement. Com-D label size is from 91% to 95% smaller than LSDX label size. The figure also demonstrates that the storage requirement for OrderBased labels is from 91.11% to 94.94 % smaller than the storage requirement of LSDX labels. For dataset D05, OrderBased label size is the same as that of Com-D. However, for the rest of the datasets, the storage requirements are from 2.4% to 7.7% greater than the label size of Com-D.

Collision is one of the drawbacks of the LSDX and Com-D labeling scheme. For every dataset used in this performance evaluation, the two schemes give the same label for more than one XML nodes. Table 3 demonstrates the number of collisions detected while labeling using the LSDX and Com-D labeling schemes. For this reason, both LSDX and Com-D are impractical.

Table 3. Number of collisions detected

	D05	D06	D07	D08	D09	D10
Collision	57	43	34	13	30	86

In OrderBased labeling scheme, there is no collision. It avoids collision by keeping a global level based horizontal order and parent order. Both LSDX and Com-D are impractical due to the existence of collision. OrderBased is superior to the two labeling schemes for its persistence and optimal storage requirement.

4.4   Labeling Time

In this sub section, the time required to label a given XML document is studied. The time required for labeling that is seen on Fig 5 above is the average labeling time taken from five tests done on each dataset. The labels are generated by a depth first traversal for the three labeling schemes.

Fig 5 stipulates that for all the six datasets, LSDX is at 7.99 to 15.74 times faster than Com-D. With regard to labeling time, OrderBased labeling scheme is approximately 2.2 to 3.9 and 17.28 to 51.8 times faster than LSDX and Com-D labeling schemes respectively.

The labeling time performance hit of OrderBased over LSDX is due to LSDX's larger label size (Fig 4: the total label size of LSDX is more than 100 to 400 times larger than the total label size of OrderBased). Even though Com-D labels need the minimum storage requirement, it takes the longest labeling time. This decrease in labeling performance results from compression overhead.

The labeling time test set shows that OrderBased labeling scheme takes the least labeling time compared to LSDX and Com-D labeling schemes. This labeling time performance hit of OrderBased is because of the optimal label size. From this result it can be concluded that compression degrades labeling time performance more than large label size does.

4.5   Query

In this performance evaluation part, a query which returns all descendants of the root node is run. Finding descendant of a given node depends on the time required for Parent-Child, and Sibling-Order queries.

Given an ancestor finding its descendants is one of the structural queries found in XML querying. These types of queries are usually seen in XPath statements. The query for retrieving all descendant of a root node is equivalent to the XPath expression Site/*(since the root node of the data sets used in this performance evaluation is site).

For a reasonably small size and small number of nodes of a given XML data set, LSDX and OrderBased take nearly the same time. However, OrderBased executes faster as the data size and the number of nodes increase. In addition, both LSDX and OrderBased labeling scheme are incomparably faster than Com-D. This performance variation comes from decompressing overhead for Com-D. Com-D querying involves decompressing of each label. It can be seen from Fig 6 that decompressing degrades query performance than label size does.

OrderBased labeling scheme is superior to LSDX and Com-D with respect to querying time. Such a performance hit is due to its optimized size of labels.

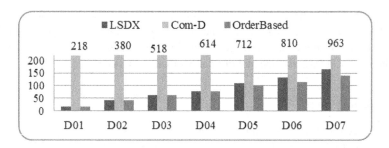

Fig. 6. Time required for retrieving all descendants of a given node

4.6   Updates

In this update performance evaluation of the study, the time needed to insert a sub tree, and delete a sub tree for the three schemes is analyzed. The most profound problem with most XML labeling schemes is that they are designed with an assumption of static document. Whenever a deletion or an insertion is done on the XML document, relabeling of all or part of the XML tree is inevitable. However, in real world applications, updating an XML document is an important and necessary operation.

Inserting a Sub Tree
In this performance evaluation part of the study, the time to insert a sub tree which is an XML by itself is seen. For this study, an XML dataset D01 of 11.3 MB is generated by giving 0.01 to the factor parameter of the xmlgen generator. Inserting D01 at different part of the XML tree produces same time. Thus, for convenience for all the datasets the D01 is inserted as the child of the root node.

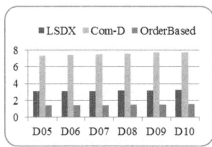

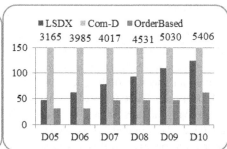

Fig. 7. Insertion time (sec)   **Fig. 8.** Deletion time (ms)

Fig 7 shows that the time of insertion of DO1 to the six datasets is nearly constant irrespective of their size. Moreover, insertion time mainly depends on the size of the inserted sub tree.

Com-D takes more than two times and four times longer time than that of LSDX and OrderBased labeling schemes. These performances degrade is resulted from the time needed for compression, since all labels have to be compressed. Fig 7 illustrates that OrderBased is superior to the rest of the schemes with respect to insertion time in that it is twice faster than LSDX and four times faster than Com-D. OrderBased insertion time performance hit is due to its reasonable small size.

Deleting a Sub Tree
In this part of the performance evaluation, the time needed to delete a sub tree is studied. All the three schemes avoid relabeling after deletion. The spaces and the labels deleted can be used for future insertions.

For the B+ tree used to store the labels of XML tree nodes, a mechanism of lazy deletion is employed. Lazy deletion does not rebalance the B+ tree on deletion. Avoiding rebalancing on deletion has been justified empirically [12, 13 and 14].

Delete site/closed_auctions: delete the node with name closed_auctions.

Fig 8 depicts that Com-D takes the longest time to delete in all the six datasets. This is because decompressing is necessary to determine whether the nodes are descendants of the deleted node. OrderBased labeling scheme deletion is 1.5 to 2.33 faster than LSDX.

4.7   Discussion on Results

In this performance evaluation study we have seen the storage requirement, labeling time, querying time, insertion time and deletion time for OrderBased, LSDX, and Com-D labeling schemes.

The first test set for storage requirement, LSDX labels need the largest storage requirement .Com-D labels need the least space. The storage requirement for Order-Based labels is nearly as good as the storage requirement for Com-D labels (2.34% to 7.7% greater than Com-D).

The second test set for labeling time requirement shows that OrderBased needs the least labeling time whereas Com-D takes the longest labeling time because of compression overhead. From this result it can be concluded that the larger the label size, the faster the labeling is. On the other hand, the compression reduces the label size; it degrades labeling time more than large label size does.

For querying performance, for small data sets, it seems LSDX and OrderBased take equal time. However, as the data size increases, it becomes clear that Order-Based needs the least time. Com-D has the least performance because of the need of decompression.

In the fourth test, update performance (insertion and deletion) time requirement is studied. With regard to insertion, OrderBased needs the least time. Again Com-D needs the longest time because of compression overhead. For deletion time requirement test, OrderBased needs the least time.

5   Conclusion

This paper pointed out the challenges of dynamic labeling scheme for XML documents. Large storage requirement, inefficient labeling or querying time and complexity are challenges of dynamic labeling schemes. To address these problems, a fully dynamic labeling scheme called OrderBased labeling scheme is proposed. Performance evaluation studies show that OrderBased labeling scheme outperforms LSDX and Com-D with respect to labeling time, query performance, and update performance. It is also shown that the total label size for OrderBased labels from 91.1% to 91.95% smaller than label size of LSDX. Even though OrderBased label size is from 2.4% to 7.1% greater than that of Com-D, its efficient querying, labeling and update performance makes it preferable.

References

1. Boag, S., Chamberlin, D., Fernandez, M.F., Florescu, D., Robie, J., Simeon, J.: XQuery 1.0: An XML Query Language. W3C working draft (2001)
2. Clarke, J., DeRose, S.: XML Path Language (XPath) version 1.0. W3C Recommendation (1999)
3. Diets, P.F.: Maintaining Order in a Linked Lists. In: Proceedings of the ACM Symposium on Theory of Computing (1982)
4. Li, Q., Moon, B.: Indexing and Querying XML Data for Regular Path Expressions. In: Proceedings of the VLDB (2001)
5. Yun, J.H., Chung, C.-W.: Dynamic Interval-based Labeling Scheme for Efficient XML Query and Update Processing. The Journal of Systems and Software (2008)
6. Cohen, E., Kaplan, H., Milo, T.: Labeling Dynamic XML Trees. In: Proceedings of the ACM SIGMOD- SIGACT- SiGART (2002)
7. Tatarinov, I., Viglas, S., Beyer, K., Shanmugasundaram, J., Shekita, E., Zhang, C.: Storing and Querying Ordered XML Using a Relational Database System. In: Proceedings of ACM SIGMOD (2002)
8. ONeil, P.E., et al.: ORDPATHs: Insert-Friendly XML Node Labels. In: Proceedings of the ACM SIGMOD (2004)
9. Duong, M., Zhang, Y.: LSDX: New Labeling Scheme for Dynamically Updating XML Data. In: Proceedings of 16th Australian Database Conference (2005)
10. Duong, M., Zhang, Y.: Dynamic Labelling Scheme for XML Data Processing. In: Meersman, R., Tari, Z. (eds.) OTM 2008. LNCS, vol. 5332, pp. 1183–1199. Springer, Heidelberg (2008)
11. Schmidt, A., Waas, F., Kersten, M., Carey, J., Manolescu, I., Busse, R.: XMark: A Benchmark for XML Data Management. In: Proceedings of VLDB (2002)
12. Gray, J., Reuter, A.: Transaction Processing: Concepts and Techniques. Morgan Kaufmann (1993)
13. Mohan, C., Levine, F.: ARIES/IM, An Efficient and High Concurrency Index Management Method Using Write-Ahead Logging. SIGMOD Record 21(2), 371–380 (1992)
14. Olson, M.A., Bostic, K., Seltzer, M.I.: Berkeley DB. In: USENIX Annual, FREENIX Track, pp. 183–191 (1999)
15. Ying, L., Jun, M., Yuyin, S.: Applying Dewey Encoding to Construct XML Index of Path and Keyword Query. In: Proceedings of IEEE First International Workshop on Database Technology and Applications (2009)
16. Kha, D.D., Yoshikawa, M., Uemura, S.: A Structural Numbering Scheme for XML Data. In: Chaudhri, A.B., Unland, R., Djeraba, C., Lindner, W. (eds.) EDBT 2002. LNCS, vol. 2490, pp. 91–108. Springer, Heidelberg (2002)

17. Xu, L., Bao, Z., Ling, T.-W.: A Dynamic Labeling Scheme Using Vectors. In: Wagner, R., Revell, N., Pernul, G. (eds.) DEXA 2007. LNCS, vol. 4653, pp. 130–140. Springer, Heidelberg (2007)
18. Xu, L., Ling, T.W., Wu, H.: Labeling dynamic XML Documents: An Order-centric Approach. IEEE Transactions on Knowledge and Data Engineering (2012)
19. Wu, X., Lee, M.L., Hsu, W.: A Prime Number Labeling Scheme for Dynamic Ordered XML Trees. In: Proceedings of the 20th Int. Conference on Data Engineering (2004)
20. Gabillon, A., Fansi, M.: A Persistent Labeling Scheme for XML and tree Database. In: Proceedings of ACI (2006)
21. Damien, K., Franky, F., William, L., Shui, M., Wong, R.K.: Dynamic Labeling Schemes for Ordered XML Based on Type Information. In: Seventeenth Australasian Database Conference Technology, vol. 49 (2006)
22. Silberstein, A., et al.: BOXes: Efficient Maintenance of Order-Based Labeling for Dynamic XML Data. In: Proceedings of International Conference on Data Engineering (ICDE). IEEE CS Press (2005)
23. Thonangi, R.: A Concise Labeling Scheme for XML Data. In: International Conference on Management of Data, COMAD 2006, Delhi, India (2006)
24. Xu, L., Ling, T.W., Wu, H., Bao, Z.: DDE: From Dewey to a Fully Dynamic XML Labeling Scheme. In: Proceedings of the 35th SIGMOD International Conference on Management of Data, Providence, Rhode Island, USA, June 29-July 02 (2009)
25. Yun, J.H., Chung, C.W.: Dynamic Interval-Based labeling Scheme for Efficient XML Query and Update Processing. Journal of Systms and Sofware 81, 56–70 (2008)
26. Haw, S.C., Lee, C.S.: Extending Path Summary and Region Encoding for Efficient Structural Query Processing in Native XML Databases. Journal of Systems and Software (2009)
27. Fomichev, A., Grinev, M., Kuznetsov, S.: Sedna: A Native XML DBMS. In: Wiedermann, J., Tel, G., Pokorný, J., Bieliková, M., Štuller, J. (eds.) SOFSEM 2006. LNCS, vol. 3831, pp. 272–281. Springer, Heidelberg (2006)
28. Jagadish, H.V., Al-Khalifa, S., Chapman, A., Lakshmanan, L.V.S., Nierman, A., Paparizos, S., Patel, J.M., Srivastava, D., Wiwatwattana, N., Wu, Y., Yu, C.: TIMBER: A Native XML Database. The VLDB Journal (December 2002)
29. Pal, S., Cseri, I., Seeliger, O., Rys, M., Schaller, G., Yu, W., Tomic, D., Baras, A., Brandon, B., Denis, C., Eugene, K.: XQuery Implementation in a Relational Database system. In: Proceedings of the 31st International Conference on VLDB (2005)
30. Nicola, M., Linden, V.D.: Native XML Support in DB2 Universal Database. In: Proceedings of the 31st International Conference on VLDB (2005)
31. Guangjun, X., Cheng, Q., Jarek, G., Calisto, Z.: Some Rewrite Optimizations of DB2 XQuery Navigation. In: CIKM 2008 (2008)
32. Lu, J., Ling, T.-W., Yu, T., Li, C., Ni, W.: Efficient Processing of Ordered XML Twig Pattern. In: Andersen, K.V., Debenham, J., Wagner, R. (eds.) DEXA 2005. LNCS, vol. 3588, pp. 300–309. Springer, Heidelberg (2005)
33. Jiang, Z., Luo, C., Hou, W.-C., Zhu, Q., Che, D.: Efficient Processing of XML Twig Pattern: A Novel One-Phase Holistic Solution. In: Wagner, R., Revell, N., Pernul, G. (eds.) DEXA 2007. LNCS, vol. 4653, pp. 87–97. Springer, Heidelberg (2007)
34. Li, J., Wang, J.: Fast Matching of Twig Patterns. In: Bhowmick, S.S., Küng, J., Wagner, R. (eds.) DEXA 2008. LNCS, vol. 5181, pp. 523–536. Springer, Heidelberg (2008)

A 16-Intersection Matrix
for the Polygon-Polyline Topological Relation
for Geographic Pictorial Query Languages

Anna Formica, Mauro Mazzei, Elaheh Pourabbas, and Maurizio Rafanelli

National Research Council
Instituto di Analisi dei Sistemi ed Informatica "Antonio Ruberti"
Viale Manzoni 30, I-00185, Rome, Italy
{anna.formica,mauro.mazzei,elaheh.pourabbas,
maurizio.rafanelli}@iasi.cnr.it

Abstract. In this paper we address the problem of formalizing qualitative topological relationships between geographical objects in a Geographical Pictorial Query Language (GeoPQL) in order to completely
capture the semantics of the user queries. We focus on the polygon-
polyline topological relation and we define a 16-intersection matrix that
has been conceived to enhance and distinguish the semantics of cells'
content with respect to the well-known 9-intersection matrix. On the basis of such distinctions, we revise the geographic operators of GeoPQL
and we give their formal semantics. In order to implement our proposed
16-matrix, we invoked in GeoPQL the open source Java libraries JTS
Topology Suite, which conforms to the Simple Features Specification for
SQL published by the Open GIS Consortium-OGC. Finally, the proposed
16-intersection matrix is illustrated through some query examples.

Keywords: Pictorial query languages, topological relationships, intersection matrix.

1 Introduction

Human knowledge about spatial world is necessarily approximate, and *spatial
reasoning* is an area where humans consistently reason approximately with good
results [11]. Approximate qualitative spatial reasoning is a research area that
has been conceived to represent commonsense reasoning and to incorporate such
reasoning techniques in computer systems [16]. In particular, this research area
deals with the development of techniques and tools for reasoning with non-
metrical and incompletely specified spatial knowledge [6]. In this context, most
studies focused on fundamental aspects of space such as topology, orientation,
size, and shape. These topics have been extensively investigated since more than
one decade both at a mathematical level [7], and within Geographic Information
Systems (GIS) [20] [22] [23] [27]. The remarkable amount of studies in these
directions aimed at including qualitative reasoning methods in standard GISs in
order to overcome the key limitations of these systems which are entirely based

G. Quirchmayr et al. (Eds.): CD-ARES 2012, LNCS 7465, pp. 302–316, 2012.
© IFIP International Federation for Information Processing 2012

on numerical methods [6] [21]. Indeed, numerical approaches for representing and reasoning on spatial information are ineffective to process imprecise or uncertain data [30]. For this reason, advanced GISs must provide an effective and accessible query system to appropriately capture a user's desired search criteria and a user's mental query model [17] [18]. Specifically, the user's query mental model is the user's perception regarding the semantics of the query in his/her mind.

In general, geographic queries can be better expressed by using graphical metaphors in query languages. They are powerful to express the user's query mental model [24], and to exploit the semantics of data models in order to facilitate query formulation. In the field of spatial databases many authors studied the way to formulate queries using graphical configurations, and to embed them into query languages, for instance [18] [28]. In particular, in [18] the authors proposed a pictorial query language, called *Geographical Pictorial Query Language* (GeoPQL), to address the user's query mental model and to answer to his/her queries. They defined a set of Symbolic Graphical Objects (SGOs) to graphically represent the spatial configurations of geographic entities (i.e., *point, polyline,* and *polygon*), the spatial relationships of pairs of SGOs, as well as the spatial operators based on an Object-Calculus. In this paper, we refer to GeoPQL. Indeed, the formalization of qualitative topological relationships between spatial objects is one of the main topics in the representation and manipulation of spatial data. In order to characterize such topological relationships, the well-known 9-Intersection matrix is extensively used [12].

Suppose the user wants to find all the Italian regions which are passed through by a river. This query can be graphically represented in the GeoPQL working area, for instance, by means of one of the pictorial queries shown in Figures 1 and 2, where regions and rivers are represented by polygons and polylines, respectively. With respect to the pictorial query shown in Figure 1, the one given in Figure 2 also requires that an internal part of the river is on the boundary of (touches) the region. The 9-Intersection matrices related to these figures differ for only one value, i.e., in correspondence to the intersection between the boundary of the polygon and the interior of the polyline. In particular, according to the standard notation in the OGC environment [3], in the case of Figure 1, it is 0, meaning that the dimension of the intersection is a point, whereas in the case of Figure 2, it is 1 meaning that this dimension is a line.

However, often the abstractions of spatial relationships defined in the literature cannot efficiently capture the variety of semantics associated with the user queries. For instance, in the case of Figure 2, the intersection between the boundary of the polygon and the interior of the polyline consists of three points and one line. This level of detail can not be incorporated in a unique 9-intersection matrix. For this reason, in [9], [10], three different 9-intersection matrices, representing point, polyline, and polygon intersection results, respectively, have been introduced.

In this paper, we focus on this problem and we propose a 16-intersection matrix, which is the main contribution of this paper, which enables us to embed in a unique matrix the point, polyline, and polygon intersection results. Essentially

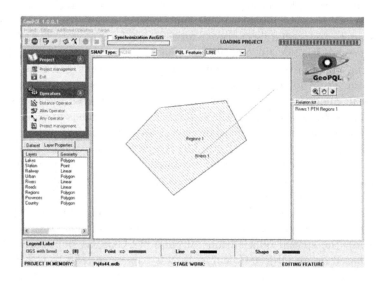

Fig. 1. A pictorial representation of a pass through relationship in GeoPQL

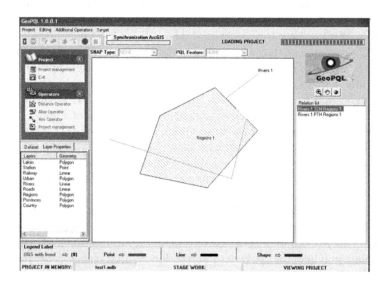

Fig. 2. A pictorial representation of pass through and touch relationships in GeoPQL

in our proposed matrix, we enhance the semantics of the interior and boundary of a polyline and a polygon, respectively. Specifically, the interior of a polyline is decomposed into *isolated single interior points* $(\mathcal{L}_{i_p})$ and *interior lines* $\mathcal{L}_{i_l}$. Similarly, the boundary of a polygon is decomposed into *isolated single boundary points* $(\mathcal{P}_{b_p})$ and *boundary lines* $(\mathcal{P}_{b_l})$. In particular, with respect to the well-known matrices proposed in the literature where for each cell only null or non-null intersections are given, the 16-intersection matrix provides, for a given topological relationship, the number of connected components that are in the intersection of the pair of SGOs. On the basis of such distinctions, we revise the geographic operators of GeoPQL and we give their formal semantics. These formalizations allow us not only to precisely distinguish each operator but also to define *composite* operators that correspond to the combination of different topological relationships. For instance, in both the aforementioned figures, the geo-operator corresponding to the topological relationship is "pass-through" but, in the case of Figure 2, it is also combined with the "touch" operator. In order to implement our proposal, we invoked in GeoPQL the open source Java libraries JTS Topology Suite [4], which conforms to the Simple Features Specification for SQL published by the Open GIS Consortium-OGC.

The paper is structured as follows. In Section 2, the GeoPQL operators are revised. In Section 3, the 16-intersection matrix is formally defined and some examples are given in order to clarify it from a graphical point of view. In the same section, a query example is provided in order to show our proposal. In Section 4, we illustrate the implemented 16-intersection matrix in GeoPQL. In Section 5 the related work follows, and in Section 6 the conclusion is given.

2   Revised GeoPQL Operators

In this paper, among the possible geographical pictorial languages proposed in the literature, we focus on GeoPQL [18]. Below, we start by recalling the notion of Symbolic Geographical Objects (SGOs).

Definition 21 [SGO]. *Given a Geographic Information System, a Symbolic Geographical Object (SGO) is a 5-tuple* $\psi = \langle id, geometric\_type, objclass, \Sigma, \Lambda \rangle$ *where:*

- *id is the SGO identifier assigned by the system to uniquely identify the SGO in a query;*
- *geometric_type can be a point, a polyline or a polygon;*
- *objclass is the geographical concept name belonging to the database schema and iconized by the SGO, identifying a geographical class (set of instances) of the database;*
- Σ *represents the set of typed attributes of the SGO which can be associated with a set of values by the user;*
- Λ *is an ordered set of pairs of coordinates, which defines the spatial extent, and position of the SGO with respect to the coordinate reference system of the working area.*

The GeoPQL algebra consists of 12 binary geo-operators, which are *logical* (Geo-union (UNI), Geo-any (ANY), Geo-alias (ALS)), *metrical* (Geo-difference (DIF), and Geo-distance (DIS)), and *topological* (Geo-disjunction (DSJ), Geo-touching (TCH), Geo-inclusion (INC)[1], Geo-crossing (CRS), Geo-pass-through (PTH), Geo-overlapping (OVL), Geo-equality (EQL)). Our focus is on the polygon-polyline relation, therefore in this paper we will consider a subset of the topological operators, namely, disjoint (DSJ), inclusion (INC), touch (TCH), and pass through (PTH). Indeed, the remaining operators are not considered because in the case of the polygon-polyline relation they are not applicable (see for instance CRS which is defined between two polylines, OVL which is defined between two polygons, or EQL which is defined for two polylines or two polygons).

The formal semantics of the above mentioned operators is formally given in the Definition 22 below. Before introducing it, we have to present the notation we use in our approach, which differs from the one usually adopted in the literature as explained below.

Given a polygon $\mathcal{P}$ and a polyline $\mathcal{L}$, in our approach, $\mathcal{P}_i$, $\mathcal{P}_{b_p}$, $\mathcal{P}_{b_l}$, $\mathcal{P}_e$ denote the interior, single boundary points, boundary lines and exterior of the polygon $\mathcal{P}$, respectively, and $\mathcal{L}_{i_p}$, $\mathcal{L}_{i_l}$, $\mathcal{L}_b$, $\mathcal{L}_e$, denote single interior points, interior lines, boundary points (or end points) and exterior of the polyline $\mathcal{L}$.

With respect to the existing literature, where there is no distinction between isolated single boundary points and boundary lines of a polygon, and between isolated single interior points and interior lines of a polyline, in our approach the different notations, namely $\mathcal{P}_{b_p}$, $\mathcal{P}_{b_l}$ for a polygon, and $\mathcal{L}_{i_p}$, $\mathcal{L}_{i_l}$ for a polyline, are respectively introduced. They allow us to distinguish different configurations, as for instance the ones shown in Figure 3, where the intersection between a polygon and a polyline consists of one isolated point, case (a), or a line, case (b). These configurations correspond to two different pictorial queries that the user can draw to represent the TCH geo-operator but they have different computational models, as we will see in the next section.

(a)   (b)

Fig. 3. Boundary point vs boundary line intersections

---

[1] Note that in our approach the operators *cover* and *covered-by*, extensively used in the literature, can be represented by using the INC geo-operator.

For the sake of simplicity, in the rest of this paper we will consider the *geometric_type* component of a SGO. In particular, due to the focus of our paper, we will concentrate on the *polygon* and *polyline* geometric types.

Definition 22 [Geo-operators]. *Let $\mathcal{SGO}$ be the set of all possible SGOs. Given a polygon $\mathcal{P}$, and a polyline $\mathcal{L}$ both in $\mathcal{SGO}$, the binary geo-operations DSJ, INC, TCH, and PTH are formally defined as follows, where $k \in \{i, b_p, b_l, e\}$, and $j \in \{i_p, i_l, b, e\}$:*

- *DSJ (geo-disjunction):*
  $\mathcal{P}$ *DSJ* $\mathcal{L}$ *iff* $\mathcal{P}_k \cap \mathcal{L}_j = \emptyset$ $j, k \neq e$
- *INC (geo-inclusion):*
  $\mathcal{P}$ *INC* $\mathcal{L}$ *iff* $\mathcal{P}_k \cap \mathcal{L}_j = \mathcal{L}_j$, $k = i, j = i_p$
- *TCH (geo-touching):*
  assume $S = \mathcal{L}_j \cap \mathcal{P}_k \neq \emptyset$ *where* $j \neq e$ *and* $k = b_l, b_p$. $\mathcal{P}$ *TCH* $\mathcal{L}$ *iff* $\forall x \in S$, *and* $\forall I(x)$, *where* $I(x)$ *is a neighborhood of* x, *the following holds:*
  $I(x) \cap \mathcal{L}_j \cap \mathcal{P}_e = \emptyset$ *or* $I(x) \cap \mathcal{L}_j \cap \mathcal{P}_i = \emptyset$, $j \neq e$.
- *PTH (geo-pass-through):*
  $\mathcal{P}$ *PTH* $\mathcal{L}$ *iff* $\mathcal{P}_k \cap \mathcal{L}_{i_l} \neq \emptyset$, $k = i, e$.

According to the definition above, for instance, both the configurations given in Figure 3 correspond to the TCH operator, where in the case (a) one single interior point of the polyline is in common to the boundary of the polygon, and in case (b) one interior line of the polyline is in common to the boundary of the polygon. Note that, in the case (b) we assume that the number of isolated single points which are in common between the boundary of the polygon and the polyline is zero.

In our approach, it is possible to have pictorial queries by combining two geo-operators, i.e., TCH + PTH, and TCH + INC. In such cases, the semantics of the *composite* geo-operators requires that the above definition holds for both the involved geo-operators.

3   The 16-Intersection Matrix

In this section we introduce the *16-intersection calculi* matrix (*16-intersection matrix* for short) which is on the basis of our approach. The 16-intersection matrix differs from the classical 9-intersection matrix for two main reasons. First, it extends the 9-intersection matrix by introducing the distinction between isolated single boundary points ($\mathcal{P}_{b_p}$) and boundary lines ($\mathcal{P}_{b_l}$) of the polygon, as well as the distinction between isolated single interior points ($\mathcal{L}_{i_p}$) and interior lines ($\mathcal{L}_{i_l}$) of the polyline. Second, each cell in the matrix contains a number providing additional information with respect to the 9-intersection matrix, corresponding to the number of connected components that are in the intersection between the pair of SGOs. Below, the formal definition of the 16-intersection matrix is given.

Definition 31 [16-intersection matrix]. *Given a polygon $\mathcal{P} \in \mathcal{SGO}$, and a polyline $\mathcal{L} \in \mathcal{SGO}$, the 16-intersection matrix is defined by the following 4x4 matrix:*

$$
\begin{array}{c}
\begin{array}{cccc} \mathcal{P}_i & \mathcal{P}_{b_p} & \mathcal{P}_{b_l} & \mathcal{P}_e \end{array} \\
\begin{array}{c} \mathcal{L}_{i_p} \\ \mathcal{L}_{i_l} \\ \mathcal{L}_b \\ \mathcal{L}_e \end{array}
\left(
\begin{array}{cccc}
- & 0\ldots n & - & - \\
0\ldots n & - & 0\ldots n & 0\ldots n \\
0,1,2 & 0,1,2 & - & 0,1,2 \\
1\ldots n & - & 1\ldots n & 1\ldots n
\end{array}
\right)
\end{array}
$$

where each element $(\mathcal{L}_j, \mathcal{P}_k)$, $j \in \{i_p, i_l, b, e\}$ and $k \in \{i, b_p, b_l, e\}$ is defined as follows:

$$
(\mathcal{L}_j, \mathcal{P}_k) = \begin{cases} |\,I\,| & (j = i_p, k = b_p), (j = b, k \neq b_l) \\ |\,C\,| & (j = e, i_l,\ k \neq b_p) \\ - & incomparable \end{cases}
$$

and:

- I is the set of isolated single points in $\mathcal{L}_j \cap \mathcal{P}_k$;
- C is the set of connected components in $\mathcal{L}_j \cap \mathcal{P}_k$.

Note that, since the end points of a polyline are two, in any 16-intersection matrix the sum of the numbers in the third row is always equal to two.

For instance, the element $(\mathcal{L}_e, \mathcal{P}_i)$ of the matrix above denotes the number of connected components (polygons) contained in the intersection between the interior points of the polygon and the external points of the polyline. Similarly, the element $(\mathcal{L}_{i_p}, \mathcal{P}_{b_p})$ denotes the number of isolated single points contained in the intersection between single interior points of the polyline and single boundary points of the polygon.

In six cases the elements of the matrix are incomparable. In fact, in three cases, namely $(\mathcal{L}_{i_p}, \mathcal{P}_{b_l})$, $(\mathcal{L}_{i_l}, \mathcal{P}_{b_p})$, $(\mathcal{L}_b, \mathcal{P}_{b_l})$, the comparison is performed between isolated single points and lines, and in the other three cases, namely $(\mathcal{L}_{i_p}, \mathcal{P}_i)$, $(\mathcal{L}_{i_p}, \mathcal{P}_e)$, $(\mathcal{L}_e, \mathcal{P}_{b_p})$, the comparison is between isolated single points and portions of the $\mathcal{R}^2$ space.

In order to further clarify the issue, in the following subsection a query example is shown.

3.1 A Query Example

Consider the following user query q:

Find all the Italian regions that are passed through by a river.

As already mentioned in the Introduction, this query, which involves the PTH operator, can be specified by using different pictorial representations. For instance, the one shown in Figure 4 (a) is a possible pictorial query of q. The 16-intersection matrix corresponding to this configuration is the following:

$$
(m_1)\ \begin{array}{c}
\begin{array}{cccc} \mathcal{P}_i & \mathcal{P}_{b_p} & \mathcal{P}_{b_l} & \mathcal{P}_e \end{array} \\
\begin{array}{c} \mathcal{L}_{i_p} \\ \mathcal{L}_{i_l} \\ \mathcal{L}_b \\ \mathcal{L}_e \end{array}
\left(
\begin{array}{cccc}
- & 6 & - & - \\
3 & - & 0 & 4 \\
0 & 0 & - & 2 \\
4 & - & 6 & 3
\end{array}
\right)
\end{array}
$$

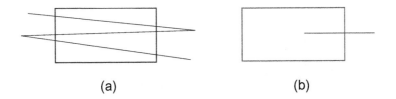

Fig. 4. Two possible pictorial representations of q

In fact, we have:

- six points which are single boundary points of the polygon and single interior points of the polyline (element $(\mathcal{L}_{i_p}, \mathcal{P}_{b_p})$ of the matrix, see Figure 5-(a));
- three connected components (polylines) which belong to the polyline and interior of the polygon (element $(\mathcal{L}_{i_l}, \mathcal{P}_i)$ of the matrix, see Figure 5-(b));
- four connected components (polylines) which belong to the polyline and the exterior of the polygon (element $(\mathcal{L}_{i_l}, \mathcal{P}_e)$ of the matrix, see Figure 5-(c));
- two boundary points of the polyline which are exterior points of the polygon (element $(\mathcal{L}_b, \mathcal{P}_e)$ of the matrix, see Figure 5-(d));
- four connected components (polygons) that are internal to the polygon and external to the polyline (element $(\mathcal{L}_e, \mathcal{P}_i)$ of the matrix, see Figure 5-(e));
- six connected components (polylines) that are external to the polyline and are the boundary lines of the polygon (element $(\mathcal{L}_e, \mathcal{P}_{b_l})$ of the matrix, see Figure 5-(f));
- three connected components (polygons) that are external to the polygon and external to the polyline (element $(\mathcal{L}_e, \mathcal{P}_e)$ of the matrix, see Figure 5-(g)).

A simpler pictorial representation of q is, for instance, shown in Figure 4 (b). Indeed q can be represented in an equivalent way by one of the two pictorial queries shown in Figures 4 (a) and (b) representing the PTH operator, but the corresponding 16-intersection matrices are different. The 4x4 matrix corresponding to the simpler pictorial query of Figure 4 (b) is shown below:

$$(m_2) \quad \begin{array}{c} \\ \mathcal{L}_{i_p} \\ \mathcal{L}_{i_l} \\ \mathcal{L}_b \\ \mathcal{L}_e \end{array} \begin{array}{cccc} \mathcal{P}_i & \mathcal{P}_{b_p} & \mathcal{P}_{b_l} & \mathcal{P}_e \\ \left(\begin{array}{cccc} - & 1 & - & - \\ 1 & - & 0 & 1 \\ 1 & 0 & - & 1 \\ 1 & - & 1 & 1 \end{array} \right) \end{array}$$

In the next section, the GeoPQL system will be presented and the 16-intersection matrices related to both the pictorial representations of the query q of Figure 4 (a) and (b) will be further illustrated.

4   The GeoPQL System

GeoPQL is a stand alone tool, in which the developed pictorial functions are integrated with ESRI-ArcView® [2] in order to exploit its basic browsing and

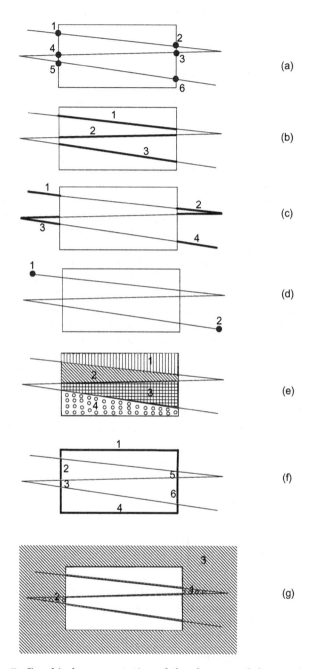

Fig. 5. Graphical representation of the elements of the matrix m_1

drawing functions as well as its underlying geographical database called ArcMap [1]. ArcMap represents geographic information as a collection of layers, where each layer corresponds to a particular dataset overlayed in the map. GeoPQL allows users to formulate their queries using drawing facilities and correctly interprets the query syntax and semantics on the basis of its underlying sound algebra (for details, see [18]).

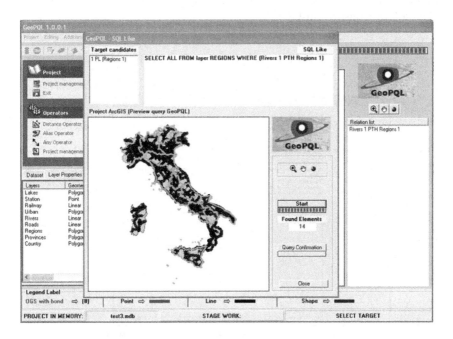

Fig. 6. Answer to the pictorial query shown in Figure 1, as highlighted regions

For instance, in the Introduction, Figure 1 illustrates the pictorial formulation of the query shown in Figure 4 (b) in the GeoPQL working area, on the geographical database of Italy. As we can see in Figure 1 in the "Relation list" on the right side of the working area, GeoPQL correctly identifies the spatial relationship between the SGOs (*Rivers 1 PTH Regions 1*). Then, this query is translated and visualized to the user in a SQL like language [18], as shown on the top of Figure 6. Note that during the drawing phase which involves modifications, deletions and shifting of the pictorial representation, the textual query is continuously updated. The query is executed on ArcMap and the result is shown in Figure 6, where the highlighted regions are the answer. The 16-intersection matrix m_2 given in Section 3, corresponding to this example, is shown on the bottom left of Figure 7. As we can observe, the content of the 16-intersection matrix illustrated on the top left of the above mentioned figure represents the *type* of the intersections results, i.e. 0, 1, and 2 which stand for point, line, and polygon, respectively, according to the native representation of the OGC environment. The matrix indicated on the bottom, instead, is our proposed one, and contains in each cell the number of connected components that are in the intersection between the pair of SGOs.

Note that, in order to implement our proposed 16-intersection matrix we invoked in GeoPQL the open source Java libraries JTS Topology Suite [4]. JTS Topology Suite is an API of 2D spatial predicates and functions and provides a complete, consistent, robust implementation of fundamental 2D spatial analysis methods. It conforms to the Simple Features Specification for SQL published by the Open GIS Consortium-OGC® [3].

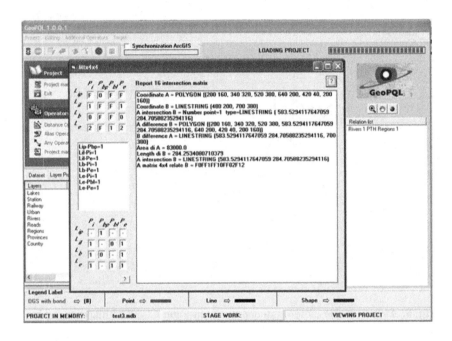

Fig. 7. 16-intersection matrices corresponding to the query shown in Figure 1

Note that in Figure 7, which represents a simple PTH relationship, the matrix on the bottom left does not essentially add information to the matrix given on the top left. The 16-intersection matrix corresponding to Figure 2 is shown in Figure 8. In this figure, a different scenario, where the matrices illustrate a composite PTH+TCH between SGOs. In fact, as anticipated in the Introduction, our proposed matrix provides, for instance, the *number* of points $((\mathcal{L}_{i_p}, \mathcal{P}_{b_p}) = 3)$, and the *number* of polylines $((\mathcal{L}_{i_l}, \mathcal{P}_{b_l}) = 1)$ that are in the intersection between the interior of the polyline and the boundary of the polygon. This is not the case of the matrix on the top left of the same figure, which simply provides the values 0, and 1, simply indicating the *type* of the intersection values respectively. Note that in the OGC environment the F (FALSE) notation corresponds to *incomparable* and 0 in our 16-intersection matrix notation.

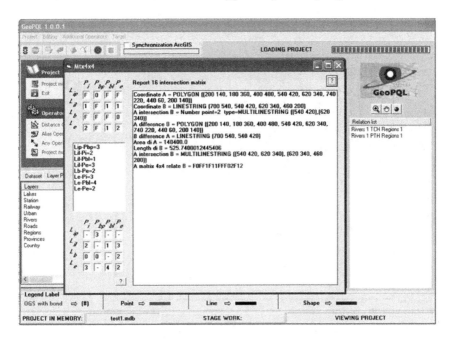

Fig. 8. 16-intersection matrices corresponding to the query shown in Figure 2

Finally, in Figure 9, the matrices related to the pictorial representation of the query q of Figure 4 (a) are shown, where the matrix on the bottom left of the figure corresponds to the matrix m_1 given in Section 3. The level of detail of these matrices differs, for instance, in the case of the element $(\mathcal{L}_{i_p}, \mathcal{P}_{b_p})$. In fact, the number of isolated interior points of the polyline which are also isolated boundary points of the polygon are six, whereas the standard OGC notation only provides the value zero, standing for an intersection of type point. Similarly, in the case of the element $(\mathcal{L}_e, \mathcal{P}_{b_l})$, the number of boundary lines of the polygon that are external to the polyline are six whereas, according to the standard OGC notation, the corresponding cell of the matrix provides the value one, simply standing for an intersection of type polyline. Note that the answers to both the queries shown in Figures 8 and 9 are null.

5   Related Work

In the last few years, a number of proposals focused on the problems regarding the topological relations between SGOs. Some papers studied the conceptual neighborhood of topological relations between polylines [29] or between regions [15]. Similarly, other proposals discussed qualitative spatial reasoning [30], models [25] [26]. With regard to the operators and algebras for geographical data, in [19] the authors introduced the oriented polylines, and extended the set of operators proposed in [17] [18]. With regard to binary topological relations, the

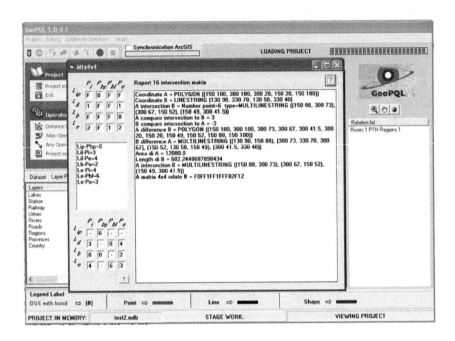

Fig. 9. 16-intersection matrices corresponding to the query shown in Figure 4 (a)

4-Intersection and 9-Intersection models [12] have been proposed, and a comparison between them has been made [13]. Regarding the 9-intersection model, the definition of binary topological relationships based on the interior ($A°$), boundary (∂A), and exterior (A^-) of a 2-dimensional point set embedded in $\mathcal{R}^2$ have been introduced [14].

Concerning the topological relationships between geographical features, there is a number of different proposals in the literature, see for instance [5] [26] [8] [9] [10]. For instance, in [5] the authors refer to a calculus-based method, and investigate 17 relationships between polyline-polygon relations. In the mentioned paper some configurations, such as the relationship between a polyline entirely lying on the boundary of the polygon, are not considered. In [26] the authors present an extended model for describing topological relations between sets (objects) in GISs. However, they do not consider polygon-polyline relationships. In this paper, we consider the aforementioned relationships, and the cases in which a polyline partially or totally overlaps the boundary of the polygon.

In [8] the authors focus on six kinds of topological relations between a polyline and a polygon, and illustrate a hierarchical representation of these relations. They propose sixteen polyline-polygon topological relations as well as a conceptual neighborhood graph. However, the topological operators and their possible combinations are not discussed.

In [9] [10], starting from the Geographical Pictorial Query Language (GeoPQL) proposed in [18], a preliminary study has been proposed which regards constraint relaxation on topological operators in the case of queries which produce null answers. As already clarified in the Introduction, in the aforementioned papers, given a topological relationship, three 9-intersection matrices have been defined that necessarily require to compute 27 matrix elements. In this paper, the 16-intersection matrix allows us to significantly reduce the number of elements to be evaluated to 10.

6 Conclusion

In this paper, we addressed the polygon-polyline topological relation and we defined a 16-intersection matrix that has been conceived to enhance and distinguish the semantics of cells' content with respect to the well-known 9-intersection matrix. In order to implement our proposed 16-matrix, we invoked in GeoPQL the open source Java libraries JTS Topology Suite, which conforms to the Simple Features Specification for SQL published by the Open GIS Consortium-OGC. The cases related to the polygon-polygon and polyline-polyline topological relations will be investigated in future work.

References

1. http://www.esri.com/software/arcgis/
2. http://www.esri.com/software/arcview/
3. http://www.opengeospatial.org/standards
4. http://www.vividsolutions.com/jts/JTSHome.htm
5. Clementini, E., Di Felice, P., van Oosterom, P.: A Small Set of Formal Topological Relationships Suitable for End-user Interaction. In: Abel, D.J., Ooi, B.-C. (eds.) SSD 1993. LNCS, vol. 692, pp. 277–295. Springer, Heidelberg (1993)
6. Cohn, A., Hazarika, S.: Qualitative spatial representation and reasoning: an overview. Fundamenta Informaticae 46(1-2), 1–29 (2001)
7. Cui, Z., Cohn, A.G., Randell, D.A.: Qualitative and Topological Relationships in Spatial Databases. In: Abel, D., Ooi, B.C. (eds.) SSD 1993. LNCS, vol. 692, pp. 296–315. Springer, Heidelberg (1993)
8. Deng, M.: A hierarchical representation of line-region topological relations. The International Archives of the Photogrammetry, Remote Sensing and Spatial Information Sciences XXXVII(Pt. B2), 25–30 (2008)
9. D'Ulizia, A., Ferri, F., Grifoni, P., Rafanelli, M.: Relaxing Constraints on GeoPQL Operators to Improve Query Answering. In: Bressan, S., Küng, J., Wagner, R. (eds.) DEXA 2006. LNCS, vol. 4080, pp. 728–737. Springer, Heidelberg (2006)
10. D'Ulizia, A., Ferri, F., Grifoni, P., Rafanelli, M.: Constraint relaxation on topological operators which produce a null value as answer to a query. In: IRMA 2007, Canada (2007)
11. Dutta, S.: Approximate spatial reasoning. In: IEA/AIE 1988, vol. 1 (1988)
12. Egenhofer, M.J., Franzosa, R.D.: Point-set topological spatial relations. International Journal of Geographical Information Systems 5(2), 161–174 (1991)
13. Egenhofer, M.J., Sharma, J., Mark, D.M.: A critical comparison of the 4-intersection and 9-intersection models for spatial relations: formal analysis. In: McMaster, R., Armstrong, M. (eds.) Autocarto 11 (1993)

14. Egenhofer, M.J., Mark, D.M.: Modeling conceptual neighborhoods of topological line-region relations. International Journal of Geographical Information Systems 9(5), 555–565 (1995)
15. Egenhofer, M.J.: The Family of Conceptual Neighborhood Graphs for Region-Region Relations. In: Fabrikant, S.I., Reichenbacher, T., van Kreveld, M., Schlieder, C. (eds.) GIScience 2010. LNCS, vol. 6292, pp. 42–55. Springer, Heidelberg (2010)
16. Escrig, M.T., Toledo, F.: Qualitative Spatial Reasoning: Theory and Practice. Frontiers in Artificial Intelligence and Applications. IOS Press (1998)
17. Ferri, F., Pourabbas, E., Rafanelli, M.: The Syntactic and semantic correctness of pictorial configurations to query geographic databases by PQL. In: ACM SAC 2002, Spain (2002)
18. Ferri, F., Rafanelli, M.: GeoPQL: A Geographical Pictorial Query Language That Resolves Ambiguities in Query Interpretation. In: Spaccapietra, S., Zimányi, E. (eds.) Journal on Data Semantics III. LNCS, vol. 3534, pp. 50–80. Springer, Heidelberg (2005)
19. Ferri, F., Grifoni, P., Rafanelli, M.: A Pictorial Human Computer Interaction to Query Geographical Data. In: Bozanis, P., Houstis, E.N. (eds.) PCI 2005. LNCS, vol. 3746, pp. 317–327. Springer, Heidelberg (2005)
20. Frank, A.U.: The Use of Geographical Information Systems: the User Interface Is the System. In: Medyckyj-Scott, D., Hearnshaw, H.M. (eds.) Human Factors in Geographical Information Systems, pp. 15–31. Belhaven Press (1993)
21. Frank, A.U.: Qualitative Spatial Reasoning: Cardinal Directions as an Example. Geographic Information Systems 10(3), 269–290 (1996)
22. Gould, M.D.: Human Factors Research and Its Value to GIS User Interface Design. In: GIS/LIS, Orlando, Florida, USA, pp. 541–550 (1989)
23. Grudin, J.: Utility and Usability: Research Issues and Development Contexts. Interacting with Computers 4(2), 209–217 (1992)
24. Kuhn, W.: Metaphors Create Theories for Users. In: Frank, A.U., Campari, I. (eds.) COSIT 1993. LNCS, vol. 716, pp. 366–376. Springer, Heidelberg (1993)
25. Li, S.: A complete classification of topological relations using 9-intersection method. International Journal of Geographical Information Science 20(6), 589–610 (2006)
26. Liu, K.F., Shi, W.Z.: Extended model of topological relations between spatial objects in geographic information systems. International Journal of Applied Earth Observation and Geoinformation 9, 264–275 (2007)
27. Medyckyj-Scott, D., Hearnshaw, H.M. (eds.): Human Factors in Geographical Information Systems. Belhaven Press (1993)
28. Papadias, D., Sellis, T.: A Pictorial Query-by-Example Language. Journal of Visual Languages and Computing 6(1), 53–72 (1995)
29. Pereira Reis, R.M., Egenhofer, M.J., Matos, J.: Conceptual neighborhoods of topological relations between lines. In: SDH 2008, France, July 23-25, pp. 557–574 (2008)
30. Schultz, C.P.L., Clephane, T.R., Guesgen, H.W., Amor, R.: Utilization of Qualitative Spatial Reasoning in Geographic Information Systems. In: Riedl, A., Kainz, W., Elmes, G.A. (eds.) Proc. of Int. Symposium on Spatial Data Handling: Progress in Spatial Data Handling, pp. 27–42. Springer (2006)

Usage Control in Inter-organisational Collaborative Environments – A Case Study from an Industry Perspective

Åsmund Ahlmann Nyre[1] and Martin Gilje Jaatun[2]

[1] Norwegian University of Science and Technology
nyre@idi.ntnu.no
[2] SINTEF ICT
martin.g.jaatun@sintef.no

Abstract. Sharing information between collaborators without relinquishing control of that information has for many years been a tantalizing goal in the research community, but despite application support, the concept of usage control has failed to take hold in the business community. In this paper we present the results of a case study in the Norwegian oil & gas domain. The purpose of the study is to better understand the reasons for the slow adoption rate of usage control technology to control shared information. To this end we investigate risk perception, existing control measures and the attitude towards usage control technology. The study shows that although participants in the case study do not think their information is properly protected, there are several practical challenges that prevent them from adopting usage control technology as a means to improve protection.

1 Introduction

The extensive collaboration across system boundaries facilitated by the Internet is unfortunately also increasing the potential for misuse of shared information. While mechanisms to protect assets from active attackers (such as firewalls, intrusion detection systems and anti-virus software) are commonplace, the availability of commercial software to protect information from misuse remains limited.

From the research community, *usage control* has been proposed as a potential remedy to let businesses retain control of information beyond their systems' boundaries [1]. Since the initial proposition from Park and Sandhu [1], several usage control models have been proposed, with different strategies of enforcement. Some of the models have even been implemented as prototypes and tested for computational overhead [2]. From a researcher's perspective, it seems obvious that usage control would help those that share potentially sensitive information with others. There are even some commercially available products that offer some of the concepts of usage control. Examples in this respect include the EMC[2] Documentum Information Rights Management client[1], which basically

---

[1] http://www.emc.com/products/detail/software/information-rights-management.htm

G. Quirchmayr et al. (Eds.): CD-ARES 2012, LNCS 7465, pp. 317–331, 2012.
© IFIP International Federation for Information Processing 2012

extends the access control policy of the Documentum repository to include all receiving devices. The client verifies in real time that the subject has access to the documents, regardless of whether the document is a copy or not. Similarly, the Microsoft Information Rights Management system for the Office suite integrates with Sharepoint server and offers the same kind of functionality.

However, despite the belief of researchers and the fact that there are commercially available tools to help, the industry seems to be reluctant to adopt usage control technologies. A natural response therefore would be to ask "why"? What is it that makes this seemingly attractive technology not attractive enough? It is exactly this question that formed the basis for our case study.

This paper contributes new knowledge on the perceived usefulness of usage control technology within the oil and gas sector. More specifically, the target of investigation is the vision of *Integrated Operations* of the oil and gas sector, and thus this is the domain where we will elicit requirements for such mechanisms to ease the transition to technology-based enforcement of usage control. To this end, the study will identify the current measures used to control and restrict shared information together with the perceived threats and opportunities provided by usage control enforcement mechanisms.

The remaining parts of this paper is organised as follows: Section 2 provides a brief introduction to the concept of usage control and distributed enforcement. Section 3 gives an overview of the context of the study - Integrated operations in the oil and gas industry. The design of the case study is detailed in Section 4, including procedures on data collection, analysis and measures to mitigate threats to validity. Section 5 presents our analysis and findings from the study, before we give our concluding remarks and possible future directions in Section 6.

2   Usage Control

Usage control has been proposed as a means to remedy the information misuse problem by extending common security mechanisms beyond single systems such as PCs, servers or entire corporate systems. The idea is to provide a model for expressing and enforcing restrictions on how the information is to be *used* . Current mechanisms such as access control, Digital Rights Management, confidentiality and privacy protection all attempt to restrict information in one way or the other. The focus of usage control is to create a holistic approach to restricting information, and thus it may be used for any of the purposes listed above.

When introducing usage control Park and Sandhu stressed the notion of a continuous access decision and mutability of attributes as the two most important factors of what they called the $UCON_{ABC}$-model [1]. Later, Pretschener et al. included *obligations* as a fundamental concept of distributed usage control [3]. Unlike the UCON model, the authors define obligations to be concerned with the future, e.g. "data d must not be further distributed" [3]. For the purpose of this study, we focus on the enforcement of usage control policies, particularly with respect to these three central aspects of usage control:

- *Continuity of access decision*: The decision on whether the subject should be granted access to the requested object is not considered a discrete-time event when requesting access to the object. Instead, the access decision is considered to be continuous, so that any context change (e.g. attribute values) may immediately affect the access decision.
- *Mutability of attributes*: The usage decision may alter attribute values of both subject and object. This will allow for frequency limitations on usage, such as "use at most 3 times".
- *Obligations*: Upon granting usage rights to an object, constraints may be imposed on future usage. Examples include having to delete the information within x days, not being able to forward the information, etc.

One of the fundamental questions when identifying users' attitudes towards usage control is how to enforce it? How can the aspects described above be enforced for distributed information? While there are several proposed enforcement models [2], we focus on the two main strategies of enforcement: *proactive* and *reactive* enforcement [2]. That is, whether enforcement should attempt to prevent misuse of information or merely detect it. The proactive approach is the predominant strategy for current access control mechanisms as well as commercial Digital Rights Management (DRM) systems, and since usage control may be viewed as an extension of both, proactive enforcement is a natural choice. However, unlike common DRM systems, usage control may also be reactive. The analogy to law enforcement is apparent and also companies' use of Non-Disclosure Agreements (NDAs) follow this principle. Hence, the industry is well acquainted with the reactive approach from existing protection measures. Usage control may contribute a more accurate and cost-effective way of detecting violations.

3   Context – Integrated Operations

Integrated Operations is a term used in the oil and gas industry in Norway to denote a future state in which work processes, information and people are integrated across geographical and organizational boundaries. Thus, information can flow without unnecessary obstacles from one organisation to another. This is not to say that everything should be open and accessible to everyone; on the contrary, the vision is that the flow of information is secure and only accessible to authorized personnel.

To reach this state of collaboration is not trivial, especially since the relationships between companies are extremely complex and dynamic. To provide a glimpse of this complexity, we provide a brief overview of the main categories of companies.

1. *Operators* are commonly oil companies and are responsible for the actual production of an oil or gas field. Due to the specialised expertise required for oil field development and production, operators to a large extent use *integrators* and suppliers to perform specified tasks.

2. *Licence owners* are oil companies that own a share of the license to develop an oil field. Commonly licences are shared between several oil companies. Thus both costs, risks and future revenue are divided according to the license share.
3. *Integrators* (sometimes called *contractors*) deliver complete products and services to operators by combining solutions from different *suppliers*.
4. *Suppliers* develop and deliver a specialised product or service for specific tasks, sometimes by incorporating products or services from other suppliers. The distinction between integrators and suppliers is blurred, however the term supplier is used when most of the development effort is done in-house.
5. *Consultancies* or consultancy firms may be used by any of the above-mentioned actors as support for their activities. For example as ICT developers, technical assessments or advisors.

These categories are by no means exhaustive nor mutually exclusive, and therefore there may be companies that do not fit any description, while others fit several. Still, they serve the purpose of illustrating the complex business relations that currently exist in the oil and gas sector. For example oil companies are competing to gain market share, but at the same time they are collaborating to explore and produce oil. There are even circumstances in which the Norwegian government demands cooperation in order to exploit minor oil fields, that would not be profitable if requiring a separate installation. Similarly, there are several companies that interchangeably between projects acts as both suppliers and integrators. Hence, integrators often find themselves in the position that they are dependent on one of their competitors for delivering according to their contract.

> *There are certainly other sectors where situations occasionally occur where you have to collaborate with your competitors, but here, this happens constantly. We both cooperate and compete with them simultaneously.*
>
> *(Engineer from the study)*

In addition to the constant collaboration with competitors, there is also a struggle among the companies to extend their product portfolio to get a bigger slice of the cake. With the amount of money involved in the industry, both oil companies, suppliers and integrators may be looking to increase their share of the operation at the others' expense, making the climate for trust a very fragile one.

4   Case Study Design

4.1   Research Questions

The main goal of this study is to *identify the factors influencing adoption of usage control enforcement mechanisms in collaborative environments.*

1. What are the main perceived threats to shared information?
2. Which measures are currently deployed to protect shared information from misuse?

3. To what extent are the current protection schemes believed to be adequate?
4. What are the main opinions on usage control enforcement technology?

These research questions are inspired by the main principle of the Protection Motivation Theory [4,5]. That is, the perceived risk and the perceived efficacy of the mitigating measures influence the decision to adopt the mitigating measures, which in our case is usage control technology. However, since we anticipate that there may be existing mechanisms in place, we have also considered the *relative advantage* of usage control technology compared to the existing measures [6]. As the focus of this paper is the case study outcome, we will not elaborate more on theoretical underpinnings of the study. For a more complete discussion of the relations to existing theory on technology adoption, we refer to [7].

4.2   Rationale for Case Selection

A case selected for a case study is often either a *typical* case or an *extreme* case. With our goal of attempting to understand why companies adopt (or don't adopt) usage control technologies in collaborative environments, we chose the extreme case. The rationale behind this was the idea that companies that extensively share potentially sensitive information are more likely to have a conscious opinion on the risks involved. Hence, we assume that in the extreme cases we are more likely to actually identify factors influencing adoption, than in more moderate settings. Indeed, as described in the previous section, the oil and gas industry in Norway in general (and Integrated Operations in particular) fits this description.

4.3   Data Collection Procedure

This study has used interviews as the data collection method. Other options we considered were workshops and focus group interviews. However, requiring people to participate at a certain time and place seemed to be a major obstacle to recruiting participants. This, coupled with our worry that group interviews potentially could prevent people from being sincere about their perception of risk, caused us to settle for individual interviews. We followed a semi-structured interview type on four main topics; shared information, risk perception, current security measures and attitude towards usage control enforcement technology. The interview guide given in Appendix A was used both as a starting point of discussion and as a means to ensure that all four topics were addressed.

Six companies, both national and international, within the oil and gas industry in Norway were selected to ensure a good coverage of categories of actors. Table 1 shows the distribution of participants with respect to both company category and the role of the participants in their company. We sought to cover the three different viewpoints from Engineers, Security Professionals and Management. However, it may sometimes be difficult to separate these three, especially for intermediate managers within R&D departments. The interviews were all held during the winter and spring of 2012, nearly half were conducted face-to-face

Table 1. Distribution of participants with respect to company category and participant role

(a) Number of organisations and interviews per category of actor

Category	Companies	Interviews
Operator	1	3
Licence owner	1*	1*
Integrator	1	3
Suppliers	3	5
Consultancy	1	1
Total	6	12

(b) Number of interviews for each participant role

Role	Interviews
Engineer	6
Security professional	2
Manager	4

*) The operator was also a licence owner. Hence these numbers are duplicates of the above

while the rest were done by telephone interview. Although we initially tried to avoid telephone interviews, it turned out to be difficult to schedule multiple interviews on a single day, as would have been required due to travel costs and time.

4.4 Analysis Procedure

All interviews were recorded and later transcribed in full. The transcribed interviews were then analyzed and coded using the constant comparison method [8] to extract the collective view on risks, existing measures and attitude towards usage control enforcement. The process of coding and labeling text was assisted by the use of NVivo^{TM}, a software tool for qualitative analysis.

4.5 Validity, Bias and Limitations of the Study

There are several aspects of this study that potentially could have a negative impact on the result. Here we outline the most important ones, and describe our efforts to neutralize the negative effect they would have.

Bias from theory may result in a bias in favour of data supporting the theory on the expense of the data contradicting it [9]. We have therefore refrained from detailing our theoretical framework in advance, in order to reduce the likelihood of theory bias in the interpretation of the results.

Truthfullness of participants' answers may be questioned since the topic of information security by many is regarded as sensitive. There is a chance that participants restrain themselves from revealing problems or anything that might be bad for their reputation. We have therefore made it clear up front that neither participants nor companies would be identified when publishing results. Additionally, since the interviewer is a security , there is a chance that participants may adapt answers to what they believe the interviewer would like to hear or seek confirmation from the interviewer. We have therefore stressed to participants in advance, that the important part of this study is their subjective beliefs. During the interviews we have also strived to remain as neutral as possible (without appearing uninterested), to any of the statements made by the interviewees.

The generalisability of the case may be limited since, as described in Section 4.2, it is an extreme case of sharing sensitive information. That being said, we argue that the size of the oil and gas industry could still provide a great impact even if only considering internal generalisation [9], i.e. generalization within the setting of the study. Admittedly, generalizing on the basis of a relatively small study is not without danger, which is why we have chosen to interpret most of our findings as *views* rather than *facts*. A larger scale study or survey based on our findings are likely to provide more statistically sound data for generalization.

5 Analysis

In this section we present our findings from the case study on the four main topics addressed; information sharing, risk perception, existing security measures and attitude towards usage control enforcement technology. In order to assess the outcome of this study, we also provide a profile of the interviewed participants.

5.1 Participant Profiles

Table 1b provides an overview of the participants according to the roles they currently have in their company. Notice however, that the distinction between the three types of roles are in some cases a bit blurred. For example, within the engineering discipline there are also managers, and hence separating managers from engineers may not be trivial. We have however attempted to distinguish managers as the ones whose primary role is to manage others. The same table also indicates that only two people interviewed were considered security professionals, i.e. where information security was their primary task. That being said, there were several of both the engineers and managers that had prior experience from securing information systems as part of product development.

Participants' experience from the oil and gas industry ranged from 2 to 20 years, with an average of approximately nine years. Further, all participants had at least a bachelor's degree or equivalent, while the majority additionally held master's degrees.

In terms of security awareness, the participants reported they would rate their security awareness in the upper end of the scale. As one of the managers stated "I am professionally paranoid".

5.2 Shared Information

The kind of information that is shared among partners within Integrated Operations vary considerably depending on the production phase and the type or category of company. Although the information in itself is perhaps not essential to understand attitudes towards usage control enforcement technology, it does help to understand the risk perception of participants.

For integrators and suppliers the most sensitive information is shared either prior to a project contract or in the planning phase of the project. The most important information shared is information on pricing, offers and technical details required by the operators or partners in the bidding process. Additionally, integrators and suppliers may be required to share technical details and product information in order to integrate their solutions with others.

For operators and license owners, the most sensitive information is shared during the operational phase of the project, whether it is exploration or production of oil fields. Integrators and suppliers will often collect a vast amount of data on the operational status through their systems and transport this information to the operator. Although the data in several cases originates from suppliers and integrators, the data is still considered owned by the operators and is shared with other partners at the operators' discretion. Thus, integrators and suppliers consider it to be information shared by the operators, rather then by them. There is a tremendous amount of real-time data on the status of the operation, such as production volumes, pipeline capacities, disruptions or other events, and status of sensors and actuators and for exploration activities also geological information. Some of which may influence stock prices for oil companies while others may be devastating in terms of company reputation.

5.3   Risk Perception

Users' perception of risk is believed to influence their motivation for protecting themselves and therefore constitutes the cornerstone of the Protection Motivation Theory [5]. The idea is that without any risks, there is no need for protection either. In this section we aim to identify the specific risks related to sharing potentially sensitive information with business partners.

Potential Impact. There are fundamentally four kinds of potential impact from misusing shared information that seem to be causing concern:

– *Reduced competitive power* - Shared information on products and technology may be utilized by competitors to improve their products and technology, and thereby reducing the competitive power of the owner of the information.
– *Reduced market share* - Shared information on pricing, tender details and strategies may be utilised by competitors to adapt their pricing in order to gain an advantage in the bidding process.
– *Reduced reputation in the industry* - Especially suppliers and integrators are concerned with the devastating effect it would have if they were responsible for leaking information obtained from customers and partners. Operators also see this as a concern, since it could reduce their suppliers willingness to collaborate to solve future problems. The industry is very much built on trust, and thus if the basis for this trust should disappear, the effects could be dramatic.

 — *Reduced reputation in general* - Security incidents resulting from lack of control of information could potentially be very damaging to the reputation of a company from the viewpoint of citizens, government and the world at large. This is particularly due to the potential environmental hazard of oil production.

Table 2. Identified threats, agents, sources and their potential impact

Threat	Threat agents	Threat sources	Potential impact
Industrial espionage	Competitors, Intelligence agencies	Information on products, solutions and technology	Reduced competitive power
Corporate espionage	Competitors, Suppliers, customers	Information on pricing, bidding and strategies	Reduced market share
Economic espionage	Employees, general public	Information on operational situation, production and field development	Reduced reputation
Terrorism and activism	Hackers, environmental activists	Information on incidents, status and business	reputation, production
Unintentional disclosure	Own and partner employees	Any information	Any of the above
Intentional disclosure	Own and partner employees	Any information	Any of the above

Table 2 lists the main threats with corresponding threat agents (attackers), threat source and potential impact as seen by the participants. Industrial espionage is the single threat that is mentioned most frequently by the participants. It occurs when companies take advantage of technology or product specific information received directly or indirectly from its competitors. The primary effect is that companies lose their competitive advantage relative to their competitors and thus potentially also their market share. For integrators and suppliers, the degree of severity vary with the kind of information abused. According to one of the participants, even interface descriptions might reveal functionality that can be copied. However, acknowledging the need for open interfaces in a competitive industry, the effort is placed on preventing descriptions of the inner workings of their products from being misused by their competitor. Some of the participants have even experienced attempts from foreign national intelligence agencies trying to steal sensitive information.

Participants also highlight the threat of corporate espionage, which is not about IPR or theft of new technology, but rather information on bids, pricing and strategies. Thus, for competitors to gain market share they can adapt their product pricing, bid requirements and strategy to their competitors. While on the one hand participants argued the probability of this occurring, they simultaneously argued that this kind of information was treated with the utmost discretion. Even project members in a bidding process did not know the pricing of the products they were to deliver.

Economic espionage is when the actors exploit operational data and other knowledge of the companies to predict future pricing in the stock market. While participants noted that this threat meant that the operational data was treated as sensitive data, none of them argued that it would be particularly devastating for the company.

Similarly, hacking and activism was not seen as a great threat, at least not to shared information. While this could cause some reputation problems, it was considered to be improbable. One participant noted however that although a lot of the sensitive information would be impossible for hackers to exploit, they could potentially sell the information to competitors that could exploit it.

Several participants however argued both for the probability and possible impact of unintended disclosure of information. That is, that authorized personnel, either in their own company or their partners, would release sensitive information by mistake. For instance by releasing an entire specification rather than just the interface specification to customers. One of the subjects even claimed that *"if we could only get rid of the human mistakes, we would probably reduce the incident occurences by 80%"*, although not all of these incidents would be related to shared information. Another stated that when treating sensitive information *"What is really challenging for me is to keep track of the people that already know the secret, and with whom I can discuss matters"*. Hence, unintentional disclosure may result from simple mistakes, not necessarily lack of security awareness. For integrators and suppliers, it is perhaps even worse if this should occur with an operator's data. As noted earlier, during the production phase much of the data shared by these companies are actually owned by the operator. Being liable for misuse of information is potentially more damaging to companies as it may damage the trust of the customers they are dependent on.

5.4   Current Security Measures

In order to properly assess the *relative advantage* of any new security measures it is important to know existing mechanisms and understand their strengths and limitations. Thus, we asked respondents to name existing mechanisms for controlling shared information usage.

> We have no control, as far as I know, of information and what happens to it, other than agreements and mutual trust.
>
> *(Participant in the study)*

This statement is representative for all participants in the study. As one of them noted *"there are access control mechanisms, but once you have access we have no [usage] control, technical control that is"*. The predominant strategy is the use of

Non-Disclosure Agreements (NDAs) or other contractual agreements restricting the usage of information. Some company policies will not even allow discussions of cooperation without a signed NDA. They are therefore used extensively, and particularly whenever companies share product information. However, for integrators and suppliers this tends to be less important towards new customers.

NDAs used within Integrated Operations are to a large extent kept general and signed on management level, but occasionally, depending on the sensitivity of the data, NDAs are also signed by individual employees for a certain specific project. Needless to say, the employees' knowledge of the actual content of an NDA signed at the company level is not very good. Still, participants claim to have a fairly good idea about what is acceptable and what is not, and that this to a large extent boils down to common sense and contents of security policies.

Within research and development projects, where new technology is developed in collaboration, descriptions of Intellectual Property Rights (IPR) is an important part of the contracts. By explicitly stating the owners of IPR for each component in the system any doubts regarding the ownership are removed and the climate for sharing expertise considerably improved.

Contractual measures seem to be the norm throughout the industry, since only one of the participants had ever experienced that other partners had required any form of usage control technology to be used prior to information disclosure. That being said, one of the companies have introduced usage control technology internally, but this has thus far not been widely used.

The contractual measures are in general viewed to be appropriate and not excessive. However, the process of getting NDAs signed can be time-consuming and tedious, particularly in situations were there are disagreements between companies. And although they provide legal protection from misuse, most participants state that it is not enough. It is considered very difficult to get someone convicted for violating an NDA. As one of the participants argue that *"you would have to misuse patentable techology if you were to be convicted in court for telling your new employer"*. This is also backed up by the fact that none of the participants had ever been involved in either prosecuting or being prosecuted for violation of NDAs or other such contracts. To some extent they therefore do question the practical consequences of protecting information using solely *"social and legal measures"*. That being said, utilizing sanctions as a means to coax people into complying with policies has been shown to effective [10].

5.5   Attitude towards Usage Control Enforcement Technology

I want to help protect the information by helping users so that they do not have to think for themselves. Use technology in such a way that end-users cannot make mistakes.   (Security specialist)

Based on an introduction to the concept of usage control enforcement, similar to that of Section 2, participants were asked to provide their opinion as to whether this could actually improve the control of shared information.

Apparent Benefits. Most participants state that usage control enforcement technology definitely would improve control of information, but that these benefits always must be viewed in context with the challenges introduced. We treat the risks and challenges of usage control technology below, but first we outline the main benefits of the technology, as seen by the participants.

- Relieve employees of the need to think.
- Prevents employees from being tempted to misbehave or take short-cuts.
- Ease the process of invalidating obsolete information.
- Revoke usage rights automatically.
- Restrict actual usage of information as opposed to mere access to it.
- Effective detection/prevention of usage policy violations.

Several participants mention that the reliance on employees to enforce usage policy is not optimal. Therefore, it is no surprise that allowing for automatic enforcement is seen as a benefit. Also, participants seem to think that people might be tempted by circumstances to take short cuts or circumvent systems for convenience. Revoking usage rights of potentially distributed information is something that several participants find interesting, since it reduces the gap between centralized and local information. The exact same functionality may be exploited to invalidate obsolete information distributed to partners. Several participants state that one of the fundamental problems of shared information is ensuring that all collaborating partners have the latest revision of it. Hence, if one could invalidate information that would force people to obtain the latest revision. Restricting usage (e.g. printing, forwarding, copying) is also mentioned as a clear benefit together with the improved effectiveness of detecting or preventing (depending on the type of enforcement) usage policy violations.

Some participants argue that although the benefit is clear, there are other things that are more pressing than usage control enforcement. For instance access control policies could be improved. Participants have experienced collaboration projects where the entire document repository was accessible to all, since managing access control policies was considered a burden. As a result, a lot of sensitive information could not be stored in the repository, and hence alternative parallel systems had to be established for this kind of information exchange.

Risks and Challenges

There are a few strengths, but there are also some extreme inconveniences
(Engineer in the study)

The greatest potential risk of utilising usage control enforcement technology, according to participants, is that information may not be available to personnel when they need it. That is, that usage rights have been revoked, or network connectivity prevents you from obtaining necessary authorizations. There is a fear that such a system would be more strict than existing access control systems and additionally extended with ubiquitous enforcement. Since the technology to some extent resembles Digital Rights Management (DRM) systems, many also draw parallels to some of the unfair restrictions that commonly apply to downloadable media files. Thus, participants foresee information lock-in as a direct consequence of adopting usage control technology.

And then there is the management of usage rights. Participants point to the management overhead and costs of specifying, maintaining and deleting usage rights and usage policies. In the event that authorised personnel cannot access information, then either the assigned usage rights are wrong or the policy is incorrect. One of the participants stated that even with their current four-scale classification scheme for sensitive information "... *the probability that a document is correctly classified is about 50%*".

Another serious issue with usage control technology is the handling of real-time data and legacy systems. Operational data collected at an oil field need to travel through a wide range of different systems for analysis, some of which are legacy systems that are difficult, not to say impossible, to change. As illustrated by one of the security specialists: "*We have state of the art systems, but it is state of the art from 1985 in some cases*". Additionally, with real-time remote control of operations, there is a general fear that latencies caused by the additional security may be intolerable.

While using information in unforeseen ways or contexts are commonly regarded a threat, it is also how creative solutions to difficult problems come about. One of the participants fear that creativity may suffer as a result of stricter usage control enforcement.

On a general basis, the lack of flexibility that participants see in usage control technology is of great concern and many fear that as a result employees will go to great lengths to bypass the technology.

Regarding whether the enforcement strategy should be proactive or reactive, the participants tend to disagree. To some, the entire value in the technology lies in the prevention of information misuse. The majority however sees the reactive strategy as a way to mitigate most of the challenges identified above, particularly regarding information being unavailable. This of course comes at the price of not being able to prevent misuse. Additionally, by introducing logging mechanisms for all handling of sensitive information, several participants express great concern of being subject to surveillance by both their own and collaborating companies. Furthermore, by being held accountable for their actions, some employees fear that if being ordered to violate a policy, they are accepting the responsibility of the commanding officer.

6   Conclusions and Future Work

Through this case study of a collaborative environment with extensive sharing of sensitive information, we have shed some light on the reasons why usage control technology adoption is not picking up the pace. From our analysis it seems clear that the participants are conscious about the risks and the shortcomings of existing measures to restrict usage of shared information. Still, the study demonstrates some of the practical challenges that needs to be tackled in order for the industry to embrace the technology. Some of this might be alleviated through adding flexibility to the enforcement mechanisms, while others require other enabling technology such as decision support on policy specifications.

It seems however, that there is no *silver bullet* for usage control technology either. There are situations in which proactive designs are superior to reactive designs, and vice versa. Still, the lessons learned from this cases study is the need to focus on practical issues that need to be addressed in order to promote all variations of this technology to great masses.

This case study forms a basis for which a more quantitative approach may be taken to gain insights into the relative importance of the different risks and features of usage control technology. Additionally, we believe that it will be worth while to investigate further the effect of decision support systems for both policy specifications and handling of sensitive information.

Acknowledgements. We would like to express our sincerest gratitude to the participants in this study. As part of the research project Integrated Operations in the High North (IOHN), this study has received funding from the Research Council of Norway.

References

1. Park, J., Sandhu, R.: The $UCON_{ABC}$ usage control model. ACM Trans. Inf. Syst. Secur. 7, 128–174 (2004)
2. Nyre, Å.A.: Usage Control Enforcement - A Survey. In: Tjoa, A.M., Quirchmayr, G., You, I., Xu, L. (eds.) ARES 2011. LNCS, vol. 6908, pp. 38–49. Springer, Heidelberg (2011)
3. Pretschner, A., Hilty, M., Basin, D.: Distributed usage control. Communications of the ACM 49, 39–44 (2006)
4. Norman, P., Boer, H., Seydel, E.R.: Protection motivation theory. In: Conner, M., Norman, P. (eds.) Predicting Health Behaviour: Research and Practice with Social Cognition Models, pp. 81–126. Open University Press, Maidenhead (2005)
5. Rogers, R.W.: A protection motivation theory of fear appeals and attitude. Journal of Psychology 91 (1975)
6. Rogers, E.M.: Diffusion of Innovations, 5th edn. Free Press (2003)
7. Nyre, Å.A., Jaatun, M.G.: On the adoption of usage control technology in collaborative environments. In: Proceedings of the 12th International Conference on Innovative Internet Community Systems, Trondheim, Norway (accepted for publication, 2012)
8. Seaman, C.B.: Qualitative methods. In: Shull, F., Singer, J., Sjøberg, D.I.K. (eds.) Guide to Advanced Empirical Software Engineering, pp. 35–62. Springer, London (2008)
9. Robson, C.: Real World Research, 3rd edn. John Wiley & Sons (2011)
10. Siponen, M., Pahnila, S., Mahmood, A.: Employees' Adherence to Information Security Policies: An Empirical Study. In: Venter, H., Eloff, M., Labuschagne, L., Eloff, J., von Solms, R. (eds.) New Approaches for Security, Privacy and Trust in Complex Environments. IFIP, vol. 232, pp. 133–144. Springer, Boston (2007)

A   Interview Guide

Introduction

1. What is your age, education and professional background?
2. What is your current position in the company?
3. Do you have experience from securing information systems?
4. For how long have you been working within the oil and gas industry?
5. How would you rate yourself regarding general information security awareness on a scale from 1(very conscious) to 7 (completely oblivious)?

Shared information

6. With which partners do you (most often) share information?
7. What kind of information do you (most often) share?

Risk perception

8. How do you think information shared with partners can be misused/abused?
9. What kinds of misuse/abuse do you consider to be the most harmful to your organisation?
10. What kinds of misuse/abuse do you consider most likely to happen?
11. Which actors do you think pose the greatest threat of misusing/abusing information?

Current security measures

12. What security measures do you (or your organisation) currently use in order to control how information is used when shared with partners?
13. What security measures do your partners currently use in order to control usage of information they share with your organisation? (security policies, NDAs, contracts)
14. Are there any situations where you find these security measures to be unnecessary?
15. Are there any situations where you find a lack of protection alarming?
16. Do you believe that the current security measures overall are adequate?

Enforcement technology

17. How do you see enforcement technology improving the control of information?
18. What enforcement strategy (proactive/reactive) would you have preferred for your company?
19. What would you consider the greatest risk in adopting enforcement technology?

Stock Market Multi-Agent Recommendation System Based on the Elliott Wave Principle

Monica Tirea[1], Ioan Tandau[2], and Viorel Negru[1]

[1] West University of Timisoara, Timisoara Romania
{tirea.monica,vnegru}@info.uvt.ro
[2] Green Mountain Analytics, Cary, North Carolina, USA
tandauioan@gmail.com

Abstract. The goal of this paper is to create a hybrid recommendation system based on a Multi-Agent Architecture that will inform the trader about the future stock trend in order to improve the profitability of a short or medium time period investment.

We proposed a Multi-Agent Architecture that uses the numbers of the Fibonacci Series and the Elliott Wave Theory, along with some special Technical Analysis Methods (namely Gap Analysis, Breakout System, Market Modes and Momentum Precedes Price) and Neural Networks (Multi-Layer Perceptron) and tries to combine and / or compare the result given by part / all of them in order to forecast trends in the financial market. In order to validate our model a prototype was developed.

Keywords: Multi-Agent Systems, Elliott Wave Theory, Technical Analysis Methods, Neural Networks, Fibonacci Series.

1 Introduction

Stock Market Forecasting has gained an important place in the research area due to its attractive benefits and its commercial applications. Due to the fact that the stock market is noisy, non-linear, chaotic, dynamic, very complicated and influenced by many macro-economical factors it is almost impossible to make a perfect prediction of which is the best moment to buy / sell a stock or to forecast a market trend. During the last decades researchers have tried to combine a series of techniques in order to alleviate the insurmountable prediction problem and provide better decision guidelines and optimized forecasting tools.

The most common techniques used are Fundamental and Technical Analysis [4,5,11]. Technical Analysis computes some indicators/oscillators, based on a stock historical data, which have the aim to signal a buy / sell moment. Fundamental Analysis takes in consideration the macro-economical factors that influence the market in order to also signal a buy/sell moment. Another approach is the use of Artificial Neural Networks [2,3,8] because of their ability to capture patterns and relationships based on the historical data and to cope with the environmental changes that may occur in the market in order to help in determining a future stock trend or a good moment to buy / sell.

G. Quirchmayr et al. (Eds.): CD-ARES 2012, LNCS 7465, pp. 332–346, 2012.

In the field of Technical Analysis, there are a series of methods that are considered to be profitable such as Gap Analysis, Breakout Systems, Market Modes and Momentum Precedes Price. Another complex and comprehensive Technical Analysis Method is the Elliott Wave Theory [6,7].

The Elliott Wave Theory plays an important part in the stock market research area because of its ability to interpret the psychological aspect that may appear on a market behavior. Taking in consideration that stock prices are following a trend is very important to know which is the direction of the current trend and when this direction will change.

In completion to the Wave Analysis Stock Prediction Model proposal, which is based on Fuzzy Logic Theory, Neural Network, and the Elliott Wave Theory [1], we add an agent based system that uses some special Technical Analysis Methods, for a better detection of a good buy / sell moment and a better forecast of a market trend.

Based on this information we developed a framework (Stock Market Multi-Agent Recommendation System - SMMARS) in which we will combine the result of these Technical Analysis Methods with the Neural Network Methods (Multi-Layer Peceptron) into a Multi-Agent Architecture in order to make a better forecast on the future trend of a stock in a stock market.

This framework's goal is to compare, to find a correlation between the result from three different techniques and to combine them in order to improve the final results and to make a better forecast on the market future trend. We defined a hybrid system whose aim is to find a better solution to how we can manipulate a portfolio in order to have a substantial gain on the stock market. These methods are applied on the Bucharest Stock Exchange Market (BSE).

In Section 2 we describe the Elliott Wave Principle and the methods associated with it along with the Technical Analysis Methods that we will use in order to forecast a stock trend. Section 3 presents the proposed model of the agent architecture. Section 4 presents an analysis of our model on the Bucharest Stock Exchange, the results obtained along with the comparison of our model's results with other similar models. Conclusions and future work is presented in the last section.

2   Elliott Wave Principle and Stock Market Forecasting

2.1   Profitable Methods Based on Technical Analysis

Stock Market prediction has been an interest area of research for many years. Researchers have played with Technical Analysis indicators and oscillators in order to find a better way to predict an important moment to buy / sell on a stock market. The profitable methods [7] based on the Technical Analysis are considered to be Gap Analysis Patterns, Breakout Systems, the Market's Mode and the Momentum Precedes Price concept.

Gap Analysis Method

We define a gap as the area on which no trades occurred. These methods can signal an important event on the stock market based on the fundamental data or on the psychology of the crowd that accompanies this market movement. Taking in consideration the breaking news or changes that may appear in the market's conditions, this method signals that something important happened [7,9].

In the case that this information is true and the price of a stock evolves in the direction of the gap, then we can take in consideration two possible moves: we buy when the market gaps down below the low on the open and then crosses above yesterday's close and sell when the market opens above yesterday's high and crosses below yesterday's close; or we buy/sell if the market gaps up / down at some percentage of yesterday's range above the open/ bellow the open. Gaps are good tools for forecasting short and medium trends.

We distinguish four basic categories of gaps : *Common* (appears in a trading range or congestion area, and reinforces the apparent lack of interest in the stock at that time); *Breakaway* (occurs when the price action is breaking out of their trading range or congestion area); *Runaway* (occurs when an increased interest in the stock appears); and *Exhaustion* (occurs when a high volume and large price difference between the previous day's close and the new opening price appears).

Breakout Systems

There are considered to be one of the best methods from the Technical Analysis because of their ability to carry the stock beyond the breakout point in order for the user to have a gain on the market. We distinguish two categories of breakout systems: the channel breakout (occurs when a stock was trading in a given channel and the trading starts at a price higher than the top of that channel) and the volatility breakout (buy / sell when the market breaks above/below its open / previous close by a given percentage of the previous day's range) [7,12].

Market Mode

This method has an interest in identifying the status of the market: if is trending, will continue to trend or will consolidate. In order to make such assumption we use a series of Technical Analysis indicators. One of the most used indicators is the Average Directional Movement (ADX) which signal the market status when it goes above / below a set level. A market is considered to be trending when the indicator goes above 25, is consolidating when it goes below 20 [7].

Momentum Precedes Price

This method indicates whether or not a possible price change will occur. Based on the market movement in one direction it is possible that the price will continue further in the same direction. A signal of buy / sell moment will appear if the momentum oscillator sets a new high / low and the oscillator is above / bellow zero [7].

2.2   Elliott Wave Principle

The market moves in ratios and patterns that reflects the human behavior of a stock price's trend. Taking this fact into consideration, the Elliott Wave Principle is defined as a two direction waves (impulse wave and corrective wave) [1,6,7].

The impulse wave is defined as a five wave sequence (noted $1 - 2 - 3 - 4 - 5$) that follow the trend direction and the corrective wave is defined as a three wave sequence (noted $a - b - c$) in the opposite direction of the impulse wave. This type of waves can be used in short-term and long-term prediction because of their construction from similar patterns on a large or short scale.

Elliott defined a hierarchy of waves based on their degree: Grand Supercycle, Supercycle, Cycle, Primary, Intermediate, Minor, Minute, Minuette, Subminuette. In this study we take into consideration the last four of them in order to forecast the stock market trend for short and medium term period.

Looking at a trend on the stock market we can identify on which position of the pattern we are by taking in consideration some rules :

1. The second wave in the Elliott Wave Pattern must not exceed the length of the first wave and cannot return a price lower than the one set at the beginning of the first wave.
2. The third wave must not have the shortest length compared to the first and the fifth waves.
3. The fourth wave must not return a lower price than the closing price of the first wave.
4. Wave two and four usually have alternate forms.
5. Wave 1, 2, and 3 must have the same direction and wave 2, and 4 must be in the opposite direction

The impulse waves are categorized as follows: extended wave (this means that one of the waves 1, 3, and 5 can be extended into an Elliott Wave sub-wave structure), diagonal triangle (occurs when wave 5 is in the same line with wave 2 and 4 causing a diagonal triangle), fifth wave failure (occurs when the length of wave five doesn't exceed the length of wave 3, causing a double top in the trend).

The Corrective Wave are also categorized as follows: *Zig-Zag* ($5 - 3 - 5$ sub-wave structure); *Flat* ($3 - 3 - 5$ sub-wave structure, a and b wave having the same length); *Irregular* ($3 - 3 - 5$ sub-wave structure, with b longer than a); *Horizontal Triangle* (5-wave triangular pattern composed of $3 - 3 - 3 - 3 - 3$ sub-wave structure); *Double Three* (any combination of the above having the form *abcxabc* where x is the link wave); *Triple Three* (any combination of the above having the form *abcxabcxabc* where x is the link wave).

2.3   Fibonacci Mathematics in Financial Markets

The wave principle discovered by Elliott, has in practice a connection with the Fibonacci sequence [13] due to the fact that this series defines the static and dynamic characteristics of a natural system. The Fibonacci sequence is defined as a sequence of derived numbers starting from two initial values

$$(1, 1, 2, 3, 5, 8, 13, 21, 34, 55, 89, 144, 233 \dots).$$

We take in consideration four ratios computed from the Fibonnacci Sequence. Starting from the fifth element, if we divide the current number with the previous number we get a ratio of 1.618. If we divide the current number with the next number in the series we get a ratio of 0.618. If we divide the current number with the number on the previous two position we get a ratio of 2.618. If we divide the current number with the number in the series that precedes it with two position we get a ratio of 0.382. These are called the Fibonacci ratios and in the Elliott Wave Theory, this ratios are the primary factor of the extent of price and time movements in a stock market.

These ratios are used in order to explain the market behavior and to spot a wave. Applied on the Elliott Wave Principles, this ratios have the following behavior: wave 2 corrects up to 50% or 62% of wave 1; wave 4 corrects up to 24% to 28% of wave 3; wave 3 has the length 1.62, 2.62, 4.25 of the length of wave 1; wave 5 depends either on the wave 1 or on the length of the parallel from the start of the wave 1 until the end of the wave 3.

3 Agent Based Architecture

We propose the system architecture described in Figure 1 based on three main agents. The first one combines a series of technical analysis methods based on breaking news or changes in the market conditions along with historical data information in order to find a better moment to buy / sell a stock on the market and to identify a market's status. The second one takes in consideration the hierarchical patterns of the market prices and interprets the psychological aspect of the markets behavior in order to forecast the trend of a stock. The third one uses Neural Networks Methods (more precisely Multi-Layer Perceptron) that searches and recognizes pattern from historical data in order to make a better forecast on the current data.

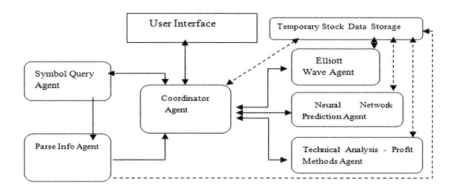

Fig. 1. System Architecture

Coordinator Agent (CA)

The backbone of our proposed system is the Coordinator Agent, who is responsible with the coordination of the agent signals and actions which are presented in Figure 2.

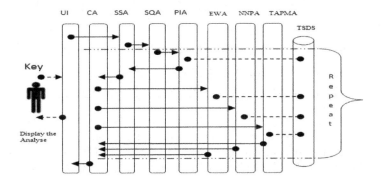

Fig. 2. Agent's signals and actions

All other agents are passing the results gathered to this agent for a more accurate interpretation, meaning that these agents are not interpreting the results, but just send it to CA. The main goal of this agent is to generate buy/sell signal at an earlier time as well as to generate predictions of the trend, so that the gain of the investor approaches maximum.

The signal generating principle is considered to be the following: each analyzing agent has a weight of 0.33% in the final result, if the final result has a probability greater than 50% then CA will trigger the appropriate buy/sell signal. Each analyzing agent will return to CA an integer value in the range of [-1, 1]: 1 for 100% probability for a buy signal, -1 for 100% probability for a sell signal. If the sum of the returned value is greater than 1.5 then a buy signal is triggered and if is lower than -1.5 a sell signal is triggered. Our system provides a probability of 100% that the next day price will rise if all three analyzing agents return +1 value to CA. In Table 1 and Table 2 we present the weights for computing the return value for CA.

For Technical Analysis - Profit Methods Agent we have weight(y) = 0.25 for each analyzing method. These weights are multiplied with +1 if we have a buy signal, 0 if we cannot distinguish a signal, and -1 if we have a sell signal. The result of this multiplication is then returned by each analyzing agent to CA.

Symbol Query Agent (SQA)

CA starts the analysis by signaling SQA to query the stock database servers about a particular share. Our system uses the services provided by SSIFBroker.ro, due to its simple method for downloading the historical data form BSE

Table 1. Neural Network Prediction Agent Weight Distribution

Forecasted Price Difference (diff)	0<|diff|<2.5%	2.5%<|diff|<5%	5%<|diff|<10%	10%<|diff|<15%
Weight(y)	0.25	0.5	0.75	1

Table 2. Elliott Wave Agent Weight Distribution

Elliott Wave Number	1	2	3	4	5	a	b	c
Weight(y)	-	0.5	1	0.66	0.33	-1	-0.66	-0.33

by using the HTTP portal and Comma-Separated Variables (CVS) files. The symbol market and period can be specified in the HTTP address. Also this agent can be modified for downloading data directly from BSE web server.

Parse Info Agent (PIA)

The data downloaded is then used by PIA in order to parse the essential information and will save the data into Temporary Stock Data Storage. This Stock Data can be then used by the other agents for analyze. When PIA is complete, CA signals Elliott Wave Agent, Technical Analysis Profitable Methods Agent and Neural Network Prediction Agent for a parallel analysis of the historical data.

Elliott Wave Agent (EWA)

After receiving the Begin Analysis signal from CA, the EWA will start to analyze the data gathered by PIA on cycles and try to forecast market trends, by searching for extremes values in investor psychology, highs and lows in prices. The Elliott Wave patterns link to form five and three-wave structures which can be predicted, regardless of the size or lengths. By distinguishing the waves and wave structures, the application of the wave principle is a form of pattern recognition.

Neural Network Prediction Agent (NNPA)

NNPA uses Multi-Layer Perceptron Method with variable number of layers in order to predict tomorrow's change. Due to the variable number of layers we can calculate more accurately the predicted values. We discovered, on previous research, that we have a better prediction of stock price if we let the neural network to compute which is the necessary number of hidden layers that it should use, not to give it a fix number of hidden layers.

We set as the maximum difference value between today close value and today generated value to be 1%, meaning that:

$$(|Today\,Generated\,Value \setminus Today\,Close\,Value - 1|) < 0.01. \qquad (1)$$

Starting from 1 hidden layer, NNPA will forecast Today's Value. If (1) is not satisfied than the number of hidden layers will be incremented with one.

For example different stock share, from different industry type, could need a different number of layers to calculate today's value. Also this value is then used for forecasting tomorrow's value.

Technical Analysis - Profit Methods Agent (TAPMA)

TAPMA uses data interpreters and other tools to search for times when a security is having a rise period or a fall period, meaning that it predicts what is could happen in the next period by analyzing the historical data and not by searching patterns. The data interpreters are: Gap Analysis Patterns (GAP), Breakout Systems (BreakS), the Market's Mode (MM) and the Momentum Precedes Price concept (MPP). Each of them works in a parallel mode, and don't interact with each other.

1. GAP analysis will trigger a buy/sell signal under these conditions:
   - Buy: (Today Open > Yesterday High) & (price = Today Open+0.3* Average (TrueRange, 3))
   - Sell: (Today Open < Yesterday Low) & (price = Today Open+0.3* Average (TrueRange, 3))
2. BreakS analysis will trigger a buy/sell signal under these conditions:
   - Buy: (price =Highest (High, 20))
   - Sell: (price =Lowest (Low, 20))
3. MM analysis will trigger a trending/consolidating signal under these conditions:
   - Trending: (Today ADX>25) & (Yesterday ADX<25)
   - Trending: (Today ADX>25) & (Yesterday ADX<25)
   - Consolidating: (Today ADX<20) & (Yesterday ADX>20)
   - Consolidating: (Today ADX<45) & (Yesterday ADX<45)
4. MPP analysis will trigger a buy/sell signal under these conditions:
   - Buy: (MO >0) & (MO=Highest (MO, 32))
   - Sell: (MO<0) & (MO=Lowest (MO, 32)),
   where ADX represents Average Directional Movement , MO represents Momentum Oscillator and TrueRange is the larger of the following:
   - The distance between today's High and today's Low.
   - The distance between today's High and yesterday's Close, or
   - The distance between today's Low and yesterday's Close.

After each method finishes the analysis, TAPM agent is responsible with the interpretation of the intermediate result. GAP analysis signals an important event, BreakS analysis signals if it is a good moment to buy / sell, MM analysis signals if the market is trending or consolidating and MPP analysis signals if the price will continue further in the same direction. Together these four data interpreters can trigger a strong signal to buy or sell.

4   Results

Our architecture uses JAVA Agent Development (JADE) framework for implementing our system agents. By using JADE we can fully distribute the resources, the information and the control on a computer or mobile terminals. The data used by SMMARS framework are downloaded from the services offered by ssif-brocker.ro, which is a founding member of the Bucharest Stock Exchange.

We test our proposed system on two Bucharest Stock Exchange symbols: OLT and TLV, based on a time frame of one month (March 2012).

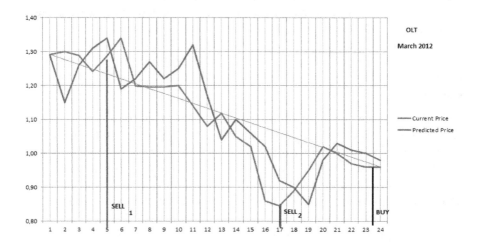

Fig. 3. OLT symbol analysis during March 2012

Figure 3 shows the analysis performed by our system on a short time frame for a descending trend. The system had generated two sell signals at day 5 and day 17 and a buy signal at day 23. The first sell signal is generated by the GAP analysis and the second one by BreakS, who is acting like a Stop Loss indicator. The buy signal is generated by MPP. We should follow the next period to see if the market had reverted the price trends as the MPP predicted. On these analysis we considered a time period of 14 days for calculating temporary technical indicators that were used by our system: Average Directional Index, Momentum Oscillator, Exponential Moving Average and Average True Range. From the chart we can also notice that our system is generating the sell signal at almost the highest price of the month (1.27 p.u / share) and the buy signal after the price tried to break the current trend (at 0.96 p.u / share), meaning a net difference of +32%.

Starting from the current data of a stock, we can predict the tomorrow's value and by using the special Technical Analysis methods the system can give a buy / sell signal. (Table 3)

Figure 4 presents the system analysis on a rising trend; it generates five buy signals (at day 3, 5, 9, 14 and 22) and two sell signals (at day 8 and 20).

Table 3. Stock Price, Predicted Price and Buy / Sell Signals for TLV symbol analysis during March 2012

Current data	Predicted data	Gap Analysis Signal	Breakout System Signal	Momentum Precedes Price
1.030	1.030			
1.080	1.051		Buy	Buy
1.100	1.090			
1.130	1.160			Buy
1.135	1.126			
1.065	1.093	Sell		
1.100	1.090	Buy		
1.100	1.231	Buy		
...	...	...	...	...
1.081	1.064	Sell		
...	...	...	...	...
1.090	1.090	Buy		
1.141	1.060			Buy
1.126	1.120			
1.150	1.150		Buy	Buy
1.150	1.190		Buy	Buy
1.169	1.160			
...	...	...	...	...

We can easily notice that the first sell signal (generated by GAP analysis) is not correctly placed, because at day 10 the price is having an increase. This increase is correctly predicted by 3'th buy signal. Also the second sell signal is generated yet again by BreakS, which is acting such as a Stop Loss Indicator. The net gain in this situation for buying at day 3 (1.08 p.u/share) and selling at day 20 (1.141 p.u/share) is +5.6%. The time period used for the technical indicator is 14 days.

In Figure 5 we present the analysis for a long period of time (1 year) performed by Elliot Wave Agent. As we can notice, this agent is best suited for sell signals, as it generates six major sell signals during the time period. We can also notice that there are two type of wave that an agent is able to distinguish: up trend (sell signals 1, 2 and 5) and down trend (signals 3, 4 and 6). By using this analysis we can maximize our profit by selling at the highest price during an Elliot Wave. The up-trend waves are generating the maximum profit for us, as the sell signal is generated at the moment when the 5'th wave is changing the trend. The down-trend waves sell signals are considered to be such as Stop-Loss signals, because the signals are generated at the moment when 4'th wave is changing the trend. Related to the buy signals, the system is generating four buy signals, each after a down-trend Elliot Wave. Buy signals 2 and 3 are confirmed by the price movement in the next period and more, our system will forecast a buy signal at the moment when 5'th wave from sell signals number 6 is changing the trend.

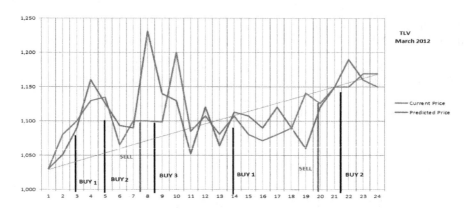

Fig. 4. TLV symbol analysis during March 2012

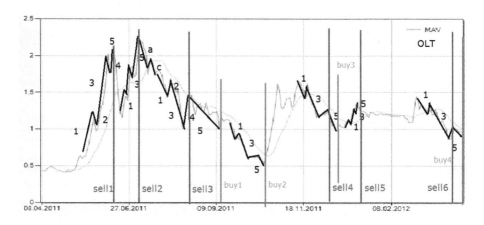

Fig. 5. Elliott Wave Agent Analysis

We will compare our system's results with "Multi-Agent Stock Trading System". We instructed each model to perform it's analysis based on the same time-frame (March 2012) and o the same symbol (OLT).

We can notice that our system is generating the sell signal 3 days ahead of MASTS system, and at a higher price (1.28 p.u / share vs 1.2 p.u / share) meaning a net gain of +6% ; also the BreakS analysis will generate the Stop-Loss signal at the end of the down trend (0.8 p.u / share). The buy signal is generated by MASTS right after changes had occurred in the trend at 0.95 p.u / share. Because our system is using Elliot Wave analysis, we can that now detect if the buy signal is defected before the 5'th Elliot wave is finished, meaning that the buy signal detected by MASTS is not a valid buy signal. Our system will generate a buy signal at the moment when the 5'th wave is finished and the price trend will reverse in an up direction. We can conclude that both systems

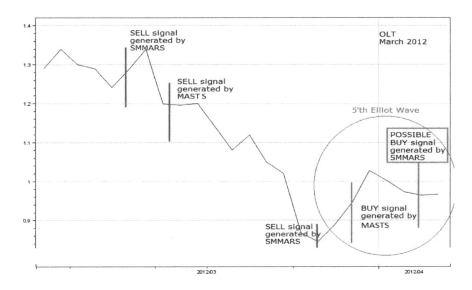

Fig. 6. Comparison between the Stock Market Multi-Agent Recommendation System (SMMARS) and Multi-Agent Stock Trading System (MASTS) buy / sell signals

can detect buy/sell signals at good price/share ratio, but because our proposed system is implementing the Elliot Wave principle, we can detect if non-valid signals appear. Also our system is implementing a Stop-Loss mechanism which is able to save future losses.

Figure 7 presents the recommendation system based on NNPA and TA for TLV symbol for a medium time frame of 100 days. If the recommendation value is +0.1 then the system will trigger a BUY signal and if it is -0.1 it will trigger a SEL signal. These signals will then be filtered by EWA for a more accurate prediction.

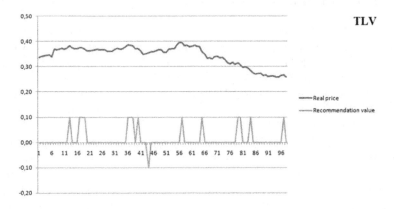

Fig. 7. Recommendation System based on NNPA and TA for TLV Symbol for a Medium Time Frame of 100 Days

Figure 8 presents the recommendation system based on NNPA and TA for OLT symbol for a short time frame of 60 days. The signals are triggered the same as described above.

We quantify the gain/loss in Tabel 4 based on Figure 8:

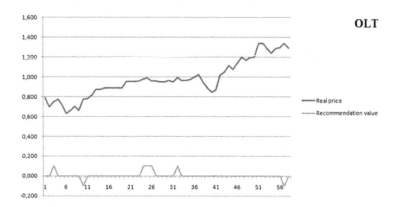

Fig. 8. Recommendation System based on NNPA and TA for OLT Symbol for a Short Time Frame of 60 Days

Table 4. Gain/Loss quantification of OLT Symbol Data

Day	3	10	25	32	57
BUY Price	0.77	-	0.9	0.9	-
SELL Price	-	0.8	-	-	1.37
Gain/Loss per share	-	0.8-0.77=+0.03	-	-	1.37-0.9=+0.47
Gain/Loss in % per share	-	+3%	-	-	+52%

5   Conclusion and Future Work

With this system architecture we proposed a new approach of analyzing the historical data of stock market, by combining pattern recognition software like Neural Network and Elliot Wave with Technical Analysis methods that proved they can be used in predicting buy / sell signals and trends.

By adding both type of Neural Network we can forecast the next day price movement as well as the buy / sell signal, maximizing the profit because the buy/sell at the lowest / highest price.

Also, by adding the Elliot Wave capability, we added a Stop-Loss mechanism; so that the price trend enters in down period, the user can be warn at the beginning of 5'th wave. By adding a Multi-Agent Architecture we can better integrate the pattern recognition agents, who communicate with each other.

After comparing the result given by SMMARS and the one's of the MASTS, we conclude that SMMARS gives a more appropriate result in order to have a gain on the stock market.

As a future work, we propose to solve the risk management problems in order to minimize the losses on a portfolio and to take decision based on noises, how much and in which circumstances these noises can influence the market trend.

This system can be used in order to generate forecasts based on historical data in tourism domain such as the number of specific utilities and the service demands that must be used in order to attract tourist in a region.

Acknowledgment. This work was partially supported by the strategic grant POSDRU/CPP107/ DMI1.5/S/78421, Project ID 78421 (2010), co-financed by the European Social Fund – Investing in People, within the Sectorial Operational Program Human Resources Development 2007 – 2013.

And, partially supported by the grant of the European Commission FP7-REGPOT-CT-2011-284595 (HOST) and Romanian national grant PN-II-ID-PCE-2011-3-0260(AMICAS).

References

1. Atsalakis, G.S., Dimitrakakis, E.M., Zopounidis, C.D.: Elliott Wave Theory and neuro-fuzzy systems, in stock market prediction: The WASP system. Expert Systems with Applications 38, 9196–9206 (2011)
2. Chang, P.-C., Liu, C.-H., Lin, J.-L., Fan, C.-Y., Ng, C.S.P.: A neural network with a case based dynamic window for stock trading prediction. Expert Systems with Applications 36(3, Pt. 2), 6889–6898 (2009)
3. Guresen, E., Kayakutlu, G., Daim, T.U.: Using artificial neural network models in stock market index prediction. Expert Systems with Applications 38(8), 10389–10397 (2011)
4. Tirea, M., Tandau, I., Negru, V.: Multi-Agent Stock Trading Algorithm Model. In: SYNASC - 13th International Symposium on Symbolic and Numeric Algorithms for Scientific Computing, Timisoara, September 26-29, pp. 365–372 (2011)
5. Lam, M.: Neural network techniques for financial performance prediction: integrating fundamental and technical analysis. Decision Support Systems 37(4), 567–581 (2004)
6. Poser, S.W.: Applying Elliott Wave Theory Profitably. Wiley & Son (2003)
7. Ruggiero Jr., M.: Cybernetic Trading Strategies - Developing a Profitable Trading System with State-of-the-Art Technologies. John Wiley & Son (1997)
8. Khan, Z.H., Alin, T.S., Hussain, M.: Price Prediction of Share Market using Artificial Neural Networks (ANN). International Journal of Computer Applications 22(2), 42–47 (2011)
9. Schumakera, R.P., Chenb, H.: A quantitative stock prediction system based on financial news. Information Processing & Management 45(5), 571–583 (2009)
10. Alsubaiea, A., Najand, M.: Trading volume, time-varying conditional volatility, and asymmetric volatility spillover in the Saudi stock market. Journal of Multinational Financial Management 19(2), 139–159 (2009)

11. Wanga, J.-L., Chan, S.-H.: Stock market trading rule discovery using pattern recognition and technical analysis. Expert Systems with Applications 33(2), 304–315 (2007)
12. Pierdziocha, C., Döpkeb, J., Hartmanna, D.: Forecasting stock market volatility with macroeconomic variables in real time. Journal of Economics and Business 60(3), 256–276 (2008)
13. Boroden, C.: Fibonacci Trading: How to Master the Time and Price Advantage. McGraw-Hill (2008)

Similarity of Transactions
for Customer Segmentation

Ke Lu and Tetsuya Furukawa

Department of Economic Engineering, Kyushu University,
Hakozaki 6–19–1, Higashi-ku, Fukuoka 812–8581 Japan
{looker,furukawa}@en.kyushu-u.ac.jp

Abstract. Customer segmentation is usually the first step towards customer analysis and helps to make strategic plans for a company. Similarity between customers plays a key role in customer segmentation, and is usually evaluated by distance measures. While various distance measures have been proposed in data mining literature, the desirable distance measures for various data sources and given application domains are rarely known. One of the reasons lies in that semantic meaning of similarity and distance measures is usually ignored. This paper discusses several issues related to evaluating customer similarity based on their transaction data. Various set distance measures for customer segmentation are analyzed in several imaginary scenarios, and it is shown that each measure has different characteristics which make the measure useful for some application domains but not for others. We argue that no measure always performs better than other measures, and suitable measures should be adopted for specific purposes depending on applications.

Keywords: Customer Segmentation, Transaction Similarity, Set Distance.

1 Introduction

Intense commercial competition induces companies to pay increasing attention to understand their customers more deeply in order to support decision making. For example, e-commerce companies usually offer distinct home pages and recommend relative products to customers based on predictive models built on customer data. Most financial companies construct their own risk models based on the analysis of customer data to prevent customer credit risk.

Data mining techniques have been widely applied in customer relationship management (CRM) [10]. As an important topic in CRM, customer segmentation, which is based on analysis of customer similarity, has drawn increasing attention, and the similarity between customers is an unavoidable issue. While customer segmentation is highly expected to help companies make commercial plans, it does not seem that existing analysis methods work well enough. Consumers still receive significant amount of mails recommending products that they are not interested in, and online recommendations are still far from acceptable [14].

G. Quirchmayr et al. (Eds.): CD-ARES 2012, LNCS 7465, pp. 347–359, 2012.
© IFIP International Federation for Information Processing 2012

An important reason is that customers are segmented improperly due to unsuitable similarity measures. In order to make customer segmentation more adaptable and flexible, it is necessary for companies to understand their target of customer segmentation and which similarity measure is needed for a specific application.

Clustering is usually employed to segment customers, and it is critical to find suitable distance measures to evaluate the similarity between customers with various types of data sources. Customer data is the corner stone of customer segmentation, and can be briefly separated into two categories. The one is demographic data, which is relatively static in long term. Demographic data may include customers' natural properties, *e.g.*, age and gender, or social properties, *e.g.*, marital status and income. The other one is transaction data, which is relatively dynamic compared with demographic data. Generally, transaction data may include much information in purchasing action. Other types of data, *e.g.*, lifestyle data, psychographic data and marketing action data, can be derived from demographic data and transaction data through some statistic methods. Transaction data is merely available for current customers, so that it is necessary to utilize demographic characteristics that are observable in advance for targeting potential customers who are similar to current customers. It has been found that transaction data is the most powerful and reliable data for predicting future customer purchase behavior [8][15]. This paper focuses on the issues of segmenting customers base on transaction data and the issues related to demographic data are not included.

Considerable efforts in finding appropriate distance measures for transaction data have been conducted throughout different applications, because distance measures are fundamentally important for clustering data. However, such endeavors pay little attention to the problem: for a similarity that is evaluated from certain perspective, which distance measures are desirable. For example, some similarities are desired to be evaluated by proportion of affinity items to transactions, while other may require a specific distance. Without explicit understanding the meaning of similarity between customers, it is difficult to select the adaptable distance measures against diverse types of customer data and applications. This paper presents formal discussion on several possible perspectives of measuring the similarity between transactions. Set distances are introduced for evaluating the similarity between transactions. Some measures partially focus on pairwise item distance, while others are affected by assignment of items greatly. It is argued that for different applications, different measures should be adopted and various segmentation results may come out. To the best of our knowledge, this is the first paper that introduces set distances to evaluate the similarity between transactions.

The rest of this paper is organized as follows. Section 2 discusses some preliminary problems and gives some description about the data mentioned in this paper. Similarity between transactions based on *Affinity Items* is discussed in Section 3. Section 4 concerns about the application of set distance measures partially focusing on pairwise item distance. Section 5 refers to the discussion of set distance measures that take assignment of items into consideration. The conclusion of this paper is presented in Section 6.

2 Preliminaries

Customer data is the first word to segment customer. The description of transaction data mentioned in this paper is formally given as follows. Let a customer transaction database D contain all of transactional records of customers. Let $I = \{i_1, i_2, ..., i_r\}$ be the set of product items included in D, where i_k $(1 \leqslant k \leqslant r)$ is the identifier for the k_{th} item. For items i_1 and i_2, let the distance be denoted by $d(i_1, i_2)$. This paper assumes that the distance between pairwise items is given in advance [1][3]. A transaction, denoted by T, is a subset of I. For a distance measure and a threshold σ, if the distance between two transactions is shorter than σ, they are said similar to each other. Customers can be segmented by analyzing the similarity between their transactions.

Segmenting customers based on transaction data has been a long overdue issue for a public debate. Motivated by [9], the so called Customer-Oriented Catalog Segmentation problem, which concerns the problem of segmenting customer based on transactions, has been discussed in [2][6]. The issues related to segmenting customers by transaction data with concept hierarchy have been addressed in [7][12]. As an important association study, clustering transactions has drawn increasing attention [14][16].

The literature mentioned above measures the similarity between transactions based on co-occurrence items. Intuitively, two transactions are deemed to be similar if most items in one transaction have the same item in the other transaction. Hence, counting the co-occurrence items of two transactions is a general method to evaluate the similarity between two transactions, and follows the conventional understanding of similarity. However, it may face a predicament of differentiation dilemma and overlook the relationship between individual items. Nowadays, companies differentiate their products to tackle the problem of homogenization, so that the total kinds of items in transactions are doubled in the past decadeswhile different items may denote very similar products or highly related products. Therefore, what is needed is the error-tolerant measure, s.t., if two items are similar to some predefined extent, they can be regarded as equal to each other in certain sense.

Based on pairwise distance between items, set distance measures are introduced to evaluate the similarity between transaction. Some topics related to set distance measure have been deeply discussed in [5][13].

From the mathematical point of view, distance is defined as a quantitative degree of how far two entities are from each other. The concept of distance mentioned in this paper, both pairwise item distance and transaction distance, obeys the following mathematical meaning of distance.

Definition 1. *Given a set S, a real-valued function $d(x, y)$ on the Cartesian product $S \times S$ is a distance if for any $x, y \in S$, it satisfies the following conditions:*

1. $d(x, y) \geq 0$ (non-negativity),
2. $d(x, y) = d(y, x)$ (symmetry),
3. $d(x, y) = 0$ *if and only if* $x = y$ (self-identity).

A great number of distance measures have been proposed for various applications [4], and the selection of distance measures should depend on specific data and applications. Employing set distance to evaluate the similarity between transactions can give us more precise information than the similarity given by co-occurrence based methods.

3   Transaction Similarity Based on Affinity of Items

The degree of how similar two items are can be evaluated simply by the distance between them. When the distance is short within a certain range, they are called *Affinity Items* in this paper. The definition of *Affinity Items* is formally given as follows.

Definition 2. *If* $d(i_1, i_2) \leqslant \sigma$, *where* σ *is a threshold given in advance,* i_1 *and* i_2 *are regarded as Affinity Items to each other, denoted by* $Aff(i_1, i_2)$.

Compared with co-occurrence, employing distance measures enriches the meaning of similarity between transactions. For example, both substitutes and complements can be deemed similar to each other, or highly related to each other in other words, *e.g.*, both the distance between *Coke* and *Pepsi* (as substitutes) and the distance between *computer* and *software* (as complements) can be deemed very short. Transaction T_1 can be treated similar to transaction T_2 that consists of substitutes or another transaction T_3 that consists of complements. The details of this problem are not considered in this paper, because this paper assumes that the pairwise distance is given in advance.

Example 1. Tom and Jerry meet at a super market and found that they bought *Coke* and *Pepsi*, respectively. Even though *Coke* and *Pepsi* are different product items, Tom and Jerry may improve the identity between them mentally, because *Coke* and *Pepsi* are both soft drink.

The above scenario may appear in our daily life, and this mental phenomenon promotes the following definition about similarity.

Definition 3. *Transactions* T_1 *and* T_2 *are loosely similar to each other if* $\exists i_1 \in T_1$, $\exists i_2 \in T_2$, *s.t.*, $Aff(i_1, i_2)$.

Similar product items, even the same item, appear in different transactions occasionally is a general phenomenon. However, how two customers are said to be similar to each other, is from the perspective of their purchase behavior, which indicates that all of the items in a transaction should be taken into consideration. Similar customers may used to buy some products together. Motivated by this analysis, the definition that two transactions are similar to each other in the strictest term is given as follows.

Definition 4. *Transactions* T_1 *and* T_2 *are strictly similar to each other if* $\forall i_1 \in T_1$, $\exists i_2 \in T_2$, *s.t.*, $Aff(i_1, i_2)$, *and* $\forall i_2 \in T_2$, $\exists i_1 \in T_1$, *s.t.*, $Aff(i_1, i_2)$.

Example 2. Consider the example with two transactions T_1 and T_2 shown in Figure 1 whose items are denoted by $\times$ and $\bigcirc$, respectively. If two items are circled by dotted line together, they are *Affinity Items* for each other. In (a), even there is only a pair of item are *Affinity Items*, they can be deemed loosely similar to each other. While in (b), every item in T_1 has at least one *Affinity Item* in T_2, and vice versa, so that they are strictly similar to each other.

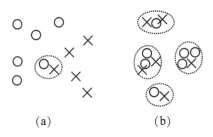

(a)   (b)

Fig. 1. Loose Similarity and Strict Similarity

In practical applications, transactions that satisfy strict similarity come out from time to time, and loose similarity is not so acceptable well enough. In most cases, companies concern about the fraction of items that have *Affinity Items* in another transaction, the following measure is an acceptable one.

Definition 5. *Let* $|R(T_1, T_2)|$ *denote the total number of items in transaction* T_1 *that have* Affinity Items *in transaction* T_2. *The Cardinal Transaction Similarity between transactions* T_1 *and* T_2, *denoted by* $S_c(T_1, T_2)$, *is the fraction of items in either transaction that has* Affinity Items *in the other transaction, i.e.,* $S_c(T_1, T_2) = \frac{|R(T_1,T_2)|+|R(T_2,T_1)|}{|T_1|+|T_2|}$. *For a specified similarity threshold* δ, T_1 *and* T_2 *are cardinally similar to each other, if* $S_c(T_1, T_2) \geqslant \delta$.

Clearly, alternative definitions of measures are possible and the above measure, though intuitive, is only one among possibly several reasonable similarity definitions between sets of itemsets. Cardinal Transaction Similarity is a simple and straightforward measure. However, it may lose some other important information about the similarity between transactions.

4   Transaction Similarity Based on Distance of Items

While Cardinal Transaction Similarity can approximately reflect how similar two transactions are, the specific distance between items is not involved in evaluating the similarity. The measures, which just vaguely evaluate similarity between transactions, can not satisfy diverse practical application in daily scenarios of companies.

Example 3. Let $\times$ and $\bigcirc$ denote the items of T_1 and T_2, respectively. In the example shown in Figure 2, items are *Affinity Items* for each other if they are circled by dotted lines. Cardinal Similarities between transactions T_1 and T_2 are all 0.67 in (a), (b), (c) and (d). However, there are also some differences between them should not be ignored. In (a), there is only one item of T_1 that does not have *Affinity Items* in T_2, and in (b), there are nearly half of items in T_1 that does not have *Affinity Items*. In both (a) and (c), for every item, there is at most one *Affinity Items*, while in both (b) and (d), an item may have several *Affinity Items*. Even for (a) and (c), there is an obvious difference. In (a), all of items in either T_1 or T_2 are relatively similar to each other, while in (c), there is an item in T_2 is far from the rest items in T_1 or T_2.

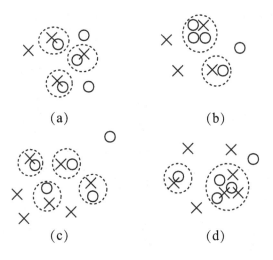

(a)   (b)

(c)   (d)

Fig. 2. Examples of Different Conditions for the Same Cardinal Similarity

As shown in above example, Cardinal Transaction Similarity is not well suitable for applications that require precise information about similarity between transactions. It is very desirable to find measures that at least take the following two factors into consideration:

1. The pairwise distance between items.
2. The assignment determining pairs of items that are involved in calculating the distance between transactions.

This section introduces set distance measures, which determine distance from the perspectives corresponding to those two factors mentioned above, to measure the similarity between transactions. The following discussion starts by introducing the general form of set distance measures. Referencing some concepts of bipartite graph, if two items are assigned together and the distance between them is involved in calculating the distance between two transactions, it is said that they are connected and there is an edge between these two items. For two transactions T_1 and T_2, the general form of set distance measures between them can be written in the following way

$$\mathcal{D}_s(T_1, T_2) = F\left(\frac{\sum_{(i_1, i_2) \in M} d(i_1, i_2)}{|M|}\right),$$

where $M \subseteq T_1 \times T_2$ defines an assignment between T_1 and T_2, $|M|$ denotes the number of edges in M, and F is an aggregation function against the normalized sum of pairwise distance. Maximum, minimum and average are the general options for F. By combining different assignments and aggregation functions, we can get various set distance measures referring to divers factor options.

Assignment is not necessary to be considered together with pairwise distance. Companies may prefer pairwise distance while ignore the assignment in some cases. Consider the following scenario.

Scenario 1
For a given transaction T_1, companies hope to find a transaction T_2 in which there is an item that has the shortest distance to an item in T_1 than any item in other transactions, and deem T_1 and T_2 similar to each other. Corresponding to this scenario, Single-link Distance [11] introduced as follows is a good choice.

Single-link Distance

$$D_{sl}(T_1, T_2) = \min_{i_1 \in T_1, i_2 \in T_2} d(i_1, i_2)$$

In Scenario 1, companies only require one pair of items to satisfy a given constraint. On the opposite, the following scenario need that every items satisfy some conditions.

Scenario 2
For a given transaction T_1, companies hope to find a transaction T_2, s.t., distances of every pairwise items between T_1 and T_2 shorter than a given threshold, and deem T_1 and T_2 similar to each other. Corresponding to this scenario, Complete-link Distance [11] introduced as follows is suitable.

Complete-link Distance

$$D_{cl}(T_1, T_2) = \max_{i_1 \in T_1, i_2 \in T_2} d(i_1, i_2)$$

Another well known distance measure is Hausdorff Distance.

Hausdorff Distance

$$D_h(T_1, T_2) = \max(h(T_1, T_2), h(T_2, T_1)),$$

where $h(T_1, T_2)$, the so-called one-sided Hausdorff distance from T_1 to T_2, is formally defined as follows.

$$h(T_1, T_2) = \max_{i_1 \in T_1} (\min_{i_2 \in T_2} d(i_1, i_2))$$

$h(T_1, T_2)$ and $h(T_2, T_1)$ are asymmetric.

If two transactions are deemed similar based on Complete-link Distance, the distances of every pair of items are within a constrained range. Compared with Complete-link Distance, Hausdorff Distance only guarantees every item in one transaction can find an item in the other transaction, s.t., the distance between two items is in a limited range. However, they may cause another type of ambiguous result. Two transactions may be deemed dissimilar to each other due to a pair of items that are distant to each other, while the rest of pairwise distances are very short. If a new constraint is added to calculate Complete-link distance and Hausdorff distance, which requires every pair of items involved in calculating those two distances must be *Affinity Items*, it seems more reasonable. New measures are formally given as follows.

Affinity Complete-link Distance

$$D_{acl}(T_1, T_2) = \max_{i_1 \in T_1, i_2 \in T_2, Aff(i_1, i_2)} d(i_1, i_2)$$

Affinity Hausdorff Distance

$$D_{ah}(T_1, T_2) = \max(h(T_1, T_2), h(T_2, T_1)),$$

where $h(T_1, T_2)$, the so-called one-sided Affinity Hausdorff distance from T_1 to T_2, is formally defined as follows.

$$h(T_1, T_2) = \max_{i_1 \in T_1} (\min_{i_2 \in T_2, Aff(i_1, i_2)} d(i_1, i_2))$$

$h(T_1, T_2)$ and $h(T_2, T_1)$ are asymmetric.

These five measures do not take much information about the items into consideration, and are determined by the distance of certain pair of items with extreme condition. For example, two transactions may be deemed similar if there is a pair of items that are very similar while the rest of pairwise distances are far apart from each other. Different from those five measures that are determined by certain pairwise items, Average Distance takes the distances of pairwise items into consideration. For two transactions, the upper limit and lower limit of their Average Distance are Complete-link Distance and Single-link Distance, respectively.

Average Distance

$$D_{avg}(T_1, T_2) = \frac{\sum_{i_1 \in T_1, i_2 \in T_2} d(i_1, i_2)}{|T_1||T_2|}$$

Despite various weaknesses, the set distance measures mentioned in this section are very straightforward, and adhere to conventional thinking way of clustering.

5   Assignment of Items between Transactions

It is obvious that there is not fixed structure for transaction, *e.g.*, the size of different transactions may be different, and items are not necessary to be corresponding to any attribute. This characteristic induces assignment to be a noteworthy factor in calculating set distance between transactions. Actually, assignment refers to structures of transactions, *e.g.*, a transaction may mainly consist of soft drinks and alcoholic drinks, while another transaction may conclude pastry and vegetable. The original intention of assignment is to connect items that are as similar as possible.

Example 4. As shown in Figure 3, let □, ○ and × indicate the items of three different transactions, respectively. If the assignment of items is not taken into consideration, for transactions denoted by □ and ×, Single-link Distance, Complete-link Distance and Hausdorff Distance between transaction denoted by ○ and them are the same as shown in Figure 3(a). However, if assignment of items requires that every item must be connected to at least one item in another transaction, the transaction denoted by □ is closer to the one denoted by ○ than the one denoted by × as shown in Figure 3(b).

This is just a simple example that every transaction has equal size. It becomes more complicated when the size of various transactions are different.

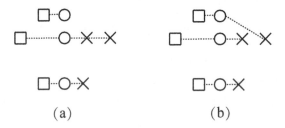

(a)   (b)

Fig. 3. Examples of Assignment in Set Distance

This section discusses set distance measures that take assignment of items into consideration. The following discussion goes with various scenarios which companies may encounter.

Scenario 3
Companies have a target transaction T_1 which consists of some picked up products. They hope to find another transaction T_2 in which there is at least one distinct similar item for as many as possible items in T_2, and the average pairwise distance is as short as possible. Corresponding to this scenario, Matching Distance introduced as follows is a good choice.

Matching Distance

For two transactions T_1 and T_2, if every item in T_1 is connected to at most one item in T_2, and vice versa, it is said that there is a matching between T_1 and T_2. For a matching ζ between two transactions T_1 and T_2, if $\nexists$ matching ζ' s.t. $|\zeta'| > |\zeta|$, ζ is a maximum matching of T_1 and T_2, and $\min\{|T_1|, |T_2|\} \geqslant |\zeta|$. It should be noted that there is not necessarily only one maximum matching for two transactions. The Matching Distance measure is given as follows and it actually refers to the minimum-weighted maximum matching problem.

Definition 6. *Let ζ be a maximum matching between T_1 and T_2, Matching Distance between T_1 and T_2 is defined as follows.*

$$D_m(T_1, T_2) = \min_{\zeta} \frac{\sum_{(i,j) \in \zeta} d(i,j)}{\min\{|T_1|, |T_2|\|}$$

Matching Distance does not take all of items into consideration. Especially, when the difference of size between two transactions is very large, a large proportion of items in the large transaction are not involved in calculation. It is desired to find some other measures that take all of items into consideration. Consider the following scenario.

Scenario 4

For two transactions T_1 and T_2, suppose $|T_1| \geqslant |T_2|$. Companies hope to find a similarity measure by which every item in T_1 is compared with the most similar item in T_2 and every item in T_2 is compared with at least one item in T_1. The items that are far from any items in the other transaction are also taken into consideration of similarity between transactions as a penalty. Surjection Distance is introduced to against this scenario.

Surjection Distance

For two transactions T_1 and T_2, here suppose $|T_1| \geqslant |T_2|$, if every item in T_1 is only connected to one item in T_2, and every item in T_2 is connected to at least one item in T_1, it is said that there is a surjection between T_1 and T_2. Based on the distance between items, Surjection Distance is given as follows.

Definition 7. *Let η be a surjection between transactions T_1 and T_2. Surjection Measure between T_1 and T_2 is defined as follows.*

$$D_s(T_1, T_2) = \min_{\eta} \frac{\sum_{(i,j) \in \eta} d(i,j)}{\max(|T_1|, |T_2|)}$$

In Surjection Distance measure, every item in the transaction that has a larger size is constrained to be connected to at most one item in the other transaction. However, in practical application, an item in the transaction with larger size may be very similar to some items in the other transaction. This application requires that a measure should take all of items into consideration while an item can be connected to multiple items in another transaction. Link Distance measure is such a measure that satisfies above requirements.

Link Distance

Link is another assignment that every item in one transaction is connected with the other transaction. For two transactions T_1 and T_2, if every item in T_1 is connected to at least one item in T_2, and vice versa, it is said that there is a link between T_1 and T_2. Link Distance [5] is given as follows.

Definition 8. *Let τ be a link between T_1 and T_2, Link Distance between T_1 and T_2 is*

$$D_l(T_1, T_2) = \min_{\tau} \sum_{(i,j) \in \tau} d(i,j).$$

It should be noted that Link Distance is not normalized in definition in order to avoid being effected by some items that have many similar items in another transaction. Link Distance must be normalized before we employ Link Distance to compare the distance between diverse transactions.

Example 5. As shown in Figure 4, transactions T_1 and T_2 are denoted by $\times$ and $\bigcirc$, respectively. According to the definition of Link Distance, the link τ that determines the assignment of items is described by the dotted line in Figure 4(a). If Link Distance is normalized before it is applied to compare the similarity between transactions, adding some other pairwise link, *e.g.*, the solid line shown in 4(b), can shorten the Link Distance between transactions. However, it disobeys the original intention of assignment.

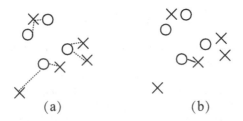

(a)   (b)

Fig. 4. Why Link Distance cannot be normalized in advance

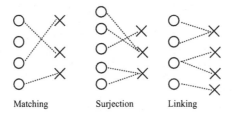

Matching   Surjection   Linking

Fig. 5. Examples of Matching, Surjection and Linking

Some examples of Matching, Surjection and Linking are visualized as examples in Figure 5. Set Distance measures that take assignment into consideration enrich the meanings the similarity between transactions. Employing Set Distance measures flexibly can help companies solve various problems in their daily business.

6   Conclusion

This paper refers to the issue that how to evaluate the similarity between customers based on various customer data. Various measures helping to segment customers based on transaction data were discussed. Set distance measures were introduced to evaluate the similarity between transactions from two perspectives: (1) the pairwise distance between items and (2) the assignment of items. The applications of set distances were discussed under various imaginary business scenarios for companies. No similarity measure performs better over all of other measures, and understanding the semantic meaning of similarity measures is critical for customer segmentation.

An obvious limitation of this paper is that we have not yet verified our analysis on real transaction data. The future work includes verifying the results of this paper, and proposing specific methods for segmenting customers based on transaction data.

References

1. Aggarwal, C.C., Procopiuc, C.M., Yu, P.S.: Finding Localized Associations in Market Basket Data. IEEE Trans. Knowl. Data Eng. 14(1), 51–62 (2002)
2. Amiri, A.: Customer-oriented Catalog Segmentation: Effective Solution Approaches. Decision Support Systems 42(3), 1860–1871 (2006)
3. Das, G., Mannila, H.: Context-Based Similarity Measures for Categorical Databases. In: The 4th European Conference on Principles and Practice of Knowledge Discovery in Databases, Bilbao, pp. 201–210 (2000)
4. Deza, E., Deza, M.: Dictionary of Distances. North-Holland, Amsterdam (2006)
5. Eiter, T., Mannila, H.: Distance Measures for Point Sets and Their Computation. Acta Inf. 34(2), 109–133 (1997)
6. Ester, M., Ge, R., Jin, W., Hu, Z.J.: A Microeconomic Data Mining Problem: Customer-oriented Catalog Segmentation. In: The 10th ACM SIGKDD International Conference on Knowledge Discovery and Data Mining, Seattle, pp. 557–562 (2004)
7. Hsu, F.M., Lu, L.P., Lin, C.M.: Segmenting Customers by Transaction Data with Concept Hierarchy. Expert Syst. Appl. 39(6), 6221–6228 (2012)
8. Kim, S.Y., Jung, T., Suh, E.H., Hwang, H.S.: Customer Segmentation and Strategy Development based on Customer Lifetime Value: A Case Study. Expert Syst. Appl. 31(1), 101–107 (2006)
9. Kleinberg, J.M., Papadimitriou, C.H., Raghavan, P.: A Microeconomic View of Data Mining. Data Min. Knowl. Discov. 2(4), 311–324 (1998)
10. Ngai, E.W.T., Li, X., Chau, D.C.K.: Application of Data Mining Techniques in Customer Relationship Management: A Literature Review and Classification. Expert Syst. Appl. 36(2), 2592–2602 (2009)

11. Niiniluoto, I.: Truthlikeness. D. Reidel Pub. Comp., Dordrecht (1987)
12. Wang, M., Hsu, P.-Y., Lin, K.C., Chen, S.: Clustering Transactions with an Unbalanced Hierarchical Product Structure. In: Song, I.-Y., Eder, J., Nguyen, T.M. (eds.) DaWaK 2007. LNCS, vol. 4654, pp. 251–261. Springer, Heidelberg (2007)
13. Woznica, A., Kalousis, A.: Adaptive Distances on Sets of Vectors. In: The 10th IEEE International Conference on Data Mining, Sydney, pp. 579–588 (2010)
14. Yang, Y.H., Padmanabhan, B.: Segmenting Customer Transactions Using a Pattern-Based Clustering Approach. In: The 3th IEEE International Conference on Data Mining, Florida, pp. 411–418 (2003)
15. Yen, S.F., Lee, Y.S.: An Efficient Data Mining Approach for Discovering Interesting Knowledge from Customer Transactions. Expert Syst. Appl. 30(4), 650–657 (2006)
16. Yun, C.H., Chuang, K.T., Chen, M.S.: Clustering Item Data Sets with Association-Taxonomy Similarity. In: The 3th IEEE International Conference on Data Mining, Florida, pp. 697–700 (2003)

Challenges in Using Linked Data within a Social Web Recommendation Application to Semantically Annotate and Discover Venues

Jakub Dzikowski, Monika Kaczmarek,
Szymon Lazaruk, and Witold Abramowicz

Department of Information Systems,
Faculty of Informatics and Electronic Commerce,
Poznan University of Economics
al. Niepodleglosci 10, 61-875 Poznan, Poland
{j.dzikowski,m.kaczmarek,s.lazaruk,w.abramowicz}@kie.ue.poznan.pl
http://www.kie.ue.poznan.pl

Abstract. This paper focuses on a semantically-enhanced Social Web Recommendation application, called *Taste It! Try It!* It is a mobile restaurants' review and recommendation application based on a Linked Data source and integrated with a social network. The application is consuming Linked Data (while creating the reviews), producing semantic annotations (about the reviewed entities) and then, querying the gathered data in order to offer personalized recommendations. In this paper, we focus only on the consumption and usage of Linked Data for the needs of social recommendation system and point out the challenges and shortcomings that need to be addressed.

Keywords: Linked data application, semantic annotations, semantic content creation tool.

1 Introduction

The Semantic Web paradigm constitutes a major step in the evolution of the Web. It is to enable machines to understand the meaning of information on the WWW. It is done via extending the network of hyper-linked human-readable web pages by inserting machine-readable meta-data, i.e., semantic annotations, about the Web content and information on how they are related to each other, thus, enabling automated reasoning [Berners-Lee et al., 2001]. A semantic annotation is machine processable, if it is explicit, formal, and unambiguous and this goal is usually reached by using ontologies [Uschold and Grüninger, 1996].

The Web has evolved into the Web of Data [Bizer et al., 2009] by using a set of best practices for publishing and connecting structured data on the Web, known as Linked Data. The content of the Linked Data cloud is diverse in nature [Bizer et al., 2009], comprising, e.g., data about geographic locations, people, companies, radio programmes, genes, proteins, census results, and reviews. Since 2007, the Linking Open Data cloud has expanded considerably. However, apart

G. Quirchmayr et al. (Eds.): CD-ARES 2012, LNCS 7465, pp. 360–374, 2012.
© IFIP International Federation for Information Processing 2012

of some initiatives showing how to build applications using it, there is still plenty of space for more end-user applications operating on the Linked Data.

The above trends constitute a motivation for the development of a *Taste It! Try It!* application focusing on the creation of semantically annotated restaurants' reviews using concepts from DBpedia. The mentioned application is not only consuming the Linked Data (while creating the reviews), but also produces additional semantic annotations (about the reviewed entities) using either the mobile or WWW interface. As we are following the faceted-based approach to the review creation, we benefit from the additional information within the disambiguation process. That is why for the needs of the *Taste It! Try It!* application, a distinct disambiguation solution has been designed, adjusted to the specific needs of a mobile device. *Taste It! Try It!* is a real-world application and during the performed experiments it has been used by 180 users.

The goal of the paper is twofold. On the one hand, it is to show the user-friendly way of creating semantic annotations using Linked Data, and on the other, is to start a discussion on the consumption and usage of Linked data within the applications such as *Taste It! Try It!* and point the challenges and shortcomings that need to be addressed. Although the issues related to the efficiency of application of semantic technologies (reasoners, integration of data) are well investigated in the literature, there is still a number of issues left to be addressed. Thus, with this paper we aim at starting a discussion on the maturity of both the semantic data sources as well as tools that are to facilitate the Semantic Web and the Linked Data adoption. In addition, as the application is also integrated with the Facebook portal, the privacy related issues are also discussed.

In order to meet the above mentioned goal, the paper is structured as follows. We start with a short summary of the related work and position our application towards the work of others. Then, the vision of the tool, along with its architekture is shortly presented. Next, we focus on the interactions with the Linked Data sources within the *Taste It! Try It!* application and provide information on the semantic annotations' creation and usage process. Then, the challenges tackled in the context of DBpedia[1] and Facebook are discussed. The paper concludes with final remarks.

2 Related Work

Recommender Systems (RS) are information search tools that have been proposed to cope with the information-overload problem, i.e, the typical state of a consumer, having too much information to make a decision [Adomavicius and Tuzhilin, 2005, Burke, 2007]. Recommender Systems can be either [Pu et al., 2012]: *rating-based* (content-based or social/collaborative-based) – users explicitly express their preferences by giving binary or multi-scale scores to items that they have already experienced, or *feature-based* (case-based, utility-based, knowledge-based and critiquing-based) – evaluating the match between a user's need and the set of options available [Burke, 2002].

---

[1] http://dbpedia.org

Recommender systems normally use software instead of users for the information filtering tasks [Peis et al., 2008]. This approach, however, has some disadvantages. The communications process, either between agents and users or agents only, is complicated because of the heterogeneity of information representation, which in turn leads to incapability of its reuse in other processes and applications. Thus, Semantic Web technologies are more and more often used within the recommender systems.

A particularly interesting example of ontology-based system has been introduced by Cantador and Castells in [Cantador and Castells, 2006] and extended in [Cantador et al., 2011]. In this work, a multi-layer semantic social network model has been proposed, based on a hypothesis that since user's interests are not made of a single piece, any approach that deals with them as such would have inevitable limitations. Thus, the system has been defined from different perspectives, splitting user profiles according to meaningful groups/layers of preferences shared among users, so that the similarities between users are to be established based on sub-profiles, rather than the global ones. This approach is also continued in the *Taste It! Try It!* application.

Semantic Web technologies have been introduced almost a decade ago, and yet, their real-life impact has been considerably limited for first few years. The situation has changed dramatically by an initiative called a Linked Data project. Based on the simple semantic technologies, like RDF and URIs, used along with Linked Data principles[2], a number[3] of datasets have been made available in a machine-understandable manner, eg., Wikipedia's resources are available on the Web of Data in the form of DBpedia.

Linked Data sets are used in more and more real-world application. Examples include [Hausenblas, 2009]:

- Faviki[4] – social bookmarking tool, utilizing semantic tags stemming from Wikipedia (via DBpedia) so that all concepts are ambiguously identified;
- DBpedia mobile[5] – mobile, location-based application presenting information from DBpedia on a map;
- Revyu[6] – a generic reviewing site based on the Linked Data principles and the Semantic Web technology stack.

Linked Data lowers the entry barrier for data providers by focusing on publishing structured data rather than, on the ontological level or inferencing, hence fosters a wide spread adoption. However, there exists some challenges that need to be tackled by developers of real-world linked open data applications, not least of which include resource discovery, consolidation and integration across a distributed environment. Another group of challenges arise from the fact that building application based on foreign resources under control of third parties

---

[2] http://www.w3.org/DesignIssues/LinkedData.html
[3] 295 datasets up to 2011 - source: http://lod-cloud.net/
[4] http://faviki.com
[5] http://wiki.dbpedia.org/DBpediaMobile
[6] http://revyu.com/

leads to unresolved issues regarding potentially dynamic nature of dataset content, meaning that they can be changed or even disappear [Umbrich et al., 2010]. Furthermore, problems of co-reference, ontology mapping, aggregation from distributed sources, resource discovery, queries spanning multiple datasets are also to be tackled [Millard et al., 2010].

The *Taste It! Try It!* application benefits from the already developed semantic technologies and tools, and offers an added value through their integration and usage in order to, on the one hand, contribute to the Linked Data by producing semantic annotations, and on the other, to offer personalized advanced discovery and clustering possibilities. For the needs of the *Taste It! Try It!* application, a distinct disambiguation solution has been designed, adjusted to the specific needs of a mobile device. All of these features together, make the *Taste It! Try It!* application a distinct solution.

3   Taste It! Try It! Application

Taste It! Try It! has been designed as a Web 2.0 application supporting the creation of semantic annotations describing various places and locations. It is targeted at end-users, among which two groups may be distinguished: data producers (contributors) – users providing reviews of places, i.e., people creating semantically annotated reviews, and data consumers (beneficiaries) – users interested in the content produced by the application, i.e., people looking for opinions about various places. Therefore, on the one hand, *Taste It! Try It!* enables data producers to contribute to a semantic content creation process using their mobile devices[7] or a WWW interface, and on the other, provides data consumers with personalized, semantic, context-aware recommendation process (i.e., offer a personalized semantic search mechanism).

3.1   Storyboard

The storyboard supported by the system is as follows. A user goes to a restaurant. While being at the restaurant, the user decides to share his opinion on the restaurant with other members of the community. He uses Taste It! Try It! to express this opinion and creates a review by providing values to selected features suggested by the application. In particular, the review edition screen is divided into 3 tabs:

Main tab. containing basic and obligatory information such as: name of the place being reviewed; type of location; GPS location which is to be provided using the mobile devices built-in GPS module; and star ratings that allow the user to express his Overall, Service, Atmosphere, Food impression in the quantitative manner, by assigning from 1 to 5 stars in each category.

---

[7] The application is developed to work with the Android system.

Details tab. allowing the user to assess a wide range of qualitative features of the place, which are grouped in intuitive categories such as: Dining options, Entertainment or Good for. In this tab, the user is also able to select the cuisine type and best dishes/drinks served. Values of those fields are suggested from DBpedia.

More tab. containing some additional star ratings and features together with a free-text comment field.

The review is then uploaded to a *Taste It! Try It!* server and in the background, the semantic representation is created. Based on the quantity and quality of created annotations, the user may be awarded with a special title e.g., *Polish-cuisine expert*, *International-food expert*. This title is visible to his friends at the Facebook portal, with which the application is integrated. Moreover, a user may check the ranking among his friends on Facebook.

In addition, based on the user behaviour and data made available by the Facebook portal, the user profile is created, which is then used in the personalization process.

3.2   Architecture

Taste It! Try It! consists of three main components: an Android client, a Facebook client and a Server. Moreover the *Taste It! Try It!* application communicates with three other components: Facebook (FB), the INSEMTIVES platform and DBpedia (see fig. 1). The first three components are to provide basic functionalities of the application. Communication with the other ones is to connect the application with Web 2.0 services (the social aspect) and Linked Data (the semantics).

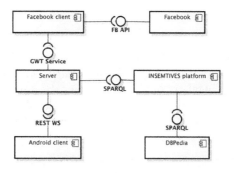

Fig. 1. UML component diagram of *Taste It! Try It!*

The Android client provides a user with a front-end to manage reviews. For communication with the Server a RESTful Web Service interface is used. The Facebook client is a web front-end embedded in the Facebook canvas[8] and

---

[8] http://developers.facebook.com/docs/guides/canvas/

written with the use of Google Web Toolkit framework[9]. Via the FB API interface[10] the Facebook client authenticates and authorises the user, as well as retrieves basic information about the user (name, gender, list of friends). The GWT Service interface provided by the Server is to retrieve and store informations about user's interaction with the application, including restaurant reviews and user's personal information.

To support the semantic content creation process, the *Taste It! Try It!* application integrates with the INSEMTIVES platform and DBpedia. The INSEMTIVES platform is a tool created by the INSEMTIVES consortium[11] on top of the OWLIM semantic repository[12], which uses native RDF engines implemented in Java and both Sesame[13] and Jena[14] frameworks. Among others it consists of a SPARQL endpoint, that is used to store and retrieve RDF triples. A part of semantic data is retrived and cached from DBpedia via the DBpedia SPARQL endpoint.

3.3   Semantic Annotations Based on Linked Data

An ontology is a formal, explicit specification of a shared conceptualization [Gruber, 1995]. It provides a data model, i.e., shared vocabulary that may be used for describing objects in the domain (their type, properties and relations). The important part of every ontology are the instances forming a knowledge base. Instances refer to a concrete object being an instantiation of an object type represented by the ontology.

After conducted analysis of the coverage and popularity of the currently available semantic contents providers, the decision was taken to consume data from DBpedia while creating the reviews in order to provide unambiguous values to the reviewed features of a venue. After the careful analysis of the structure of relevant concepts from DBpedia and schema.org, as well as types of assigned properties to the Restaurant concept, and comparing it to the Data model used by the *Taste It! Try It!* application, we have noticed that values of only few elements/fields require disambiguation (e.g., features expressed using stars or having binary value can be directly mapped to DBpedia concepts within the application model and no-aid from a user is necessary). Thus, only the following facets from the review need to be linked to the concepts from DBpedia by users of the application: category of restaurant, type of cuisine, food and drinks served. Values of all other features are mapped automatically.

As a consequence of this decision, users while filling in the above mentioned aspects of a review, are pointing to the concepts from DBpedia. As the process of assigning semantic annotations to the created reviews was to be on the one

---

hand, user-friendly and almost invisible to users, and on the other, work well on a mobile device (specific way of introducing data), we have decided to take advantage of an auto-completion mechanism suggesting possible tags to be used. The auto-completion mechanism is shown in figure 2.

Fig. 2. Autocompletion mechanism

As we are following the faceted-based approach to the review creation, we can benefit from the additional knowledge in order to disambiguate and limit the potential tags (concepts from DBpedia) to be presented to users as an option to choose from. This becomes even more important in case of a mobile device – the presented list of tags to choose from, should not be too long. Therefore, for the needs of the *Taste It! Try It!* application, a distinct disambiguation solution has been designed. It works as follows – once a user starts to type in the first characters of the tag for the selected feature, the disambiguation takes place in the following steps:

- an appropriate SPARQL query limited to the branch of interest (e.g., in case a user is providing a tag to the *best dishes* feature, only the concepts related to Food and drinks are suggested) is created automatically by the application,
- the obtained result is filtered using the preferred language of the user as well as the first characters typed in and as a result the list of concepts with their labels is retrieved from DBpedia,
- the proposed list of suggestions is sorted by Levenshtein distance between suggestions and typed characters and presented to the user.

The SPARQL queries used to gather the relevant concepts for auto-completion, depending on the type of field being annotated, needed to be created in a semi-automated manner – using appropriate scripts to generate queries based on the manual analysis of the structure of DBpedia.

The reviews provided by users are stored on the server and then serialized into the RDF format, so that they can be later on published as linked dataset.

In order to check, whether such a venue is already defined within the ontology (i.e., in order to disambiguate the object being reviewed), the server performs the following steps:

- Taking into account the data provided by a user, i.e., the geographical coordinates of the location, the SPARQL query is formulated automatically by the application in order to retrieve all already described places of interest (restaurants and all subcategories) within specific radius from the coordinates provided. As a result a set of objects is being retrieved.
- If the set is not null, the Levenshtein measure is applied to the name of the concepts being retrieved and the name provided in the review in order to identify similar objects (e.g., in case of a typo in a name of the place).
- Based on the above, the ranking list is created. In case only one object reaches the defined similarity threshold, the disambiguation is automatically performed, in all other cases – the system is assuming it is a new concept as long as a user being presented with the ranked list of restaurants will not decide otherwise.

Once we know whether the RDF triples will concern a new or already existing concept, the further serialization is performed.

Another issue that needs to be addressed while creating the RDF triples is reaching the consensus in case contradictory information is provided by different users on the same venue. Therefore, the tool needed also to incorporate a feature supporting consensus creation while providing annotations. It is worth noting that the created semantic annotations that are to be made available outside the *Taste It! Try It!* application, are anonymous (no information about the author of the review is revealed outside the *Taste It! Try It!* application) and the subjective evaluation of the venue is expressed in an aggregated form (e.g., by showing an average number of assigned stars).

A new venue is being added to the database as soon as it reaches the limit of 3 reviews being assigned. Each new review added about the already existing venue within the knowledge base, may result in updating the information on the restaurant stored there. The created RDF triples are then uploaded to the INSEMTIVES platform via the SPARQL interface and stored in the local RDF repository.

Although our application exploits semantic datasets, the complex semantic nature of the underlying information is hidden to the end users who do not interact directly with the Semantic Web languages and technologies such as RDF or SPARQL. It is also visible while performing the search of a restaurant of interest. The following scenarios are currently supported:

- Searching for a restaurant with some quantitative criteria (non-semantic, e.g., number of stars assigned (not less than...)).
- Searching for a restaurant with some qualitative (non-semantic) criteria added, e.g., wi-fi zone, live sport events transmissions etc.
- Searching restaurants near some location – a map and coordinates (see fig 3).
- Searching for a restaurant with some criteria requiring reasoning (semantic ones from DBpedia) – type of cuisine and type of dishes (see fig 3).

Fig. 3. *Taste It! Try It!*– searching for a restaurant – choosing location, cuisine and dishes

Additionally the *Taste It! Try It!* application enables personalisation in the searching process. Thus, the following personalisation-enhanced search scenarios are supported:

- Searching for a restaurant I may like, i.e., recommended by people with a similar profile.
- Searching for a restaurant that my friends from the Facebook recommended (criteria – author of the review).
- Searching for a restaurant that one specific persons (that I trust) likes.
- Hang-out (recommend a restaurant for n-number of *Taste It! Try It!* users).

When it comes to specifying the semantic criteria, a user searches for it by typing characters in the corresponding text field, as indicated on fig 3. The application returns an auto-complete list of suggested concepts retrieved from DBpedia. Once the list has been populated, the user can select one (or more) of the suggested concepts.

As already mentioned, while returning the search results, the additional personalization may be applied. Thus, in fact while searching, the personalized recommendation exploits both the knowledge base – information gathered by the *Taste It! Try It!* application and DBpedia (content-based approach), and the similarities between users (collaborative-filtering approach).

4   Challenges

Implementation of scenarios and functionalities described shortly in the previous section, required addressing several issues. In the case of integration with DBpedia we had to deal with poor reliability of public SPARQL endpoints while trying to find an efficient solution to a well known problem of querying semantic data coming from various repositories. In the case of integration with the Facebook, we had to handle problems resulting from a restricted Facebook privacy policy.

In order to test our application and evaluate the usability of the developed tool, experiments with 180 participants were conducted during December 2011 and January 2012. The conducted experiments not only allowed to improve the application and verify its performance, but also as a result, 2274 reviews on approximately 900 different restaurants with 5667 semantic concepts coming from DBpedia were created. The challenges presented below encompass also few selected findings from the experiments, however, due to the limited space the experiments themselves are not further described.

4.1   Integration with DBpedia

During the process of searching for restaurants both the original concepts from DBpedia and the ones created by the *Taste It! Try It!* application need to be considered. As already mentioned in the previous section, search criteria include e.g., cuisine types and dishes from DBpedia (being used within the created reviews) as well as restaurants, which could be already defined within DBpedia or constitute new venues added by the *Taste It! Try It!* application. In this case two approaches may be followed: (1) performing a federated query to DBpedia and our local SPARQL endpoint or (2) storing part of the data from DBpedia in our endpoint. We decided to test both of them.

At the time of writing, neither DBpedia nor the SPARQL enpoint in the IN-SEMTIVES platform supports federated queries. It is possible to query DBpedia and the INSEMTIVES platform using another endpoint supporting federated queries[15]. However, there are only few public endpoints of that kind and we find their performance unsatisfactory.

After unsuccessful experiments with Virtuoso[16] and Sesame[17] we have decided to use – Apache Jena Fuseki[18]. An instance of the endpoint has been deployed and tested as an interface to perform federated queries. The endpoint itself turned out to be a feasible solution, however, the following performance issues have occurred:

- Because of the obscure structure of DBpedia, queries for retrieving cuisine or dishes types had to be quite complex. Performing these queries took long time and often led to time-out errors.
- The performance of the DBpedia SPARQL endpoint depends of its current usage and often is very poor (participants of experiments complained having to wait up to 30 seconds or more for a result). Sometimes the endpoint is not available at all.

---

[15] For example http://sparql.org/query.html
[16] http://virtuoso.openlinksw.com/
[17] http://www.openrdf.org/
[18] http://incubator.apache.org/jena/documentation/serving_data/

– The way SPARQL federated queries work is not efficient enough. For example a federated query (as shown in listing 1.1) is performed as follows. The first sub-query is performed on the first endpoint (in our case the INSEMTIVES platform). Then, for every result of the sub-query further sub-queries are performed on the second endpoint (the DBpedia). At the end the results of the queries are integrated by the endpoint that supports federated queries (Apache Jena Fuseki).

The first of the issues enumerated needs to be stressed. An important finding from the conducted experiments is the poor quality of information provided by DBpedia (mainly the lack of consistency regarding the structure to which concepts of the same type are being assigned). The coverage of DBpedia was deemed as unsatisfactory by most of the users. It does not necessarily result from the fact that the required concept is not present in the data gathered by DBpedia, but the concept could have been assigned to a not-intuitive place in the structure, which makes it difficult to be discovered

As a consequence, we decided to follow the second approach and to duplicate the part of DBpedia. Although all the data from DBpedia is available to download[19], required by our application RDF triples (covering such concepts as dishes, cuisine types and restaurants) are defined in multiple files. Thus, the whole English version of DBpedia has been downloaded and integrated with the RDF repository in our instance of the INSEMTIVES platform. During the first launch of the platform indexing of 111 GB text files with RDF triples in the NT format took about 3.5 day. Additionally, the response-time of the copy of DBpedia was too long (because of the large amount of data to process and complex queries to handle). Thus, we decided to retrieve via the DBpedia SPARQL endpoint only required concepts, generate *.nt files and insert them to our RDF repository.

Listing 1.1. SPARQL federated query to retrieve from DBpedia `skos:broader` concepts of dishes from the INSEMTIVES platform

```
select ?uriBroader {
  { service <http://insemtives.example.com/sparql>
    { select ?uri where {
    <http://insemtives.eu/tasteit/DishesType>
    <http://insemtives.eu/tasteit/instance>
    ?uri .    } } }
  { service <http://dbpedia.org/sparql>
    { select ?uriBroader ?uri where {
    ?uri
    <http://www.w3.org/2004/02/skos/core#broader>
    ?uriBroader .  } } } }
```

To retrieve only relevant concepts and relations the public DBpedia SPARQL endpoint, our instance of the INSEMTIVES platform and our instance of the Apache Jena Fuseki were used. At first queries for restaurants, dishes and cuisine

---

[19] http://wiki.dbpedia.org/Downloads37

types were performed on the DBpedia. Then, we generated RDF triples to store them in our repository in the INSEMTIVES platform. The example of the triples is shown in listing 1.2.

Listing 1.2. An example of generated RDF triples for dishes types (NT format)

```
. . .
<http :// insemtives .eu/ tasteit / DishesType >
    <http :// insemtives .eu/ tasteit / instance >
        <http :// dbpedia .org/ resource / Pasta_salad >  .
<http :// insemtives .eu/ tasteit / DishesType >
    <http :// insemtives .eu/ tasteit / instance >
        <http :// dbpedia .org/ resource / Waldorf_salad >  .
. . .
```

Storing presented RDF triples in our repository enabled us to display in the application auto-suggestions for cuisine types and dishes, in efficient manner. Instead of complex query to the DBpedia SPARQL endpoint, a simple query to our local endpoint is being performed to retrieve a list of suggestions.

Additionally, our reasoning mechanism requires an access to all concepts C and C' that fulfil the following conditions:

- A given cuisine type, dish or restaurant is in the relation skos:broader with C.
- A given cuisine type, dish or restaurant is in the relation dcterms:subject with C.
- C is in the relation skos:broader with C'.

To retrieve appropriate RDF triples we performed federated queries to the DBpedia and the INSEMTIVES platform on our Apache Jena Fuseki endpoint. An example of the query is presented in listing 1.1.

However, the presented example is still too complex to perform it as one query. The public DBpedia SPARQL endpoint was not able to handle about 10,000 sub-queries (for all pre-fetched dishes types) without time-out. In consequence, we had to put limits and offsets after first sub-query and generate queries automatically. We have prepared UNIX/Linux shell scripts to generate and perform queries to count entities from the first sub-queries, retrieve concepts for particular subsets of concepts for the sub-queries and generate appropriate RDF triples in the NT format. A part of the script is presented in listing 1.3. The parameter LIMIT contains limit for the results in the first sub-query. In our case value of this parameter differs according to the complexity of the query (from 1 to 50). It had to be adjusted to the DBpedia endpoint performance for particular queries. The COUNT variable contains a number of results of the first sub-query and the s-query is included in Fuseki distribution Ruby script for querying SPARQL endpoints.

Listing 1.3. Part of a shell script to perform federated queries

```
for OFFSET in 'seq 0 $LIMIT $COUNT'
do
    QUERY="""
select ?uri ?uriBroader {
{ service <http://insemtives.example.com/sparql>
   { select ?uri where {
       <http://insemtives.eu/tasteit/DishesType>
       <http://insemtives.eu/tasteit/instance>
       ?uri . }
   limit $LIMIT offset $OFFSET   } }
  { service <http://dbpedia.org/sparql>
     { select ?uriBroader ?uri where {
        ?uri
        <http://www.w3.org/2004/02/skos/core#broader>
        ?uriBroader . } } } }
    """
    ../s-query --output=tsv --service $FUSEKI_URL "$QUERY"
done
```

Thus, the implementation of two possible scenarios proved that neither of them works fully in practice, in this way limiting the potential usage of the Linked Data. Although, all of the content of DBpedia is available to download and free to use, a number of issues needs to be considered in order to take advantage of it.

4.2   Integration with the Facebook

In addition, the restrictions resulting from the Facebook privacy policy – the user's personal data is not allowed to be stored by other applications – needed to be tackled. In consequence, in case user's data needs to be utilised, two independent requests to two components (the Facebook and the Server) are required. In figure 4 we present an UML sequence diagram of displaying statistics of the user's friends. This is a good example of the enforced redundancy in HTTP calls. The first call occurs when the user visits the appropriate *Taste It! Try It!* webpage. The user has to be authorised by the Facebook, so the first call occurs when the Facebook client requests Facebook for user credentials. Therefore, the Facebook client uses FB API interface to request Facebook for user authentication and authorisation (see fig. 1 and 4).

When the user is authorised, the Facebook client uses the Google Web Toolkit client-server communication interface to retrieve a user profile from the Server. These two calls have to be performed each time – it is significantly slowing down the loading of particular web pages (user profile, review list, search form, friends statistics and user settings). Although these calls are inherently asynchronous, the application has to wait for the results of the former call to perform the latter one. Thus, they are executed as if they were synchronous.

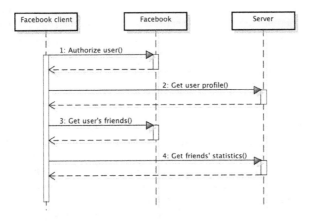

Fig. 4. UML sequence diagram of retrieving statistics of friends using the *Taste It! Try It!* application

As has been already mentioned, according to the Facebook privacy policy the application is not allowed to store a list of user's friends. Thus, the list as well has to be retrieved each time from the Facebook portal. During the third call the Facebook client uses the FB API to obtain the list of friends' Facebook IDs. The fourth call, when the Facebook client calls the Server, is to retrieve statistics of user's Facebook friends, who are using the *Taste It! Try It!* application.

A similar sequence of calls occurs each time the application requires additional information from the Facebook portal and Server.

5 Conclusions

The *Taste It! Try It!* application, presented in this paper, is a semantic content creation tool for a mobile device. It is to support users in the process of creation of semantically annotated reviews of various venues. It uses DBpedia as a source of data and is integrated with the Facebook portal. In this paper, we have shown how the application is consuming the Linked Data, and how additional semantic annotations are created. As they are to be made available outside the *Taste It! Try It!* application, they are anonymous and the subjective evaluation of the venue is expressed in an aggregated form.

In order to verify the mechanisms applied within the application as well as evaluate the usability of the developed tool, experiments with 180 participants were conducted. The evaluation of the proposed solution has shown that the application constitutes a good compromise between the power of semantic annotations and the difficulty of creating and maintaining them, and in addition, allowed to identify new directions of the application evolution.

During the implementation of the application, a number of problems related to the lack of maturity of the semantic technologies has been encountered. They show that apart of the already well known problems with the federated queries, also the problems related to the quality of the linked data, its coverage, as well as the performance of the semantic technologies, hamper greatly the evolution of the Web. Users will not accept fully the Semantic Web paradigm, if semantic applications will burden them with additional interactions with RDF or SPARQL technologies, or will exhibit lower performance than the traditional applications.

References

[Adomavicius and Tuzhilin, 2005] Adomavicius, G., Tuzhilin, A.: Toward the next generation of recommender systems: A survey of the state-of-the-art and possible extensions. IEEE Trans. on Knowl. and Data Eng. 17, 734–749 (2005)

[Berners-Lee et al., 2001] Berners-Lee, T., Hendler, J., Lassila, O.: The semantic web. Scientific American 284(5), 34–43 (2001)

[Bizer et al., 2009] Bizer, C., Heath, T., Berners-Lee, T.: Linked data - the story so far. International Journal on Semantic Web and Information Systems 5(3), 1–22 (2009)

[Burke, 2002] Burke, R.: Hybrid recommender systems: Survey and experiments. User Modeling and User-Adapted Interaction 12, 331–370 (2002)

[Burke, 2007] Burke, R.: Hybrid Web Recommender Systems. In: Brusilovsky, P., Kobsa, A., Nejdl, W. (eds.) Adaptive Web 2007. LNCS, vol. 4321, pp. 377–408. Springer, Heidelberg (2007)

[Cantador and Castells, 2006] Cantador, I., Castells, P.: Multilayered Semantic Social Network Modeling by Ontology-Based User Profiles Clustering: Application to Collaborative Filtering. In: Staab, S., Svátek, V. (eds.) EKAW 2006. LNCS (LNAI), vol. 4248, pp. 334–349. Springer, Heidelberg (2006)

[Cantador et al., 2011] Cantador, I., Castells, P., Bellogín, A.: An enhanced semantic layer for hybrid recommender systems: Application to news recommendation. Int. J. Semantic Web Inf. Syst. 7(1), 44–78 (2011)

[Gruber, 1995] Gruber, T.: Toward principles for the design of ontologies used for knowledge sharing. International Journal of Human-Computation Studies 43, 907–928 (1995)

[Hausenblas, 2009] Hausenblas, M.: Exploiting linked data to build web applications. IEEE Internet Computing 13, 68–73 (2009)

[Millard et al., 2010] Millard, I., Glaser, H., Salvadores, M., Shadbolt, N.: Consuming multiple linked data sources: Challenges and experiences. In: Proceedings of the First International Workshop on Consuming Linked Data (COLD 2010), Shanghai, China (2010)

[Peis et al., 2008] Peis, E., del Castillo, J.M.M., Delgado-López, J.A.: Semantic recommender systems. analysis of the state of the topic. Hipertext.net 6 (2008) (online)

[Pu et al., 2012] Pu, P., Chen, L., Hu, R.: Evaluating recommender systems from the user's perspective: survey of the state of the art. User Modeling and User-Adapted Interaction, 1–39 (2012), 10.1007/s11257-011-9115-7

[Umbrich et al., 2010] Umbrich, J., Hausenblas, M., Hogan, A., Polleres, A., Decker, S.: Towards dataset dynamics: Change frequency of linked open data sources. In: Proceedings of the WWW 2010 Workshop on Linked Data on the Web, LDOW 2010 (2010)

[Uschold and Grüninger, 1996] Uschold, M., Grüninger, M.: Ontologies: principles, methods, and applications. Knowledge Engineering Review 11(2), 93–155 (1996)

Pay-As-You-Go Data Integration
Using Functional Dependencies

Naser Ayat[1], Hamideh Afsarmanesh[1], Reza Akbarinia[2], and Patrick Valduriez[2]

[1] Informatics Institute, University of Amsterdam, Amsterdam, Netherlands
{s.n.ayat,h.afsarmanesh}@uva.nl
[2] INRIA and LIRMM, Montpellier, France
Firstname.Lastname@inria.fr

Abstract. Setting up a full data integration system for many application contexts, e.g. web and scientific data management, requires significant human effort which prevents it from being really scalable. In this paper, we propose IFD (Integration based on Functional Dependencies), a pay-as-you-go data integration system that allows integrating a given set of data sources, as well as incrementally integrating additional sources. IFD takes advantage of the background knowledge implied within functional dependencies for matching the source schemas. Our system is built on a probabilistic data model that allows capturing the uncertainty in data integration systems. Our performance evaluation results show significant performance gains of our approach in terms of recall and precision compared to the baseline approaches. They confirm the importance of functional dependencies and also the contribution of using a probabilistic data model in improving the quality of schema matching. The analytical study and experiments show that IFD scales well.

Keywords: Data integration, uncertain data integration, functional dependency.

1 Introduction

Data integration systems offer uniform access to a set of autonomous and heterogeneous data sources. Sources may range from database tables to web sites, and their numbers can range from tens to thousands. The main building blocks of a typical data integration application are mediated schema definition, schema matching and schema mapping. The mediated schema is the schema on which users pose queries. Schema matching is the process of finding associations between the elements (often attributes or relations) of different schemas, e.g. a source schema and the mediated schema in the popular Local As View (LAV) approach [1]. Schema mapping (also referred to as semantic mapping) is the process of relating the attributes of source schemas to the mediated schema (sometimes using expressions in a mapping language). The output of schema matching is used as input to schema mapping algorithms [1].

Setting up a full data integration system with a manually designed mediated schema requires significant human effort (e.g. domain experts and database

G. Quirchmayr et al. (Eds.): CD-ARES 2012, LNCS 7465, pp. 375–389, 2012.
© IFIP International Federation for Information Processing 2012

designers). On the other hand, there are many application contexts, e.g. web, scientific data management, and personal information management, which do not require full integration to provide useful services [2]. These applications need to start with a data integration application in a complete automatic setting for reducing human effort and development time and put more effort on improving it as needed. Let us present a motivating example from the scientific data management context.

Example 1. Consider a researcher who is interested in the less-known or yet unknown functions of the protein ABCC8 related to diabetes. While biological experiments are the ultimate means for verifying predicted functions, she must first discover and suggest such functions. For doing this, she should perform manual exploratory searches over numerous online sources. For example, she should consider both well-known databases such as EntrezGene, EntrezProtein and less-known databases of other research labs as well. Having a data integration system with approximate answers can considerably save the time and reduce the research cost in this domain. It is sufficient to set up such a system in a complete automatic setting and spend more effort to improve it only if it is necessary. This recent setting, referred to by pay-as-you-go data integration, has attracted considerable attention, e.g. [2–5]. The ultimate goal of this setting is to reduce human burden, and thereby reduce the time and cost of data integration while providing sufficient integration [2].

The goal of our work is to provide a pay-as-you-go data integration system that deals with the uncertainty arising during the matching process. To capture the uncertainty, we generate Probabilistic Mediated Schemas (PMSs) which have shown to be promising [6]. The idea behind PMSs is to have several mediated schemas, each one with a probability that indicates the closeness of the corresponding mediated schema to the ideal mediated schema.

The closest related work to ours is that of Sarma et al. [3] which based on PMSs proposed UDI (Uncertain Data Integration), an uncertain data integration system. However, UDI may fail to capture some important attribute correlations, and thereby produce low quality answers. Let us clarify this by an example which is the same as the running example in [3].

Example 2. Consider the following schemas both describing people:
$S_1(name, hPhone, hAddr, oPhone, oAddr)$
$S_2(name, phone, address)$

In S_2, the attribute *phone* can either be a home phone number or an office phone number, and the attribute *address* can either be a home address or an office address.

An ideal data integration system should capture the correlation between *hPhone* and *hAddr* and also between *oPhone* and *oAddr*. Specifically, it must generate schemas which group the *address* and *hAddr* together if *phone* and *hPhone* are grouped together. Similarly it should group the *address* and *oAddr* together if *phone* and *oPhone* are grouped together. In other words either of the following schemas should be generated (we abbreviate $hPbone, oPhone, hAddr, oAddr$ as $hP, oP, hA,$ and oA respectively):

$M_1(\{name, name\}, \{phone, hP\}, \{oP\}, \{address, hA\}, \{oA\})$
$M_2(\{name, name\}, \{phone, oP\}, \{hP\}, \{address, oA\}, \{hA\})$

Although these schemas are generated by UDI, they are overwhelmed by schemas in which the attribute correlations are not respected. Thus, by producing a large number of schemas which can easily be exponential, the desirable schemas get a very low probability. This occurs because UDI does not consider attribute correlations. Most attribute correlations are expressed within Functional Dependencies (FDs). For example let F_1 and F_2 be the set of FDs of S_1 and S_2 respectively:

$F_1 = \{hPhone \rightarrow hAddr, oPhone \rightarrow oAddr\}$
$F_2 = \{phone \rightarrow address\}$

These FDs show the correlation between attributes. For example, $hPhone \rightarrow hAddr$ indicates that the two attributes $hPhone$ and $hAddr$ are correlated. Considering the pairs of FDs from different sources can help us extracting these correlations and achieving the goal of generating mediated schemas that represent these correlations. For example, the FD pair $phone \rightarrow address$ and $hPhone \rightarrow hAddr$ indicates that if we group $phone$ and $hPhone$ together, we should also group $address$ and $hAddr$ together, as well as $oPhone$ and $oAddr$.

In this paper, we propose IFD (Integration based on Functional Dependencies), a pay-as-you-go data integration system that takes into account attribute correlations by using functional dependencies, and captures uncertainty in mediated schemas using a probabilistic data model. We model the schema matching problem as a clustering problem with constraints. This allows us to generate mediated schemas using algorithms designed for the latter problem. In our approach, we build a custom distance function for representing the knowledge of attribute semantics which we extract from FDs. We also propose a new metric (i.e. FD-point) for ranking the generated mediated schemas in the clustering process, and selecting high quality ones. IFD allows integrating a given set of data sources, as well as incrementally integrating additional sources, without needing to restart the process from scratch. To validate our approach, we implemented IFD as well as baseline solutions. The performance evaluation results show significant performance gains of our approach in terms of recall and precision compared to the baseline approaches. They confirm the importance of FDs in improving the quality of uncertain mediated schemas.

The rest of the paper is organized as follows. In Section 2, we make our assumptions precise and define the problem. In Section 3, we propose IFD, and describe its architecture, components and algorithms. We also analyze the execution cost of IFD's algorithms. Section 4 describes our performance validation. Section 5 discusses related work, and Section 6 concludes.

2   Problem Definition

In this section, we first give our assumptions and some background about PMSs. Then, we state the problem we address in this paper.

For the applications which we consider (e.g., scientific data management), we assume the availability of functional dependencies for the attributes of sources. This is a reasonable assumption in the applications which we consider, in particular scientific applications, because the data source providers are willing to provide the full database design information, including functional dependencies. However, there are contexts such as the web in which functional dependencies are not available. For these applications, we can use one of the existing solutions, e.g. [7, 4] to derive functional dependencies from data. Another assumption, which we make for ease of presentation, is that the data model is relational.

Now, we define some basic concepts, e.g. functional dependencies and mediated schemas, and then state the problem addressed in this paper. Let S be a set of source schemas, say $S = \{S_1, \ldots, S_n\}$, where for each $S_i, i \in [1, n], S_i = \{a_{i,1}, \ldots, a_{i,l_i}\}$, such that $a_{i,1}, \ldots, a_{i,l_i}$ are the attributes of S_i. We denote the set of attributes in S_i by $att(S_i)$, and the set of all source attributes as A. That is $A = \cup_i att(S_i)$. For simplicity, we assume that S_i contains a single table. Let F be the set of functional dependencies of all source schemas, say $F = \{F_1, \ldots, F_n\}$. For each $S_i, i \in [1, n]$, let F_i be the set of functional dependencies among the attributes of S_i, i.e. $att(S_i)$, where each $fd_j, fd_j \in F_i$ is of the form $L_j \to R_j$ and $L_j \subseteq att(S_i), R_j \subseteq att(S_i)$. In every F_i, there is one fd of the form $L_p \to R_p$, where $R_p = att(S_i)$, i.e. L_p is the primary key of S_i.

We assume that every attribute in the data sources can be matched with at most one attribute in other data sources, which means we only consider one-to-one mappings. We do this for simplicity and also because this kind of mapping is more common in practice. For a set of sources S, we denote by $M = \{A_1, \ldots, A_m\}$ a mediated schema, where $A_i \subseteq A$, and for each $i, j \in [1, m], i \neq j \Rightarrow A_i \cap A_j = \emptyset$. Each attribute involved in A_i is called a mediated attribute. Every mediated attribute ideally consists of source attributes with the same semantics.

A probabilistic mediated schema (PMS) for a set S of source schemas is the set $N = \{(M_1, P(M_1)), \ldots, (M_k, P(M_k))\}$ where $M_i, i \in [1, k]$, is a mediated schema, and $P(M_i)$ is its probability. For each $i, j \in [1, k], i \neq j \Rightarrow M_i \neq M_j$, i.e. M_i and M_j are different clusterings of $att(S)$; and $\sum_{i=1}^{k} P(M_i) \leq 1$.

Since each mediated schema corresponds to a clustering of source attributes, we can measure its quality by computing the F-measure of the clustering.

Let us now state the problem we address. Suppose we are given a set of source schemas S, and a set of functional dependencies F and a positive integer number k as input. Our problem is to efficiently find a set of k probabilistic mediated schemas which have the highest F-measure.

3   Data Integration Based on Functional Dependencies

In this section, we describe IFD, a data integration system that automatically performs the tasks of mediated schema generation and the attribute matching, by taking advantage of functional dependencies among the source attributes. In the rest of this section, we first briefly describe the architecture of our data integration system. Then, we describe our approach for schema matching.

3.1   System Architecture

Figure 1 depicts the architecture of our system, which consists of two main parts of schema matching and query processing, in part A and part B respectively. The components of part A operate during the set-up time of the system and the components of part B operate at query evaluation time. In this paper, our focus is on the schema matching part (part A) but we include components of part B in the architecture of our system to provide a complete picture of a data integration system. A more detailed description of the components is available in the extended version of this paper [8].

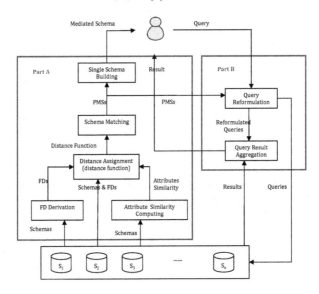

Fig. 1. Architecture of our data integration system

To build the mediated schema automatically, we cluster the source attributes by putting semantically equivalent attributes in the same cluster. We use a clustering algorithm that works based on a *distance matrix* (i.e. the distance between every two attributes). Specifically we use the single-link CAHC (Constrained Agglomerative Hierarchical Clustering) algorithm [9]. To assign the distances between the attributes, we use the attributes' name similarity as well as some heuristics we introduce about FDs.

3.2   FD Heuristics

We use heuristic rules related to FDs in order to assign the distance of attributes. Before describing our heuristics, let us first define *Match* and *Unmatch* concepts. Consider a_1 and a_2 as two typical attributes. If we want to increase their chance of being put in the same cluster, we set their distance to MD (i.e. Match Distance) which is 0 or a number very close to 0. In this case, we say that we matched a_1 with a_2, and we show this by $Match(a_1, a_2)$. In contrast, if we want to decrease their chance of being put in the same cluster, then we set their distance to UMD (i.e. Un-Match Distance) which is 1 or a number very close to 1. In this case, we say that we *unmatched* a_1 and a_2 and we show this by $Unmatch(a_1, a_2)$. Now, Let us use the following example to illustrate the heuristics.

Example 3. Consider two source schemas, both describing a university course schedule. In this example, primary keys are underlined; F_1 and F_2 are the sets of FDs of S_1 and S_2 respectively:

$S_1(\underline{term}, \underline{c\#}, \underline{section\#}, coursename, instructor, name, time, room)$
$S_2(\underline{semester}, \underline{course}, \underline{sec\#}, name, instructor, ins\_name, location)$
$F_1 = \{c\# \rightarrow coursename, instructor \rightarrow name\}$
$F_2 = \{course \rightarrow name, instructor \rightarrow ins\_name\}$

Heuristic 1. *Let S_p and $S_q, p \neq q$, be two source schemas. Then,*

$$Match(a_{p,i}, a_{q,k}) \Rightarrow unmatch(a_{p,i}, a_{q,l}) \wedge unmatch(a_{q,k}, a_{p,j})$$

where $a_{p,i} \in att(S_p), a_{p,j} \in att(S_p) \setminus \{a_{p,i}\}, a_{q,k} \in att(S_q), a_{q,l} \in att(S_q) \setminus \{a_{q,k}\}$.

The reason behind heuristic 1 is that each attribute can be matched with at most one attribute of the other source.

Heuristic 2. *Let $fd_p : a_{p,i} \rightarrow a_{p,j}$ and $fd_q : a_{q,k} \rightarrow a_{q,l}$ be two FDs, where $fd_p \in F_p, fd_q \in F_q, p \neq q$. Then, $similarity(a_{p,i}, a_{q,k}) > t_L \Rightarrow Match(a_{p,j}, a_{q,l})$ where t_L is a certain threshold and similarity is a given similarity function.*

The reason behind heuristic 2 is that we consider the set of facts that the two sources are assumed to be from the same domain, and both attributes $a_{p,j}$ and $a_{q,l}$ are functionally determined by the attributes $a_{p,i}$, and $a_{q,k}$ respectively, which themselves have close name similarity. Thus, we heuristically agree that: the probability of $Match(a_{p,j}, a_{q,l})$ is higher than that of $Match(a_{p,j}, a_{q,s})$ and $Match(a_{q,l}, a_{p,r})$, where $a_{q,s} \in att(S_q) \setminus \{a_{q,l}\}$ and $a_{p,r} \in S_p \setminus \{a_{p,j}\}$. Therefore, in such a case we match $a_{p,j}$ with $a_{q,l}$ to reflect this fact. Note that this heuristic has a general form in which there are more than one attribute on the sides of the FDs (see Section 3.3).

By applying heuristic 2 on Example 3, we have the FD $instructor \rightarrow name$ from S_1, and $instructor \rightarrow ins\_name$ from S_2. There is only one attribute at the left side of these FDs, and their name similarity is equal to 1 that is the maximum similarity value. Thus, we match the $name$ with the ins_name which appear on the right side of these FDs. Notice that in this example, FDs guided us to recognize that the $name$ in S_2 is in fact the instructor's name, and not the course's name. This kind of mistake is typically made by approaches which only rely on name similarity for attribute matching.

Heuristic 3. *Let PK_p and $PK_q, p \neq q$, be the primary keys of S_p and S_q respectively. Then,*

$$(\exists a_{p,i} \in PK_p, a_{q,j} \in PK_q \mid (a_{p,i}, a_{q,j}) = \underset{a_p \in PK_p, a_q \in PK_q}{\arg \max} \; similarity(a_p, a_q)) \wedge$$

$$(similarity(a_{p,i}, a_{q,j}) > t_{PK}) \Rightarrow Match(a_{p,i}, a_{q,j})$$

where t_{PK} is a certain threshold and similarity is a given similarity function.

The reason behind heuristic 3 is simple. Since we assume sources are from the same domain, there are a number of specific attributes which can be part of the primary key. Although these attributes may have different names in different sources, it is reasonable to expect that some of these attributes from different sources can be matched together. Obviously, we can set t_{PK} to a value less than the value we set for t_L because typically the probability of finding matching attributes in the primary key attributes is higher than the other attributes. After matching $a_{p,i}$ with $a_{q,j}$, we remove them from PK_p and PK_q respectively, and continue this process until the similarity of the pair with the maximum similarity is less than the threshold t_{PK} or one of the PK_p or PK_q has no more attributes to match.

Now we apply heuristic 3 to Example 3. It is reasonable to match the attributes: *term*, *c#*, and *section#* of S_1 with *semester*, *course*, and *sec#* of S_2 rather than with other attributes of S_2, and vice versa. The attribute pair with the maximum similarity is *(section#, sec#)*. If we choose a good threshold, we can match these attributes together. The similarity of other attribute pairs is not high enough to pass the wisely selected threshold values.

Heuristic 4. *Let PK_p and $PK_q, p \neq q$, be the primary keys of S_p and S_q respectively. Then,*

$$(\exists a_{p,i} \in PK_p, a_{q,j} \in PK_q, fd_p \in F_p, fd_q \in F_q \mid$$

$$fd_p : a_{p,i} \to R_p, fd_q : a_{q,j} \to R_q) \Rightarrow Match(a_{p,i}, a_{q,j}) \quad (1)$$

and also

$$(RHS(1) \wedge R_p = \{a_{p,r}\} \wedge R_q = \{a_{q,s}\}) \Rightarrow Match(a_{p,r}, a_{q,s}) \quad (2)$$

We can apply heuristic 4 when we have two attributes in two primary keys which each of them is the single attribute appearing at the left side of a FD. In this case, we match these attributes with each other(rule 1). We also match the attributes on the right sides of the two FDs if there is only one attribute appearing at the right side of them (rule 2).

By applying heuristic 4 on Example 3, we match *c#* with *course* which is a right decision. We do this because of the two FDs: $c\# \to coursename$ and $course \to name$. We also match *coursename* with *name* which are the only attributes appearing at the right side of these FDs. Had we used name similarity only, we would have very likely matched *coursename* with *course* for example, which is a wrong decision.

Algorithm 1. Distance Assignment

Input: 1) Source schemas $S_1, \ldots, S_n$; 2) The sets of FDs $F_1, \ldots, F_n$ (the FDs related to PK are omitted); 3) $P = \{PK_1, \ldots, PK_n\}$ The set of primary keys of all sources.
Output: Distance matrix $D[m][m]$.
1: compute $A = \{a_1, \ldots, a_m\}$ the set of all source attributes
   // match attributes on the right sides of FDs
2: **for all** FD pair $fd_i \in F_k, fd_j \in F_l, k \neq l$ **do**
3:     **if** $IsMatch(L_i, L_j)$ **then**
4:         make local copies of fd_i, fd_j
5:         find the attribute pair $a_p \in R_i, a_q \in R_j$ with the maximum similarity s
6:         **if** $s > t_R$ **then**
7:             $DoMatch(a_p, a_q)$
8:             $R_i \leftarrow R_i \setminus \{a_p\}; R_j \leftarrow R_j \setminus \{a_q\}$
9:             **if** $| R_i | > 0$ and $| R_j | > 0$ **then**
10:                go to 5
    // match PK attributes
11: **for all** pair $PK_i, PK_j \in P$, where they are PKs of S_i and S_j respectively **do**
12:     make local copies of PK_i and PK_j
13:     **for all** pair $a_p \in PK_i, aq \in PK_j$ **do**
14:         **if** $\exists fd_k \in F_i$ and $fd_l \in F_j$ such that $L_k = \{a_p\}$ and $L_l = \{a_q\}$ **then**
15:             $DoMatch(a_p, a_q)$
16:             $PK_i \leftarrow PK_i \setminus \{a_p\}; PK_j \leftarrow PK_j \setminus \{a_q\}$
17:             **if** $R_k = \{a_s\}$ and $R_l = \{a_t\}$ **then**
18:                 $DoMatch(a_p, a_q)$
19:     find the attribute pair $a_p \in PK_i$ and $a_q \in PK_j$ with maximum similarity s
20:     **if** $s > t_{PK}$ **then**
21:         $DoMatch(a_p, a_q)$
22:         $PK_i = PK_i \setminus \{a_p\}; PK_j = PK_j \setminus \{a_q\}$
23:         **if** $| PK_i | > 0$ and $| PK_j | > 0$ **then**
24:             go to 19
25:     **if** $PK_i = \{a_p\}$ and $PK_j = \{a_q\}$ **then**
26:         $DoMatch(a_p, a_q)$
27: **for all** attribute pair $a_i, a_j \in A$ which $D[a_i][a_j]$ has not been computed yet **do**
28:     **if** $a_i, a_j \in S_k$ (the same source) **then**
29:         $D[a_i][a_j] \leftarrow UMD$
30:     **else**
31:         $D[a_i][a_j] \leftarrow similarity(a_i, a_j)$
32: $\forall a_i, a_j, a_k \in A$ if $(D[a_i][a_k] = MD$ and $D[a_k][a_j] = UMD)$ **then** $D[a_i][a_j] \leftarrow UMD$
33: $\forall a_i, a_j, a_k \in A$ if $(D[a_i][a_k] = MD$ and $D[a_k][a_j] = MD)$ **then** $D[a_i][a_j] \leftarrow MD$
34: $\forall a_i, a_j \in AD[a_i][a_j] \leftarrow D[a_j][a_i]$

Heuristic 5. *Let PK_p and $PK_q, p \neq q$, be the primary keys of S_p and S_q respectively. Then,*

$$(\forall a_{p,r} \in PK_p \setminus \{a_{p,i}\}, \exists a_{q,s} \in PK_q \setminus \{a_{q,j}\} \mid Match(a_{p,r}, a_{q,s})) \wedge$$
$$(|PK_p| = |PK_q|) \Rightarrow Math(a_{p,i}, a_{q,j})$$

We can apply heuristic 5 when all attributes of PK_p and PK_q have been matched, and only one attribute is left in each of them. We match these two attributes with each other hoping that they are semantically the same. Coming back to Example 3, there is only one attribute left in each of the primary keys that we have not yet matched (i.e. *term, semester*) that we can match using this heuristic.

3.3   Distance Assignment Algorithm

Algorithm 1 describes how we assign distances to attribute pairs and build the distance matrix that is used in schema matching. Steps 2-10 of the algorithm find

FD pairs from different sources which their left sides match together and then try to match attribute pairs on the right sides of these FDs. Steps 5-7 find the attribute pairs (a_p, a_q) whose similarity is maximum. If the similarity of a_p and a_q is more than threshold t_R, their distance is set to MD (Match Distance), and the distances between each of them and any other source-mates are set to UMD (Unmatch Distance). The algorithm uses the $DoMatch$ procedure for matching and unmatching attributes. It gets the attributes which should be matched as parameter, matches them, and unmatches every one of them with the other ones' source-mates. Generally, whenever the algorithm matches two attributes with each other, it also unmatches the two of them with the other one's source-mates because every attribute of a source can be matched with at most one attribute of every other source. Steps 8-10 remove the matched attributes from the list of unmatched attributes, and repeat the matching process if there are still some attributes remaining for matching.

Step 3 uses the $IsMatch$ function. This function takes as parameter the left sides of two FDs and returns true if they can be matched together, otherwise it returns false. It first checks whether the input parameters are two sets of the same size. Then, it finds the attribute pair with maximum name similarity and treats it as matched pair by removing the attributes from the list of unmatched attributes if their similarity is more than threshold t_L. It repeats the matching process until there is no more attribute eligible for matching. After the matching loop is over, the function returns true if all attribute pairs have been matched together, otherwise it returns false which means the matching process has not been successful.

Notice that we do not reflect the matching of attributes of the left sides of FDs in the distance matrix. The reason is that for these attributes (in contrast to those on the right side), the matching is done just based on attribute name similarity and not the knowledge in FDs.

In this algorithm, we use three different similarity thresholds (i.e. t_L, t_R, and t_{PK}). We do this to have more flexibility in the matching. The discussion on setting these parameters is available in the extended version of this paper[8].

Coming back to Algorithm 1, steps 11-26 apply PK heuristics to every PK pair and try to match their attributes based on these heuristics. Steps 13-18 check every attribute pair of two PKs to see if they are the only attributes at the left sides of two FDs. If yes, then these attributes are matched together. Steps 19-24 find the attribute pair with the maximum name similarity and if it is more than threshold t_{PK}, the attributes are matched together. The matching process continues until there is at least one attribute in every PK and the similarity of the attribute pair with the maximum similarity is more than threshold t_{PK}. After the matching process, if each of the two PKs has only one attribute left, their attributes are matched with each other by steps 25-26.

Steps 27-31 set the distances of attribute pairs which have not been computed by the heuristic rules. Step 28 checks if the attributes are from the same source, in which case their distance is set to UMD; otherwise the distance is set to their name similarity by step 31.

Steps 32-33 perform a transitive closure over the match and unmatch constraints. Step 34 deals with the symmetric property of the distance function to ensure that the returned distance is independent from the order of attributes.

Algorithm 2. Schema Matching

Input: 1) Source schemas $S_1, \ldots, S_n$; 2) Distance matrix $D[m][m]$; 3) Number of needed mediated schemas k.
Output: A set of probabilistic mediated schemas.
1: compute $A = \{a_1, \ldots, a_m\}$ the set of all source attributes
2: let C be the set of clusters c_i such that $c_i = \{a_i\}, a_i \in A, i \in [1, m]$
3: $M \leftarrow C$
4: find two clusters $c_i, c_j \in C$ having the minimum distance d_{min} while distance d_{ij} between c_i and c_j is computed as follows:
5:     **if** $\exists a_k \in c_i, a_l \in c_j, a_k, a_l \in S_p$ **then**
6:         $d_{ij} \leftarrow \infty$
7:     **else**
8:         $d_{ij} \leftarrow Min(D[a_k][a_l]), a_k \in c_i, a_l \in c_j$
9: **if** $d_{min} \neq \infty$ **then**
10:     merge c_i with c_j
11:     Add the newly added mediated schema to M
12:     go to 4
13: **for each** $C_i \in M$ compute the $FDpoint_i$ as the number of attribute pairs recommended by distance matrix and respected by C_i
14: $FDpoint_{max} \leftarrow Max(FDpoint_i), C_i \in M$
15: $M \leftarrow \{C_i \mid C_i \in M, FDpoint_i = FDpoint_{max}\}$
16: **if** $k < |M|$ **then**
17:     select k mediated schemas randomly from M
18:     assign probability $\frac{1}{k}$ to every selected mediated schema and return them
19: **else**
20:     assign probability $\frac{1}{|M|}$ to every $C_i \in M$ and return them

---

3.4   Schema Matching Algorithm

The distances between attributes are used for computing the distance between clusters in the clustering method, i.e. CAHC. Algorithm 2 describes how we create probabilistic mediated schemas. This algorithm takes as input the source schemas, distance matrix, and the needed number of mediated schemas (k) which is specified by the user. Steps 1-2 create the first mediated schema by putting every attribute in a cluster. The algorithm stores all created mediated schemas in the set M, and so does for the first created mediated schema in step 3.

Steps 4-8 look for the two clusters with the minimum distance while the distance between two clusters is defined as follows: if the clusters have two attributes from the same source, the distance between them is infinity; otherwise the minimum distance between two attributes, each from one of the two clusters, is regarded as the distance between the two clusters. Steps 9-12 merge these clusters together and store this newly created mediated schema in M and continues this process by going to step 4. The necessary condition for merging clusters is that their distance should not be equal to infinity. We get the infinity as the minimum distance between clusters when every two clusters have attributes from the same source. In such a case, we stop creating the mediated schemas.

Since for all generated mediated schemas we do not let unmatched attributes to be put in the same cluster, we count the number of matched pairs which has been respected by the mediated schema, as a metric for ranking mediated schemas. We call this metric the FD-point. For every created mediated schema, Step 13 computes its FD-point, which is a metric for measuring the quality of mediated schemas and for selecting only the high quality ones. Distance matrix recommends some attribute pairs to be put in the same cluster by returning their distance as MD. FD-point is defined as the number of these recommendations which are respected by the mediated schema. Steps 14-15 select the mediated schemas with the maximum FD-point. We call them as eligible mediated schemas.

Steps 16-20 return k randomly selected mediated schemas to the user. Since the algorithm has no means for differentiating between eligible mediated schemas, it assigns equal probabilities to all returned mediated schemas.

Let m be the number of the attributes of all sources, then the running time of algorithms 1 and 2 together is $\theta(m^3)$. The details about the complexity analysis of our algorithms are available in the extended version of this paper [8]).

IFD starts with a given set of sources and ends up generating several PMSs from these sources. A useful property of IFD is that it allows new sources to be added to the system on the fly. The details of this process are available in the extended version of this paper [8].

4   Performance Evaluation

In this section, we study the effectiveness of our data integration solution. In particular, we show the effect of using functional dependencies on the quality of generated mediated schemas. We compare our solution with the one presented in [3] which is the closest to ours. To examine the contribution of using a probabilistic approach, we compare our approach with two traditional baseline solutions that do not use probabilistic techniques, i.e. they generate only one single deterministic mediated schema.

The rest of this section is organized as follows. We first describe our experimental setup. Then we compare the performance of our solution with the competing approaches.

4.1   Experimental Setup

We implemented our system (IFD) in Java. We took advantage of Weka 3-7-3 classes [10] for implementing the hierarchical clustering component. We used the SecondString tool[1] to compute the Jaro Winkler similarity [11] of attribute names in pair-wise attribute comparison. We conducted our experiments on a Windows XP machine with Intel core 2 GHz CPU and 2GB memory.

In our experiments, we set the number of mediated schemas (denoted as n) to 1000, which is relatively high, in order to return all eligible mediated schemas. Our experiments showed similar results when we varied n considerably (e.g. n = 5). The default values for the parameters of our solution are as follows.

---

[1] Secondstring. http://secondstring.sourceforge.net/

We set similarity threshold for PK attributes (t_{PK}) to 0.7, similarity threshold for attributes on the left side of functional dependencies (t_L) to 0.9, similarity threshold for attributes on the right side of functional dependencies (t_R) to 0.8, the distance between attributes being matched (MD) to 0, and the distance between attributes being unmatched (UMD) to 1.

We evaluated our system using a dataset in the university domain. This dataset[2] consists of 17 single-table schemas which we designed ourselves. For having variety in attribute names, we used Google Search with "computer science" and "course schedule" keywords and picked up the first 17 related results. For every selected webpage, we designed a single-table schema which could be the data source of the course schedule information on that webpage and we used data labels as attribute names of the schema. Also, we created primary key and functional dependencies for every schema using our knowledge of the domain.

To evaluate the quality of generated mediated schemas, we tested them against the mediated schema which we created manually. Since each mediated schema corresponds to a clustering of source attributes, we measured its quality by computing the precision, recall, and F-measure of the clustering. We computed the metrics for each individual mediated schema, and summed the results weighted by their respective probabilities.

To the best of our knowledge, the most competing approach to ours (IFD) is that of Sarma et al. [3] which we denote by UDI as they did. Thus, we compare our solution with UDI as the most competing probabilistic approach. We implemented UDI in Java. We used the same tool in our approach for computing pair-wise attribute similarity as in UDI. Also, we set the parameters edge-weight threshold and error bar to 0.85 and 0.02 respectively. Since the time complexity of UDI approach is exponential to the number of uncertain edges, we selected the above values carefully to let it run.

To examine the performance gain of using a probabilistic technique, we considered two baseline approaches that create a single mediated schema:

- FD1: creates a deterministic mediated schema as follows. In Algorithm 2, we count the number of FD recommendations and obtain the maximum possible FD-point, then we stop at the first schema which gets this maximum point.
- SingleMed: creates a deterministic mediated schema based on Algorithm 4.1 in [3]. We set frequency threshold to 0 and the edge weight threshold to 0.85.

Also, to evaluate the contribution of using functional dependencies in the quality of generated mediated schemas, we considered Algorithm 2 without taking advantage of the FD recommendations (WFD) and compared it to our approach.

4.2   Results

Quality of Mediated Schemas. In this section, we compare the quality of mediated schemas generated by our approach (IFD) with the ones generated by UDI and other competing approaches.

---

[2] The dataset is available at http://www.science.uva.nl/CO-IM/papers/IFD/ IFD-test-dataset.zip

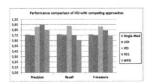

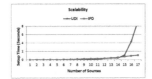

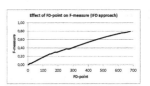

Fig. 2. Performance comparison of IFD with competing approaches

Fig. 3. Execution time comparison of IFD and UDI (seconds)

Fig. 4. Effect of FD-point on F-measure in IFD approach

Figure 2 compares the results measuring precision, recall, and F-measure of IFD, UDI, Single-Med, FD1, and WFD. It shows that IFD obtains better results than UDI. It improves precision by 23%, recall by 22%, and F-measure by 23%.

Figure 2 also shows the contribution of using FD recommendations in the quality of the results. WFD (Without FD) shows the results of our approach without using FD recommendations. It is obvious that using these recommendations has considerable effect on the results.

Furthermore, Figure 2 shows the performance gain of using a probabilistic approach rather than a single deterministic schema approach. FD1 applies all of the FD recommendations to obtain the mediated schema with the maximum FD-point, then stops and returns the resulted mediated schema. On the other hand, IFD does not stop after applying all FD recommendations but since there is no further FD recommendation, it starts merging clusters based on the similarity of their attribute pairs. This increases recall considerably, but reduces precision a little because some pairs are clustered wrongly. Overall, IFD improves F-measure by 8% compared to FD1. On the other hand, this Figure shows that UDI does not get such performance gain compared to Single-Med which creates a single deterministic schema. This happens because UDI cannot select the high quality schemas among the generated schemas.

Scalability. To investigate the scalability of our approach, we measure the effect of the number of sources (n) on its execution time. By execution time, we mean the setup time needed to integrate n data sources. For IFD, the execution time equals to the execution time of computing distances using Algorithm 1 plus the execution time of generating mediated schemas using Algorithm 2. For UDI, we only consider the time needed to generate mediated schemas to be fair in our comparison. For UDI, the execution time is the time needed to create the mediated schemas.

Figure 3 shows how the execution times of IFD and UDI increase with increasing n up to 17 (the total number of sources in the tested dataset). The impact of the number of sources on the execution time of IFD is not as high as that of UDI. While in the beginning, the execution time of UDI is a little lower than IFD, it dramatically increases eventually. This is because the execution time of IFD is cubic to the number of the attributes of sources (see Section 3.4). But, the execution time of UDI is exponential to the number of uncertain edges. This shows that IFD is much more scalable than UDI.

Effect of FD-Point. In this section, we study the effect of FD-point on F-measure. Figure 4 shows how F-measure increases with increasing FD-point up to 680 which is the maximum possible value in the tested dataset. The starting point is when we have one cluster for every attribute. We have not used any recommendation at this point yet; as a result, $FD - point = 0$. Also it is clear that $precision = 1$ and $recall = 0$, thus $F - measure = 0$. As we begin merging clusters using recommendations, FD-point increases and this increases the F-measure as well. The increase in FD-point continues until it reaches its maximum possible value in the tested dataset. We consider all generated mediated schemas with maximum FD-point value as schemas eligible for being in the result set.

5   Related Work

There has been much work in the area of automatic schema matching during the last three decades (see [12] for a survey). They studied how to use various clues to identify the semantics of attributes and match them. An important class of approaches, which are referred to by constraint matchers, uses the constraints in schemas to determine the similarity of schema elements. Examples of such constraints are data types, value ranges, uniqueness, optionality, relationship types, and cardinalities. Our approach is different, since we use an uncertain approach for modeling and generating mediated schemas. Thus, the heuristic rules we use as well as the way we decrease the distance of the attributes is completely different. In addition, we take advantage of FDs. The proposals in [13] and [14] also consider the role of FDs in schema matching. However, our heuristic rules and the way we combine it with attribute similarity is completely different with these proposals.

The closest work to ours is that of Sarma et al. [3] which we denote as UDI in this paper. UDI creates several mediated schemas with probabilities attached to them. To do so, it constructs a weighted graph of source attributes and distinguishes two types of edges: certain and uncertain. Then, a mediated schema is created for every subset of uncertain edges. Our approach has several advantages over UDI. The time complexity of UDI's algorithm for generating mediated schemas is exponential to the number of uncertain edges (i.e. attribute pairs) but that of our algorithm is PTIME (as shown in Section 3.4), therefore our approach is much more scalable. In addition, the quality of mediated schemas generated by our approach has shown to be considerably higher than that of UDI. Furthermore, the mediated schemas generated by our approach are consistent with all sources, while those of UDI may be inconsistent with some sources.

6   Conclusion

In this paper, we proposed IFD, a data integration system with the objective of automatically setting up a data integration application. We established an advanced starting point for pay-as-you-go data integration systems. IFD takes advantage of the background knowledge implied in FDs for finding attribute correlations and using it for matching the source schemas and generating the mediated schema. We built IFD on a probabilistic data model in order to model the uncertainty in data integration systems.

We validated the performance of IFD through implementation. We showed that using FDs can significantly improve the quality of schema matching (by 26%). We also showed the considerable contribution of using a probabilistic approach (10%). Furthermore, we showed that IFD outperforms UDI, its main competitor, by 23% and has cubic scale up compared to UDI's exponential execution cost.

References

1. Özsu, M.T., Valduriez, P.: Principles of Distributed Database Systems, 3rd edn. Springer (2011)
2. Madhavan, J., Cohen, S., Dong, X.L., Halevy, A.Y., Jeffery, S.R., Ko, D., Yu, C.: Web-scale data integration: You can afford to pay as you go. In: Proc. of CIDR (2007)
3. Sarma, A.D., Dong, X., Halevy, A.Y.: Bootstrapping pay-as-you-go data integration systems. In: Proc. of SIGMOD (2008)
4. Wang, D.Z., Dong, X.L., Sarma, A.D., Franklin, M.J., Halevy, A.Y.: Functional dependency generation and applications in pay-as-you-go data integration systems. In: Proc. of WebDB (2009)
5. Akbarinia, R., Valduriez, P., Verger, G.: Efficient Evaluation of SUM Queries Over Probabilistic Data. TKDE (to appear, 2012)
6. Dong, X.L., Halevy, A.Y., Yu, C.: Data integration with uncertainty. VLDB J. 18(2), 469–500 (2009)
7. Huhtala, Y., Kärkkäinen, J., Porkka, P., Toivonen, H.: Tane: An efficient algorithm for discovering functional and approximate dependencies. Comput. J. 42(2), 100–111 (1999)
8. Ayat, N., Afsarmanesh, H., Akbarinia, R., Valduriez, P.: Uncertain data integration using functional dependencies. Technical report, http://www.science.uva.nl/CO-IM/papers/IFD/ifd.pdf
9. Davidson, I., Ravi, S.S.: Using instance-level constraints in agglomerative hierarchical clustering: theoretical and empirical results. Data Min. Knowl. Discov. 18(2), 257–282 (2009)
10. Hall, M., Frank, E., Holmes, G., Pfahringer, B., Reutemann, P., Witten, I.H.: The weka data mining software: an update. SIGKDD Explorations 11(1), 10–18 (2009)
11. Cohen, W.W., Ravikumar, P.D., Fienberg, S.E.: A comparison of string distance metrics for name-matching tasks. In: Proc. of IIWeb (2003)
12. Rahm, E., Bernstein, P.A.: A survey of approaches to automatic schema matching. VLDB J. 10(4), 334–350 (2001)
13. Biskup, J., Embley, D.W.: Extracting information from heterogeneous information sources using ontologically specified target views. Inf. Syst. 28(3), 169–212 (2003)
14. Larson, J.A., Navathe, S.B., Elmasri, R.: A theory of attribute equivalence in databases with application to schema integration. IEEE Trans. Software Eng. 15(4), 449–463 (1989)

Analyzing Recommender System's Performance Fluctuations across Users

Charif Haydar, Azim Roussanaly, and Anne Boyer

Université de Lorraine, Laboratoire Loria, Bâtiment C, Equipe KIWI
615, rue de jardin botanique
54600 Vandœuvres-lès-Nancy, France
{charif.alchiekhhaydar,azim.roussanaly,anne.boyer}@loria.fr
http://kiwi.loria.fr

Abstract. Recommender systems (RS) are designed to assist users by recommending them items they should appreciate. User based RS exploit users behavior to generate recommendations. As a matter of fact, RS performance fluctuates across users. We are interested in analyzing the characteristics and behavior that make a user receives more accurate/inaccurate recommendations than another.

We use a hybrid model of collaborative filtering and trust-aware recommenders. This model exploits user's preferences (represented by both item ratings and trusting other users) to generate its recommendations.

Intuitively, the performance of this model is influenced by the number of preferences the user expresses. In this work we focus on other characteristics of user's preferences than the number. Concerning item ratings, we touch on the rated items popularity, and the difference between the attributed rate and the item's average rate. Concerning trust relationships, we touch on the reputation of the trusted users.

Keywords: Recommender system, collaborative filtering, trust-aware, trust, reputation.

1 Introduction

Recommender systems (RS) [5] aim to recommend to users some items they should appreciate, over a list of items. RS exploits the user's ratings of items, and/or his explicit/implicit relationships with other users, to generate recommendations to him. Intuitively, the more the user is connected to other users and items, the better the quality of recommendation is. In this paper, we treat the question of RS performance from two different points of view. The first is the structural point of view, where we try to improve the RS performance by hybridizing two recommendation approaches. The second is the user's behavior point of view, where we study the impact of several characteristics of user behavior on the system performance.

We use the epinion.com[1] dataset. epinion.com is a consumers opinion website where users can rate items in a range of 1 to 5, and write reviews about them.

---

[1] http://www.epinion.com

G. Quirchmayr et al. (Eds.): CD-ARES 2012, LNCS 7465, pp. 390–402, 2012.

Users can also express their trust towards reviewers whose reviews seem to be interesting to them.

In [9], two recommendation approaches have been tested on this dataset separately: collaborative filtering (CF) [11] and trust-aware [9,12]. CF relies on user-item ratings to compute similarity between users, whereas trust-aware replaces this similarity by explicit trust relationships between users. Trust-aware performance surpasses that of CF, but CF is still better for some categories of users. In a previous work [27], we applied several hybridization strategies of both CF and trust-aware recommenders on this dataset. We found that hybrid models can cover a larger set of users.

In this paper, we focus on the recommendation accuracy by user. We consider its fluctuations across users as a result of user's ratings and trusting strategies. We touch on the following questions: Which type of items should user rate in order to assist the system to satisfy him? What if the user rates frequently opposite to the orientation of the community? Is trusting more users always beneficial to the user? Is there a link between the reputation of the users that a user trust and the quality of the recommendations he receives?

The outline of the paper is organized as follows: in section 2 we discuss recommendation approaches. In section 3 we explain the details of the used dataset, the context of the experiments, and both structure and user strategies based performance evaluations. Finally, the last section is dedicated to conclusion and future works.

2   State of Art

Diverse techniques were used to build recommender systems. Our current explanation is restricted to the needs of our recommendation model. We employ a hybrid RS [1] composed of Collaborative filtering (CF) [11] and trust-aware recommenders [9,12]. In the following subsections we explain both approaches and the chosen hybridization strategy.

2.1   Collaborative Filtering Recommenders

CF is the most popular recommendation approach. The prediction function in CF (which is the key element of any RS) is based on the similarity of users' preferences (usually expressed by rating items). Users' ratings are stored in a rating matrix, which is a $m \times n$ matrix, where m is the number of users, and n is the number of items. An element $v_{u_a i}$ of this matrix represents the rating given by the user u_a to the item i. This matrix assists compute the similarity between any two users. Many similarity metrics are available [7], we use Pearson correlation coefficient [11], which is one of the most popular and the most efficient in the RS domain [13], its value varies within the range $[-1, +1]$, where -1 means that the two users are completely opposite to one another, and $+1$ means that they are completely similar.

In order to predict how much the current user u_a will rate an item r, the system exploits the ratings of similar users to u_a (equation 1) out of the set of users who rated r (U_r).

$$p(u_a, r) = \overline{v_{u_a}} + \frac{\sum_{u_j \in U_r} f_{simil}(u_a, u_j) \times (v_{(u_j,i)} - \overline{v_{u_j}})}{card(U_r)} \tag{1}$$

Where:
$f_{simil}(u_a, u_j)$: the similarity between u_a and u_j.
U_r: the set of users who have rated r.
$card(U_r)$: is the number of users in U_r.
This is called Resnick formula. Neighbors in this approach are identified automatically by the prediction function, consequently the approach is sensible to the user's rating strategy. Cold start [14] is one of the essential drawbacks of this approach. It consists in the difficulty to generate recommendations to users who did not rate enough items, because it is difficult to find neighbors to them. The same difficulty can also results from certain ratings strategies such as: rating items which are not frequently rated by other users, or appreciating items that are globally detested by the community.

2.2   Trust Aware Recommenders

Trust-aware approaches have the advantages of reducing the impacts of the major weaknesses of CF recommenders such as the cold start [14], data sparsity [8], recommendation acceptability [15] and robustness to malicious attacks [16,2,17,18], without bringing the recommendation accuracy down [9].

A correlation between trust and users similarity was found in [19] and [20]. Replacing user similarity with trust relationships has been proposed by [12,25]. This approach is applied only in social systems where users can rate each other.

In order to compute recommendations, a trust-aware RS interrogates the friends of A, if the result was not satisfying the system interrogates the friends of A's friends and so on.

Trust-aware prediction function is the same as that of CF, with replacing the similarity value by trust value.

Commonly, trust propagation algorithms represent the dataset as a directed weighted graph, where users represent the nodes, the trust relationships represent the edges, and the trust values represent the weights. Trust propagation problem becomes a graph traversal problem. The main difference between those algorithms is about their strategies in traversing the graph, and selecting the path between the source and destination nodes.

In our studied case trust is a binary value. That is why we choose the model MoleTrust for our experiments. This algorithm is adapted and tested to our dataset. In MoleTrust, each user has a domain of trust where he adds his trustee users. In this context, user can either fully trust other user or not trust him at all. The model considers that trust is transitive, and that its value is inversely proportional to the distance between the source user and the destination user. The only initializing parameter is the maximal propagation distance d.

If user A added user B to his domain, and B added C, then the trust of A in C is given by the equation:

$$Tr(A, C) = \begin{cases} \frac{(d-n+1)}{d} & \text{if } n \leq d \\ 0 & \text{if } n > d \end{cases} \qquad (2)$$

Where n is the distance between A and C ($n = 2$ as there two steps between them; first step from A to B, and the second from B to C). d is the maximal propagation distance.

Consider $d = 4$ then: $Tr(A, C) = (4 - 2 + 1)/4 = 0.75$.

2.3   Hybridization

In [1] the author identifies seven strategies to hybridize multiple recommendation approaches, he argues that there is no reason why recommenders from the same type could not be hybridized.

In [28], authors propose to enhance Resnick formula by adding a global trust (reputation) value to the similarity score. To compute reputation score, they apply a CF recommender with one neighbor at a time. The global trust of a user is the number of correct recommendations that he could produce (while neighbor), divided by the global number of recommendations in which he was involved. A recommendation is considered correct when the difference between its value and the real one is smaller than a given threshold.

Authors argue that trust here represents the competence of the user to generate recommendations, i.e the usefulness of the user to the system. Trust in this model is computed implicitly. Like in CF, neighbors are still chosen automatically.

Giving more weight to users identified as more useful improves the accuracy compared to classical CF, but it has no impact neither on the coverage nor on the cold start problem (while user still needs to rate a considerable number of items before receiving good recommendations).

In [27], we applied five hybridization strategies on epinion dataset. Compared to trust-aware and CF recommenders, most hybrid models could improve the prediction coverage, without a serious decrease in the prediction accuracy. The best score was obtained by applying a weighted hybridization strategy, shown in the equation 3, with ($\alpha = 0.3$).

$$score(u_a, u_j) = \alpha \times simil(u_a, u_j) + (1 - \alpha) \times trust(u_a, u_j) \qquad (3)$$

2.4   Users Behavior Analysis

The fluctuations across users is a common issue in RSs, so the system can be accurate for some users while inaccurate for others. This is usually explained by quantitative variance of user activeness or behavior, i.e the number of ratings the user (for CF), and the number of trust phrases (in trust-aware RS).

Few studies were dedicated to qualitative evaluations of user activeness. [3] is an example where authors are interested in the popularity of rated items. They consider item's popularity as: the ratio between the number of 5 stars notes the item receives in the training corpus, and the number of 5 stars notes it receives in the whole corpus after prediction. This definition was useful to improve recommender accuracy, by orienting RS towards more popular items considering that they are more probable to be accepted by the users. At the opposite, we think that the item is popular when many people rate it regardless the value of their notes, as we shall see in 4.1.

Other factors that we propose are: ratings abnormality, number of trust relations, and reputation of trustee friends. To the best of our knowledge, no other definitions were proposed to these factors.

3   Experiments and Performance Evaluation

3.1   DataSet

Epinion dataset contains 49,290 users who rated a total of 139,738 items. users can rate items in a range of 1 to 5, the total number of ratings is 664,824. Users can also express their trust towards others (binary value), the dataset contains 487,182 trust ratings. It is important also to mention that 3,470 users have neither rated an item nor trusted a user, these users are eliminated from our statistics, thus the final number of users is 45,820 users.

In [26], authors showed on this corpus how to improve both accuracy and coverage (number of predicted ratings) by replacing similarity metrics with trust-aware metrics. The improvement of coverage was limited because of the fact that some users are active in rating items but not in rating reviewers. 11,858 users have not trusted anybody in the site (25.8% of users). Those users have made 75,109 ratings, averagely 6.3 ratings by user. This high average means that recommendations could be generated to this category by a similarity based approach. On the other hand, 5,655 users have not rated any item in the site (12.3% of the total number of users). The average of trust relationships by user in this set is 4.07 which is not negligible, those users suffer from the same problem with the similarity approachs while trust based approach can generate recommendations to them.

We divide the corpus to two parts randomly, 80% for training and 20% for evaluation (a classical ratios in the literature). We took into consideration that every user has 80% of his ratings in the training corpus and 20% in the evaluation corpus, this is important to analyse the recommendation accuracy by user.

3.2   Structural Performance Evaluation

Our test consists in trying to predict the ratings value of the test corpus. Our performance evaluation includes two aspects; accuracy and coverage.

To measure accuracy, we employ the mean absolute error metrics (MAE) [24]. MAE is a widely used predictive accuracy metrics. It measures the average absolute deviation between the predicted values and the real values. MAE is given by the following equation:

$$MAE = \frac{\Sigma_{i=1}^{N}|p_i - r_i|}{N} \tag{4}$$

Where: p_i is the rating value predicted by the recommender to the item i. r_i is the real rating value supplied by the user to the item i.

MAE focuses on ratings but not on users [25]. Take the case of a user who rated 100 items, received 20 good predictions, while other 5 users, each of whom has rated 5 items, received 1 bad prediction by user. MAE still consider the system successful in 80% of cases. Truth is; this system is able to satisfy one over 6 users. User mean absolute error (UMAE) [25] is the version of MAE which consider users' satisfaction. It consists in computing the MAE by user, before computing the average of these values. We call this average global UMAE or GUMAE.

With regard to the coverage aspect, we employ two forms of coverage metrics: Coverage of prediction is the ratio between the number of predicted ratings to the size of the test corpus. Coverage of users is the number of users who received predictions divided by the total number of users.

Table 1 illustrates the MAE, GUMAE and both forms of coverage for the three recommendation approaches (CF, Trust and hybrid). It is obvious that the hybrid model surpasses both CF and trust-aware approaches in both forms of coverage, without a serious lose in accuracy. This is because hybrid system uses each approach to predict ratings unpredictable by the other approach.

Table 1. Accuracy and coverage of RS

Strategy	MAE	coverage	GUMAE	users coverage
Pearson correlation	0.84	61.15%	0.8227	47.46%
MoleTrust	0.8165	69.28%	0.8079	52.21%
Weighted ($\alpha = 0.3$)	0.8210	76.38%	0.8124	62.22%

Intuitively, the more the user rates items, the more the CF is able to recommend items to him. The same role is applied for the trust-aware recommender and the number of users a user trusts.

As for a hybrid recommender, both roles are applied. Nevertheless, we note that some users who have a considerable number of ratings/trust relation still have a larger UMAE than others who have less number of ratings/trust relations. This lead us to analyze their ratings/trusting strategies in order to answer this question.

4   User Strategies Analysis

In this section we analyze many characteristics of user behavior and rating strategy. The aim of which is to explain the recommendation accuracy fluctuation across users. In this context, we represent user behavior by four criteria, one of which is quantitative (number of trusted friends), and the three others are qualitative. We need also to say that the first two criteria (user Ratings' popularity and abnormality) consider the quality of user's item ratings. The last two criteria (number of trusted friends and their reputation) are dedicated to the social influence and the quality of trust relation that the user does.

In the four following subsection, we illustrate the relations between of each criterion and the UMAE value of users, trying to explain the impact of this criterion on the performance of RS.

4.1   User Ratings' Popularity

We define item's popularity as the number of ratings that the item gets. Users tend to rate popular items more than unpopular item [3], this behavior creates an important bias in items popularity. By consequence, RS tends to recommend popular items more than others. This can limit the choices of users and reduce the serendipity in the RS.

The question here is about the user choice of items to rate, and how can this influence the performance of the recommender.

Now we define user's ratings' popularity as the average of the popularity of items who have been rated by this user. We compute the user's ratings popularity value for all users, then in figure 1 we show the relation between it and UMAE.

In order to have a readable figures, we categorize the population into 20 categories, users are grouped in function of their increasing ratings' popularity value, with regarding that every category contains about 5% of the population. This percentage is not fix, because we are conscious to keep users having the same ratings' popularity value in the same category. We compute, then, the average of UMAE of the members of the category. Therefor every point in the curve represent the average of UMAE of nearly 5% of the whole population.

Note that in figure 1, the more UMAE is low the more accurate are the recommendations. Thus we can find that users who have a high ratings' popularity value (more than 100) are receiving the less accurate recommendations. This results from the fact that those very popular items are usually less discriminant and less informative to RS because they are appreciated by almost everybody.

4.2   Abnormality Coefficient

This measurement distinguish users with particular taste. we tend to study user's rating strategies versus the global orientation of the community.

Formally: we compute the average rate of the item, then the difference between the rate supplied by the current user and this average. The Abnormality

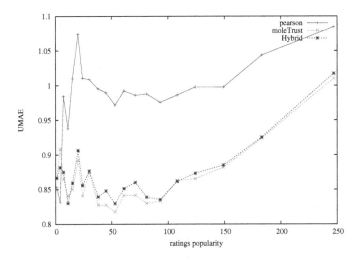

Fig. 1. UMAE and ratings popularity

coefficient of the user is the average of differences between his ratings and the average rate of each item he rates.

$$abn(u) = \sum_{i}^{N} \left(\frac{|r_{ui} - \overline{r_i}|}{N} \right) \tag{5}$$

Where: N: is the number of items rated by the user u.
r_{ui}: is the rate given by the user u to the item i.
$\overline{r_i}$: is the average rate of the item i.

Figure 2 has the same structure as figure 1 with one difference is that users' categorizing is done in function of their increasing abnormality coefficient.

Regarding to figure 2 [A], UMAE is relatively very high for users with large abnormality coefficient, which means that users whose ratings are close to the average rates of the rated items receive more accurate recommendations than those whose ratings is opposite to the tendency of the community. The part [B] of the same figure illustrates the distribution of average number of ratings in the abnormality categories. Users in categories with high abnormality (more than 1.4) and categories with low abnormality (less than 0.4) have nearly the same number of ratings. Looking at those same categories in the figure [A], we notice that they are on both extremes of UMAE. It is obvious here that, for users with small quantity ratings, abnormality is a discriminant factor of RS performance, rather than number of ratings.

4.3   Number of Trusted Users

This factor links the number of trusted users with the UMAE. It is intuitive that the more the user trusts people, the more the system can recommend items to

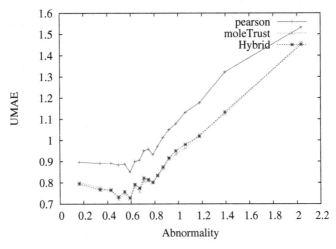

[A]

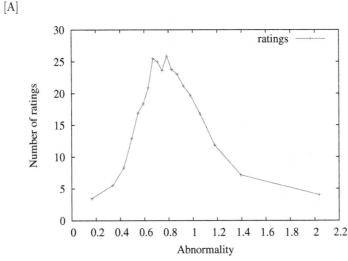

[B]

Fig. 2. Abnormality and UMAE

him. Even though, we find it is important to have a close look on the details of
this correlation. The curve in figure 3 represents a Hyperbolic cosecant function.
This means that trusting more users is in general beneficial for any user, but it is
more beneficial for users with a low number of trust relations, while it becomes
slightly beneficial for those with numerous relations.

4.4   Reputation of Trusted Users

In 4.3, we discussed the number of people the user trusts, but we think that
this is not the only factor, derived from a trust relationships, to influence the
performance of RS. The reputation of the trusted persons is a key issue for RS.

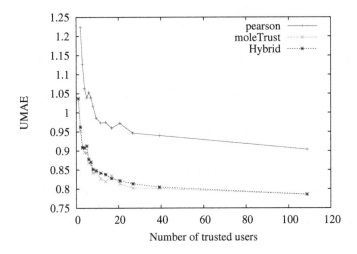

Fig. 3. Number of trusted users and UMAE

In this section, we illustrate the impact of trusting reputed /not reputed people on the quality of recommendations.ted /not reputed people on the quality of recommendations.

We consider a primitive metrics of reputation; the reputation of a user is the number of users who trust him.

$$Rep(u_i) = Nb.trusters_{u_i} \qquad (6)$$

Where: $Nb.trusters_{u_i}$ is the number of people how trust u_i.

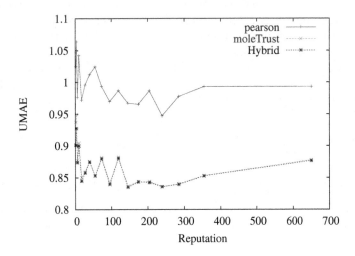

Fig. 4. Reputation of trusted users

We think that even when a user trusts few people, this can be more informative to RS when these people are well reputed. Therefore, our current factor $Trep(u_a)$ is the average of the reputations of users that the user u_a trusts, shown in the equation 7. Figure 4 illustrates the relationship between this average and the UMAE. Like precedent factors, users are categorized in groups. This categorization is based on the values of our $Trep$ value metrics.

$$Trep(u_a) = \frac{\sum_i^N Rep(u_i)}{N} \tag{7}$$

$u_i \in D(U_a)$ (the group of users who are trusted by u_a).

The curve in figure 4 shows that UMAE is relatively high when average of reputation is very low (less than 10), whereas it is almost stable after that. This shows that gaining reputation is not a complicated issue in this context, it is sufficient that the user shows positive intention to a few users to have a sufficient reputation in the community.

5   Conclusion and Future Works

In this paper we showed that, even though trust-aware recommenders improve the accuracy of CF recommenders, the hybrid model can, once again, make use of both approaches to surpass their performances, and generate recommendation to a wider set of users community without a serious decrease in accuracy.

We also showed that it is important to analyze the performance of the system regarding to various users behavior, which can lead in the future to build a model aware to different users ratings and trusting strategies.

In this paper, we analyzed the behavior criteria separately, it will be interesting in the future to elaborate an analysis by clustering users according all criteria together, and to build user profile in function of his own strategies.

Even though epinion is a known corpus in the literature, we think that is important to test our model on other corpora, and to elaborate the same analysis in order to generalize our results.

The nature of current corpus restricted our choice of trust metrics. We hope that upcoming tests be done on datasets with numeric trust values, which allow to test other trust metrics.

References

1. Burke, R.: Hybrid Web Recommender Systems. In: Brusilovsky, P., Kobsa, A., Nejdl, W. (eds.) Adaptive Web 2007. LNCS, vol. 4321, pp. 377–408. Springer, Heidelberg (2007)
2. Burke, R., Mobasher, B., Zabicki, R., Bhaumik, R.: Identifying attack models for secure recommendation. In: Beyond Personalization: A Workshop on the Next Generation of Recommender Systems (2005)
3. Steck, H.: Item popularity and recommendation accuracy. In: Proceedings of the Fifth ACM Conference on Recommender Systems (RecSys 2011), pp. 125–132. ACM, New York (2011)

4. Steck, H.: Training and testing of recommender systems on data missing not at random. In: Proceedings of the 16th ACM SIGKDD International Conference on Knowledge Discovery and Data Mining (KDD 2010), pp. 713–722. ACM, New York (2010)

5. Resnick, P., Varian, H.R.: Recommender systems. Commun. ACM 40(3), 56–58 (1997)

6. Ben Schafer, J., Konstan, J., Riedi, J.: Recommender systems in e-commerce. In: Proceedings of the 1st ACM Conference on Electronic Commerce (EC 1999), pp. 158–166. ACM, New York (1999)

7. Candillier, L., Meyer, F., Fessant, F.: Designing Specific Weighted Similarity Measures to Improve Collaborative Filtering Systems. In: Perner, P. (ed.) ICDM 2008. LNCS (LNAI), vol. 5077, pp. 242–255. Springer, Heidelberg (2008)

8. Miller, B.N., Konstan, J.A., Riedl, J.: PocketLens: Toward a personal recommender system. ACM Trans. Inf. Syst. 22(3), 437–476 (2004)

9. Massa, P., Bhattacharjee, B.: Using Trust in Recommender Systems: An Experimental Analysis. In: Jensen, C., Poslad, S., Dimitrakos, T. (eds.) iTrust 2004. LNCS, vol. 2995, pp. 221–235. Springer, Heidelberg (2004)

10. Basu, C., Hirsh, H., Cohen, W.: Recommendation as classifcation: using social and content-based information in recommendation. In: Proceedings of the Fifteenth National/Tenth Conference on Artifcial Intelligence/Innovative Applications of Artifcial Intelligence (1998)

11. Resnick, P., Iacovou, N., Suchak, M., Bergstrom, P., Riedl, J.: GroupLens: an open architecture for collaborative filtering of netnews. In: Proceedings of the 1994 ACM Conference on Computer Supported Cooperative Work (CSCW 1994), pp. 175–186. ACM, New York (1994)

12. Golbeck, J., Hendler, J.: FilmTrust: movie recommendations using trust in web-based social networks (2006)

13. Shardanand, U., Maes, P.: Social information filtering: algorithms for automating "word of mouth". In: Katz, I.R., Mack, R., Marks, L., Rosson, M.B., Nielsen, J. (eds.) Proceedings of the SIGCHI Conference on Human Factors in Computing Systems (CHI 1995), pp. 210–217. ACM Press/Addison-Wesley Publishing Co., New York (1995)

14. Maltz, D., Ehrlich, K.: Pointing the way: active collaborative filtering. In: Katz, I.R., Mack, R., Marks, L., Rosson, M.B., Nielsen, J. (eds.) Proceedings of the SIGCHI Conference on Human Factors in Computing Systems (CHI 1995), pp. 202–209. ACM Press/Addison-Wesley Publishing Co., New York (1995)

15. Herlocker, J.L., Konstan, J.A., Riedl, J.: Explaining collaborative filtering recommendations. In: Proceedings of the 2000 ACM Conference on Computer Supported Cooperative Work (CSCW 2000), pp. 241–250. ACM, New York (2000)

16. Mobasher, B., Burke, R., Bhaumik, R., Williams, C.: Toward trustworthy recommender systems: An analysis of attack models and algorithm robustness. ACM Trans. Internet Technol. 7(4), Article 23 (October 2007)

17. Lam, S.K., Riedl, J.: Shilling recommender systems for fun and profit. In: Proceedings of the 13th International Conference on World Wide Web (WWW 2004), pp. 393–402. ACM, New York (2004)

18. O'Mahony, M., Hurley, N., Kushmerick, N., Silvestre, G.: Collaborative recommendation: A robustness analysis. ACM Trans. Internet Technol. 4(4), 344–377 (2004)

19. Ziegler, C.-N., Lausen, G.: Analyzing Correlation between Trust and User Similarity in Online Communities. In: Jensen, C., Poslad, S., Dimitrakos, T. (eds.) iTrust 2004. LNCS, vol. 2995, pp. 251–265. Springer, Heidelberg (2004)

20. Lee, D.H., Brusilovsky, P.: Does Trust Influence Information similarity? In: Proceedings of Workshop on Recommender Systems & the Social Web, the 3rd ACM International Conference on Recommender Systems, New York, NY, USA, October 22-25 (2009)
21. Golbeck, J.: Personalizing applications through integration of inferred trust values in semantic web-based social networks. In: Semantic Network Analysis Workshop at the 4th International Semantic Web Conference (November 2005)
22. Kuter, U., Golbeck, J.: Using probabilistic confidence models for trust inference in Web-based social networks. ACM Trans. Internet Technol. 10(2), Article 8, 23 pages (2010)
23. Ziegler, C.-N., Lausen, G.: Spreading Activation Models for Trust Propagation. In: Proceedings of the 2004 IEEE International Conference on e-Technology, e-Commerce and e-Service (EEE 2004), pp. 83–97. IEEE Computer Society, Washington, DC (2004)
24. Herlocker, J.L., Konstan, J.A., Terveen, L.G., Riedl, J.T.: Evaluating collaborative filtering recommender systems. ACM Trans. Inf. Syst. 22(1), 5–53 (2004)
25. Massa, P., Avesani, P.: Trust-Aware Collaborative Filtering for Recommender Systems. In: Meersman, R., Tari, Z. (eds.) CoopIS/DOA/ODBASE 2004. LNCS, vol. 3290, pp. 492–508. Springer, Heidelberg (2004)
26. Massa, P., Avesani, P.: Trust-aware Bootstrapping of Recommender Systems. In: ECAI Workshop on Recommender Systems (2006)
27. Haydar, C., Boyer, A., Roussanaly, A.: Hybridising collaborative filtering and trust-aware recommender systems (2012)
28. O'Donovan, J., Smyth, B.: Trust in recommender systems. In: Proceedings of the 10th International Conference on Intelligent User Interfaces (IUI 2005). ACM, New York (2005)
29. McNally, K., O'Mahony, M.P., Smyth, B.: Models of Web Page Reputation in Social Search. In: Third IEEE International Conference on Social Computing (SocialCom 2011). MIT, Boston (2011)
30. Kamvar, S.D., Schlosser, M.T., Garcia-Molina, H.: The Eigentrust algorithm for reputation management in P2P networks. In: Proceedings of the 12th International Conference on World Wide Web (WWW 2003), pp. 640–651. ACM, New York (2003)
31. Levien, R., Aiken, A.: Attack-resistant trust metrics for public key certification. In: Proceedings of the 7th Conference on USENIX Security Symposium, SSYM 1998, vol. 7, p. 18. USENIX Association, Berkeley (1998)

A Secure Distributed Video Surveillance System Based on Portable Devices

Pietro Albano[1], Andrea Bruno[1], Bruno Carpentieri[1], Aniello Castiglione[1],
Arcangelo Castiglione[1], Francesco Palmieri[2],
Raffaele Pizzolante[1,*], and Ilsun You[3]

[1] Dipartimento di Informatica "R.M. Capocelli"
Università degli Studi di Salerno
I-84084, Fisciano (SA), Italy
pietro.albano@gmail.com, andrea.bruno@antaresnet.org,
bc@dia.unisa.it, castiglione@ieee.org,
arccas@lug-ischia.org, rpizzolante@unisa.it
[2] Dipartimento di Ingegneria dell'Informazione
Seconda Università degli Studi di Napoli
I-81031, Aversa (CE), Italy
fpalmier@unina.it
[3] Korean Bible University
16 Danghyun 2-gil, Nowon-gu
Seoul, Republic of Korea
isyou@bible.ac.kr

Abstract. In this work a distributed video surveillance system based on a Client-Server architecture is presented. The proposed system is accessible from portable devices such as tablets, smartphones, etc. In a typical real-world scenario, for example in homeland security, it is useful to have portable devices that can receive in real-time a frame or a sequence of frames coming from a selected camera to prevent or to detect attacks (i.e. terrorist attacks, etc.). In the proposed system, a portable device knows only the address of the server (repository), and the repository sends to the portable device the list of the clients (nodes) which are connected with one or more cameras. When the portable device obtains the list of the nodes, it connects directly to a specific node and requests the images of its connected cameras. The whole system provides secure communication channel between all its components. The security of both the node-repository and the repository-portable devices communications is guaranteed by using a secure connection. The security of the node-portable devices interconnection is provided by a digital invisible watermarking algorithm that affects each image before sending it from the node to the portable devices. Each portable device can extract the watermark and verify the identity of the node.

Keywords: Video Surveillance, Remote Video Surveillance, Remote Personal Security, Mobile Video Surveillance, Remote Homeland Security.

---

* Corresponding author.

G. Quirchmayr et al. (Eds.): CD-ARES 2012, LNCS 7465, pp. 403–415, 2012.

1   Introduction

Video surveillance has become increasingly important in everyday use and video surveillance systems have become sophisticated and are increasingly accessible and usable by the general public. Important applications of video surveillance are the identification of individuals and objects as well as the prevention and the detection of abnormal activities. Video surveillance is also helpful in other fields such as agriculture (for the prevention of fires), etc.

With the diffusion of advanced *portable devices*, now it is possible to perform surveillance and monitoring activities using them.

Hence, in this work we propose a secure distributed system for video surveillance, based on a Client-Server paradigm, that introduces the possibility of remote connections from *portable devices* for real-time monitoring. The system architecture is based on several basic entities: a central server (or *repository*), which knows the locations of some collector *nodes*, connected with one or more *cameras*.

The *portable devices* accessing the system know only the location of the *repository*. When the connection is established, the *repository* sends to the *portable device* a list of *nodes* and, as a second step, the device connects directly with a *node* and receives from it the image frames or multimedia contents obtained by its camera(s). There is an high degree of security both in the communication among the system parts and in the video frames.

The remainder of this work is organized as follows: Section 2 discusses the distributed architecture of the proposed system. Section 3 focuses on the security aspects and describes the approaches for the engineering and development of the prototype we have developed. In Section 4 we describe the system from the point of view of the end user and in Section 5 we present our conclusions and highlight future work directions.

2   The Distributed Architecture

The main task of the *repository* is to allow the localization of the *nodes*. It interacts with them and with the *portable devices* accessing the system by maintaining a list of all the *nodes* that joined the system.

A collector *node* is connected with at least a camera and interacts with the *portable devices* interested in monitoring the areas covered by its associated camera(s). The *portable devices* need to know only the IP address of the *repository* that provides the IP addresses of the list of the available collector *nodes* and other descriptive information about them. When a *portable device* connects to a *node* it receives, at regular intervals, the images obtained by the specific camera(s) connected to the *node*.

Figure 1 shows a graphical representation of the proposed system architecture.

In the following, we discuss the interaction among *node-repository* (see Section 2.1), *repository-portable device* (see Section 2.2) and *node-portable device* (see Section 2.3).

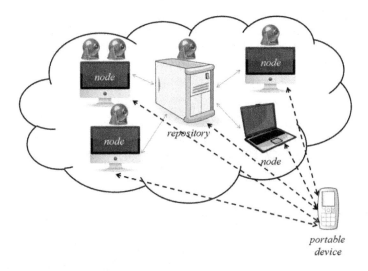

Fig. 1. The architecture of the proposed system

2.1   Interaction *Node-Repository*

The communication between these two entities takes place through a TCP connection over TLS/SSL. Its security is essential, since without a secure connection a fake *node* could easily enter into the system and send manipulated/tampered images to the accessing *portable devices*.

There are three types of messages exchanged between a *node* and the *repository*: *Login*, *Register*, and *Disconnect*. These messages are encoded by XML markup sequences. Figure 2 shows an example of a complete interaction between the above entities, including each of the three messages.

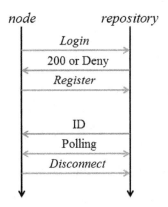

Fig. 2. An example of a complete interaction between a *node* and the *repository*

The *Login* message is used by a *node* to authenticate itself to the *repository*. If the authentication succeeds, the *repository* answers with a return code "200", otherwise the *repository* denies the access for that *node*. Figure 3 shows an example of *Login* message from a *node* to the *repository*.

```xml
<?xml version="1.0" encoding="UTF-8"?>
<properties>
  <entry key="type">LOGIN</entry>
  <entry key="usr">username</entry>
  <entry key="pwd">password</entry>
</properties>
```

Fig. 3. An example of a *Login* message from a *node* to the *repository*

The *Register* message is used by a *node* to send its descriptive information to the *repository*. When the *repository* receives the information about the *node* it replies with an *ID*. The *ID* is also used by the *node* during the disconnection process. Figure 4 shows an example of *Register* message from a *node* to the *repository*.

```xml
<?xml version="1.0" encoding="UTF-8"?>
<properties>
  <entry key="type">REGISTER</entry>
  <entry key="descr">description</entry>
  <entry key="name">name</entry>
</properties>
```

Fig. 4. An example of a *Register* message from a *node* to the *repository*

When a *node* want to disconnect itself from the *repository*, it sends *Disconnect* message as shown in Figure 5.

```xml
<?xml version="1.0" encoding="UTF-8"?>
<properties>
  <entry key="type">DISCONNECT</entry>
  <entry key="id">idStr</entry>
</properties>
```

Fig. 5. An example of a *Disconnect* message from a *node* to the *repository*

2.2   Interaction *Repository-Portable Device*

As previously, the interaction between the *repository* and the *portable devices* is based on a TCP connection over TLS/SSL. There are three new commands associated respectively to three different XML messages: *ListServer*, *Update* and

Desc. The *ListServer* message requests the server to download the list of *nodes* currently registered. The reply of the *repository* can be either the "530" return code in case of error, or a string having this form:

$$//n\%ts\%\%ID_1\%Name_1\%IPAddress_1\%\%...\%\%ID_n\%Name_n\%IPAddress_n\%\%//$$

where:

n is the number of the entries;
ts is a timestamp which is used for indicate when the request has been sent and is also used with *Update* command;
ID$_i$ is an unique identifier associated to *node i*;
Name$_i$ is the alias or the name of the *node i*;
IPAddress$_i$ is the IP address of the *node i*.

The *Update* message is used by the *node* to communicate to the *repository* its intention to update the local list. The command *Update* takes as parameter the timestamp, used by the *repository* to verify if the list of *nodes* maintained by the *portable device* has been updated. The possible replies of the *repository* can be: a "400" return code if there isn't updates or, alternatively, a string structured as:

$$//n\%ts\%\%[+|-]ID_1\%Name_1\%IPAddress_1\%\%...$$
$$\%\%[+|-]ID_n\%Name_n\%IPAddress_n\%\%//$$

where:

n is the number of the entries (n);
ts is a timestamp which is used to indicate when the request has been sent;
+ID$_i$ is the *node* with the identifier ID*i* has been registered after the last request of update, *or*
-ID$_i$ is the *node* with the identifier ID*i* has been disconnected after the last request of update;
Name$_i$ is the alias or the name of the *node i*;
IPAddress$_i$ is the IP address of the *node i*.

2.3   Interaction *Node-Portable Device*

The communication between these two entities is performed through the use of TCP sockets which adopt a FTP-like protocol for exchanging messages and data. The main difference between the FTP protocol and the proposed ad-hoc protocol is that in the former the client opens two communication channels (one for the messages and one for the data), in the latter, *portable device*, using a GPRS/UMTS connection, cannot open more than one channel due to commonly closed mobile operators policies.

   In the proposed protocol the server (*node*) opens two sessions (with two different channels) and the client (the *portable device*) opens just one. The *node* communicates to the client the port of the other opened channel , resulting in two communication options. The three message used are: *Login*, *List*, and *MGet*.

The *Login* message is used by the *portable device* to authenticate. The Login operation can succeed or not. In the first case the *node* replies to the *portable device* with a message with return code "200" and the communication continues normally. On the contrary, the *portable device* receives an alert message on the display.

The *List* message is used by the *portable device* to request a snapshot of all the environments monitored by the *node*. When a *node* receives this message, it takes a snapshot from each of its camera(s) and sends it to the *portable device*.

The *MGet* message is used by the *portable device* to request the monitoring of a specific area, identified by an unique identifier. When this message is received by the *node*, it opens a data channel that is able to send the multimedia frames at regular intervals.

3   System Security

The development of secure architectures, providing controlled access, privacy protection, content confidentiality and authenticity, is one of the most challenging issues in the video surveillance area, and several solutions, based on the use of cryptography have been proposed (e.g. [1, 2, 3]). Furthermore, the existence of a surveillance system strongly depends on legal boundaries [4] that states what is allowed to be monitored, what is not, and also who is authorized to perform monitoring. In these cases the data produced by surveillance activities must be properly secured against unauthorized accesses or misuses of the collected images.

The proposed system has two important security aspects: the first one concerns the communication channel between a *node* and the *repository*, while the second one concerns the communication channel between a *node* and a *portable device*.

In the first case the secure connection between the *repository* and a *node* is guaranteed by using a SSL/TLS connection, providing privacy through symmetric cryptography and message reliability through keyed message authentication codes. Asymmetric cryptography is also used to protect each key exchange. This ensures the prevention against any type of eavesdropping and tampering.

However, some *portable devices* could not be able to implement, fully or partially, the aforementioned cryptographic mechanisms and primitives. For this reason we decided to use Digital Watermarking techniques to further guarantee security between a *node* and a *portable device*.

Therefore, each *node*, before sending an image modifies it with an invisible digital watermark. On the other hand, when the *portable device* receives the image, it extracts the watermark in order to verify the authenticity of each image.

3.1   Digital Watermarking to Improve the Security of the Proposed System

Digital Watermarking is one of the techniques generally used to insert hidden data into digital contents. When a signal is protected by a robust digital watermark, then the associated hidden information will be also carried in its copies. Watermarking is also used to prevent unauthorized copy of digital media.

There are different embedding methods: such as Spread-Spectrum [5, 6, 7], or Amplitude Modulation [8].

In the first one, the signal affected by digital watermark is obtained by an additive modification. Also in the case of amplitude modulation the marked signal is obtained by an additive modification, like in Spread-Spectrum embedding, but the watermark is only embedded in the spatial domain.

Before sending the images, the *node* embeds in them a digital invisible watermark. When the *portable device* receives the image it extracts the watermark in order to verify the trueness of each image.

The watermarking algorithm used in this work has been proposed in [9], and it is based on a modified version of the one proposed in *Langelaar et al.* [10].

It takes as input the source image, the watermark string, a seed and a threshold T.

The watermark string is converted in a bit matrix where each character is converted in a 5x8 sub-matrix of bits (an example is reported in Figure 6). The resulting bit string is obtained by reading the bit matrix line-by-line from left-top corner. The *seed* represents an ID (such as numeric PIN) that is used to embed the watermark, and in second instance to extract it from the watermarked image. The threshold T is a real number that indicates the robustness of the watermark that will be embedded.

The algorithm used for embedding a digital invisible watermark in an image is sketched as follows:

1. The image is converted from the **RGB** domain to the **YUV** domain.
2. The watermark string is converted to a matrix of bits. Each character is converted in a 5x8 matrix of bits (see the example in Figure 6).
   The resulting matrix will be embedded in the original image line-by-line from left-top corner.
3. A block B of 8x8 pixels is pseudo-randomly selected from the image to embed one bit of the watermark string.
4. A fixed binary pseudo-random pattern of the same size of B is generated.
5. The I_0, I_1 and D quantities are calculated from B. I_0 and I_1 are obtained by calculating the averages of the luminance values in B, respectively where the random pattern is 0 and where the random pattern is 1. D is the difference $I_1 - I_0$.
6. B' is a reduced quality block obtained by applying the quantization and the 8x8 DCT transform.
7. The I'_0, I'_1 and D' quantities are calculated from B'. I'_0 and I'_1 are obtained by calculating the averages of the luminance values in B', respectively where the random pattern is 0 and where the random pattern is 1. D' is the difference $I'_1 - I'_0$.
8. If the bit to embed has value 1 the go to step 11.
9. In order to embed the **bit with value** 0, the binary pseudo-random pattern is subtracted from the block B, if D and D' are greater than the threshold T. The steps 6-8, and 10 are repeated iteratively until both differences are less or equal than $-T$. Go to step 12.

10. In order to embed the **bit with value** 1, the binary pseudo-random pattern is added from the block B, if D and D' are less or equal than the threshold T. The steps 6-8, and 11 are repeated iteratively until both differences are greater than T.
11. The steps from 4 to 11 are applied to all pseudo-randomly selected blocks until all bits of the watermark string are embedded.
12. The image in **YUV** domain is converted back to the **RGB** domain.

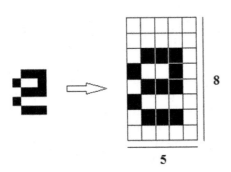

Fig. 6. Example of conversion from the character 'e' to the matrix of bits composed by 5x8 (40 bits). The white cells are represented by the value 0 and the black cells are represented by the value 1.

Figure 7(a) and Figure 7(b) show respectively the original "Lena" image and the "Lena" image affected by a digital invisible watermark of 200 bits (the string "SeCAM") with the previously described watermarking algorithm.

(a)   (b)

Fig. 7. (a) The original "Lena" image; (b) The "Lena" image affected by a digital invisible watermark

Analogously, the algorithm for extracting the digital invisible watermark is reported below:

1. The image is converted from the **RGB** domain to the **YUV** domain.
2. A block B of 8x8 pixels is pseudo-randomly selected from the image to read one bit of the watermark string.
3. A fixed binary pseudo-random pattern of the same size of B is generated.
4. I_0, I_1 and D are calculated from B. I_0 and I_1 are then obtained by calculating the averages of the luminance values in B, respectively where the random sequence is 0 and where the random sequence is 1. D is the difference $I_1 - I_0$.
5. If $D > 0$ then the embedded bit has value 1 else the embedded bit has value 0.

4 The End User Interface

From the end user point of view, there are three main system components:

- The *repository* GUI (described in Section 4.1)
- The *node* GUI (described in Section 4.2)
- The *portable device* GUI (described in Section 4.3)

4.1 The *Repository* GUI

The *repository* GUI is very intuitive and simple, it is subdivided in two parts: the first one provides a panel to configure its starting options (Username and Password), the second one provides a panel which allows the *repository* to operate as a *node*. An example is shown in Figure 8.

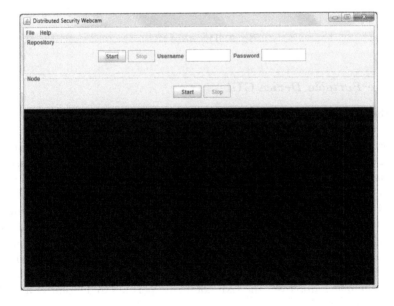

Fig. 8. The *repository* GUI

4.2   The *Node* GUI

The *node* GUI takes as input from the user: the Username and the Password, obtained during the registration process, the Name (or the alias) of the *node*, the Hostname (that is the IP address of the *repository*) and the Description of the *node*. Figure 9 shows an example of the *node* GUI.

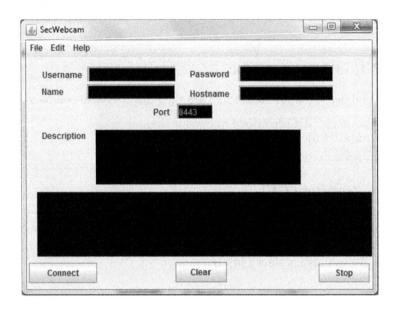

Fig. 9. The *node* GUI

4.3   The *Portable Device* GUI

As in the case of the *repository* GUI, also the one of *portable device* is subdivided in two parts. In the first step (Figure 10(a)) the end user must insert the information associated to the connection with the *repository*. In details, the required information are: Username, Password and Host respectively used for authentication and connection.

In the second step (Figure 10(b)) the application shows the list of *nodes* obtained from the *repository*. For each *node*, the application has three commands: Details, Update and Connect. The Details command permits to obtain a detailed description of the *node*. The Update command permits to request the update of the local list of the *nodes*. The Connect command permits to connect with the *node* and to obtain the sequences of frames captured by the camera(s) (Figure 10(c)) of the *node*. Moreover, the Exit command permits to disconnect and close the application.

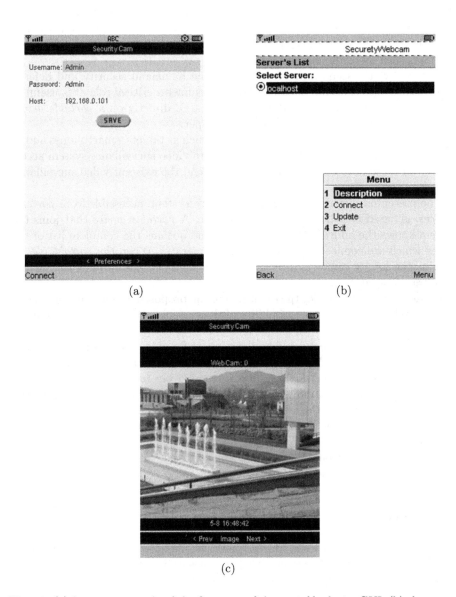

Fig. 10. (a)shows an example of the first step of the *portable device* GUI; (b) shows an example of the *portable device* GUI with the list of the *nodes*; (c) shows an example of the image obtained by the selected camera of the *node*

5   Conclusion and Future Works

In recent years, video surveillance has become an important system for the monitoring of areas, environments, etc. One of the more important application of the video surveillance is the security, but video surveillance is used also for other purposes such as traffic monitoring, etc.

In a real-world scenario, as for instance the homeland security and defense issues, where the video surveillance systems assumes a critical role, it is useful to receive real-time images from different camera(s), directly on a *portable device* as allowed by the presented system in this paper.

With the wide diffusion of *portable devices* such as tablets, smartphones and so on, it is now meaningful to have a really secure video surveillance system accessible from these devices, to reinforce or to extend the existent video surveillance systems.

The presented distributed video surveillance system, accessible from *portable devices*, is based on Client-Server architecture. A *portable device* that joins the system knows the address of the *repository* and obtains the complete list of the *nodes* which are connected to one or more camera(s). When the *portable device* obtains the list, it connects directly to a specific *node* and obtains the images from the camera(s).

Future work will consider the extension of the proposed architecture to a *peer-to-peer* architecture to allow scalability of the system with an increasing number of *nodes*.

Another research aspect could be the support for video-streaming from a *node* to the *portable devices*. Video streaming could allow advanced commands such as *Play, Pause, Stop* and *FrameCapture* respectively to indicate to *node* that can start the video streaming, that can temporarily stop the streaming, that can stop and deallocate the resources of the video streaming and to indicate to save a frame during the streaming, that, in second time, could send it to the *portable device*.

Moreover, it could be of interest to consider the sending from a *node* to a *portable device* a compressed short video with audio.

References

[1] Castiglione, A., Cepparulo, M., De Santis, A., Palmieri, F.: Towards a Lawfully Secure and Privacy Preserving Video Surveillance System. In: Buccafurri, F., Semeraro, G. (eds.) EC-Web 2010. LNBIP, vol. 61, pp. 73–84. Springer, Heidelberg (2010)

[2] Castiglione, A., De Santis, A., Palmieri, F.: Ensuring privacy and confidentiality in digital video surveillance systems. In: Yee, G.O.M. (ed.) Privacy Protection Measures and Technologies in Business Organizations: Aspects and Standards, pp. 245–267. IGI Global (2012)

[3] Fleck, S., Straßer, W.: Towards secure and privacy sensitive surveillance. In: Proceedings of the Fourth ACM/IEEE International Conference on Distributed Smart Cameras, ICDSC 2010, pp. 126–132. ACM, New York (2010)

[4] Hunker, J., Probst, C.W.: Insiders and insider threats - an overview of definitions and mitigation techniques. Journal of Wireless Mobile Networks, Ubiquitous Computing, and Dependable Applications (JoWUA) 2(1), 4–27 (2011)

[5] Liang, Q., Ding, Z.: Spread spectrum watermark for color image based on wavelet tree structure. In: 2008 International Conference on Computer Science and Software Engineering, vol. 3, pp. 692–695 (December 2008)

[6] Wang, Y.P., Chen, M.J., Cheng, P.Y.: Robust image watermark with wavelet transform and spread spectrum techniques. In: Conference Record of the Thirty-Fourth Asilomar Conference on Signals, Systems and Computers (October 29-November 1), vol. 2, pp. 1846–1850 (2000)

[7] Bender, W., Gruhl, D., Morimoto, N., Lu, A.: Techniques for data hiding. IBM Systems Journal 35(3.4), 313–336 (1996)

[8] Kutter, M., Jordan, F.D., Bossen, F.: Digital watermarking of color images using amplitude modulation. Journal of Electronic Imaging 7, 326–332 (1998)

[9] Pizzolante, R., Carpentieri, B.: Copyright protection for images on mobile devices. In: Proceedings of IMIS 2012 (2012)

[10] Langelaar, G.C., van der Lubbe, J., Biemond, J.: Copy protection for multimedia data based on labeling techniques. In: 17th Symposium on Information Theory in the Benelux (1996)

Network Profiling:
Content Analysis of Users Behavior in Digital
Communication Channel

Clara Maria Colombini[1], Antonio Colella[2,*],
Marco Mattiucci[3], and Aniello Castiglione[4]

[1] External Researcher at University of Milan, University of Milan, I-20100 Italy
cmcolombini@email.it
[2] Italian Army, Italian Army General Staff
Via XX Settembre, 123
I-00187 Rome, Italy
antonio.colella@esercito.difesa.it
[3] Raggruppamento Carabinieri Investigazioni Scientifiche (RaCIS)
Caserma "Palidoro", Viale di Tor di Quinto, 119 I-00191 Rome, Italy
marco.mattiucci@carabinieri.it
[4] Dipartimento di Informatica "R.M. Capocelli" - University of Salerno
Via Ponte Don Melillo I-84084 Fisciano (SA), Italy
castiglione@ieee.org

Abstract. In this paper, we focus on a method of analysis of data in a
digital communication channel, using the Digital Profiling technique. We
believe, in fact, that the massive use of cloud computing and pervasive
technology compels us to improve the results of investigative analysis,
in case of cyber-crime, reducing the times of job and maximizing the
outcome. The method suggested highlights relationships between flowing
data in a digital communication channel and the behavioral models of a
possible intruder that threaten that communication. We have chosen to
use the two typical approaches adopted in literature: the *Top-down* to
confirm the facts and the *Bottom-up* to to construct the hypotheses.

Keywords: Digital Profiling, Channel Profiling, Intrusion Protection
System, User Behavior, Network Profiling.

1 Introduction

It is now known that technology development is pushing the communication
means towards prompted use of the network. This causes, in the event of an investigation, that Digital Forensics experts are forced to manage enormous masses
of data that flow in the channel, in a very short time. Moreover, the growing
trend of pervasive computing technology increases the need to tightly control
the networks that provide access to servers, storage and databases. An important mean for monitoring the networks is the control of network performance

---

* Corresponding author.

G. Quirchmayr et al. (Eds.): CD-ARES 2012, LNCS 7465, pp. 416–429, 2012.
© IFIP International Federation for Information Processing 2012

and, in particular, the profiling of the network itself, in order to collect and analyze information of flowing traffic that are generated by routers, firewalls and all other network equipment. In this scenario, we believe that additional method of analysis of the data stream is necessary and that this new method should be able to improve the results of investigation, reducing the times at the same time. What we propose here is to apply the technique of analysis of digital profiling [1] to a communication channel in order to extrapolate the patterns useful to find the profiling of user's digital behavior. From these patterns we can obtain a raw "sample profile" that can be used for the automatic comparison during the monitoring operations of the channel. This approach allows to obtain the immediate detection of any "abnormal behavior" that might reveal the implementation of illegal operations. To better present our research we chose to make a brief overview on profiling of cyber-criminals, Network Security and Intrusion Detection System in order to describe the scenario wherein our model has been applied.

2   Cyber-Crime and Profiling

The application of Digital Profiling (DP) technique in the cyberspace is not easy, especially in terms of appropriate investigation method [2]. The main causes can be summarized as follows:

- inappropriate and incomplete documentation on this subject;
- difficulties to combine the human nature with Computer Science paradigms;
- manifested distrust towards traditional criminal profiling and in general psychological investigations.

Behavior of offender can be the same every attack, but it can also be unique to the individual under analysis, and may occur only sporadically. From the offender's point of view, most of what they do when they are committing a crime is acting normally, for them. From another point of view, they are acting out on needs and patterns developed over the life course, some of which may be abnormal needs and patterns. If there are repeated crime scenes (as with a serial or repeat offender), it is much more likely, with proper examination, that any unique behavior, need, and pattern will be uncovered.

Three elements link crimes in a series:

- method of operation (*modus operandi*);
- ritual (signs of fantasy or psychological need);
- signature (unique combinations of behaviors).

Signature, in a hacker behavior for instance, is a sort of "trademark" and reflects a compulsion on the part of criminals to go beyond just committing the crime to "express themselves", reflecting in some way their personality. In a defacing attack, for instance, this aspect is more evident than in others because the acting of hack is visible to everyone. Anyway, the motivations, actions, and modus operandi of traditional crimes respect to cyber-crimes are different.

For example, it appears that as of 2009, we have entered a new era where organized cyber-criminals can operate identity theft and resale operations, as well as, engaged in cyber-war. The approach to hacking as multi-stage process leads to individuate three main stages, that are: casing, scanning, and enumeration. For example, the time of action can change from 48/72 hours of constantly working during a network intrusion, to a longer period such as the operations performed by pedophiles. However, hackers have found ways to streamline the efficiency of the classic methodology. In particular, the most recent development has been the use of viruses and trojans as part of the modus operandi. The difference with the past is that the "new" method uses a virus or trojan that is either custom made or standard and has the same effect as one had been hacked into the target system to install a keylogger. Clearly, the new method is considered easier than the old one.

3 Network Security

Before focusing the new approach to DP we should recall some notions of Network Security to better cover the topics useful to face cyber-criminal challenges. Security of a complex system is an active process that have at least four steps. The process can be considered as a circular structure. These steps are generically as follows [3].

- *Estimation of possibilities*: that is concerning the evaluation of policies, procedures, laws, internal regulations, financial availability, technical skills, etc.. All these possibilities are important to determine if the system is able to defend itself.
- *Implementation of protective barriers*: the barriers to intruders, for instance, are implemented by hardware, software, human factor and security policies. They are built in order to carry out a form of prevention from possible damage and, at same time, to increase the perception of the security degree.
- *Intrusion detection system*: that implies identification of violations of security policies and management system.
- *System Response*: that is the step in which is possible to remedy the problem by classifying the solutions and by finding available means in order to not allow that these problems happen in the future.

Thus, the purpose of the cycled structure is to minimize the risk of loss of resources arising from complexity of system. This risk depends mainly on three factors: the possible threats, the potential vulnerabilities as well as the intrinsic value of the resource.

3.1 Network Intrusion

"*A wise man always walks with his head down, humble as the dust - it does not matter how smart you are, how many years you studied, how many accomplishments you have already had, one day you will challenge someone with more knowledge than you, with more cunning, with more skills ...* " [4].

An intrusion is a violation of security policies and/or of a secure system management. An intruder in a computer system is primarily a curious person [5]. Just such attitude, in fact, guides the early stages of the intrusion even from a technical standpoint. He seeks to identify, by means just apparently with little risky, system vulnerabilities and other data, such as connections, active services, applications, accessible, available ports, the type of operating system, etc.. After this activity, having had determined the vulnerabilities, the attacker can initiate its action of intrusion revealing his true nature through one of the following activities:

- use of a service available to enter the system apparently;
- use of a service, within the limits of its abilities, making him perform functions not budgeted;
- use of a service in order to determine the fall and to eventually assume the privileges at the wake.

At this point the intrusion can actually be accomplished in several ways:

- Copy, alteration and/or removal of data (files, logs, databases, etc..);
- appropriation of other services;
- ownership of privileges and password(s);
- alteration of the software and creation of backdoors;
- creation of a tunnel to the system being attacked and/or to other systems;
- installation of bots/worms for remote communications or surveys.

All this may continue for some time, at least until the intruder or his tracks are not detected or the intruder itself loses interest and ceases to employ resources or damages the system permanently.

4   Intrusion Detection System - IDS

In order to better introduce the authors claims, it is important to recall what is written in the field of network analysis and in particular on the Intrusion Detection System (IDS). These are, in fact, main tools for carrying out an inquiry either for incident response or digital network investigation. The examination of how IDS works and is classified. In fact, allow us to present a new approach based on behavioral profiling of users linked with the device traces left (e.g., a common PC) in a digital communication channel. Obviously, our goal is very difficult to achieve and can not find conclusion in this paper, but further studies needs to be conducted in the near future. Saying that, now we can move to IDS examination.

The intrusion detection can be considered as the "*problem of identifying those users or malware and bots that are using (or attempting to use) the resources of a computer system without having the required privileges.*" [6]. In the process IDS the symptoms highlighted by the system or data in digital communications are used to realize that the intrusion has occurred or is occurring. The purpose of the ID is to identify evidence of cyber-attack in order to ensure effective protection of the system. IDS systems can be classified according to the following functional attributes [7] [8]. However, current intrusion detection systems are able to recognize and generate alarms in presence of already known menaces or phenomena, characterized by a specific protocol or communication patterns whose templates should be preconfigured in the IDS attacks knowledge base. This can severely limit their effectiveness in presence of completely new (and unknown) menaces, the so called 0-day attacks. To cope with this problem new ID systems are emerging, based on the concept of anomaly detection, and based on the on-line examination of several linear or nonlinear statistic properties of the ongoing traffic, aiming at inferring the occurrence of anomalous phenomena characterized by some deviance from the "normal" (or baseline network traffic behavior [10].

4.1 Classification According to the Source of Data

a. Network based IDSs (NIDSs) [9]: intercept and analyze packets that travel over the network using a "stealth" network card, active real-time and whose use is restricted to the administrator of the network.
b. Host based IDSs (HIDSs) [11]: monitor and analyze predetermined log file and in particular the operating system audit log. Operate in either real time or periodically.
c. Application-based IDSs (AIDSs): Special HIDS that focus on particular audit log of specific applications.
d. Stack-based IDSs (SIDSs) [8] operate directly on the TCP/IP stack by monitoring the passage of packets through the layers of network protocol.

4.2 Classification According to the Method of Analysis

a. Fingerprint based IDSs are based on a database of classes of attacks. When a match between an event and a recently recorded class of features is found (or at least match only in part) there is an high probability that the IDS has detected an intrusion in progress.
b. Historical profile based IDSs: IDSs commercial and experimental attempt to determine an average profile over the period of use of the controlled system. If the IDS detects an abrupt change in this profile then a possible intrusion or at least an irregular operation is going to occur [12].

4.3 Classification According to the Type of Reaction

a. Active IDSs react to the abnormal situation of specific applications running under administrative privileges, changing the system environment (for example, isolating resources) and sometimes, if unable to identify the intrusion, even acting directly responsible for the attack on isolating and recording accurately subsequent actions and communications.
b. Passive IDSs: report alarms to the system administrator who is responsible for deciding what action to take.

At last, IDSs, while providing an important input to prevent, block and contrast attacks against Digital Forensics analysis, unfortunately, are still very "rigid" in their activities referring to precise patterns and pre-packaged, and also show a marked sensitivity to parameter settings. This means that the implementation of an IDS with a firewall to anticipate barriers in a network system is absolutely valid, but what if it does not follow a long period of evaluation, observation and analysis of statistics on the data provided, the cost of employing be too high compared to the benefits. Without fear of contradiction, an IDS must be chosen with different intervention policies at home and various parameters that can be selected and reviewed at least every 6 months based on precise analytical observations of the behavior of the network system.

In any case, the last goal of modern IDS systems is the timely generation of sufficiently accurate alerts that can be used to trigger automatic protection countermeasures such as the determination and distribution of the proper filtering rules [13] to defeat the detected attacks. In the near future, these mechanism will be properly orchestrated to cooperate in a structured organization working as self-learning distributed security solution [14] or operating like a kind of network immune systems [15] where firewalls and detectors play the roles of network antibodies.

5   Network Profiling of Digital Communication Channel

In order to test the application of the method of behavioral analysis offered by the Digital Profiling of a digital communication channel, and to extrapolate the patterns of behavior, you chose to take a sample analysis of log files for access to a corporate web server on which they are resident, on the web portal and the Intranet.

The web server log files record the values for each request received from the server itself. The data are collected in text: when a user accesses a web page, the browser makes a request to the server resources, the system of allocation and management of the web site from which the page is called. The resources required may consist of web files (HTML, PHP,. ASP, etc..), image files or graphics, sound files, video files, and special applications. The web server accesses resources and sends them to your browser, so you can view them. This exchange activities between browser and web server is recorded in the log file, and creates a log of requests to a server by browsers of the users and the resulting responses [16]. The information contained in log files are normally stored in the format known as the *Common Log File Format*, a text file in which each request from browser to web server corresponds to a string. The log file records only the web pages needed and the resources associated with them as audio files, graphics files, etc.. Each server response - indicating success, error, timeout (i.e. no response) - is recorded by the server log file. Table 1 is a typical line of a log file in the Common Log File Format:

82.68.58.90 - user [01/Feb/1998:10:10:00 +0100] "GET /ind.htm HTTP/1.0"
200 4839

Where each field expresses a particular value.

Table 1. Log file in the Common Log File Format

Field	Definition	Description
82.68.58.90	REMOTEHOST	Fully qualified domain name or IP address of the applicant.
-	RFC931	Server authentication.
User	Auth user	Username with which the user is authenticated.
01/Feb/1998:10:10:00 +0100	DATA	Date and time zone for the request.
GET /ind.htm HTTP/1.0	REQUEST	Type of request.
200	Status	Classification code of the result, identified by the HTTP server sends in response to the client. Indicates whether the file has been traced.
4839	Byte	Number of bytes of the response..

The specific type chosen for the log file was created by experimentation in order to maintain control of accesses to the public for statistical purposes(number of users in different periods of the year, attendance at different hours of the day, pages most viewed, etc...). It also records the accesses to the Intranet, reserved for employees through authentication, where a number of users employees own the publishing rights in areas dedicated to each business structure that provides its own documentation. In particular, the control has been implemented following the discovery of a leak of confidential information, in the published literature within the Intranet. This site discusses and summarizes the application of the method of Digital Profiling used to out line the behavior of digital users in order to detect any misconduct.

5.1   The Method of Analysis

In the analysis of log files, depending on the purpose it is intended, are used to highlight relationships between data and build a result of behavioral models that describe two types of approach:

- Top down: search for confirmation of facts already known or assumed (eg, an action resulting from an intrusion has already occurred).
- bottom-up: to find information useful to construct hypotheses (e.g., the most likely causes that produce a particular result).

This research proposes to apply the method of Digital Profiling [1] with both bottom-up and top-down approach. The cycle of analysis takes place in 6 phases.

Step 1 - Identification of the target.

Step 2 - Collection of data log files.

Step 3 - Identification of characteristic properties (features) from the mass of data collected from log files and collect this information (indicators) contained the features detected.

Step 4 - Detection of possible subjects to which it is possible to attribute behavior Digital.

Step 5 - Analysis of information and construction of the behavior of digital accesses.

Step 6 - Construction of the user profile and usage of digital information obtained, depending on the objective.

5.2   Application of Method: A Case Study

Phase 1 - Objective. In the case study,the goal is extrapolation of the profile of users accessing the portal/intranet via the digital reconstruction of the behavior of the various requests that come to the web server. The collection of log files has been confined here in a span of 90 days, identified as the period in which the intrusion occurred.

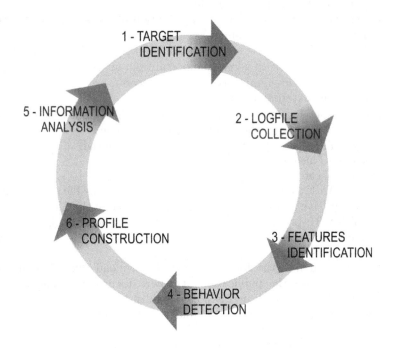

Fig. 1. Network profiling cycle of analysis

Phase 2 - Data Collection. Log files are chosen as standard for access to the IP address of a web portal resident on the web server with one part open to the public and a private Intranet to employees, consisting of an enterprise document repository with access through authentication(username+ password unique to each individual user). These special log files are specifically configured by the company to perform statistics on areas of greatest influx both by external users to the portal by employees in the documentary Intranet, in order to improve the efficiency of the service offered in terms of both external and internal communications. They were chosen for this analysis because of their relative simplicity makes it an ideal sample for a more agile and easy illustration of the application being tested. Log files are structured in records consisting of 8 fields, according Table 2.

2012-04-16 02:35:34 document document.pdf visualization john.smith
10.6.301.0 yes /intranet/office01/data/

Phase 3 - Identification of Properties Characteristic, Features, and Relative Values, Indicators. Each field is an ENTITY that has one or more characteristic properties(FEATURES), each of which contains a set of possible values, which are characteristic or factual information(INDICATORS), which will build the behavioral model of each entity.

1. DATE: gives information on the distribution of accesses in the days of the week: year-month-day (in yyy.mm.dd).
2. TIME: provides information on the distribution of accesses in the daytime: hour.minutes.seconds (in hh.mm.ss).
3. USERNAME: contains information on the identity of the user-employee or as an alternative means to access the portal from an external user.
   - firstname.lastname (employee - internal access).
   - anonymous (external access).
4. IP: provides the identification number of the machine from which the user/ employee has logged on, where indicator is IP number.
5. OBJECT TYPE: provides the type of file being accessed:
   - Document: means access to a file;
   - folder: indicates access to a folder or area.
6. OBJECT NAME: contains the name the extension of the file or folder name to which you have access: Name.extension-full name of the file.
7. OBJECT PATH: provides the entire path to the object sought within the web site or Intranet.
8. ACTION: shows actions performed by the user:
   - Display: visualizes the document in read/download, allowed to all users;
   - creation: allows the publication of a new document or folder (action reserved for users with permission to publish);
   - edit: edits a new document or folder (action reserved for users with permission to publish);
   - delete: allows deletion of a new document or folder (action reserved for users with permission to publish).

Table 2. Log files are structured in records consisting of 8 fields

Field	Definition	Description
01/Feb/1998:10:10:00 +0100	Data Time	Date and time for the request.
Document	Object Time	Type of object searched by the user, consisting of a document (text / spreadsheet / image, etc..), from an area of the site or the Intranet..
Document.pdf	Object Name	Name of the file object of the request.
Visualization	ACTION	Type of action taken by the user on the file or folder / area sought..
John.smith	USERNAME	Contains the user name, consisting of first-name.lastname and kept in the Active Directory enterprise, with which the user-employee makes the request for access to the portal, which allows him access to the Intranet. In the case of access by a user not recognized by the system, the field describes it as anonymous, with the right of access only to the public.
10.6.301.0	IP	identifies the IP address of the machine, inside the company domain, from which the user has logged-dependent. When accessing from outside the corporate domain, the field identifies it as N.D.
IS	INTRANET	Access to employees or less restricted area by the user.
/intranet/uffice01/data/	OBJECT PATH	Location of the file / folder that the user has accessed.

Phase 4 - Conduct of Digital Extrapolation. Depending on the original purpose, each ENTITY detected can be considered the main actor in which to disclose the information (indicators) derived from the Feature of the other elements of the log file, for the delineation of their digital behavior.

It then considers the set log file L, which belong to the entity E:

$L = E_1 \cdots E_n$

Each entity E is formed in turn by one or more Features f, properties that characterize it: $E = f_1 \cdots f_n$

Each Feature f contains a value that represents the indicator i, i.e., characterizing the information. The goal of the set of indicators is to form the behavior of each Entity. $E = i_1 \cdots i_n$

We discuss here briefly the extrapolation of the behavior pattern of entities subject to company analysis after successful intrusion. Within the log file of the case to identified ENTITIES interest, each of which has its own digital personal behavior. The application of the method can be implemented with two different approaches of cited. In this case we assume knowledge of an intrusion already occurred, and we use a top-down approach, identifying the ENTITIES primary object of the intrusion, i.e. the file containing the stolen information, indicated by the field OBJECT NAME.

Entity OBJECT - Digital model of behavior: the Feature which characterize its behavior contain digital indicators with which it is possible to build the model behavior of the follow Entities.

- OBJECT NAME: indicates not only the file on which the action was done, but how many times it has been accomplished in the time interval considered.
- PATH: identifies the area where the object is contained (in this case within the Intranet with the subfolders), the indicators that they extract provides guidance on:
  - Vulnerabilities in the implementation of security measures for the affected area;
  - presence of other types of confidential documents also present in the object of intrusion.
- ACTION: the type of action that was performed on the object-target:
  - Display (ie the download file);
  - create (upload a file or creating a folder);
  - edit (edit the file as its replacement, moving, renaming the file);
  - delete (delete a file or a folder of files).
- DATE and TIME: the date and time when the operation was performed on the object. Indicators are also obtained from extracts statistical information on the days and hours of the day when the shares were the most frequently performed.
- IP: The IP address of the machine you are logged on (whether fixed or Domain) or IP address of the source provider (if dynamic). It also indicates how many times the same IP has made other actions.

Similarly, but with a bottom-up approach, we can apply the same method of profiling the log file from the user anonymous, useful if you want a model to study the behavior of users who access the web server from outside domain, in order to implement security measures with the aim of preventing any abnormal behavior. In this way we can create a primary entity (USERANONYMOUS), using the primary USER ENTITY, filtered with Feature "Anonymous" from the USERNAME field. The Feature which characterize its behavior contain digital indicators with which it built its digital model of behavior: ACTION, OBJECT NAME, DATE and TIME, IP.

Phase 5 - Analysis of Information and Construction of the Behavior Profile of Digital Accesses. The information derived from the measured indicators are the behavioral profile of the subject being treated as the main entity. In the case of the Entity OBJECT, that is, the file object intrusion, with reference to the time period examined (90 days), the indicators have revealed that it has been shown, by an anonymous user, with an IP not identified, for 5 times in one month:

- 3, Saturday morning, at 10:12 am;
- 4, Sunday morning, at 11:05 am;
- 10, Saturday morning, at 9:55 am;
- 11, Sunday morning, at 10:00 am;
- 17, Saturday morning, at 10:47am.

Similarly,the behavioral profile was obtained USERANONYMOUS, which connects mainly in the evening after 18, Saturday and Sunday morning browsing documents information on services and products offered by the company.

Phase 6 - Comparisons of the Obtained Profiles and Usage of Given Digital Information, Depending on the Objective. Last operation is the comparison between the obtained profiles in order to reveal affinity in the digital behavior. Using connection dates as a filter, we selected users access to anonymous on Saturday and Sunday morning, in the 3 month period. The comparison with the dates reserved for the display of files allowed to isolate two anonymous users online on the dates and times in which the confidential file with the same IP address was downloaded.

5.3 Considerations

In this paper it is shown the possibility to apply the Digital Profiling to a data stream with the aim to extrapolate the profile of the entity of interest by looking at a set of log files resulting as the access log of a web server in a given time interval. The application of the method is also possible on any other entity within a log file, in order to extrapolate the digital behavior of "someone" (or "something") of interest. A second factor to be considered is that it is also possible to make a comparison between different behaviors in order to build broader profiles, composed of different behaviors of the "actors" who populate the data flow. Indeed, where there is no availability of specific log files, it is possible to reconstruct the profile by comparing different behaviors of the different entities available in a given log file.

6   Conclusions

The Digital Profiling of a set of log file could be very useful for the identification of a perpetrators of a cyber-crime (e.g., phishing, attacks on servers, etc.), where the extrapolation of the digital behavior of selected entities, as subject of a set of log file, can make the reconstruction and subsequent analysis of the modus operandi of the offender (i.e., the intruder in case of a network intrusion). The proposed approach is able to reveal information about:

- Target of the attack (fraud, Denial of Service, political attack, etc.);
- tools and techniques used for intrusion (rootkits, shells, worms, social engineering, etc.);

- technical skills used;
- possible correlation with measures of social engineering;
- time chosen for the attack (day/night, intra/end of week, etc.);
- duration of the attack and possible frequency (single or fragmented in pre-determined time intervals, etc.);
- correlation of the moment chosen for the attack with external events;
- choices of victims (national or foreign government institution, bank, commercial organization, etc.);
- typology of (eventual) anti-forensic techniques adopted;
- achievement of goal.

References

1. Colombini, C., Colella, A.: Digital Profiling: A Computer Forensics Approach. In: Tjoa, A.M., Quirchmayr, G., You, I., Xu, L. (eds.) ARES 2011. LNCS, vol. 6908, pp. 330–343. Springer, Heidelberg (2011)
2. Colombini, C., Colella, A.: Digital scene of crime: technique of profiling users. To appear in Journal of Wireless Mobile Networks, Ubiquitous Computing, and Dependable Applications, JoWUA (2012)
3. Aterno, S., Cajani, F., Costabile, G., Mattiucci, M., Mazzaraco, G.: Computer Forensics e Indagini Digitali. Manuale Tecnico-giuridico e Casi Pratici, Experta srl (2011)
4. Bejtlich, R.: The Tao of network security monitoring. Addison-Wesley (2005)
5. Shinder, D.L., Cross, M.: Scene of the Cybercrime, 2nd edn. Syngress Publishing (2008)
6. Mukherjee, B., Heberlein, T.L., Levitt, K.N.: Network Intrusion Detection. IEEE Network 8(3), 26–41 (1994)
7. Bace, R., Mell, P.: Intrusion Detection Systems. National Institute of Standards and Technology Special Publication on IDS (2001)
8. Laing, B.: How to guide: implementing a network based intrusion detection system (2001)
9. Roesch, M.: Snort - Lightweight Intrusion Detection System for Networks. In: 13th System Administration Conference - LISA 1999, Seattle, WA (1999)
10. Francesco, P., Ugo, F.: Network anomaly detection through nonlinear analysis. Computers & Security 29(7), 737–755 (2010)
11. Crosbie, M.J., Kuperman, B.A.: A building block approach to Intrusion Detection. In: RAID (2001)
12. Stephenson, P.R.: The application of Intrusion Detection Systems in a Forensic Environment. In: Recent Advances in Intrusion Detection - Raid, Toulose, France (2001)
13. Francesco, P., Ugo, F.: Containing large-scale worm spreading in the Internet by cooperative distribution of traffic filtering policies. Computers & Security 27(1-2), 48–62 (2008)

14. De Santis, A., Castiglione, A., Fiore, U., Palmieri, F.: An intelligent security architecture for distributed firewalling environments. Journal of Ambient Intelligence and Humanized Computing, 1–12 (2011),
    http://dx.doi.org/10.1007/s12652-011-0069-8
15. Francesco, P., Ugo, F.: Automated detection and containment of worms and viruses into heterogeneous networks: a simple network immune system. Int. J. Wire. Mob. Compututer 2(1), 47–58 (2007)
16. Farinella, T.: Tecnologia database per l'analisi di log file di Web Server. Universita' degli Studi di Modena e Reggio Emilia (2005)

How to Forge a Digital Alibi on Mac OS X

Aniello Castiglione[1], Giuseppe Cattaneo[1], Roberto De Prisco[1],
Alfredo De Santis[1], and Kangbin Yim[2]

[1] Dipartimento di Informatica, Università di Salerno
84084 Fisciano (SA), Italy
[2] Dept. of Information Security Engineering, Soonchunhyang University
Asan, Chunknam, 336-745, Korea

Abstract. *Digital evidence* is increasingly being used in court cases. It
consists of traces left on digital devices from which one can infer information about the actions performed on those digital devices. Digital
evidence can be on computers, phones, digital cameras belonging either
to an alleged offender or to third parties, like servers operated by ISPs
or by companies that offer web services, such as YouTube, Facebook and
Gmail. Digital evidence can either be used to prove that a suspect is indeed guilty or to prove that a suspect is instead not guilty. In the latter
case the digital evidence is in fact an alibi.

However digital evidence can also be forged giving an offender the
possibility of creating a *false digital alibi*. Offenders can use false digital
alibi in a variety of situations ranging from ordinary illegal actions to
homeland security attacks.

The creation of a false digital alibi is system-specific since the digital
evidence varies from system to system. In this paper we investigate the
possibility of creating a false digital alibi on a system running the Mac OS
X 10.7 Lion operating system. We show how to construct an automated
procedure that creates a (false) digital alibi on such a system.

1 Introduction

Modern technology permeates everyday life. Computers, tablets, smart-phones,
GPS and other digital devices are widespread and are used in all sorts of activities: editing a spreadsheet, downloading a document, listening to a song,
watching a TV program, browsing the Internet, paying a bill, chatting on a
social network, and much more.

As the use of digital devices increases also the number of criminal or illegal
actions perpetrated by using, or at least involving, such devices is growing. The
use of digital devices often leaves digital traces. Many computer activities normally leave several traces of what has happened; mobile phones equipped with
GPS might record the GPS coordinates of the locations that have been visited
carrying the device; Internet activities leave traces in the logfile of the servers
and in this last case the servers can be located anywhere in the world. These are
just a few example of digital evidence. Any digital device can contain traces of
activities performed using the device.

G. Quirchmayr et al. (Eds.): CD-ARES 2012, LNCS 7465, pp. 430–444, 2012.

Digital evidence can be involved in court debates and can be used to provide evidence of crimes or more in general of illegal actions. There are several court debates where digital evidence has played a crucial role.

Digital evidence can consist of histories files, emails, content of computer memory, pictures on a digital camera, data on a mobile device. Generally speaking, digital evidence is information stored in a digital device. The online US legal definitions and legal terms dictionary [17] defines digital (or electronic) evidence as any probative information stored or transmitted digitally that can be used during the court trial.

However, digital evidence might also constitute an *alibi* for the defense of an alleged offender. The Latin word *alibi* literally means *"in or at another place"*. The Merriam-Webster online dictionary [22], explains *alibi* as "the plea of having been, at the time of the commission of an act, elsewhere than at the place of commission". Digital evidence that somebody was using a specific computer located far away from the place where the offender acted might constitute an alibi for the user of the computer.

There are several examples of legal proceedings in which digital evidence has been considered an alibi that contributed to exonerate the alleged offender. Among these, an interesting case is the one that involved Rodney Bradford [18,19], accused of armed robbery and released thanks to digital evidence proving that the alleged offender performed activities on his Facebook account at the same time when the crime was committed. The Erb Law Firm, a corporation of lawyers in Philadelphia, emphasized that "Facebook Can Keep You Out of Jail" [25]. Another example is the Italian case named "Garlasco" [20], in which the sentence of the first trial acquitted the alleged murder. The defendant's laptop contained digital evidence of work activity at the time the crime was committed. Offenders can use false digital alibi in a variety of situations. Homeland security attacks might also be performed exploiting a false digital alibi to cover the offender.

Digital evidence is *immaterial*. That is, the traces are bits stored in some storage device (hard disk and similar). Being bits stored somewhere, digital evidence can be modified by whoever has permission to access the memory storage where the bits are stored. For example, the administrator of a server can modify the logfiles that store information regarding all the accesses to the server.

Moreover, it is difficult, if not impossible, to identify the true originator of the digital evidence. Indeed even though we have digital evidence of some activities on a specific device, the digital evidence itself does not provide any information about *who* has produced it. For example, Bob claims that at a given time he has been at home working with his computer and he even posted some comments in a public blog and that there is digital evidence of these activities on his computer; if we are able to assert without any doubt that Bob's computer has indeed been used at the time Bob indicated and the activities performed are those claimed by Bob, we cannot be sure that really was Bob to use his computer. Bob might have asked somebody else to use his computer on his behalf, perhaps providing the password to access the computer.

As a matter of fact, Bob does not even need to ask somebody to use the computer on his behalf. Indeed it is possible to set up a sequence of automated actions that simulate a real user performing activities on a computer leaving digital evidence of the actions but without leaving any trace of the automation. Any action performed by an individual on a computer can be simulated by means of automated tools, including mouse clicks, pressure of keys, writing of texts, web browsing, and so on. Automating Internet accesses also produces traces in the servers that can be considered trusted third parties. This means that it is possible to forge a *false* digital alibi. However, care must be taken in order to not leave digital evidence of the automation.

The digital evidence left on a particular device is strongly dependent on the device and on the operating system running on the device. Hence the construction of a false digital alibi is system-dependent. For example, in a Windows based system the Windows Registry contains a wealth of information about the activities performed on the computer (e.g., [11]). Knowing the details of how the operating system stores information about the activities performed by the user is clearly crucial both for the analysis, for which we are interested in finding the information stored in the system, and for the construction of a digital alibi, for which we want to delete the information about the activities performed on the system. Many other technical details, like the type of filesystem, the use of virtual memory, the presence of automatic backup software play a crucial role.

In a recent paper [6] an automated procedure for the construction of a false digital alibi on systems running Microsoft Windows XP with Service Pack 3 and Microsoft Windows Vista has been described. In this paper we focus the attention on a system running Mac OS X 10.7 Lion and show how to construct an automation procedure for the construction of a false digital alibi.

2   Forging a Digital Alibi

To create a false digital alibi we design an automated procedure that can be scheduled to run on the chosen computer at a given time (in the absence of the user of the computer, which might be elsewhere at that time). The automated procedure will simulate the use of the computer with some activities that are normally performed by the user, such as text editing, web surfing and other Internet actions, leaving the normal digital evidence of such activities – the exact same digital evidence that would be left if the user performed those actions. To forge the digital alibi the user of the computer needs only to schedule (or run with an appropriate delay) the automated procedure before leaving the place where the computer is located.

Creating the automated procedure is not difficult. There are many tools available that make the task easy to accomplish also for non-expert users. However, the problem is not that of creating the automated procedure but that of deleting the digital evidence of the use of the automated procedure, leaving only the digital evidence of the "normal" actions.

2.1   Unwanted Evidence

An automation can leave traces on the system that allow an inspector to realize that the automated procedure was used making void the alibi (actually in this case the false alibi can become evidence against the suspected person). Traces of the automation is referred to as *unwanted evidence*, and should be avoided or removed after the automation. Unwanted evidence can be left, for examples in the execution traces or logon traces. Often the digital evidence is stored in system logfiles. For example, almost all operating systems provide mechanisms to trace the execution of all the processes that get run on the machine, writing in specific logfiles information such as the executable name, the time it was started, the amount of CPU that was allocated during the execution, the maximum resident size for virtual memory and so on. Depending on the OS, the execution of an automation generated with tools like AutoIt also leaves this kind of traces. For example, Windows stores a lot of information in the Registry. In Linux, system logs are stored in the */var/logs* directory and memory map of processes is maintained in the */proc* directory. In a Mac OS X computer system logs are stored in the */private/var/log* directory. Most of recent OSs implement techniques like "Virtual Memory Allocation" and "Prefetch", which also store data about programs on the filesystem. Application specific data can also contain digital evidence. If a specific application used for the automation leaves unwanted evidence we must be careful in using that application. For example, if when using a OS X based system we decide to use an Applescript for the automation we have to be sure that the fact the Applescript gets executed is not logged somewhere (for example, in the shell history if we use a shell to launch the script).

2.2   Avoiding or Removing Unwanted Evidence

In order to avoid traces of the automation one can take several precautions. The specific precautions depend on the particular system that one is using. If, in order to execute the automation, we are forced to create evidence of the automation, then it is necessary to remove the unwanted evidence. Whenever it is not possible either to avoid or to securely remove an unwanted trace (for example, when its location is write-protected), an a-priori obfuscation strategy could be adopted in order to avoid any logical connections between unwanted evidence and the automation procedure, in a way that the unwanted evidence could have been produced by a "normal" system operation.

While wiping unwanted evidence can be easily achieved using several wiping techniques (e.g., [10] [9] [21]), the actual problem is "how to erase the eraser". In [10] several methods that can be exploited to implement an automatic, selective and secure deletion/self-deletion are shown.

2.3   Iterative Refinement

The automation needed to construct a false digital alibi can be constructed with an iterative techniques consisting of two phase:

1. development of the automation and
2. testing of the procedure on the target system.

The automation can be refined at every iteration by fine tuning the simulated actions and the wiping of the unwanted evidence. The process will stop when it produces an automated procedure that leaves only the wanted evidence.

Both activities could leave many traces in the target system and thus one must be very careful during the construction of the automation. The best solution is to construct the automation on a completely separated, but identical, system, like another computer or a virtual machine with the same characteristic of the target system. If the automation is constructed on the target system then one must take care also of unwanted evidence relative to the construction of the automation.

The specific strategy that we have used is the following. We started with a first version of the automation procedure, call it $automation_0$. Then we proceeded in constructing refined versions $automation_1$, $automation_2$, ... and so on by using the following technique to decide the refinements. Given version $automation_i$, run it starting from a pre-determined state of the system, say $S0$ and call $S1$ the corresponding final state of the system. Then, starting again from $S0$ perform manually the actions of the automation and call $S2$ the corresponding state of the system. Notice that when performing several actions there are delays between actions. Clearly, it is impossible to match the delays used in the manual execution of the actions with those of the automated execution. However, it is possible to use reasonable random delays in the automation. Having produced state $S1$ (automated execution of the actions) and state $S2$ (manual execution of the actions) we can compare the two states. In particular we can check all the files that have been either accessed or modified. By a careful inspection of the modified or accessed file list for the two states we can infer where the automation has left unwanted evidence. Then we can refine the automation in order to avoid the unwanted evidence. It is necessary to repeat the whole process because the modifications might create new unwanted evidence. The process stops when the states $S1$ and $S2$ obtained for a specific version $automation_n$ of the automated procedure are indistinguishable in the sense that there is no evidence of the use of the automation but only the evidence of the actions. That is, there is no way of telling that it was an automated procedure to execute the actions and not a real user.

3   Case Study for Mac OS X 10.7 Lion

In this section we describe the construction of a false digital alibi on a Mac running OS X 10.7 Lion. The construction of a false digital alibi needs an automated tool that simulates the behaviour of a user working at the computer and a mechanism that deletes any evidence of the use of the automated tool. Writing a program or script that simulates a real user using the computer is quite simple. Avoiding to leave traces or deleting all the traces that are left by the program/script can be tricky. The difficulty of wiping all the evidence of the use of the automated tool depends also on how we implement the automation and this, in turn, can make the automation itself not so easy. In the following section we explain how to create an automated tool for a Mac running OS 10.7 Lion and how to erase any trace left by the automation.

3.1 Unwanted Traces on a Mac

It is important that no information is left about the execution of the automation scripts. Hence it is necessary to pay attention to a few things that can potentially leave traces. On the particular system that we are using, we have identified the following potential source of information leakage.

- *Logfiles.* As it happens in other systems, whenever the user executes programs or takes other actions, information about the actions executed gets written in specific files. These files are usually logfiles but any other type of file can be involved. As we will explain in more details in the next sections, we have identified a set of system files that get modified and can potential contain digital evidence of the taken actions. System wide logfiles are stored in */private/var/log*. Application specific logfiles can be anywhere.
- *Virtual memory.* If virtual memory is being used it is possible that a copy of the scripts gets saved in the virtual memory. Virtual memory swap files are written in */private/var/vm/*. To avoid a potential leakage of information the automated procedure will have to make sure that no new swapfile will be left in the directory.
- *Time machine.* Another potential leakage of information derives from the use of the Time Machine backup software. If during the execution of the scripts there is a planned backup session it is possible that relevant files will be copied on the Time Machine backup disk, potentially revealing the execution of the automation. So, it is necessary to disable the backup software so that no backup will be performed during the time when the automated scripts will run. Disabling the Time Machine can raise suspicion only if the user never disables the backup software. It will be enough to disable it randomly in order to not raise suspicions. Alternatively one can modify the backup schedule to obtain the wanted effect (that is, no backup will be performed during the time when the automated scripts will run).
- *Journaled filesystem.* A journaled filesystem could also potentially leave traces due to the storage of metadata about the files. If the chosen Mac does use a journaled filesystem (e.g. HFS+) then it is necessary to use an external device with a non journaled filesystem (e.g., FAT32). For this reason, we use a USB external pendrive to store the scripts needed for the automation procedure; the pendrive uses a FAT32 filesystem.

3.2 The Sequence of Simulated Actions

We start by setting up a pre-determined sequence of actions that we wish to simulate, that is, the sequence of actions that the automated procedure will take leaving the same evidence that would be left if the user itself takes the actions. These actions have been chosen with two goals: leave on the system digital evidence that constitutes the false digital alibi and facilitate the removal of unwanted evidence (the digital evidence of the execution of the automated procedure).

The specific set of actions that we used is shown in Listing 1.1. Clearly one can decide any arbitrary set of actions. As we will explain later, some of these actions have been chosen because they help in not creating or in removing the unwanted evidence.

```
1  Delay the execution (wait an appropriate time)
2  Launch iTunes and start playing a playlist
3  Launch Safari and use it to post a twit on twitter
4  Launch Pages and start writing a document
5  Go back to Safari and make a Google search
6  Visit a website in the list returned by the search
7  Launch Mail, write and send an email
8  Close iTunes
9  Go back to Page and finish the document, saving it to disk
10 Shutdown the computer
```

Listing 1.1. Simulated actions

3.3 The Automated Procedure

The automated procedure comprises three files:

1. the *launcher*, an Applescript that simply launches the scheduler-wiper.
2. the *scheduler-wiper*, a Python script that is responsible of launching the simulator and of deleting the traces of the execution of the simulator (clearly not those relative to the simulated activities but only those that might reveal the use of the script to perform the activities).
3. the *simulator*, an Applescript script that simulates the behaviour of a real user using the computer.

The launcher script is needed only to avoid the direct execution of the scheduler-wiper since executing directly the Python script would leave traces of its execution. Indeed, in order to directly launch the scheduler-wiper script, a Python script, we would need to use a shell. Normally the commands executed within a shell are saved in a shell history. Although it is possible to disable the shell history, such a choice is not common and can raise suspicion. So, we decided to avoid running commands directly from the shell. To run the Python script we use an Applescript that simply launches the Python script. The Applescript can be launched through the graphical interface, without opening a shell (and thus without saving any commands in the shell history).

All these files will be stored on an external storage device, such as USB pendrive, to avoid problems with either a journaled filesystem or with a backup software like Time Machine. Moreover, the script have been saved as *.app* files, which are stand-alone executables. This is especially important for the Python script because no Library function will be called at the time of the execution.

We have chosen Applescript for the simulation because Applescript makes easy to create an automation, as we will explain in the sequel. Python has been chosen because the execution of a Python scripts leaves very few traces so there is little unwanted evidence to delete or to avoid. Moreover, the use of Python is preferable to other interpreted languages (like Java bytecode) since it does not require additional software not already shipped with the operating system (like the Java Virtual Machine).

The launcher Applescript. The launcher is a very simple Applescript since the only action that it has to perform is launching the scheduler-wiper script (which is written in Python). The entire code is a single line and is shown in Listing 1.2:

```
do shell script ''python /Volumes/PENDRIVE/helloWorld.py''
    with administrator privileges
```

Listing 1.2. The launcher Applescript code

Notice that the scheduler-wiper needs to be run with administrator privileges since in order to delete the traces of its own execution it will have to modify some files not accessible to a regular user. As we have already said we use this script only to avoid launching directly the Python scheduler-wiper script.

The Scheduler-Wiper Python Script. The scheduler-wiper script has two functionalities: running the simulator and deleting all the unwanted evidence relative to the execution of the entire automation. Clearly, all the traces that are relative to the simulated activities have to be left on the system. However, no traces of the three scripts and of their execution have to be left on the system.

The first action that the scheduler-wiper takes is that of checking the status of some relevant system files. These files will be modified by the execution of the simulator and by the execution of the wiper, so they will need to be "touched" after the simulation in order to delete the traces of the existence of the scheduler and the wiper.

```
# list of files to restore
listOfFiles=["/usr/bin/srm",
"/System/Library/Frameworks/OSAKit.framework/...",
"/System/Library/Frameworks/ServerNotification.framework
    /...",
...
...
"/System/Library/ScriptingDefinitions/CocoaStandard.sdef"]

size=len(listOfFiles) # n. of paths

# init arrays
```

```
12 atimes = [0] * size  # access times
13
14 # get last access time of each file
15 for i in range(size) :
16     atimes[i]=os.path.getatime(listOfFiles[i])
17
18 ### AUTOMATION ###
19
20 # run the applescript file
21 os.system("/Volumes/PENDRIVE/helloWorld.app/Contents/MacOS
      /applet")
```

Listing 1.3. Snippet 1 of the scheduler-wiper

Listing 1.3 provides a snippet of code of the scheduler-wiper Python script. The last line of this snippet contains the call to the simulator script which performs all the wanted actions (that is, the ones listed in Listing 1.1) for which we want to leave the digital evidence needed for the false alibi. In the next section we provide more details about the simulator script.

Then the scheduler-wiper deletes in a secure way, using the *srm*, command, the 3 files containing the scripts, which are on the external USB pendrive. Notice that it is possible to delete these files even though the system is executing the scheduler-wiper because the Python language is interpreted and the entire file is loaded by the interpreter when the file gets executed; hence the physical copy can be removed without affecting the execution of the script.

Then the wiper goes through the list of system files that could potentially reveal that the simulation scripts have been executed and restores the initial status of those files in such a way that there is no trace of the execution of the simulation scripts. Also the swapfiles are deleted.

Listing 1.4 shows the relative snippet of code.

```
1 # delete the applescript launcher
2 os.system("srm -r /Volumes/PENDRIVE/launcher.app")
3 # delete the applescript simulator
4 os.system("srm -r /Volumes/PENDRIVE/simulator.app")
5 # delete the python script
6 os.system("srm -r /Volumes/PENDRIVE/helloWorld.app")
7
8 #delete the swap file modified during the script's
      execution
9 for root,dirs,files in os.walk("/var/vm") :
10     for f in files :
11         if f!="sleepimage" :
12             swapFilePath=os.path.join(root,f)
13             mtime=os.path.getmtime(swapFilePath)
14             if(mtime>nowMilliseconds) :
15                 os.system("srm "+ swapFilePath)
16
17 ### Reset access time ###
```

```
18
19  for i in range(size):
20      atime=os.path.getatime(listOfFiles[i])
21      touchTime = millsToDate(atimes[i])
22      if(atime>atimes[i]) :
23          os.system("touch -c -t " + touchTime + " \"" +
                listOfFiles[i] + "\"") # set both last access and
                last modified time (-c do not create file , -t
                specified time)
24
25  ### Turn off the system ###
26
27  os.system("sudo shutdown -h now")
```

Listing 1.4. Snippet 2 of the scheduler-wiper

The wiper deletes also any swap file left in the */private/var/vm* directory.

The Simulator. To simulate a user working at the computer we can use an Applescript. Applescript is a scripting language, integrated in the Mac operating system, specifically designed to control other applications. Using Applescript is very easy to schedule user actions, since it allows to launch specific applications and execute specific actions within the applications. It even allows to simulate keyboard typing. For example, the following code snippet written in Applescript simulates the use of iTunes for listing a playlist:

```
1  tell application "iTunes"
2      delay 3.47
3      play playlist 1
4  end tell
```

Listing 1.5. Applescript code snippet for using iTunes

Note that the *delay* command does not make any guarantees about the actual length of the delay, and it cannot be more precise than 1/60th of a second. However, this is enough to simulate random delays between user actions.

A slightly more complicated code snippet is required to simulate an access to Twitter, by means of Safari, and the posting of a comment:

```
1   tell application "Safari"
2       activate
3       open location "https://twitter.com/"
4       delay 30
5       tell application "System Events"
6           keystroke "USER"
7           delay 5.12
8           keystroke tab
9           delay 7.3
10          keystroke "PASSWD"
11          delay 3.8
```

```
12        keystroke return
13        delay 15.6
14        keystroke tab
15        delay 8.21
16        keystroke tab
17        delay 7.48
18        keystroke "What a nice day!!!"
19        delay 3.21
20        keystroke tab
21        delay 5.45
22        keystroke return
23     end tell
24 end tell
```

Listing 1.6. Applescript code snippet for posting on Twitter

By properly writing the simulator we can simulate almost any real behaviour. Some actions can be more complicated than others. However, the Applescript language is powerful enough to allow the simulation of almost any action.

Particular attention has to be paid to the scheduling of the actions: the timing should be reasonable in order to not create any suspicion. For example, if we are simulating the writing of a long document, then we should leave enough time between the launching of the text editor and the saving of the file so that in the elapsed time a real user can actually type all the necessary keystrokes.

4   Testing

In order to test the automation we have operated in a virtual environment. We have created a virtual machine and installed the Mac OS X 10.7 Lion operating system. The disk for the virtual machine is an external USB hard disk previously formatted with a low-level writing procedure. Beside the operating system we installed the iWork software in the virtual machine and we copied some mp3 files to be used with iTunes. Moreover, we configured the following applications: Mail, iTunes and Pages. After the setting phase the virtual machine has been shut down and the external hard disk containing its filesystem has been copied bit by bit on an another external hard disk having the same physical dimension. We will refer to this disk image as the *initial disk state*. At this point we proceeded with two copies of the virtual machine starting from the initial state.

In the first copy we plugged in the USB pendrive with the scripts that accomplish the automation and we executed them as described earlier in the paper. The *launcher.app* script has been run with a double click. The script requested the administrator password and after that it executed all the actions that we described in the previous sections, without any further human intervention. At the end the virtual machine was automatically shut down. We will call the resulting disk state *automated disk state* (this is the disk state after the automation).

In the second copy, starting again from the initial state, we manually executed the set of actions that the automation comprises and we shut down the machine.

For this case, we will call the resulting disk state *manual disk state* (this is the disk state after the manual execution of the actions).

4.1   Iterative Refinement

In order to produce the final version of the automation scripts we have used the technique described in Section 2.3, where $S1$ is the automated disk state and $S2$ is the manual disk state. As an example, we describe in the following one specific iteration.

A file by file analysis of the two states, the automated disk state and the manual disk state, revealed all the files that were either accessed or modified in each of the two cases. The vast majority of the files accessed or modified for both cases were relative to the use of the applications. For example, sending the email causes the creation of files in */Users/userName/Library/Mail*. From these file it is impossible to tell whether they were created by the manual execution or by the automation.

Among the files that were accessed only by the automated procedure we found the following list of files (the dots mean that we specified only the directory under which there are a number of files accesses by the automation):

```
1  /System/Library/Frameworks/OSAKit.framework/...
2  /System/Library/Frameworks/ServerNotification.framework
      /...
3  /System/Library/PrivateFrameworks/AOSKit.framework/...
4  /System/Library/PrivateFrameworks/AOSNotification.
      framework/...
5  /System/Library/PrivateFrameworks/SyncServicesUI.framework
      /...
6  /System/Library/ScriptingDefinitions/CocoaStandard.sdef
```

Listing 1.7. Accessed files

We are not sure that one can infer the use of the automation by the fact that these files have been accessed, but to be on the safe side the automation script has been refined in order to restore the access time of these files as in the initial disk state.

Among the files not relative to the set of simulated actions we found the following list of files:

```
1   /private/var/log/asl/2012.05.29.G80.asl
2   /private/var/log/asl/2012.05.29.U0.G80.asl
3   /private/var/log/asl/2012.05.29.U501.asl
4   /private/var/log/asl/AUX.2012.05.29
5   /private/var/log/asl/AUX.2012.05.29/44545
6   /private/var/log/asl/AUX.2012.05.29/44547
7   /private/var/log/asl/AUX.2012.05.29/44549
8   /private/var/log/asl/BB.2013.05.31.G80.asl
9   /private/var/log/asl/StoreData
10  /private/var/log/DiagnosticMessages/2012.05.29.asl
```

```
11 /private/var/log/DiagnosticMessages/StoreData
12 /private/var/log/opendirectoryd.log
13 /private/var/log/secure.log
14 /private/var/log/system.log
```

Listing 1.8. System-wide log files

A manual inspection of these files showed no traces of the automation (this in fact depends on the fact that in previous refinement we have taken steps to avoid unwanted evidence). In particular there were no traces relative to the use of Applescript which is the main evidence of the use of an automation.

Clearly we kept refining the scripts until we obtained a version of the automation for which no unwanted evidence was left in the system.

4.2 Forensic Analysis

The iterative refinement technique has been used to improve to automation scripts up to the point of obtaining a script that behaves exactly as a real user and does not leave any evidence of the automation. However, to validate the false digital alibi we have to execute a forensic analysis of the state of the system after the automation. For example, it is necessary that there be no unwanted evidence of the automation not only in the files of the filesystem but also on the erased portion of the disk. To cope with leakage of information in deleted files we always use secure deletion. We will provide more details about the forensic analysis in the extended version of this paper.

5 Conclusions

Digital evidence contains information about actions taken on a computer, like logon data, the use of specific applications, web histories, command histories, and much more. Digital evidence is becoming relevant as a consequence of the widespread use of digital devices. Many court cases nowadays involve digital evidence. However, digital evidence can be fake: a *false digital alibi* can be constructed. A false digital alibi can be constructed by setting up an automated procedure that executes actions (writing a document, visiting websites, posting comments, etc) without the physical presence of the user who can be elsewhere when the actions are automatically performed on his computer. The automation can leave digital evidence of itself. However by carefully crafting the automated process one can either avoid the digital evidence of the automation or delete it afterwords. In [6] it has been shown how to set up an automated procedure to create a false digital alibi for a Windows based system (the specific OS considered are Windows XP with Service Pack 3 and Windows Vista). The creation of a false alibi heavily depends on the particular operating system as the digital evidence left is system specific. In this paper we have showed how to construct a false digital alibi on a system running Mac OS X (specifically, 10.7 Lion).

The false digital alibi constructed as a case study comprises a specific set of actions ranging from using iTunes for listening to a playlist to surfing the web using Safari and posting comments on public website. The set of actions was carefully chosen in order to not leave digital evidence of the automation. Further study might include the investigation of which actions can be safely simulated and which ones create trouble for the deletion of the digital evidence of the automation. The case study has used a specific version of the Mac OS X operating system. An interesting deeper investigation would be that of understanding whether the false digital alibi can be constructed with different versions of the operating system. We believe that this should be doable, perhaps with some modifications to the automated procedure.

Acknowledgements. We would like to thank Dario Di Nucci, Fabio Palomba and Stefano Ricchiuti for helping with the testing of the automated procedure.

References

1. Albano, P., Castiglione, A., Cattaneo, G., De Maio, G., De Santis, A.: On the Construction of a False Digital Alibi on the Android OS. In: Proceedings of the Third International Conference on Intelligent Networking and Collaborative Systems (INCoS 2011), Fukuoka Institute of Technology, Fukuoka, Japan, November 30-December 2, pp. 685–690. IEEE (2011)
2. Carvey, H.: Windows Forensics Analysis, 2nd edn. Syngress (2009)
3. Chandola, V., Banerjee, A., Kumar, V.: Anomaly detection: A survey. ACM Computing Surveys 41(3) (July 2009)
4. Craig, W., Dave, K., Shyaam, S.R.S.: Overwriting Hard Drive Data: The Great Wiping Controversy. In: Sekar, R., Pujari, A.K. (eds.) ICISS 2008. LNCS, vol. 5352, pp. 243–257. Springer, Heidelberg (2008)
5. Castiglione, A., Cattaneo, G., De Santis, A., De Maio, G.: Automatic and Selective Deletion Resistant Against Forensics Analysis. In: Proceedings of the 2011 International Conference on Broadband, Wireless Computing, Communication and Applications (BWCCA 2011), Barcelona, Spain, pp. 392–398. IEEE (2011)
6. De Santis, A., Castiglione, A., Cattaneo, G., De Maio, G., Ianulardo, M.: Automated Construction of a False Digital Alibi. In: Tjoa, A.M., Quirchmayr, G., You, I., Xu, L. (eds.) ARES 2011. LNCS, vol. 6908, pp. 359–373. Springer, Heidelberg (2011)
7. De Maio, G., Castiglione, A., Cattaneo, G., Costabile, G., De Santis, A., Epifani, M.: The Forensic Analysis of a False Digital Alibi. In: Proceedings of the Sixth International Conference on Innovative Mobile and Internet Services in Ubiquitous Computing (IMIS 2012), Palermo, Italy, July 4-6, IEEE (2012)
8. Fierer, N., Lauber, C.L., Zhou, N., McDonald, D., Costello, E.K., Knight, R.: Forensic identification using skin bacterial communities. Proceedings of the National Academy of Sciences, Abstract (March 2010), http://www.pnas.org/content/early/2010/03/01/1000162107.abstract
9. Gutmann, P.: Data Remanence in Semiconductor Devices. In: 2001 Usenix Security Symposium, Washington DC (August 2001), http://www.cypherpunks.to/~peter/usenix01.pdf
10. Gutmann, P.: Secure Deletion of Data from Magnetic and Solid-State Memory. In: Sixth USENIX Security Symposium Proceedings, San Jose, California, July 22-25 (1996)

11. Mee, V., Tryfonas, T., Sutherland, I.: The Windows Registry as a forensic artefact: Illustrating evidence collection for Internet usage. Digital Investigation 3, 166–173 (2006)
12. Poisel, R., Tjoa, S., Tavolato, P.: Advanced File Carving Approaches for Multimedia Files. Journal of Wireless Mobile Networks, Ubiquitous Computing, and Dependable Applications (JoWUA) 2(4), 42–58 (2011)
13. Salem, M.B., Stolfo, S.J.: Combining Baiting and User Search Profiling Techniques for Masquerade Detection. Journal of Wireless Mobile Networks, Ubiquitous Computing, and Dependable Applications (JoWUA) 3(1/2), 13–29 (2012)
14. Shelton, D.E.: The 'CSI Effect': Does It Really Exist? National Institute of Justice Journal (259) (March 17, 2008)
15. Silberschatz, A., Galvin, P.B., Gagne, G.: Operating System Concepts, 7th edn. Wiley (2004)
16. Internet world stats (June 30, 2010), http://www.internetworldstats.com/stats.htm
17. U.S. Legal, Inc. Legal Definitions and Legal Terms Dictionary, http://definitions.uslegal.com
18. The New York Times, I'm Innocent. Just Check My Status on Facebook (November 12, 2009), http://www.nytimes.com/2009/11/12/nyregion/12facebook.html?_r=1
19. CNN, Facebook status update provides alibi (November 12, 2009), http://www.cnn.com/2009/CRIME/11/12/facebook.alibi/index.html
20. Xomba: A Writing Community. Garlasco, Alberto Stasi Acquitted (December 2009), http://www.xomba.com/garlasco_alberto_stasi_acquitted
21. U.S. Department of Defense, DoD Directive 5220.22, National Industrial Security Program (NISP) (February 28, 2010)
22. Merriam-Webster online dictionary, http://www.merriam-webster.com/
23. Wikipedia, KVM switch, http://en.wikipedia.org/wiki/KVM_switch
24. NIST Special Publication 800-88: Guidelines for Media Sanitization, p. 7 (2006)
25. The Erb Law Firm, Facebook Can Keep You Out of Jail (November 2009), http://www.facebook.com/note.php?note_id=199139644051
26. Wikipedia. Five Ws, http://en.wikipedia.org/wiki/Five_Ws
27. U.S. Government House of Representative, Federal Rules of Evidence (December 2006), http://afcca.law.af.mil/content/afcca_data/cp/us_federal_rules_of_evidence_2006.pdf

Security-and-Privacy-Related Issues on IT Systems During Disasters

Shinsaku Kiyomoto, Kazuhide Fukushima, and Yutaka Miyake

KDDI R & D Laboratories Inc.
2-1-15 Ohara, Fujimino-shi, Saitama, 356-8502, Japan
kiyomoto@kddilabs.jp

Abstract. In this paper, we focus on security-and-privacy-related issues that confront IT systems during disasters. We summarize these security and privacy issues in the context of two major areas of operation: information gathering and system continuity management. Then we provide the results of a survey on techniques for solving these issues. Finally, we discuss outstanding issues facing these the systems.

1 Introduction

Developing emergency and disaster management systems is an important issue in our "computer society". The primary issue is how to share information about a current disaster and the status of resource allocation for emergency management. Atteih *et al.* presented a case study [3] on the implementation of an emergency management information system (EMIS) in support of emergency responders. The incident management system (IMS) [41] proposed by Perry is a tool for marshaling pre-identified and pre-assembled resources for responding to an emergency or disaster. Yao *et al.* built a system [56] that allowed virtual teams of experts to create and discuss the emergency scenario. Collabit [11] is a virtual dashboard that facilitates distributed asynchronous sharing of information in an emergency. Wickler *et al.* considered the use of new media technologies, including virtual worlds on the Internet, for collaboration in disasters [51]. Shklovski *et al.* presented evidence on ICT use [48] for reorientation toward the community and for the production of public goods in the form of information dissemination during disasters. Jang and Tsai proposed a MANET-based emergency communication and information system [29] that could support a large number of rescue volunteers during catastrophic natural disasters. Research [4] by Dilmaghani and Rao identified a set of potential network oriented problems in existing interorganizational communication protocols incorporating the information collected from several drill exercises and after interviewing first responders. Applications of geospatial information [12,7] during disaster response have been considered to use a knowledge that can be applied to action plans during future disasters.

Systems using mobile terminals for the management of a disaster must receive some consideration. Fajardo and Oppus proposed a disaster management system [14] that facilitates the logistics for rescue and relief operations. The system

G. Quirchmayr et al. (Eds.): CD-ARES 2012, LNCS 7465, pp. 445–459, 2012.

provides the optimum route for rescuing people in a disaster. Zeng *et al.* proposed a mobile communication system [57] for evacuations during emergencies. Ohya *et al.* presented a disaster-information gathering system using mobile phones [37]. However, security-and-privacy-related issues on the systems have not been discussed so far.

System continuity management is another important issue on disaster-related issue. Cloud computing environments have been considered a cost-effective solution for ensuring system continuity. Wood *et al.* performed a pricing analysis to estimate the cost of running a public cloud-based disaster-recovery service and showed significant cost reductions compared to using privately owned resources [53]. Cloud computing environments are also robust in the context of wide-area disasters, and cloud services have been used for system contiunuity management. The Japanese Ministry of Internal Affairs and Communications has assembled a budget of 40 million dallar and has supported to develop cloud computing technologies for wide-area disasters.

In this paper, we focus on the security-and-privacy-related issues that confront IT systems during disasters. We summarize security and privacy issues for two major areas of operation: information gathering and system continuity management. Then we provide the results of a survey on techniques for solving these issues. Finally, we discuss outstanding issues facing these systems.

2   Security and Privacy Issues

In this section, we consider the security-and-privacy-related issues that confront information systems during disasters or other emergencies. Two major functions for IT systems during disasters are system continuity management and information gathering and broadcasting. These items are summarized as follows:

- System Continuity Management. To use a cloud service is a cost-effective solution for system continuity management. However, when a cloud service is used as a backup system, some security issues need to be solved.
- Information Gathering/Broadcasting. During a disaster, information gathering and broadcasting are major issues. In particular, govermental organizations that manage resources for disaster recovery need to gather information, and another organization has the responsibility of broadcasting informartion to users. Concerns about privacy breaches should be considered even during disasters.

We discuss security-and-privacy-related issues on the above two functions in the later subsections.

2.1   System Continuity Management

There is always a risk that servers will be physically damaged in a disaster. To use open cloud architecture is an efficient and cost-effective solution [53] to improve the availability of systems during a disaster. However, several security

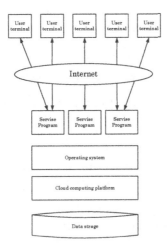

Fig. 1. Cloud Architecture

risks that could affect cloud computing services have been pointed out[36,25]. It is impossible for users to verify the trustworthiness of all cloud computing environments, and the concern is that operations in cloud computing may be carried out in the absence of trusted environments. The dynamic and fluid nature of the environments will make it difficult to maintain consistent security and ensure the ability to audit records. Thus, moving critical programs and sensitive data to a public and shared cloud computing environment is a major concern for service providers [42]. Now, we consider a model for cloud computing. Figure 1 shows typical architecture of cloud computing. In PaaS services, the platform provider supplies a software development kit (SDK) and service providers develop service programs for the platform. Users can access the services by executing these programs from a user terminal via the Internet. The program can be executed by any server in the cloud environment; thus, system continuity is still maintained even when some cloud servers are damaged.

We discuss three security issues when cloud environments are used to ensure system continuity: secure computation, data backup, and user authentication.

Secure Computation. A program that runs on its own servers has to be moved to a cloud environment in the event of a disaster. It is assumed that three kinds of entities try to attack the program on the cloud environment. External attackers can eavesdrop or modify Internet communications between a user terminal and service program. Malicious users try to attack other users to steal secret information or use a service without the correct permission. Furthermore, we have to consider malicious platform providers as an insider threat [24,47,30]. However, if the ability of the malicious platform provider is unlimited, we have to assume all possible attacks by the provider, which makes it a very difficult task to realize secure cloud computing. We consider a reasonable adversary model as follows; the platform provider honestly executes user requests and cannot obtain any information from the execution environment such as physical memory. The platform provider may try to use the user's program maliciously or try to obtain information from data storage. This model is a reasonable model in the situation where we assume that the attacker is the system manager of the platform.

We should consider the following threats to secure cloud computing.

– Malicious users or malicious platform providers may access a service program and execute it on the platform.
– Malicious users or a malicious platform provider may steal user's information stored in the service program.
– External attacker may modify a communication between a user terminal and the platform, or steal user's information from communication data.

Security issues in disaster situations are considered to be security problems for cloud services. Thus, we should find a solution to protect the program against the above threats.

Secure Data Backup. If we assume that a database is compromised by a disaster, data backup is another issue that IT systems need to resolve for ensuring system continuity. There are many backup services that allow outsourcing of data backups; however, security concerns should be considered. Chow *et al.* suggested that a major concern [9] for cloud computing is lack of control in the cloud and thus cloud users are for the most part putting only their less sensitive data in the cloud. If a database is compromised and data on an outsourced backup service are used as a temporary system for workflows, an access control mechanism should be prepared. For example, take a data backup service, which is one of the most common services provided by cloud environments, and consider a situation wherein a company backs up their data in the storage service on a cloud environment. If the cloud service is vulnerable or the cloud provider has a malicious/curious administrator, the private information of users and corporate confidential information may be leaked. Furthermore, where a database on a cloud service is shared by users, a fine-grained access control mechanism is a mandatory function. Hence, how to realize data encryption and access control without additional implementation on the cloud environment should be considered.

Authentication of Users. User authentication is a key component for IT systems in a disaster. In particular, the capacity to respond to a request from disaster victims, such as issuing disaster-victim certificates that is based on an authentication mechanism, has to be resumed as soon as possible. Generally, many IT systems have an authentication mechanism based on an authentication token, ID/PW, and biometric information. There are two serious situations regarding authentication mechanisms as follows;

– Users have lost their authentication tokens due to the disaster.
– Information such as the biometric templates of users has been lost due to the disaster.

If the above situations occur, the IT system cannot authenticate each user, even supposing that the IT system has resumed functioning by using a backup system. One possible solution is to backup all data and programs to a cloud environment and run the programs on the cloud environment. However, this solution may be accompanied by a new security risk and it violates security policy. Another solution is to use a fuzzy encryption [43] for a biometric authentication; The fuzzy encryption can generate a key from biometric information and authenitcate users using the key, but it requires a huge computational cost fo each authentication. It is not a realistic solution to delegate local authentication/identification of users to an outsourced cloud service. Thus, we restore a local authentication/identification system without help from cloud services.

2.2 Information Gathering /Broadcasting

Fraunhofer Gesellschaft conducted a study on disaster and emergency management systems and suggested that timeliness and updating of information is a major requirement for the systems [32]. Mobile terminals are key devices to gather timeliness information for planning emergency responses. There are two key issues for information gathering and broadcasting: privacy control and information accuracy. We discuss the two issses in the following subsections.

Privacy Control. A special issue during a major disaster and/or emergency is how an organization responsible for disaster management gathers reliable and useful information. Internet search engines are not an effective means for searching for information about a disaster, and sometimes an information overflow occurs. There are several studies that have examined how to construct a disaster management system using computer networks. The main topic is how to support sharing of information about the current disaster and the status of resource allocation for emergency management. Currently, user-centric systems using mobile terminals are seen as new approaches to achieving a more efficient information-sharing system. It has been suggested that SNS and micro-blogs are effective systems for communication and sharing information during a major disaster. A simple solution for setting up an information-gathering system is to construct a server to which information is uploaded and published. However, such a centralized approach is not flexible and nor is it robust. For example, it is often difficult to find an appropriate system to which the user can upload information in a disaster, and the centralized server may be down because of overload or has been physically destroyed. We must consider a distributed and dynamic architecture for the platform.

How to control the privacy level is an important issue when gathering information during disasters. For example, where a rescue worker is searching for a person who has a mobile phone, it is very helpful if that mobile phone is able to automatically distribute detailed information on the location of the terminal. On the other hand, privacy should be protected in the reconstruction phase; for example, detailed personal information should be kept secret but people can obtain personalized information that is customized to each person. Figure 2 shows

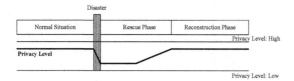

Fig. 2. Privacy Level

variations in the privacy level according to the phase of the disaster. Thus, technology that flexibly changes privacy levels is required.

Information Accuracy. False information may spread in a major disaster, and an attacker may try to confuse governmental organizations or users by broadcasting false or fake information to them. Furthermore, the information may be altered during communications and a masquerading entity may broadcast information to users. Thus, how to ensure the trustworthiness of the information sent from user terminals is an important issue. Generally, it is very difficult for an organization and users to judge whether the information is correct or not. A possible solution is to compare the information with other information; that is, the information is trusted where many messages from many users include the same information. The organization may be able to identify a person who sends a message by tracing logs. This fact may work as a deterrent against the dissemination of false information. However, it is still an open issue as to how to measure the reliability of gathered information.

In a disaster situation, a local and temporary broadcasting service is an effective way to convey emergency messages. It can be realized using a PC and small antennas mounted on a car. The problem is how to confirm that the broadcasting content is sent by an authorized organization. Appending a digital signature to data is a simple answer. A receiver of the data checks the validity of sender of information. However, how to compute a digital signature for content broadcast via a lossy channel is an important issue.

3   Solutions

In this section, we survey the current research aimed at solving security and privacy issues in a disaster situation. Especially, we focus on practical solutions for the issues.

3.1   Solution for System Continuity Management

We have three existing technologies for secure system continuity management.

Software Protection Scheme for Cloud Computing. There are several secure computation methods based on cryptographic primitives. Garbled circuits

(GC) [54,55] allow secure computation with encrypted functions, and a fully homomorphic encryption scheme [17] allows arbitrary functions to be computed over encrypted data without a decryption key. Bugiel *et al.* proposed an architecture [8] for secure computing, which uses GC as a primitive component. However, their scheme imposes a heavy computation load on cloud environments.

Fukushima *et al.* presented a practical software protection scheme [15] for cloud computing. Their scheme transforms a target program into a protected program and a user program. The protected program is executed on the platform and only handles encoded data. The program receives encoded input and sends back the encoded output to the user program. The user program is executed on the user terminal. This function encodes the input by the user and sends it to the protected program. After receiving the encoded output, the user program checks the validity of the output. If it is valid, the function returns the decoded execution result to the user. The user program encodes the input using encoding rules and checks the validity of the data received from the protected program using a non-trivial relation. Finally, it decodes the execution result of the whole program using a decoding rule.

Another approach to ensure secure computation is monitoring insider activities. Khorshed *et al.* presented evaluation results [26] of popular machine learning techniques, where the techniques are applied to the detection of insider threats.

Attribute-Based Encryption. Attribute-based encryption (ABE) schemes are an efficient way to realize both encryption of data and fine-grained access control. Sensitive user data are encrypted under an access policy in ABE schemes, and a user who does not satisfy the access policy cannot decrypt the data. An access policy is described by a user's attributes; for example, appointments, departments, or work location etc.

Attribute-based encryption (ABE) has been extensively researched as a cryptographic protocol [6,50,21]. In Ciphertext-Policy ABE (CP-ABE) systems [6], a user encrypts data with descriptions of an access policy. The access policy defines authorized users, their statements consisting of attributes and logical relationships such as **AND**, **OR**, or **M of N** (threshold gates); for example, users who have the attributes *"Project manager"* and *"Control department"* can access the data, where the access policy is defined as *"Project manager ∧ Control department"*. It is possible to prevent a cloud service provider or an adversary from accessing the secret information. Another type of ABE is a Key-Policy ABE (KP-ABE) [21]. In KP-ABE, a user's personal key is described as a combination of attributes *"Project manager ∧ Control department"*.

Generally, ABE schemes require a huge amount of computation such as numerous pairing computations. Some papers have dealt with the implementation of pairing computation on different devices [46,1]. As shown in these papers, one pairing computation can be completed in less than a few msec on a current PC. However, more computation time is required on other devices that have less computational power, such as smart phones. It is an essential issue for practical use that the computational power of ABE increases according to the increase in the number of attributes.

Delegated Authentication. Delegated authentication is one possible way to solve the problem where a local authentication mechanism is lost. The delegated authentication uses other authentication mechanisms and receives an authentication result from other authentication mechanisms. For example, if a local authentication mechanism has been lost, an authentication mechanism of an internet service provider, which performs the duties of the local authentication, is used instead. A local IT system authenticates a user to receive the result from the Internet service provider. Single-Sign-On schemes lend themselves to delegated authentication, even though some existing protocols have been shown to have vulnerabilities by security analyses[2,49]. Gomi *et al.* [20] introduced a delegation model for federated identity management systems and proposed a delegation framework that is an extension of Security Assertion Markup Language (SAML). Santos and Smith developed a Web-based delegated authentication system [44] using proxy certificates that empowers a user to unambiguously specify a limited subset of his/her privileges to pass to another user. This scheme is also applicable to delegated authentication between two entities, and there are similar existing schemes for delegated authentication.

We have realized a delegated authentication scheme based on existing techniques; however, how to ensure the same security level between two authentication schemes is an issue awaiting resolution.

3.2   Solution for Information Gathering/Broadcasting

We are pursuing several research directions for solving security and privacy issues in relation to information gathering and broadcasting in a disaster situation.

Location Data Management. Obfuscation of location information is an effective way to protect user privacy. There are several approaches to obfuscating location information to provide *privacy-aware* location-based services [34,45]: Kido *et. al.* proposed a *false dummy method* [27], where a user sends n different locations to a location database server, with only one of them being correct (the rest are "dummies" that mask the true location). Hong and Landay introduced an architecture based on *landmark objects* [23], where users refer to the location of a significant object (landmark) in their vicinity, rather than sending an exact location. This scheme makes it difficult to control the granularity of location information and thus may not be suitable for some types of location-based services. For many service providers it is sufficient to provide *approximate*, rather than *exact* location information. The objective of *location perturbation* is to blur the exact location information. Various location perturbation techniques have been suggested for obfuscating location information. Gruteser and Grunwald [22] suggested "blurring" the user's location by subdividing space in such a way that each subdivision has at least $k-1$ other users. Gedik and Liu [16] adapted this to allow users to have personalized values of the masking parameter k. Mokbel *et. al.* presented a hierarchical partitioning method to improve the efficiency of location perturbation [35]; however it was shown in [18] that this fails to provide location anonymity under non-uniform distribution of user locations. Selection of optimal subdivision spaces was investigated in [31,5]. Finally, in [18] a decentralized approach without an anonymizer was considered in order to realize good load balancing; however communication between users is required to calculate anonymized location information. Recent research [34] has focused on establishing location anonymity in a spatial domain. This approach uses a *location anonymizer*, which is a trusted server that anonymizes location information within a defined *anonymizing spatial region* (ASR). Location anonymity is provided to the extent that an attacker cannot determine precisely where a given user is in the ASR (although they do know that they are located in the ASR). Existing schemes can control granularity of location information by changing parameters for location anonymization.

Privacy Preserving Information Gathering System. Kiyomoto *et al.* proposed the information gathering system [28] shown in Figure 3. They suggested that security and privacy concerns should be addressed when providing information from user's mobile terminals using their platform. If the identity of users can be kept anonymous from governmental organizations, users will find it acceptable to send information to such organizations. They summarize three security and privacy requirements for information gathering systems as follows. Messages on the mobile terminal should be encrypted to protect the privacy of communications. User consent is needed to transfer messages to a governmental organization; thus, the user is required to configure which information is acceptable to send to governmental organizations, so a tagging process should be executed on user terminals. Location information is important for choosing the appropriate governmental organization; however, location information is personal information that may be sensitive in terms of user privacy. Thus, attached location information should be anonymized.

Their system adds a label to messages sent from user mobile terminals and automatically transfers messages to an appropriate governmental organization. In a disaster, messages to a commercial SNS or micro-blog system are copied and transferred to systems of corresponding organizations, where the user accepts the responsibility of providing information to these organizations. The messages have a tag that describes the type of information, and the control server selects the appropriate system according to the tag. The organizations can gather information about the disaster and about people who need support. To improve usability, the tag for each message is selected automatically from among several categories in the mobile terminal. All message content is encrypted by the public key of the governmental organizations, thereby avoiding privacy leakage to intermediate entities. The control server is distributed in mobile networks and checks the current status of the systems by frequently accessing the system. If the system of a governmental organization is damaged by a disaster or the organization has insufficient human resources to help people, the control server automatically selects a system from another organization. Their system is designed in accordance with the following principles;

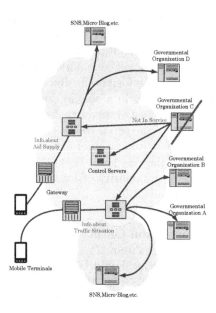

Fig. 3. Information Gathering System

- Tag information is needed for each emergency message in order to deliver it. To avoid leakage of message contents, we execute a categorization mechanism that makes the tag on each mobile terminal.
- Messages should be kept secret from intermediate entities between users and governmental organizations. Thus, messages are encrypted on each mobile terminal.

They assumed the following scenarios as examples;

- **Scenario 1.** Users upload traffic information to the SNS or micro- blog services; for example, some trains have stopped running or stations are closed, there are traffic jams, or there are obstructions on the roads that make it hard to walk or drive. In this situation, the information is copied and transferred to the governmental organizations responsible for traffic control in order to provide support for evacuation of a disaster area.
- **Scenario 2.** A user updates information to SNS or micro-blog services about shortages of aid supplies. The information is copied and transferred to the nearest governmental organization responsible for aid supplies. If the governmental organization does not have such supplies, the information is transferred to other governmental organizations near the location of the user.
- **Scenario 3.** If a user discovers an emergency involving the collapse of a house and gas leaks, the user would upload such information to the SNS or micro-blog services. In this case, the information is copied and transferred to the governmental organizations (rescuer or police) responsible for the area near the location.

Authenticated Broadcasting. Various schemes have been proposed to achieve strong authentication of streaming data on a lossy channel. Wong and Lam proposed two approaches [52] for digital signature schemes tolerating arbitrary loss patterns on received data packets; a group of consecutive packets is signed in the star-chaining technique, and the digital signature is attached to each packet along with hashed values of all other packets in the group. The tree-chaining technique uses a balanced tree of hashed values of packets pertaining to a group. Each intermediate node contains a combination of all hashed values of the child nodes, and the hash value of the root node is signed and the digital signature is included in each packet. Piggy Backing [33] uses a group that is partitioned in a subgroup of packets. A generalization of the simple hash-chaining method has been presented by Golle and Modadugu [19]. Two efficient schemes [40], timed efficient stream loss-tolerant authentication (TESLA) and the efficient multichaining stream signature (EMSS) scheme have been proposed by Perrig *et al.*. The TESLA uses only symmetric cryptgraphic primitives and it is based on timed release of keys by the sender. In EMSS, each packet contains a fixed number of hash values of other packets and the final packet contains the digital signature. Park *et al.* adopted Rabin's information dispersal algorithm to construct a streaming authentication scheme that amortizes a group authentication data over all the group packets [39,38]. Cucinotta *et al.* presented redundancy techniques [10] in order to avoid losses of packets including a digital signature. Eltaief and Youssef proposed a multi-layer connected chain structure [13] for streaming authentication. Lightweight streaming authentication schemes are ready for practical use; however, how to implement them to commercial products such as mobile phones should be addressed.

4   Concluding Remarks

In this paper, we highlighted two important goals for IT systems operating in a disaster situation: system continuity management and information gathering/broadcasting, and discussed security and privacy techniques for approaching the goal. We can develop secure and privacy-aware IT systems based on existing technologies, but some open issues remain. We these remaining issues will be the subject of future research:

- *Feasibility study of a total cloud system.* We can solve a system continuity problem to use a cloud environment in a disaster, and existing technologies are used as basic components for construction of a secure cloud environment. We implement all security components on a commercial cloud environment and evaluate the feasibility of the system.
- *Rebuilding of local authentication systems.* Delegated authentication is a temporary solution that can be used during an emergency. How to rebuild local authentication systems is an open issue. We also address peer-to-peer authentication that a person authenticates/authorizes other persons in an ad-hoc manner in a disaster.

– *Correctness of Information.* It is still an open question how we prevent fake information from being distributed during a disaster. Several alert systems are running on commercial network services; a message authentication mechanism should be implemented on client devices.

We hope that this survey is helpful for solving current issues on IT systems during disasters.

Acknowledgment. This work has been supported by the Japanese Ministry of Internal Affairs and Communications funded project, "Study of Security Architecture for Cloud Computing in Disasters."

References

1. Aranha, D.F., López, J., Hankerson, D.: High-Speed Parallel Software Implementation of the η_T Pairing. In: Pieprzyk, J. (ed.) CT-RSA 2010. LNCS, vol. 5985, pp. 89–105. Springer, Heidelberg (2010)
2. Armando, A., Carbone, R., Compagna, L., Cuellar, J., Tobarra, L.: Formal analysis of saml 2.0 web browser single sign-on: breaking the saml-based single sign-on for google apps. In: Proc. of the 6th ACM Workshop on Formal Methods in Security Engineering, FMSE 2008, pp. 1–10 (2008)
3. Atteih, A.S., Algahtani, S.A., Nazmy, A.: Emergency management information system: Case study. In: GM, Unicom for Communication Technologies, http://www.unicomg.com/Home/
4. Dilmaghani, R.B., Rao, R.R.: A systematic approach to improve communication for emergency response. In: Proceedings of the 42nd Hawaii International Conference on System Sciences, IEEE HICSS 2009, pp. 1–8 (2009)
5. Bamba, B., Liu, L., Pesti, P., Wang, T.: Supporting anonymous location queries in mobile environments with privacygrid. In: Proc. of 17th International World Wide Web Conference (WWW 2008), pp. 237–246 (2008)
6. Bethencourt, J., Sahai, A., Waters, B.: Ciphertext-policy attribute-based encryption. In: IEEE Symposium on Security and Privacy, pp. 321–334 (2007)
7. Bhaduri, B., Bright, E.A., Vijayraj, V.: Towards a geospatial knowledge discovery framework for disaster management. In: Proc. of ESA-EUSC 2008 (2008)
8. Bugiel, S., Nurnberger, S., Sadeghi, A., Schneider, T.: Twin clouds: An architecture for secure cloud computing. In: Proc. of Workshop on Cryptography and Security in Clouds, ECRYPT-II (2011)
9. Chow, R., Golle, P., Jakobsson, M., Shi, E., Staddon, J., Masuoka, R., Molina, J.: Controlling data in the cloud: outsourcing computation without outsourcing control. In: Proceedings of the 2009 ACM Workshop on Cloud Computing Security, CCSW 2009, pp. 85–90 (2009)
10. Cucinotta, T., Cecchetti, G., Ferraro, G.: Adopting redundancy techniques for multicast stream authentication. In: Proc. of the The Ninth IEEE Workshop on Future Trends of Distributed Computing Systems, FTDCS 2003 (2003)
11. de Lanerolle, T.R., Anderson, W., DeFabbia-Kane, S., Fox-Epstein, E., Gochev, D., Morelli, R.: Development of a virtual dashboard for event coordination between multipul groups. In: Proc. of 7th International Conference on Information Systems for Crisis Response and Management, ISCRAM 2010 (2010)

12. DeCapua, C., Bhaduri, B.: Applications of geospatial technology in international disasters and during hurricane katrina. Available at the Project Site of Capturing Hurricane Katrina Data For Analysis and Lessons-Learned Research (2007)

13. Eltaief, H., Youssef, H.: Efficient sender authentication and signing of multicast streams over lossy channels. In: Proc. of 2010 IEEE/ACS International Conference on Computer Systems and Applications (AICCSA), pp. 1–7 (2010)

14. Fajardo, J.T.B., Oppus, C.M.: A mobile disaster management system using the android technology. International Journal of Communications 3, 77–86 (2009)

15. Fukushima, K., Kiyomoto, S., Miyake, Y.: Towards secure cloud computing architecture - a solution based on software protection mechanism. Journal of Internet Services and Information Security (JISIS) 1(1), 4–17 (2011)

16. Gedik, M., Liu, L.: A customizable k-anonymity model for protecting location privacy. In: Proc. of the 25th International Conference on Distributed Computing Systems (ICDCS 2005), pp. 620–629 (2005)

17. Gentry, C.: Fully homomorphic encryption using ideal lattices. In: Proc. of the 41st Annual ACM Symposium on Theory of Computing, STOC 2009, pp. 169–178 (2009)

18. Ghinita, G., Kalnis, P., Skiadopoulos, S.: PRIVÉ: Anonymous location-based queries in distributed mobile systems. In: Proc. of 16th International World Wide Web Conference (WWW 2007), pp. 371–380 (2007)

19. Golle, P., Modadugu, N.: Authenticating streamed data in the presence of random packet loss (extended abstract). In: ISOC Network and Distributed System Security Symposium, pp. 13–22 (2001)

20. Gomi, H., Hatakeyama, M., Hosono, S., Fujita, S.: A delegation framework for federated identity management. In: Proc. of the 2005 Workshop on Digital Identity Management, DIM 2005, pp. 94–103 (2005)

21. Goyal, V., Pandey, O., Sahai, A., Waters, B.: Attribute-based encryption for fine-grained access control of encrypted data. In: Proceedings of the 13th ACM Conference on Computer and Communications Security, CCS 2006, pp. 89–98. Algorithms and Computation in Mathematics (2006)

22. Gruteser, M., Grunwald, D.: Anonymous usage of location-based services through spatial and temporal cloaking. In: Proc. of the 1st International Conference on Mobile Systems, Applications, and Services (MobiSys 2003), pp. 163–168 (2003)

23. Hong, J.I., Landay, J.A.: An architecture for privacy-sensitive ubiquitous computing. In: Proc. of the 2nd International Conference on Mobile Systems, Applications, and Services (MobiSys 2004), pp. 177–189 (2004)

24. Jansen, W.A.: Cloud hooks: Security and privacy issues in cloud computing. In: Proc. of 44th Hawaii International Conference on System Sciences (HICSS), pp. 1–10 (2011)

25. Hamlen, K., Kantarcioglu, M., Khan, L., Thuraisingham, B.: Security issues for cloud computing. International Journal of Information Security and Privacy 4(2), 39–51 (2010)

26. Khorshed, M.T., Ali, A.S., Wasimi, S.A.: Monitoring insiders activities in cloud computing using rule based learning. In: Proc. of 2011 IEEE 10th International Conference on Trust, Security and Privacy in Computing and Communications (TrustCom), pp. 757–764 (2011)

27. Kido, H., Yanagisawa, Y., Satoh, T.: An anonymous communication technique using dummies for location-based services. In: Proc. of IEEE International Conference on Pervasive Services 2005 (ICPS 2005), pp. 88–97 (2005)

28. Kiyomoto, S., Miyake, Y., Tanaka, T.: On designing privacy-aware data upload mechanism - towards information-gathering system for disasters. In: Proc. of The 11th IEEE International Conference on Ubiquitous Computing and Communications, IUCC 2012 (2012)

29. Lien, Y.-N., Jang, H.-C., Tsai, T.-C.: A manet based emergency communication and information system for catastrophic natural disasters. In: 29th IEEE International Conference on Distributed Computing Systems Workshops, ICDCS Workshops 2009, pp. 412–417 (2009)

30. Lu, Y., Tsudik, G.: Privacy-preserving cloud database querying. Journal of Internet Services and Information Security (JISIS) 1(4), 5–25 (2011)

31. Mascetti, S., Bettini, C.: A comparison of spatial generalization algorithms for lbs privacy preservation. In: Proc. of the 1st International Workshop on Privacy-Aware Location-Based Mobile Services (PALMS 2007), pp. 258–262 (2007)

32. Meissner, A., Luckenbach, T., Risse, T., Kirste, T., Kirchner, H.: Design challenges for an integrated disaster management communication and information system. In: Proc. of DIREN 2002 (co-located with IEEE INFOCOM 2002 (2002)

33. Miner, S., Staddon, J.: Graph-based authentication of digital streams. In: Proc. of 2001 IEEE Symposium on Security and Privacy, pp. 232–246 (2001)

34. Mokbel, M.F.: Towards privacy-aware location-based database servers. In: Proc. of the 22nd Internationl Conference on Sata Engineering Workshops (ICDEW 2006), pp. 93–102 (2006)

35. Mokbel, M.F., Chow, C.Y., Aref, W.G.: The new casper: Query processing for location services without compromising privacy. In: Proc. of the 32nd International Conference on Very Large Data Bases (VLDB 2006), pp. 763–774 (2006)

36. National Institute of Standard Technology (NIST). Us government cloud computing technology roadmap, vol. ii, release 1.0 (draft). NIST SP500-293 (2011)

37. Ohya, M., Asada, J., Harada, N., Matsubayashi, R., Hara, M., Takata, R., Naito, M., Waga, M., Katada, T.: Disaster information-gathering system using cellular phone with a global positioning system. In: Proc. of the International Symposium on Management System for Disaster Prevention 2006 (2006)

38. Park, J.M., Chong, E.K.P., Siegel, H.J.: Efficient multicast stream authentication using erasure codes. ACM Trans. Inf. Syst. Secur. 6(2), 258–285 (2003)

39. Park, J.M., Chong, E.K.P., Siegel, H.J.: Efficient multicast packet authentication using signature amortization. In: Proc. of 2002 IEEE Symposium on Security and Privacy, pp. 227–240 (2002)

40. Perrig, A., Canetti, R., Tygar, J.D., Song, D.: Efficient authentication and signing of multicast streams over lossy channels. In: Proc. of 2000 IEEE Symposium on Security and Privacy, pp. 56–73 (2000)

41. Perry, R.W.: Incident management systems in disaster management. Journal of Disaster Prevention and Management 12(5), 405–412 (2003)

42. Popovic, K., Hocenski, Z.: Cloud computing security issues and challenges. In: MIPRO, 2010 Proceedings of the 33rd International Convention, pp. 344–349 (2010)

43. Sahai, A., Waters, B.: Fuzzy Identity-Based Encryption. In: Cramer, R. (ed.) EUROCRYPT 2005. LNCS, vol. 3494, pp. 457–473. Springer, Heidelberg (2005)

44. Santos, N., Smith, S.W.: Limited delegation for client-side ssl. In: Proc. of the 6th Annual PKI R & D Workshop, pp. 76–90 (2007)

45. Scipioni, M.P., Langheinrich, M.: Towards a new privacy-aware location sharing platform. Journal of Internet Services and Information Security (JISIS) 1(4), 47–59 (2011)

46. Scott, M.: On the efficient implementation of pairing-based protocols. Cryptology ePrint Archive, Report 2011/334 (2011), http://eprint.iacr.org/
47. Sengupta, S., Kaulgud, V., Sharma, V.S.: Cloud computing security–trends and research directions. In: Proc. of 2011 IEEE World Congress on Services (SERVICES), pp. 524–531 (2011)
48. Shklovski, I., Palen, L., Sutton, J.: Finding community through information and communication technology in disaster response. In: Proceedings of the 2008 ACM Conference on Computer Supported Cooperative Work, CSCW 2008, pp. 127–136 (2008)
49. Wang, R., Chen, S., Wang, X.: Signing me onto your accounts through facebook and google: a traffic-guided security study of commercially deployed single-sign-on web services. In: Proc. of 2012 IEEE Symposium on Security and Privacy (to appear, 2012)
50. Waters, B.: Ciphertext-Policy Attribute-Based Encryption: An Expressive, Efficient, and Provably Secure Realization. In: Catalano, D., Fazio, N., Gennaro, R., Nicolosi, A. (eds.) PKC 2011. LNCS, vol. 6571, pp. 53–70. Springer, Heidelberg (2011)
51. Wickler, G., Potter, S., Tate, A., Hansberger, J.: The virtual collaboration environment: New media for crisis response. In: Proc. of 8th International Conference on Information Systems for Crisis Response and Management, ISCRAM 2011 (2011)
52. Wong, C.K., Lam, S.S.: Digital signatures for flows and multicasts. IEEE/ACM Transactions on Networking 7(4), 502–513 (1999)
53. Wood, T., Cecchet, E., Ramakrishnan, K.K., Shenoy, P., van der Merwe, J., Venkataramani, A.: Disaster recovery as a cloud service: economic benefits & deployment challenges. In: Proceedings of the 2nd USENIX Conference on Hot Topics in Cloud Computing, HotCloud 2010 (2010)
54. Yao, A.C.: Protocols for secure computations. In: 23rd Annual Symposium on Foundations of Computer Science, pp. 160–164 (1982)
55. Yao, A.C.-C.: How to generate and exchange secrets. In: 27th Annual Symposium on Foundations of Computer Science, pp. 162–167 (1986)
56. Yao, X., Turoff, M., Hiltz, R.: A field trial of a collaborative online scenario creation system for emergency management. In: Proc. of 7th International Conference on Information Systems for Crisis Response and Management, ISCRAM 2010 (2010)
57. Zeng, Q.-A., Wei, H., Joshi, V.: An efficient communication system for disaster detection and coordinated emergency evacuation. In: Proc. of Wireless Telecommunications Symposium, WTS 2008, pp. 329–333 (2008)

Semantic Techniques of Image Retrieval – The Example of a Structural Analysis of Coronary Arteries

Mirosław Trzupek and Marek R. Ogiela

AGH University of Science and Technology,
Department of Automatics and Biomedical Engineering,
al. A. Mickiewicza 30, 30-059 Krakow
{mtrzupek,mogiela}@agh.edu.pl

Abstract. Specialised medical databases currently play a major role in archiving and searching for comparable data acquired by different modalities of medical imaging. In the context of storing and searching for data in medical databases, it is of immense importance to find a method of extracting and representing the contents found in the image that would ensure the rapid access and satisfactory results of searches for image information records. What is important, this representation should also be independent of the form of the image. The wide spread of multimedia medical databases that can store not just single images but also video sequences has shown that the problem of effectively searching for images containing specific disease cases that are significant for medical diagnostics is still fraught with great difficulties. This article presents a semantic retrieval methods in medical imaging databases using graph formalisms of syntactic image recognition which contribute to solving these problems. The proposed methods although they are mainly predestined for medical applications can also provide a base for other solutions, particularly for the acquisition and sophisticated semantic analysis of complex image patterns for security and defence reasons.

Keywords: Semantic image retrieval, content-based image retrieval (CBIR), image understanding systems.

1 Introduction

In recent years, digital images have become a constant part of our life, while in the field of medical imaging they significantly contribute to saving this life. It is hard to imagine making a medical diagnosis and treating many disorders without such basic medical imaging apparatuses as X-ray, CT, USG or MRI equipment. Image data obtained by various medical imaging modalities makes it possible to non-invasively look into the patient's body, which means that the popularity of such diagnostic methods is constantly increasing. On the other hand, the increasing availability of medical imaging apparatuses and, as a direct result, the rapidly growing set of images generated by these apparatuses lead to a major glut of image data used in medical diagnostics. In order to fully utilise its potential, this data must be stored in the right

G. Quirchmayr et al. (Eds.): CD-ARES 2012, LNCS 7465, pp. 460–467, 2012.

way, particularly so that it is easily accessible. In this context, it is worth noting that proposed methodology may also be used in the area that combines security and defence aspects in designing advanced systems for the retrieving, acquisition, storing and sophisticated semantic analysis of complex image patterns and group behaviours. In the case of medical diagnostics, this field is currently dominated by systems for archiving medical image data, such as PACS (Picture Archiving and Communication Systems). In particular, these systems are now responsible for the correct and secure transmission, storage and retrieval of image data. The way in which single image is searched in a huge set of image data collected in these databases is the major weakness of these systems. Most frequently, this data is searched for by filling out the appropriate fields with search criteria in the form of alphanumeric data (text and numbers), such as: the patient's personal data, the examination date, the examination description or the selection of the appropriate image modality. Figure 1 shows a typical screen shot from a PACS system.

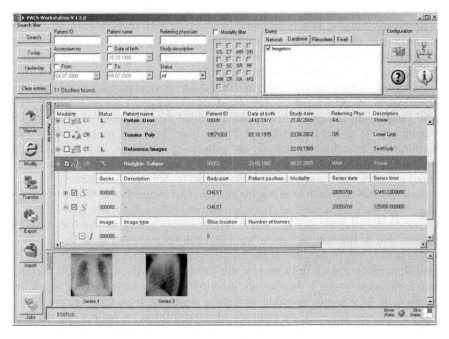

Fig. 1. The main window of the K-PACS system supporting viewing a medical database and searching in it [source: K-PACS V1.6.0 DICOM Viewing Software]

The search criteria are entered as attributes in the alphanumeric format mainly because the images stored in such specialised databases also contain alphanumeric information (describing these images) saved, *inter alia*, in the headers of the archived files (e.g. DICOM files). Certain inaccuracies or ambiguities in the descriptions are more probable where human factor comes into play during inputting the search information. Those inaccuracies may lead to incorrectly assigning the description to a given image what, in extreme cases, leads to increasing the risk of mistakes.

In addition, describing images textually is labour- and time-intensive, and in the case of medical images requires great experience in interpreting their contents, thus posing a risk of important information being omitted in the description. On the other hand, the clear upside of this method of medical data storage is that image information records of interest can be relatively quickly and effectively found in huge resources of specialised medical databases.

2   Development of Systems for Context-Indexing Images

Systems for indexing images with their contents date back to the 1970s, but very intensive work on developing such systems was done in 1990s and resulted from the rapidly growing quantity of digital image data which made it necessary to look for effective methods of storing, indexing and accessing it [1,2]. Another, no less important factor was the rapid development of computer technology, which, in medicine, directly contributed to the design of new, increasingly advanced medical diagnostic apparatuses. This trend could be observed both in the area of professional equipment (e.g. used in medical imaging) and in everyday life (all kinds of devices for capturing images). In addition, the constantly rising computing power of computers made it possible to undertake problems of digital image analysis which could not be solved before due to their high computational complexity (e.g. morphological transformations). The rapid development of computer methods of digital image analysis and processing which started then has now led not only to the accumulation of a huge quantity of image data, but also to elaborating many algorithms for the computer analysis and processing of images. This means that the great volume of data kept in specialised medical databases requires the creation of increasingly effective algorithms for indexing and finding specific cases.

The traditional approach to managing resources of image data is based on indexing images with their alphanumeric descriptions, but if the sets of this type of data are huge, problems arise because the search results are often very far from optimal. This is mainly due to the vast amount of data that can be contained in an image (this is obvious particularly in the case of medical images), as a result of which even the best verbal description cannot fully present the contents of a given image ("a picture is worth a thousand words"). Neither are descriptions using key words of much help, regardless of their incontrovertible advantage stemming from their brevity. This is mainly due to the fact that the elements of interest (areas of interest) of the image greatly depend on the context, so key words that can be used to describe a given image may be different and not necessarily as expected. This demonstrates the importance of researches in the field of image managing and predefined criteria based searching algorithms. What helps in this regard are CBIR (content-based image retrieval) systems based on the idea of finding images according to their contents. The technique most frequently used in these systems is the query by image content (QBIC), in which the user inputs (or draws) an example image, and the system finds images kept in the database that are similar to this set pattern. CBIR systems such as the QBIC [3] allow images retrieving according to their visual features such as e.g. their colour, texture, and shape features, etc. The interface of a typical CBIR system is shown in Figure 2.

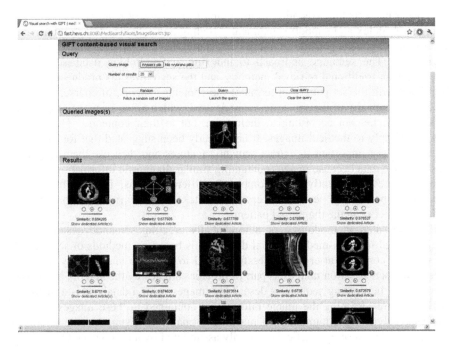

Fig. 2. A screen shot of the MedSearch interface [source: MedGIFT Content-based medical image retrieval]

Another, more refined method of searching within image data sets consists in an attempt to explore the contents of the image using its semantic characteristics (e.g. the type of object or event shown in the image). This is of major importance for medical images, as in their specific case, the computer has to try to explore the meaning of the lesions observed in the image and not just to analyse their form. This 2 level distinction (primitive image features and semantic features) is introduced in article [4] in connection with looking for effective methods of automatically retrieving, archiving and semantically categorising image data in multi-media databases. The author of article [5] go a step further and distinguish 3 levels (primitive features, logical features, abstract attributes), which, in addition, can then be split into more sub-levels.

This article presents methods of semantic image retrieval in medical databases using semantic features of images. There are still a number of unsolved problems associated with the subject defined above, so the authors are presenting a proposal that applies to a certain class of images, specifically images of the coronary vascularisation obtained from diagnostic examinations with the use of computed tomography (CT).

3   Technologies of Semantic Image Retrieval – Example of CT Images of Coronary Vascularisation

This paper presents the possibility to use graph formalisms of mathematical linguistic to organise, index and support semantically finding and selecting image information. The set of image data consists of images originating from computed tomography (CT) diagnostics. The semantic approach to indexing and searching databases is more effective than traditional retrieval methods, and the search results produced are more correlated with the set pattern in terms of the contents. This is, of course, due to the descriptive capacity of the semantic methods used, which allow images to be grouped semantically, i.e. not according to their form, but to their contents. The methods presented apply to medical images. It has already been suggested that for this image class, it is very important to extract semantic features and then use them to manage sets of image data because images containing similar diagnostic information about the disease process frequently have completely different forms. In such images, the specific shapes of the lesions observed may take many forms due to individual differences between the diagnosed patients.

The presented methodology of automatically creating semantic descriptions of images stored in multi-media medical databases is based on methods of semantically interpreting coronary arteries, successfully used to describe and identify lesions in coronary vascularisation images as part of previous studies by the authors [6-9]. What is important in creating sequences describing images from a database is a method of effectively transforming the image information contained in these images (which is easily perceived by a human) to a machine format which supports the intelligent, semantic selection of a specific case (easily assimilated by a computer). One possible method consists in the proposed grammar formalisms for the structural analysis of images, in which the analysed image is treated as a hierarchical structure composed of so-called picture primitives. In their previous publications, the authors proposed using graph grammars to describe and model the spatial relations of coronary vascularisation reconstructions [6-9]. Grammars of this type generate a formal language in the form of graphs which can model the images considered here, and then the graphs obtained can be represented in the form of their characteristic descriptions. So the mechanism presented makes it possible to transform image information contained in images into a machine format, namely a characteristic description of graphs modelling the coronary vascularisation. What is more, this description can be additionally complemented by sequences generated by sequential grammars [9] that are used to represent the width graphs of individual coronary vessels (represented by the edges of the graph modelling the coronary vascularisation). Of course, the use of grammar formalisms also offers a number of other possibilities available when indexing with the use of the grammars applied. Apart from characteristic descriptions representing the graph modelling the given structure enhanced with sequences generated by sequential grammars, it is also possible to use mechanisms provided by the introduced grammar, e.g. in the form of a sequence of numbers of derivation rules of this grammar, defined by the set of their productions. The general diagram of retrieving images from a semantically indexed specialised medical database with the use of the above methodology is presented in Figure 3.

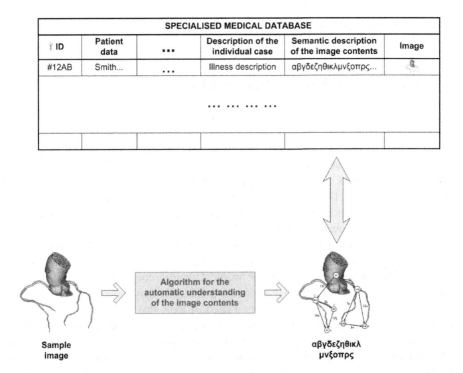

SPECIALISED MEDICAL DATABASE					
⌕ ID	Patient data	•••	Description of the individual case	Semantic description of the image contents	Image
#12AB	Smith...	...	Illness description	αβγδεζηθικλμνξοπρς...	🐟

Fig. 3. Using the above methodology to search for information in a semantically-indexed specialised medical database by reference to a set pattern

In this case, semantic searching boils down to comparing the sequence of semantic descriptions representing the contents of individual images stored in the database to the sequence representing the semantic description of the set pattern (the semantic description of the input image which constitutes the set pattern must also be semantically described in accordance with the presented methodology). As the mechanism thus defined should generate results which accurately correspond to the set pattern, there is a risk that these results will include only a few images. To avoid this, a certain threshold of similarity between the semantic description sequence representing the data in the database and the sequence representing the set pattern should be defined. Although this will increase the risk of obtaining results that are not fully satisfactory, it will also raise the number of results similar to the set pattern, which number can be controlled by adjusting the similarity threshold as necessary. In the case of medical images, additional similar results may help the physician in his/her work. The formal definition of the similarity threshold of sequences of indexing keys will form the subject of further research.

To conclude, it is worth noting that in the case of medical databases, a structural description of image contents with the use of the presented linguistic formalisms is more unambiguous than the traditional description methods using e.g. the colour or texture. This is significant because it has direct impact on the results of searches for images similar to the set pattern in multi-media databases, thus producing more results which strongly correlate with the set pattern in terms of the contents of these images.

4   Summary and Further Research Directions

Image indexing systems currently in use have several major shortcomings, and therefore cannot be fully utilised. First of all, the majority of them is based on an alphanumeric description written by a human, which can be imperfect. It frequently omits information that is significant from an objective point of view, and often contains errors. Also the headers of DICOM files can contain a relatively high proportion of errors [11], and this can hinder the correct retrieval of all the images looked for. What is more, systems whose operation is based on visual characteristics can usually process low-level attributes (the colour, texture, shape etc.) without being able to identify high-level features (relationships between objects, object types etc.), or they are able to do this only for a very narrow class of images.

Here it should also be stressed that medical images constitute a special class of images in which images completely different graphically may have the same contents, so particularly for these images there is a need of tools that can correctly extract the image contents masked by varied forms. A doctor following diagnostic guidelines frequently wants to review images showing a similar disorder so that the decision he/she takes is based on many premises and is therefore optimal. In this situation, the attempt to find an image that is similar (in terms of its contents, not form) in large alphanumerically indexed databases leads to retrieving a large number of images whose contents may not be correlated with the set pattern. Hence it is obvious that providing the doctor with the appropriate tools allowing databases to be semantically indexed using an example image pattern can contribute to improving the precision of that physician's diagnostic decisions. In this context, the methods of semantically indexing and retrieving images from medical databases, presented in this article using the example of CT images of coronary vascularisation, significantly contribute to solving at least some of the problems associated with the effective storage, indexing and access to this data. It is also obvious that the proposed mathematical linguistic formalisms offer great potential. Of course, the solutions proposed apply only to a selected class of diagnostic images showing coronary vascularisation, but it is possible to adapt the above solutions to another class of images, especially for complex image patterns (e.g. research that combines security and defence aspects) [12].

It is also worth noting that the solutions described in the literature are frequently dedicated only to a narrow class of images or are limited only to a specific database [13]. An ideal system would be able to combine these databases and search through a much greater number of available sources of medical images. What is more, sometimes a system, even though dedicated to a broader group of images, does better with patterns from one class and worse with those from another class for which the implemented mechanisms are less suitable. These and many other problems discovered during research on such systems will also form the subject of further intense work by the authors.

Acknowledgments. This work has been supported by the Ministry of Science and Higher Education, Republic of Poland, under project number N N516 478940.

References

1. Eakins, J.P.: Towards intelligent image retrieval. Pattern Recognition 35, 3–14 (2002)
2. Müller, H., Michoux, N., Bandon, D., Geissbuhler, A.: A review of content-based image retrieval systems in medical applications-clinical benefits and future directions. I. J. Medical Informatics 73(1), 1–23 (2004)
3. Niblack, W.R., et al.: The QBIC project: querying images by color, texture and shape. IBM Research Report RJ-9203 (1993)
4. Gudivada, V.N., Raghavan, V.V.: Content-based image retrieval systems. IEEE Comput. 28(9), 18–22 (1995)
5. Eakins, J.P.: Techniques for image retrieval. Library and Information Briefings 85, British Library and South Bank University, London (1998)
6. Ogiela, M.R., Tadeusiewicz, R., Trzupek, M.: Picture grammars in classification and semantic interpretation of 3D coronary vessels visualizations. Opto-Electronics Review 17(3), 200–210 (2009)
7. Trzupek, M.: Semantic Interpretation of Heart Vessel Structures Based on Graph Grammars. In: Bolc, L., Tadeusiewicz, R., Chmielewski, L.J., Wojciechowski, K. (eds.) ICCVG 2010, Part I. LNCS, vol. 6374, pp. 81–88. Springer, Heidelberg (2010)
8. Trzupek, M.: Linguistic approach in intelligent image content analysis of heart vessel structures. In: Barolli, L., et al. (eds.) The Fourth International Conference on Complex, Intelligent and Software Intensive Systems, CISIS 2010, February 15-18, pp. 856–859. IEEE Computer Society, Krakow (2010)
9. Trzupek, M., Ogiela, M.R., Tadeusiewicz, R.: Intelligent image content semantic description for cardiac 3D visualizations. Engineering Applications of Artificial Intelligence 24, 1410–1418 (2011)
10. Poisel, R., Tjoa, S., Tavolato, P.: Advanced File Carving Approaches for Multimedia Files. Journal of Wireless Mobile Networks, Ubiquitous Computing, and Dependable Applications 2(4), 42–58 (2011)
11. Güld, M.O., Kohnen, M., Keysers, D., Schubert, H., Wein, B.B., Bredno, J., Lehmann, T.M.: Quality of DICOM header information for image categorization. In: Proceedings of the International Symposium on Medical Imaging, San Diego, CA, USA, vol. 4685, pp. 280–287 (2002)
12. Wolter, P.: Representing humans in system security models: An actor-network approach. Journal of Wireless Mobile Networks, Ubiquitous Computing, and Dependable Applications 2(1), 75–92 (2011)
13. Ghosh, P., Antani, S., Long, L.R., Thoma, G.R.: Review of medical image retrieval systems and future directions. In: CBMS, pp. 1–6 (2011)

Evaluation of Carotid Artery Segmentation with Centerline Detection and Active Contours without Edges Algorithm

Tomasz Hachaj[1] and Marek R. Ogiela[2]

[1] Pedagogical University of Krakow, Institute of Computer Science and Computer Methods, 2 Podchorazych Ave., 30-084 Krakow, Poland
tomekhachaj@o2.pl
[2] AGH University of Science and Technology, 30 Mickiewicza Ave., 30-059 Krakow, Poland
mogiela@agh.edu.pl

Abstract. The main contribution of this article is a new method of segmentation of carotid artery based on original authors inner path finding algorithm and active contours without edges segmentation method for vessels wall detection. Instead of defining new force to being minimized or intensity metric we decide to find optimal weight of image – dependent forces. This allows our method to be easily reproduced and applied in other software solutions. We judge the quality of segmentation by dice coefficient between manual segmentation done by a specialist and automatic segmentation performed by our algorithm. We did not find any other publication in which such approach for carotid artery bifurcation region segmentation has been proposed or investigated. The proposed algorithm has shown to be reliable method for that task. The dice coefficient at the level of 0.949±0.050 situates our algorithm among best state of the art methods for those solutions. That type of segmentation is the main step performed before sophisticated semantic analysis of complex image patterns utilized by cognitive image and scene understanding methods. The complete diagnostic record (Electronic Health Record – EHR) obtained that way consists private biometric data and its safety is essential for personal and homeland security.

Keywords: Active contours without edges, lumen segmentation, carotid bifurcation, computed tomography angiography, brain perfusion maps, computer - aided diagnosis.

1 Introduction

Extracting vessels from computed tomography angiography (CTA) is a key requirement for the display and analysis that type of modality [1]. CTA is a popular medical imaging method that is often used beside standard computed tomography (CT) in acute stroke imaging. Imaging of the carotid arteries is important for the evaluation of patients with ischemic stroke or Transient Ischemic Attack (TIA). There are many automatic methods to perform the task of segmentation that have been yet proposed in literature. That methods can be divided into two groups: model – based and intensity

G. Quirchmayr et al. (Eds.): CD-ARES 2012, LNCS 7465, pp. 469–479, 2012.

– based. The first group analysis the geometric specificity of vessels, in particular the notions of orientation and tubular shape. The common approach is utilizing some tube detection filters based on analysis of volume Hessian matrix eigenvalues [2]. Those methods are capable to detect any local tubular structure but are sensitive to noises and scanning artifacts. Algorithms among the second group are dedicated mainly for detailed extraction of continues tubular structures. Many of those algorithms are two – step procedures: at first algorithm finds the path within examined vessel, than detects its boundary. In [3] authors finds minimal cost paths between the Common Carotid Artery (CCA) and both the External Carotid Artery (ECA) and the Internal Carotid Artery (ICA). Then the cylindrical tube around each path is created with a radius of 0.5mm that is later used for the level set evolution algorithm with proper function of the image intensity. Method in [4] is based on a variant of the minimal path method that models the vessel as a centerline and boundary. This is done by adding one dimension for the local radius around the centerline. The crucial step of method is the definition of the anisotropic metric giving higher speed on the center of the vessels and also when the minimal path tangent is coherent with the vessels direction. Segmentation is refined using a region-based level sets.

The main contribution of this article is a new method of segmentation of carotid artery based on original authors inner path finding algorithm and active contours without edges segmentation method for vessels wall detection. Instead of defining new force to being minimized or intensity metric we decide to find optimal weight of image – dependent forces. This allows our method to be easily reproduced and applied in other software solutions. We judge the quality of segmentation by dice coefficient between manual segmentation done by a specialist and automatic segmentation performed by our algorithm. We did not find any other publication in which such approach for carotid artery bifurcation region segmentation has been proposed or investigated.

That type of segmentation is the main step performed before sophisticated semantic analysis of complex image patterns utilized by cognitive image and scene understanding methods. The complete diagnostic record (Electronic Health Record – EHR) obtained that way consists private biometric data and its safety is essential for personal and homeland security.

The results presented in this article are extension of our previous work. Our latest researches were concentrated on automatic analysis of dynamic perfusion computed tomography maps (CTP) in the event of brain stroke [5]. We decided to widen the area of our interest on CTA because the examination of carotid arteries is an important step during assessing the risk of brain stroke [6].

2   Methods

The proposed lumen segmentation method is consisted of two sub-algorithms. After preprocessing step the first algorithm detects the possible path between the start and the end point (it is similar to typical region growing algorithm). In the second step it performs the thinning of previously obtained path. The generated path between the start and point becomes 1 voxel width keeping the same length as path from first step. The second algorithm is an active contours without edges segmentation method. The role of this procedure is to segment the whole lumen of considered vessel. The active contours is computed in axial slices and the starting counter is the sphere with radius of 5 voxels. The center point of each sphere is a voxel taken from path from Algorithm I. The algorithm requires manual indication of two initial points inside both sides of vessel to be segmented. In order to detect bifurcated structures (like CCA – ICA – ECA) three points have to be chosen and the path detection algorithm have to be run two times, ones for CCA – ICA part than for CCA – ECA. After computing both paths the further analysis is performed on all voxels from both obtained paths.

List of symbols used in algorithm description:

Freezed points:= $\emptyset$ – already visited points.
Narrow band$_i$:= $\emptyset$ – points, that are visited in i-th step.
Start point – starting point of the path. $\emptyset$
End point – end point of the path.
Delta value:=0 - maximal accepted difference between neighbor points.
S(x_j) - Surrandings of point x_j with radius 1 (26 voxels).
V(x_j) - Value of vexel density in point x_j.
Path length - the length of the path (in voxels).
Delta value - maximal accepted difference between two voxel densities. If the difference is greater than Delta value, the considered voxel is not included into the path.

In the preprocessing step of first algorithm the volumetric image is convoluted with Gaussian kernel in order to remove noises and scanning artifacts. The image is then thresholded in order to remove voxels that density do not belongs to range:

[min(V(Start point), V(End point)) – 40, max(V(Start point), V(End point)) + 200]

That step eliminates the uncontrolled propagation of path detection algorithm in regions where tissues has too low or too high density to be part of examined vessel.

Algorithm I, step I – detection of path between *Start point* and *End point*.

```
Delta value:=-1
While (End point∉Freezed points)
  Delta value:=Delta value+1
i:=0
Narrow band:= ∅
Narrow band₀:={Start point}
Freezed point:={(Start point, I)}
While ( #Narrow bandᵢ>0 ∧ End point ∉Freezed points)
i:=i+1
∀xⱼ∈Narrow bandᵢ
∀yₖ∈S(xⱼ)
  if(|V(xⱼ)- V(yₖ)|<Delta value)
    Narrow bandᵢ:= Narrow bandᵢ∪ yₖ
    Freezed point:= Freezed pointᵢ∪ (yₖ,i)
Path length:=i
End algorithm I, step I
```

Because the algorithm stops immediately after detecting the end point it will not generate paths that are too long and it is unnecessary to add any penalization term of path length to the edges weighting function.

Algorithm I, step II – thinning of path obtained in step I. The path generated in second step has the same length as previous path but is only one voxel width.

```
Path:= ∅ - path from End point to Start point
Path:=Path∪End point
k:=Path length -1
i:=0
x_i:=End point
While(Start point ∉ Path)
    X_{i+1}:=(y_j: |V(y_j)-V(x_i)|=min|V(y_i)-V(x_i)|, (y_i,k) ∈Freezed
points, y_i∈S(x_i))
    Path:= Path∪x_{i+1}
    i:=i+1
    k:=k-1
End Algorithm I, step II
```

The second algorithm is based on active contours without edges segmentation procedure [7]. The method requires rescaling the CT volume ISO values (densities) so that it does not consist any negative values of voxels. Beside of that the active contours algorithm does not require any preprocessing and is performed on "raw" CT volume data

The basic idea in active contours models or snakes is to evolve a curve, subject to constraints from a given image in order to detect objects in that image [7]. Let Ω be a bounded open subset of R^2. The algorithm is driven by optimization procedure of energy term:

$$F_1(C,c_1)+F_2(C,c_2)= \int_{inside(C)}(I(x,y)-c_1)^2 + \int_{outside(C)}(I(x,y)-c_2)^2 \qquad (1)$$

Where:
C is the curve that represents the boundary of segmented region in Ω.
I(x,y) is pixel intensity value of image to be segmented with coordinates x, y.
c_1 is average value of pixels intensity inside region with boundary C.
c_2 is average value of pixels intensity outside region with boundary C.

The equation (1) may also consist regularization terms [7] and becomes:

$$F(c_1,c_2,C) = \mu \cdot Length(C)+v \cdot Area(inside(C))$$
$$+ \lambda_1 \int_{inside(C)}|I(x,y)-c_1|^2 dxdy$$
$$+ \lambda_2 \int_{outside(C)}|I(x,y)-c_2|^2 dxdy \qquad (2)$$

The first term depends on length of the curve, the second on area inside it. Parameters μ, v, λ_1 and λ_2 ($\mu, v \geq 0$, $\lambda_1, \lambda_2 > 0$) are constants.

In [8] the authors proposed an effective implicit representation for evolving curves and surfaces, which has found many applications, because it allows for automatic change of topology such as merging and breaking, and the calculations are made on a fixed rectangular grid. A given curve C is represented by zero level set of a scalar Lipschitz continuous function $\phi : \Omega \to R$ such that:

$$
\begin{cases}
C = \partial \omega = \{(x, y) \in \Omega : \phi(x, y) = 0\} \\
inside(C) = \omega = \{(x, y) \in \Omega : \phi(x, y) > 0\} \\
outside(C) = \omega = \{(x, y) \in \Omega : \phi(x, y) < 0\}
\end{cases}
\tag{3}
$$

The energy from (2) might be rewritten as:

$$
\begin{aligned}
F(c_1, c_2, \phi) = {} & \mu \int_\Omega \delta(\phi(x, y)) |\nabla \phi(x, y)| dxdy \\
& + v \int_\Omega H(\phi(x, y)) dxdy \\
& + \lambda_1 \int_\Omega |I(x, y) - c_1|^2 H(\phi(x, y)) dxdy \\
& + \lambda_2 \int_\Omega |I(x, y) - c_2|^2 (1 - H(\phi(x, y))) dxdy
\end{aligned}
\tag{4}
$$

Where:

$$
H(z) = \begin{cases} 1 & if \quad z \geq 0 \\ 0 & if \quad z < 0 \end{cases}
\tag{5}
$$

H is the Heaviside function

$$
\delta_0(z) = \frac{d}{dz} H(z)
\tag{6}
$$

Dirac measure.

In numerical solution the non-zero value of δ_0 is defined in range $(z - \varepsilon, z + \varepsilon)$, where ε is a small $\varepsilon > 0$ value.

In the rest of this article we assume that $v = 0$ and we do not consider area regularization term into calculations.

In order to minimize $F(c_1, c_2, \phi)$ with respect to ϕ we have to solve Euler-Lagrange equation for ϕ [9].

$$\frac{\partial \phi}{\partial t} = \delta(\phi)\left[\mu \cdot div\left(\frac{\nabla \phi}{|\nabla \phi|}\right) - \lambda_1(I - c_1)^2 + \lambda_2(I - c_2)^2 \right] = 0 \quad \text{in} \quad t \geq 0 \quad \text{and in } \Omega$$

$$\phi(0, x, y) = \phi_0(x, y) \quad \text{in } \Omega \tag{7}$$

$$\frac{\delta(\phi)}{|\nabla \phi|}\frac{\delta\phi}{\delta n} = 0 \quad \text{in } \delta\Omega$$

Where:

$\overline{n}$ is the exterior normal of the boundary $\delta\Omega$

$\frac{\delta\phi}{\delta n}$ is the normal derivative of ϕ at the boundary.

The parameters ν (curve smoothing term), λ_1 and λ_2 affects results of optimization procedure. In our case we wanted to verify the hypothesis that term λ_1 should have the higher value than λ_2 to perform proper lumen segmentation. That is because we wanted to restrain the excessive grown of segmented area especially when the borders between area of interest and another tissue with similar density is very narrow. In our experiment the smoothing term is set to $\mu = 0.55$ that we assumed proper for considered segmentation task.

3   Results

The proposed algorithm was tested on a set of four CTA volumes of carotid artery with size 512x512x415, 512x512x425, 512x512x432 and 512x512x433 voxels scanned by SOMATOM Sensation 10 CT scanner. The distance between axial slices was 0.7 mm. The segmentation was performed on left and right carotid artery separately. Because of that the experimental set was consisted of eight tubular structures.

The volume to be segmented was determined similarly as in comparison protocol in [10]. It is defined around the bifurcation slice, which was marked as the first (caudal to cranial) slice where the lumen of the CCA appears as two separate lumens: the lumen of the ICA and the lumen of the ECA (external carotid artery). The segmentation contain the CCA, starting at least 20 mm caudal of bifurcation slice, the ICA, up to at least 40 mm cranial of bifurcation slice, and the ECA, up to between 10 and 20 mm cranial of the bifurcation slice. The segmentation was performed at first on CCA – ICA section, than on CCA – ECA, the final segmentation result is the common part of those two. The λ_1 that we took into account was: 1, 2, 4, 6, 8 and 10. In figure 1 the carotid arteries segmentation results of all considered CTA volumes are presented ($\lambda_1 = 10$).

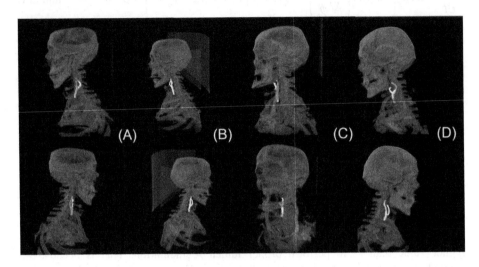

Fig. 1. The carotid arteries segmentation results of all considered CT volumes ($\lambda_1 = 10$). Each column consists different CTA volume. Top row visualize left carotid artery, the bottom the right one.

The TP, FP, TN and FN coefficients values as the function of λ_1 parameter for CTA from figure 1 (B), bottom row (right artery) are shown in table 1. The visualized results of the same artery are presented in figure 2 and figure 3.

Table 1. The TP, FP, TN and FN coefficients values as the function of λ_1 parameter for CTA from figure 1 B, bottom row (right artery).

λ_1	TP	FP	TN	FN
1	12596	5380	116111768	48
2	12496	3538	116113610	148
4	12542	2042	116115106	102
6	12516	1223	116115925	128
8	12446	617	116116531	198
10	12427	238	116116910	217

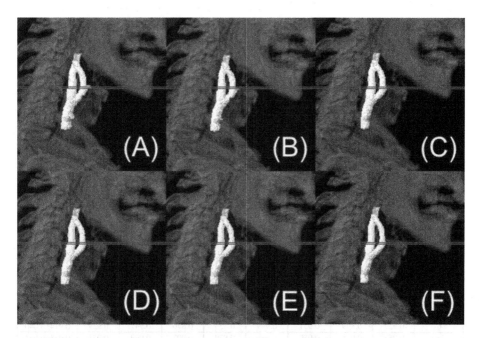

Fig. 2. Detailed view of segmentation results for CTA from figure 1 B, bottom row (right artery). Red line marks the axial slice that is presented later in figure 3.

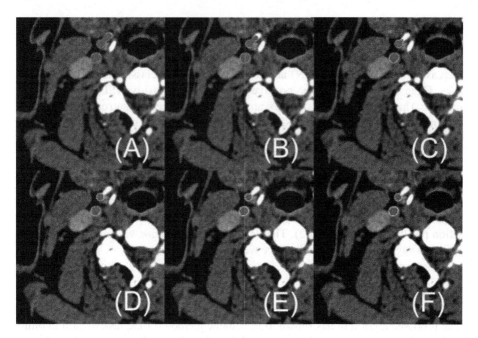

Fig. 3. Detailed view of segmentation results for CTA from figure 1 B, bottom row (right artery). Red regions are the segmented ICA and ECA tissues.

The volume lumen segmentations is evaluated using the dice similarity measure:

$$D_{si} = \frac{2 \cdot |pv_r \cap pv_p|}{|pv_r| + |pv_p|} \tag{8}$$

Where pv_r and pv_p are the reference and an algorithmically determined arteries tissues. Table 2 presents values of dice coefficient between manual segmentation performed by specialist and automatic segmentation performed by our algorithm. The last column consists average value of coefficient for all considered CTA volumes for given λ_1 value ($\pm$ standard deviation).

Table 2. Values of dice coefficient between manual segmentation performed by specialist and automatic segmentation performed by our algorithm. The last column consists average value of coefficient for all considered CTA volumes for given λ_1 value ($\pm$ standard deviation).

$\lambda 1$\case	1	2	3	4	5	6	7	8	AVG
1	0.648	0.535	0.835	0.823	0.764	0.785	0.806	0.745	0.743±0.096
2	0.765	0.649	0.879	0.872	0.795	0.825	0.863	0.829	0.810±0.071
4	0.879	0.823	0.924	0.921	0.822	0.886	0.913	0.903	0.884±0.039
6	0.927	0.899	0.951	0.949	0.835	0.876	0.947	0.929	0.914±0.040
8	0.953	0.945	0.959	0.968	0.829	0.907	0.969	0.953	0.935±0.044
10	0.977	0.970	0.956	0.982	0.827	0.923	0.986	0.973	0.949±0.050

4   Discussion

The detail analysis of segmentation results (table 1) shows that increasing of λ_1 causes increasing of true negative (TN) and false negative (FN) classification of vessel tissues. From the other hand true positive (TP) and false positive (FP) coefficient decreases. That is because less voxels are captured into region surrounded by active contours during algorithms second step. That behavior is also clearly visible in figure 2 if we compare (A) and (F). The segmented region in (F) is thinner and it also does not consist additional false segmented tissue region. The same situation in the axial view is visualized in Figure 3 (A) and (F). The increasing of λ_1 parameter causes also as expected increase of dice coefficient as it is shown in table 2. From the value of λ_1 above 6 we observe the increasing of standard deviation between averaged results. That is because not always the higher value of λ_1 causes the improvement of segmentation results (case 5 in table 2). That is because above some value the expansion of counters might be stopped by the force weighted by λ_2.

5   Conclusions

The proposed algorithm has shown to be reliable method for the task of carotid bifurcation region segmentation. The dice coefficient at the level of 0.949±0.050 situates our algorithm among best state of the art methods for those solutions. What is more our proposition can easily be implanted using popular image processing libraries that consists parameterizes active contours without edges algorithm. The proposed method has some drawbacks. The first is that the value of λ_1 that results in optimal from medical point of view solution may differ between examined CTA. The second one is long performance time of the segmentation procedure. What is more the first part of the algorithm – the path finding procedure may be difficult to parallelize on SIMD machines (like GPU processors) because that algorithm is highly sequential (not parallel). It is difficult to predict how the region growing procedure will evolve in each step.

Our method requires further investigation in order to find optimal value not only for λ_1 but also λ_2 and curvature – steering μ. The validation of the segmentation should be performed on bigger set of control data. If the result of evaluation will be on acceptable rate we will use this algorithm as the baseline for the further researches on automatic diagnosis of carotid structures. In order to accomplish this task we are planning to create appropriate semantic description of carotid artery similarly to those proposed in [11], [12]. After correct identification of possible lumen abnormality we will try to integrate the results with already developed by us CTP diagnosis framework. That approach will allow us to create more complex and complete diagnostic records (Electronic Health Record – EHR) that might be very helpful for radiologist in decision - making process. Nowadays EHR becomes a standard in hospital information systems and in the future might be accessed by wireless personal devices in the area of hospital using low-power personal area networks [13]. The proper information flow policy model will forbid a doctor from mixing the personal medical details of the patients [14]. What is more EHR consists private biometric data and its safety is essential for personal and homeland security.

Acknowledgments. We kindly acknowledge the support of this study by a Pedagogical University of Krakow Statutory Research Grant.

References

1. Josephson, S.A., Bryant, S.O., Mak, H.K., Johnston, S.C., Dillon, W.P., Smith, W.S.: Evaluation of carotid stenosis using CT angiography in the initial evaluation of stroke and TIA. Neurology 63(3), 457–460 (2004)
2. Hachaj, T., Ogiela, M.R.: Segmentation and Visualization of Tubular Structures in Computed Tomography Angiography. In: Pan, J.-S., Chen, S.-M., Nguyen, N.T. (eds.) ACIIDS 2012, Part III. LNCS, vol. 7198, pp. 495–503. Springer, Heidelberg (2012)
3. Krissian, K., Arencibia Garcia, S.: A Minimal Cost Path and Level Set Evolution Approach for Carotid Bifurcation Segmentation. In: Proc. of MICCAI 2009 Workshop: Carotid Lumen Segmentation and Stenosis Grading Challenge (2009)
4. Mille, J., Benmansour, F., Cohen, L.: Carotid Lumen Segmentation Based on Tubular Anisotropy and Contours Without Edges. In: Proc. of MICCAI 2009 Workshop: Carotid Lumen Segmentation and Stenosis Grading Challenge (2009)
5. Hachaj, T.: Pattern Classification Methods for Analysis and Visualization of Brain Perfusion CT Maps. In: Ogiela, M.R., Jain, L.C. (eds.) Computational Intelligence Paradigms. SCI, vol. 386, pp. 145–170. Springer, Heidelberg (2012)

6. Steinman, D.A., Poepping, T.L., Tambasco, M., Rankin, R.N., Holdsworth, D.W.: Flow Patterns at the Stenosed Carotid Bifurcation: Effect of Concentric versus Eccentric Stenosis. Annals of Biomedical Engineering 28(4), 415–423 (2000), doi:10.1114/1.279
7. Chan, T.F., Vese, L.A.: Active contours without edges. IEEE Transactions on Image Processing 10(2), 266–277 (2001)
8. Osher, S., Sethian, J.A.: Fronts propagating with curvature dependent speed: Algorithms based on Hamilton-Jacobi formulation. JCP 79, 12–49 (1988)
9. Chan, T.F., Vese, L.A.: A Multiphase level set framework for image segmentation using the Mumford and Shah model. International Journal of Computer Vision 50(3), 271–293 (2002)
10. Hameeteman, R., Zuluaga, M., Joskowicz, L., Freiman, M., Van Walsum, T.: Carotid lumen segmentation and stenosis grading challenge (May 2009), 4.2, 5.1, http://cls2009.bigr.nl/download/evaluationframework2009.pdf
11. Trzupek, M., Ogiela, M.R., Tadeusiewicz, R.: Intelligent image content semantic description for cardiac 3D visualisations. Engineering Applications of Artificial Intelligence 24, 1410–1418 (2011)
12. Trzupek, M.: Semantic Modelling of Coronary Vessel Structures in Computer Aided Detection of Pathological Changes. In: Tjoa, A.M., Quirchmayr, G., You, I., Xu, L. (eds.) ARES 2011. LNCS, vol. 6908, pp. 220–227. Springer, Heidelberg (2011)
13. Jara, A.J., Zamora, M.A., Skarmeta, A.F.G.: An Initial Approach to Support Mobility in Hospital Wireless Sensor Networks based on 6LoWPAN (HWSN6). Journal of Wireless Mobile Networks, Ubiquitous Computing, and Dependable Applications 1(2/3), 107–122 (2010) ISSN: 2093-5374
14. Viet Triem Tong, V., Clark, A., Mé, L.: Specifying and enforcing a fine-grained information flow policy: model and experiments. Journal of Wireless Mobile Networks, Ubiquitous Computing, and Dependable Applications 1(1), 56–71 (2010)

Automatic Image Annotation
Using Semantic Text Analysis

Dongjin Choi and Pankoo Kim[*]

Dept. Of Computer Engineering Chosun University, Gwangju, South Korea
dongjin.choi84@gmail.com, pkkim@chosun.ac.kr

Abstract. This paper proposed a method to find annotations corresponding to given CNN news documents for detecting terrorism image or context information. Assigning keywords or annotation to image is one of the important tasks to let machine understand web data written by human. Many techniques have been suggested for automatic image annotation in the last few years. Many researches focused on the method to extract possible annotation using low-level image features. This was the basic and traditional approach but it has a limitation that it costs lots of time. To overcome this problem, we analyze images and theirs co-occurring text data to generate possible annotations. The text data in the news documents describe the core point of news stories according to the given images and titles. Because of this fact, this paper applied text data as a resource to assign image annotations using TF (Term Frequency) value and WUP values of WordNet. The proposed method shows that text analysis is another possible technique to annotate image automatically for detecting unintended web documents.

Keywords: Image annotation, Text analysis, WUP measurement, Semantic analysis.

1 Introduction

In the last decade, images and videos are the most common contents on the web documents due to the fact those digital cameras and other digital devices became popular over the world. Moreover, lots of Social Network Services (SNS) have been emerged into digital devices especially, Smartphone. The SNS have completely changed human life style into a person who is willing to share his/her current activities through digital photos. However, it has become more difficult to distinguish which data is reliable or not due to huge amount of textural and image data on the web. Moreover, there is a high possibility of leaking personal information of users. Users are able to send any types of data to anyone in anywhere and anytime. This is a serious problem of insider security. The 'insider threat' is an individual with privileges who misuses them or shoes access results in misuse [16]. In order to prevent leakage of personal data, many researchers have been studying recently. [17] proposed a new model of differential privacy for evaluating tables with k-anonymity

---

[*] Corresponding author.

G. Quirchmayr et al. (Eds.): CD-ARES 2012, LNCS 7465, pp. 479–487, 2012.

to prevent leakage of personal information. The growing bulk of unstructured data such as text, images and video is needed to be formed into specific predefined manners. In order to satisfy this fact, automatic image annotation method is the first requirement for making structured web data for detecting unintended malicious data such as terrorism. There are two main approaches for image annotation task. First is supervised learning method which was tagged by human hands [1], [2], [3]. These researches applied probabilistic method and ontology scheme to determine which keywords will be precise annotations. The given images were labeled with a common semantic label and classify into corresponding group. These supervised methods guarantee high precision rates though, it requires lots of time and human efforts for labeling manually. For example, if we have an image for animal 'tiger', the system has to discover hypernym and hyponym of 'tiger' concepts. The second approach is an unsupervised automatic image annotation using low-level image features. [4] proposed a method to separate regions of images for detecting objects and describe into small vocabulary of blobs. Automatic image annotation is a popular task in computer vision. Many approaches have been introduced using lots of distinct learning algorithms [7], [8], [9]. Because of the image processing techniques, it is possible to obtain objects in given images. Despite these researches applied different algorithms, all works essentially attempt to learn the correlation between image features and keywords. However, it is still an expensive and challenging task for machine. Hence, automatic image annotation techniques are starting to apply high-level features especially text data [5], [6]. The text data which is surrounding given images and their co-occurring texts have great evidence to discover relevant keywords. This is based on the fact that the surrounding text data of images is likely to describe the given images. For example, let us we have a news document or Wikipedia document. The surrounding texts of images in these web documents explain not only for the given image but also main purpose of documents. It is no doubt that web text data has lots of noisy information. We hereby propose a method to remove irrelevant keywords which were extracted by using Term Frequency (TF) value through WUP similarity in WordNet. WordNet was developed by the Cognitive Science Laboratory of Princeton University and it defines approximately 81,000 noun concepts [10]. WordNet is one of the most well-known Knowledge Base (KB) over the world. So it has been applied to many different fields for finding semantic similarity between terms. Hwang has been studied to grasp semantic similarities and context information from abstract in Wikipedia documents [11], [18]. His research proved that WordNet has valuable information to build semantic network between words for semantic retrieval system. For this reason, we applied modified WUP similarity in WordNet to measure semantic relations between titles and candidate annotations. This paper is organized as follows: Section 2 explains what WUP similarity is. The proposed automatic annotation algorithm is introduced in Section 3. Finally, Section 4 concludes with discussion of future work in this area.

2   WUP Similarity Measurement

WUP similarity [19] is one of the popular methods to measure similarity of nodes. It is a function of the path length from the least common subsumer (LCS) of the two given concepts C_1 and C_2, which is the most specific concept that they share as an ancestor. This similarity value is scaled by the sum of the path lengths from the individual concepts to the root. For example, if C_1 was 'China.n.01[1]' and C_2 was 'Xinjiang.n.01[2]' then the LCS would be 'administrative district.n.01[3]'. The WUP similarity between node C_1 and C_2 is calculated by following formula 1.

$$sim_{wup} = \frac{2 \times depth(LCS(C_1,C_2))}{depth(C_1)+depth(C_2)} .$$ (1)

where, $depth(C)$ is the depth of concept C in the WordNet hierarchy. The value of this method goes to thigh when two concepts share an ancestor with long depth. The semantic relations between sense 'China.n.01' and sense 'Xinjiang.n.01' defined in WordNet are shown in following Figure 1.

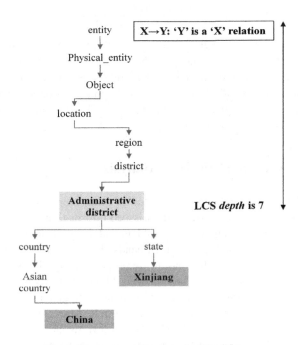

Fig. 1. The concept hierarchy in WordNet

The similarity between 'China.n.01' and 'Xinjiang.n.01' is 0.7368 which means that these two words share many ancestors so, it can be considered as a relevant concept each other. In order to grasp lexical similarities or semantic similarities between concepts, lots of studies have been applied WordNet hierarch for building

[1] A communist nation that covers a vast territory in eastern Asia, the most populous country in the world.
[2] An autonomous province in far northwestern China on the border with Mongolia and Kazakhstan.
[3] A district defined for administrative purposes.

semantic relations. [12] proposed new similarity measurement method for analyzing web documents based on WordNet sense network to make computer can understand human language. Also, [13] tested a semantic similarity using diverse measurement method and compared their accuracy, precision and recall rate, respectively. This research shows that there is no best technique to discover semantic similarities for machine like human does. For example, human can easily distinguish differences between 'bat.n.01[4]' and 'bat.n.02[5]' but machine cannot. Also, human can understand 'jaguar' as a 'vehicle' but computer may misunderstand 'jaguar' as a 'big cat'. This is a major problem when machine tried to understand human language because natural human language is still complicated for machine. In order to overcome this limitation, we applied modified WUP measurement to find most relevant annotation from extracted candidates. The following formula 2 indicates modified WUP similarity.

$$sim_{wup} = \frac{2 \times depth((LCS(C_1, C_2)))^2}{depth(C_1) + depth(C_2)} \ .$$

(2)

when the sim_{wup} value is higher than 0.5, $depth$(LCS) will be multiplied again to the numerator. When WUP value goes higher than 0.5, it means that given two concepts are sharing half of all concept hierarchies. So we can emphasize relevant concepts using modified WUP measurement. Eventually, the standard deviation of similarities between two given concepts using $m\_$WUP value will be higher than simple WUP value [15].

3   Automatic Semantic Text Analysis

Consider we have news documents consisted of titles, images and surrounding texts. Each of news documents describes current issued information corresponding to given titles and images. There is a traditional problem that the given images are not labelled. If so, annotations were labelled by human hands. This is a disturbing task for human so it has to be automated. For this reason, we propose an algorithm to analyze images and their co-occurring text data. The following Figure 2 shows proposed process for automatic image annotation system. In order to annotate given images automatically, titles of news documents have to be extracted, at first. After extracting a title of given document, stopwords will be deleted. The stopwords are terms that appear so frequently in text that they lose their usefulness as search terms. The stopping is a simple task of removing common words from the stream of token. The most common words are typically function words that help form sentence structure but contribute little on their own to the description of the topics covered by the text [14]. The most popular "the," "a," "an," "that," and "those" are *determiners*. These words are part of how we describe nouns in text, and express concepts like location or quantity. After stopping process, we extract only noun type of words due to the fact that nouns or proper nouns have significant meaning and they are subjects or objects of sentences.

---

[4] Nocturnal mouselike mammal with forelimbs modified to form membranous wings and anatomical adaptations for echolocation by which they navigate.

[5] A turn trying to get a hit.

Finally, we can obtain title word list $title_t = \{t_1, \ldots, t_n\}$. Following Table 1 shows the extracted title word lists compare to the original title sentences.

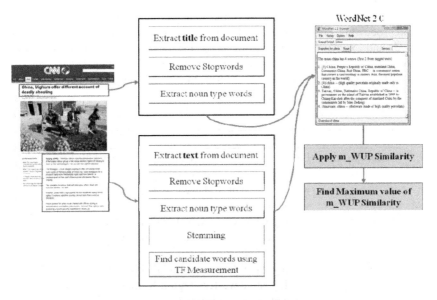

Fig. 2. The proposed system architecture

Table 1. Extracted word list from title

No.	Title	$title_t$
1	China Uighurs offer different account of deadly shooting	{China, Uighurs, offer, account}
2	Donations pour into Philippines in wake of deadly storm	{Donations, Philippines, wake, storm}
3	Top U.S. diplomat to visit North Korea's neighbors	{Top, US, diplomat, North, Korea, neighbors}
4	China Uighurs offer different account of deadly shooting	{China, Uighurs, offer, account}
...	...	...

The next step is extracting surrounding text from documents. In this step we applied *TF* value to determine candidate words. This weight is a value often used in information retrieval and text mining. This weight is a statistical measure used to evaluate how important a word is to a document in a corpus. It is followed by given formula 3.

$$Term\ Frequency\ w(x) = \frac{tf(x)}{\max tf(n)} \ . \tag{3}$$

where, n is a total number of word and max $tf(n)$ denotes the maximum frequency of the given document. Thus, the expression computes a term ratio for each term in a surrounding text.

Table 2 shows how surrounding text was changed into candidate annotation. This is the preprocessing step to find candidate terms through removing special characters, stopwords and extracting noun types of words list $text_t = \{k_1, ..., k_n\}$. Now, we are ready to calculate TF weigh of filtered surrounding text. Following Table 3 shows the result of TF weight. The total number of terms in new document number 1 is 122.

Table 2. Results processed by each step

Step	Result
Surrounding Text	Beijing (CNN) -- Chinese officials said they killed seven members of the Uighur ethnic group in the restive western region of Xinjiang in order to free two hostages -- an account the Uighurs disputed.
Remove Special Characters	Beijing CNN Chinese officials killed seven Uighur ethnic restive western region Xinjiang free hostages account Uighurs disputed …
Remove Stopwords	Beijing CNN Chinese officials killed seven Uighur ethnic restive western region Xinjiang free hostages account Uighurs disputed …
Extract noun type words	Beijing CNN Chinese officials Uighur western region Xinjiang hostages Uighurs …

Terms which appeared more than twice were shown in Table 3. It is clear that most relevant terms appeared in surrounding text more often. However, this is not always true. The term 'rescue' is close to the title "China Uighurs offer different account of deadly shooting' even though its occurring frequency is two. Moreover, a word 'terror' was discarded due to the fact that it only appeared once although 'terror' was relevant to given title. In order to overcome this drawback, we multiplied WUP value between t_i and k_j to the TF value. Following formula 4 express the semantic weight.

Table 3. TF results of news documents #1

Terms	TF	Terms	TF
Uighur	13/122	Pakistan	2/122
security	4/122	city	2/122
Xinjiang	3/122	government	2/122
crackdown	3/122	hostages	2/122
region	3/122	militants	2/122
Beijing	2/122	operation	2/122
Chinese	2/122	police	2/122
Han	2/122	population	2/122
Hotan	2/122	rescue	2/122

$$SW_{t_i k_j} = w(x) \times Sim_{m\_wup} \tag{4}$$

So, we are able to compare t_i and k_j and determine how much they are closed to. Eventually, we can obtain final annotation for given image through proposed process. The following Table 4 the news images and its annotation grasped automatically.

The annotations are different from other traditional research that described object in given images. Recognizing an object in images is not cover major meaning of images. The proposed approach in this paper focused on the annotations which describe core meaning of given image. Hence, annotated words are semantically related to titles and images. We believe that this annotation can represent not only documents but also images. However, traditional approaches only can detect object in image so, results will be 'human,' 'apple,' 'boy,' 'girl,' and so on for first image in Table 4.

Table 4. Extracted annotation using proposed method

Image		
Annotation	Uighurs, security, Xinjiang, China, terrorism, Asian, crackdown, police, Beijing, Pakistan	Philippines, storm, donation, Asia, Children, China, rain, flood, Australia, Europe

4   Conclusion

The amounts of data which are a mixture of different media have been dramatically increasing. Also the there is a high possibility of personal information leakage. This is a big issue and has to be protected in advance. Automated way to index text, images, audio, and video data is necessary for not only homeland security but also future semantic services. Future semantic web has to annotate image automatically and build semantic relationships between documents and surrounding images to prevent insider threat. Semantic annotation allows us concept search instead of keyword search. In order to make further step for getting close to semantic web and homeland security issues, this paper proposed semantic image annotation approach to analyze images and co-occurring text. We applied modified WUP similarity measurements when values satisfy the predefined condition. The proposed method is simple though still gives possible approach for building semantic image annotation. The costing time of our suggested method is cheaper than traditional annotation system using image recognition techniques. Also it can be applied to another system directly and easily. The most common methods to extract annotation were image object recognition. So, they gave only names of the objects in images. Our approach not only gives context information of documents but also support semantic relationship between title, images, and surrounding text. The weakness of this research is that it is hard to prove whether our approach is adequate or not. For this reason, we have to apply different semantic measurements to enhance reliability of this research. Moreover, when we combine image object recognition technique over our proposed method, the results will be more faithful than current work.

Acknowledgments. This research was financially supported by the Ministry of Education, Science Technology (MEST) and National Research Foundation of Korea (NRF) through the Human Resource Training Project for Regional Innovation.

References

1. Carneiro, G., Chan, A.B., Moreno, P.J., Vasconcelos, N.: Supervised Learning of Semantic Classes for Image Annotation and Retrieval. IEEE Transactions on Pattern Analysis and Machine Intelligence 29, 394–410 (2007)
2. Scheiber, A.T., Dubbeldam, B., Wielemaker, J., Wielinga, B.: Ontology-Based Photo Annotation. IEEE Intelligent Systems 16, 66–74 (2001)
3. Hollink, L., Schreiber, G., Wielemaker, J., Wielinga, B.: Semantic Annotation of Image Collections. In: Workshop on Knowledge Markup and Semantic Annotation, KCAP 2003 (2003)
4. Jeon, J., Lavrenko, V., Manmatha, R.: Automatic Image Annotation and Retrieval using Cross-Media Relevance Models. In: Proceedings of the 26th Annual International ACM SIGIR Conference on Research and Development in Information Retrieval (2003)
5. Feng, Y., Lapata, M.: Topic Models for Image Annotation and Text Illustration. In: The 2010 Annual Conference of the North American Chapter of the Association for Computational Linguistics, pp. 831–839 (2010)
6. Tirilly, P., Claveau, V., Gros, P.: News image annotation on a large parallel text-image corpus. In: 7th Language Resources and Evaluation Conference, pp. 2564–2569 (2010)
7. David, M.B., Jordan, M.I.: Modeling annotated data. In: Proceedings of the 26th Annual International ACM SIGIR Conference on Research and Development in Information Retrieval, pp. 127–134 (2003)
8. Lavrenko, V., Manmatha, R., Jeon, J.: A Model for Learning the Semantics of Pictures. In: Advances in Neural Information Processing Systems 16 NIPS (2004)
9. Barnard, K., Johnson, M.: Word sense disambiguation with pictures. Journal Artificial Intelligence 167, 13–30 (2005)
10. Deselaers, T., Ferrari, V.: Visual and Semantic Similarity in ImageNet. In: CVPR 2011 (2011)
11. Hwang, M., Choi, C., Kim, P.: Automatic Enrichment of Semantic Relation Network and Its Application to Word Sense Disambiguation. IEEE Transactions on Knowledge and Data Engineering 23(6), 845–858 (2011)
12. Hwang, M., Choi, D., Choi, J., Kim, H., Koo, P.: Similarity Measure for Semantic Document Interconnections. An International Interdisciplinary Journal 13(2), 253–267 (2010)
13. Fern, S., Stevenson, M.: A Semantic Similarity Approach to Paraphrase Detection. In: Computer and Information Science (2008)

14. Croft, W.B., Metzler, D., Strohman, T.: Search Engines: Information Retrieval in Practice
15. Choi, D., Kim, J., Kim, H., Hwang, M., Kim, P.: A Method for Enhancing Image Retrieval based on Annotation using Modified WUP Similarity in WordNet. In: 11th WSEAS International Conference on Artificial Intelligence, Knowledge Engineering and Data Bases (2012)
16. Hunker, J., Probst, C.W.: Insiders and Insider Threats-An Overview of Definitions and Mitigation Techniques. Journal of Wireless Mobile Networks, Ubiquitous Computing and Dependable Applications 2(1), 4–24 (2011)
17. Kiyomoto, S., Martin, K.M.: Model for a Common Notion of Privacy Leakage on Public Database. Journal of Wireless Mobile Networks, Ubiquitous Computing and Dependable Applications 2(1), 50–62 (2011)
18. Hwang, M., Choi, D., Kim, P.: A Method for Knowledge Base Enrichment using Wikipedia Document Information. An International Interdisciplinary Journal 13(5), 1599–1612 (2010)
19. Wu, Z., Palmer, M.: Verb Semantics and Lexical Selection. In: ACL 1994 Proceedings of the 32nd annual meeting on Association for Computational Linguistics, pp. 133–138 (1994)

Routing Algorithm Based on Nash Equilibrium against Malicious Attacks for DTN Congestion Control

Chengjun Wang, Baokang Zhao, Wanrong Yu,
Chunqing Wu, and Zhenghu Gong

School of Computer Science, National University of Defense Technology,
Changsha, Hunan, China
cjwmhd@gmail.com, {bkzhao,wlyu,wuchunqing,gzh}@nudt.edu.cn

Abstract. In Delay-Tolerant Network(DTN), certain malicious node might generate congestion in attack to reduce the overall performance of the whole network, especially the target of message successful delivery ratio. In this paper, a novel Nash equilibrium based congestion control routing algorithm with the function of security defense (NESD) is proposed. In the process of message delivery, node can use Nash equilibrium to compute the largest proportion of transfer messages occupancy to node memory capacity. This mechanism constrains the attack from malicious node and guarantees the message transfer of regular node. This congestion control routing algorithm for security defense is evaluated by experiment. It is important application in the field of homeland defense. The results show that related key parameters are significantly improved in DTN scenario.

Keywords: Delay-Tolerant Network Routing, Congestion Control, Gaming theory, Nash equilibrium.

1   Introduction

DTN [1] is widely applied in the obscure or tragedy district [2], vehicle network [3], satellite communication [4] and other wireless network environment.These fields mostly have close relationship with homeland defense.It resolves the problem of intermittent connection, high latency, low data transfer speed, high packet loss rate in DTN by adding a bundle layer [5] between the traditional transmission and application layer and designing storage transfer protocol [6].

As a special wireless network environment, the chief goal of DTN is to guarantee the message successful delivery ratio. The previous algorithms mostly adopt the mechanism of increasing message replicas [7] or leverage the historical information of node's encounter probability [8] as the criterion of transfer node selection in the message delivery.

Meanwhile, limit of DTN resource causes the congestion which also affects the message successful delivery ratio in some extent. Previous congestion control algorithms mostly adopt the passive message delete [9] or migration [10] when

G. Quirchmayr et al. (Eds.): CD-ARES 2012, LNCS 7465, pp. 488–500, 2012.

congestion happens, or adjust message generation ratio and sending speed by feedback control system [11]. This kind of method usually is passive and lagging. In some extent, it results in the frequent jitter of traffic and unstable network environment.

These methods mostly assume that network nodes are regular and it doesn't consider the presence of malicious nodes. Malicious node tends to forge the probability of its encounter with the target node. High encounter probability is forged by malicious node (Blackhole Attack) [12]. Message transfer request is accepted and then received message is discarded. Or malicious node forges the low probability of its encounter with the target node (Resource-Misuse Attack) [13] which occupies the memory of transfer node and causes network congestion. Two attack methods both block the communication between the other nodes and target nodes and this reduces message successful delivery ratio. The impact of attack is visible in the field of homeland defense.

The presence of malicious nodes causes the failure of the past mechanism which passively controls congestion in order to guarantee the message successful delivery ratio. The active congestion control mechanism to deal with the attack of malicious nodes should be adopted. This paper leverages the Nash equilibrium in game theory [14] to allocate node memory appropriately that makes the fair sharing of local node memory between existing messages in this node and messages which are about to be transferred to this node. This mechanism not only satisfies the essential message transfer operation for message successful delivery and but also avoids the arbitrary message delivery from malicious node to regular nodes. This attack behavior of malicious node makes regular node's whole memory is occupied by malicious node's transfer message which causes the congestion and packet loss in the regular node. It reduces the overall message successful delivery ratio in the network.

2 Related Work

To increase message successful delivery ratio, the simplest way to leverage message replica is the flooding routing [7]. This unrestricted duplication of message is a great waste of bandwidth resource. In [15], the authors improve this mechanism by transferring message replicas to all the neighbor nodes in the first communication. Then, these nodes deliver message directly which decreases the amount of replicas, but the successful delivery ratio is obviously affected. In[16], the authors comprehensively consider the tradeoff of resource utilization and successful delivery ratio. It provides message replicas to the successive transfer nodes with the decreasing probability until the message is delivered to destination node at last.

The most popular message delivery strategy is routing algorithm based on the historical information of node encounter probability [8]. This algorithm adopts custody transfer protocol and node carries message until it encounters the node which has larger probability to meet destination node. This is just the common measure which malicious node uses to attack in DTN. It forges its encounter probability with destination node to destroy usual transfer of message in DTN. Thus, the successful delivery ratio of message is reduced.

To assign different functions for nodes, they are classified as regular node and ferry node. In [17], regular node use random movement and ferry node move in a constant path to assist message delivery of the regular node. This resolves many issues in the traditional DTN network. But the path selection of ferry node is still a hard problem to researchers. This motivates the idea of social network [18] applications in DTN. DTN network is divided into multiple regions. The routing in a region and between regions is different.

For the congestion control, the most common method in message process is to delete new arrival message or previous old message stored in the node [9]. In [19], the authors add the probability management for the operation of message deleting that adopts the predefined constant threshold to control the new arrival message's deleting ratio. In [20], the authors introduce the migration algorithm that means when congestion happens, and then the message is transferred to the nearby nodes. Migration will result in the increase of message transfer overhead, the decrease of message successful delivery ratio and increase of message delivery latency.

In the aspect of message sending speed adjustment, the authors [21] define threshold to implement Additive Increase Multiplicative Decrease (AIMD) which is first proposed in [22] to adjust message sending rate dynamically. The constant threshold sometimes can't reflect the network current status which might cause the inaccuracy of control. The authors in [23] use ACK as the sign to adjust the message sending speed. When node derives the feedback of message loss, it directly rollbacks the sending speed to that the message was successful delivered recently.

The above two aspects both can't control congestion from the overall situation which needs to build the global feedback control system [24]. Due to the latency as the specific attribute in DTN, control effect of ACK always has the lag phenomenon and congestion identification mistake. Meanwhile, it might cause the severe jitter of message sending speed which leads to the instability of DTN data transfer speed. If the Nyquist Criterion [25] is used in the feedback control system , the instability of message transfer speed in system is mostly resolved. Moreover, some other issues can be considered, including the localization [26,27], human mobilities [28].

In conclusion, the above congestion control mechanisms assume all the nodes are regular. In the process of message delivery, the forge of node's attribute is not considered. Meanwhile, when congestion happens, passive method is adopted to control congestion. If there is active attack from malicious node in the network, limited storage resource would be consumed. This passive control method always can't reach the expected effect. This demands the algorithm which can actively control congestion and guarantee the message successful delivery ratio has the capacity to do active defense.

3   NESD Congestion Control Routing Algorithm

3.1   Problem Description

Node in DTN network is distributed discretely and adopts random routing. Random routing results in randomness of node's encounter to a large extent which makes the message successful delivery ratio unpredictable. The previous solutions usually select transfer node based on historical encounter record to improve the message successful delivery ratio. But the network security is not considered which has no active defense capacity to the active attack of malicious node. Once history record based on encounter probability is leveraged by malicious node, the consumption attack is implemented to the memory resource of network node which causes network congestion, and the network message successful delivery ratio is lessened as well.

3.2 Algorithm Idea

In most cases, the resource is limit which inevitably leads to competition of individuals for public resources in the same system. How to balance the interests of all parties and reach a win-win situation in some extent facilitates the emergence of game theory. This theory adopts formal language derivation to compute the optimal combination of the interests of all parties. Under this combination, each individual would not deviate from this balance for the interest temptation. Thus, it avoids the loss of one individual's interest or the non-optimal situation of overall individuals' interest caused by the individual's competition for public resources.

Memory resource is very rare in DTN node. If presence of malicious nodes is considered, active defense measures must be taken to constrain its active consumption attack for the resource of the node in DTN. Meanwhile, regular occupation demand for memory resource should be guaranteed for the message delivery of regular node. If malicious node attack and regular node demand can't be distinguished, we can adopt the game theory for trade-off. Memory resource of each node should be allocated appropriately. The memory occupation during the regular delivery of regular node message is guaranteed. Meanwhile, malicious occupation of malicious node is avoided.

3.3 Algorithm Implementation

The memory of each node in DTN is mostly occupied by two types of messages: existing messages in this node and messages which are about to be transferred to this node. Malicious node always unlimitedly demands other nodes to transfer its brought messages. The memory of attacked nodes is wholly occupied. The memory of attacked party is used out which results in congestion. The method to deal with congestion always deletes the oldest messages. It makes attacked node drop all existing messages in memory.

We adopt Nash equilibrium [14] in gaming theory to tradeoff the share of node memory between existing messages in this node and messages which are about to be transferred to this node. In conditions that malicious node and regular node are not differentiated, active defense is adopted to guarantee the message delivery of regular node. Meanwhile, the attack from malicious node is weakened in some extent and congestion is avoided.

The key of NESD is to leverage Nash equilibrium. The optimal combination of node memory occupancy for existing messages in this node and messages which are about to be transferred to this node is computed. The memory of node is fully shared by two kinds of messages, but not excessively occupied by one party.

The message transfer scenario under malicious node attack is applied to gaming theory. To make use of Nash equilibrium, we assume:

Attendee: existing messages in this node and messages which are about to be transferred to this node.

Action: node memory occupancy of existing messages in this node and messages which are about to be transferred to this node.

Preference:existing messages in this node and messages which are about to be transferred to this node all hope to obtain more opportunities to be transferred unitl reaching the destination node.

Table 1. Symbols Used in Theorems

Symbol	Description
L_x	Preference of X type message
p_x	Memory size occupied by type X message
1	Messages which are about to be transferred to this node
2	Existing messages in this node
b	Size of node memory
c	Node congestion degree
S_x	Spare memory size allocated in proportion to type X message
T_x	Node memory ratio already occupied by type X message
R	Spare memory size of node
D_x	Drop-off message amount of type X caused by congestion

Theorem 1. When L_1 and L_2 both reach maximum, based on the characteristic of Nash equilibrium [14], p_1 and p_2 can reach the same reasonable value.

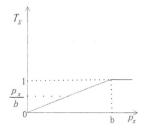

Fig. 1. T_x

Proof.

$$L_x = S_x + p_x - D_x \tag{1}$$

$$S_x = T_x \times R \tag{2}$$

$$T_x = \begin{cases} \frac{p_x}{b} & , & p_x \le b \\ 1 & , & p_x > b \end{cases} \tag{3}$$

Figure 1 is derived from formal (3)

$$R = \begin{cases} b - p_1 - p_2 & , & p_1 + p_2 \le b \\ 0 & , & p_1 + p_2 > b \end{cases} \tag{4}$$

Figure 2 is derived from formal (4)

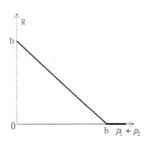

Fig. 2. R

$$D_x = cp_x(0 \le c \le 1) \tag{5}$$

The setting of D_x represents the idea that more occupancy means more responsibility. More memory consumption by certain kind of message results in larger packet drop-off probability for the messages when congestion happens.

According to formal (1) to (5):

$$L_1 = \begin{cases} \frac{p_1}{b} \times (b - p_1 - p_2) + p_1 - cp_1 & , & p_1 + p_2 \le b \\ p_1 - cp_1 & , & p_1 + p_2 > b \end{cases} \tag{6}$$

$$L_2 = \begin{cases} \frac{p_2}{b} \times (b - p_1 - p_2) + p_2 - cp_2 & , & p_1 + p_2 \le b \\ p_2 - cp_2 & , & p_1 + p_2 > b \end{cases} \tag{7}$$

Figure 3 is derived from formal (6)

When $p_1 + p_2 \le b$ and $p_2 = 0$, L_1 achieves maximum under formula (8)

$$p_1 = b - \frac{bc}{2} \tag{8}$$

When $p_1 + p_2 \le b$ and $p_2 > 0$, L_1 achieves maximum under formula (9)

$$p_1 = b - \frac{p_2}{2} - \frac{bc}{2} \tag{9}$$

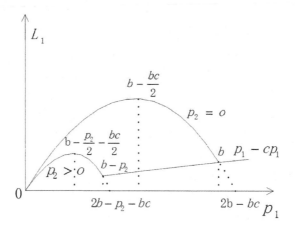

Fig. 3. Preference of L_1

When $p_1 + p_2 \leq b$ and $p_1 = 0$, L_2 achieves maximum under formula (10)

$$p_2 = b - \frac{bc}{2} \tag{10}$$

When $p_1 + p_2 \leq b$ and $p_1 > 0$, L_2 achieves maximum under formula (11)

$$p_2 = b - \frac{p_1}{2} - \frac{bc}{2} \tag{11}$$

According to (9), we argue that when y-axis L_1 adopts the maximum value, x-axis depends on p_2

$$f_1(p_2) = \begin{cases} b - \frac{p_2}{2} - \frac{bc}{2} & , & p_2 \leq b \\ 0 & , & p_2 > b \end{cases} \tag{12}$$

According to (11), we argue that when y-axis L_2 adopts the maximum value, x-axis depends on p_1

$$f_2(p_1) = \begin{cases} b - \frac{p_1}{2} - \frac{bc}{2} & , & p_1 \leq b \\ 0 & , & p_1 > b \end{cases} \tag{13}$$

Based on Nash equilibrium, Figure 4 is derived from formal (12) and formal (13).When L_1 and L_2 adopt maximum at the same time, we have.

$$p_1^* = p_2^* = \frac{2}{3}b - \frac{bc}{3} \tag{14}$$

According to the Theorem 1 and verification, We configure the concrete threshold for the node memory occupancy by two kinds of messages as $p_1^* = p_2^*$. This mechanism realizes the full share of node memory resource between existing messages in this node and messages which are about to be transferred to this

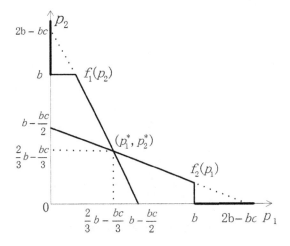

Fig. 4. Nash Equilibrium

node. It also makes the resource not overused by one party. This effectively defenses the attack of memory occupancy from malicious node. The active control to congestion caused by malicious node memory occupancy increases the system global message successful delivery ratio.

4   Evaluation

We leverage DTN-dedicated simulator THE ONE to do the simulation. NESD congestion control routing algorithm and encounter history based regular routing algorithm is compared in this paper. Meanwhile, network congestion ratio, message successful delivery ratio and the cost of message successful delivery are analyzed under the situation that memory is attacked through active consumption by a small quantity of malicious nodes.

The parameters in routing algorithm are set as table 2.

Table 2. Simulation parameters

Parameter	Value
Scenario length and width	10000m
Hotspot area length and width	4000m
Node number	20
Node memory	3 MB
Node speed	10 m/s
Communication radius	50m
Message generation rate	20 seconds per message
Message size	500KB
Message transfer speed	5000KB/s

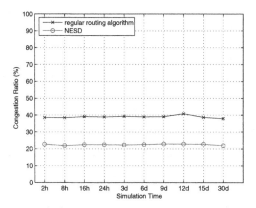

Fig. 5. Congestion ratio

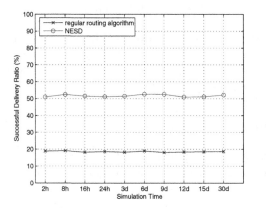

Fig. 6. Successful delivery ratio

In order to prove the advantages of this algorithm in a limited testing time, we set more nodes, smaller nodes memory, faster node speed, more frequent message generation rate and larger message transfer speed. Thus, congestion control performance can be exhibited in short experiment time. And whether message is successfully delivered also can be exhibit promptly. It's beneficial to our evaluation to the algorithm performance.

By the comparison of congestion ratio shown in Figure 5, we found that NESD congestion control routing algorithm significantly improves DTN network congestion compared to regular routing algorithm based on historical encounter information. It sets the concrete threshold for node memory occupancy to limit the node memory consumption from malicious node. The exhaustion of the encounter node memory in the attack of malicious node compels the attacked node to accept all the messages for transfer from malicious node. Since we set the same memory size for each node, this inevitably causes attacked node lose

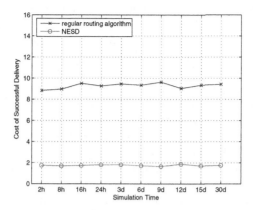

Fig. 7. Cost of successful delivery

its' all messages for accepting all the messages from malicious node which results in congestion. The algorithm we design avoids the emergence of this problem and reduces the network congestion ratio.

By the comparison of successful delivery ratio shown in Figure 6, we found that NESD congestion control routing algorithm significantly increases message successful delivery ratio. Node's message delivery in DTN mainly depends on the assistance of message transfer operation. More than one hop is needed to complete the successful delivery. But in the network with memory consumption attack from malicious node, messages are always forcefully deleted before arrival at the destination node due to the memory exhaustion by malicious node's attack. This inevitably lessens the message successful delivery ratio. The algorithm we design limits the attack from malicious node and guarantees the necessary transfer operation of regular node for message delivery and the successful delivery ratio is also insured.

By the comparison of the cost for message successful delivery in Figure 7, NESD congestion control routing algorithm significantly lessens the cost of message successful delivery. In this experiment, we define the cost of message successful delivery as the overall number of messages transferred to the un-destination node divided by the overall number of messages transferred to the destination node. Obviously, congestion and packet loss caused by malicious node attack increases the overall delivery number to un-destination node and lessens overall delivery number to destination node which increases the cost of message successful delivery. The constraint operation to the malicious node attack inevitably reduces the cost of message successful delivery.

5   Conclusion

Based on the conclusion of the main research work for DTN congestion control routing, this paper proposes NESD congestion control routing algorithm under the premise that there is memory consumption attack from malicious node. These also have significant application values in the field of homeland defense.This algorithm leverages Nash equilibrium in game theory by setting concrete threshold to tradeoff the node memory occupancy between existing messages in this node and messages which are about to be transferred to this node. The transfer operation for successful message delivery of regular node is guaranteed. Meanwhile, illegal occupancy of node memory from malicious node is constrained effectively. This algorithm improves the congestion ratio and enhances message successful delivery ratio. This paper in detail proves existing messages in this node and messages which are about to be transferred to this node both can be transferred continually with high probability until coming into contact with the destination node. At the same time, the concrete threshold for the share of node memory by two-class messages is computed for achieving this target. And the high performance of this algorithm is proved by experiment.

We will continue the research on active defense mechanism to all kinds of attacks from malicious node. Message successful delivery ratio should be guaranteed. The mechanism also should perfect congestion control, optimize the defense result and effectively decrease the delivery latency of messages. In next step, we will discuss the effect of other attack behavior to DTN from malicious node and propose the corresponding defense measurement. The message successful delivery ratio should be guaranteed and congestion should be controlled effectively.

Acknowledgement. The work described in this paper is partially supported by the grants of the National Basic Research Program of China (973 project) under Grant No.2009CB320503, 2012CB315906; the National 863 Development Plan of China under Grant No. 2009AA01A334, 2009AA01A346, 2009AA01Z423; and the project of National Science Foundation of China under grant No. 61070199, 61003301, 60903223, 60903224, 61103189, 61103194, 61103182; and supported by Program for Changjiang Scholars and Innovative Research Team in University of the Ministry of Education("Network Technology",NUDT), the Innovative Research Team in University of Hunan Province("Network Technology",NUDT), and the Innovative Research Team of Hunan Provincial natural science Foundation(11JJ7003).

References

1. DTNRG: Delay-tolerant networking research group, http://www.dtnrg.org
2. Pentland, A.S., Fletcher, R., Hasson, A.: DakNet: Rethinking Connectivity in Developing Nations. Computer 37, 78–83 (2004)
3. Burgess, J., Gallagher, B., Jensen, D., Levine, B.N.: Maxprop: Routing for Vehicle-Based Disruption-tolerant Networks. In: Proceedings of INFOCOM, Barcelona, Spain, pp. 1–11 (2006)
4. Burleigh, S., Hooke, A., Torgerson, L., Fall, K., Cerf, V., Durst, B., Scott, K.: Delay-tolerant Networking: an Approach to Interplanetary Internet. IEEE Communications Magazine 41(6), 128–136 (2003)
5. Scott, K., Burleigh, S.: Bundle Protocol Specification. Internet RFC 5050 (2007)

6. Fall, K., Hong, W., Madden, S.: Custody Transfer for Reliable Delivery in Delay Tolerant Networks. Technical Report, IRB-TR-03-030, Intel Research at Berkeley (2003)
7. Vahdat, A., Becker, D.: Epidemic routing for partially connected ad hoc networks. Technical Report, CS-2000-06, Duke University (2000)
8. Lindgren, A., Doria, A., Schelén, O.: Probabilistic routing in intermittently connected networks. SIGMOBILE Mobile Computing Communications Review 7(3), 19–20 (2003)
9. Jain, R., Ramakrishnan, K.K.: Congestion Avoidance in Computer Networks with a Connectionless Network Layer: Concepts, Goals, and Methodology. In: Proc. IEEE Comp. Networking Symp., Washington, D.C., pp. 134–143 (1988)
10. Seligman, M., Fall, K., Mundur, P.: Storage routing for DTN congestion control. Wireless Communications and Mobile Computing, 1183–1196 (2007)
11. Hollot, C.V., Misra, V., Towsley, D., Gong, W.B.: A Control Theoretic Analysis of RED. In: IEEE INFOCOM (2001)
12. Feng, L., Jie, W., Avinash, S.: Thwarting Blackhole Attacks in Distruption-Tolerant Networks using Encounter Tickets. In: IEEE INFOCOM (2009)
13. Vivek, N., Yi, Y., Sencun, Z.: Resource-Misuse Attack Detection in Delay-Tolerant Networks. In: 2011 IEEE 30th International Performance Computing and Communications Conference, IPCCC (2011)
14. Martin, J.O.: An Introduction to Game Theory. Oxford University Press (2004)
15. Spyropoulos, T., Psounis, K., Raghavendra, C.S.: Spray and Wait: An Efficient Routing Scheme for Intermittently Connected Mobile Networks. In: Proceedings of the 2005 ACM SIGCOMM Workshop on Delay-tolerant Networking (WDTN 2005), pp. 252–259. ACM, New York (2005)
16. Spyropoulos, T., Psounis, K., Raghavendra, C.S.: Efficient routing in intermittently connected mobile networks: the multiple-copy case. IEEE/ACM Trans. on Network 16(1), 77–90 (2008)
17. Zhao, W., Ammar, M., Zegura, E.: A message ferrying approach for data delivery in sparse mobile ad hoc networks. In: Proc. of the ACM Mobihoc, pp. 187–198 (2004)
18. Costa, P., Mascolo, C., Musolesi, M., Picco, G.P.: Socially-Aware routing for publish-subscribe in delay-tolerant mobile ad hoc networks. IEEE Journal of Selected Areas in Communication 26(5), 748–760 (2008)
19. Floyd, S., Jacobson, V.: Random Early Detection Gateways for Congestion Avoidance. IEEE/ACM Transactions on Networking (1993)
20. Seligman, M., Fall, K., Mundur, P.: Alternative Custodians for Congestion Control in Delay Tolerant Networks. In: SIGCOMM Workshops, Pisa, Italy (2006)
21. Nishiyama, H., Ansari, N., Kato, N.: Wireless Loss-tolerant Congestion Control Protocol Based on Dynamic Aimd Theory. IEEE Wireless Communications, 1536–1284 (2010)
22. Chiu, D.M., Jain, R.: Analysis of the Increase and Decrease Algorithms for Congestion Avoidance in Computer Networks. Comput. Networks ISDN Sys. 17, 1–14 (1989)
23. Godfrey, P.B., Schapira, M., Zohar, A., Shenker, S.: Incentive Compatibility and Dynamics of Congestion Control. In: SIGMETRICS, New York, USA (2010)
24. Firoiu, V., Borden, M.: A Study of Active Queue Management for Congestion Control. In: IEEE INFOCOM (2000)
25. Paganini, F., Wang, Z.K., Doyle, J.C., Low, S.H.: Congestion Control for High Performance, Stability, and Fairness in General Networks. IEEE/ACM Transactions on Networking 13, 43–56 (2005)

26. Andersson, K.: Interworking Techniques and Architectures for Heterogeneous Wireless Networks. Journal of Internet Services and Information Security 2, 22–48 (2012)
27. Charles, J.Z., Turgay, K.: A Comparative Review of Connectivity-Based Wireless Sensor Localization Techniques. Journal of Internet Services and Information Security 2, 59–72 (2012)
28. Sun, J., Wang, Y., Si, H., et al.: Aggregate Human Mobility Modeling Using Principal Component Analysis. Journal of Wireless Mobile Networks, Ubiquitous Computing, and Dependable Applications 1, 83–95 (2010)

Managing Urban Waste Collection through Timed Automata Based Fuzzy Cognitive Maps

Giovanni Acampora[1], Vincenzo Loia[2], and Autilia Vitiello[2]

[1] School of Industrial Engineering, Information Systems,
Eindhoven University of Technology,
P.O. Box 513, 5600 MB, Eindhoven, The Netherlands
g.acampora@tue.nl
[2] Department of Computer Science,
University of Salerno,
Fisciano, Salerno, 84084, Italy
{loia,avitiello}@unisa.it

Abstract. In the last years, the increasing urbanization has constrained to face the dramatic growth of the urban waste production and the consequent socio-economical and environmental impact. The relevance of finding an optimal waste management further increases when it involves hazardous materials, since they represent a vulnerable infrastructure sector for homeland defense. Although there is a general agreement on the best strategies for solving urban garbage problem, an opportune waste management seems far due to its intrinsic complexity arising from necessity of dealing with several factors which are often in conflict each other. Over the years, several computerized waste management systems, including deterministic models and fuzzy approaches, have been developed aimed at addressing this complex problem. However, all these approaches do not consider relevant factors which could affect decision policies related to waste treatment, i.e., the rapid evolutions and modifications occurring in a complex scenario such as the urban environment. In order to overcome this drawback, this paper presents an innovative waste management simulation system based on a new timed cognitive inference engine, named Timed Automata based Fuzzy Cognitive Map (TAFCM). A TAFCM is able to simulate the dynamic features of a waste management environment thanks to its temporal benefits due to its ability of dealing with the concept of time in a direct way. As shown in the experimental section, TAFCMs represent a suitable and efficient methodology to manage the waste production problem.

Keywords: Urban Waste Management System, Computational Intelligence, Cognitive Modeling, Fuzzy Cognitive Maps, Timed Automata, Timed Automata based Fuzzy Cognitive Maps.

1 Introduction

In last years, urbanization has been one of the most strong and clear changes affecting all the world. The rapid and constant growth of urban population has led

G. Quirchmayr et al. (Eds.): CD-ARES 2012, LNCS 7465, pp. 501–515, 2012.

to a dramatic increase in urban waste production, with a crucial socio-economic and environmental impact [1]. The importance of finding an optimal waste management further increases when it involves hazardous garbage including any radioactive material manufactured, used, transported, or stored by industrial, medical, or commercial processes. Indeed, hazardous waste represents an environmental infrastructure sector vulnerable to attacks and, for this reason, its treatment goes into homeland defense missions. In the last years, legislation and regulations have been instituted in order to guide the management of waste, hazardous and not, and improve waste policies. Nowadays, there is a general agreement on the best strategies for sustainable management of urban waste which consists in minimising waste production and optimizing waste recovery. Indeed, it is proved that the recovery of the waste is an essential way to reduce the natural resource depletion and create alternative energy sources. Moreover, it is necessary to decrease the use of landfill sites which lead to damage human mental and physical health and represents a more suffered problem in big cities where there is no appropriate land filling zones.

However, an appropriate waste management seems far from being attained [1], due, above all, to the intrinsic complexity of the problem. Indeed, an optimal urban waste management involves various relative factors, which are often in conflict. The most important factors are mainly economic (e.g., system cost and system benefit), environmental (air emission, water pollution) and technological (the maturity of the technology). This complexity has led to the necessity of developing integrated, computerized systems for obtaining more generalized, optimal solutions for the management of urban waste collection [2]. In last years, there have been many solutions developed for the implementation of a waste management system which would monitor and manipulate the generated waste. The theoretical approaches in literature refer to issues concerning the conflict between urban residents and the municipality for the selection of sites for waste treatment, transshipment stations and disposal, or the issue of waste collection and transport as well as its impact to human health due to noise, traffic, etc [2]. Several deterministic models, including Linear Programming (LP) [3][4][5], have been exploited for optimizing sitting and routing aspects of waste collection networks. However, uncertainty often plays a prominent role in dealing waste management problems. Possible sources of uncertainty are the random nature of waste production and the vagueness in planning objectives and constraints. For this reason, fuzzy mathematical programming approaches [6][7][8] have been introduced in the waste collection management.

However, all these approaches do not consider relevant factors which could affect decision policies related to waste treatment, i.e., the rapid evolutions and modifications occurring in a complex scenario such as the urban environment. The aim of this paper is to present a waste management simulation system capable of supporting a municipal government in their dynamic decisions related to waste treatment and safe disposal. In detail, our proposal is aimed at simulating a waste management environment by using an extension of Fuzzy Cognitive Maps (FCMs), named *Timed Automata based Fuzzy Cognitive Maps (TAFCMs)*

[9]. FCMs can be viewed as inference networks that use cyclic, directed graphs to represent the fuzzy causal relationships among fuzzy concepts. FCMs' inference engine is based on an easy, iterative and numeric process and, consequently, FCMs are able to represent knowledge and implement inference operators with greater flexibility as compared to many other available methods. Nevertheless, in spite of these benefits, conventional FCMs are not capable of dealing with the concept of time in a direct way. For this reason, a new timed cognitive inference engine, i.e., TAFCMs, has been introduced for improving FCMs' time representation of qualitative system dynamics. Thanks to this feature, TAFCMs represent a promising method for implementing a waste management simulation system where decisions to be made are usually dependent on the temporal events. The rest of the paper is devoted to present this new model and show how it is efficiently able to simulate a dynamic waste management environment.

2   Timed Automata Based Fuzzy Cognitive Maps: Basic Concepts

This section discusses about the methodology, i.e., the Timed Automata based Fuzzy Cognitive Maps (TAFCMs), exploited in this work to simulate a dynamic waste management environment. TAFCMs are new inference engines able to model dynamic changes in cognitive representation of a system and, consequently, perform a more realistic and coherent temporal computation. They achieve this aim by exploiting a synergic approach which combines traditional Fuzzy Cognitive Maps (FCMs) and *Timed Automata* theory [10]. Indeed, a TAFCM can be informally defined as a pair of a timed automaton, used to describe the dynamic evolution of a system, and a FCM, modeling the cognitive behaviour of the system during the first phase of its existence. Therefore, for a complete understanding, it is necessary to know TAFCMs' basic components which, for this reason, will be briefly discussed below before describing TAFCMs in a more detailed way.

2.1   Basic Components of TAFCMs: Fuzzy Cognitive Maps and Timed Automata

FCMs are directed graphs with feedback capable of modeling systems through of collection of concepts and causal relations among them. In detail, in the graph, nodes represent concepts, whereas, edges reflect the causal influences among them. The value of a node, contained in the range $[0, 1]$, is the degree to which the concept is active in the system at a particular time, whereas, the value of the weights, positioned on the edges and contained in the interval $[-1, 1]$, represents the amount of influence existing between two concepts incident on an edge. In particular, the casual relationship between two concepts C_i and C_j can be: *positive* which means that an increase in the value of concept C_i leads to the increase of the value of concept C_j, whereas a decrease in the value of concept C_i leads to the decrease of the value of concept C_j; or *negative* which means that an increase in the value of concept C_i leads to the decrease of the value of concept C_j and vice versa. A graphical representation of a FCM is presented in Fig. 1. Associated with the graphical representation there is a mathematical model that consists of a $1 \times n$ state vector A which includes the values of the n concepts and an $n \times n$ weight matrix W which gathers the weights W_{ij} of the interconnections between the n concepts of the FCM. In this model, the value A_i for each concept C_i is computed by the following rule:

$$A_i = f(\sum_{\substack{j=1 \\ j \neq i}}^{n} A_j W_{ij} + A_i^{old}), \tag{1}$$

where A_i is the activation level of concept at iteration $t+1$, A_j is the activation level of the concept C_j at iteration t, A_i^{old} is the activation level of concept C_i at iteration t (it is clear that the variable t just represents the iteration number between two successive FCM matrix computation), and W_{ji} is the weight of the interconnection between C_j and C_i, and f is a threshold function, i.e, a function used to reduce unbounded inputs to a strict range (typically, a sigmoidal function). FCMs have been used in different research [11] and application fields for decision analysis [12] and for distributed cooperative agents [13]. However, in spite of their wide applicability, FCMs could be not flexible enough to deal with dynamic systems that change their configurations over time, like social and economical environments and the same urban waste management influenced by government decisions occurring in different and unpredictable moments. Hence, the introduction of TAFCMs capable of enhancing the temporal expressive power of FCMs through the exploitation of a timed automaton.

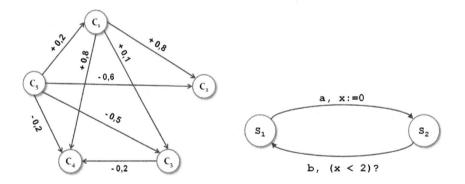

Fig. 1. An example of a simple FCM   **Fig. 2.** A Timed Automaton

Timed automata are standard finite-state non-deterministic automata extended with a finite collection of real-valued clocks providing a straightforward way to represent time related events. The transitions of a timed automaton are labeled with a *guard* (a condition on clocks), an *action* or *symbol* on alphabet Σ, and a *clock reset* (a subset of clocks to be reset). Timed automata start computations with all clocks set to zero and clocks increase simultaneously and uniformly with time while the automaton state is located in a given node. Different from standard non-deterministic machine, transitions in timed automata can be taken if the clocks fulfill the related guards. By taking transition, all clocks belonging to the clock reset collection will be set to zero, whereas the remaining keep their values [14]. The transitions occur instantaneously. A simple example [10] of a timed automaton is reported in Fig. 2. The start state of the automaton is S_1. There is a single clock, named x. The annotation $x := 0$ on an edge corresponds to the action of resetting the clock x when the edge is traversed. Instead, the annotation $(x < 2)$? represents a clock constraint which means that the edge can be traversed only if the value of the clock x is less than 2. In general, the behavior of the automaton is as follows. The automaton starts in the state S_1 and moves to state S_2 reading the symbol input a. The clock x gets set to 0 along with this transition. While in state S_2, the value of the clock x shows the time elapsed since the occurrence of the last symbol a. The transition from the state S_1 to state S_2 is enabled only if the value of the clock x is less than 2. The whole cycle repeats when the automaton moves back to state S_1.

The set of behaviors expressed by a system modeled by means of a timed automaton is defined by a *timed language*, i.e., a collection of *timed words*. A timed word is a pair (σ, τ), where $\sigma = \sigma_1 \sigma_2 \ldots$ is an infinite word and $\tau = \tau_1 \tau_2 \cdots$ is an infinite sequence of time values $\tau_i \in \mathbb{R}$ with $\tau_i > 0$, satisfying constraints of *monotonicity* and *progress* (see [10]). In detail, if a timed word $w = (\sigma, \tau)$, it presents the symbol σ_i at time τ_i. Therefore, if σ_i is an event occurrence then the corresponding component τ_i is interpreted as the time of occurrence of σ_i. As for the timed automaton presented in Fig. 2, the timed language is represented by all words in which a and b alternate and the delay between a and the following b is always less than 2. Therefore, a possible word is $w = (\sigma, \tau)$, where $\sigma = abab$ and $\tau = 0.0, 1.8, 2.2, 3.7$. Given the word $w = (a, 0.0) \rightarrow (b, 1.8) \rightarrow (a, 2.2) \rightarrow (b, 3.7)$, the automaton starts in the state S_1 and moves to state S_2 reading the symbol input a at time 0.0. The clock x gets set to 0 along with this transition. While in state S_2, the value of the clock x increases. When the symbol b is read at time 1.8, the automaton moves from the state S_2 to state S_1 since the clock x has the value 1.8 which satisfies the guard present on the edge. The automaton moves again to the state S_2 when the second symbol a is read at time 2.2. Finally, the automaton moves to state S_1, when the final symbol b is read at time 3.7. Indeed, at time 3.7, the x value is 1.5, and then, the clock satisfies again the guard.

Formally, this timed behavior is captured by introducing the *run* concept. Intuitively, a run is a collection of sequential discrete transitions, where each transition denotes an event releasing a task and the guard on the transition (i.e. a temporal constraint) specifies all the possible arriving times of the event. Therefore, by considering the automaton in Fig. 2, the run which corresponds to word $w = (a, 0.0) \rightarrow (b, 1.8) \rightarrow (a, 2.2) \rightarrow (b, 3.7)$ is as follows:

$$r : \langle S_1, [0] \rangle \xrightarrow[0]{a} \langle S_2, [0] \rangle \xrightarrow[1.8]{b} \langle S_1, [1.8] \rangle \xrightarrow[2.2]{a} \langle S_2, [0] \rangle \xrightarrow[3.7]{b} \langle S_1, [1.5] \rangle.$$

See [10] for more details about the run concept, and, in general, timed automata.

2.2 TAFCMs: Merging of Timed Automata and Fuzzy Cognitive Maps

TAFCMs are new timed cognitive inference engines capable of modeling dynamic complex systems. They enhance the modeling power of FCMs by adding three new timing mechanisms, named *Top-time* (T-Time), *cognitive era* and *cognitive configuration*. In detail, the exploitation of these new cognitive concepts enables FCMs to represent a generic system as a biological entity that lives its existence by crossing a sequence of time periods (cognitive eras), each one representing the longest interval time in which the system does not change its cognitive configuration, i.e., its concepts and causal relationships. In order to implement this new mechanism, TAFCMs exploit a timed automaton whose possible behaviors define all the potential sequences of cognitive eras (and the related cognitive configurations) that the system could cover during its life-cycle. More in detail, TAFCMs improve FCMs by associating each state in a timed automaton with a cognitive configuration which describes the behavior of a system in a time interval. Therefore, informally (see [9] for a mathematical definition), a TAFCM has two components: a timed automaton T_M that describes the dynamic evolution of a system and a FCM F^0 modeling the cognitive behavior of the system during first phase of its existence. Once that the automaton computation starts over a given timed word, the state transitions will adaptively modify the initial FCM in order to model time-dependency of the system. In order to transform the structure of a FCM representing a cognitive configuration, the following collection of operators has been introduced:

- To add concepts ($\oplus$);
- To add causal relationships ($\boxplus$);
- To remove concepts ($\ominus$);
- To remove causal relationships ($\boxminus$);
- To magnify/reduce the strength of a causal relationships ($\dotplus$ for an additive modification and $\boxdot$ for a multiplicative modification);
- To magnify/reduce the level of system concept († for an additive modification and ‡ for a multiplicative modification).

The mapping between the states of timed automaton T_M and the collection of cognitive configurations computable starting from F^0 by applying different sequence of operators is called *cognitive evolution*, whereas, the progression of the cognitive eras is performed by using the so called *cognitive run*, i.e., a cognitive extension of the initial idea of the run of a timed automata. As aforesaid, intuitively, a run is a collection of sequential discrete transitions, where each transition denotes an event releasing a task and the guard on the transition (i.e.

a temporal constraint) specifies all the possible arriving times of the event. In the context of the cognitive representation, the ith discrete transition can be used to move a system among cognitive eras and release a task changing the cognitive configuration of the system, i.e., transforming the FCM that represents the cognitive configuration during i^{th} cognitive era into a new one modeling the system during $(i+1)^{th}$ cognitive era. Both the cognitive evolution and the cognitive run are potentially based on the infinite concept in the system. In fact, the cognitive evolution can exploit an infinite application of cognitive operators to compute the mappings between the automaton states and the FCMs representing cognitive configurations, whereas, the cognitive run uses a timed word, defined as a infinite sequence of ordered pairs, to describe the cognitive/dynamic behavior of the system. Consequently, in order to simulate the behavior of a TAFCM during the first n cognitive eras, the annotation of nth-order cognitive evolution and n^{th}-cognitive run has been introduced.

See [9] for a formal definition of cognitive evolution, cognitive run and T-Time, whereas, our discussion about TAFCMs ends with an example taken by [9]. In this sample, a timed cognitive system describing the behavior of an ecosystem formed by three initial elements, *predators* (P_2), *preys* (P_1) and *grass for preys* (G)) is given. Figs. 3 and 4 show, respectively, the initial cognitive configuration F^0 of proposed system and the modified timed automaton T_M that defines the dynamic behavior. In order to show how a TAFCM allows to dynamically modify the cognitive concepts of the system, let us consider, for instance, the transition from the state s_0 to s_2. When the automaton traverses this transition, the new concept *hunter (H)* is added to system to modify the cognitive concepts, G, P_1 and P_2 in a novel and unpredicted way. This transformation is denoted by the operator $\oplus$ present on the transition. Moreover, by considering the timed word $w = (\sigma, \tau) = (a, 0.2) \to (b, 0.4)$, we can compute the 3th-order cognitive run r_c^3 (with the clock period $k = 0.1$) as follows:

$$r_c^3 : \langle s^0, [0] \rangle \xrightarrow[0.2]{a, \oplus} \langle s^1, [0.2] \rangle \xrightarrow[0.4]{b, \boxplus} \langle s^2, [0.4] \rangle, \tag{2}$$

which defines three cognitive eras, respectively starting at time 0, 0.2 and 0.4. Fig. 5 shows the three corresponding cognitive configurations.

3   A TAFCM for Urban Waste Management

In this section, we show how a TAFCM can be exploited to simulate and evaluate the behavior of a dynamic waste management system. In general, it is the municipality's responsibility to manage waste including its collection, treatment, and safe disposal. During the term of a municipal government, in its effort to improve the waste management, it may make several decisions in order to modify its political plan. Such decisions are very complex due to great number of the involved factors, often in conflict each other, and usually dependent on the time in which they are taken. In particular, this last feature denotes a dynamic nature of urban waste management problem. Therefore, thanks to its ability

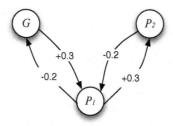

Fig. 3. The initial cognitive configuration of ecosystem sample

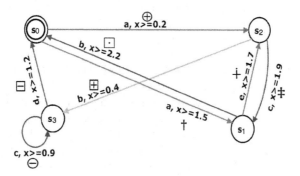

Fig. 4. The cognitive timed automaton that describes the dynamic behavior of the ecosystem sample

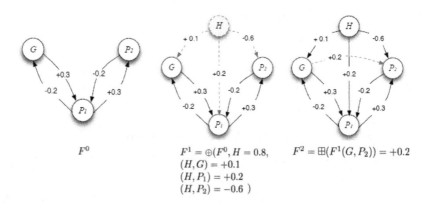

Fig. 5. Three cognitive configurations of ecosystem sample. The graph (a) shows the first cognitive configuration F^0; the graph (b) shows the cognitive configuration F^1 related to the state s_2, obtained by applying the $\oplus$ operator over the FCM F^0; the graph (c) shows the cognitive configuration F^2 related to the state s_3, obtained by applying the $\boxplus$ operator over the FCM F^1.

to model systems evolving over time, a TAFCM could represent a promising methodology for efficiently designing an urban waste management simulation system. Our idea is to use a TAFCM for comparing different political strategies so to allow municipality to make the most opportune decisions at beginning of its government mandate.

As aforesaid, factors involved in the urban waste management are a lot, but above all, characterized by different nature: economical, social and environmental. In particular, in this work, we consider the following factors:

- *population*: this factor refers to number of residents in the city at issue. It is very important to estimate the amount of produced waste;
- *migration into city*: this factor refers to degree of migration which affects the city. It is relevant over years in order to estimate the increasing of the population;
- *modernization*: this factor includes all municipality activities aimed at improving life quality of people. For instance, they involve infrastructure and transportation improvements;
- *waste per area*: this factor refers to average amount of waste per area produced by population. It represents a critical value which should be maintained under control and minimized;
- *sanitation facilities*: this factor includes all activities of municipality and not only devoted to improve health quality of people.
- *disease percentage*: this factor refers to number of deseases per 1000 residents. It is a critical value which should be monitored because its increasing may lead to an sanitation alarm;
- *bacteria per area*: this factor refers to average amount of bacteria per area. It represents a critical value which, obviously, should be minimized in order to improve life quality of people;
- *economical funds*: they represent the money reserved to urban waste management. Therefore, for instance, they can be used to build new incinerators, to look for location for new landfills, to promote educational plans or recycling programs, to pay workers responsible for collecting waste door to door or cleaning streets. These municipality's funds could be increased by periodical or one-off government payments.

Starting from all involved factors, there are several possible strategies which the municipality could follow. They belong to these four categories:

- *waste disposal*: it includes all disposal methods such as dumping, landfilling and incineration of waste;
- *waste recycling*: it refers to recycling of all materials that can be reprocessed either into the same material (closed loop) or a new product (open loop). Therefore, recycling is not only an alternative to disposal, but it allows also the reduction of the amount of virgin materials used for the manufacture of new products;
- *waste processing*: it includes all activities devoted to the treatment and recovery of materials or energy from waste through thermal, chemical, or biological procedures;

- *waste minimization*: it is aimed at decreasing the generation of waste by means of education and optimized production process rather than enhancing technology for handling waste. In detail, minimizing waste production is viewed as result of a maximization of the efficiency of available resources, and as a consequence, it may lead to decrease costs to treat waste to be disposed.

In order to simulate the application of different strategies, a TAFCM composed of the initial FCM F^0 (see Fig. 6) and the timed automaton T_M (see Fig. 7) is introduced. In particular, F^0 models the collection of concepts related to waste management, before possible strategies are applied. The mapping between the considered factors and the cognitive concepts is as follows: $c_1 \equiv$ population, $c_2 \equiv$ migration into city, $c_3 \equiv$ modernization, $c_4 \equiv$ waste per area, $c_5 \equiv$ sanitation facilities, $c_6 \equiv$ disease percentage, $c_7 \equiv$ bacteria per area, $c_8 \equiv$ economical funds. The weights characterizing the relations among concepts had been defined by an expert of domain. Instead, the timed automaton T_M allows to model municipality strategies by transforming F^0 at right opportunities. However, for sake of simplicity, the reported T_M models only two possible strategies belonging to the first presented category (see section 4). The timed automaton T_M considers only a clock named x. Each edge of T_M is labeled with a *symbol*, representing an occurred event, a *guard*, indicating the temporal constraint which x must satisfy to cross transition and a *sequence of transformation operators* which allows to opportunely modify the initial FCM. In particular, each operator takes in input concepts which are affected by the change and, according to the kind of operator, a real value representing the amount of modification. In this work, the temporal constraint for cognitive transitions is in the unit of Year, whereas, the simulated time duration is equal to a complete municipality mandate (5 years). However, in spite of the implemented TAFCM, the exploited methodology represents a general framework able to efficiently simulate also other, more expanded, waste management scenarios characterized by a greater number of factors, new strategies and a different temporal constraint.

4   Experimental Results

In this section, we demonstrate how a TAFCM can efficiently simulate a dynamic waste management system. Indeed, our experiment will show how a TAFCM can be used to support municipality's decisions by providing a temporal simulation of all involved factors. In particular, our experiment illustrates how the implemented TAFCM to succeed in supporting municipality's decisions by detecting the best strategy (between the considered strategies) to be followed in order to minimize the waste and bacteria per area with a good use of government funds reserved for urban waste management.

In detail, the experiment involves the evaluation of two strategies, named *program I* and *program II*. The scenario is the following one. Let us consider a city which is not equipped with technological tools for waste treatment, and hence, the municipality decides to build one of them. Besides, the municipality plans

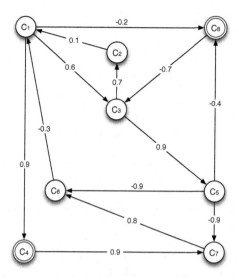

Fig. 6. The cognitive map F^0

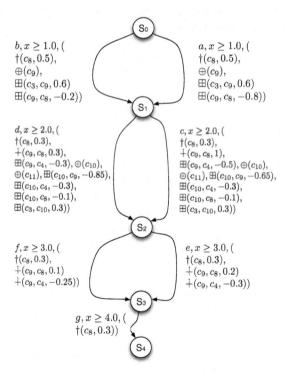

Fig. 7. The cognitive timed automaton T_M

to promote some educational plans in order to teacher people how to minimize the production of waste. The municipality annually receives a fixed amount of economical funds by the central government, and, occasionally, it receives a further economical support. In this scenario, the two considered strategies dissent because of the use of different kinds of technologies:

- *program I* provides to build high quality and expensive technologies that are characterized by a slow aging and cheap maintenance costs;
- *program II* provides to build low quality and cheap technologies.

Starting from this description, it is clear the necessity to introduce new factors over time to deal with urban waste management. In detail, they are:

- *technology*: this factor represents technological tools aiding waste treatment such as incinerators;
- *educational plans*: this factor refers to a collection of educational programs promoted by the municipality to raise citizen awareness;
- *aging*: this factor refers to aging which may affect technological tools.

With the help of the implemented TAFCM (F^0, T_M), it is possible to decide the best strategy among *program I* and *program II*. By taking into account our TAFCM, the two considered strategies correspond, respectively, to two different timed words of the exploited timed automaton T_M:

$$
\begin{aligned}
w_1 &= (\sigma_1, \tau) = (a, 1) \to (c, 2) \to (e, 3) \to (g, 4) \\
w_2 &= (\sigma_2, \tau) = (b, 1) \to (d, 2) \to (f, 3) \to (g, 4)
\end{aligned}
\tag{3}
$$

Both timed words evolve F^0 through the five years by crossing four cognitive eras whose cognitive configurations are defined, respectively, by cognitive transitions labeled with symbols *aceg* and *bdfg*. w_1 and w_2 generate a 4th-order cognitive evolution with the corresponding 4th-order cognitive run which represents the application of opportune decisions in a given time.

Now, let's analyze the effects of application of w_1 and w_2 on the initial map F^0 in order to highlight benefits/drawbacks provided by corresponding strategies. During the cognitive runs related to w_1 and w_2, the TAFCM (F^0, T_M) evolves through such events as receiving funds from the central government, improving technologies and educational plans. During their cognitive evolutions, both timed words allow to add new concepts to F^0: $c_9 \equiv$ technology, $c_{10} \equiv$ educational plans, $c_{11} \equiv$ aging.

The whole municipality's behavior with respect to the timed words w_1 and w_2 is showed, respectively, in Tables 1 and 2.

As highlighted by Figs. 8 and 9, *program I* associated with w_1 produces a more effective behavior of the whole municipality decisions because they decrease the value of concepts c_4 and c_7, respectively, related to waste per area and bacteria per area, and at the same time, it allows municipality to save economical funds (concept c_8). Therefore, thanks to the exploitation of a TAFCM, it has been possible to identify the best strategy to be followed.

Table 1. Description of the 4th-order Cognitive Evolutions related to timed word w_1

	Operator	Description
I cognitive era	$\oplus(c_9)$	High quality (HQ) Technology is added
	$\dagger(c_8, 0.5)$	Municipality increases by 50% its funds
	$\boxplus(c_3, c_9, 0.6)$	Modernization positively supports Technology Maintenance (60%)
	$\boxplus(c_9, c_8, -0.8)$	HQ technology reduces by 80% the municipality funds
II cognitive era	$\dagger(c_8, 0.3)$	Municipality increases by 30% its funds
	$\dotplus(c_9, c_8, 1)$	HQ Technology positively increases municipality funds
	$\boxplus(c_9, c_4, -0.5)$	HQ Technology strongly decreases garbage per area
	$\oplus(c_{10})$	Municipality starts Educational Plans
	$\oplus(c_{11})$ $\boxplus(c_{11}, c_9, -0.65)$	Technology aging starts
	$\boxplus(c_{10}, c_4, -0.3)$	Educational Plans reduce waste per area
	$\boxplus(c_{10}, c_8, -0.1)$	Educational Plans reduce municipality funds
	$\boxplus(c_3, c_{10}, 0.3)$	Modernization positively influences Educational Plans
III cognitive era	$\dagger(c_8, 0.3)$	Municipality increases by 30% its funds
	$\dotplus(c_9, c_8, 0.2)$	HQ Technology positively increases municipality funds
	$\dotplus(c_9, c_4, -0.3)$	HQ Technology decreases waste per area
IV cognitive era	$\dagger(c_8, 0.3)$	Municipality increases by 30% its funds

Table 2. Description of the 4th-order Cognitive Evolutions related to timed word w_2

	Operator	Description
I cognitive era	$\oplus(c_9)$	Low quality (LQ) Technology is added
	$\dagger(c_8, 0.5)$	Municipality increase by 50% its funds
	$\boxplus(c_3, c_9, 0.6)$	Modernization positively supports Technology Maintenance (60%)
	$\boxplus(c_9, c_8, -0.2)$	LQ technology reduces by 20% the municipality funds
II cognitive era	$\dagger(c_8, 0.3)$	Municipality increases by 30% its funds
	$\dotplus(c_9, c_8, 0.3)$	LQ Technology slowly increases municipality funds
	$\boxplus(c_9, c_4, -0.3)$	LQ Technology slowly decreases waste per area
	$\oplus(c_{10})$	Municipality starts Educational Plans
	$\oplus(c_{11})$ $\boxplus(c_{11}, c_9, -0.85)$	Technology aging starts
	$\boxplus(c_{10}, c_4, -0.3)$	Educational Plans reduce waste per area
	$\boxplus(c_{10}, c_8, -0.1)$	Educational Plans reduce municipality funds
	$\boxplus(c_3, c_{10}, 0.3)$	Modernization positively influences Educational Plans
III cognitive era	$\dagger(c_8, 0.3)$	Municipality increases by 30% its funds
	$\dotplus(c_9, c_8, 0.1)$	LQ Technology increases municipality funds
	$\dotplus(c_9, c_4, -0.25)$	LQ Technology decreases garbage per area
IV cognitive era	$\dagger(c_8, 0.3)$	Municipality increases by 30% its funds

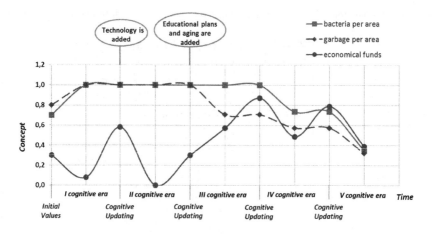

Fig. 8. Concept values (c_4, c_8, c_7) evolution related to 4th-order cognitive run of w_1

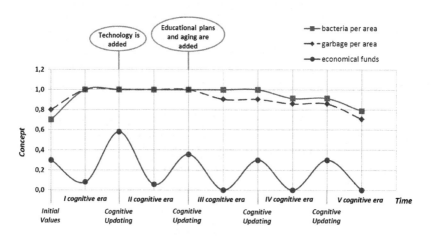

Fig. 9. Concept values (c_4, c_8, c_7) evolution related to 4th-order cognitive run of w_2

5   Conclusions

The management of hazardous and not waste is a significant problem due to socio-economical and environmental impact and the relative homeland defense issues. This paper presents a new method to simulate a dynamic waste management system able to support municipality's decisions by identifying the best strategies to be followed. In particular, the exploited methodology, named Timed Automata based Fuzzy Cognitive maps (TAFCMs), is capable of efficiently managing the waste production problem thanks to its cognitive approach. In detail, TAFCMs allow to model complex systems characterized by a temporal uncertainty, like urban environments, through the exploitation of a double-layered temporal granularity based on the concepts of cognitive configuration, cognitive era and cognitive run. As shown by an experiment, TAFCMs are a promising framework for simulating a dynamic waste management system.

However, TAFCMs introduced in this work exploit expert knowledge to design the collection of cognitive eras and configurations representing the temporal behavior of the system under design. Therefore, in the future, our idea is to investigate some machine learning approaches such as evolutionary computation to automatically find suitable cognitives era and configurations for improving the system behavior.

References

1. Karadimas, N.V., Orsoni, A., Loumos, V.: Municipal Solid Waste Generation Modelling Based on Fuzzy Logic. In: ECMS 2006 – Proceedings of the 20th European Conference on Modelling and Simulation, pp. 309–314 (2006)
2. Karadimas, N.V., Kouzas, G., Anagnostopoulos, I., Loumos, V.: Urban Solid Waste Collection and Routing: the Ant Colony Strategic Approach. International Journal of Simulation: Systems, Science and Technology 6, 45–53 (2005)
3. Gnoni, M.G., Mummolo, G., Ranieri, L.: A mixed-integer linear programming model for optimisation of organics management in an integrated solid waste system. Journal of Environmental Planning and Management 6(51), 833–845 (2008)
4. Hsieh, H.N., Ho, K.H.: Optimization of solid waste disposal system by linear programming technique. J. Resour. Management Technology 4(21), 194–201 (1993)
5. Lund, J.R., Tchobanoglous, G.: Linear programming for analysis of material recovery facilities. J. Environ. Eng., ASCE 5(120), 1093–1095 (1994)
6. Jin, L.: A type-II fuzzy optimization model for municipal solid waste management. In: 2011 Eighth International Conference on Fuzzy Systems and Knowledge Discovery (FSKD), pp. 55–59 (2011)
7. Huang, G.H., Baetz, B.W., Patry, G.G.: A grey integer programming for solid waste management planning under uncertainty. European J. Oper. Res. 83, 594–620 (1995)
8. Chang, N.B., Wang, S.F.: A fuzzy goal programming approach for the optimal planning of metropolitan solid waste management systems. European J. Oper. Res. 99, 287–303 (1997)
9. Acampora, G., Loia, V.: On the Temporal Granularity in Fuzzy Cognitive Maps. IEEE Transactions on Fuzzy Systems 19, 1040–1057 (2011)
10. Alur, R.: A theory of timed automata. Theoretical Computer Science 126, 183–235 (1994)
11. Miao, Y., Liu, Z.-Q.: On causal inference in fuzzy cognitive maps. IEEE Transactions on Fuzzy Systems 1(8), 107–119 (2000)
12. Zhang, W.R., Chen, S.S., Bezdek, J.C.: Pool2: a generic system for cognitive map development and decision analysis. IEEE Transactions on Systems, Man and Cybernetics 1(19), 31–39 (1989)
13. Zhang, W.-R., Chen, S.-S., Wang, W., King, R.S.: A cognitive-map-based approach to the coordination of distributed cooperative agents. IEEE Transactions on Systems, Man and Cybernetics 1(22), 103–114 (1992)
14. Ericsson, C., Wall, A., Yi, W.: Timed automata as task models for event-driven systems. In: Proceedings of Nordic Workshop on Programming Theory (1998)

Mobile Malware Threats and Defenses
for Homeland Security

Seung-Hyun Seo[1], Kangbin Yim[2], and Ilsun You[3]

[1] Korea Information and Security Agency (KISA),
IT Venture Tower, 78 Garak, Songpa, Seoul, 138-950 Korea
seosh@ewhain.net
[2] Dept. of Information Security Engineering, Soonchunhyang University,
646 Eupnae, Shinchang, Asan, 336-745 Korea
yim@sch.ac.kr
[3] School of Information Science, Korean Bible University,
214-32 Dongil, Nowon, Seoul, 139-791 Korea
isyou@bible.ac.kr

Abstract. As the population of mobile users grows rapidly, mobile malware targeting smartphones are becoming a new threat to homeland security. So far, many kinds of malicious malwares including monetizing, stealing credentials or rooting have emerged. The latest mobile malwares are especially posing a serious threat to homeland security, because they can zombify phones to be controlled by their command and conquer servers. In this paper, we survey the threats and malicious behaviors of current mobile malwares. Then, we study the defense mechanisms of mobile malware and introduce a cooperative system for mobile security in South Korea. We also discuss the possible future of mobile malware and attack techniques.

1   Introduction

Recent large scale acts of terror such as the September 11, 2001 attacks have awakened national governments to the needs for supporting homeland security[10]. The original scope of homeland security includes: Emergency preparedness and response (for both terrorism and natural disasters), emergency management, Critical infrastructure and perimeter protection, Border security, Transportation security, Biodefense, etc. However, due to dramatic advances in IT technology, most *Supervisory Control And Data Acquistion* (SCADA)[18] systems and other official forms of networked computer system have been utilized over the last decade to control power grids, gas and oil distribution, water supply, telecommunications and etc. These computer-controlled and network-connected systems can be potential targets for hackers or hacking groups with malicious intent such as a crime or terrorist organization. As the government's critical systems increasingly rely on IT technology, the threats of cyber attacks increase. So far, hackers have performed cyber attacks using information exploitation tools including computer viruses, malwares, worms, or eavesdropping sniffers.

G. Quirchmayr et al. (Eds.): CD-ARES 2012, LNCS 7465, pp. 516–524, 2012.
© IFIP International Federation for Information Processing 2012

As the population of smartphone users rapidly increases, hackers are converting their target systems of choice towards smartphones. Smartphones have a wide variety of feature-rich applications, commonly referred to as "apps". These apps include user-friendly content such as *Social Network Service* (SNS), navigation, banking and stock trading based on accessibility to public networks at anytime and anywhere.

Unlike computer applications, the smartphone platform vendors provide centralized marketplaces such as Apple's App Store or Google's Android Market in order to allow for smartphone users to conveniently browse and install their smartphone apps. However, some markets such as Google's Android market or the third-party app markets deal with illegitimately modified free versions of paid apps. This allows some apps to be posted without proper security checks, and allows the distribution of mobile malware at an increasing rate within these markets. Moreover, most users without security expertise install these apps unaware of its vulnerability. This has lead to the explosive growth of mobile malwares numbering at about 12,000 malicious apps in 2011 since the appearance of the mobile malware Cabir in 2004[13]. Especially, since the smartphones store sensitive data, if hackers infect a user's smartphone with mobile malware, they can steal sensitive data. If the infected smartphone were to be used at work in a company, hackers can obtain corporate secrets. Governments and public service offices which actively introduce the technology "Mobile Office" where employees are all equipped with smartphones connected to company servers and Intranet, have a greater security risk.

In order to prevent a cyberwar through mobile malware, *Korea Internet & Security Agency* (KISA)[15] of South Korea has organized a cooperative mobile security defense group. KISA also operates a hot line for response and defense against a mobile cyber war. In this paper, we first present the threats of mobile malware and attack scenarios against homeland security. Then, we show countermeasures for mobile security and introduce KISA's cooperative system against mobile cyber war. The remainder of this paper is organized as follows: In Section 2, we present threats of mobile malware. In Section 3, we present countermeasures for mobile security and introduce response and defense systems against mobile cyber war. We expect the possible future of mobile attack technique in Section 4 and conclude in Section 5.

2   Threats of Mobile Malware

In this section we first discuss about mobile malware threats and attack scenario for homeland security. Then, we give some examples of mobile malwares which recently emerged.

2.1   Threat Model and Infection Techniques

In order to obtain sensitive financial information, hackers have recently developed and spread mobile malwares. Mobile malwares achieve their malicious goals or profits by infecting the Operating System (OS) of smartphones. Usually, mobile malwares steal information stored on users' smartphone or send SMS to premium numbers for hackers' monetary profit. Stolen information can include *International Mobile Equipment Identity* (IMEI) numbers, *International Mobile Subscriber Identity* (IMSI) numbers, *Subscriber Identity Module* (SIM) serial number, user credentials for future misuse, contacts or *Global Positioning System* (GPS) location. Some mobile malware changes the infected phone into a bot that can be remotely controlled by the *Command and Conquer* (C&C) server.

We can categorize the infection techniques of mobile malware into Repackaging, Malvertising, and Browser Attacks[13].

- **Repackaging**: Repackaging is one of the most popular techniques to deceive users into installing malware. Hackers repackage legitimate apps after embedding malicious code and upload the modified apps to an unregulated market. These repackaged apps are distributed via the marketplace and downloaded by unwary users. The repackaged apps not only feature the same functionality as the original apps, but also include malicious code to collect sensitive information or to obtain monetary profit.
- **Malvertising**: Malvertising uses genuine looking advertisements that link back to fraudulent websites that can download malware to users' smartphones. Originally malvertising was one of the hacking techniques used on the Internet for many years. Now it is beginning to target mobile devices.
- **Browser Attacks**: There are two types of smartphone apps such as web apps and native apps. Mobile users fall for a hacker's browser-based malware, the hacker can trick a mobile user into visiting one of their URLs and essentially control any content they receive. This type of attack is far more dangerous and pervasive because it is not limited to strictly the unregulated Android marketplace.

2.2   Mobile Attack Scenarios against Homeland Security

Cyberthreat presents a real risk in loss of property and could threaten the lives of people. Recently, threats to industrial infrastructure networks such as SCADA systems have increased because of the lack of information security. So, in this section, we present the mobile attack scenarios against industrial SCADA systems using mobile malware.

The overview of an attack scenario is shown in Fig.1. It is supposed that employees can connect to a SCADA operating server using their smartphone. The employees can check the status of the SCADA system and control the SCADA server by inputting commands through their smartphone.

We also assume that hackers have repackaged a popular game app by including a malicious root exploit code and uploaded the repackaged game app both to the official Android market and unregulated third party market. Some of the employees download the repackaged apps from the market. Once these game apps are successfully installed, their malicious code can obtain root privileges while allowing hackers to control the infected smartphone. This attack can be

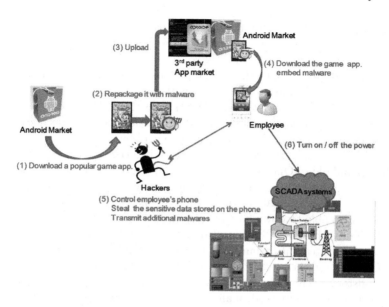

Fig. 1. Overview of Mobile Attack Scenario to the SCADA system

divided into two types: (i) sending command to control the SCADA system and (ii) transmitting additional malware to steal sensitive data. For example, if hackers send the command of "turn off the power" of a hypothetical SCADA system such as a national water utility, the employee's infected phone will shut off the power. If the SCADA system is compromised, a serious disaster could occur. If hackers send an additional malware which steals sensitive information, they could gather all the information about monitoring and controlling. Afterwards, they could launch more attacks towards the SCADA system using this stolen information. For instance, with stolen usernames and passwords, the hacker can access the remote network to gain access to the utilities network and cause the system to turn on and off repeatedly, until the water pump burned out.

2.3   Recent Mobile Malware

The mobile malware has many types of malicious behaviors such as leaking sensitive data or stealing credentials for unauthorized users, sending SMS to premium numbers for monetary loss, restricting device usage, mobile *Distributed Denial of Service* (DDoS) attacks and etc. These types of damages tend to appear in a complex manner in actual mobile malware incidents. Recent mobile malwares include root exploits(or jailbreak exploits) that gain extra privileges and execute commands from the C&C server. These mobile malwares can convert the infected smartphone into a bot. Once a exploit malware obtains root-level access, its powers are potentially unlimited. So, if these malwares are distributed and downloaded in the smartphone apps market place, hackers can remotely control users' smartphones. Root exploit malwares are especially dangerous compared to other types of malware.

DroidDream[3] in March, 2011, GingerMaster in August, 2011 and RootSmart in Feburary, 2012 are major root exploits malware for Android OS. DroidDream uses the "rageagainstthecage" and "exploid", and is functional for Android OS versions 2.2 and older. More than 50 apps have been found to contain Droid-Dream in the official Android Market. DroidDream can root a users phone and send sensitive information (IMEI and IMSI) from the phone to a remote server. DroidDream-infected phone can download additional malwares without a user's knowledge as well as open the phone up to control by hackers.

GingerMaster[8] and RootSmart[17] using "GingerBreak" run on Android OS versions 2.3 and older. Once the GingerMaster is installed, it creates a backdoor root shell and gains root privileges. It silently runs a service in the background which gathers information about the infected phone and transmits it to the C&C server. It is also able to download and install further malwares.

Unlike "GingerBreak", RootSmart does not directly include the root exploit inside the app. Instead, it dynamically fetches the GingerBreak root exploit from the C&C server and then executes it to escalate its privilege. RootSmart-infected phones register system-wide receivers and lie dormant until a system event activates it. After being activated, malicious actions run in the background. Then, RootSmart-infected phone connects to the C&C server with various information collected from the phone such as the Android OS version number, IMEI number, as well as the package name.

3   Countermeasures for Mobile Security

In this section, we present countermeasures for mobile security. Firstly, we discuss various detection mechanisms proposed in academic research and security mechanism for smartphone platform. Then, we introduce KISA's collaborative defense system against mobile cyber war.

3.1   Mobile Malware Detection Mechanism

Enck et al.[4] proposed TaintDroid system. It is an information flow tracking system for realtime privacy monitoring on smartphone and demonstrates potential privacy threats from third-party apps in Android platform. Chin et al.[2] proposed Comdroid system that analyzes the vulnerability in inter app communication in Android apps and finds a lot of exploitable vulnerability. Grace et al.[9] presented Woodpecker which exposes capability leaks on stock Android phones by analyzing preloaded apps in the phone firmware. Stowaway tool by Felt et al.[6] detects whether an app is overprivileged. Stowaway identifies the set of API calls used in an app and then maps it to the corresponding permissions. It examines 940 apps and finds that one-third apps are overprivileged.

Xie et al.[19] proposed pBMDS, a behavior-based malware detection system for cellphone devices. pBMDS utilized a probabilistic-based approach that correlates a user's input with system call events to detect abnormal behaviors in smartphones. Liu et al.[12] proposed virusMeter that detects mobile malware based on abnormal power consumption caused by mobile malware. Burguera et al.[1] presented Crowdroid that collects ststem calls of running apps on smartphones and applies clustering algorithms to differentiate between normal and malicious apps. Zhou et al.[20] proposed DroidMOSS that detects repackaged apps in unregulated third-party Android markets. Zhou et al.[21] presented DroidRanger that performs offline analysis to detect mobile malware in current Android Markets.

3.2 Security Mechanism for Smartphone Platform

ScanDroid by Fuchs et al.[7] is an automated security certification of Android apps. It extracts app specific security specifications and applies data flow analysis for their consistency in the app code. Enck et al.[5] proposed Kirin that is lightweight mobile phone app certification. The goal of Kirin is to block the installation of potential unsafe apps if they have certain dangerous permission combination. Nauman et al.[14] revised the current Android framework. Apex by Nauman et al. provides fine-grained controls of resources accessed by third-party untrusted apps. L4Android by Lange et al.[11] isolates smartphone OS for different usage environments in different virtual machines.

3.3 KISA's Collaborative System

In South Korea, KISA has organized a cooperative mobile security defense group which is consisted of Korea government office, telecommunication company, security research institute, virus vaccine company, smartphone device vendors and etc. KISA has also organized the response and defense process for mobile security and operates a hot line for response and defense against a mobile cyber war. KISA's collaborative response and defense process for mobile security is divided into 5 steps: the monitoring, beginning response, analysis and information sharing, recovery, and improvement steps.

1) Monitoring step: In this step, each member of the cooperative mobile security defense group monitors infection routes of mobile malwares and gathers the information of mobile security issues and report of smartphone users' damages.
2) First action step: In this step, KISA blocks the distribution sites of mobile malwares to prevent additional damages and notifies the security threat of mobile malwares. Then, each member of the cooperative group collects the mobile malware sample.
3) Analysis and information sharing step: In this step, malware analysts of the cooperative group analyze the collected malware sample and grasp malicious functions of the malware. Then, they classify the types of the mobile accident and share the analysis information.
4) Recovery step: According to the analysis results, in this step, KISA blocks IP addresses of hacker's C&C servers and virus vaccine companies update vaccine patterns. Service centers of smartphone device vendors recover the users' infected smartphones.

5) Improvement step: In this step, the cooperative group analyzes the features and trends of mobile accidents and forecasts the possible future mobile security accidents. Then, they try to improve the response and defense process.

4   Future of Mobile Attacks and Defenses

Most malwares were usually organized in a static code frame and they could not change their patterns. Because these malwares were packaged with the whole body, it was deterministic whether they would have vulnerabilities or not and a security assessment outside the mobile platform was effective to find malicious patterns or behaviors and save its computing resources. Therefore, it was reasonable to prepare the lab-based security framework to analyze mobile apps. This type of framework may consist of massive multicore servers and provide an enough performance to analyze a number of malwares in parallel. Two common functions of this framework are abstracting signatures from new malwares through a dynamic analysis and scanning the existing malwares to find the signatures through a static analysis.

On the other hand, recent malwares have become facilitated with the ability to root the kernel and started placing a backdoor to download additional codes to extend themselves. Because the initial base code of these malwares may have no differences with that of normal apps, it is difficult for the lab-based framework to decide if they are malicious. The downloadable part can also make themselves highly polymorphic, thus confusing the security framework. Furthermore, they will incorporate the ability to hide themselves from or make immune to analysis by manipulating the kernel structures similarly to the self-defensive malwares in the stationary PC environment.

Due to these reasons, another security framework inside the mobile platform is getting focused as a counterpart of the lab-based framework to neutralize the self-defensive malwares. Because a sequence of a dynamic analysis and the signature-based vaccination are performed in a virtualized environment of the lab-based framework, the main objective of the mobile security framework is to disinfect the kernel. The objects targeted are various kernel structures such as the task structure, which should be repeatedly investigated. The disinfection also should be performed out of the scheduling to make sure these kernel structures are exclusively accessed by the security framework.

5   Conclusion

Due to the advent of mobile device technology such as smartphones, the threat to homeland security using mobile malware is rapidly expanding. Motivated by this, we studied the possible securuty threats of mobile malwares as well as the infection techniques. In addition, we presented a feasible serious attack scenario against SCADA systems through mobile malware, and then focused on the existing countermeasures, one of which KISA has organized as a mobile cooperative security systems against mobile cyber war. Finally, we provided the possible attack techniques of mobile malwares in the future.

References

1. Burguera, I., Zurutuza, U., Nadjm-Tehrani, S.: Crowdroid: Behavior-Based Malware Detection System for Android. In: Proceedings of the 1st Workshop on Security and Privacy in Smartphones and Mobile Devices, CCSSPSM 2011 (2011)
2. Chin, E., Felt, A.P., Greenwood, K., Wagner, D.: Analyzing Inter-Application Communication in Android. In: Proceedings of the 9th Annual Symposium on Network and Distributed System Security, MobiSys 2011 (2011)
3. DroidDream, http://blog.mylookout.com/blog/2011/03/01/security-alert-malware-found-in-official-android-market-droiddream/
4. Enck, W., Gilbert, P., Chun, B.-G., Cox, L.P., Jung, J., Mc- Daniel, P., Sheth, A.N.: TaintDroid: An Information-Flow Tracking System for Realtime Privacy-Monitoring on Smartphones. In: Proceedings of the 9th USENIX Symposium on Operating Systems Design and Implementation, USENIX OSDI 2010 (2010)
5. Enck, W., Ongtang, M., McDaniel, P.: On Lightweight Mobile Phone Application Certification. In: Proceedings of the 16th ACM Conference on Computer and Communications Security, CCS 2009 (2009)
6. Felt, A.P., Chin, E., Hanna, S., Song, D., Wagner, D.: Android Permissions Demystied. In: Proceedings of the 18th ACM Conference on Computer and Communications Security, CCS 2011 (2011)
7. Fuchs, A., Chaudhuri, A., Foster, J.: SCanDroid: Automated Security Certification of Android Applications,
http://www.cs.umd.edu/avik/projects/scandroidascaa
8. GingerMaster, http://www.csc.ncsu.edu/faculty/jiang/GingerMaster/
9. Grace, M., Zhou, Y., Wang, Z., Jiang, X.: Systematic Detection of Capability Leaks in Stock Android Smartphones. In: Proceedings of the 19th Annual Symposium on Network and Distributed System Security, NDSS 2012 (2012)
10. Homeland Security, http://en.wikipedia.org/wiki/Homeland_security
11. Lange, M., Liebergeld, S., Lackorzynski, A., Warg, A., Peter, M.: L4Android: A Generic Operating System Framework for Secure Smartphones. In: Proceedings of the 1st Workshop on Security and Privacy in Smartphones and Mobile Devices, CCS-SPSM 2011 (2011)
12. Liu, L., Yan, G., Zhang, X., Chen, S.: VirusMeter: Preventing Your Cellphone from Spies. In: Proceedings of the 12th International Symposium on Recent Advances in Intrusion Detection, RAID 2009 (2009)
13. McAfee, Threats Report: Second Quarter 2011 (2011)
14. Nauman, M., Khan, S., Zhang, X.: Apex: Extending Android Permission Model and Enforcement with User-Defined Runtime Constraints. In: Proceedings of the 5th ACM Symposium on Information, Computer and Communications Security, ASIACCS 2010 (2010)
15. KISA, Korea Internet and Security Agency, http://www.kisa.or.kr
16. Kim, H., Smith, J., Shin, K.G.: Detecting Energy-Greedy Anomalies and Mobile Malware Variants. In: Proceeding of the 6th International Conference on Mobile Systems, Applications, and Services, MobiSys 2008 (2008)
17. RootSmart, http://www.csc.ncsu.edu/faculty/jiang/RootSmart/
18. SCADA, Supervisory Control and Data Acquisition,
http://en.wikipedia.org/wiki/SCADA
19. Xie, L., Zhang, X., Seifert, J.-P., Zhu, S.: pBMDS: A Behavior-based Malware Detection System for Cellphone Devices. In: Proceedings of the 3rd ACM conference on Wireless Network Security, WiSec 2010 (2010)

20. Zhou, W., Zhou, Y., Jiang, X., Ning, P.: DroidMOSS: Detecting Repackaged Smartphone Applications in Third-Party AndroidMarketplaces. In: Proceedings of the 2nd ACM Conference on Data and Application Security and Privacy, CODASPY 2012 (2012)
21. Zhou, Y., Wang, Z., Zhou, W., Jiang, X.: Hey, You, Get Off of My Market: Detecting Malicious Apps in Official and Alternative Android Markets. In: Proceedings of NDSS 2012 (2012)

Facial Identity Encryption with Kinoform and Phase-Key Watermarking for Homeland Security Agencies

Muhammad Naveed Iqbal Qureshi[1], Jin-Tae Kim[2,*], and Sang-Woong Lee[1,*]

[1] Computer Vision and Multimedia Laboratory, Department of Computer Engineering,
Chosun University, Gwangju, 501-759, South Korea
[2] Laser Applications Laboratory, Department of Photonic Engineering,
Chosun University, Gwangju, 501-759, South Korea
`mniqureshi@hotmail.com, {kimjt,swlee}@chosun.ac.kr`

Abstract. Internet has made it easy to access and transfer copyrighted material like facial ID to unauthorized users. In order to maintain confidentiality of any classified documents, especially, facial identity; their security and integrity are essential requirements for all law enforcement and homeland security agencies. We propose a new method to make the facial identity more secure and intact by using encrypted kinoform facial identity tags for sensitive image document such as passport, identity card, security clearance gate passes, etc. Our method to use encrypted phase-key watermarking on the kinoform facial identity- tags makes them more secure.

Keywords: Face Recognition, Kinoform, Optical Security, Image Encryption, Phase-key watermarking.

1 Introduction

Document forgeries with false and duplicate facial identity are big threats for any law enforcement agencies. Face recognition security systems are in market for more than half century. However, there is no absolutely secure and fail proof face recognition system developed up to date. The available systems mainly rely on computer vision based algorithms, such as principal component analysis, independent component analysis, linear discriminant analysis, evolutionary pursuit, elastic bunch graph matching, kernel method, trace transform, active appearance model, support vector machine, hidden Markov models and Bayesian framework, etc.

A Machine readable passport (MRP) system that usually installed on the immigration counter of international airport uses electronic scanning techniques, particularly optical character recognition.

Most worldwide travel passports are MRPs with a special machine readable zone (MRZ), usually at the bottom of identity page at the beginning of a passport. The MRZ of passport spans of two lines and each line is 44 characters long. Following information has to be provided in this zone: name, passport number, nationality, date of birth, sex, passport expiration date and personal identity number. There is a space for optional, often country dependent and supplementary information [1].

---

* Corresponding authors.

G. Quirchmayr et al. (Eds.): CD-ARES 2012, LNCS 7465, pp. 525–533, 2012.

A biometric passport known as an e-passport or digital passport contain biometric information in an electronic chip. It is used to authenticate the identities of travelers. It uses contactless smart card technology including a microprocessor chip (computer chip) and antenna (for both power to the chip and communication) embedded in the front or back cover, or center page of the passport. The critical information is printed on the data page of the passport and stored in the chip. Public key infrastructure is used to authenticate the data which is stored electronically in the passport chip. The chip makes it expensive and difficult to forge when all security mechanisms are fully and correctly implemented [2].

Much remarkable work is already done in the field of document security and authentication. However, we present combined approach of optics and computer vision to embed the encrypted kinoform facial identity on next generation of passports, identity cards, security clearance passes and all the confidential image documents that are sensitive in order to keep the homeland security intact.

A kinoform has inherent resistance against damage either natural or intentional, such as scratches and humidity. This feature makes its embedding more feasible on important documents.

2   Previous Work

In 1996, Stepien *et al.* proposed an idea about a distributed kinoform in optical security applications [3]. That method was comprised on optically variable devices, diffraction and interference. Their work mainly relied on the use of very expensive and sophisticated optical equipment.

In 2003, Zhai *et al.* stated that non-cascade phase retrieval kinoform converges quickly and account for less data amount, which not only ensured good imperceptibility, but also reconstructed without conjugate images [4].

In 2003, Cable *et al.* stated an idea of recording kinoform optically generated hologram typically made on a photosensitive material by laser beams [5]. Recorded kinoform images can be retrieved by a reconstruction beam. It is reconstructed optically to the original data through a Fourier transform lens.

In 2010, Hye *et al.* presented a technique for application of kinoform computer generated holograms (CGHs) to an identity tag system [6]. Their idea comprehended on 11-level kinoform CGH image generated on the tag sample by modified simulated annealing method at a low quantization error rate of 0.4% compared with the original data. In the retrieval process they used a commercial digital camera to take image of the kinoform ID tag. It is then reconstructed through computer to the original data with about 4 % reconstruction error rate.

In 2011, Deng *et al.* stated that kinoform accounts for much less data amount to be embedded than regular CGH [7]. A kinoform can be extracted with only right phase key and right fractional order, and reconstructed to represent original watermark without original cover image. They use random fractional Fourier transform in the kinoform generation process.

Optical reconstruction of kinoform can be easily explained by the following figure.

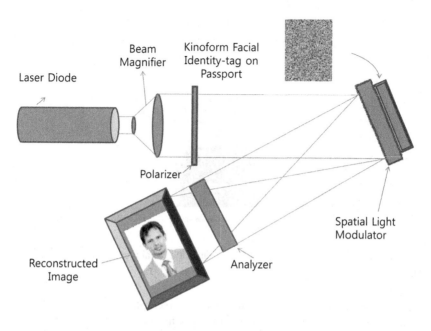

Fig. 1. Electro-optical reconstruction of kinoform [9]

3   Robustness of Kinoform Identity-Tag against Natural and Intentional Damage

A kinoform is phase-only reference of input data and does not contain information about amplitude. We can suggest that these identity tags are more robust and damage tolerant than conventional identification tags. The kinoform can be reconstructed with high accuracy even if it is damaged by fire up to 50%, scratched or kept under extreme weather conditions such as rain or damp environment. Information in these identification tags is encoded in frequency domain. Watermarking is done in spatial domain. Collectively our identification tag is more robust as compared to other secure identification-tags such as barcodes, etc.

Robustness of kinoform had been investigated and proved in the work of Hye *et al.* [6]. According to them, even if we lose 50 % of the entire kinoform identity-tag, we can reconstruct the original identity with 12.5% error. They used kinoform (CGH) tags in which one has 25% damage, and the other has 50% damage physically. Both tags were detected optically and recovered on the same condition, have the same light intensity, the same camera angle, and so on. The recovered data were compared in terms of error rates with the original data.

We propose to use kinoform instead of facial identity. It makes the document more robust against damage and corruption. If, in case of scratch or fire we lose 50 % of the entire identity tag, we can recover the original identity from it with a maximum error of 13 %.

Following are the experimental results of reconstruction with 50% of data loss on kinoform identity tag. We can easily verify the facial identity with the reconstructed image.

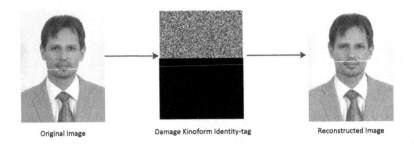

Original Image   Damage Kinoform Identity-tag   Reconstructed Image

Fig. 2. Original input data and its reconstructed data for a facial identity kinoform tag with 50% damage

Fig. 2 shows that the facial identity kinoform reconstructs of original data at an error rate of 13% for the 50% tag loss in the experiments.

4   Overview of Proposed System

We propose a method of making travel document like a passport safer than earlier from forgery. Kinoform facial identity-tags are impossible to reconstruct and fabricate without knowledge of actual identity and exact phase-key as well as the complex optical phenomenon details. Without highly normalized cross correlation value, original information cannot be retrieved from the kinoform identity tag unless we know the exact phase key.

5   Construction of Kinoform Identity-Tag

We construct kinoform identity tag of the facial identity photograph by optical instruments. After optical construction, we took a photograph of the kinoform of the object with an ordinary digital camera. We do Encryption of the phase-key by using substitution cipher database in next step. Then by using least significant bit method of watermarking, we hide phase-key along-with error correcting codes in kinoform identity tag. We do watermarking with standard image processing tools. After watermarking, our encrypted kinoform facial identity tag becomes ready to be printed on passport.

Fig.3 describes our proposed system and workflow stepwise for the construction of encrypted phase-key watermarked kinoform facial identification tags.

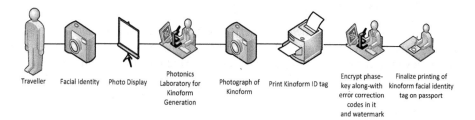

Traveller   Facial Identity   Photo Display   Photonics Laboratory for Kinoform Generation   Photograph of Kinoform   Print Kinoform ID tag   Encrypt phase-key along-with error correction codes in it and watermark   Finalize printing of kinoform facial identity tag on passport

Fig. 3. Kinoform facial identity tag generation process

In rest of the section 5 we will discuss each step of the Kinoform construction process in more detail.

5.1   Kinoform

A phase-only reference-less optically generated Fourier hologram, which gives a non-symmetrical image in the reconstruction process, is known as kinoform [3]. Although it can be generated by CGH method but we used optical instruments for its construction. Kinoform is a phase only optical element and its amplitude should either be kept constant or unity. In reconstruction if we use only phase information of kinoform of the input image, it may contain noise because of the amplitude negligence. The kinoform is designed in such a manner that maximum phase modulation of the incident light is 2π.

Our idea is to embed encrypted watermark of person specific phase information in the face image kinoform.

Fig. 4. Facial identity photograph and its corresponding kinoform identity tag developed in our photonic engineering laboratory

5.2   Watermarking

From previous works in the field of watermarking we already know that size of secret message should not exceed more than 25% of cover image. If we hide only encrypted phase-key information in the cover image, we can avoid this limit violation.

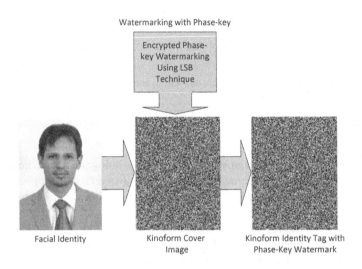

Fig. 5. Our proposed idea to generate kinoform facial identity tag with phase-key watermarking

In 2000 Chang and Orchard stated that a watermarking scheme has two operations; engraving and detection [8]. It is convenient to represent these two operations as two subsets in the image space, the Kernel K and the set of watermarked images W. Given the original image I, engraving embeds a watermark into an image I, resulting in another image I', which is the image in K closest to I. The detection takes an image I' and declares it to be watermarked if and only if I' belongs to W.

We propose to use least significant bit (LSB) watermarking technique to hide the phase-key inside the cover image. The cover image is itself a secure identity because it is a kinoform of original facial identity and it cannot be reconstructed easily. Fig. 5 describes this phenomenon.

Phase-key encryption adds another fold of security to the identity-tag. It is described in detail in the following sub-section.

5.3   Phase-key Encryption

To enhance the security of kinoform identity-tag, we propose to embed another fold of safety by using substitution cipher encrypted phase-key as a watermark instead of the original phase-key.

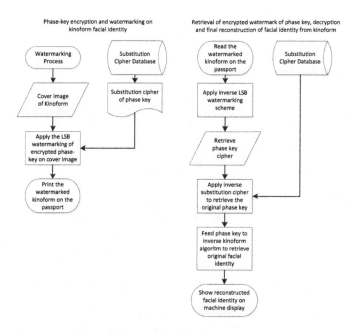

Fig. 6. Process of encryption and decryption of phase-key watermarking

Database of substitution cipher should be kept as a top secret material under surveillance of government agencies to make this scheme more reliable and secure. The same reference database of substitution cipher should be embedded in the memory of passport reading device for reconstruction of original facial identity. Since the passport reading devices are only available at the immigration counters of airport under strict surveillance, we can assume that it is safe to embed the substitution cipher database in their memory. Fig. 6 explains this encrypted watermarking process stepwise both at the construction and reconstruction phases.

6   Reconstruction of Facial Identity from Kinoform Identity-Tag

In the reconstruction process of encrypted kinoform identity-tag, device should work in the following steps:

- Read the encrypted kinoform facial identity-tag on passport
- Retrieve phase-key watermark from kinoform identity-tag
- Decrypt phase-key with substitution cipher embedded in the memory of reading device
- Check phase-key for errors by using the error correcting algorithm

Reading machine will run error correction algorithm to make phase-key retrieval process more reliable.

After retrieving the correct phase key our facial identity reconstruction device will supply it to inverse kinoform generation algorithm. We propose to use function of inverse fractional Fourier transform with the correct decrypted phase key which is retrieved and decrypted from the watermark.

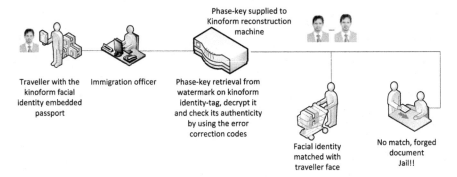

Fig. 7. Reconstruction of facial identity from kinoform tag at airport immigration counters

Since in the construction of Kinoform we only preserve the phase information and make the amplitude of source object either as a constant or unity, we do not need to care about amplitude information at the reconstruction.

We do not need much processing power for computing inverse fractional Fourier transform of the kinoform. The whole reconstruction algorithm can be easily embedded in 32-bit SoC for digital image and signal processing.

7   Conclusion and Future Work

We can claim that this technique is very secure because once the kinoform is watermarked with the encrypted phase key; it cannot be reconstructed by optical instruments. If we try to reconstruct it with optical instrumentation, only noise will be generated in result. It is impossible to retrieve the phase-key watermark by any optical process. Moreover, the substitution cipher is another fold of security that we have embedded in encryption of phase-key watermarking on kinoform identity-tag. Our proposed reconstruction method is the only way to reconstruct original facial identity.

The idea of kinoform based facial identity tag implementation can effectively reduce the document forgery. This system has 3-fold security and this feature makes it almost absolutely secure. We have seen that the reconstruction of original data is impossible without original phase key information. Even if the phase key is extracted from the watermark, it is not very easy to decrypt it. Reconstruction of the original facial identity image from the kinoform identity tag is extremely difficult unless we do know the exact reconstruction algorithm.

This idea can be implemented on any image document. We can further conclude that kinoform based security solutions are much better and more secure as compared to the conventional identity-tag verification systems.

Acknowledgement. This work was supported by the National Research Foundation of Korea(NRF) grant funded by the Korea government(MEST)(no.2009-0075968).

References

1. Machine readable passport, http://en.wikipedia.org/wiki/Machine-readable_passport
2. Biometric passport, http://en.wikipedia.org/wiki/Biometric_passport
3. Stepien, P., Gajda, R., Szoplik, T.: Distributed Kinoform in optical security applications. Optical. Engineering 35, 2453–2458 (1996)
4. Zhaia, H., Liua, F., Yanga, X., Mua, G., Chavel, P.: Improving binary images reconstructed from Kinoform by amplitude adjustment. Optical Communication 219, 81–85 (2003)
5. Cable, A., Mesh, P., Wilkinson, T.: Production of computer-generated holograms on recordable compact disc media using a compact disk writer. Optical Engineering 42, 2514–2520 (2003)
6. Kim, H.-R., Pak, K.-M., Jun, K.-W., Choi, H.-W., Lim, J.-S., Won, Y.-H.: Application of Kinoform CGHs to an ID Tag System. IEEE Photonics Journal, 553–562 (2010)
7. Deng, K., Yang, G., Xie, H.: A blind robust watermarking scheme with non-cascade iterative encrypted kinoform. Optical Express 19, 10241–10251 (2011)
8. Chang, E.-C., Orchard, M.: Geometric properties of watermarking schemes. Proceedings International Conference on Image Processing 3, 714–717 (2000)
9. Zheng, H., Yu, Y., Qian, H., Asundi, A.: Reduction of speckle noise by multi-kinoform in holographic three-dimensional display. In: Proceedings of Ninth International Symposium on Laser Metrology, pp. 7155–7155 (2008)

Detecting Unusual User Behaviour to Identify Hijacked Internet Auctions Accounts*

Marek Zachara[1] and Dariusz Pałka[2]

[1] AGH University of Science and Technology, Poland
mzachara@agh.edu.pl
[2] Pedagogical University of Cracow, Poland
dpalka@up.krakow.pl

Abstract. For over 15 years auction services have grown rapidly, constituting a major part of e-commerce worldwide. Unfortunately, they also provide opportunities for criminals to distribute illicit goods, launder money or commit other types of fraud. This calls for methods to mitigate this threat. The following paper discusses the methods of identifying the accounts of users participating in internet auctions that have been hijacked (taken over) by malicious individuals and utilised for fraudulent purposes. Two primary methods are described, monitoring users' activities (e.g. the number of auctions created over time) with EWMA and clustering similar auction categories into groups for the purpose of assessing users' sellers profiles and detecting their sudden changes. These methods, utilised together allow for real-time detection of suspicious accounts. The proposed models are validated on real data gathered from an auction web site.

Keywords: internet auctions, identity theft, anomaly detection.

1 Internet Auctions - Introduction

Since the launch of eBay in 1995, internet auctions have become an important part of the global marketplace. According to the eBay annual report, their income from transactions amounted to 7.7 billion dollars in 2009. Assuming an average fee for a transaction to be below 10%, the total sales through eBay would amount to around 100 billion dollars, compared to 135 billion dollars of total e-commerce retail sales in the US [19] during the same year. There are certainly other auction services beside eBay, but even considering only the numbers related to eBay (which is certainly the largest one), the importance of this transaction medium is obvious.

One of the primary reasons for the success of auction services is the low cost of entry. A person does not need any specific tools nor formalities to start selling their products (or information services). This results in a large number of both sellers and buyers registered with auction sites. A large user-base of

---

* This work is partially supported by NCBiR grant 0021/R/ID2.

G. Quirchmayr et al. (Eds.): CD-ARES 2012, LNCS 7465, pp. 534–546, 2012.
© IFIP International Federation for Information Processing 2012

the sellers means statistically high chances of users with weak passwords or otherwise vulnerable to hacking methods. A huge amount of buyers, on the other hand, provide an excellent opportunity to find those interested in illicit goods or susceptible to various scam methods. As a result, auction systems are an important medium for criminals, granting them means of expanding their illegal activities, including fraud and/or the provision of prohibited goods. Left unmitigated, this would constitute a serious threat to public security.

Although most readers are probably familiar with how internet auctions work, a brief explanation will be provided here fore reference purposes. A person willing to sell an item, posts its description (often with photos) and an initial asking price at an auction site. Other users can view the offer, may ask additional questions and may also bid a certain sum for the item. Auctions usually end after a specific time (e.g. 14 days), with the item sold to the highest bidder. There might be other types of offers (e.g. a fixed price, multiple items, etc.), but in all cases the transaction is concluded between two registered users of the auction service.

After each transaction the parties have a chance to evaluate it by posting their comments and ratings of the other party. Such ratings for each user are usually aggregated into an overall reputation rating (e.g. a person with 96 positive and 3 negative 'comments' would have a rating of 93).

The reputation system. i.e. the method of calculating the reputation rating and the actual numbers are vital to an auctions system. Contrary to traditional sales scenario, where both parties meet in person and the goods are exchanged for money at the same time, purchases made over the internet usually take much longer, with money often being paid up-front and the goods delivered after a few days. Buyers are therefore likely to make the buying decision based on their trust that sellers will keep their part of the bargain. This trust is likely to be higher if a lot of other users have already concluded transactions with this particular seller, and were satisfied with them, which would be reflected in the sellers reputation rating. Similarly, the seller is more likely to offer e.g. a CoD option to a buyer with a good reputation standing. Although the reputation rating is valuable to every user, it is vital to sellers, as it will directly affect their business and profit.

The reputation system and the 'snowball effect' of an increasing number of buyers and sellers using the auction systems for their needs have motivated many merchants who were selling their products via their own web service to integrate with an auction system and use it as their primary sales channel, resulting in such a large volume of trade as mentioned at the beginning of the article.

1.1 Auction-Related Fraud

The volume of transactions made via internet auctions make it a valuable target for criminals and abusers. According to [9], auction frauds can be split into three major categories:

- *Pre-auction fraud*, which includes misrepresentation, the sale of illegal goods or triangulation. The former two are not specific to auctions or e-commerce in general, while the later (triangulation) is the sale of goods purchased with stolen credit card for cash - leaving the fraudster with cash and transferring the risk of seizure to the recipient [9].

- *In-auction fraud*, which is used to disrupt competitors' sales (e.g. by placing a high bid via a fraudulent account with no intention of buying the item, or by inflating the price by bidding on one's own items.
- *Post-auction fraud*, consisting mainly of non-delivery of the purchased item, the delivery of a broken or inferior item or stacking the buyer with additional fees.

More details about auction fraud can be found in [11] and [9]. However, of all the possible options, the most profitable to a fraudster are the ones which include up-front payment and non-delivery of the item, or the delivery of an item inferior to the offered one. Unfortunately for a fraudster, the reputation system does not al-low this scenario to be exploited for long, as negative feedback from the buyers will soon warn other users and effectively prevent the fraudster from using his/her ac-count with the auction system for this purpose. On the other hand, having access to an account with a high reputation allows for a larger numbers of buyers to be attracted to the fraudster's offer, allowing him/her to gather more money before negative feedback starts pouring in. Developing the means to abuse or circum-vent the reputation system is therefore vital to a fraudster. It is a broad subject discussed e.g. in [18], but can be narrowed down to two most often used methods:

- *Building up a fraudulent reputation*, often utilizing a 'Sybil Attack' [2] where positive feedback for a specific account is generated via dummy accounts controlled by the fraudster
- *Gaining access to a legitimate account*, and exploiting it for own purposes (e.g. fraudulent offers/sales), leaving the original account owner with un-happy customers and, potentially, a legal struggle.

Of these two methods, the first one is more deterministic, although it requires a certain amount of effort and time to reach the stage when the fraudster can execute his/her schema, after which the account is basically unusable and a new one needs to be prepared. The second method is less reliable, as it depends on certain circumstances, often outside the fraudster's control (e.g. carelessness of a certain user or the auction system operator), but provides the fraudster with an account that can be utilized on the spot and with possible less risk as the original user will be the primary target of the claims.

1.2   Existing Fraud Prevention and Detection Techniques

It was not long after eBay launched that fraudsters noticed the new options it provided. An initial analysis of auction fraud and its prevention appeared as early as 2000 [3]. By 2006, online auction fraud was the most offen reported offence in Australia, according to a government report [21].

So far, most of the research focus has been applied to identifying the fraudulent accounts that were used to build up a reputation score based on the distribu-tion of accumulated feedback in time [4], decision trees [5] or belief propagation and Markov random fields [25]. Also, there are proposals to utilize non-technical methods (i.e. social groups and their collective expertise) to combat some specific forms of auction fraud [7]. There is, however, substantially less interest in identifying hacked or stolen auction accounts. Although the issue (also named an 'identity theft') is very important to financial industry, as outlined in [17],[23], there is little specific research related to auction accounts, even though, as will be demonstrated in this article, this specific environment provides opportunities to utilize various techniques based on specifically available data.

2   An Overview of the Proposed Method

In this paper we propose a multi-model approach to detecting anomalies in the behaviour of sellers participating in the internet auctions. For each seller a different behaviour model is created, which is next constantly matched against the current profile (offers and transactions performed). The model consists of a number of features and procedures which are used to evaluate the users' behaviour.

The primary task of the model is to assign a probability value to the current behaviour of the seller. This probability value reflects the probability of the occurrence of the given feature value with regards to an established seller profile. The assumption is that feature values with a sufficiently low probability indicate potentially abnormal behaviour, which in turn my be the result of an account hijacking by a malicious individual. Based on the model outputs, the user's behaviour may be reported as abnormal. This decision is reached by calculating a number of anomaly scores. The current user's behaviour is reported as anomalous if at least one of these anomaly scores is above the corresponding detection threshold. This approach shares some concepts with intrusion detection systems (IDS) [16], however, it operates on different types of data and behaviour models, as IDS operates on the network traffic level - detecting anomalies in network packets.

Similar multi-model approaches were successfully used for detecting potential attacks on web applications [15], [13]. Sample models of the seller's behaviour are described in the following section.

The real data about users' activities presented in this article have been gathered by the authors by monitoring Polish largest auction service (allegro.pl). This service consistently hosts over 1 million active auctions at any given time, and has an important advantage over eBay from the research point of view, as it allows for the retrieval of users' history (past auctions).

3   EWMA of the User's Activity

The proposed model is based on measuring the total number of items offered for auction in all categories on any given day. To restrict the model sensitivity to temporary fluctuations in the number of items offered daily, the model utilizes an exponentially weighted moving average. This average ($S(t)$) is calculated according to a recursive formula:

$$S(t) = \begin{cases} \alpha \cdot y(t-1) + (1-\alpha) \cdot S(t-1) & \text{if } t > 2 \\ y(1) & \text{if } t = 2 \end{cases} \tag{1}$$

Where:

- t is discrete time (the number of the day), in which we calculate the average number of auctions; the mean is calculated from the initial time $t = 2$
- $y(t)$ is users' activity (e.g. the number of items offered by a seller) on the day t
- α is the smoothing constant (filter factor)

Additionally, the variance is calculated recursively:

$$V(t) = \alpha \cdot (y(t) - S(t-1))^2 + (1-\alpha) \cdot V(t-1) \tag{2}$$

Where:

- $V(t)$ is the variance at the moment t

Applying Chebyshev's inequality

$$P(|x - E(x)| > \varepsilon) < \frac{V(x)}{\varepsilon^2} \tag{3}$$

and substituting $E(x) = S$ and $\varepsilon = |y(t) - S|$, we obtain:

$$P(|y - S| > |y(t) - S|) < \frac{V(t)}{|y(t) - S|^2} \equiv P(y(t)) \tag{4}$$

The Chebyshev's inequality imposes an upper bound on the probability, i.e. that the difference between the value of a random variable x and $E(x)$ exceeds a certain threshold ε, for an arbitrary distribution with variance $V(x)$ and mean $E(x)$. The inequality is very useful because it can be applied to various arbitrary distributions with finite variance.

The formula (4) calculates the probability value $P(y(t))$ if the amount of user's activity (e.g. the number of items put up for auctions) at any given time $y(t)$ exceeds the current value of $S(t)$. If the number of items is smaller then or equal to $S(t)$, it is assumed that $P(y(t)) = 1$. The value of $P(y(t))$ is the value returned by this model.

Figure 1 illustrates a typical scenario, with varying but consistent user's activity over time. Although the activity is changing substantially, the value of the $dV(t)/dt$ function does not reach significant levels.

In another scenario, illustrated in Fig. 2 the user's activity includes a significant peak at a certain time (around 40th day). This is promptly signalled as a suspicious activity by the change in variation exceeding the value of 10. The proposed model proves also its usefulness in Fig. 3, when an activity of a specific user is illustrated. This user apparently puts up items for sale in weekly 'batches'. As can be seen in this figure, the model does not alert of a suspicious activity in this case, which is a desired outcome, as such behaviour is consistent and unsurprising.

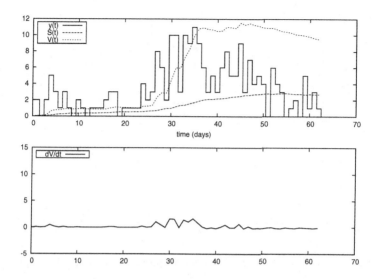

Fig. 1. Non suspicious activity of a selected user. The values of moving average, variance and variance's derivative are presented. The values calculated for ($\alpha = 0.02$).

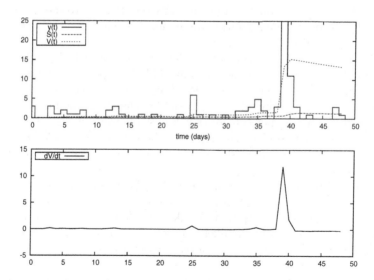

Fig. 2. Example of suspicious activity ($\alpha = 0.02$)

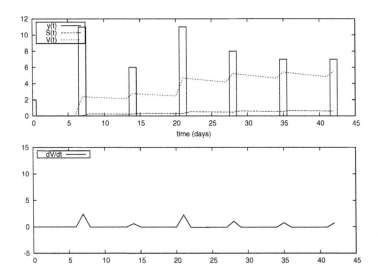

Fig. 3. Insensitivity of the detection to periodical activity ($\alpha = 0.02$)

4   'Thematic' Category Clusters

Although the proposed model of user's activity performs up to the expectations, it is usually better to have multiple detection systems (at least two) for the confirmation of a suspicious case.

Another criterion of the suspicious seller's behaviour (which might indicate a takeover of an account) is a sudden change of the types of items provided by the seller. Since all auction services allow the sellers to assign the offered item with a category (from a provided list), a sudden change in the number of items offered (or transactions) per categories is a possible warning sign. For example, a user who so far has sold items mostly in the categories *for children → toys* and *books → comics* suddenly starts to sell in the category *jewellery for men* and *jewellery for women*.

In order to detect such changes in the profile of categories for a given seller, it is necessary to cluster all categories of an auction service into thematic groups. By 'thematic' we mean groups that are likely to share similar items across several categories. Such clusters are likely to group together the already mentioned *jewellery for men* and *jewellery for women* as well as e.g. *books → guidebooks* and *car → manuals*.

This clusterization allows to build and observe sellers' activity profiles within given thematic categories. Unfortunately, the hierarchy of categories offered by auction services often does not suit this purpose, as similar items can be offered in distant categories (according to the hierarchy tree).

In order to create useful clusters of categories, they were grouped on the basis of similarity of the names of items present. This is done as follows:

In given time intervals (one month in the existing implementation), the names of all objects offered in all categories are acquired. For each category pair the probability is calculated using the formula:

$$s(c_a, c_b) = \frac{\sum_{i=1}^{n} \max_{1 \leq j \leq m} \tilde{f}(p_{ca}(i), p_{cb}(j))}{n} \tag{5}$$

where

- n the number of auctions in the category c_a
- m the number of auctions in the category c_b
- $p_{ca}(i)$ - the name of the object with the number and in the category c_a
- $p_{cb}(j)$ - the name of the object with the number and in the category c_b

next, the similarity factor is calculated:

$$\tilde{f}(p_{ca}(i), p_{cb}(j)) = \begin{cases} 0 & \text{if } f(p_{ca}(i), p_{cb}(j)) < 0.5 \\ f(p_{ca}(i), p_{cb}(j)) & \text{if } f(p_{ca}(i), p_{cb}(j)) \geq 0.5 \end{cases} \tag{6}$$

$$f(p_{ca}(i), p_{cb}(j)) = \frac{1 - L_{dist}(p_{ca}(i), p_{cb}(j))}{\max(|p_{ca}(i)|, |p_{cb}(j)|)} \tag{7}$$

where

- $L_{dist}(p_{ca}(i), p_{cb}(j))$ - the Levenshtein distance betwen name $p_{ca}(i)$ and $p_{cb}(j)$
- $|p_{ca}(i)|$ - size (number of characters) of name $p_{ca}(i)$
- $|p_{cb}(j)|$ - size (number of characters) of name $p_{cb}(j)$

The similarity $\tilde{f}$ shown in equation (6), represents the percentage distance between names (i.e. the minimum number of edits needed to transform one name into another divided by the length of the longest name multiplied by 100%). If it exceeds 50%, the value of similarity $\tilde{f}$ is assigned the value of 0 to limit the influence on the similarity of the category $s(c_a, c_b)$ of the objects significantly differing in names (the suggested cut off threshold at 50% is arbitrary, but has proven to be a reasonable value).

Before calculating the Levenshtein distance [14] L_{dist} between the names of the items, p_{ca} and p_{cb} are normalized:

- all 'marketing' marks used by sellers in order to attract buyers such as: '#', '!', '*' are removed
- white spaces and the following signs ",;.-" are concatenated to a single space
- all letters are transformed to lower case.

Such normalization of names is necessary to achieve a meaningful distance between the names, as sellers tend to utilize numerous ways of modifying the names in order to stand out with their offers. As can be observed, due to the way of defining the similarity S between categories, $0 \leq s(c_a, c_b) \leq 1$ as well as self-similarity of categories $s(c_a, c_a) = 1$.

On the basis of the similarity s between categories the symmetrical similarity measure is defined as:

$$s_{sym}(c_a, c_b) = \frac{s(c_a, c_b) + s(c_b, c_a)}{2} \tag{8}$$

On the basis of the symmetrical similarity measure s_{sym}, an undirected graph is built which represents the similarity between categories. In this graph the vertices represent given edges, and edges represent the similarity between given categories. The weight of the edges connecting vertices c_a and c_b equals $s_{sym}(c_a, c_b)$. If $s_{sym}(c_a, c_b) = 0$, the edge is discarded.

During the next step, the graph constructed undergoes a clusterization in order to group thematically similar categories together. The clusterization algorithm used is a recursive spectral algorithm described in [12]. This algorithm was chosen because of its many advantages, including its speed and the fact that it can be successfully applied in a variety of contexts [1], [8], [20], [22], [10], [24].

The specific algorithm used in the reference implementation was based on [6] and is described in (Algorithm 1).

Algorithm 1. Clustering of the categories

Input: Matrix n x n containing weights of undirected weighted graph representing categories similarity

Output: A tree whose leaves are the row indexes of A representing clusters

1. Initialize
   - Let $R^2 \in \Re^{n \times n}$ be a diagonal matrix whose diagonal entries are the row sums of AA^T
2. Compute Singular Vector
   - Compute the second largest right singular vector v' of the matrix $A^T R^{-1}$
   - Let $v = R^{-1}v'$
3. Cut
   - Sort v coordinates so that $v_i <= v_{i+1}$
   - Find the value t that minimizes the conductance of the cut:
     $(S, T) = (\{v_1, ..., v_t\}, \{v_{t+1}, ..., v_n\})$
   - Let A_S, A_T be the submatrices of A whose rows are those in S, T
4. Normalize
   - Adjust the selfsimilarities
     $$A_{ii}^2 := A_{ii}^2 + \begin{cases} \sum_{j \in T} A_{(i)} \cdot A_{(j)} \; if \; i \in S \\ \sum_{j \in S} A_{(i)} \cdot A_{(j)} \; if \; i \in T \end{cases}$$
5. Recurse
   - Recurse steps 2-4 on the submatrices A_S and A_T

The conductance of a cut $(S, V \setminus S)$ is calculated as follows:

$$cond(S, V \setminus S) = \frac{d(S, V \setminus S)}{min(d(S), d(V \setminus S))} \qquad (9)$$

where

- $d(A, B) = \sum\limits_{i \in A, j \in B} A_{(i)} \cdot A_{(j)}$
- $d(A) = d(A, V)$
- $A_{(i)}$ is i-th row vector in matrix A

The results of the clusterization can be seen in Fig. 4, which illustrates how all activities of two users really belong to one primary specific cluster of categories, with some marginal activity in other category clusters.

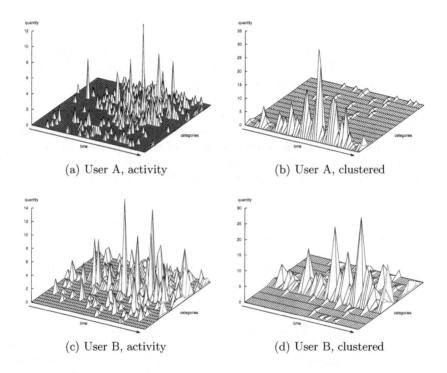

(a) User A, activity   (b) User A, clustered

(c) User B, activity   (d) User B, clustered

Fig. 4. Illustration of User's activity (the quantity of daily transactions) for two different accounts. The graphs on the right illustrate activity aggregated into 'thematic' clusters.

5   Detecting Unusual Activities

After the clusterization into thematic category groups, the probability of a certain number of offers appearing in a given group on a given day is calculated. The probability is calculated in the same way as the EWMA model described above. The probability of correct (non anomalous) behaviour yielded by this model $P(y(t))$ is described as the minimum of probabilities in particular clusters:

$$P(y(t)) = min(P_c(y(t)))$$ (10)

where

- $c \in C$ (set of all clusters)

After calculating the probability of non anomalous behaviour at a given time t using particular models expressed as $P_m(t)$, it is possible to calculate the following parameters:

$$anomaly\_score_w = \sum_{m \in M} w_m \cdot (1 - P_m)$$
$$anomaly\_score_{max} = max(1 - P_m)$$ (11)

The first one represents a weighted sum of anomalous behaviour calculated by each model, while $(1 - Pm)$ denotes the probability of anomalous behaviour according to the model m, and w_m represents the weights associated with this model. The second parameter specifies a maximum probability of anomalous behaviour yielded by all models.

Finally, it is possible to select thresholds k_w and k_{max} respectively for calculated anomaly scores in such a way that after exceeding them, the system will report a possibility of unauthorized usage of the suspicious account. The thresholds needs to be be adjusted manually in order to minimize the number of false positive alerts while preserving the sensitivity of the system to anomalous behaviour.

6   Conclusion

The models proposed in this paper for the assessment of the user's activity behaviour have proven very effective against the provided set of data. The data used for validating the models were gathered by daily retrieval of all the auctions from their web site for a period of one month. There were several millions of auctions retrieved during that time. Unfortunately, due to legal and privacy concerns, we were not able to receive data on real accounts taken over by criminals, so the model was validated with the data manually reviewed which deemed to be suspicious (e.g. Fig. 2). The clusterization of the categories has also proved to yield extraordinary results, with significant portion of users having most of their transactions in just a few (or even one) primary category groups. Interestingly, with the total number of groups equal to approximately a quarter of all categories, some groups consisted of over 200 categories, while the others were single-membered.

The most computationally expensive part of the proposed process is the grouping of categories, which can fortunately be done quite rarely (e.g. once a month) and off-line. Other algorithms are lightweight and can easily be utilized for a real-time monitoring on any scale of users. Implementing such solutions will not eliminate the possibility of fraudulent use of a hijacked account, but will at least greatly limit the benefits, as an alert can be risen very quickly and the suspicious account suspended for evaluation. As has been mentioned before, auction fraud is a considerable aspect of public security, therefore, its mitigation is of interest to both auction service providers and security forces (e.g. police).

Although the proposed model proves to be effective, it can be further enhanced with other detection factors (e.g. the assessment of the value of items offered instead of their number). This may further improve its ability to distinguish anomalies in users' behaviour.

References

1. Alpert, C., Kahng, A., Yao, Z.: Spectral partitioning: the more eigenvectors the better. Discrete Applied Mathematics 90, 3–26 (1999)
2. Beranek, L.: Auditing Electronic Auctions Systems. ISACA OnLine Journal 4 (2010), http://www.isaca.org/Journal/Past-Issues/2010/Volume-4/Pages/default.aspx
3. Boyd, C., Mao, W.: Security Issues for Electronic Auctions. Technical Report, Hewlett Packard (2000)
4. Chang, J.S., Chang, W.H.: An Early Fraud Detection Mechanism for Online Auctions Based on Phased Modeling. In: Proceedings of Joint Conferences on Pervasive Computing (JCPC), Taipei, pp. 743–748 (2009)
5. Chau, D., Faloutsos, C.: Fraud Detection in Electronic Auction. In: Proceedings of EWMF 2005: European Web Mining Forum, Porto (2005)
6. Cheng, D., et al.: On a recursive spectral algorithm for clusterin from pairwise similarities. MIT LCS Technical Report MIT-LCS-TR-906 (2003)
7. Chua, C., Wareham, J.: Fighting Internet Auction Fraud: An assessment and proposal. IEEE Computer 37(10), 31–37 (2004)
8. Dhillon, I.: Co-clustering documents and words using bipartite spectral graph partitioning. In: Knowledge Discovery and Data Mining, pp. 269–274 (2001)
9. Dong, F., Shatz, S., Zu, H.: Combating Online in-Auction Fraud: Clues, Techniques and Challenges. Computer Science Review 3(4), 245–258 (2009)
10. Fowlkes, C., et al.: Spectral Grouping Using the Nyström Method. IEEE Transactions on Pattern Analysis and Machine Intelligence 26, 214–225 (2004)
11. Gavish, B., Tucci, C.: Reducing Internet Auction Fraud. Communications of the ACM 51(5), 89–97 (2008)
12. Kannan, R., Vempala, S., Vetta, A.: On clusterings: good, bad and spectral. In: Proceedings of the 41st Annual Symposium on Foundations of Computer Science, California, pp. 367–380. IEEE Computer Society (2000)
13. Kruegel, C., Vigna, G., Robertson, W.: A multi-model approach to the detection of web-based attacks. Computer Networks 48, 717–738 (2005)
14. Levenshtein, V.I.: Binary codes capable of correcting deletions, insertions and reversals. Soviet Physics Doklady 10, 707–710 (1966)
15. Pałka, D., Zachara, M.: Learning Web Application Firewall - Benefits and Caveats. In: Tjoa, A.M., Quirchmayr, G., You, I., Xu, L., et al. (eds.) ARES 2011. LNCS, vol. 6908, pp. 295–308. Springer, Heidelberg (2011)
16. Pietro, R., Mancini, L. (eds.): Intrusion Detection Systems. Springer (2008) ISBN: 978-0-387-77265-3

17. Putting an End to Account-Hijacking Identity Theft. Federal Deposit Insurance Corporation (2004)
18. Reichling, F.: Effects of Reputation Mechanisms on Fraud Prevention in eBay Auctions. Thesis, Stanford University (2004)
19. Quaterly Retail E-commerce Sales (2009),
    http://www.census.gov/retail/mrts/www/data/pdf/09Q4.pdf
20. Shi, J., Malik, J.: Normalized cuts and image segmentation. IEEE Transactions on Pattern Analysis and Machine Intelligence 22(8), 888–905 (2000)
21. The risk of criminal exploitation of online auctions. Australian Institute of Criminology (2007)
22. Weiss, Y.: Segmentation using eigenvectors: a unifying view. In: Proceedings of IEEE International Conference on Computer Vision, pp. 975–982 (1999)
23. Wheeler, R., Aitken, S.: Multiple algorithms for fraud detection. Knowledge-Based Systems 13, 93–99 (2000)
24. Xiang, T., Gong, S.: Spectral clustering with eigenvector selection. Pattern Recognition 41(3), 1012–1029 (2008)
25. Zhang, B., Zhou, Y., Faloutos, C.: Toward a Comprehensive Model in Internet Auction Fraud Detection. In: Proceedings of Hawaii International Conference on System Sciences, pp. 79–87. IEEE Computer Society (2008)

A Formal Support
for Collaborative Data Sharing*

Fabio Martinelli, Ilaria Matteucci, Marinella Petrocchi, and Luca Wiegand

Istituto di Informatica e Telematica, CNR, Pisa, Italy
`firstname.surname@iit.cnr.it`

Abstract. Collaborating entities usually require the exchange of personal information for the achievement of a common goal, including enabling business transactions and the provisioning of critical services. A key issue affecting these interactions is the lack of control on how data is going to be used and processed by the entities that share it. To partially solve the issue, parties may have defined a set of data sharing policies regulating the exchange of data they own, or over which they have jurisdiction. However, distinct set of policies, defined by different authorities, may lead to conflicts once enacted, since, *e.g.,* different subjects may have defined different permissions on the same data set. This paper focuses on policy analysis and offers a formal support for coming up with a conflict-free set of data sharing policies. We illustrate the methodology on the example of an emergency management.

1 Introduction

An effective, speedy, and continuous data exchange is essential for todays life. In a collaborative fashion, several parties usually interact one with each other, for the achievement of a common goal. As an example, heating our houses is possible since a series of gas producers and gas distribution providers have agreed in cooperating to let the final product reach us. Such collaboration leads, with high probability, to a massive data exchange, that should be enabled in a safe way, avoiding the risks of violating privacy and confidentiality that may be associated with the data. In this scenario, it is of utmost importance to ensure that data exchange happens in accordance with well defined and automatically manageable policies. Data Sharing Agreements (DSA), which are formal agreements regulating how parties share data, enable secure, controlled, and collaborative data exchange. Consequently, infrastructures based on DSA become an increasingly important research topic and promise to be a flexible mechanism to ensure protection of critical data.

As the name itself recalls, a data sharing agreement is a contract signed by parties that mutually *agree* on its contents. According to the number of authors,

---

* The research leading to these results has received funding from the European Union Seventh Framework Programme (FP7/2007-2013) under grant no 257930 (Aniketos) and under grant no 256980 (NESSoS), and from the IIT internal project Mobi-Care.

G. Quirchmayr et al. (Eds.): CD-ARES 2012, LNCS 7465, pp. 547–561, 2012.

we may distinguish between agreements with only one author, *unilateral* DSA, and agreements with more than one author, *multilateral* DSA.

The core of a unilateral DSA consists of a list of rules regulating the sharing of information typically owned by the author of the contract. As an example, a unilateral DSA may dictate the set of privacy policies that an individual define on her own sensitive data, *e.g.,* medical or bank account data. To some extent, a contract edited by a service provider, and regulating the management of personal data of service consumer, could be considered as an unilateral DSA too. Indeed, accepting such a contract, service consumers implicitly agree on the data management policies dictated by the service provider. Whereas the client does not agree with the terms of the provider's data policies, she can always chooses another provider that best satisfies their privacy requirements. In [1], we presented a design phase for unilateral DSA, defining and developing two tools for DSA authoring and analysis.

On the other hand, a multilateral DSA consists of a document edited and signed by several parties. Each party has a set of privacy policies over a set of data. Data may be owned by the party itself, *e.g.,* the previous mentioned medical data of a patient, or the marketing strategical view of a company for the next five years. Also, some organization could have rights to express policies over data which it does not directly own, but over which it may have jurisdiction (*e.g.,* traffic policemen have usually rights to ask for driver licenses). Since each entity has its own rules regulating data sharing, and since data that are subjects of different policies may overlap, the design phase for multilateral DSA is quite more complex than the one for unilateral DSA. Drawing up a multilateral DSA requires, for instance, a definition phase in which policies dictated by different organizations over the same set of data are checked to be conflict-free.

In this paper, we extend the analysis framework presented in [1] to deal with multilateral DSA. We propose an analysis methodology, decorated by an analysis tool, as a formal support for the creation of a well-defined, conflict-free multilateral DSA. The analysis examples and results are presented through a set of reference policies related to a scenario in which a set of individuals/organizations need to share data in a urgent but controlled way, for the successful management of an emergency situation.

The paper is structured as follows. Section 2 describes the reference structure of a data sharing agreement. Section 3 shows the reference scenario. Sections 4 and 5 present our analysis framework. Section 6 discusses related work in the area. Finally, Section 7 concludes the paper.

2   Multilateral Data Sharing Agreements

From the analysis of samples of real DSA, *e.g.,* [2–4] we derived a general structure for an agreement. A DSA consists of various parts, among which a *Title*, a validity *Period*, the list of *Data* covered by the agreement, the list of involved *Subjects*, their respective *Signatures*, and *Data Sharing Policies* sections.

For the sake of classification, such policies can be divided into *Authorizations*, *Obligations*, and *Prohibitions*, indicating which actions are authorised, obliged, or denied on which data by which subject.

The following general assumptions hold throughout the paper:

1. if no obligation policies are explicitly expressed, then subjects are not required to make any actions on any data;
2. everything that is not explicitly expressed by an authorization or an obligation policy is prohibited.

From the second assumption, we can also derive that, if neither authorization nor obligation policies are explicitly expressed, then the following implicit prohibition holds: "all entities (users, groups, etc.) belonging to *Subjects* are not authorized/required to make any action on *Data* during *Period*".

Some sections in a DSA are optional: *Purpose* stating the purpose of the DSA in layman's language; *Definitions* defining terms used in the agreements; *Data quality* describing the degree of commitment to data quality; *Custodial responsibility* describing who is responsible for the data and the confidentiality requirements stated in the DSA; *Trust domain* defining the pre-existent trust relationships among the *Subjects*; and *Security infrastructure requirements* describing any requirement related to the security infrastructure, *e.g.,* : encryption algorithms, length of encryption keys, etc.

Hereafter, we suppose that a common ontology exists among the *Subjects* and we focus on the analysis of the authorizations, obligations, and prohibition sections.

3   Scenario

Let us consider an emergency scenario in which several vehicles are involved in an accident, including a tanker. Both firemen and Red Cross paramedics and toxicologists spring to the victims aid. We generically refer to firemen and Red Cross representatives as Rescue Time, or rescuers.

Managing the emergency with timeliness and accuracy implies to share information regarding the context in which rescuers operate. Examples of sensitive information the rescuers need to exchange are personal and medical information of victims, information on the tanker's content, and information on the alert state of the accident.

Reasonably, all the entities at stake, both individuals and organizations, have their own rules for sharing sensitive information, even within an emergency. Below, we list a series of plausible data sharing policies, in terms of authorizations A, obligations O, and prohibitions P.

Fire Brigade

A_{F1} Firemen can access both personal and medical data of the victim.
A_{F2} Firemen can access the personal data of drivers involved in an accident.
A_{F3} Firemen can access the delivery notes of any trucks involved in accidents. In particular, firemen can access the current delivery note and delivery notes of the past ten days.

A_{F4} Firemen can define the alert state of the accident.

P_{F1} If the alert state of the accident is greater than five, then rescue team members cannot communicate the alert state to the population living in the surrounding area.

Red Cross

A_{R1} Red Cross members (toxicologists plus paramedics) can access the alert state of the accident.

A_{R2} Paramedics can access medical data of the victim.

A_{R3} Toxicologists can access the delivery note of the trucks involved in the accident.

O_{R1} After that Red Cross members access the alert state of the accident, then, if the alert state is greater then five, then Red Cross members must communicate the alert state to the population living in the surrounding area.

Victim

P_{V1} People belonging to medical organizations cannot access my medical data if I am not in peril of my life.

Tankers company

P_{T1} Individuals not covering the role of firemen cannot access the current delivery notes of tankers.

4   Policy Specification

In order to specify information sharing policies, we adopt a controlled natural language called CNL4DSA [5]. The language aims at formally specifying such policies without loosing simplicity of use for end-users. Peculiarity of the language is the use of contexts, specifying attributes of *Subjects* and *Data* (like the subjects' roles, or the data category), plus attributes of environmental factors (like time and location). With the help of contexts, authorizations, obligations, and prohibitions are enriched with the capability to express under which set of conditions a subject is *allowed*, *obliged*, or *not allowed* to perform an action on a data object.

The core of CNL4DSA is the notion of *fragment*, a tuple $f = \langle s, a, o \rangle$ where s is the subject, a is the action, o is the object. The fragment expresses that "the subject s performs the action a on the object o", *e.g.*, "Bob reads Document1". It is possible to express authorizations, obligations, and prohibitions by adding the *can/must/cannot* constructs to the basic fragment. Fragments are evaluated within a specific *context*. In CNL4DSA, a *context* is a predicate c that evaluate either to *true* or *false*. Some examples of simple contexts are "date is more than 1 year ago" or "location is inside the building". In order to describe complex policies, contexts need to be composable. Hence, we use the Boolean connectors *and, or,* and *not* for describing a *composite context C* which is defined inductively as follows:

$$C := c \mid C \text{ and } C \mid C \text{ or } C \mid \text{not } c$$

The syntax of a *composite fragment*, denoted as F, is inductively defined as follows:

$$F := nil \mid can/must/cannot \; f \mid F; F \mid if \; C \; then \; F \mid after \; f \; then \; F \mid (F)$$

The intuition is the following:

- *nil* can do nothing.
- *can/must/cannot f* is the atomic fragment that expresses that f is permitted/required/not permitted. $f = \langle s, a, o \rangle$. Its informal meaning is *the subject s can/must/cannot perform the action a on the object o.*
- *F; F* is a list of composite fragments (*i.e.,* a list of authorizations, obligations, or prohibitions).
- *if C then F* expresses the logical implication between a context C and a composite fragment: if C holds, then F is permitted/required/not permitted.
- *after f then F* is a temporal sequence of fragments. Informally, after f has happened, then the composite fragment F is permitted/required/not permitted.

CNL4DSA has an operational semantics based on a modal transition system, able to express *admissible* and *necessary* requirements to the behaviour of the CNL4DSA specifications [5, 6].

4.1 Examples

With reference to the scenario in Section 3, we show some examples of CNL4DSA policies.

A_{F1} *if* hasRole(user1, fireman) *and* hasDataCategory(data, personal) *or* hasDataCategory(data, medical) *and* isReferredTo(data, user2) *and* isInvolvedIn(user2, accident) *then can* access(user1, data)

where hasRole(user1, fireman) *and* hasDataCategory(data, personal) *and* hasDataCategory(data, medical) *and* isReferredTo(data, user2) *and* isInvolvedIn(user2, accident) is a composite context and *can* access(user1, data) is a composite authorization fragment.

A_{F3} *if* hasRole(user1, fireman) *and* hasDataCategory(data, deliveryNote) *and* isReferredTo(data, truck) *and* isInvolvedIn (truck, accident) *then can* access(user1, data) where hasRole(user1, fireman) *and* hasDataCategory(data, deliveryNote) *and* isReferredTo(data, truck) *and* isInvolvedIn (truck, accident) is a composite context and *can* access(user1, data) is a composite authorization fragment.

O_{R1} *if* hasRole(user1, RedCross) *and* hasDataCategory(data, alertState) *then after that* access(user1, data) *then if* isGreaterThan(alertState,five) *then must* communicate(user1,data)

where hasRole(user1, RedCross) *and* hasDataCategory(data, alertState) is a composite context, access(user1, data) is the simple fragment representing the pre-condition of the obligation, isGreaterThan(alertState,five) is a second composite context, and *must* communicate(user1,data) is a composite obligation fragment.

P_{T1} *if not* hasRole(user1,fireman) *and* hasDataCategory(data,deliveryNote) *and* isReferredTo(data,truck) *then cannot* access(user1, data)

where *not* hasRole(user1,fireman) *and* hasDataCategory(data,deliveryNote) *and* isReferredTo(data,truck) is a composite context and *cannot* access(user1, data) is a composite prohibition fragment.

5   Policy Analysis

In this section, we perform a series of analyses over a set of data sharing policies. The analysis process allows i) to detect conflict between policies; ii) to answer questions related to single clauses; and iii) to visualize a table of access.

- *Conflict detection.* After defining a set of contextual conditions, the analysis process is able to check if the set of policies is conflict-free, under those contextual conditions. Conflicts are searched either between an authorization and a prohibition clause, or between an obligation and a prohibition clause. Suppose that the user defines a certain context, *e.g.,* she defines the category of the data to be medical, and the role of the user to be a toxicologist. Looking for conflicts in the available policies means to check if

  1. there exists an authorization and a prohibition that, at the same time, allows and denies the toxicologist to perform the same action on those medical data;
  2. there exists an obligation and a prohibition that, at the same time, obliges and denies the toxicologist to perform the same action on those medical data.

  It is worth noticing that we do not check conflicts between an authorization and an obligation because our assumption is that any obliged action is implicitly authorized, see Section 2.

- *Questions related to single queries.* The analysis process is also able to answer several questions regarding authorizations, obligations, and prohibitions, like "is it true that subject x is authorised to perform action z on object y, under a set of contextual conditions?" and "is it true that subject x is required to perform action z on object y, after that subject w performs action t on object q, under a set of contextual conditions?". In the last sentence, possibly x=w, z=t, y=q.
- *Table of access.* This table shows all the authorised actions in the investigated set of policies, under a set of contextual conditions.

Answers to these questions are obtained with standard Maude built-in commands, such as *red*, *rew*, and *search* that basically allow to find all the possible traces, or a particular trace, in a specification written in Maude. The interested reader can refer to the Maude Manual, available online.

In [1] we verified that the policies of a unilateral DSA have been specified according to the author's intent. Hereafter, we exploit our analysis framework for detecting possible conflicts that can arise dealing with multiple policies to be deployed according to a multilateral DSA.

5.1   The Analysis Tool

The analysis tool consists of two parts:

- a formal engine that actually performs the analysis of the policies;
- a graphical user interface that allows the user to dynamically load contextual conditions and launch the analysis of the set of policies.

The Engine CNL4DSA has been designed with precise formal semantics rules, regulating states and transitions between these states. This allows for a precise translation of CNL4DSA in Maude. Maude is an executable programming language that models distributed systems and the actions within those systems [7]. Systems are specified by defining algebraic data types axiomatizing systems states, and rewrite rules declaring the relationships between the states and the transitions between them.

The choice of using Maude for DSA analysis is driven by the fact that rewrite rules are a natural way to model the behaviour of a distributed system, and we see a DSA exactly as a process where different subjects may interact with each other, possibly on the same set of objects. Maude is executable and comes with built-in commands allowing to search for allowed traces, *i.e.*, sequence of actions, of a policy specified in CNL4DSA. These traces represent the sequences of actions that are authorised, or required, or denied by the policy. Also, exploiting the implementation of modal logic over the CNL4DSA semantics, as done in [8, 9] for CCS-like languages, it is possible to prove that a modal formula, representing a certain query, is satisfied by the Maude specification of the DSA.

Also, a Maude related toolkit allows a series of formal reasoning about the specifications produced, including real-time and probabilistic model checking [10, 11].

These additional facilities allow to deal with DSA whose policies are also based on probability and time-out.

CNL4DSA has been made executable by translating its syntax and formal semantics in Maude and the translation has been presented in [1].

The Graphical User Interface. The GUI is deployed as a Web Application and it allows the user to query the analysis engine and visualize its results. The analysis engine exposes its functionalities as Web Service methods. The GUI is in charge of retrieving the set of policies that a user wants to analyse and the related vocabulary. Each vocabulary is implemented as an ontology and the inner logic of the GUI exploits it in order to create and show a set of menus whose information is consistent with the vocabulary. We assume that all the organizations agree on a common ontology for expressing their policies. We leave the phase of negotiation of this common ontology as a future work.

The interface helps the user to create dynamic contexts, which represent the environment under which the analysis will be performed. The inner logic of the GUI updates the information according to the selected context. Furthermore, it is possible to compose different types of queries, related to authorizations, obligations, and prohibitions. Once the user selected the context and, possibly, the queries, the GUI sends all the inputs, *i.e.*, the vocabulary, the high level description of the policies, the context defining the conditions on which the policies have to be evaluated, and the set of queries to the engine that performs the analysis. When the analysis has been performed, the results are shown through the GUI.

5.2   Analysis Example

Here, we show some example analyses over our reference policies. The GUI is available at `http://dev4.iit.cnr.it:8080/DsaAnalyzerWebGUI-0.1/?dsaID=CI.xml`. The interested reader should press the *Submit for the Analysis* button in order to load our reference policies and the related vocabulary. The vocabulary is pre-loaded, *stitched* on the reference policies.

First, the user can select the contextual conditions under which the analysis is carried out.

The user selects the context from a drop-down menu. The menu is dynamically created according to the vocabulary of the loaded policies. All the selected contexts are automatically set to *true*. We assume that everything that is not explicitly specified does not hold. Hence, the user shall select each context that is supposed to be true.

Once the context has been defined, the user has three possibilities (see Figure 2). Either she can ask for conflict detection, or she can compose a query and perform successive elaboration on it, or she can ask for the table of access.

In the following, we show how to compose a query and some analysis results when a conflict is detected.

Composition of queries. If the user selects the analysis *Compose a query*, a form appears through which it is possible to compose queries representing either authorizations, or obligations, or prohibitions, see Figure 3.

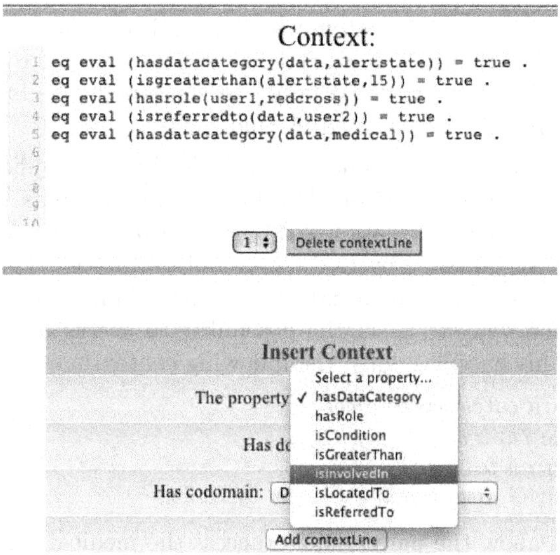

Fig. 1. Screenshot of the context insertion box

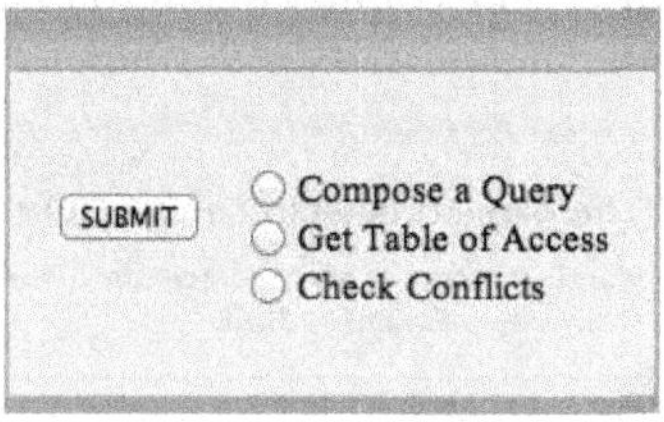

Fig. 2. Alternative analyses

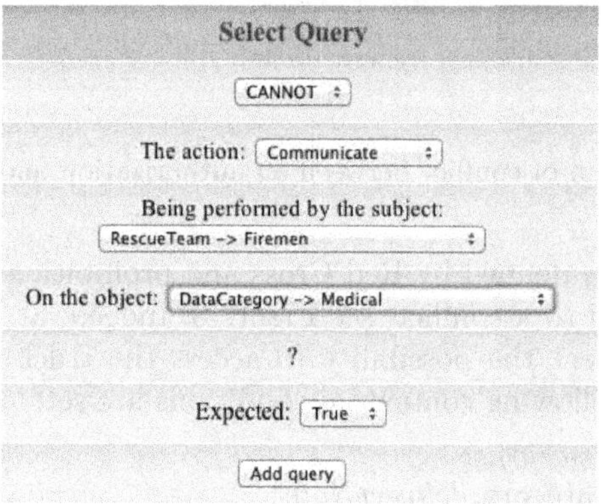

Fig. 3. Screenshot of the query insertion box

Once that the user has selected both context and queries, she can start the analysis process by pressing the Submit button. This launches the inner analysis engine. At the end of the process, the GUI shows the analysis result to the user. In particular, the answer is true if a policy exists, among the loaded policy set, that satisfies the request represented by that query.

Conflict detection. We show some analysis examples where a conflict is detected between two data sharing policies defined by distinct organizations. The first conflict is detected between an authorization and a prohibition of our reference scenario.

Authorization A_{R2} defined by Red Cross and prohibition P_{V1} defined by an individual being involved in the accident lead to a conflict. Indeed, at the same time they give and deny to user1 the possibility to access the medical data of the individual. This happens when the following contextual conditions are set:

- data have data category *medical*
- user1 has role *paramedic*
- data are referred to *user2*
- *user2* is involved in *accident*

These conditions allow the paramedic to access the medical data (according to authorization A_{R2}). On the other hand, the individual is not in peril of her life. This is due to the fact that the context *user2 hascondition critical* is not true. The lack of this context activates prohibition P_{V1} according to which the paramedic is not allowed to access the data. The conflict detection is shown in Figure 4.

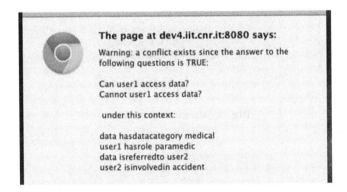

Fig. 4. Detection of conflict between an authorization and a prohibition

Authorization A_{R3} defined by Red Cross and prohibition P_{T1} defined by the tanker company lead to a conflict, see Figure 5. Indeed, at the same time they give and deny to user1 the possibility to access the truck delivery note. This happens when the following contextual conditions are set:

- user1 has role *toxicologist*
- data have data category *deliveryNote*
- data are referred to *truck*
- *truck* is involved in *accident*

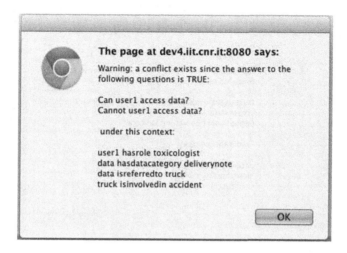

Fig. 5. Detection of conflict between an authorization and a prohibition

Conflicts may also raise between obligations and prohibitions. Indeed, it is possible that some actions are prohibited by an organization and obliged by another one. This is the case of obligation O_{R1} by Red Cross and prohibition P_{F1} by Fire brigade. The Fire Brigade does not permit to communicate the alert state to people not belonging to the rescue team while Red Cross members are obliged to communicate the alert state, *e.g.*, to people living in the area surrounding the accident. The conflict detection raises with the following contextual conditions set to true:

- data have data category *alertState*
- *alertState* is greater than *level 5*
- user1 has role *RedCross*

Under this context, user1 is obliged to communicate the alert state, but, according to prohibition P_{F1} and since the Red Cross member is also a member of the rescue team, user1 cannot communicate the alert state. The conflict detection is shown in Figure 6.

Through the user interface it is possible to save the current configuration (*i.e.*, a set of contextual conditions and a set of queries) for successive elaborations (see Figure 7). This functionality allows to load a saved session without redefining contexts and queries. This is useful when the user, that possibly detects a conflict among the policies, modifies those policies. When checking the correctness of the modified clauses, there is no need to reformulate the contextual conditions and the queries.

Finally, the GUI is decorated with a help on line facility, for guiding the user through the capabilities of the analyser.

Fig. 6. Detection of conflicts between an obligation and a prohibition

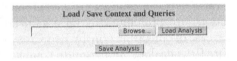

Fig. 7. Screenshot of the load and save box

6 Related Work

Data protection in critical infrastructures has been discussed in the past recent years and several documents depict generic guidelines for secure data sharing in an informal way, *e.g.,* [12–15]. Often, such generic guidelines remain inaccessible from the software architecture supporting the data sharing itself, mainly because such guidelines are often written in natural language, which is difficult to parse and prone to ambiguity. Multilateral Data Sharing Agreements promise to be a flexible mean to fill the gap between a traditional legal contract regulating the sharing of data among different domains, and the software architecture support-ing it. However, to come up with a consistent enforceable DSA, there is the need to check that data sharing policies deployed by different organizations/individ-uals are conflict-free.

The work presented in this paper mainly focuses on conflict detection among a set of data sharing policies originally defined by different authorities. In the liter-ature, there exist other work related to the authoring, analysis, and enforcement of data sharing policies. Here, we revise our analysis framework with existing work in the area.

Binder [16] is an open logic-based security language that encodes security authorizations among components of communicating distributed systems. It has a notion for context and provides flexible low-level programming tools to express delegation, even if Binder does not directly implement higher-level security concepts like delegation itself. Also, the Rodin platform provides animation and model-checking toolset, for developing specifications based on the Event-B language (www.event-b.org). In [17], it is shown that the Event-B language can be used to model obliged events. This could be useful in the case of analysing obligations in DSA. In [18], the authors present a formalization of DSA clauses in Event-B and the ProB animator and model checker are exploited in order to verify that a system behaves according to its associated DSA. The main difference with our approach is that CNL4DSA captures the events (or actions) that a system can perform, the order in which they can be executed and it can be easily extended for dealing with other aspects of this execution, such as time and probabilities. On the other hand, in [18] the analysis of the agreement clauses is performed without considering a direct association between the set of clauses and the system functionality. Hence, Event-B language models the clauses that hold in a certain state of a system rather than its transition.

Also, a relevant work in [19] proposes a comprehensive framework for expressing highly complex privacy-related policies, featuring purposes and obligations. Also, a formal definition of conflicting permission assignments is given, together with efficient conflict-checking algorithms. Finally, the Policy Design Tool [20] offers a sophisticated way for modeling and analysing high-level security requirements in a business context and create security policy templates in a standard format.

To conclude, there exists generic formal approaches that could *a priori* be exploited for the analysis of some aspects of DSA. As an example, the Klaim family of process calculi [21] provides a high-level model for distributed systems, and, in particular, exploits a capability-based type system for programming and controlling access and usage of resources. Also, work in [22] considers policies that restrict the use and replication of information, *e.g.,* imposing that a certain information may only be used or copied a certain number of times. The analysis tool is a static analyser for a variant of Klaim.

Related to the sharing of data, but not strictly related to analysis, [23, 24] present on opportunistic authority evaluation scheme for sharing data in a secure way in a crisis management scenario. The main idea is to combine two already existing data sharing solutions in order to share data in a secure way through opportunistic networks. Finally, even if not specifically DSA-related, [25] presents a policy analysis framework which considers authorizations and obligations, giving useful diagnostic information.

7   Conclusions and Future Work

We focused on the analysis phase of a set of data sharing policies, originally defined by separate authorities for the management and the protection of data owned, or governed, by these authorities.

The achievement of a common goal, such as the management of an emergency, let such authorities interact and collaborate. Interactions may lead to the disclosure of possibly sensitive information whose sharing need to be regulated. Increasingly used, data sharing agreements are a usual way to regulate the sharing of information. In this paper, we propose a formal analysis framework to support several authorities to come up with the definition of a conflict-free multilateral DSA. The framework consists of a user-friendly interface that exploits capabilities of a background analysis tool in such a way to guide the user to detect conflicts on a multilateral DSA.

We leave some work for the future. Currently, the vocabularies collecting the terms used in a DSA do not carry semantic information, but we plan to evolve them towards more formal ontological definition of terms in such a way to enable the management of different vocabularies in which syntactically different terms are semantically equivalent, *e.g.,* in which two different terms refer to the same subject, or object. Also, our tool is able to detect conflicts, but no strategy is being defined and enforced to solve them. We are currently working on a classification of different kind of conflicting policies and on the definition of a set of strategies for supporting the user in solving conflicts, once detected. Finally, as it is common for tools based on state exploration, the underlying analysis engine suffers from the problem of the state explosion. Thus, it may be convenient to further investigate the feasibility of using this engine for more complex DSA specifications.

References

1. Matteucci, I., Petrocchi, M., Sbodio, M.L., Wiegand, L.: A Design Phase for Data Sharing Agreements. In: Garcia-Alfaro, J., Navarro-Arribas, G., Cuppens-Boulahia, N., de Capitani di Vimercati, S. (eds.) DPM 2011 and SETOP 2011. LNCS, vol. 7122, pp. 25–41. Springer, Heidelberg (2012)
2. Oklahoma Health Care Authority: Interagency Agreement, http://www.okhca.org/provider/contracts/ffs/pdflib/mhcm_over21.pdf (last access April 11, 2012)
3. National Research Network: Data Sharing Agreement Template, www.researchtoolkit.org/primer/docs/AAFP-NRNDUA.pdf (last access April 11, 2012)
4. National Collaborative on Workforce and Disability: Sample Inter-Agency Data Sharing Agreement, http://www.ncwd-youth.info/assets/guides/assessment/sample_forms/data_share.pdf (last access April 11, 2012)
5. Matteucci, I., Petrocchi, M., Sbodio, M.L.: CNL4DSA: a Controlled Natural Language for Data Sharing Agreements. In: SAC: Privacy on the Web Track, pp. 616–620. ACM (2010)
6. Larsen, K.G., Thomsen, B.: A modal process logic. In: LICS, pp. 203–210 (1988)
7. Clavel, M., Durán, F., Eker, S., Lincoln, P., Martí-Oliet, N., Meseguer, J., Talcott, C. (eds.): All About Maude - A High-Performance Logical Framework. LNCS, vol. 4350. Springer, Heidelberg (2007)
8. Verdejo, A., Martí-Oliet, N.: Implementing CCS in Maude 2. ENTCS, vol. 71 (2002)

9. Colombo, M., Martinelli, F., Matteucci, I., Petrocchi, M.: Context-aware analysis of data sharing agreements. In: Advances in Human-Oriented and Personalized Mechanisms, Technologies and Services (2010)
10. Ölveczky, P.C., Meseguer, J.: Semantics and pragmatics of Real-Time Maude. Higher-Order and Symbolic Computation 20(1-2), 161–196 (2007)
11. AlTurki, M., Meseguer, J.: PVeStA: A Parallel Statistical Model Checking and Quantitative Analysis Tool. In: Corradini, A., Klin, B., Cîrstea, C. (eds.) CALCO 2011. LNCS, vol. 6859, pp. 386–392. Springer, Heidelberg (2011)
12. North American Electronic Reliability Corporation: Critical infrastructure protection: Security guidelines, http://www.nerc.com (last access April 19, 2012)
13. U.S. Department of Justice: Justice information sharing, http://it.ojp.gov/default.aspx (last access April 19, 2012)
14. Natural Resources Canada: Best practices for sharing sensitive environmental geospatial data (2010), www.geoconnections.org
15. US Fire Administration: Critical infrastructure protection – information sharing and analysis center, http://www.usfa.fema.gov/fireservice/subjects/emr-isac/ (last access April 19, 2012)
16. Abadi, M.: Logic in Access Control. In: LICS, p. 228. IEEE (2003)
17. Bicarregui, J., Arenas, A.E., Aziz, B., Massonet, P., Ponsard, C.: Towards Modelling Obligations in Event-B. In: Börger, E., Butler, M., Bowen, J.P., Boca, P. (eds.) ABZ 2008. LNCS, vol. 5238, pp. 181–194. Springer, Heidelberg (2008)
18. Arenas, A.E., Aziz, B., Bicarregui, J., Wilson, M.D.: An Event-B Approach to Data Sharing Agreements. In: Méry, D., Merz, S. (eds.) IFM 2010. LNCS, vol. 6396, pp. 28–42. Springer, Heidelberg (2010)
19. Ni, Q., et al.: Privacy-aware Role-based Access Control. ACM Transactions on Information and System Security 13 (2010)
20. Policy Design Tool (2009), http://www.alphaworks.ibm.com/tech/policydesigntool
21. De Nicola, R., Ferrari, G.-L., Pugliese, R.: Programming Access Control: The KLAIM Experience. In: Palamidessi, C. (ed.) CONCUR 2000. LNCS, vol. 1877, pp. 48–65. Springer, Heidelberg (2000)
22. Hansen, R.R., Nielson, F., Nielson, H.R., Probst, C.W.: Static Validation of Licence Conformance Policies. In: ARES, pp. 1104–1111 (2008)
23. Scalavino, E., Gowadia, V., Lupu, E.C.: PAES: Policy-Based Authority Evaluation Scheme. In: DBSec, pp. 268–282 (2009)
24. Scalavino, E., Russello, G., Ball, R., Gowadia, V., Lupu, E.C.: An Opportunistic Authority Evaluation Scheme for Data Security in Crisis Management Scenarios. In: ASIACCS (2010)
25. Craven, R., et al.: Expressive Policy Analysis with Enhanced System Dynamicity. In: ASIACCS (2009)

Tool-Supported Risk Modeling and Analysis of Evolving Critical Infrastructures

Fredrik Seehusen and Bjørnar Solhaug

SINTEF ICT
{fredrik.seehusen,bjornar.solhaug}@sintef.no

Abstract. Risk management is coordinated activities to direct and control an organization with regard to risk, and includes the identification, analysis and mitigation of unacceptable risks. For critical infrastructures consisting of interdependent systems, risk analysis and mitigation is challenging because the overall risk picture can be strongly affected by changes in only a few of the systems. In order to continuously manage risks and maintain an adequate level of protection, there is a need to continuously maintain the validity of risk models while systems change and evolve. This paper presents a risk analysis tool that supports the modeling and analysis of changing and evolving risks. The tool supports the traceability of system changes to risk models, as well as the explicit modeling of the impact on the risk picture. The tool, as well as the underlying risk analysis method, is exemplified and validated in the domain of air traffic management.

Keywords: Risk analysis, interdependencies, critical infrastructures, ATM.

1 Introduction

Critical infrastructures is a term that is commonly used to refer to assets and facilities that are highly essential for the functioning of a society. Such infrastructures include, for example, electricity and power generation and supply, gas and oil production and distribution, telecommunication, public health, and public security and emergency services. Clearly, the disruption of services that are provided by these infrastructures can be severe or even catastrophic. Critical infrastructures are therefore the subject of the strongest requirements to protection from hazards and risks. They are moreover often characterized by strong interdependencies, which means that the safety, security and reliability of some critical infrastructures strongly rely on such properties of several other.

Governments are both nationally and internationally taking measures to safeguard critical infrastructures. For example, at EU level the European Programme for Critical Infrastructure Protection (EPCIP) was created as a result of the European Commission's Directive EU COM(2006) [5]. The objective is to maintain a list of critical infrastructures across the EU, including the set of assets for which protection and incident preparedness is required. The directive stresses the strong interdependencies and the need to identify these in order to achieve

G. Quirchmayr et al. (Eds.): CD-ARES 2012, LNCS 7465, pp. 562–577, 2012.
© IFIP International Federation for Information Processing 2012

the EPCIP objectives. It moreover prescribes risk management and risk assessment as necessary means to identify and document threats, vulnerabilities, risks and countermeasures. Clearly, such risk assessments need to systematically take into account the identified infrastructure interdependencies [3,9].

Risk management is coordinated activities to direct and control an organization or a system with regard to risk, and includes the identification, analysis and mitigation of unacceptable risks [8]. For critical infrastructures, risk analysis is particularly challenging because the overall risk picture can be strongly affected by changes in only a few of the systems; in order to continuously manage risks and maintain an adequate level of protection, there is a need to continuously maintain the validity of risk models while systems change and evolve. For this purpose the risk analysis process should be supported by methods and tools that cope with interdependencies in a systematic way, allowing traceability of changes from system to risk. However, established risk management guidelines, standards and methods [1,2,8,11,14,16] largely view systems in a monolithic way and provide little support for handling change [10,12].

This paper presents a risk analysis tool that supports the modeling and analysis of changing and evolving risks. The tool supports traceability of system changes to risk models, as well as the explicit modeling and assessment of the impact of the changes on the overall risk picture. The tool is developed to support the method and the risk modeling language presented in [12], and has been validated in the air traffic management (ATM) domain [17]. ATM systems are critical infrastructures with strong dependencies on other critical infrastructures such as communication, electricity and energy, positioning and satellite systems, transportation systems and emergency. Moreover, interdependencies in ATM are becoming even more relevant and critical with the ATM 2000+ Strategy [6] and the SESAR initiative (http://www.sesarju.eu/) as traditionally quite closed systems at national level are integrated at transnational, European level.

The structure of the paper is as follows. In Section 2 we give some background to risk analysis in general and to the risk analysis method and language that the tool presented in this paper is developed to support. In Section 3 we present the most important requirements to the tool, and in Section 4 we give an example-driven presentation of the most important functionalities. In Section 5 we discuss the tool with respect to the identified requirements. Finally, in Section 6, related work is discussed before we conclude.

2   Background

According to the ISO 31000 risk management standard [8] risk analysis should be regularly conducted in order to assess and mitigate risks. The standard defines risk analysis as an iterative process consisting of five consecutive steps. *Establish the context* is to define the external and internal parameters to be accounted for when managing risk, and to set the scope and risk criteria for the risk management policy. *Risk identification* is to find, recognize and describe risks. *Risk estimation* is to comprehend the nature of risk and to determine the risk level.

Risk evaluation is to compare the risk estimation results with the risk criteria to determine whether the risk and its magnitude are acceptable or tolerable. *Risk treatment* is the process of modifying the risk.

The purpose of the standard is to provide methodological advice on how to manage risk, and it offers no specific techniques for how to conduct the activities in practice. Nor does the standard prescribe any support or advice on how to identify and document risk, for example by means of risk modeling techniques and languages. Most of the established risk analysis methods have activities that generally follow the principles laid out by the standard, and commonly they also provide techniques and come with tools to support the activities. CORAS [11] is an approach to model-driven risk analysis that is closely based on ISO 31000. It is self-contained in the sense that it offers a method that comes with concrete, practical guidelines, it comes with a language with modeling support and analysis techniques, and it comes with a tool that supports all activities.

In order to handle change, interdependencies and traceability in a systematic and methodic way, each activity must be supported by specialized guidelines and techniques. For this purpose the ISO 31000 process is in [12] generalized to include such guidelines throughout the whole process, and this generalization is in turn instantiated in CORAS. At the same time the CORAS language is extended and generalized to offer risk modeling support for the traceability techniques and for explicitly modeling and assessing changes to risks. The reader is referred to [12] for the details about the generalized method and language. In the following we highlight the most important principles, focusing on risk identification.

A part of establishing the context is to make a description of the target of analysis. The target description includes the documentation and models of the target of analysis, and serves as the basis for the subsequent risk assessment. It is therefore important that all relevant aspects of the target of analysis are properly documented. Moreover, dependencies to other systems and infrastructures must be included in the description of the environment in order to capture how external factors may affect the risks. An important aspect of the generalized process is that possible changes and evolutions are explicitly taken into account during context establishment and documented as part of the target description.

The risk identification involves identifying and documenting unwanted incidents with respect to the target of analysis and the identified assets. In the generalized approach, a further objective is to identify and document the changing risks given the description of change in the target of analysis. A main principle is that to the extent that we have identified and documented the risks for the target of analysis before changes, we only address the parts of the target that are affected by the change. The methodological guidelines are summarized as follows. 1) Identify and document risks by using as input the target description before changes have been taken into account. 2) Establish and document the traceability between the target description before change and the risk documentation resulting from the previous step. 3) Based on the traceability and the description of the changed target, identify the parts of the risk documentation that are persistent under change. 4) Conduct the risk identification of the

Fig. 1. Elements of CORAS threat diagrams

changed target only with respect to the parts of the target and the risks that are affected by the change.

In conducting these activities we make active use of three model artifacts, namely the target model, the risk model and the trace model. The target model needs to capture the relevant aspects of the target of analysis and can be built using any suitable notation, such as the UML [15]. For risk modeling CORAS threat diagrams are used. Threat diagrams document risks by describing how threats exploit vulnerabilities to initiate threat scenarios and unwanted incidents. A risk is the likelihood of an unwanted incident and its consequence for a specific asset. Risks are estimated by annotating each identified unwanted incident with a likelihood and a consequence. The graphical language constructs are shown in Figure 1, and an example diagram is depicted in Figure 5.

The trace model is part of the generalized CORAS approach and is used to build links between elements of the target model and elements of the risk model. The links are depicted in CORAS diagrams by means of the target segment construct which is an extension of the standard CORAS language. A further extension is the support for the explicit modeling of risk changes. Each CORAS language element can be assigned one of the three modes *before*, *after* and *before-after*. The mode *before* captures elements of the risk picture that become obsolete after change and are depicted in gray. The mode *after* captures elements that emerge after change and are depicted in the standard way with colors. The mode *before-after* captures elements that are persistent under change and are depicted using a double layer. Moreover, because the likelihoods and consequences of the latter elements may change these values are annotated in pairs, where the former is the value before change and the latter is the value after change. Examples of the use of these modes are shown in Figure 7.

A full risk analysis will typically result in a large number of threat diagrams covering the various parts of the target description. Without any automated tool support the task of tracing changes from the target model to the risk model must be conducted manually. Moreover, keeping track of how changes percolate, and correctly and consistently assigning modes to the risk elements, can be challenging. Hence, making efficient use of the generalized risk analysis method and the traceability requires proper tool support.

3   Tool Requirements

The tool is mainly a diagram editor that is designed to support on-the-fly risk modeling during structured brainstorming. The brainstorming sessions involve one or two risk analysts as well as four to seven people with expert knowledge about the target of analysis. The tool is operated by a risk analyst who draws diagrams that are displayed to the participants while the discussions proceed. There are of course many requirements that apply for such a tool to adequately support the whole risk analysis process. In this section we focus on the requirements that are relevant for handling dependencies, traceability and change.

First and foremost, for the tool to fulfill its purposes it should support the specification of all kinds of CORAS diagrams using the language generalized to capture the three different modes with respect to change. Next, in order to deal with traceability the tool must support the specification of traceability links from elements of the target model to elements of the risk model. This, in turn, requires the tool to import (a representation of) the target model. CORAS does not prescribe a specific notation to be used for the target modeling, as different languages may be suitable in different risk analyses, so the tool should be able to import models irrespective of the chosen language.

Whereas we have generalized the CORAS language to explicitly model change, we cannot assume the corresponding expressiveness in the language chosen for the target modeling. Instead we assume that the target model is modified to reflect the changes, such that we have one model before the changes and one model after the changes. The specific parts of the target of analysis that have changed must then be determined by comparing the two models and generating the diff. For detecting changes and supporting traceability, this should be conducted automatically by the tool. Based on the specified traceability links and the diff, the system changes can now be traced to the parts of the risk model that may be affected. This should also be supported by the tool by automatically flagging the affected diagrams of the risk model.

When reassessing the risks the threat diagrams are updated by assigning modes of change to the elements. While the generalized language is useful for the documentation of and the reasoning about risk changes, it may be challenging to keep track of how changes percolate through the threat diagrams and to maintain consistency with respect to change. For this purpose there should be automatic support for detecting and resolving inconsistencies in the diagrams.

In the following the requirements to the tool that are relevant for handling dependencies and change are summarized.

- The tool should support on-the-fly modeling of syntactically correct CORAS diagrams with change.
- The tool should support the importing of the target models irrespective of the chosen language for target modeling.
- The tool should support the specification of traceability links between elements of the target model and elements of the risk model.
- The tool should automatically generate the diff between the target model before changes and the target model after changes.
- The tool should automatically flag all elements of the risk model that are affected by the system changes and therefore have to be reassessed.
- The tool should provide support for detecting and resolving inconsistencies with respect to change.

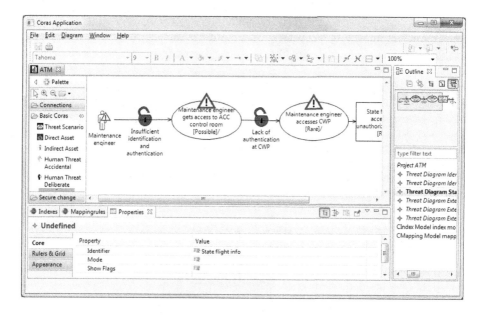

Fig. 2. Creating CORAS diagrams

4   Tool Functionality and Features

In this section we describe and exemplify the most important functionality and features of the tool regarding the support for handling traceability and change. The tool has been developed as a plugin to Eclipse such that it can be easily extended with new features and easily integrated with other Eclipse-based tools. To ensure that the models that are created using the tool are stored in a standard format, it is based on Eclipse Modeling Framework (EMF). The examples that we use are from the ATM domain and have been extracted from validation activities involving experts on ATM and on secure system engineering [17].

The main use of the tool is as a diagram editor for creating CORAS diagrams. The interface is shown in Figure 2 with the drawing canvas in the middle. The palette to the left contains all language elements and relations, and diagrams are created easily by drag-and-drop. For each diagram that is created, the user must first choose the kind of CORAS diagram. The syntactically correct diagram is defined by the meta-model of the language, and the tool automatically prevents the user from making diagrams that are grammatically incorrect.

As mentioned above, the risk identification and the creation of the threat diagrams are conducted by systematically going through the target model trying to determine where things can go wrong and how. The ATM validation activities addressed the initial phases of a system engineering process for the development of ATM services provided by an Air Navigation Service Provider (ANSP) in Area Control Centers (ACCs). The requirements were captured in collaboration

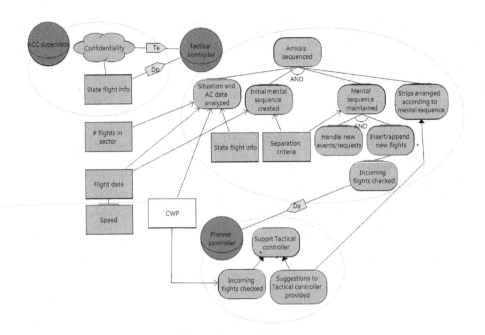

Fig. 3. Modeling the target of analysis

with the ANSP and modeled as SI* goal models [13]. A small fragment of the requirement model, which served as the target model, is shown in Figure 3.

SI* models show the goals (rounded rectangles) that actors/roles (circles) seek to achieve, as well as the resources (rectangles) that are needed for achieving the goals. Non-functional requirements, such as security goals, are captured by soft goals (clouds). A delegation marks a passage of responsibility for achieving a goal (delegation execution, De) or of authority with respect to a resource (delegation permission, Dp). Trust is a relation between actors/roles representing the expectations of the trustor about the capabilities of the trustee (trust execution, Te) or about the behavior of the trustee with respect to a permission (trust permission, Tp). Figure 3 shows three air traffic controllers (ATCOs) and some of their goals in the sequencing of flights during arrival management. The ACC supervisor is supervising the ATM activities, and is also responsible for protecting the confidentiality of State Flight info. A State Flight is any flight involving military, customs, police or other law enforcement services of a state, or any flight declared as such by state authorities. ATCOs need access to State Flight info since these flights are sequenced differently than commercial flights, but at the same time the information must be kept confidential to prevent misuse by potential adversaries. The Tactical controller is responsible for sequencing the arriving flights, and is supported by the Planner controller in achieving some of the sub-goals. The latter two ATCOs rely on several resources, such as the controller working position (CWP), which is their workstation.

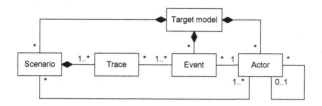

Fig. 4. Meta-model for generic target model

The risk analysis tool is designed to import the target model independent of the language that is chosen for making the target description. To this end, all target models must conform to a meta-model, *TM*, for the representation of the target model in the tool. This meta-model is shown in Figure 4 (somewhat simplified to focus on the conceptual aspects), and is defined to capture the parts of the target of analysis that are relevant for reasoning about risk, namely actors (which can be human and non-human), events that may occur, and scenarios that may unfold. Because the tool can take arbitrary target models as input, the user needs to define a mapping from the meta-model, *MM*, of the target model to the meta-model, *TM*, of the tool. The only requirement is that *MM* is defined according to an Ecore meta-model, which is the EMF specification of meta-models. The mapping is defined by a set of transformation rules that apply to elements, element attributes and element references. In the ATM case study with the use of SI*, we have, for example, mapped actor/role to actor and goal to scenario, including the names and the goals that are attributed to the actor/role. The specification of the transformation is a one-off task for the selected target modeling language; it is stored in a text file that is loaded by the tool together with the meta-model of the target model (here the SI* meta-model).

The tool is now ready to import the target model that is used. The purpose of importing the target model to the tool is to be able to specify traceability links, not to view or edit the target models, which instead is conducted separately in a designated tool. In order to be able to uniquely refer to the separate elements of the target model the tool creates an index of all elements, where each index is represented by a tuple (*ID, Name, Category, Description, Mode*). *ID* is a unique automatically generated identifier, *Name* is the name of the element as specified in the target model, *Category* is the kind of target model element (*Actor, Event* or *Scenario*), and *Mode* specifies the mode of the target model element with respect to change. *Description* is an initially empty field that can be filled in by the user if further explanation is desired or needed. The set of index tuples are represented in the tool in the table format shown at the bottom of Figure 5. Note that the mode of all target elements are currently *before* since no changes have yet been specified for the target system.

Given the threat diagrams and the index of the target model, traceability between them can be specified by defining mapping rules. Basically, a mapping rule is a pair of a target model element and a risk model element. Additionally, each mapping rule is given a tag with a chosen name for the mapping rule. In the visualization of the mapping rule in the threat diagrams, the name of the tag

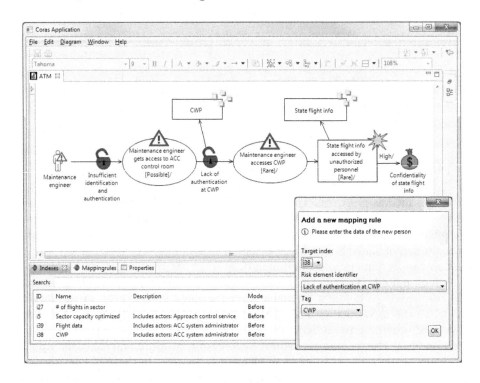

Fig. 5. Defining mapping rules

is automatically inserted. For example, in Figure 5 a mapping rule pairs target element with index *i38* (*CWP*) with the vulnerability *Lack of authentication at CWP*. A further purpose of using the tag is that it allows several mapping rules to be clustered. For example, all three actors in Figure 3 are ATCOs, and for elements of the risk model to which all three are related we can create three mapping rules with the same tag, *ATCO*.

Given the target model, the finalized risk model, and the trace model, the process is ready to proceed with handling changes that may occur. Two of the changes that were addressed in the ATM case study were the introduction of the AMAN and the SWIM. AMAN (Arrival Manager) is a decision support tool that automates the sequencing of flights in arrival management. The AMAN therefore needs to be fed with all relevant flight data, including State Flight info. SWIM (System Wide Information Management) is an information network that will integrate information systems and facilitate the flow of information between entities such as aircrafts, airports, ACCs, ATCOs, ANSPs, etc. Previously, State Flight info did not have to be digitally stored and shared, but could be kept separate from flight data (cf. Figure 3). With the AMAN introduction, however, this information needs to be part of the general flight data and shared over the SWIM network. This raises new security threats, for example with respect to the confidentiality of State Flight info, which is an asset in our case study.

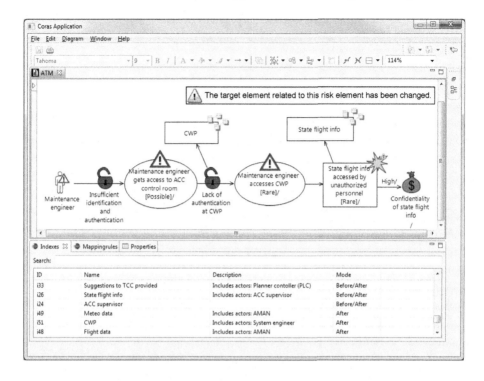

Fig. 6. Automatic flagging of changes

The first step in addressing the changes is to update the target model. As a result we have two target models, one for the situation before changes and one for the situation after changes. To determine what has changed we need to compare the two models. This is supported by the tool by the automatic generation of the diff, which is done by comparing two target model files as specified by the user. In practice, the tool first transforms the two models to its own target model representation and generates the diff based on this. It thereafter updates the index to include the changes and setting the correct change mode to each target model element. Due to space constrains we do not show the updated SI* model after change, but at the bottom of Figure 6 we see some of the new indexes with their mode. For example, System engineer is an actor that was included after the changes, whereas ACC supervisor is in the target model both before and after.

Due to the changes in the target of analysis, some parts of the risk analysis may have to be conducted anew. The tool supports the identification of the affected threat diagrams by flagging all risk model elements that are related to changes in target model elements. This is shown in Figure 6 with the warning sign on the unwanted incident *State flight info accessed by unauthorized personnel* and the pop-up message on the screen.

In reassessing the risks that are documented in the flagged threat diagrams, we need to determine which parts become obsolete and which parts are persistent, and we also need to identify new risks that may arise. The explicit modeling

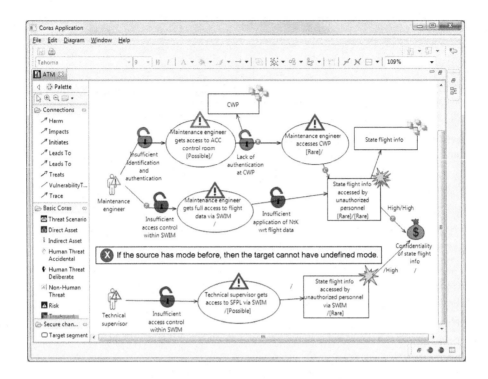

Fig. 7. Modeling change and resolving inconsistencies

and assessment of such changes are supported by the generalized language and by the tool by assigning one of the modes *before*, *after* and *before-after* to each element. This is exemplified in Figure 7, where, for example, the threat scenario *Maintenance engineer gets access to ACC control room* has mode *before*, the threat scenario *Technical supervisor gets access to SFPL via SWIM* has mode *after*, and the unwanted incident *State flight info accessed by unauthorized personnel* has mode *before-after*. Note that the default mode is *undefined*, i.e. when a new element is inserted there is no mode assigned to it.

While the generalized language supports the assessment and documentation of changing risks, the increased complexity makes it more challenging to keep diagrams consistent. For example, a threat diagram element of mode *before* cannot be related to an element of mode *after* as they do not coexist. Moreover, a threat diagram element should not have an undefined mode when it is related to elements where the mode has been specified. To support the user in modeling risk changes the tool does automatic consistency checking, and warnings pop up whenever an inconsistency in introduced. Each inconsistency is flagged with a red circle with a white cross, for example on the relation between the threat *Maintenance engineer* and the threat scenario *Maintenance engineer gets full access to flight data via SWIM*. This is, as the shown pop-up explains, because the former is assigned mode *before* and the latter has undefined mode. A further example is on the relation between the unwanted incident (in mode *before-after*) and the asset (in undefined mode); the latter should also be in mode *before-after*.

In addition to detecting errors, the automatic consistency checking is very useful for systematically tracing changes through the threat diagrams. For example, when starting from the left and assigning a mode to the threat, warnings will immediately be flagged on the relations to the adjacent elements. When resolving this inconsistency these warnings disappear, and new ones emerge one step further to the right. The user can in this way update the diagram step by step while maintaining the consistency.

Finally, when all threat diagrams are updated, finalized and consistent, new mapping rules should be defined to establish the traceability with respect to the updated target model. This ensures that all documentation is ready for any further future changes that need to be dealt with in the same way.

5   Discussion

In this section we discuss the tool with respect to the requirements identified in Section 3. As mentioned before, these requirements focus on the need for tool support for handing dependencies, traceability and change. For a more general evaluation that also takes into account the methodological support and the language support, the reader is referred to [17].

The tool should support on-the-fly modeling of syntactically correct CORAS diagrams with change. The tool is a diagram editor with all language constructs immediately available by drag-and-drop from the palette. Relations between the elements can moreover easily be attached by click-and-drag, where the tool automatically selects the syntactically correct relation. Moreover, as the tool implements the meta-model of the CORAS language, the user is prevented from making diagrams that are grammatically incorrect. An exception from the latter is the use of the extended notation to enable the modeling of risk changes; instead of preventing the user from making inconsistencies with respect to change, the tool automatically flags all such errors. However, this is intended as diagrams are updated in a stepwise manner when change is brought into the picture. If inconsistencies with respect to change was prevented, the users would have to build all the diagrams from scratch instead of updating them.

The tool should support the importing of the target models irrespective of the chosen language for target modeling. The tool is designed to import target models of arbitrary languages, since different notations are suitable for different kinds of target systems and since different communities can have different modeling preferences. The tool therefore uses one common and generic meta-model for all target models. This is at the cost of users having to specify the transformation from the meta-model of the chosen language to the meta-model used by the tool, which requires some expertise in language design. However, this is a one-off task for a given target modeling language, and the benefit is of course that the use of the risk analysis method and tool is not restricted to only one target modeling language. Still, one restriction with respect to the choice of target modeling language is that the its meta-model must be an Ecore meta-model.

The tool should support the specification of traceability links between elements of the target model and elements of the risk model. This is supported by the functionality of defining mapping rules. In order to be able to specify all possible mapping rules, it is necessary that all elements of the target model are indexed by the tool. This in turn requires that the transformation rules mapping the meta-model of the target modeling language to the meta-model in the tool is complete, i.e. that it covers all elements of the target model. For some languages, it may be that the meta-model of the tool is not rich enough, resulting in dependencies that cannot be captured automatically.

The tool should automatically generate the diff between the target model before changes and the target model after changes. This is supported by the tool by comparing the two models and generating the diff between them, identifying elements that are deleted, added or modified. The diff is generated by comparing the representation of the target models in the tool, i.e. according to the target meta-model of the tool. As for the traceability, this means that if there are target elements that are not captured by this meta-model, changes to these are not captured. As an alternative to using a generic target meta-model in the tool, the tool could be customized for one specific target modeling language, such as the UML or SI*. The tool would then use the meta-model for this specific language, and all elements and changes would be captured. Moreover, the user would not have to specify the transformation rules for the meta-model. When designing the tool we aimed for flexibility and general applicability, which explains our design choice. However, customized versions could be developed by replacing the generic target meta-model with any specific one.

The tool should automatically flag all elements of the risk model that are affected by the system changes and therefore have to be reassessed. This is supported by the tool, but the extent to which all affected threat diagrams are flagged depends on two things. First, the generated diff must be able to capture all system changes as discussed above. Second, the users of the tool of course need to specify mapping rules that cover all system changes that occur.

The tool should provide support for detecting and resolving inconsistencies with respect to change. This is supported by the flagging of inconsistencies as discussed above. Resolving the inconsistencies must be conducted manually, but the user can immediately see when consistency is restored.

6   Related Work and Conclusion

Model Versioning and Evolution (MoVE) (http://move.q-e.at/) [4] is an approach to build an infrastructure to maintain the validity, mutual consistency and interdependencies between models as they evolve over time within model engineering. The approach does not target security and risk in particular, but rather builds a tool-supported infrastructure for versioning of several interdependent models, for example for software architecture and design, business processes, services, security and risk. Similar to our approach, the underlying idea is to provide support for tracing changes from one model to another so as to ensure that they are globally up-to-date and mutually consistent. However, although the infrastructure can support the handling of dependencies and change in risk analysis, as exemplified in a case study, there is no specific modeling or methodological support for this. Instead the user chooses the models and notations, such as CORAS or UML, to be managed by MoVE.

ProSecO [7] is a model-based approach to risk analysis with support for dependency identification and modeling. The approach relates risk elements to elements of a functional model of the target of analysis. Moreover, the model elements are related to security objectives and security requirements, and risks are related to threats and security controls. Although risk assessment is supported, there is no risk modeling support other than a description of incidents and their likelihood and consequence.

Dependent CORAS [3,11] is an extension of the CORAS language to support modular risk analysis, as well as the modeling and reasoning about interdependencies. However, the purpose is not to capture and model dependencies of the risk models on the target system, but rather interdependencies between different risk models. This is in particular relevant for mutually dependent critical infrastructures, where the risks and risk level of one can strongly depend on the risks and risk level of the other. Tool support is provided for creating and editing Dependent CORAS diagrams, but there is no automation of dependency analysis. In [9] a method is proposed to capture and monitor the impact of service dependencies in interdependent systems of systems. The dependencies between system services are explicitly modeled, and subsequently taken into account during risk identification and modeling. However, the problem of tool-supported traceability between system elements and risk elements is outside the scope.

In [17] an approach to integrate risk assessment and modeling with system development and modeling to aid the handling of dependencies and change between the two domains is presented. The former is supported by the Rinforzando tool and the latter by the SOA Modelling Suite (SMS). The tool supports tight integration between the system model and the risk model in several ways. For example, in the risk models assets and supporting equipment, technologies, work processes, etc. can be selected directly from the SMS target models. Moreover, dependencies are continuously maintained such that modifications in one model is either automatically propagated to the other model, or warning flags appear as pop-ups. This integration of system and risk model is tighter than in our approach, but it requires the use of SMS for system modeling. Furthermore, explicit modeling of risk changes is not supported as the objective is rather to maintain the mutual consistency between models.

In this paper we have presented a tool to support the method and language presented in [12], enabling the traceability from the target of analysis and/or its environment to the risks. The tool gives automated support for tracing changes and identifying risks that need to be reassessed in order to maintain the validity of risk models, as well as automated support for maintaining consistency of risk models. The tool has been validated in the ATM domain, which is a critical infrastructure with strong dependencies on other infrastructures.

Further work is required for evaluating and validating the tool with the use of different modeling languages for capturing the target of analysis, although the results have been promising in case studies so far. A further topic for future work is to develop a tighter integration between the target model and the risk model to support mutual consistency and automated updates of model elements in case of changes.

Acknowledgments. This work has been partially funded by the European Commission via the NESSoS (256980) network of excellence.

References

1. Alberts, C.J., Davey, J.: OCTAVE criteria version 2.0. Technical report CMU/SEI-2001-TR-016, Carnegie Mellon University (2004)
2. Barber, B., Davey, J.: The use of the CCTA risk analysis and management methodology CRAMM in health information systems. In: 7th International Congress on Medical Informatics (MEDINFO 1992), pp. 1589–1593. North-Holland (1992)
3. Brændeland, G., Refsdal, A., Stølen, K.: Modular analysis and modelling of risk scenarios with dependencies. Journal of Systems and Software 83(10), 1995–2013 (2010)
4. Breu, M., Breu, R., Löw, S.: MoVEing forward: Towards an architecture and processes for a Living Models infrastructure. International Journal On Advances in Life Sciences 3(1-2), 12–22 (2011)
5. Communication from the Commission on a European programme for critical infrastructure protection. In: The European Commission, COM, 786 final (2006)
6. EUROCONTROL: Air traffic management strategy for the years 2000+ (2003)
7. Innerhofer-Oberperfler, F., Breu, R.: Using an enterprise architecture for IT risk management. In: Information Security South Africa Conference, ISSA 2006 (2006)
8. International Organization for Standardization: ISO 31000 Risk management – Principles and guidelines (2009)
9. Ligaarden, O.S., Refsdal, A., Stølen, K.: Using indicators to monitor security risk in systems of systems: How to capture and measure the impact of service dependencies on the security of provided services. In: IT Security Governance Innovations: Theory and Research. IGI Global (to appear, 2012)
10. Lund, M.S., Solhaug, B., Stølen, K.: Evolution in relation to risk and trust management. Computer 43(5), 49–55 (2010)
11. Lund, M.S., Solhaug, B., Stølen, K.: Model-Driven Risk Analysis – The CORAS Approach. Springer (2011)
12. Lund, M.S., Solhaug, B., Stølen, K.: Risk Analysis of Changing and Evolving Systems Using CORAS. In: Aldini, A., Gorrieri, R. (eds.) FOSAD VI. LNCS, vol. 6858, pp. 231–274. Springer, Heidelberg (2011)

13. Massacci, F., Mylopoulos, J., Zannone, N.: Security Requirements Engineering: The SI* Modeling Language and the Secure Tropos Methodology. In: Ras, Z.W., Tsay, L.-S. (eds.) Advances in Intelligent Information Systems. SCI, vol. 265, pp. 147–174. Springer, Heidelberg (2010)

14. Microsoft Solutions for Security and Compliance and Microsoft Security Center of Excellence: The Security Risk Management Guide (2006)

15. Object Management Group: OMG Unified Modeling Language (OMG UML), Superstructure. Version 2.2, OMG Document: formal/2009-02-02 (2009)

16. Peltier, T.R.: Information Security Risk Analysis, 2nd edn. Auerbach Publications (2005)

17. Report on the industrial validation of SecureChange solutions. SecureChange project deliverable D1.3 (2012)

A Secure Data Encryption Method by Employing a Feedback Encryption Mechanism and Three-Dimensional Operation

Yi-Li Huang, Fang-Yie Leu, and Cheng-Ru Dai

Department of Computer Science, TungHai University, Taiwan
{yifung,leufy}@thu.edu.tw

Abstract. Currently, electronic documents are commonly exchanged between/among government offices in many countries. When a government office would like to transmit a high-security-level-electronic document to another office, the sending end officer needs to encrypt it so as to protect the document from being known to hackers. AES and DES have been commonly and widely invoked to protect documents in recent years. However, the two algorithms have so far faced the threats of Brute-Force cracks. To avoid the threats, in this study, we proposed a new data encryption approach, called the Secure Data Encryption Method (SeDEM for short), in which plaintext and system keys are encrypted by using a sequential-logic style encryption approach which further employs a three-dimensional operation and a feedback encryption mechanism to effectively protect encrypted data from brute-force and cryptanalysis attacks. The feedback encryption mechanism is a feedback process in which each of its calculation iteration generates three internally-used dynamic feedback keys for the next calculation iteration. The purpose is to effectively improve the security level and unpredictability of generated ciphertext. The three-dimensional operation is employed to further increase the computational complexity of the encryption technique so as to enhance the security level of the ciphertext, and difficulty of cracking the keys.

Keywords: DES, AES, symmetric encryption, Feedback Encryption, three-dimensional computing, dynamic feedback keys.

1 Introduction

Recently, many governments have adopted electronic documents to substitute traditional paper documents, aiming to achieve a paperless homeland and environment. So before a high-security-level document is transmitted through networks or the Internet, for security consideration, an encryption mechanism [1-3] is often required. Also, when a military office delivers a command to one of its subordinates, for example, to attack an enemy group sometime later, the command must be encrypted [4] before being sent out, particularly when the delivery goes through a wireless communication system.

G. Quirchmayr et al. (Eds.): CD-ARES 2012, LNCS 7465, pp. 578–592, 2012.

On the other hand, owing to the popularity of wireless communication, wireless systems have been quickly developed, and mobile devices have been commonly used in our everyday life. However, owing to the wireless transmission nature, hackers can easily eavesdrop and crack those messages sent through wireless channels. That is why security problems have been more serious and attracted many more researchers' attention than before. Presently Data Encryption Standard (DES) and Advanced Encryption Standard (AES) are two of the cryptographic techniques most widely used to protect transmitted messages. But their keys are relatively short, and current computer processing speeds have been significantly improved. DES encryption algorithm was successfully cracked in 1999 [4-7], implying that DES is no longer a high security encryption mechanism. Although AES has not been successfully cracked, no one dares to say that AES is always secure enough to protect transmitted data. In the following, we will use documents and messages interchangeably since documents are carried in messages.

Both AES and DES block ciphering requires complicated calculation on their own parent keys so as to generate a certain number of sub-keys to encrypt plaintext. But the combinatorial-logic style calculation is quite a problem since its outputs only rely on current inputs, without employing previous outputs as a part of the inputs to increase the security level of its ciphertext. Hence, their ciphertext may be cracked relatively easier by hackers by using cryptanalysis attacks, like chosen plaintext attack, and attacks by statistical methods and by Brute-force methods [5]. Namely, security levels of this style of encryption techniques are not as high as expected. So how to improve their security levels has been one of the focuses of security researchers.

The principles of modern encryption mechanisms are that even though the encryption process of a technique has been disclosed, as long as the hackers do not know all the encryption keys, the plaintext (i.e., the delivered documents) is still safe since without acquiring all keys, it is almost impossible for hackers to crack the ciphertext. On the other hand, if a ciphertext is generated by using a combinatorial-logic block encryption technique, the sub-keys produced by the parent key given when the system starts up are the same, i.e., no matter how complicate the encryption process is, the same plaintext block will generate the same ciphertext block. In this case, hackers can analyze the relationship between plaintext blocks and their corresponding ciphertext blocks by using Brute-force cracking methods. Hence, due to high speed of current computer systems, a symmetric encryption mechanism may be no longer secure.

So, in this study, we propose a new encryption approach, called the Secure Data Encryption Method (SeDEM for short), in which plaintext and system keys are encrypted by using a sequential-logic style encryption method which further employs the Feedback Encryption mechanism and Three-dimensional Operation (FETDO for short) to solve the abovementioned problems. Here feedback encryption is an encryption technique, in which a computational result of an encryption round R is fed back to the encryption mechanism for the next encryption round, i.e., Round R+1, as a part of (R+1)'s inputs, thereby increasing the unpredictability of ciphertext. The three-dimensional operation, referring to three different computations, includes an addition (+) [8,9], exclusive-or ($\oplus$), and exclusive-and ($\odot$), when encrypting a plaintext block. The purpose is to increase the encryption complexity so as to reduce the probability of cracking the encryption process by hackers.

The rest of this paper is organized of follows. Section 2 briefly introduces the DES and AES. Section 3 describes the feedback encryption mechanism and the three-dimensional operation. Security analyses are presented and discussed in Section 4. Section 5 concludes this paper and addresses our future research.

2   Research Related

Block cipher refers to the process in which a fixed length plaintext is cryptographically manipulated by a series of operations so as to produce the corresponding secure ciphertext, often the length of which is the same as that of the plaintext.

2.1   Data Encryption Standard (DES)

DES is a typical block cipher technique, the block size of which is 64 bits. But in practice, the keys used by the DES algorithm to encrypt plaintext blocks are only 56 bits in length [4,5]. The remaining 8 bits are parity bits or unused, implying the ciphertext generated by this technique is not as secure as expected since a longer key's security level is generally higher than a shorter key's.

2.1.1   DES Structure

The DES encryption structure as shown in Fig. 1 consists of the initial permutation (IP for short), 16 processing stages (called 16 rounds) and the final permutation (IP^{-1} for short). IP and IP^{-1} are the mutual inverse arrays. Each of the 16 rounds contains a Feistel-function operation [4,5], denoted by F, and an $\oplus$ operation.

Before the first round, a plaintext block (64-bit) follows the given IP table to permute their bits. After that, the new 64-bit block is divided into two 32-bit subblocks. Let the right subblock be $IP_{1,1}$ which is directly input to the first Feistel function, named round-1 Feistel function which receives another input, called subkey1, to generate a result, $result_{1,1}$ (i.e., round1's 1st result). Let the left subblock be $IP_{1,2}$ which is exclusive-ored with $result_{1,1}$ to generate $result_{1,2}$ (i.e., round1's 2nd result). Let $IP_{2,1} = result_{1,2}$ and let $IP_{2,2} = IP_{1,1}$. The rounds continue. The general rule is that round i's Feistel function receives the two inputs subkey i and $IP_{i,1}$ to generate $result_{i,1}$ which is then exclusive-ored with $IP_{i,2}$ to generate $result_{i,2}$. After that, $IP_{(i+1),2}=IP_{i,1}$ and $IP_{(i+1),1} = result_{i,2}$, for all i= 1, 2,... ...,16. Lastly, $IP_{17,1}$ is the right half and $IP_{17,2}$ is the left half of the 64-bit result of round 16. We input the right and left halves to IP^{-1} to produce the 64-bit ciphertext.

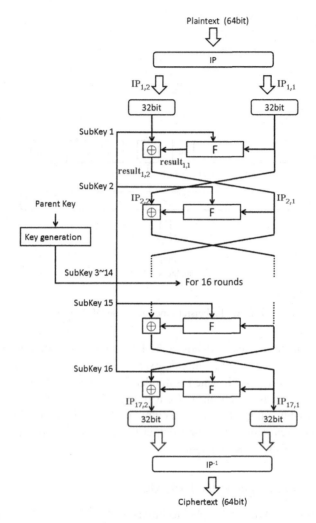

Fig. 1. The DES encryption structure [4,5]

2.1.2   Feistel Function

The Feistel function's architecture, as shown in Fig. 2, consists of four main functions, including expansion, key mixing, substitution, and permutation, respectively, denoted by E, ⊕, S (named S-Box) and P.

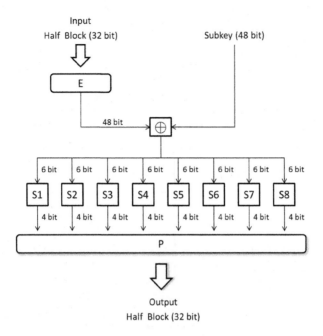

Fig. 2. The Feistel function of the DES [4,5]

Expansion transforms and extends a 32-bit pattern into 48 bits by using the expansion permutation [4,5]. Key mixing exclusive-ors E's output and a 48-bit sub-key to generate a 48-bit result which is divided into 8 6-bit patterns as the inputs of 8 S-boxes. Each S-box as a non-linear form transformation mechanism transforms a 6-bit input to a 4-bit output, implying the output of the 8 S-boxes is 32 bits long. After that, permutation rearranges the 32-bit output based on a fixed permutation process. The final result is also 32 bits in length.

2.2   Advanced Encryption Standard (AES)

The AES is also a kind of block cipher technique with block size 128 bits long. But its key length can be 128, 192 or 256 bits when necessary. The longer the length of the keys, the higher the security level of the system being considered. The AES uses a parent key to generate sub-keys.

Fig. 3 shows the AES encryption process which is performed on a 4×4 matrix, e.g., M, in which an element is 8 bits in length. The initial M contains a plaintext block, i.e., 128 bits (=4×4×8) in length. The AES encryption has 10 rounds. Each round, except the last one, comprises four stages:

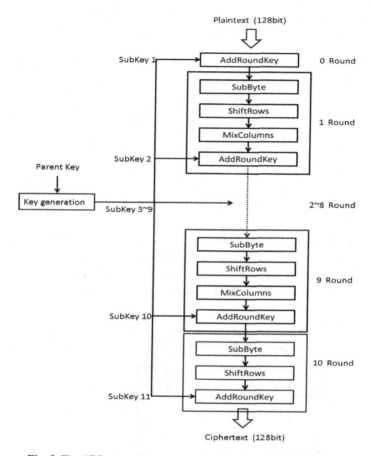

Fig. 3. The AES encryption process when key length is 128 bits [5]

Stage1: SubBytes. In this stage, an element of M, e.g., $a_{i,j}$, as shown in Fig. 4 is substituted by its corresponding element $a'_{i,j}$ which is retrieved from a pre-generated table, called Rijndael S-box [10-12], the elements of which are produced beforehand by invoking a non-linear function.

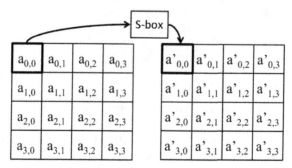

Fig. 4. The SubBytes stage [5,6]

Stage2: ShiftRows. In this stage, all elements of row r_i in M as illustrated in Fig. 5 are left rotated i times, $0 \leq i \leq 3$, even though the name of this stage is ShiftRows.

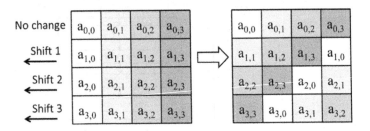

Fig. 5. The ShiftRows stage [5,6]

Stage3: MixColumns. The MixColumns stage as shown in Fig. 6 linearly converses a column $(a_{0,i}, a_{1,i}, a_{2,i}, a_{3,i})^T$, which is four bytes in length, to $(a'_{0,i}, a'_{1,i}, a'_{2,i}, a'_{3,i})^T$ by invoking the method of the Rijndael mix columns [10-12], implying an element of the matrixes in Fig. 6 is one byte in length. The conversion process is shown in Fig. 7.

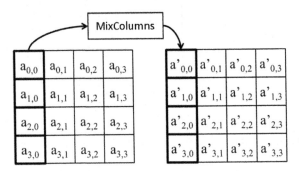

Fig. 6. The MixColumns stage [5,6]

$$\begin{pmatrix} a'_{0,x} \\ a'_{1,x} \\ a'_{2,x} \\ a'_{3,x} \end{pmatrix} = \begin{pmatrix} 02 & 03 & 01 & 01 \\ 01 & 02 & 03 & 01 \\ 01 & 01 & 02 & 03 \\ 03 & 01 & 01 & 02 \end{pmatrix} \begin{pmatrix} a_{0,x} \\ a_{1,x} \\ a_{2,x} \\ a_{3,x} \end{pmatrix} \quad 0 \leq x < 4;$$

Fig. 7. Column conversion of MixColumns stage [5]

In fact, it invokes an "xtime" function [5,10] whose inputs and outputs are all 1 byte in length, and which left shifts each input for one bit with the least significant bit being filled by a 0. If the input's most significant bit before shift is 1, the shift result will exclusive-or with $\{1b\}_{hex}$.

That means the square matrix on the right hand side of the matrix calculation shown in Fig. 7 is the MixColumus function illustrated in Fig. 6. Hence,

$$a'_{0,0} = (\{02\} \bullet a_{0,0}) \oplus (\{03\} \bullet a_{1,0}) \oplus a_{2,0} \oplus a_{3,0}$$
$$a'_{1,0} = a_{0,0} \oplus (\{02\} \bullet a_{1,0}) \oplus (\{03\} \bullet a_{2,0}) \oplus a_{3,0}$$
$$a'_{2,0} = a_{0,0} \oplus a_{1,0} \oplus (\{02\} \bullet a_{2,0}) \oplus (\{03\} \bullet a_{3,0})$$
$$a'_{3,0} = (\{03\} \bullet a_{0,0}) \oplus a_{1,0} \oplus a_{2,0} \oplus (\{02\} \bullet a_{3,0})$$

in which

$$\{02\} \bullet a_{i,j} = a_{i,j} \bullet \{02\} = xtime(a_{i,j})$$
$$\{03\} \bullet a_{i,j} = a_{i,j} \bullet (\{01\} \oplus \{02\}) = a_{i,j} \bullet xtime(a_{i,j})$$

Stage4: AddRoundKey. In this stage, each $a_{i,j}$ in M is exclusive-ored with $k_{i,j}$ where $k_{i,j}$ is an element of a given round sub-key table used to convert $a_{i,j}$ to $a'_{i,j}$, $0 \leq i, j \leq 3$. Fig. 8 gives an example. The parent key is used by Rijndael's key schedule [10-12] to generate round sub-keys for each round.

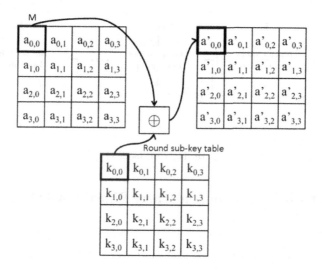

Fig. 8. The AddRoundKey stage [5,6]

2.3   Output Feedback and Cipher Feedback

Output Feedback (OFB for short) [13] and Cipher Feedback(CFB for short) [13] as two commonly used block cipher modes of operation provide feedback mechanisms to resist the plaintext-ciphertext pair statistics attack. They can also invoke other block cipher techniques, e.g., DES and AES, to further improve their security level.

The technical aspects of OFB and CFB are very similar. Both of them need an Initialization Vector together with a key K to trigger a block cipher encryption mechanism. The output of the mechanism, denoted by R, is then XORed with a plaintext block p_i to produce the corresponding ciphertext block c_i, no matter whether OFB or CFB is invoked.

With the OFB, R as shown in Fig. 9 is directly fed back as a key of the next block cipher encryption mechanism. With the CFB, the feedback parameter as shown in Fig. 10 is c_i, rather than R, i.e., the inputs of the CFB include Initialization Vector IV, plaintext p, key K, and ciphertext C where $C=c_1,c_2,c_3\ldots\ldots c_n$.

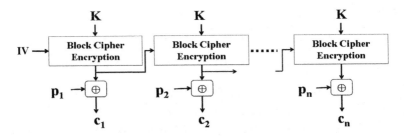

Fig. 9. The OFB mode [13]

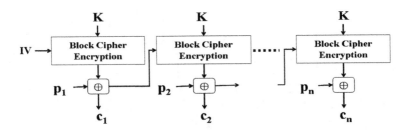

Fig. 10. The CFB mode [13]

3   Feedback Encryption and Three Dimensional Operations

The parameters and functions employed in this study are defined below.

Plaintext：p_i ,$1 \leq i \leq n$, (n is the total number of the blocks of the plaintext)
System key：K_i ,$1 \leq i \leq 7$
Dynamic key：$a_i, b_i, d_i, 1 \leq i \leq n$
Dynamic Feedback key：a_{i-1} , b_{i-1} , d_{i-1} , $1 \leq i \leq n$
Initial feedback key：$a_0 = K_8$, $b_0=K_9$, $d_0=K_{10}$
Ciphertext block：$c_i, 1 \leq i \leq n$

Fig. 11 illustrates the FETDO architecture in which before the first round, the values of the system feedback keys (a_{i-1}, b_{i-1}, and d_{i-1}) are all null. That means a_0, b_0 and d_0 require initial values.

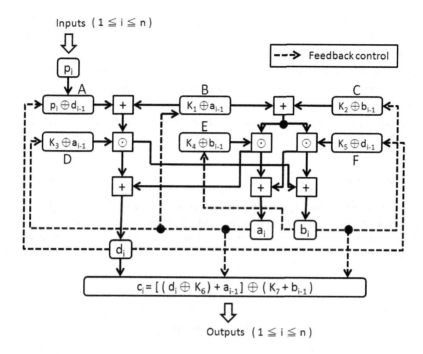

Fig. 11. The architecture of the FETDO Encryption Method

3.1   Encryption

The encryption process of the SeDEM is as follows.

Let ($p_i \oplus d_{i-1}$), ($K_1 \oplus a_{i-1}$), ($K_2 \oplus b_{i-1}$), ($K_3 \oplus a_{i-1}$), ($K_4 \oplus b_{i-1}$) and ($K_5 \oplus d_{i-1}$) are respectively denoted by A, B, C, D, E and F to simplify the expressions of the following equations.

$$d_i = [(A+B) \odot D] + [(B+C) \odot E] \tag{1}$$

$$a_i = [(B+C) \odot E] + [(B+C) \odot F] \tag{2}$$

$$b_i = [(A+B) \odot D] + [(B+C) \odot F] \tag{3}$$

$$c_i = [(d_i \oplus K_6) + a_{i-1}] \oplus (K_7 + b_{i-1}) \tag{4}$$

The feedback encryption mechanism has two stages, preparation stage and encryption stage. In the preparation stage, the equations being employed include Eqs.(1)~(3) in which d_i, a_i and b_i are used to encrypt plaintext blocks into ciphertext blocks.

Before the start of the i_{th} encryption iteration, named round i, a_{i-1}, b_{i-1} and d_{i-1} are known or have been calculated in round i-1. Superficially, the complexities of the expressions deriving d_i, a_i, b_i and c_i are high. In fact, the costs of the required operations are lower than those of the DES and AES.

Basically, Eqs.(1), (2) and (3) are produced almost at the same time after A~F are calculated. The total number of operations for deriving A~F is six $\oplus$s (see Fig. 11)). Calculating, a_i, b_i, and d_i needs extra eight operations (i.e., five +s and three $\odot$s, even though the numbers of +s and $\odot$s in Eqs. (1)~(3) are nine and six, respectively, since several $\odot$s and +s in the three equations are the same operations).

After that, the number of operations used to derive c_i is four (two +s and two $\oplus$s). Hence, the total number of operations in generating a_i, b_i, and d_i are eighteen ($= 6+8+4$, in which there are eight $\oplus$s, seven +s, and three $\odot$s).

3.2   Encryption

To decrypt c_i to p_i, the receiving site needs to first calculate A~F, Eq.(2), and Eq.(3). From Fig. 11, we can see that the number of operations required to generate a_i and b_i is thirteen (i.e., six $\oplus$s, three $\odot$s and four +s, excluding the + operation right above d_i).

Let

$$G = (B+C)\odot E \tag{5}$$

and

$$H = c_i \oplus (K_7+b_{i-1}) \tag{6}$$

Then

$$d_i = \begin{cases} (H - a_{i-1}) \oplus K_6 & ; \text{if } H \geq a_{i-1} \\ (H + \bar{a}_{i-1} + 1) \oplus K_6 & ; \text{if } H < a_{i-1} \end{cases} \tag{7}$$

$$p_i = \begin{cases} [(d_i - G)\odot D - B]\oplus d_{i-1}, if\ d_i \geq G\ and\ (d_i - G)\odot D \geq B \\ [(d_i - G)\odot D + (\bar{B} + 1)]\oplus d_{i-1}, if\ d_i \geq G\ and\ (d_i - G)\odot D < B \\ [(d_i + \bar{G} + 1)\odot D - B]\oplus d_{i-1}, if\ d_i < G\ and\ (d_i + \bar{G} + 1)\odot D \geq B \\ [(d_i + \bar{G} + 1)\odot D + (\bar{B} + 1)]\oplus d_{i-1}, if\ d_i < G\ and\ (d_i + \bar{G} + 1)\odot D < B \end{cases} \tag{8}$$

Here, G can be obtained before acquiring a_i (see Fig. 11). So no extra operations are required. To derive H, two operations, i.e., one $\oplus$ and one +, are needed. When deriving d_i (see Eq.(7)), in worst case i.e., when $H<a_{i-1}$, three operations, i.e., two +s, one $\oplus$, and one judgment are required. On calculating p_i, also in worst case, i.e., when $d_i<G$ and $(d_i+\bar{G}+1)\odot D<B$, two times of judgment and six operations (i.e., four +s, one $\odot$ and one $\oplus$) are needed since $(d_i+\bar{G}+1)\odot D$ in $p_i=((d_i+\bar{G}+1)\odot D+(\bar{B}+1))\oplus d_{i-1}$ can reuse the one calculated in the judgment $(d_i+\bar{G}+1)\odot D<B$, no extra cost is required. But calculating $\bar{G}$, $\bar{B}$ and $\bar{a}_{i-1}$ consumes three $-$s since they are respectively the one's complement of G, B, and a_{i-1}. Namely, in worst case, deriving d_i consumes four operations (rather than three), including two $+$s, one $\oplus$, one $-$, and one judgment, and deriving p_i needs eight operations (rather than six), including four $+$s, one $\odot$, one $\oplus$, two $-$s and two times of judgment.

In summary, to decrypt c_i to p_i, in worst case, we need three judgments and twenty seven (=13+2(for H)+4(for d_i)+8(for p_i)) operations.

4   Safety Analysis and Comparison

A well-designed encryption mechanism must be one with high security level to effectively protect a system from being attacked by hackers, and with high performance and low cost to efficiently perform encryption and decryption [14]. In the following, we will analyze FETDO mechanism and compare it with other cryptographic methods.

4.1   Brute-Force and Cryptanalysis

It is very inefficient if someone wishes to solve the FETDO's ten system keys (including seven system keys $K_1 \sim K_7$, and three dynamic keys a_i, b_i, and d_i) by using a brute force method because the ten keys are not directly generated by the given parent key, and they have $2^{(n \times 10)}$ combinations where n is the key length. The probability of correctly guess their current values on one trial is $1/(2^{(n \times 10)})$ which is approximate to zero, even if n=64.

With the FETDO, current ciphertext is not only a function of current plaintext, but also affected by previous inputs. Its first ciphertext block (c_1) has five unknown variables which are calculated by using two-dimensional operations, i.e., $\oplus$ and +. The computational complexity is high. Therefore, if hackers would like to analyze d_1 from c_1, they have to first solve a_0 and b_0 (see Eq.(4)). Without a_{i-1} and b_{i-1}, they cannot solve the ciphertext blocks c_i, i=1,2,... ...n, implying the ciphertext blocks $c_1, c_2, c_3, ...$ ...c_n are securely protected.

For security consideration, the ten keys as parameters are built in the developed program so as to significantly reduce the burden of hardware. Hackers cannot crack the keys by using differential cryptanalysis and analyze the key generation process. Further, the three-dimensional operation is a non-linear computation so it is difficult for hackers to solve the operation by using differential and linear cryptanalyses.

4.2   Flexible Design on Plaintext Blocks and Keys

CPU processing speeds of recent computers are faster day by day. The 128-bit blocks and 128-bit keys of the AES must be expanded someday. Once they are expanded, the encryption system of the AES has to be redesigned to meet the expansion, e.g., S-box required in the SubBytes stage and the Round sub-key table used in the AddRoundKey stage need to be expanded. But the FETDO still works because the sizes of a key and a block are equal, and can be dynamically adjusted when necessary.

Table 1. Security Analysis

	DES	AES	FOTDO
Operation structure	Combination logic	Combination logic	Sequential logic
Operator	1	1	3
Round	16	10, 12, 14	1
Key	1	1	10
Block and Key Flexible design	Low	Low	High
Computing Complexity	*Middle*	High	Low
Security level	Low	Middle	High

4.3   Comparison

Table 2. Cost of Encryption / Decryption processes

	Encryption	Decryption
DES(64-bit block)	$32 \oplus s + 1$ IP $+ 1$ IP^{-1} + 128 S-BOX + 16Expansion + 16 Permutation.	The same number of operations as that of the encryption process.
AES(128-bit block, 128-bit key)	$176 \oplus s$ (AddRoundKey) + 160 Substitutions (SubBytes), + 30 ShiftRows (ShiftRows), + (576(at least 432) $\oplus s$ + 144 time of judgment + 144 ShiftRows) (MixColumns).	The same number of operation as those of the encryption process for AddRoundKey, + SubBytes, and + ShiftRows MixColumns: 116(at least 684)$\oplus s$ +432 time of judgment + 432 ShiftRows.
FCTDO	$18 = (8 \oplus s + 3 \odot s + 7 + s,)$	MAX $27 = (9 \oplus s + 4 \odot s + 11 + s + 3 - s)$

Table 1 summarizes the features of the DES, AES and FETDO. In order to improve data delivery security, the AES and DES encryption methods improve their security levels by adding an option of encryption feedback, e.g., the CFB[13,15] mode and OFB[13,15] mode. But due to the following reasons they are still not secure enough.

The feedback values of the ciphertext blocks are relatively easier to be cracked and known. Although the OFB does not expose the feedback value, when the first ciphertext block is cracked, it will face the same problem of the CFB.

The FETDO does not have this problem since it has three internal feedback keys, i.e., a_i, b_i and d_i, and does not expose the feedback values as a part of its output. To achieve this, it uses two keys, i.e., K_6 and K_7, and two-dimensional operators, i.e., $\oplus$ and $+$, to protect the output. Hackers cannot acquire the feedback keys, consequently highly improving its security level for transmitted data.

Table 2 summarizes the cost of the encryption and decryption processes of the three schemes, AES, DES and FETDO. We can see the FETDO outperforms the other two.

5   Conclusion and Future Work

In this paper, we discussed and analyzed two encryption algorithms, including DES and AES, which employ combinatorial-logic style monotonic encryption operations, i.e., only keys are used to encrypt plaintext. Hence, their ciphertext is relatively easier to be cracked compared to that of the FETDO. The FETDO solves this problem by using a feedback encryption mechanism to increase the unpredictability of the ciphertext, and a three-dimensional operation and multiple keys to increase the cracking complexity so as to improve its system security level which is higher than those of the AES and DES, and decrease its encryption/decryption cost which is lower than those of the AES and DES.

In fact, the security level of employing multiple keys is similar to that of using lots of one-time-keys [16]. Generally, the encryption mechanism of a security system requires a large number of calculation for the keys exchanged before its data communication begins. The purpose is to increase its security level. However, all the keys as parameters used by our mechanism are built in the developed program, thus consuming a small hardware space to store the key. Today, security technologies advance quickly. Increasing the number of encryption keys (space factor) does not seriously impact the encryption and decryption costs (timing factor). On the contrary, this can exploit low cost and high security, and is suitable for being used by current applications.

When documents need to be securely protected during their delivery, like transmitting military secrets [1] or UIDs and passwords for e-commerce transactions [17], we can distribute the three dynamic keys, a_i, b_i, and d_i, to three key men. Before encrypting documents, the values of the three keys have to be input to the cryptographic system. The user's responsibility is only preparing the documents. But on the receiving end, the three key men have to participate in the decryption. As a result, even if there is a spyware invasion, the documents are still effectively and confidentially protected.

However, the FETDO does not provide fault tolerance and parallel encryption/decryption. If it can provide a non-linear dynamic substitution operation, i.e., a dynamic S-box [18], which provides random S-boxes, i.e., different S-boxes for different rounds, the system will be more secure than it was. Also, we would like to derive its reliability model so that users can predict the reliability of the system before using it. These constitute our future research.

References

1. Huang, Y.L., Leu, F.Y.: Constructing a Secure Point-to-Point Wireless Environment by Integrating Diffie-Hellman PKDS RSA and Stream Ciphering for Users Known to Each Other. Journal of Wireless Mobile Networks, Ubiquitous Computing, and Dependable Applications 2(3), 96–107 (2011)
2. Lee, S.M., Kim, D.S., Park, J.S.: A Survey and Taxonomy of Lightweight Intrusion Detection Systems. Journal of Internet Services and Information Security 2(1/2), 119–131 (2012)
3. Pandey, S.K., Barua, R.: Efficient Construction of Identity Based Signcryption Schemes from Identity Based Encryption and Signature Schemes. Journal of Internet Services and Information Security 1(2/3), 161–180 (2011)
4. http://zh.wikipedia.org/wiki/DES
5. Yang, C.H.: Network Security: Theory and Practice. XBOOK MARKETING Co. Ltd. (September 2008)
6. http://en.wikipedia.org/wiki/Advanced_Encryption_Standard
7. Hunker, J., Probst, C.W.: Insiders and insider threats—an overview of definitions and mitigation techniques. Journal of Wireless Mobile Networks, Ubiquitous Computing, and Dependable Applications 2(1), 4–27 (2011)
8. Huang, Y.F., Leu, F.Y., Chiu, C.H., Lin, I.L.: Improving Security Levels of IEEE802.16e Authentication by Involving Diffie-Hellman PKDS. Journal of Universal Computer Science 17(6), 891–911 (2011)
9. Moore, A.P., Cappelli, D.M., Carony, T.C., Shaw, E., Spooner, D., Trzeciak, R.F.: A preliminary model of insider theft of intellectual property. Journal of Wireless Mobile Networks, Ubiquitous Computing, and Dependable Applications 2(1), 28–49 (2011)
10. Barkan, E., Biham, E.: In How Many Ways Can You Write Rijndael? In: Zheng, Y. (ed.) ASIACRYPT 2002. LNCS, vol. 2501, pp. 160–175. Springer, Heidelberg (2002)
11. Federal Information Processing Standards Publication 197. Announcing the ADVANCED ENCRYPTION STANDARD (AES) (November 26, 2001)
12. Daemen, J., Rijmen, V.: AES Proposal: Rijndael. In: The First Advanced Encryption Standard Candidate Conference (September 1999)
13. http://en.wikipedia.org/wiki/Block_cipher_modes_of_operation
14. Eisenbarth, T., Kumar, S., Uhsadel, L., Paar, C., Poschmann, A.: A Survey of Lightweight-Cryptography Implementations. IEEE Design & Test of Computers, 522–533 (December 2007)
15. Dworkin, M.: Recommendation for BlockCipher Modes of OperationMethods and Techniques. Natl. Inst. Stand. Technol. Spec. Publ. 800-38A 2001 ED, 66 pages (December 2001)
16. Mils Electronic, One Time Key Encryption, http://www.mils.com/
17. Yang, F.Y., Liu, Z.W., Chiu, S.H.: Mobile Banking Payment System. Journal of Wireless Mobile Networks, Ubiquitous Computing, and Dependable Applications 2(3), 85–95 (2011)
18. El-Ramly, S.H., El-Garf, T., Soliman, A.H.: Dynamic Generation of S-boxes in Block Cipher Systems. In: Radio Science Conference, pp. 389–397 (August 2002)

Discussion on the Challenges and Opportunities of Cloud Forensics

Rainer Poisel and Simon Tjoa

Institute of IT Security Research
St. Poelten University of Applied Sciences
St. Poelten, Austria
{rainer.poisel,simon.tjoa}@fhstp.ac.at
http://www.fhstp.ac.at

Abstract. Cloud Forensics refers to digital forensics investigations performed in Cloud Computing Environments. Nowadays digital investigators face various technical, legal, and organizational challenges to keep up with current developments in the field of Cloud Computing. But, due to its dynamic nature, Cloud Computing also offers several opportunities to improve digital investigations in Cloud Environments. Digital investigators may utilize Cloud Computing setups and process complex tasks in cloud infrastructures. Thus they can take advantage of the enormous computing power at hand in such environments.

In this paper we focus on the current State-of-the-Art of affected fields of Cloud Forensics. The benefit for the reader of this paper is a clear overview of the challenges and opportunities for scientific developments in the field of Cloud Forensics.

Keywords: Cloud Forensics, digital forensics, evidence.

1 Introduction

In recent years, Cloud Computing has gained vastly in importance. It has been introduced to optimize the general usage of IT infrastructures. Cloud Computing is a technology that evolved from technologies of the field of distributed computing, especially grid computing [28]. According to NIST [48], "Cloud Computing is a model for enabling ubiquitous, convenient, on-demand network access to a shared pool of configurable computing resources (e. g. networks, servers, storage, applications, and services) that can be rapidly provisioned and released with minimal management effort or service provider interaction".

There will be substantial market growth in the field of Cloud Computing over the next few years. According to Kazarian and Hanlon [35], 40% of small and medium businesses (SMBs) from different countries are expected to use three or more cloud services and migrate their data into the cloud. In 2010, Gartner [31] released a study which forecasted the cloud service revenues to reach 148.8 billion in 2014 (compared to 58.6 billion in 2009). Carlton and Zhou [18] state that Cloud Computing is, from a technical point of view, a combination of existing

G. Quirchmayr et al. (Eds.): CD-ARES 2012, LNCS 7465, pp. 593–608, 2012.

technologies. People have difficulties to capture the big picture: for managers and customers of cloud services the idea is similar to exchanging information through web-based user interfaces. Others view the concept as being an extension of the timesharing concept from the 1960s.

Cloud providers sell services based on different business models (also referred to as "service models"): Software-as-a-Service (SaaS), Platform-as-a-Service (PaaS), and Infrastructure-as-a-Service (IaaS) [47,26]. With SaaS, the customer uses applications which are provided by the service seller (e. g. web-based e-mail services). With PaaS, the service seller then provides his infrastructure (servers, operating systems, network, etc.). The customer is able to write/use his own applications using the application programming interface made available by the provider. IaaS enables the user to use and run software of his choice (e. g. operating systems). The service seller provides the customer with the necessary infrastructure (servers, network, storage facilities, etc).

Depending on the level of access to the underlying cloud infrastructure the following types of clouds have been categorized [47,39]: private clouds, community clouds, public clouds, and hybrid clouds. In "private clouds" the infrastructure is operated on behalf of a single entity. Usually the infrastructure is located in the premises of the organization. "Community clouds" refer to cloud deployments where the infrastructure is shared by several organizations. In "Public Clouds" one or more providers run the infrastructure and make it available to anybody who wishes to pay for the service. "Hybrid clouds" refer to setups which are formed out of two or more cloud infrastructures. These in turn can be private, community, or public clouds. Of course, the shift in intercommunications and interaction between IT systems poses new challenges for digital forensics investigations. Cloud Service Providers (CSPs) often do not let their customers look behind their "virtual curtains" [15]. Vendor dependent implementations, multiple jurisdictions and proprietary data exchange formats [13] bring digital forensics into a deeper crisis as it is already facing [29]. Ruan et al. [58] defined Cloud Forensics as being a cross discipline between Cloud Computing and digital forensics. It is further recognized as a subset of network forensics [43]. Network forensics deals with investigating private or public networks and as Cloud Computing is based on broad network access it should follow the main phases of the network forensic process. Delport et al. [25] deem Cloud Forensics to be a subset of computer forensics as clouds consist of several nodes which are computers. This means that Cloud Forensics combines both, computer forensics and network forensics [1].

Ruan et al. [58] further extended the definition of Cloud Forensics across three major dimensions: technical, legal, and organizational. The technical dimension describes the set of procedures and tools which are utilized to carry out the digital forensics process in cloud environments. The organizational dimension refers to the fact that Cloud Computing involves at least two parties: CSPs and cloud customers. Further it is possible that CSPs outsource some of their services to other CSPs. The legal dimension refers to multi-jurisdiction and multi-tenancy challenges. Both fields have been exacerbated in cloud environments. Existing agreements and regulations have to be adopted for forensics activities to not breach any jurisdictions or confidentiality measures.

This paper is structured into two parts. First we focus on the current State-of-the-Art of affected fields of Cloud Forensics. In the second part, based on the current State-of-the-Art, related challenges and opportunities are identified in order to derive and describe open research problems.

2   State of the Art of Cloud Forensics

This chapter describes the State-of-the-Art of affected fields of digital forensics investigations in cloud environments.

2.1   Existing Digital Forensics Frameworks

Digital investigations have to consider various perspectives (e.g. legal perspective, technological perspective) in order to be successful. In order to coordinate the efforts between the various stakeholders, there exist a variety of publications dealing with procedures how to handle, analyze, document and present digital evidence. The presented work in this subsection contains well-known and well-established guidelines which are not specifically tailored to Cloud Computing. To some extent the principles introduced are also valid for cloud technology. However, an adaption of the organizational frameworks has to be considered to deal with the new challenges arising from the usage of Cloud Computing.

In the First Responder's Guide for Electronic Crime Scene Investigations [2], the forensic process is split into the four phases, (1) collection, (2) examination, (3) analysis and (4) report. The first phase is dedicated to capture electronic evidence. Thereafter, in the examination phase content and state of evidence is documented and the evidence is examined concerning hidden and obscured information. The last step of the second step is to reduce the information. In the analysis phase the evidence is analyzed concerning the relevance to the case. While examination is a technical task, analysis is usually conducted by an investigation team. Finally, in the last step reporting takes place [2].

NIST SP800-86 [34] shows how digital forensics can support incident handling. This publication focuses tackles digital forensics mainly from an IT perspective, not a legal perspective. The forensics process uses the phases of [34].

Further widely-used digital forensic frameworks include the digital forensics framework of the Association of Chief Police Officers (ACPO) [8] and the DFRWS (Digital Forensics Research Workshop) Investigative Process model [19]. Cohen proposes, in [22], a model consisting of the seven phases: identification, collection, transportation, storage, examination and traces, presentation, and destruction. Ke [36] describes the application of the SABSA model to the digital forensics process to obtain forensically sound evidence. More information on digital forensics frameworks can be found in [52].

2.2   Investigation of Cloud Infrastructures

According to Zimmerman and Glavach [66], the technology of Cloud Computing is not new. It is a new way of providing applications and computing resources on demand. Therefore the technology seems a perfect solution for smaller businesses that do not have the necessary resources to completely fulfil their IT needs [14,51]. Further, it allows private end users to utilize massive amounts of computing resources at affordable prices. However, the introduction of new technologies poses new challenges for the digital forensics investigator [65]. Grispos et al. show "how established digital forensic procedures will be invalidated in this new environment" [32]. They propose research agendas for addressing the new challenges depending on the investigation phase. As mentioned in the previous section there exist several organizational digital investigations frameworks. In the following the different investigation steps: identification, preservation, examination, and presentation are elucidated regarding their implementation for the investigation of cloud environments.

Identification, Preservation, and Acquisition: Grispos et al. outline in [32] the lack of frameworks to determine which elements were affected by IT specific crimes. The usage of conventional intrusion detection systems in the context of Cloud Computing infrastructures has been proposed by several authors [32]. The preservation and acquisition step deals with evidence collection from computer based systems. The increasing storage capacity of devices and computer systems are everlasting challenges in digital forensics investigations [32]. With the introduction of Cloud Computing systems this challenge is still ubiquitous: the elastic ability of Cloud Computing infrastructures allows the user to request additional data storage in a limitless fashion.

The chain of custody documents how evidence was handled in the context of the digital investigations process [20]. The documentation describes how evidence was collected, analyzed, and preserved to be approved in court. Due to the remote nature of Cloud Computing scenarios, assumptions that have been made with the investigation of traditional computer systems are not valid anymore [53]. Investigators usually had physical access to traditional computer systems [66]. Therefore they were able perform a live analysis or to remove storage devices for analyzing them in a forensics laboratory. Storage devices are accessed through a computer network. Digital investigators have to obtain control of cloud services before investigating them [58]. Depending on time an investigator requires to gain control of such a service, relevant evidence can be destroyed (deliberately or accidentially) by both, the service user and the cloud provider [32]. In this regard, IaaS deployments provide much more useful information for digital forensics investigations than PaaS or SaaS setups [15,16]. With PaaS or SaaS deployment scenarios, customers do not have any control of the underlying operating infrastructure. The amount of information from servers is limited and therefore, the client has to contribute to the investigation process. Besides the technical challenges, the lack of regulatory and legal frameworks complicate meeting the chain of custody requirements [63].

In Forensics, 'live' acquisitions and investigations allow to obtain data stored in non-persistent memory such as process information or active network connections [12] as well as temporary data, such as file locks or web browsing caches [15,32], RFC3227 [17] explains several best practices regarding live investigation of systems in case of security incidents.

However, traditional forensics guidelines require storage images to be forensically sound. Therefore bit-by-bit copies including a check sum are made from digital storage devices from instances in "dead" state (the system has been shutdown) to proof the unadulteratedness of digital evidence [8]. Traditional search and seizure procedures may be impractical for performing digital investigations in Cloud Computing environments. Digital evidence is stored in cloud data centres, desktop computers or mobile phones which could be out of physical control by the digital investigator [62]. As it is almost impossible to make a bit-by-bit copy of storage devices [66] the ACPO guidelines are rendered pointless when it comes to complete authenticity of digital evidence in cloud environments. Acquiring all storage devices from such a setup would be too time consuming for investigators and too disruptive for CSPs [32]. Usually cloud users are only offered remote access to the logical representation of their data. In most cases, the underlying physical infrastructure is transparent for the user. In the future, new methods will be needed to allow partial recovery of data from physical devices in accordance with accepted forensic principles. Therefore, forensics tools have to be hybrid of the current live and post-mortem analysis methods [66]. There will be a need for intelligent tools that note and predict artefacts based on heuristics. Delport et al. outline in [25] that it might be necessary to isolate cloud instances in case they have to be investigated. The problem associated with isolating cloud instances is the integrity of data intended for digital forensics investigations [14].

Basically, methods for clearing include moving uninvolved instances or suspicious instances to other nodes. This way the CIA of other instances is protected, but it might result in loss of possible evidence. However, by moving instances, evidence is protected from being tampered by these moved instances. Delport et al. [25] presented different techniques to isolate instances of cloud environments.

Instance relocation means moving an instance inside a cloud environment by moving the data logically or by creating new and destroying old instances. Server farming refers to putting up a spare instance which offers the same functionality as the instance intended for digital investigations. By Sandboxing programs can run in an environment which they cannot escape. Man in the Middle (MitM) refers to placing an entity between a sender and a receiver. In the field of digital forensics this entity is placed between the cloud instance and the hardware of the cloud. Delport et al. [25] conclude that none of their presented approaches fulfils every requirement for the investigation of cloud environments. However, depending on the case techniques may be combined to gain explicit access to a cloud instance.

The usage of cryptography in cloud environments poses additional challenges. CSPs offer encryption as a security feature to their customers. All data is encrypted on the client's side. The key to the encrypted data is never stored in the cloud environment [9].

Deleted data represents another major challenge due to the volatility and elasticity of cloud environments. On one hand, data that has remotely been requested to be deleted can be a rich source of evidence as it can still be physically existing [32]. On the other hand it depends on the CSP how to proceed in the event of a user requesting his data to be deleted [15,66] (e. g. Google's policy includes the deletion of such data from both, its active and replication servers as well as of all pointers to this data).

Reilly et al. [53] also mentioned the lack of tool support for dealing with digital investigations with cloud data centres. Currently, most tools are intended for examining data from traditional computer setups such as office or home computers. Taylor et al. [62] recommended to update existing tool suites such as EnCase or FTK to account for new developments in the field of Cloud Computing.

Examination and Analysis: Forensic tool suites such as The SleuthKit, FTK or EnCase perform "pattern matching" and "filtering" of data that is existing in different types of memory. Evidence in cloud is manifold and will likely be similar to evidence found in traditional computer setups [32]: office application documents, file fragments, digital images, emails, and log file entries [46]. Checksums are used to verify the integrity of objects (disk images, files, log entries, etc.) in the Cloud. Detecting file signatures of files in question or files which should be excluded from a digital forensics investigation are crucial for the filtering process. Hegarty et al. [33] describe a method for adapting existing signature detection techniques for their usage in cloud environments. To detect files with a specific hash value a so called "initialiser" submits the target buckets (storage units of a cloud customer) as well as the hash value to a so called "Forensic Cluster Controller" which in turn distributes the job of finding files with that has value to so called "Analysis Nodes".

In the future investigating cloud infrastructures may be a task performed by cloud deployments. However, cloud customers may access applications offered in the Cloud from a myriad of different computer setups (mobile phones of different make, desktop PCs with different operating systems, etc.) [62].

Presentation: Digital evidence can be utilized in several ways: it can be submitted to court in the form of a report [19] or it may be used by an organization to improve corporate policies and support future investigations [64]. Grispos et al. [32] highlight the need for a standard evaluation method for Cloud Forensics so that Cloud Forensics investigation results pass the Daubert principles [45]. Another challenge arises from explaining the Cloud Computing concept to a jury in court [53]. It may be difficult for a jury member to comprehend the concept as jury members will usually only have basic knowledge of how to use home PCs.

2.3   Digital Investigations Using Cloud Infrastructures

According to cloud security alliance [5], industry is heading forward to create Security-as-a-Service (SecaaS). The authors identified the following ten domains that are likely to interest consumer in the future: (1) Identity and Access

Management Services; (2) Data Loss Prevention; (3) Web Security; (4) Email Security; (5) Security Assessments; (6) Intrusion Management, Detection and Prevention (IDS/IPS); (7) Security Information and Event Management; (8) Encryption; (9) Business Continuity and Disaster Recovery; (10) Network Security. Within one of these domains the authors identify the requirement to "... provide customers with forensics support...". This opinion is also supported by Ruan et al. [58] who derive from the emerging trend to security-as-a-service that forensics-as-a-service will gain importance in cyber criminal investigations by providing massive computing power.

Reilly et al. [53] take the discussion of the usage of cloud technologies for forensic investigations one step further and highlight the benefits delivered by the usage of Cloud Computing for digital investigations. The major advantages identified by the authors include large-scale storage, high availability and massive computing power. Roussev and Richard [55,54] recognized the need for distributed forensics at an early stage. In their paper [56] they formulated the following requirements that should be satisfied by a distributed digital forensic toolkit: Scalability, platform-independence, lightweight, interactivity, extensibility and robustness. As cloud technologies can meet the abovementioned requirements, Roussev et al. evaluate in their paper [56] the feasibility and applicability of MapReduce for forensics applications. Map Reduce [24] was developed by Google in order to facilitate large scale computing. Phoenix [60] and Hadoop [4] are well known implementations of Google's MapReduce model. In their paper, the authors present their prototype, called MPI MapReduce (MMR), which is based on the Phoenix shared memory implementation. In order to test the performance of the prototype they implemented three Hadoop samples (wordcount, pi-estimator and grep) for MMR.

Cohen et al. introduce in [23] their GRR Rapid Response framework which pursues the objective to support live forensics within in an enterprise. The framework is designed to be highly scalable and is available for all common platforms. The proposed architecture is supported by an open-source prototype that is available [23].

Hegarty et al. present in their paper [33] the distributed calculation of file signatures if analyzing distributed storage platforms. Their proposed architecture consists of the three components: initializer, forensic cluster controller and analysis nodes.

Distributed computing power for password recovery or hash cracking is already well established. Various publications (e.g. [67]) and tools (e.g. Distributed Network Attack by AccessData [6,59]) are devoted to this significant subject. eDiscovery applications which are also an important component in an digital investigator's daily business are already available for cloud implementations. An example is the open source eDiscovery software FreeEd [3].

2.4   Digital Evidence in Cloud Computing Environments

The introduction of Cloud Computing provided a change of paradigms to the distributed processing of digital data. In their paper Taylor et al. [61] focuses on the legal aspects of digital forensics investigations. They concluded that due to the increasing number of interacting systems the acquisition and analysis of digital evidence in cloud deployments is likely to become more complex. The data could be encrypted before being transferred to the Cloud or it could be stored in different jurisdictions resulting in data being deleted before investigators have access to it [47].

Flaglien et al. [27] evaluated currently used formats for handling digital evidence against criteria identified in recent research literature. Recent developments with a focus on evidence exchange have been presented. Formats intended for storing evidence from highly dynamic and complex systems are characterized by incorporating additional information which can be processed by data mining tools.

Birk [15] and Wegener [16] mentioned digital evidence to be in one of three different states: at rest, in motion or in execution. Data at rest is stored on storage media. In this case it does not matter if the data is allocated to a file or if it has been deleted. Data in motion is usually data that is transferred over a computer network. Data that is neither in rest nor in motion is referred to as to be in execution. Usually this means process data that has been loaded into memory. In cloud environments evidence can be found on several sources: the virtual cloud instance (where the incident happened or originated), the network layer, and/or the client system [66,15]. Especially in SaaS setups evidence can be found on client systems.

Lu et al. [44] proposed to adopt the concept of provenance to the field of Cloud Computing. As a data object is able to report who created it and modified its contents, provenance could provide digital evidences for post investigations. However, up to now, provenance is still an unexplored area in Cloud Computing. Provenance information would have to be secured in cloud environments as leaking this information could breach information confidentiality and user privacy. Marty [46] follows a similar approach. CSPs and application providers utilize logging facilities to generate and collect relevant data to support the digital forensics investigation process. The sources for logging can be manifold: "business relevant logging covers features used and business metrics being tracked" [46]. Operational logging covers errors that concern a single cloud customer, critical conditions that impact all users, system related problems, etc. Forensics investigations are supported by security logging which focuses on login information, password changes, failed resource access and all activity that is executed by privileged accounts.

Cloud customers lose control over their data and executions in case they outsource the execution of business processes to the Cloud [21]. Accorsi [7] stated that this problem could be overcome with remote auditing. Data analytics perform traditional audits remotely by assess and report on the accuracy of financial data. This requires the introduction of an additional service model: business-process-as-a-service (BPaaS). It is based on the SaaS provision model and provides methods for modelling, utilizing, customizing, and executing business processes in cloud infrastructures. Access to the physical systems is neither possible nor necessary: external auditors will have access to both the auditee's system and the auditee's compartment in the cloud. Then it is possible for the auditors to employ remote auditing, thus addressing the inherent loss of control.

2.5 Hypervisor Forensics

Hypervisors (also referred to as "Virtual Machine Manager" or "VMM") can be understood as a host operating system which performs the allocation of computing resources such as memory, CPU, disk I/O and networking among operating systems that are running as "guest operating systems" [43]. As hypervisors build the bridge between guests and physical computer hardware, all data that is processed has to pass through the hypervisor before it can access physical devices (e. g. network interface cards, CPU . . .).

The usage of data from hypervisors to prove various actual situations has been proposed in previous research papers [30,37]. The terminology has been referred to as "virtual machine introspection" (VMI) and data gathered from this level of access supported the operation of Intrusion Detection Systems (IDS). Payne and Lee [50] focused on the development of an abstract monitoring architecture. Their programming library "XenAccess" has been released as an open-source project. Later the source-base has been forked: the project is currently released as another open-source programming library "LibVMI". The library is "focused on reading and writing memory from virtual machines" [41]. Therefore monitoring applications can access the memory state and disk activity of target operating systems in a safe and efficient manner.

Later work which was based on VM introspection and monitoring software focused mainly on the detection of and defence from malicious software. Ando et al. [10] modified Linux as guest operating system to be able to obtain event-driven memory snapshots. Heuristics developed in this project allowed the detection of unknown malware which could not be detected by characteristic signatures.

Kuhn and Taylor [40] focused on capturing exploits in virtualized environments (such as cloud infrastructures). They concluded that there is no common collective base of root-kits, applications, and kernel versions for the forensic analysis of memory in virtualized environments to form a ground-truth for cross technology comparisons. Lempereur et al. [42] presented a framework which could be used to automatically evaluate live digital forensic acquisition tools on different platform configurations. Live digital forensics techniques play an important role in the area of virtualized environments. In their work they describe three classes of digital forensic evidence: stored information (high amount, slow access), information pending storage, and operational information. Operational information can help to narrow down the amount of searches to analyze stored information. This is true for both locally stored information (e. g. within an instance) and information stored on remote systems (e. g. cloud storage).

Krishnan et al. [38] proposed a forensics platform that transparently monitored and recorded data access events within a virtualized environment by only using the abstractions which were exposed by the hypervisor. The developments focused on monitoring access to objects on disk and allowed to follow the causal chain of the accesses across processes even if objects were copied into memory. Transactions of data have then be recorded in a audit log which allowed for faithful reconstruction of recorded events and the changes that they induced. In their work the authors demonstrated how their approach could be used to obtain behavioural profiles of malware.

Current research results demonstrate the feasibility of information acquisition from virtual machine managers (Hypervisors) to support the digital forensics analysis process. However, most work is focused on smaller setups (e. g. single physical machine with several VMs). Therefore we propose that more research should be done to investigate the acquisition of digital evidence across multiple virtualized environments, as given in Cloud Computing.

3   Discussion on Challenges and Opportunities

Beside its opportunities and advantages regarding the general usage of IT infras-tructures the introduction of Cloud Computing has brought several challenges for the digital forensics investigator. Ruan et al. [58,57] explained both the chal-lenges and opportunities of digital forensics investigations in cloud environments. Based on this knowledge and the current State-of-the-Art of digital forensics in cloud environments (Section 2) we identify areas for future research. Our find-ings are visualized in kind of a Venn diagram: a sub-set of challenges can be seen as sub-set of opportunities (see Figure 1).

In the field of digital forensics, tools and procedures have to be used to cope with new technical developments. Garfinkel [29] mentioned that in this regard digital forensics is facing a crisis: advances and fundamental changes in the computer industry will lead to the loss of hard-won capabilities. Cloud Computing and the involved interconnection of computer systems are among the enumerated reasons. The following section breaks down the impacts on digital forensics investigations.

Data Volume and Performance. Appropriate capture and display filters have to be developed and set up in order to make the data volume present in Cloud Infrastructures processible. On the other hand, the elastic nature of Cloud Com-puting setups also increases the scalability and flexibility [58,53]. Complex tasks can be processed on arbitrary numbers of instances in a distributed fashion.

Complexity. The topic of Cloud Forensics is of multi-dimensional complexity [58]. Different hypervisor vendors provide different application programming in-terfaces with a short life-cycle to their customers. Different hypervisor architec-tures influence the structure of instances running in the cloud. The information exchange between multiple CSPs around the world may further complicate the forensics investigation of such systems.

Legal Situation. In cloud setups from different countries, there exists a high probability that multiple jurisdictions may apply. Another problem comes from the easy-to-use feature of most cloud deployments. Weak registration systems allow facilitating anonymity that can be easily abused by criminals to conceal their traces and identities [?].

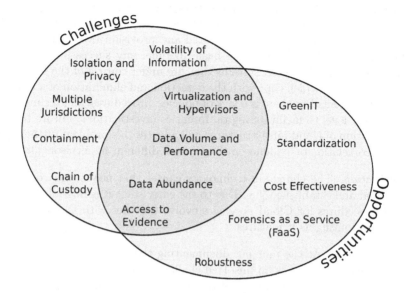

Fig. 1. Challenges and Opportunities of Cloud Forensics

Containment. It is a characteristic for cloud services that interruptions and attacks can have huge effects for a myriad of customers. An example that highlighted the strong dependence of cloud users on their providers was the outages of Amazon's and Microsoft's data centres in Dublin 2011 [49].

Isolation & Privacy. Many cloud service providers provide multi-tenant storage to their customers. Different customers that access the storage units may contaminate therefore the acquisition of forensic data before investigations can take place. Another problem resides in availability issues which can be caused by isolating instances from other instances [32].

Access to Evidence. Due to the impossibility of specifying the storage location at a high level, it may be difficult for investigators to access the data required for conducting forensics investigations [53]. Additionally CSPs intentionally hide the detail of the storage location from their customers to allow for data replication and movement across different service models [32].

Ephemeral Nature of Information in the Cloud. As storage is logical and focused on data allocated to objects (e. g. files), traditional file recovery techniques may not work with acquired images because they may not include file fragments or data from unallocated disk space [33]. Due to the cloud infrastructure being mostly under control of the cloud service provider [21], it may also be difficult to gain remote access to deleted data [58].

Virtualization and Hypervisors. Cloud deployments are often based on virtualization: CSPs implement instances of Cloud Computing in virtualized environments. Running instances are monitored and provisioned by hypervisors. In a cloud setup the hypervisor is the basic module: any successful attack may compromise the security of all systems that are under control of the hypervisor. There are strategies which cope with the detection and elimination of malware in virtual environments but there is a lack of policies, procedures, and techniques on the hypervisor level to facilitate digital forensics investigations. Future tools for the investigation of cloud infrastructures will address this problem further by allowing the correlation of evidence gathered from different hypervisors [38,42,50].

Standardization. The change in technology causes that new standards have to be developed and established [58]. Due to the early stage it is possible that standardized procedures for Cloud Forensics evolve together with the development of Cloud Computing as it matures.

Chain of Custody. At the moment documenting the chain of custody in Cloud Computing environments is an unsolved challenge. Service models such as SaaS only allow accessing a logical view of the data stored in the Cloud. Traditional methods (such as calculating hash values) that prove the integrity of data may be of no use in online scenarios. Best practices and procedures are composed into organizational frameworks. They describe the measures that have to be taken in case digital forensics investigations are conducted [32]. To overcome the problems regarding the chain of custody, an organizational framework that is suitable especially for digital forensics in Cloud Computing environments has to be implemented [22,36,63].

Cost Effectiveness. Forensics-as-a-Service (FaaS) [58] allows to plan and utilize the amount of necessary computing power required by digital forensics investigations [56].

GreenIT. Due to the scarcity of natural ressources for the production of energy required to power IT infrastructures, developments are necessary to optimize the energy consumption of nowadays devices [11]. FaaS may use idle computing resources and thus comes towards the requirements of GreenIT.

4   Conclusion and Outlook

Within this paper the current State-of-the-Art in Cloud Forensics has been presented. The subsequent discussion has shown that research has to be performed in all three subareas (technical, legal, organizational) of Cloud Forensics. Based on the results of this discussion of Cloud Forensics research we intend to focus on hypervisor forensics as both a challenge and an opportunity and the establishment of a solid organizational framework for carrying out digital forensics investigations in cloud environments. Due to the vast amount of data that has to be analyzed we intend to utilize other Cloud Computing setups to overcome the processing limits of single machines.

References

1. Children warned against net predators (2000),
   `http://news.bbc.co.uk/2/hi/uk_news/education/648156.stm`
2. Electronic crime scene investigation: An on-the-scene reference for first responders, recommendations of the National Institute of Standards and Technology (2001)
3. Freeeed.org - open-source ediscovery engine (2011), `http://www.freeeed.org/`
4. Hadoop - mapreduce (2011), `http://hadoop.apache.org/mapreduce`
5. Security guidance for critical areas of focus in cloud computing v3.0 (2011)
6. AccessData: Decryption and password cracking software,
   `http://accessdata.com/products/computer-forensics/decryption`
7. Accorsi, R.: Business process as a service: Chances for remote auditing. In: Proceedings of 35th IEEE Annual Computer Software and Applications Conference Workshops (2011)
8. ACPO: Good practice guide for computer-based electronic evidence. 7safe (August 2007), `http://www.7safe.com/electronic_evidence/ACPO_guidelines_computer_evidence_v4_web.pdf`
9. Agudo, I., Nuñez, D., Giammatteo, G., Rizomiliotis, P., Lambrinoudakis, C.: Cryptography Goes to the Cloud. In: Lee, C., Seigneur, J.-M., Park, J.J., Wagner, R.R. (eds.) STA 2011 Workshops. CCIS, vol. 187, pp. 190–197. Springer, Heidelberg (2011)
10. Ando, R., Kadobayashi, Y., Shinoda, Y.: Asynchronous Pseudo Physical Memory Snapshot and Forensics on Paravirtualized VMM Using Split Kernel Module. In: Nam, K.-H., Rhee, G. (eds.) ICISC 2007. LNCS, vol. 4817, pp. 131–143. Springer, Heidelberg (2007)
11. Baliga, J., Ayre, R.W.A., Hinton, K., Tucker, R.S.: Green cloud computing: Balancing energy in processing, storage, and transport. Proceedings of the IEEE 99(1), 149–167 (2011)
12. Barrett, D., Kipper, G.: Virtualization and Forensics: A Digital Forensic Investigator's Guide to Virtual Environments. Syngress Media, Syngress/Elsevier (2010), `http://books.google.at/books?id=QXF1kKX2za8C`
13. Beebe, N., Beebe, N.: Digital forensic research: The good, the bad and the unaddressed. In: Peterson, G., Shenoi, S. (eds.) Advances in Digital Forensics V. IFIP AICT, vol. 306, pp. 17–36. Springer, Boston (2009)
14. Biggs, S., Vidalis, S.: Cloud computing: The impact on digital forensic investigations. In: Proceedings of the International Conference for Internet Technology and Secured Transactions (ICITST) 2009, London, pp. 1–6 (November 2009)
15. Birk, D.: Technical challenges of forensic investigations in cloud computing environments. In: Proceedings of the Workshop on Cryptography and Security in Clouds, pp. 1–6 (March 2011)
16. Birk, D., Wegener, C.: Technical issues of forensic investigations in cloud computing environments. In: Proceedings of the 6th International Workshop on Systematic Approaches to Digital Forensic Engineering, Oakland, CA, USA (2011)
17. Brezinski, D., Killalea, T.: Guidelines for evidence collection and archiving. RFC 3227 (Best Current Practice) (2002)
18. Carlton, G.H., Zhou, H.: A survey of cloud computing challenges from a digital forensics perspective. International Journal of Interdisciplinary Telecommunications and Networking 3(4), 1–16 (2011)
19. Carrier, B.D., Spafford, E.H.: Getting physical with the digital investigation process. International Journal of Digital Evidence 2(2), 1–20 (2003)

20. Casey, E.: Digital Evidence and Computer Crime: Forensic Science, Computers, and the Internet. Academic Press (2011), http://books.google.at/books?id=6gCbJ4O4f-IC

21. Chow, R., Golle, P., Jakobsson, M., Masuoka, R., Molina, J.: Controlling data in the cloud:outsourcing computation without outsourcing control. In: Proceedings of the 2009 ACM Workshop on Cloud Computing Security (CCSW 2009), pp. 85–90. ACM (November 2009)

22. Cohen, F.: Digital Forensic Evidence Examination - 2nd Edn. Fred Cohen & Associates (2010)

23. Cohen, M., Bilby, D., Caronni, G.: Distributed forensics and incident response in the enterprise. Digital Investigation 8(suppl.), S101–S110 (2011)

24. Dean, J., Ghemawat, S.: Mapreduce: Simplified data processing on large clusters. In: Proceedings of the 6th Symposium on Operating Systems Design and Implementation. USENIX (2004)

25. Delport, W., Olivier, M.S., Koehn, M.: Isolating a cloud instance for a digital forensic investigation. In: Proceedings of the 2011 Information Security for South Africa (ISSA 2011) Conference (2011)

26. Dillon, T.S., Wu, C., Chang, E.: Cloud computing: Issues and challenges. In: Proceedings of the International Conference on Advanced Information Networking and Applications (AINA 2010), pp. 27–33 (2010)

27. Flaglien, A.O., Mallasvik, A., Mustorp, M., Arnes, A.: Storage and exchange formats for digital evidence. Digital Investigation 8(2), 122–128 (2011); standards, professionalization and quality in digital forensics

28. Foster, I.T., Zhao, Y., Raicu, I., Lu, S.: Cloud computing and grid computing 360-degree compared. Computing Research Repository abs/0901.0131, 1–10 (2009)

29. Garfinkel, S.L.: Digital forensics research: The next 10 years. Digital Investigation 7(suppl. 1), S64–S73 (2010); the Proceedings of the Tenth Annual DFRWS Conference

30. Garfinkel, T., Rosenblum, M.: A virtual machine introspection based architecture for intrusion detection. In: Proceedings of the Network and Distributed System Security Symposium (NDSS 2003). The Internet Society (2003)

31. Gartner: Gartner says worldwide cloud services market to surpass $68 billion in 2010 (2010), http://www.gartner.com/it/page.jsp?id=1389313 (accessed: December 30, 2011)

32. Grispos, G., Glisson, W.B., Storer, T.: Calm before the storm: The emerging challenges of cloud computing in digital forensics (August 2011), http://www.dcs.gla.ac.uk/~tws/papers/grispos11calm-rev2425.pdf, draft published for comment

33. Hegarty, R., Merabti, M., Shi, Q., Askwith, B.: Forensic analysis of distributed service oriented computing platforms (June 2011)

34. Karen, K., Chevalier, S., Grance, T., Dang, H.: Guide to integrating forensic techniques into incident response, recommendations of the National Institute of Standards and Technology (2006)

35. Kazarian, B., Hanlon, B.: SMB Cloud Adoption Study,- Global Report (December 2010), http://www.microsoft.com/Presspass/presskits/commsector/docs/SMBStudy_032011.pdf (accessed: December 30, 2011)

36. Ke, L.: Design of a Forensic Overlay Model for Application Development. Master's thesis, University of Canterbury, College of Engineering (2011)

37. Kourai, K., Chiba, S.: Hyperspector: virtual distributed monitoring environments for secure intrusion detection. In: Hind, M., Vitek, J. (eds.) Proceedings of the

1st International Conference on Virtual Execution Environments (VEE 2005), pp. 197–207. ACM (2005)

38. Krishnan, S., Snow, K.Z., Monrose, F.: Trail of bytes: efficient support for forensic analysis. In: Al-Shaer, E., Keromytis, A.D., Shmatikov, V. (eds.) Proceedings of ACM Conference on Computer and Communications Security (ACM CCS 2010), pp. 50–60. ACM (2010)

39. Krutz, R., Vines, R.: Cloud Security: A Comprehensive Guide to Secure Cloud Computing. John Wiley & Sons (2010),
   http://books.google.at/books?id=cs6Ox4CHXioC

40. Kuhn, S., Taylor, S.: A survey of forensic analysis in virtualized environments. Tech. rep., Dartmouth College, Hanover, New Hampshire (2011)

41. Sandia National Laboratories: Libvmi (2011),
   http://vmitools.sandia.gov/libvmi.html (online; Status: January 09, 2012)

42. Lempereur, B., Merabti, M., Shi, Q.: Pypette: A framework for the automated evaluation of live digital forensic techniques. In: Proceedings of the 11th Annual PostGraduate Symposium on The Convergence of Telecommunications Networking and Broadcasting (2010),
   http://www.cms.livjm.ac.uk/pgnet2010/MakeCD/index.htm

43. Lillard, T., Garrison, C., Schiller, C., Steele, J., Murray, J.: Digital Forensics for Network, Internet, and Cloud Computing: A Forensic Evidence Guide for Moving Targets and Data. Elsevier (2010),
   http://books.google.at/books?id=A4V45b2w27gC

44. Lu, R., Lin, X., Liang, X., Shen, X.S.: Secure provenance: the essential of bread and butter of data forensics in cloud computing. In: Feng, D., Basin, D.A., Liu, P. (eds.) Proceedings of the 5th ACM Symposium on Information, Computer and Communications Security (ASIACCS 2010), pp. 282–292. ACM (2010)

45. Marsico, C.V.: Computer evidence v. daubert: The coming conflict. Cerias tech report 2005-17, Center for Education and Research in Information Assurance and Security, Purdue University (2005)

46. Marty, R.: Cloud application logging for forensics. In: Chu, W.C., Wong, W.E., Palakal, M.J., Hung, C.C. (eds.) Proceedings of the 2011 ACM Symposium on Applied Computing (SAC), pp. 178–184. ACM (2011)

47. Mason, S., George, E.: Digital evidence and "cloud" computing. Computer Law & Security Review 27(5), 524–528 (2011)

48. Mell, P., Grance, T.: The nist definition of cloud computing (September 2011),
   http://csrc.nist.gov/publications/nistpubs/800-145/SP800-145.pdf

49. Miller, R.: Outage in dublin knocks amazon, microsoft data centers offline (2011),
   http://www.datacenterknowledge.com/archives/2011/08/07/lightning-in-dublin-knocks-amazon-microsoft-data-centers-offline/

50. Payne, B.D., Lee, W.: Secure and flexible monitoring of virtual machines. In: Proceedings of 23rd Annual Computer Security Applications Conference (ACSAC 2007). pp. 385–397. IEEE Computer Society (2007)

51. Pollitt, M.: Blue skies and storm clouds. Journal of Digital Forensic Practice 2(2), 105–106 (2008)

52. Pollitt, M.M.: An ad hoc review of digital forensic models. In: Proceedings Second Int. Workshop Systematic Approaches to Digital Forensic Engineering SADFE 2007, pp. 43–54 (2007)

53. Reilly, D., Wren, C., Berry, T.: Cloud computing: Forensic challenges for law enforcement. In: Proceedings of International Conference for Internet Technology and Secured Transactions ICITST 2010, pp. 1–7. IEEE (2010)

54. Richard, G.G., Roussev, V.: Next-generation digital forensics. Communications of the ACM 49, 76–80 (2006), http://doi.acm.org/10.1145/1113034.1113074
55. Roussev, V., Richard, G.G.: Breaking the performance wall: The case for distributed digital forensics. In: Proceedings of the 2004 Digital Forensics Research Workshop, DFRWS 2004 (2004)
56. Roussev, V., Wang, L., Richard, G.G., Marziale, L.: Mmr: A platform for large-scale forensic computing. In: Proceedings of the Fifth Annual IFIP WG 11.9 International Conference on Digital Forensics (2009)
57. Ruan, K., Baggili, I., Carthy, J., Kechadi, T.: Survey on cloud forensics and critical criteria for cloud forensic capability: A preliminary analysis. In: Proceedings of the 2011 ADFSL Conference on Digital Forensics, Security and Law (2011)
58. Ruan, K., Carthy, J., Kechadi, T., Crosbie, M.: Cloud forensics: An overview. Advances in Digital Forensics 7, 35–49 (2011)
59. Starcher, G.: Accessdata dna & amazon ec2 (2011), https://www.georgestarcher.com/?tag=amazon-ec2
60. Talbot, J., Yoo, R.: The phoenix system for mapreduce programming, http://mapreduce.stanford.edu/ (accessed: December 30, 2011)
61. Taylor, M., Haggerty, J., Gresty, D., Hegarty, R.: Digital evidence in cloud computing systems. Computer Law & Security Review 26(3), 304–308 (2010)
62. Taylor, M., Haggerty, J., Gresty, D., Lamb, D.: Forensic investigation of cloud computing systems. Network Security 2011(3), 4–10 (2011)
63. Wang, K.: Using a local search warrant to acquire evidence stored overseas via the internet. In: Chow, K.P., Shenoi, S. (eds.) Advances in Digital Forensics VI. IFIP AICT, vol. 337, pp. 37–48. Springer, Boston (2010), http://dx.doi.org/10.1007/978-3-642-15506-2_3
64. Wang, Y., Cannady, J., Rosenbluth, J.: Foundations of computer forensics: A technology for the fight against computer crime. Computer Law & Security Review 21(2), 119–127 (2005)
65. Wolthusen, S.D.: Overcast: Forensic discovery in cloud environments. In: Proceedings of the Fifth International Conference on IT Security Incident Management and IT Forensics, DC, USA, pp. 3–9 (2009)
66. Zimmerman, S., Glavach, D.: Cyber forensics in the cloud, the newsletter for information assurance technology professionals volume 14(1) (2011), http://iac.dtic.mil/iatac
67. Zonenberg, A.: Distributed hash cracker: A cross-platform gpu-accelerated password recovery system. Tech. rep., Rensselaer Polytechnic Institute (2009)

Towards a Logical Framework
for Reasoning about Risk

Matteo Cristani, Erisa Karafili, and Luca Viganò

Dipartimento di Informatica, Università degli Studi di Verona, Italy

Abstract. Evaluating the effectiveness of the security measures undertaken to protect a distributed system (e.g., protecting privacy of data in a network or in an information system) is a difficult task that, among other things, requires a risk assessment. We introduce a logical framework that allows one to reason about risk by means of operators that formalize causes, effects, preconditions, prevention and mitigation of events that may occur in the system. This is work in progress and we describe a number of interesting variants that could be considered.

1 Introduction

Evaluating the effectiveness of the security measures undertaken to protect a system, such as protecting privacy of data in a network or in a distributed system, is a difficult task that, among other things, requires one to carry out a *risk assessment*. To illustrate this, let us consider a real-life scenario in which privacy problems arise and security measures should be evaluated in terms of their effectiveness for risk reduction: the information system of a hospital should manage the process of hospitalizing patients coming directly from family doctors or from other wards or hospitals, where rules of access to patient data are employed to guarantee a satisfactory level of privacy within the system. We may thus look at these rules as risk reduction measures, and represent the relationships among different situations (or processes) in which the measures are taken or not.

For concreteness, let us consider a case study taken from the project *eFA* for personal health information management in hospitals [1]. All the records of a patient are stored in a *logical file* that contains a set of the *patient's medical records*, which are of three kinds: *administrative records* (*AR*) that contain the personal data of the patient, *normal records* (*NR*) that contain all the information that the doctors and nurses that attend to the patient should know, and *restricted records* (*RR*) that contain particularly sensitive information (like a record of a treatment for depression or some infectious disease).

To ensure the patient's health and simultaneously protect her privacy, the system must thus control the access to this information and enforce measures for risk reduction. The decisions about which measures of risk reduction should be adopted are based on relations among the events involved in the analyzed process; in particular, we adopt here the commonly accepted view point that assessing risk consists in managing causes and effects of a family of specific events (often also called *threats*). To enable such a decision procedure, in this paper we

G. Quirchmayr et al. (Eds.): CD-ARES 2012, LNCS 7465, pp. 609–623, 2012.

introduce a logical framework that allows one to represent the flow of time, and thereby capture the *temporal relationships* between events, and to formalize *causes*, *effects* and *preconditions* of events. Moreover, we also formalize event *prevention* (diminishing the number of occurrences of a threat) and *mitigation* (diminishing the impact of the effects of a threat).

This is work in progress and we describe a number of interesting variants that could be considered. To our knowledge, this is the first attempt at a general logical framework that accommodates causal relationships between events, as well as their prevention and mitigation. In contrast to quantitative approaches, where risk is assessed in terms of probabilities, we adopt here a *qualitative* approach in which we reason symbolically about the occurrence of events and associated risks (leaving an extension with probabilities for future work).

Risk assessment and risk reduction have been considered quite often in information security, environmental security (in the engineering context), portfolio management, and medicine. For instance, the algebraic framework RT^R given in [5] extends RT_0 [12] to provide a formal approach to risk evaluation in distributed authorization. Similarly, [2] proposes a tool for assessing risks related to policy overwrite and privacy leak; the approach is quite practical but it considers, as further work, the interesting possibility of extending the calculus of overwrite permissions "without expert intervention". A more mature investigation of risk assessment is given in [15], where, in particular, the authors consider the design of suitable experiments and analyze the effects of security enhancements within an organization, recommending methods for deciding the correct mixture of security measures to be chosen automatically. Although quite different in nature, all these investigations aim at tackling the problem of the automation of the selection process of security measures to reduce risks. The approach we propose will eventually lead to a system where such automation will be possible.

In [10,11], Lewis developed an approach to the representation of causes based on two distinct concepts: *causal dependency* and *counterfactuals*. Fundamentally, Lewis's theory describes two different causal relationships: the *precondition relation* (as developed in many temporal theories of AI, e.g., [14]) and *direct causation* (see, e.g., [4,16]). As further illustrated in [9,17], these notions can be interpreted by means of systems of possible worlds as in the Kripke semantics for modal logics. We follow a similar semantic approach to base our framework on *labeled deduction* [6,8,18]. In Section 2, we give syntax and semantics of our language and a set of tableau rules, discussing the different variants one may consider. In Section 3, we show, proof-of-concept, our framework at work on the case study. In Section 4, we conclude and discuss future work.

2   The Framework

2.1   Syntax

We consider a language structured in three layers. Given a set Π of *propositional variables* $p, q, r, \ldots$, the set of *well-formed formulas* (or, simply, *formulas*) ϕ of the first layer is defined by the grammar

$$\phi ::= p \mid \neg\phi \mid \phi \to \phi.$$

Other connectives (e.g., $\wedge$ and $\vee$) can be defined as usual. We refer to formulas ϕ also as *events* or *basic formulas* to stress that they are used by the formulas of the other two layers (we write E to denote the set of such formulas).

Formulas σ of the second layer are built from events, the two standard modal operators $\Box$ and $\Diamond$[1], and the two causal operators $\mathcal{C}$ and $\mathcal{P}$:

$$\sigma ::= \phi \mid \Box\phi \mid \Diamond\phi \mid \phi\,\mathcal{C}\,\phi \mid \phi\,\mathcal{P}\,\phi.$$

$\phi_1\,\mathcal{C}\,\phi_2$ and $\phi_1\,\mathcal{P}\,\phi_2$ are called *causal formulas*: ϕ_1 is the *cause event* and ϕ_2 is the *effect event*. $\mathcal{C}$ denotes *causation*: $\phi_1\,\mathcal{C}\,\phi_2$ denotes, intuitively, that if the cause ϕ_1 (e.g., winning a presidential election) occurs then the effect ϕ_2 (e.g., becoming the nation's president) will occur in the future. $\mathcal{P}$ denotes *precondition*: $\phi_1\,\mathcal{P}\,\phi_2$ denotes, intuitively, that if the effect ϕ_2 (e.g., suffering from a viral disease) occurs, then the cause ϕ_1 (e.g., being infected by a virus) occurred in its past.

The third layer extends the first one (so, the second and third layer are actually "side by side") by introducing formulas τ for *prevention* (or *block*) and *mitigation* of events:

$$\tau ::= \phi \mid \phi\,\mathcal{B}\,\phi \mid \phi\,\mathcal{M}\,\phi.$$

The prevention/block $\phi_1\,\mathcal{B}\,\phi_2$ denotes that the event ϕ_1 (e.g., a 100% effective prophylactic vaccine—if such a thing existed) prevents the event ϕ_2 (e.g., the illness being vaccinated against), i.e., if we have ϕ_1 then for sure we will not have ϕ_2 in the future. The mitigation $\phi_1\,\mathcal{M}\,\phi_2$ denotes that the event ϕ_1 (e.g., taking a medicine against the flu) prevents the effects of the event ϕ_2 (e.g., fever), i.e., if we have ϕ_1 then for sure we will not have in the future the effects of ϕ_2.

Note that some of the these operators can be defined in terms of standard modal operators, e.g., $\phi_1\,\mathcal{C}\,\phi_2$ could be defined as $[\Box](\phi_1 \to \Diamond\phi_2)$ and $\phi_1\,\mathcal{B}\,\phi_2$ as $[\Box](\phi_1 \to \Box\neg\phi_2)$, where $[\Box]$ denotes that this $\Box$ is optional depending on how one defines the semantics. Similarly, $\phi_1\,\mathcal{P}\,\phi_2$ could be defined as $[\Box](\phi_2 \to \blacklozenge\phi_1)$, where $\blacklozenge$ is the symbol for "$\Diamond$ in the past", which we could easily add, and $\phi_1\,\mathcal{M}\,\phi_2$ could be defined as $[\Box](\phi_1 \wedge [\Box]\forall\phi_3.\,(\phi_2\,\mathcal{C}\,\phi_3 \to \Box\neg\phi_3))$, which highlights the second-order nature of the mitigation operator. We, however, prefer to keep these operators as primitive operators in order to stress their relevance and, most importantly, to consider a number of interesting variants (e.g., there are indeed various kinds of vaccines, depending on their effectiveness or on their effects). In fact, we believe that the framework that we introduce here can be quite easily extended to encompass the several interesting variants of cause, precondition, block and mitigation that could be considered. For instance, in the following we will actually consider a more "refined" variant of block where the event ϕ_1 implies that the number of occurrences of the event ϕ_2 decreases with respect

---

[1] Note that we have here a kind of positive modal logic, in which $\Box$ and $\Diamond$ are not duals (since we have no negation in front of formulas of the second layer). This is not a problem, as positive modal logics have been well studied (see, e.g., [7,18], where different accessibility relations are considered for $\Box$ and $\Diamond$), but of course a full modal logic (in which $\Diamond A = \neg\Box A$) could be considered as well.

to the case when ϕ_1 did not hold. These choices depend on what exactly one aims to capture and thus we will now define the semantics of these formulas (actually, of their extension to labeled formulas) discussing the different options and variants that one could consider. We will also define tableaux rules for the different operators to formalize reasoning in our framework.

2.2   Time Flow, Traces and Worlds

In the systems that our framework allows us to model, we consider an underlying *time flow* $(T, <)$ where T is a non-empty set of *time instants* and $<$ is a binary relation in T that is irreflexive, transitive, dense (for all $i, j \in T$ such that $i < j$ there exists a $k \in T$ such that $i < k < j$) and linear ($i < j$ or $j < i$ for any two distinct $i, j \in T$). On top of this time flow, we may have more than one course of events, depending on the future that is in fact going to occur. We will thus define a Kripke-style model $\mathfrak{M}$ comprising of traces of possible worlds in which our events occur. Let us consider a non-empty set W of *worlds*, and the binary *adjacence* relation $\lhd \subseteq W \times W$ such that for every $w_i \in W$ there is a $w_j \in W$ for which $w_i \lhd w_j$. A *trace* is then a (possibly infinite) sequence of worlds $\vartheta = w_1 w_2 \cdots w_m w_n \cdots$ such that $w_m \lhd w_n$ for every two adjacent worlds $w_m, w_n \in \vartheta$. The traces of our framework are *discrete*: if two worlds are adjacent then there is no other world between them. We write Θ for the set of all possible traces of the system.

To go back and forth from time instants and worlds, we define the following mappings, which are illustrated in Fig. 1:

- itw : $(T \times \Theta) \to W$ maps a time instant i and a trace ϑ to a world of that trace itw$(i, \vartheta) = w \in \vartheta$. To make this mapping possible, we assume that a world may actually span different time instants until a new event occurs that makes us move to the following world.
- wi : $W \to \wp(T)$ maps a world to a set of time instants.
- iw : $T \to \wp(W)$ maps an instant of time i, to a set of subsets of W, iw$(i) = \bigcup_{\vartheta \in \Theta}$ itw(i, ϑ). This captures all the worlds in the different traces that occur in the same instants of time.
- wt : $W \to \wp(\Theta)$ maps a world to its corresponding subset of traces. This expresses that a world may occur in two (or more) traces, e.g., when they intersect or when a trace at some point diverges in two traces.

Given a trace $\vartheta = w_1 w_2 \cdots w_k w_l w_m \cdots$ and a time instant $i \geq 0$ such that $w_l = $ itw(i, ϑ), we can define the following *prefix* (sub-)traces $\vartheta|_{\leq i} = \vartheta|_{\leq w_l} = w_1 w_2 \cdots w_k w_l$ and $\vartheta|_{<i} = \vartheta|_{<w_l} = w_1 w_2 \cdots w_k$, and the following *suffix* (sub-)traces $\vartheta|_{\geq i} = \vartheta|_{\geq w_l} = w_l w_m \cdots$ and $\vartheta|_{>i} = \vartheta|_{>w_l} = w_m \cdots$.

2.3   Labeled Formulas

To be able to reason in a fine-grained way about the formulas holding in the structures providing our models, we base our framework on *labeled deduction* [6,8,18].

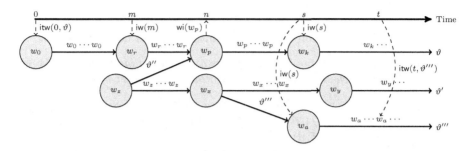

Fig. 1. Time flow, traces of worlds and mappings

We thus extend the language with a set $\mathcal{L}$ of labels and introduce the notions of labeled formula and relational formula. Our labels represent traces or pairs trace-world, which, slightly abusing notation, we will respectively denote by ϑ and (ϑ, w), possibly subscripted or superscripted.

Definition 1. *Let α be a well-formed formula (ϕ, σ or τ) and $(\vartheta, w), \vartheta \in \mathcal{L}$. Then $(\vartheta, w) : \alpha$ is a* labeled well-formed formula *(labeled formula or lwff for short), and the set of* relational well-formed formulas *(relational formulas or rwffs for short) ρ is defined as follows:*

$$\rho ::= (\vartheta, w_i) \lhd (\vartheta, w_j) \mid (\vartheta, w_i) < (\vartheta, w_j) \mid (\vartheta, w_i) \prec (\vartheta, w_j) \mid (\vartheta, w_i) \simeq (\vartheta', w_j) \mid$$
$$(\vartheta, w_i) \iota (\vartheta', w_j) \mid \vartheta \sim \vartheta'$$

Intuitively, $(\vartheta, w) : \alpha$ means that α is true at the world represented by w in the trace represented by ϑ and

- $(\vartheta, w_i) \lhd (\vartheta, w_j)$ means that the world represented by w_j is the immediate successor of the world represented by w_i in the trace represented by ϑ;
- $(\vartheta, w_i) < (\vartheta, w_j)$ means that the world represented by w_i precedes the world represented by w_j in the trace represented by ϑ, i.e., either $(\vartheta, w_i) \lhd (\vartheta, w_j)$ or there is a w_k such that $(\vartheta, w_i) \lhd (\vartheta, w_k)$ and $(\vartheta, w_k) < (\vartheta, w_j)$;
- $(\vartheta, w_i) \prec (\vartheta, w_j)$ means that the world represented by w_i precedes the world represented by w_j in the trace represented by ϑ and that in that trace there is at least one world w_k in-between w_i and w_j, i.e., there is a w_k such that $(\vartheta, w_i) \lhd (\vartheta, w_k)$ and $(\vartheta, w_k) < (\vartheta, w_j)$;
- $(\vartheta, w_i) \simeq (\vartheta', w_j)$ means that the world represented by w_i in the trace represented by ϑ is equivalent (as defined formally in Section 2.6) to the world represented by w_j in the trace represented by ϑ';
- $(\vartheta, w_i) \iota (\vartheta', w_j)$ means that the world represented by w_i in the trace represented by ϑ occurs in the same instant of time of the world represented by w_j in the trace represented by ϑ'; and
- $\vartheta \sim \vartheta'$ means that the trace represented by ϑ is equivalent to the trace represented by ϑ', i.e., $(\vartheta, w_1) \simeq (\vartheta', w_1'), (\vartheta, w_2) \simeq (\vartheta', w_2')$ and so on when $\vartheta = w_1, w_2, \cdots$ and $\vartheta' = w_1', w_2', \cdots$.

2.4   Semantics of the First Two Layers

We are now ready to give the semantics for the first two layers of our language, postponing the interpretation of block and mitigation to a later subsection.

Definition 2. *Models for the first two layers are tuples of the form* $\mathfrak{M} = (W, \Theta,$ $\mathcal{I}, \mathfrak{R}_\lhd, \mathfrak{R}_<, \mathfrak{R}_\prec, V)$, *where W is the set of worlds, Θ is the set of traces;*

- $\mathcal{I} : \mathcal{L} \to (\Theta, W)$ *is a (overloaded) function that maps every label (ϑ, w) to a pair trace-world, i.e., $\mathcal{I}((\vartheta, w)) = (\mathcal{I}(\vartheta), \mathcal{I}(w)) = (\vartheta, w)$, and every label ϑ to a single trace, i.e., $\mathcal{I}(\vartheta) = \vartheta$;[2]*
- $\mathfrak{R}_<$ *is a relation that holds true for any two worlds w_i and w_j that are in the same trace and such that w_i occurs before w_j;*
- $\mathfrak{R}_\lhd$ *is a relation that holds true for any two worlds w_i and w_j that are in the same trace and such that w_i is the immediate predecessor of w_j, i.e., $(w_i, w_j) \in \mathfrak{R}_\lhd$ iff $(w_i, w_j) \in \mathfrak{R}_<$ and there is no w_k such that $(w_i, w_k) \in \mathfrak{R}_<$ and $(w_k, w_j) \in \mathfrak{R}_<$;*
- $\mathfrak{R}_\prec$ *is a relation that holds true for any two worlds w_i and w_j that are in the same trace and such that w_i precedes w_j and is not its immediate predecessor, i.e., $(w_i, w_j) \in \mathfrak{R}_\prec$ iff there exists a w_k such that $(w_i, w_k) \in \mathfrak{R}_\lhd$ and $(w_k, w_j) \in \mathfrak{R}_<$;*
- $V : \mathcal{P} \times W \to \{\top, \bot\}$ *is a valuation function that assigns a truth value to a propositional variable p with respect to a given world w.*

Truth for a rwff or lwff in a model $\mathfrak{M}$ is the smallest relation $\models^{\mathfrak{M}}$ satisfying:

$$
\begin{aligned}
&\models^{\mathfrak{M}} (\vartheta, w_i) \bullet (\vartheta, w_j) &&\text{iff} && (\mathcal{I}((\vartheta, w_i)), \mathcal{I}((\vartheta, w_j))) \in \mathfrak{R}_\bullet \ \text{for} \ \bullet \in \{\mathfrak{R}_\lhd, \mathfrak{R}_<, \mathfrak{R}_\prec\} \\
&\models^{\mathfrak{M}} (\vartheta, w) : p &&\text{iff} && V(p, \mathcal{I}(w)) = \top \\
&\models^{\mathfrak{M}} (\vartheta, w) : \neg\phi &&\text{iff} && \not\models^{\mathfrak{M}} (\vartheta, w) : \phi \\
&\models^{\mathfrak{M}} (\vartheta, w) : \phi_1 \to \phi_2 &&\text{iff} && \models^{\mathfrak{M}} (\vartheta, w) : \phi_1 \ \text{implies} \ \models^{\mathfrak{M}} (\vartheta, w) : \phi_2 \\
&\models^{\mathfrak{M}} (\vartheta, w) : \Box\phi &&\text{iff} && \text{for all} \ (\vartheta, w_i) \in \mathcal{L}, \ \models^{\mathfrak{M}} (\vartheta, w) < (\vartheta, w_i) \ \text{implies} \ \models^{\mathfrak{M}} (\vartheta, w_i) : \phi \\
&\models^{\mathfrak{M}} (\vartheta, w) : \Diamond\phi &&\text{iff} && \text{exists} \ (\vartheta, w_i) \in \mathcal{L} \ \text{s.t.} \ \models^{\mathfrak{M}} (\vartheta, w) < (\vartheta, w_i) \ \text{and} \ \models^{\mathfrak{M}} (\vartheta, w_i) : \phi \\
&\models^{\mathfrak{M}} (\vartheta, w) : \phi_1 \, \mathcal{C} \, \phi_2 &&\text{iff} && \text{for all} \ (\vartheta, w_i) \in \mathcal{L}, \ \models^{\mathfrak{M}} (\vartheta, w) < (\vartheta, w_i) \ \text{and} \ \models^{\mathfrak{M}} (\vartheta, w_i) : \phi_1 \\
& && && \text{imply} \ \models^{\mathfrak{M}} (\vartheta, w_i) : \Diamond\phi_2 \\
&\models^{\mathfrak{M}} (\vartheta, w) : \phi_1 \, \mathcal{P} \, \phi_2 &&\text{iff} && \text{for all} \ (\vartheta, w_j) \in \mathcal{L}, \ \models^{\mathfrak{M}} (\vartheta, w) \prec (\vartheta, w_j) \ \text{and} \ \models^{\mathfrak{M}} (\vartheta, w_j) : \phi_2 \\
& && && \text{imply that there exists} \ (\vartheta, w_i) \in \mathcal{L} \ \text{s.t.} \ \models^{\mathfrak{M}} (\vartheta, w) < (\vartheta, w_i) \\
& && && \text{and} \ \models^{\mathfrak{M}} (\vartheta, w_i) < (\vartheta, w_j) \ \text{and} \ \models^{\mathfrak{M}} (\vartheta, w_i) : \phi_1
\end{aligned}
$$

2.5   Tableau Rules for the First Two Layers

In order to formalize reasoning about risk, we give a set of tableau rules. We assume that the reader is familiar with the standard tableau terminology and notation, e.g., [6]. As usual, a branch of a (possibly infinite) tableau is: *exhausted* if no more rules are applicable, *closed* if it contains the special judgment "CLOSED" and *open* if it is exhausted but not closed. A tableau is *closed* if all of its branches are closed. A rule that infers CLOSED is called a *closing rule*.

---

[2] Hence, for $\vartheta = w_1 w_2 \cdots$, we have $\mathcal{I}(\vartheta) = \mathcal{I}(\vartheta, w_1)\mathcal{I}(\vartheta, w_2) \cdots = w_1 w_2 \cdots$. Strictly speaking, we should use different symbols for labels in the syntax and traces/worlds in the semantics, but for simplicity we abuse notation and use the same symbols, and use labels and worlds/traces as synonyms.

The tableau rules for the first layer, which are shown in Fig. 2, are straightforward: they are just the labeled version of the standard rules (where ABS stands for absurdity). Rules for other connectives, such as $\wedge$ and $\vee$, can be given in the usual way. The tableau rules for the operators of the second layer are shown in Fig. 3. The positive rules ($\square$) and ($\lozenge$) mimic the semantics, whereas the closure rules ($\square$ABS) and ($\lozenge$ABS) tell us when we have a contradiction, but note that these two rules are actually derivable and could thus safely be omitted. The closure rules ($\mathcal{C}$ABS) and ($\mathcal{P}$ABS) are also derivable but we show them as their use simplifies the inferences.

The positive rule for ($\mathcal{C}$) follows the semantics, where we force the existence of the world w_k where the effect holds by requiring w_k to be fresh, i.e., different from all the worlds already present in the tableau up to that point.

Similarly, the positive rule of ($\mathcal{P}$) makes use of a fresh w_j in-between w_i and w_k, which we know must exist by the properties of $\prec$. Alternatively, we could have dispensed with the relation $\prec$ and forced our traces to be dense, but we have chosen not to do so as it would have complicated the formalization of the block and mitigation operators. Note also that we have defined ($\mathcal{P}$) to require that in-between the world where $\phi_1 \mathcal{P} \phi_2$ holds and that where ϕ_2 holds, the trace contains at least one world (where ϕ_1 holds). This basically means that if $\phi_1 \mathcal{P} \phi_2$ holds at w_i and ϕ_2 holds at its immediate successor w_j (i.e., $w_i \lhd w_j$), then $\phi_1 \mathcal{P} \phi_2$ has no "control" over ϕ_2. That is, we are modeling the situation where $\phi_1 \mathcal{P} \phi_2$ has been uttered too late in the process to have an influence on the ϕ_2 at w_j; rather, $(\vartheta, w_i) : \phi_1 \mathcal{P} \phi_2$ will require that for other occurrences of ϕ_2 holding at some future w_k, there is at least one world in-between w_i and w_k at which ϕ_1 holds.

Depending on the application, one might want to impose that causal formulas are *monotonic* in the sense that as soon as they become true, they stay true. This can be formalized by the following rules:

$$\frac{(\vartheta, w_1) : \phi_1 \mathcal{C} \phi_2 \quad (\vartheta, w_1) < (\vartheta, w_2)}{(\vartheta, w_2) : \phi_1 \mathcal{C} \phi_2} (\mathcal{C}\text{MON}) \qquad \frac{(\vartheta, w_1) : \phi_1 \mathcal{P} \phi_2 \quad (\vartheta, w_1) \prec (\vartheta, w_2)}{(\vartheta, w_2) : \phi_1 \mathcal{P} \phi_2} (\mathcal{P}\text{MON})$$

The rules in Fig. 4 formalize the properties of $<$, $\prec$ and $\lhd$; note that we give some rules schemas to save space (e.g., the rule ($\bullet$ABS) actually stands for three rules, one for each relation). We again have a number of options and variants that could be considered for these relational rules, e.g., we could introduce an explicit equality and add relational formulas of the form $(\vartheta, w_i) = (\vartheta, w_j)$ along with rules for the properties of $=$ (reflexivity, symmetry and transitivity) and extend the linearity rule ($<$ LIN) to

$$\frac{(\vartheta, w_1) \quad (\vartheta, w_2)}{(\vartheta, w_1) < (\vartheta, w_2) \mid (\vartheta, w_2) = (\vartheta, w_1) \mid (\vartheta, w_2) < (\vartheta, w_1)}$$

It is not difficult to see that these tableau rules are all sound (we omit the proof for space reasons). However, they are incomplete. Giving a complete tableau system is actually not an obvious task. As a simple example of the underlying difficulties, consider the closing rule ($\mathcal{P}$ABS) for the precondition, which is not complete as it does not represent all the possible cases for closure (in fact, as we

$$\frac{(\vartheta, w) : \neg\neg\phi}{(\vartheta, w) : \phi} \ (\neg\neg) \qquad\qquad \frac{(\vartheta, w) : \phi \quad (\vartheta, w) : \neg\phi}{\textsc{Closed}} \ (\textsc{Abs})$$

$$\frac{(\vartheta, w) : \phi_1 \rightarrow \phi_2}{(\vartheta, w) : \neg\phi_1 \quad | \quad (\vartheta, w) : \phi_2} \ (\rightarrow) \qquad \frac{(\vartheta, w) : \neg(\phi_1 \rightarrow \phi_2)}{(\vartheta, w) : \phi_1, \ (\vartheta, w) : \neg\phi_2} \ (\neg \rightarrow)$$

Fig. 2. Tableau rules for the first layer

$$\frac{(\vartheta, w_i) : \Box\phi \quad (\vartheta, w_i) < (\vartheta, w_j)}{(\vartheta, w_j) : \phi} \ (\Box) \qquad \frac{(\vartheta, w_i) : \Box\phi \quad (\vartheta, w_i) < (\vartheta, w_j) \quad (\vartheta, w_j) : \neg\phi}{\textsc{Closed}} \ (\Box\textsc{Abs})$$

$$\frac{(\vartheta, w_i) : \Diamond\phi}{(\vartheta, w_j) : \phi, \ (\vartheta, w_i) < (\vartheta, w_j)} \ (\Diamond) \ \Big(w_j \text{ fresh}\Big) \qquad \frac{(\vartheta, w) : \Diamond\phi \quad (\vartheta, w) : \Box\neg\phi}{\textsc{Closed}} \ (\Diamond\textsc{Abs})$$

$$\frac{(\vartheta, w_i) : \phi_1 \, \mathcal{C} \, \phi_2 \quad (\vartheta, w_j) : \phi_1 \quad (\vartheta, w_i) < (\vartheta, w_j)}{(\vartheta, w_k) : \phi_2, \ (\vartheta, w_j) < (\vartheta, w_k)} \ (\mathcal{C}) \ \Big(w_k \text{ fresh}\Big)$$

$$\frac{(\vartheta, w_i) : \phi_1 \, \mathcal{C} \, \phi_2 \quad (\vartheta, w_i) < (\vartheta, w_j) \quad (\vartheta, w_j) : \phi_1 \quad (\vartheta, w_j) : \Box\neg\phi_2}{\textsc{Closed}} \ (\mathcal{C}\textsc{Abs})$$

$$\frac{(\vartheta, w_i) : \phi_1 \, \mathcal{P} \, \phi_2 \quad (\vartheta, w_i) \prec (\vartheta, w_k) \quad (\vartheta, w_k) : \phi_2}{(\vartheta, w_j) : \phi_1, \ (\vartheta, w_i) < (\vartheta, w_j), \ (\vartheta, w_j) < (\vartheta, w_k)} \ (\mathcal{P}) \ \Big(w_j \text{ fresh}\Big)$$

$$\frac{(\vartheta, w_i) : \phi_1 \, \mathcal{P} \, \phi_2 \quad (\vartheta, w_i) \prec (\vartheta, w_k) \quad (\vartheta, w_k) : \phi_2 \quad (\vartheta, w_i) : \Box\neg\phi_1}{\textsc{Closed}} \ (\mathcal{P}\textsc{Abs})$$

Fig. 3. Tableau rules for the second layer

remarked above, this rule may simply be derived from $(\mathcal{P})$ and $(\textsc{Abs})$). If $(\vartheta, w_i) : \phi_1 \, \mathcal{P} \, \phi_2$ and $(\vartheta, w_k) : \phi_2$ for $(\vartheta, w_i) \prec (\vartheta, w_k)$, then by the semantics we have a contradiction if $(\vartheta, w_j) : \neg\phi_1$ for all (ϑ, w_j) such that $(\vartheta, w_i) < (\vartheta, w_j) < (\vartheta, w_k)$. The rule $(\mathcal{P}\textsc{Abs})$, however, captures the scenario where $\neg\phi_1$ is true even after the occurrence of ϕ_2, so we are missing the case in which $\neg\phi_1$ is true between (ϑ, w_i) and (ϑ, w_k) but there may be occurrences of ϕ_1 in the future worlds of (ϑ, w_k). This could be easily formalized by means of the temporal operator *until*, denoted by $\mathcal{U}$, which we apply on event pairs:

$$\models^{\mathfrak{M}} (\vartheta, w) : \phi_1 \, \mathcal{U} \, \phi_2 \text{ iff } \models^{\mathfrak{M}} (\vartheta, w) : \phi_2 \text{ or there exists } (\vartheta, w_j) \in \mathcal{L} \text{ s.t. } \models^{\mathfrak{M}} (\vartheta, w) < (\vartheta, w_j)$$
$$\text{and } \models^{\mathfrak{M}} (\vartheta, w_j) : \phi_2, \text{ and } \models^{\mathfrak{M}} (\vartheta, w_i) : \phi_1 \text{ for all } (\vartheta, w_i) \in \mathcal{L} \text{ s.t.}$$
$$\models^{\mathfrak{M}} (\vartheta, w) < (\vartheta, w_i) \text{ and } \models^{\mathfrak{M}} (\vartheta, w_i) < (\vartheta, w_j).$$

We can then represent all the possible cases of the closing rule for $\mathcal{P}$ as follows:

$$\frac{(\vartheta, w_i) : \phi_1 \, \mathcal{P} \, \phi_2 \quad (\vartheta, w_i) \prec (\vartheta, w_k) \quad (\vartheta, w_k) : \phi_2 \quad (\vartheta, w_i) \lhd (\vartheta, w_{i+1}) \quad (\vartheta, w_{i+1}) : \neg\phi_1 \, \mathcal{U} \, \phi_2}{\textsc{Closed}} \ (\mathcal{P}\textsc{Abs}^{\mathcal{U}})$$

However, this comes at the cost of having to deal with $\mathcal{U}$, which is a notoriously difficult operator, mainly due to its dual nature of being both an existential and a universal operator (in the sense that it contains both kinds of quantification). While labeled inference rules for $\mathcal{U}$ do exist, they require some technical tricks to guarantee completeness, such as the use of Skolem functions to force the existence of certain worlds [3] or the use of additional operators such as the history operator of [13]. Rather than giving such rules here as well, we observe

$$\frac{(\vartheta, w_1) \lhd (\vartheta, w_2)}{(\vartheta, w_1) < (\vartheta, w_2)} \ (\lhd <) \qquad \frac{(\vartheta, w_1) \bullet (\vartheta, w_2) \quad (\vartheta, w_2) \bullet (\vartheta, w_1)}{\text{CLOSED}} \ (\bullet \text{ABS}) \ \left(\bullet \in \{\lhd, <, \prec\} \right)$$

$$\frac{(\vartheta, w_1) \prec (\vartheta, w_2)}{(\vartheta, w_1) < (\vartheta, w_2)} \ (\prec <) \qquad \frac{(\vartheta, w_1) \bullet (\vartheta, w_2) \quad (\vartheta, w_2) \bullet (\vartheta, w_3)}{(\vartheta, w_1) \bullet (\vartheta, w_3)} \ (\bullet \text{TRANS}) \ \left(\bullet \in \{<, \prec\} \right)$$

$$\frac{(\vartheta, w_1) \quad (\vartheta, w_2)}{(\vartheta, w_1) < (\vartheta, w_2) \mid (\vartheta, w_2) < (\vartheta, w_1)} \ (< \text{LIN}) \qquad \frac{(\vartheta, w_1) \prec (\vartheta, w_2)}{(\vartheta, w_1) \lhd (\vartheta, w_3), \ (\vartheta, w_3) < (\vartheta, w_2)} \ (\prec) \ \left(\begin{matrix} w_3 \\ \text{fresh} \end{matrix} \right)$$

$$\frac{(\vartheta, w_1) < (\vartheta, w_2)}{(\vartheta, w_1) \lhd (\vartheta, w_2) \mid (\vartheta, w_1) \lhd (\vartheta, w_3), \ (\vartheta, w_3) < (\vartheta, w_2)} \ (<) \ \left(w_3 \text{ fresh} \right)$$

Fig. 4. Tableau rules for the relations (for the first two layers)

that to recover completeness for $\mathcal{P}$ (and the other operators) we can alternatively change the labeling discipline by allowing operations that work directly on the labels. For instance, we could then close for $\mathcal{P}$ as follows:

$$\frac{(\vartheta, w_i) : \phi_1 \, \mathcal{P} \, \phi_2 \quad (\vartheta, w_i) < (\vartheta, w_k) \quad (\vartheta, w_k) : \phi_2 \quad (\vartheta|_{<w_k}, w_i) : \Box \neg \phi_1}{\text{CLOSED}} \ (\mathcal{P}\text{ABS}^{lab})$$

In both these alternatives $(\mathcal{P}\text{ABS}^{\mathcal{U}})$ and $(\mathcal{P}\text{ABS}^{lab})$, the technical price to pay is quite high so, depending on the application, one might even want to stick to the sound but incomplete system given above or to select the additional rules that are best fit for the concrete example under consideration.

2.6 Semantics of the Third Layer

Since a single world $w \in W$ can also be seen as the conjunction of all the formulas that are true at it, we can define two worlds to be *equivalent*, in symbols $w_1 \simeq w_2$, iff they make true the same propositional variables. By extension, two traces are equivalent, in symbols $\vartheta_1 \sim \vartheta_2$, iff their corresponding worlds for every instant of time are equivalent, so $\text{itw}(l, \vartheta_1) \simeq \text{itw}(l, \vartheta_2)$ for every $l \in T$.

Definition 3. *Models for the third layer extend those of the first two layers (cf. Definition 2) with three relations $\mathfrak{R}_\iota$, $\mathfrak{R}_\simeq$ and $\mathfrak{R}_\sim$, where*

- *$\mathfrak{R}_\iota$ is a relation that holds true for any two worlds w_i and w_j that are not in the same trace but occur in the same instant of time;*
- *$\mathfrak{R}_\simeq$ is an equivalence relation that holds true for any two worlds w_i and w_j such that $V(p, w_i) = V(p, w_j)$ for all propositional variables $p \in \Pi$;*
- *$\mathfrak{R}_\sim$ is an equivalence relation that holds true for any two traces ϑ' and ϑ'' whose corresponding worlds in every instant of time are equivalent, i.e., $(\text{itw}(i, \vartheta'), \text{itw}(i, \vartheta'')) \in \mathfrak{R}_\simeq$ for every $i \in T$.*

Truth for these rwffs is then defined as:

$$\models^{\mathfrak{m}} (\vartheta, w) \bullet (\vartheta', w_i) \quad \textit{iff} \quad (\mathcal{I}((\vartheta, w)), \mathcal{I}((\vartheta', w_i))) \in \mathfrak{R}_\bullet \ \textit{for} \ \bullet \in \{\mathfrak{R}_\iota, \mathfrak{R}_\simeq\}$$
$$\models^{\mathfrak{m}} \vartheta \sim \vartheta' \qquad\qquad\quad \textit{iff} \quad (\mathcal{I}(\vartheta), \mathcal{I}(\vartheta')) \in \mathfrak{R}_\sim$$

$$\frac{}{\vartheta \sim \vartheta} \; (\sim \text{REFL}) \qquad \frac{\vartheta \sim \vartheta'}{\vartheta' \sim \vartheta} \; (\sim \text{SYM}) \qquad \frac{\vartheta \sim \vartheta' \quad \vartheta' \sim \vartheta''}{\vartheta \sim \vartheta''} \; (\sim \text{TRANS})$$

$$\frac{}{(\vartheta, w) \bullet (\vartheta, w)} \; (\bullet \text{REFL}) \qquad \frac{(\vartheta, w_1) \bullet (\vartheta, w_2)}{(\vartheta, w_2) \bullet (\vartheta, w_1)} \; (\bullet \text{SYM})$$

$$\frac{(\vartheta, w_1) \bullet (\vartheta, w_2) \quad (\vartheta, w_2) \bullet (\vartheta, w_3)}{(\vartheta, w_1) \bullet (\vartheta, w_3)} \; (\bullet \text{TRANS}) \qquad \frac{(\vartheta, w_1) \simeq (\vartheta', w_2) \quad (\vartheta, w_1) : \phi}{(\vartheta', w_2) : \phi} \; (\simeq \text{MON})$$

Fig. 5. Tableau rules for the relations for the third layer, where $\bullet \in \{\iota, \simeq\}$

The rules in Fig. 5 capture the properties of these relations.

Prevention. As we already remarked in Section 2.1, one can consider different forms of prevention $\phi_1 \, \mathcal{B} \, \phi_2$, varying in the strength of the blocking event. For the strongest but also less interesting form, where the blocking event ϕ_1 completely prevents the second event ϕ_2, we can define

$\models^{\mathfrak{M}} (\vartheta, w) : \phi_1 \, \mathcal{B} \, \phi_2$ iff for all $(\vartheta, w_i), (\vartheta, w_j) \in \mathcal{L}$, $(w, w_i) \in \mathfrak{R}_<$ and $(w_i, w_j) \in \mathfrak{R}_<$ and
$\models^{\mathfrak{M}} (\vartheta, w_j) : \phi_2$ imply $\not\models^{\mathfrak{M}} (\vartheta, w_i) : \phi_1$
or, alternatively: iff for all $(\vartheta, w_i) \in \mathcal{L}$, $(w, w_i) \in \mathfrak{R}_<$ and $\models^{\mathfrak{M}} (\vartheta, w_i) : \phi_1$ imply that there
does not exist $(\vartheta, w_j) \in \mathcal{L}$ s.t. $(w_i, w_j) \in \mathfrak{R}_<$ and $\models^{\mathfrak{M}} (\vartheta, w_j) : \phi_2$

to express that if ϕ_2 occurs then it cannot be that ϕ_1 occurred previously but after the blocking formula (and thus again note that we can consider variants depending on when we actually let the blocking formula and the two events occur), or that if ϕ_1 occurs then ϕ_2 cannot occur in the future. However, one might typically want to consider a more refined definition of prevention, where ϕ_1 reduces the future occurrences of ϕ_2. To that end, instead of considering worlds occurring in the same trace, we need to compare traces where ϕ_1 occurs with those where ϕ_1 does not occur. In the trace where ϕ_1 occurs, so the prevention measure is in act, the occurrences of ϕ_2 are less than the occurrences of it in the trace where ϕ_1 does not occur. More specifically, the definition of prevention that we introduce says that $\phi_1 \, \mathcal{B} \, \phi_2$ is true at a given world w of a given trace ϑ iff, for all traces ϑ' equivalent to ϑ differing only for the occurrence of ϕ_1, since in ϑ we don't have ϕ_1 and instead ϕ_1 occurs in ϑ' after $\phi_1 \, \mathcal{B} \, \phi_2$, we have that, for all occurrences of ϕ_2 in ϑ', in the same instant of time we have a world in ϑ where ϕ_2 is true, and there are some occurrences of ϕ_2 in ϑ such that in the same instant of time there is a world in ϑ' where ϕ_2 is not true:

$\models^{\mathfrak{M}} (\vartheta, w) : \phi_1 \, \mathcal{B} \, \phi_2$ iff for all $\vartheta' \in \mathcal{L}$, for all $(\vartheta, w_i) \in \mathcal{L}$, exists $(\vartheta', w_j) \in \mathcal{L}$ s.t.
$((\vartheta, w) < (\vartheta, w_i)$ and $\models^{\mathfrak{M}} (\vartheta, w_i) : \neg\phi_1$ and $(\vartheta, w_i)\iota(\vartheta', w_j)$ and
$(\vartheta, w) < (\vartheta', w_j)$ and $\vartheta|_{<(\vartheta, w_i)} \sim \vartheta'|_{<(\vartheta', w_j)}$ and $\models^{\mathfrak{M}} (\vartheta', w_j) : \phi_1)$
imply that (for all $(\vartheta', w_y) \in \mathcal{L}$, $\models^{\mathfrak{M}} (\vartheta', w_y) : \phi_2$ and $(\vartheta', w_j) < (\vartheta', w_y)$
imply that exists $(\vartheta, w_x) \in \mathcal{L}$, s.t. $\models^{\mathfrak{M}} (\vartheta, w_x) : \phi_2$ and
$(\vartheta, w_i) < (\vartheta, w_x)$ and $(\vartheta, w_x)\iota(\vartheta', w_y))$ and (exist $l > 0$ and $(\vartheta, w_{k,i})$,
$(\vartheta', w_{h,i}) \in \mathcal{L}$, where $0 < i \leq l$, s.t. $(\vartheta, w_i) < (\vartheta, w_{k,i})$ and
$\models^{\mathfrak{M}} (\vartheta, w_{k,i}) : \phi_2$ and $(\vartheta', w_j) < (\vartheta', w_{h,i})$ and $\models^{\mathfrak{M}} (\vartheta', w_{h,i}) : \neg\phi_2$ and
$(\vartheta, w_{k,i})\iota(\vartheta', w_{h,i}))$

We can then give the following tableau rules for prevention, which, however, require us to extend the labeling discipline as we described above and allow for relational formulas of the form $\vartheta|_{\leq w_0} \sim \vartheta'|_{\leq w_0}$:

$$\frac{\begin{array}{c}(\vartheta, w) : \phi_1 \, \mathcal{B} \, \phi_2 \quad (\vartheta, w_i) : \neg\phi_1 \quad (\vartheta, w_0) \lhd (\vartheta, w_i) \\ (\vartheta, w) < (\vartheta, w_i) \quad \vartheta|_{\le w_0} \sim \vartheta'|_{\le w_0} \quad (\vartheta', w_y) : \phi_2 \quad (\vartheta, w_0) < (\vartheta', w_y)\end{array}}{\begin{array}{c}(\vartheta', w_j)\iota(\vartheta, w_i), \, (\vartheta, w_0) \lhd (\vartheta', w_j), \, (\vartheta', w_j) : \phi_1, \, (\vartheta, w) < (\vartheta', w_j), \, (\vartheta, w_x) : \phi_2, \\ (\vartheta', w_j) < (\vartheta', w_y), \, (\vartheta, w_x)\iota(\vartheta', w_y), \, (\vartheta, w_i) < (\vartheta, w_x), \, (\vartheta, w_i) < (\vartheta, w_k), \\ (\vartheta', w_j) < (\vartheta', w_h), \, (\vartheta, w_k)\iota(\vartheta', w_h), \, (\vartheta, w_k) : \phi_2, \, (\vartheta', w_h) : \neg\phi_2\end{array}} \; (\mathcal{B}) \; \begin{bmatrix} w_j, \, w_x, \\ w_k, \, w_h \\ \text{fresh} \end{bmatrix}$$

$$\frac{\begin{array}{c}(\vartheta, w) : \phi_1 \, \mathcal{B} \, \phi_2 \quad (\vartheta, w_i) : \neg\phi_1 \quad (\vartheta, w_0) \lhd (\vartheta, w_i) \quad (\vartheta, w) < (\vartheta, w_i) \\ \vartheta|_{\le w_0} \sim \vartheta'|_{\le w_0} \quad (\vartheta', w_y) : \phi_2 \quad (\vartheta, w_0) < (\vartheta', w_y) \quad (\vartheta', w_j) : \Box\phi_2 \quad (\vartheta, w_0) \lhd (\vartheta', w_j)\end{array}}{\textsc{Closed}} \; (\mathcal{B}\textsc{Abs}_1)$$

$$\frac{\begin{array}{c}(\vartheta, w) : \phi_1 \, \mathcal{B} \, \phi_2 \quad (\vartheta, w_i) : \neg\phi_1 \quad (\vartheta, w_0) \lhd (\vartheta, w_i) \quad (\vartheta, w) < (\vartheta, w_i) \\ \vartheta|_{\le w_0} \sim \vartheta'|_{\le w_0} \quad (\vartheta', w_y) : \phi_2 \quad (\vartheta, w_0) < (\vartheta', w_y) \quad (\vartheta, w_i) : \Box\neg\phi_2\end{array}}{\textsc{Closed}} \; (\mathcal{B}\textsc{Abs}_2)$$

The positive rule of $\mathcal{B}$ follows the semantics, where given the ϑ-world w_i where ϕ_1 is not true, we force the existence of a fresh world w_j where ϕ_1 is true, in every other trace ϑ', equivalent to the given one, until w_j. For every world w_y in ϑ', where ϕ_2 is true, we introduce a fresh ϑ-world w_x where ϕ_2 is also true. We also introduce two fresh worlds, w_k in ϑ and w_h in ϑ', such that ϕ_2 is true at (ϑ, w_k) and it is instead false at (ϑ', w_h).

As before, these rules are sound but the two closing rules, which are used together and not as alternatives, are not complete because they do not represent all the possible cases. The rule $(\mathcal{B}\textsc{Abs}_1)$ does not capture the scenario in which there are occurrences of $\neg\phi_2$ in ϑ' and still the number of occurrences of ϕ_2 in ϑ' is bigger than the number of occurrences of ϕ_2 in ϑ. $(\mathcal{B}\textsc{Abs}_2)$ does not capture the scenario in which there are occurrences of ϕ_2 in ϑ and still the number of occurrences of ϕ_2 in ϑ' is bigger than the number of occurrences of ϕ_2 in ϑ.

We can force $\mathcal{B}$ to be monotonic over $<$ by adding a rule $(\mathcal{B}\textsc{Mon})$ analogous to $(\mathcal{C}\textsc{Mon})$.

Mitigation. As for prevention, we could consider a strong definition of mitigation $\phi_1 \, \mathcal{M} \, \phi_2$ such that ϕ_1 prevents all occurrences of the effects of ϕ_2:

$$\models^{\mathfrak{M}} (\vartheta, w) : \phi_1 \, \mathcal{M} \, \phi_2 \text{ iff } \begin{array}{l} \text{for all } w_i, w_j \in W, \, (w, w_i) \in \mathfrak{R}_< \text{ and } \models^{\mathfrak{M}} (\vartheta, w_i) : \phi_1 \text{ and} \\ (w_j, w_i) \in \mathfrak{R}_< \text{ and } \models^{\mathfrak{M}} (\vartheta, w_j) : \phi_2 \text{ imply that for all } \phi_3 \in E \text{ and} \\ \text{for all } w_x \in W \text{ s.t. } \models^{\mathfrak{M}} (\vartheta, w_x) : \phi_2 \, \mathcal{C} \, \phi_3 \text{ and } (w_x, w_j) \in \mathfrak{R}_< \\ \text{we have that } \models^{\mathfrak{M}} (\vartheta, w_j) : \Box\neg\phi_3 \end{array}$$

However, it is more interesting to consider a form of mitigation that does not block completely the occurrences of the effects of ϕ_2 but instead makes them decrease: $\phi_1 \, \mathcal{M} \, \phi_2$ means that ϕ_1 prevents all the effects of the event ϕ_2. Alternatively, we could define that it prevents only some of the effects. In both such cases, we highlight the second-order nature of this operator, which could however be pushed down to the propositional level if one were certain that such effects were finitely many. Compare, for instance, the well-known (and thus finitely enumerable) undesired effects of a commercial medicine with the still uncategorized undesired effects of an experimental treatment.

We could even define a very weak mitigation $\phi_1 \, \mathcal{M} \, \phi_2[\phi_3]$ that prevents only one effect: the event ϕ_1 mitigates the event ϕ_2 by preventing its effect ϕ_3.

As an example, we formalize the definition of mitigation that we consider the most complete: $\phi_1 \mathcal{M} \phi_2$ means that ϕ_1 prevents all occurrences of the effects of ϕ_2. This definition can easily be used to provide a more sophisticated formulation, in which we also are able to prevent the effects of a given threat that satisfy a given condition. If we write $\phi_1 \mathcal{M} \phi_2[\psi]$, we mean that ϕ_1 prevents all the effects of ϕ_2 that satisfy ψ. This extension is left for further work.

The definition of mitigation that we formalize says that $\phi_1 \mathcal{M} \phi_2$ is true in a given world w of a given trace ϑ iff, for all traces ϑ' equivalent to ϑ differing only for the occurrence of ϕ_1, since in ϑ we don't have ϕ_1 and instead ϕ_1 occurs in ϑ' after $\phi_1 \mathcal{M} \phi_2$ and ϕ_2, we have that, for all the occurrences of the event ϕ_3 in ϑ', such that ϕ_3 is an effect of ϕ_2 that comes after the occurrence of ϕ_2, which itself comes after $\phi_2 \mathcal{C} \phi_3$, in the same instant of time we have a world in ϑ at which ϕ_3 is true, and there are some occurrences of ϕ_3 in ϑ such that in the same instant of time there is a world in ϑ' at which ϕ_3 is not true.

$\models^{\mathfrak{M}} (\vartheta, w) : \phi_1 \mathcal{M} \phi_2$ iff for all $\vartheta' \in \mathcal{L}$, for all $(\vartheta, w_i) \in \mathcal{L}$, exists $(\vartheta', w_j) \in \mathcal{L}, (\vartheta, w) < (\vartheta, w_i)$
and $\models^{\mathfrak{M}} (\vartheta, w_i) : \neg\phi_1$ and $(\vartheta, w_i)\iota(\vartheta', w_j)$ and $(\vartheta, w) < (\vartheta', w_j)$ and
$\vartheta|_{<(\vartheta, w_i)} \sim \vartheta'|_{<(\vartheta', w_j)}$ and $\models^{\mathfrak{M}} (\vartheta', w_j) : \phi_1$ implies for all $\phi_3 \in E$,
for all $(\vartheta, w_p), (\vartheta, w_r) \in \mathcal{L}, \models^{\mathfrak{M}} (\vartheta, w_p) : \phi_2 \mathcal{C} \phi_3$ and $(\vartheta, w_p) < (\vartheta, w_r)$
and $(\vartheta, w_r) < (\vartheta, w_i)$ and $\models^{\mathfrak{M}} (\vartheta, w_r) : \phi_2$ implies
(for all $(\vartheta', w_y) \in \mathcal{L}, \models^{\mathfrak{M}} (\vartheta', w_y) : \phi_3$ and $(\vartheta', w_j) < (\vartheta', w_y)$ implies
exists $(\vartheta, w_x) \in \mathcal{L}, \models^{\mathfrak{M}} (\vartheta, w_x) : \phi_3$ and $(\vartheta, w_i) < (\vartheta, w_x)$ and
$(\vartheta, w_x)\iota(\vartheta', w_y))$ and (exists $l > 0$, exist $(\vartheta, w_{k,i}), (\vartheta', w_{h,i}) \in \mathcal{L}$,
where $0 < i \le l$, s.t. $(\vartheta, w_i) < (\vartheta, w_{k,i})$ and $\models^{\mathfrak{M}} (\vartheta, w_{k,i}) : \phi_3$ and
$(\vartheta', w_j) < (\vartheta', w_{h,i})$ and $\models^{\mathfrak{M}} (\vartheta', w_{h,i}) : \neg\phi_3$ and $(\vartheta, w_{k,i})\iota(\vartheta', w_{h,i}))$

We can then give the following tableau rules for mitigation, a positive rule and two closure rules, which, again, are sound but incomplete:

$$\frac{\begin{array}{c}(\vartheta, w) : \phi_1 \mathcal{M} \phi_2 \quad (\vartheta, w_i) : \neg\phi_1 \quad (\vartheta, w_0) \lhd (\vartheta, w_i) \\ (\vartheta, w) < (\vartheta, w_i) \quad \vartheta|_{\le w_0} \sim \vartheta'|_{\le w_0} \quad (\vartheta, w_p) : \phi_2 \mathcal{C} \phi_3 \quad (\vartheta, w_r) : \phi_2 \\ (\vartheta, w_p) < (\vartheta, w_r) \quad (\vartheta, w_r) < (\vartheta, w_i) \quad (\vartheta', w_y) : \phi_3 \quad (\vartheta, w_0) < (\vartheta', w_y)\end{array}}{\begin{array}{c}(\vartheta', w_j)\iota(\vartheta, w_i), \; (\vartheta, w_0) \lhd (\vartheta', w_j), \; (\vartheta', w_j) : \phi_1, \; (\vartheta, w) < (\vartheta', w_j), \\ (\vartheta', w_j) < (\vartheta', w_y), \; (\vartheta, w_x)\iota(\vartheta', w_y), \; (\vartheta, w_i) < (\vartheta, w_x), \; (\vartheta, w_i) < (\vartheta, w_k), \\ (\vartheta, w_x) : \phi_3, \; (\vartheta', w_j) < (\vartheta', w_h), \; (\vartheta, w_k)\iota(\vartheta', w_h), \; (\vartheta, w_k) : \phi_3, \; (\vartheta', w_h) : \neg\phi_3\end{array}} \; (\mathcal{M}) \begin{pmatrix} w_j, w_x, \\ w_k, w_h \\ \text{fresh} \end{pmatrix}$$

$$\frac{\begin{array}{c}(\vartheta, w) : \phi_1 \mathcal{M} \phi_2 \quad (\vartheta, w_i) : \neg\phi_1 \quad (\vartheta, w_0) \lhd (\vartheta, w_i) \quad (\vartheta, w) < (\vartheta, w_i) \\ \vartheta|_{\le w_0} \sim \vartheta'|_{\le w_0} \quad (\vartheta, w_p) : \phi_2 \mathcal{C} \phi_3 \quad (\vartheta, w_r) : \phi_2 \quad (\vartheta, w_p) < (\vartheta, w_r) \\ (\vartheta, w_r) < (\vartheta, w_i) \quad (\vartheta', w_y) : \phi_3 \quad (\vartheta, w_0) < (\vartheta', w_y) \quad (\vartheta', w_j) : \Box\phi_3 \quad (\vartheta, w_0) \lhd (\vartheta', w_j)\end{array}}{\textsc{Closed}} \; (\mathcal{M}\textsc{Abs}_1)$$

$$\frac{\begin{array}{c}(\vartheta, w) : \phi_1 \mathcal{M} \phi_2 \quad (\vartheta, w_i) : \neg\phi_1 \quad (\vartheta, w_0) \lhd (\vartheta, w_i) \\ (\vartheta, w) < (\vartheta, w_i) \quad \vartheta|_{\le w_0} \sim \vartheta'|_{\le w_0} \quad (\vartheta, w_p) : \phi_2 \mathcal{C} \phi_3 \quad (\vartheta, w_r) : \phi_2 \\ (\vartheta, w_p) < (\vartheta, w_r) \quad (\vartheta, w_r) < (\vartheta, w_i) \quad (\vartheta', w_y) : \phi_3 \quad (\vartheta, w_0) < (\vartheta', w_y) \quad (\vartheta, w_i) : \Box\neg\phi_3\end{array}}{\textsc{Closed}} \; (\mathcal{M}\textsc{Abs}_2)$$

The positive rule of $\mathcal{M}$ follows the semantics, where given the ϑ-world w_i, where ϕ_1 is not true, we force the existence of a fresh world w_j where ϕ_1 is true, in every other trace ϑ', equivalent to the given one, until w_j. For all ϑ'-worlds w_y, where ϕ_3 is true, that come after the occurrence ϕ_2, that itself comes after the occurrence of $\phi_2 \mathcal{C} \phi_3$ and before the occurrence of ϕ_1, we introduce a fresh ϑ-world w_x, where ϕ_3 is also true. We also introduce two fresh worlds w_k in ϑ and w_h in ϑ', with ϕ_3 true in w_k and not true in w_h.

The rule $(\mathcal{M}\textsc{Abs}_1)$ doesn't capture the case when there are occurrences of $\neg\phi_3$ in ϑ' and still the number of occurrences of ϕ_3 in ϑ' is bigger than the number of occurrences of ϕ_3 in ϑ, whereas the rule $(\mathcal{M}\textsc{Abs}_2)$ doesn't capture the case when there are occurrences of ϕ_3 in ϑ and still the number of occurrences of ϕ_3 in ϑ' is bigger than the number of occurrences of ϕ_3 in ϑ.

We can force mitigation to be monotonic as for the other operators.

3   A Case Study

To illustrate our framework at work, we return to the case study presented in the introduction. For simplicity, but without loss of generality, we make the standard *closed world* assumption, i.e., in a given world, every formula is false unless it is explicitly not asserted to be true. Also, we adopt a propositional language: the medical staff $\textsc{Staff} = \{d_1, d_2, \ldots\}$ and the patients $\textsc{Patients} = \{c_1, c_2, \ldots\}$ are finite sets, where d_i and c_j are propositional variables, and thus we employ $\forall$ and $\exists$ simply as abbreviations for finite conjunctions and disjunctions. We write c to denote a generic patient and d to denote a generic doctor or nurse.

When a new patient c is hospitalized, the first step is her registration $Reg(c)$, which *causes* the generation of three records:

$$Reg(c)\,\mathcal{C}\,Gen(AR_c) \qquad Reg(c)\,\mathcal{C}\,Gen(NR_c) \qquad Reg(c)\,\mathcal{C}\,Gen(RR_c).$$

The registration is a *precondition* for the assignment of a doctor to the patient and for the access of the normal records of a patient by the medical staff. The assigned doctor has full access to all the medical data of her patient (of course, the assigned doctor does not need the administrative data of the patient). The accesses made by the members of the $\textsc{Staff}$ that are not the assigned doctor cause the leak of personal information of the patient, expressed by a $Privacy.Leak$ event. All the concepts represented above are given as follows:

$$Reg(c)\,\mathcal{P}\,\exists d.Assigned(d, c) \qquad Reg(c)\,\mathcal{P}\,Access(d, NR_c)$$
$$Assigned(d, c)\,\mathcal{P}\,Access(d, NR_c) \qquad Assigned(d, c)\,\mathcal{P}\,Access(d, RR_c)$$
$$(Assigned(d, c) \wedge \exists x.(Access(x, NR_c) \wedge x \neq d))\,\mathcal{C}\,Privacy.Leak(c).$$

A patient c can be transferred, $Transfer(c)$, to another hospital (which should be a parameter but we omit it for simplicity): after the occurrence of $Transfer(c)$, the accesses to the records of c are reduced as the accesses to the patient records are made just for examination and consultation with the doctors of the new hospital of the patient, or for statistic or research aims. The transfer is made if c is registered, and when it occurs it *prevents* access to the patient's data:

$$Reg(c)\,\mathcal{P}\,Transfer(c) \qquad Transfer(c)\,\mathcal{B}\,Access(d, AR_c)$$
$$Transfer(c)\,\mathcal{B}\,Access(d, NR_c) \qquad Transfer(c)\,\mathcal{B}\,Access(d, RR_c)$$

We call *rule formulas* all of the above 12 formulas. They have to be true before the involved event takes place. If they are true after the occurrence of the event, then they can not be applied, but they can be used in the next occurrence of that event, in case they are still true. In the following scenario, we assume all these formulas to be true from the first instant of time, i.e., from the initial world (ϑ, w_0); for the sake of space we are not going to write all of them, but just the

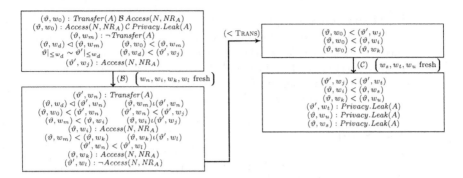

Fig. 6. Tableau fragment for the case study

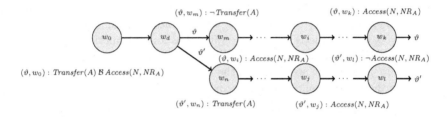

Fig. 7. The scenario for $\mathcal{B}$ in the case study

formulas we are going to use. Other rule formulas can be added to the system if they are needed.

Assume Alice (A) is a patient of the clinic and registers at time r, so $Reg(A)$ is true at world (ϑ, w) such that $\mathcal{I}(\vartheta, w) = \mathsf{itw}(r, \vartheta)$, and which comes after (ϑ, w_0). Using rule $(\mathcal{C})$, we can deduce that there is a world (ϑ, w_g) in the future of (ϑ, w), where the generation of NR_A takes place, i.e., $(\vartheta, w_g) : Gen(NR_A)$.

At time i, corresponding to (ϑ, w_i), doctor Debbie (D) modifies the restricted records of A, i.e., $(\vartheta, w_i) : Access(D, RR_A)$ and $(\vartheta, w_0) \prec (\vartheta, w_i)$. Then, given $(\vartheta, w_0) : Assigned(D, A) \mathcal{P} Access(D, RR_A)$, rule $(\mathcal{P})$ yields that there is a new world (ϑ, w_k), between (ϑ, w_0) and (ϑ, w_i), where the assignment of D to A occurs. Assume now that at world (ϑ, w_d), D decides if A needs to be transferred to another hospital. At the immediate successor (ϑ, w_m) of (ϑ, w_d), the formula $Transfer(A)$ is false. There is another branch of the trace, denoted by ϑ', that is equivalent to ϑ up to (and including) (ϑ, w_d). At world (ϑ', w_j), nurse Nancy (N) accesses the data of (A), as shown in Fig. 7. The assertion $Assigned(D, A)$ establishes that D is assigned to A. In this context, we assume that N is not assigned to A, which is anyway guaranteed by the closed world assumption. In Fig. 6, we give a significant fragment of a tableau for this scenario, where rule $(\mathcal{B})$ is used to prevent the accesses to the records of A. If the inference continues with the application of $(< \text{TRANS})$ and $(\mathcal{C})$, then we will also see that the occurrences of $Privacy.Leak(A)$ in ϑ are less than those in ϑ.

4 Concluding Remarks

In this paper, we investigated a general framework for reasoning about risks. The approach we have taken consists in designing a flexible system in order to adapt the framework to the different contexts which it may be applied to, and here we have over scratched the surface of the landscape of alternative possibilities. As we remarked, there are several ways in which this research can be taken further. We aim, in particular, at devising a complete tableau system and automating the deduction process: in addition to theorem proving, we envision a model checking procedure that would allow us to tackle concrete case studies taken from industrial practice (such as more complex scenarios for the case study discussed above).

References

1. AVANTSSAR. Deliverable 5.1: Problem cases and their trust and security requirements (2008), http://www.avantssar.eu
2. Bartsch, S.: A calculus for the qualitative risk assessment of policy override authorization. In: SIN, pp. 62–70 (2010)
3. Basin, D.A., Caleiro, C., Ramos, J., Viganò, L.: Labelled tableaux for distributed temporal logic. Journal of Logic and Computation 19(6), 1245–1279 (2009)
4. Bell, J.: A Common Sense Theory of Causation. In: Blackburn, P., Ghidini, C., Turner, R.M., Giunchiglia, F. (eds.) CONTEXT 2003. LNCS, vol. 2680, pp. 40–53. Springer, Heidelberg (2003)
5. Chapin, P.C., Skalka, C., Wang, X.S.: Risk assessment in distributed authorization. In: FMSE, pp. 33–42 (2005)
6. D'Agostino, M., Gabbay, D.M., Hähnle, R., Posegga, J. (eds.): Handbook of Tableau Methods. Kluwer Academic Publishers (1999)
7. Dunn, J.M.: Positive modal logic. Studia Logica 55, 301–317 (1995)
8. Gabbay, D.M.: Labelled Deductive Systems. Clarendon Press (1996)
9. Giunchiglia, E., Lee, J., Lifschitz, V., McCain, N., Turner, H.: Nonmonotonic causal theories. Artificial Intelligence 153(1-2), 49–104 (2004)
10. Lewis, D.: Causation. The Journal of Philosophy 70(17), 556–567 (1973)
11. Lewis, D.: Causation as influence. The Journal of Philosophy 97(4), 182–197 (2000)
12. Li, N., Mitchell, J.C.: A role-based trust-management framework. In: DISCEX-III, pp. 201–212. IEEE Computer Society (2003)
13. Masini, A., Viganò, L., Volpe, M.: A history of until. ENTCS 262, 189–204 (2010)
14. Shafer, G., Gillett, P.R., Scherl, R.B.: The logic of events. Annals of Mathematics and Artificial Intelligence 28(1-4), 315–389 (2000)
15. Singh, A., Lilja, D.J.: Improving risk assessment methodology: a statistical design of experiments approach. In: SIN, pp. 21–29 (2009)
16. Terenziani, P., Torasso, P.: Time, action-types, causation: An integrated analysis. Computational Intelligence 11, 529–552 (1995)
17. Turner, H.: A logic of universal causation. AI 113(1-2), 87–123 (1999)
18. Viganò, L.: Labelled Non-Classical Logics. Kluwer Academic Publishers (2000)

A Collaborative Approach to Botnet Protection

Matija Stevanovic[1], Kasper Revsbech[1], Jens Myrup Pedersen[1],
Robin Sharp[2], and Christian Damsgaard Jensen[2]

[1] Department of Electronic Systems
Aalborg University
{mst,kar,jens}@es.aau.dk
[2] Department of Informatics and Mathematical Modelling
Technical University of Denmark
{robin,Christian.Jensen}@imm.dtu.dk

Abstract. Botnets are collections of compromised computers which have come under the control of a malicious person or organisation via malicious software stored on the computers, and which can then be used to interfere with, misuse, or deny access to a wide range of Internet-based services. With the current trend towards increasing use of the Internet to support activities related to banking, commerce, healthcare and public administration, it is vital to be able to detect and neutralise botnets, so that these activities can continue unhindered. In this paper we present an overview of existing botnet detection techniques and argue why a new, composite detection approach is needed to provide efficient and effective neutralisation of botnets. This approach should combine existing detection efforts into a collaborative botnet protection framework that receives input from a range of different sources, such as packet sniffers, on-access anti-virus software and behavioural analysis of network traffic, computer sub-systems and application programs. Finally, we introduce ContraBot, a collaborative botnet detection framework which combines approaches that analyse network traffic to identify patterns of botnet activity with approaches that analyse software to detect items which are capable of behaving maliciously.

Keywords: Botnets, Botnet Detection, Collaborative Framework, Correlation Analysis.

1 Introduction

During the last few decades, the Internet and applications based on it have experienced a tremendous expansion to the point at which they have become an integral part of our lives, supporting a wide range of services such as banking, commerce, healthcare, public administration and education. The growing reliance on the Internet introduces a number of security challenges that require sophisticated and innovative solutions. The main carrier of malicious activities on the Internet is malicious software, i.e., malware, which includes vira, trojans, worms, rootkits and spyware.

Botnets represent a state of the art deployment of malware that combines many existing advanced malware techniques. A bot is a computer which has been infected with some form of malware which can provide a remote attacker with total, unconditional

G. Quirchmayr et al. (Eds.): CD-ARES 2012, LNCS 7465, pp. 624–638, 2012.

and imperceptible control over the compromised computer. A botnet is a (usually) large collection of such compromised computers that are infected with the specific malware instance which enables them to be controlled by the malicious third party ("botmaster"). Botnets may range in size from a couple of hundred to millions of bots, spanning over home, corporate and educational networks covering different parts of the world. Botnets provide a collaborative and highly distributed platform for a wide range of malicious and illegal activities such as sending spam, launching distributed denial of service (DDOS) attacks, malware distribution, click fraud, distribution of illegal content, collection of confidential information and attacks on industrial control systems and other critical infrastructure.

Some recent cybersecurity studies [10,28], claim that more than 40 percent of computers world-wide are infected with some kind of bot malware, thus being actively or passively involved in the malicious activities of a botnet. Additionally, these studies have shown that the average size of botnets is growing and that the biggest botnets can easily involve several million bots. The size of such botnets indicates the great potential in terms of processing power and available bandwidth. Pairing this with collaborative and coordinated action makes botnets rightfully regarded as one of the biggest threats to cybersecurity up to date.

Neutralisation of botnets involves technical, legal and political issues, and therefore requires an inter-disciplinary collaboration to achieve a successful result. At the same time, there is the challenge of raising computer users' awareness of the dangers posed by botnets as well as the challenge of persuading them to take the necessary steps to hinder the spread of botnets. Although complex in its nature, the problem of neutralisation and mitigation of botnets primarily relies on the ability to detect them. Extensive research efforts have therefore been made during the last decade to find ways to efficiently detect botnets. Many experimental systems have been reported in the literature, based on numerous technical principles and varying assumptions about bot behaviour and bot traffic patterns. However due to the dynamic nature of botnets and constant improvement of the malicious techniques, the success of the proposed detection and mitigation approaches has been limited. In this paper we present an overview of existing botnet detection techniques and we analyse their ability to cope with the challenges posed by modern botnets. We elaborate on the need for a more comprehensive detection approach in order to provide efficient and effective neutralisation of botnets. Finally, we introduce ContraBot, a collaborative botnet detection framework that combines approaches that analyse network traffic to identify patterns of botnet activity with approaches that analyse software to detect items which are capable of behaving maliciously.

The rest of this paper is organized in the following way: Section 2 examines the threat of botnets and identifies some trends in the development of botnets. A survey of earlier work on botnet detection is presented in Section 3. The need for a systematic approach to botnet protection is discussed in Section 4, which argues why combining existing approaches to botnet detection will provide better results in the fight against botnets. Section 5 presents the architecture of the ContraBot platform, which defines a collaborative framework for botnet detection and neutralization. Finally, a discussion of the ContraBot architecture and directions for future work are outlined in Section 6.

2   Threats from Botnets

As a state of the art form of malware, bots are taking advantage of multiple malicious techniques and evolve at an unprecedented speed, presenting a considerable challenge to existing botnet defence systems. Current botnets are characterized by diversity of protocols and structures, usage of advanced code obfuscation techniques and a tendency to spread to new platforms.

The essential component, and at the same time the main carrier of botnet functionality, is the C&C (Command and Control) channel that is established between the botmaster and the infected computers. Moreover, the C&C channel represent the main characteristic that distinguish bots from the other malware forms. Botmasters rely on the C&C channel to issue commands to their bots and receive information from the compromised machines. C&C infrastructure has been evolving in recent years, so that today several control mechanisms in terms of protocols and structures are used for the realization of the C&C channel.

The earliest botnets utilized a centralized C&C network architecture, where all bots in a botnet contact one (or a few) C&C server(s) owned by the botmaster. The centralized C&C channels are usually based on the IRC or HTTP protocols. IRC-based botnets are realized by deploying IRC servers or by using an IRC server in a public IRC network. The botmaster specifies a channel, which bots connect to and listen on to receive commands from the botmaster. HTTP-based botnets are similar to the IRC-based ones. After infection, bots contact a web-based C&C server and notify the server with their system-identifying information via HTTP, while the server sends back commands via HTTP responses. IRC- and HTTP-based C&C have been widely used in botnets, but both of them are vulnerable to a single point of failure. That is, once the central IRC or HTTP servers are identified and disabled, the entire botnet will be disabled. Some examples of IRC and HTTP botnets that have been observed "in the wild" (Agobot, SDbot, Zeus, etc.) have had more than a million bots and have been successfully used for malicious actions such as DDoS attacks, identity theft, etc.

In order to be more resilient to counter-measures, the attackers have recently started to build botnets using decentralized C&C infrastructures such as P2P [6] or advanced hybrid P2P structures [33], where bots belonging to a P2P botnet form an overlay network in which any of the nodes (i.e. bots) can be used by the botmaster to distribute commands to the other peers or collect information from them. In these botnets, a botmaster can join, publish commands and leave at any time at any place. While more complex, and perhaps more costly to manage compared to centralized botnets, P2P botnets offer higher resiliency, since even if a significant portion of a P2P botnet is taken down (by law enforcement or network operators) the remaining bots may still be able to communicate with each other and with the botmaster to pursue their malicious purpose.

One of the first well-known examples of a P2P botnet was the Storm botnet [18] from 2008. Storm was estimated to run on over a million compromised computers and was primarily used for sending spam emails. It utilized Kademlia [6], a decentralized Distributed-Hash-Table (DHT) protocol. Other noteworthy recent P2P botnets include Waledac [25] and Conficker [19]. Although similar to the Storm botnet they employ self-defined communication protocols based on HTTP and fast-flux techniques. This illustrates the fact that modern botnets often use additional techniques for improving resilience and robustness of communication, such as obfuscation of existing communication protocols or development of new ones, encryption of communication etc. We can conclude that botnet detection approaches designed specifically to detect and mitigate centralized botnets will be less effective for such novel, highly decentralized botnets. Also, given the range of different C&C infrastructures that the botmaster can employ, a detection method targeting only specific C&C infrastructure cannot provide sufficiently effective detection of modern botnets.

Besides the diversity in structure and protocols, current botnets commonly employ code obfuscation techniques such as polymorphism and metamorphism. These enable the bot code to mutate without changing the functions or the semantics of its payload. Usually, in the same botnet, bot binaries are different from each other. Since signature-based detection schemes look for specific data patterns within binaries, they require constant update of signatures in order to be able successfully detect bots. However even then these techniques are limited to detecting known bots.

Whereas almost all modern botnets have targeted personal computers (PCs), attackers are constantly searching for new ways of disseminating their product, such as finding new platforms to host botnets. One of the trends noticed at the beginning of 2012 was the occurrence of botnets on mobile telephones. The first mobile-based bot was Android.Counterclank, developed for the Android platform. This could be downloaded via the Android Market through several application packages. According to Symantec reports [29], this bot could carry out commands from a remote server and was capable both of stealing information from, and displaying ads on, infected Android handsets. Although promptly detected and taken down, this bot showed that botnets are slowly spreading to the smartphone domain. The popularity of smartphones and the fact they have a lot of processing power and bandwidth at their disposal will certainly continue to attract the attention of botmasters. The unique features of mobile devices such as communication via multiple technologies, like Bluetooth and NFC (Near Field Communication) in addition to the conventional IP network, could also provide mobile botnets with more stealthy and robust functioning. As existing detection techniques only cover PC-based botnets, further work is needed to counter the innovations seen in these novel botnets on smartphones and other potential new platforms.

3   Earlier Work on Botnet Detection

Botnet detection systems go back to the middle 2000s, and many experimental systems have been reported in the literature, with various aims in mind, and based on diverse technical principles and varying assumptions about bot behaviour and traffic patterns. Aims may include features such as automated operation, independence of communication topology and protocol, independence from payload content and real time detection.

Depending of the point of deployment, the detection approaches can be classified as client-based or network-based. In client-based approaches, the detection system is deployed within the client computer, and examines the computer's internal behaviour and/or traffic visible on the computers external network interfaces. Network-based detection, on the other hand, is deployed at the edge of the network (usually in routers or firewalls), providing botnet detection by passive monitoring of network traffic.

Like intrusion detection systems in general, botnet detection systems may be based on recognising characteristic patterns of code or data ("signatures") or patterns of behaviour. Likewise, they may be based on misuse detection – i.e. recognising signatures or behaviour patterns known to be associated with undesirable activities – or anomaly detection, where the idea is to detect noticeable deviations from normal behaviour. Misuse detection often gives fewer false positives, but plainly cannot be used to detect new bots or obfuscated variants of already known bots; anomaly detection is able to detect new forms of malicious activity, but may give many false positives if the pattern of normal activity changes. Thus there is a very wide range of potential combinations of approaches.

3.1   Client-Based Detection

Several client-based detection systems have been proposed. One of the earliest was BotSwat [26], which was based on a taint tracking system developed to discover programs that take advantage of received network data from an unreliable external source and to identify the potential remote control behaviour of bots. The main idea behind BotSwat is that a bot installed on the host computer has a specific pattern of behaviour that can be recognized by monitoring execution of an arbitrary executable binary, and tracing the traffic to its external source. This approach is directed at detection of individual bots by misuse detection and is independent of botnet topology and communication protocol.

The approach used by Masud et al. [15] illustrates a method for botnet traffic detection based on the assumption that bots have a different response pattern from humans and that is possible to detect them by correlating multiple network flow log files on the hosts. The approach utilizes data mining techniques to extract relevant features from these log files and detect C&C traffic. The method offers several advantages such as real-time operation, and independence from communication protocol and topology. However, the approach has two major limitations. Firstly, it requires access to payload content, so it cannot detect botnets which use encrypted communication. Secondly, as the approach relies on the assumption that the response pattern of bots differs from that of humans, it is vulnerable to evasion techniques that include mimicking of human response patterns.

EFFORT [24] is one of the most recent client-based detection approaches, and is based on intrinsic characteristics of bots from both client and network aspects. The detection framework uses a multi-module approach that correlates bot-related information gathered by inspection of client computer internals, by monitoring the computer's interaction with the human user (key strokes and mouse input) and by monitoring traffic on the computer's external interfaces. The method has a number of advantages such as independence of topology and communication protocol, and the ability to detect encrypted and obfuscated protocols. The major limitation is that each detection module within the framework that detects specific bot-related occurrences can be evaded by suitably chosen evasion techniques. Nor can this technique provide real-time detection.

3.2 Network-Based Detection

Network-based detection is a more common principle used for detecting botnets and is primarily realised by passive network monitoring. Some of the earlier approaches of this type, such as Rishi [5], Snort [21] and BotHunter [9] were based on misuse detection, using signatures of botnet malicious activity and C&C communication in order to detect them.

Rishi [5] was one of the first detection techniques to tackle the problem of IRC botnets. It uses a signature-based detection algorithm that matches the IRC nickname with typical nickname patterns of IRC bots. Rishi is based on passive traffic monitoring for suspicious IRC nicknames (Layer 7), IRC servers, and uncommon server ports (Layer 4). It uses a specially developed scoring system and n-gram analysis to detect bots that use uncommon communication channels that are commonly not detectable by classical intrusion detection systems. However this approach has not had much impact due to the fact that it does not have the ability to detect IRC botnets that use encrypted or obfuscated communication.

Snort [21] is an open source network intrusion detection system (NIDS) based on misuse detection. Snort monitors network traffic, and is configured with a set of signatures and rules for logging traffic which is deemed suspicious. This method has several advantages, such as immediate detection and the impossibility of false positives, but of course can only detect known botnets. Moreover, as it performs deep packet inspection it can easily be defeated by encryption or obfuscation of payload content.

BotHunter [9] was the first open source botnet detection system available for broad public use. It was developed as an extension of Snort, by the addition of two anomaly detection plug-ins on top of Snorts existing signature database. BotHunter defines a model of the botnet infection dialogue process, which is intended to match the life-cycle of contemporary botnets, and uses it as a guideline to recognise infection processes within the network. However, this approach suffers from many shortcomings, primarily inherited from Snort, such as the inability to detect encrypted traffic, vulnerability to various evasion techniques and attacks directed at the content of the correlation matrix. Additionally BotHunter can only identify bots whose life-cycle follows the chosen model of infection.

Other network-based detection approaches are based on detection of statistical anomalies in network traffic, such as high network latency, high volume of traffic, traffic on unusual ports and unusual system behaviour, which are exhibited as a consequence of botnet communication. Important examples are BotSniffer [7] and the approach of Karasaridis et al. [12].

BotSniffer [7] is a network-based anomaly detection approach developed to identify botnet C&C channels in a local area network without any prior knowledge of botnet signatures. It is based on the observation that, because of the pre-programmed activities related to C&C communication, bots within the same botnet will likely demonstrate spatial-temporal correlation and similar behaviour. The technique captures behavioural patterns of botnet traffic and utilizes statistical algorithms on them to detect botnets. BotSniffer was primarily developed to detect centralized IRC and HTTP based botnet C&C channels, and cannot cope with modern P2P botnets. Furthermore, the method is vulnerable to evasion techniques such as misusing whitelists, encryption, using very long or random response delays, injecting random noise packets, and evasion of the protocol matcher and etc.

Karasaridis et al. [12] used an anomaly-based botnet detection method aimed at detecting botnet controllers by monitoring transport layer data. The method was developed to detect IRC botnet controllers, i.e. IRC servers within large Tier-1 ISP networks. The approach is entirely passive and does not depend on botnet behaviour signatures or particular application layer information, so it is able to detect bots using encrypted and obfuscated protocols. However, the approach relies on an IDS to provide an indication of suspicious hosts, so it cannot detect unknown botnets or bots, and it cannot handle modern HTTP and P2P botnets.

In parallel with these efforts based on network traffic in general, a subgroup of botnet detection approaches directed at detecting anomalies of DNS traffic emerged. DNS-based detection approaches rely on detection of patterns within DNS traffic that can indicate the presence of a bot or botmaster within the network. Some of the most prominent DNS-based approaches realize botnet detection by detecting anomalies of DNS traffic as in [30], performing DNSBL (DNS Black List) counter intelligence [20], capturing DNS group behaviour [2] or building a reputation system for DNS queries [1]. Many novel classes of botnets (P2P, hybrid P2P), however, do not require a DNS service for their functioning so these approaches have a significantly limited detection scope.

Some more recent approaches to botnet detection have attempted to detect patterns of botnet traffic by employing sophisticated machine learning techniques. Machine learning is used because it offers the possibility of automated, real-time recognition of patterns within traffic without a need for traffic exhibiting specific anomalies. Several detection approaches that employ machine learning have been proposed over the years such as in Strayer et al. [27], Botminer [8], Lu et al. [13], Saad et al. [22], and Zhang et al. [36], providing more or less efficient botnet detection.

Strayer et al. [27] developed one of the first approaches that employed machine learning to detect patterns of botnet traffic within the network. Several machine learning approaches were utilized and their performance in classifying IRC traffic flows evaluated. The approach provides a real-time detection framework which has the ability to detect botnets even before a cyber-attack occurs. However, it only has the ability to detect IRC botnets with centralized topology and it requires external judgment, either by humans or machines, in order to generate reliable alarms for the existence of a botnet. This limits its practical usability.

BotMiner [8] uses an approach based on data mining, and was developed in order to successfully identify modern botnets, which can significantly differ in size, structure, communication technology and purpose. The technique assumes that bots within the same botnet will be characterized by similar malicious activity and similar C&C communication patterns. BotMiner employs clustering techniques in order to detect similarities within different hosts in the network. This technique is entirely independent of the C&C protocol, structure, infection model of botnets and it does not require prior knowledge of botnet specific signatures. However, by design it essentially targets groups of compromised machines within a monitored network, so it may not be effective at detecting individual compromised hosts. Moreover, the technique is exposed to various evasion techniques, and performs poorly in situations where stealthy P2P botnets, that mask their traffic within non-malicious P2P traffic, are present in the network.

A recent study in the field of botnet detection by Saad et al. [22] considers the problem of detecting P2P botnets by using machine learning techniques. The study evaluates the ability of commonly used machine-learning techniques to meet on-line botnet detection requirements such as adaptability, novelty detection and early detection. The study shows that machine learning algorithms have a great potential for detecting patterns of botnet traffic. However it also indicates that the performance of these techniques is highly dependent on the features selected for classification or cluster analysis and that they often have high computational requirements.

Zhang et al. [36] describe a novel botnet detection system that can identify stealthy P2P botnets, even when malicious activities may not be observable. Their approach focuses on identifying P2P bots within a monitored network by detecting their characteristic C&C communication patterns, regardless of how they perform malicious activities. To accomplish this, the system derives statistical fingerprints of the P2P communications generated by P2P hosts, and uses them to distinguish P2P bots from hosts that are part of legitimate P2P networks. This system can detect stealthy P2P botnets even when the underlying compromised hosts are running legitimate P2P applications (e.g. Skype). However, it targets only P2P bots, so it cannot cope with botnets based on IRC or HTTP. Moreover, as the method relies on numerous assumptions regarding P2P communication and P2P bot traffic patterns, it is vulnerable to evasion techniques such as using a legitimate P2P network, randomizing traffic patterns, using a malicious DNS server, or injecting P2P control messages.

Although each of the methods described above has a certain range of application, none of them can provide comprehensive botnet detection, fulfilling all of the detection requirements and providing a foundation for successful defence against modern botnets. Evidently the dynamic nature of bots and botnets requires an approach to botnet detection that would consider not just one characteristic of botnets but a variety of them, covering every aspect of the botnet life cycle. Some of the latest research efforts have therefore been directed at the development of novel combinations of detection approaches, which we look at in the next section.

4   Collaborative Botnet Detection

Faced with the many challenges of detecting modern botnets, researchers turned their efforts toward development of novel collaborative classes of detection approaches that integrate multiple principles of botnet detection. The main hypothesis behind these methods is that it is possible to provide higher efficiency and effectiveness of detection by correlating the findings of independent detection entities.

The general approach for correlating aspects of behaviour observed by various sensors is based on ideas presented by Strayer et al. [27], Oliner et al. [17] and Flaglien et al. [4], which extend older proposals made by Cuppens & Miège [3] and Ning et al. [16] for correlation of alerts in IDS systems. Using these or similar concepts, several authors have proposed botnet detection systems that correlate alerts from several detection entities. Wang and Gong have proposed frameworks for collaborative [31] and fusion [32] detection while Zeng et al. [35] proposed a combined botnet detection system.

To counteract the weaknesses of existing botnet detection architectures, Wang and Gong proposed several collaborative detection frameworks. The first framework [31] represents a hierarchical collaborative model that incorporates several independent detection systems, that use bot-related information from multiple sources such as network traffic, client computer internals and deployed honeypots. The second proposed framework [32] introduced the idea of combining multi-source information fusion with a collaborative detection framework. The framework envisions combining bot-related information originating from several sources (traffic monitors, IDSs, other botnet detection systems, firewalls) in order to determine the presence of a botnet within the monitored network. However the authors have not deployed or experimentally evaluated the proposed frameworks.

Zeng et al. proposed a hybrid detection approach [35] that achieves botnet detection by combining host- and network-level information. The approach is based on the assumption that two sources of bot-related information will complement each other in making accurate detection decisions. Their system first identifies suspicious hosts by discovering similar behaviours among hosts using network-flow analysis, and then validates the identified suspects to be malicious or not by scrutinizing their in-host behaviour. The approach promises independence from the C&C protocol, topology and content of transmitted data. The main limitation is that it operates in time windows, which prevents it from providing real-time detection and makes it vulnerable to time-based evasions. Additionally the approach did not use the opportunity of including bot-related information originating from other sources, leaving space for further improvements.

The systems reported on by these research groups and others, although mainly proofs of concept, demonstrated that systems which combine information from multiple sources can achieve significantly increased accuracy in recognising malicious behaviour on a network wide scale. This sets a milestone for a new direction in the field of malware detection informally known as a collaborative detection.

5   The ContraBot Framework

The ContraBot framework represents a novel systematic approach to the detection and mitigation of botnets. Following the principles considered by the research groups presented in the previous section [27,17,4,31,32], ContraBot belongs to the emerging class of collaborative botnet detection approaches that integrate multiple principles of botnet detection, in order to provide more efficient and effective detection. The basic scientific hypothesis behind our method is that correlating the observations and analyses from client and network entities combined with in-depth analysis of harvested code will significantly improve the botnet classification ability, in comparison to todays state-of-the-art methods.

The ContraBot framework utilises several functional entities, as illustrated in Figure 1. A set of network sniffers placed within the network collect and pre-process network traffic data, while a set of activity monitors within the clients collect and pre-process information about client activity. The pre-processing is necessary in order to reduce the amount of data and also to allow selective analysis of particular traffic and/or client behaviour patterns. The output of this pre-processing is passed to a set of one or more Correlators, where it is analysed to reveal patterns of similar behaviour in different hosts and different parts of the network. Unusual patterns of activity, which may indicate an attack, will lead to the harvesting of portions of code from the hosts (and the associated network traffic), so that these can be further analysed by entities which investigate the code for malicious effects. In a similar way, Client distribution analysis entities analyse modules, apps and other forms of software fetched by the Clients from the network, so that well-known malicious software can be disabled or removed as in a traditional AV (anti-virus) system.

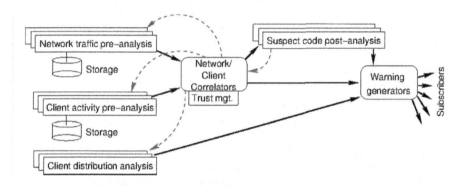

Fig. 1. Architecture of the proposed analysis system

The ContraBot framework will require input from a wide range of sources, including sensors installed by end users, ISPs and backbone network providers. The producers and consumers of this input often belong to different, possibly competing, organisations that employ different types of sensors, so it is important that all parties can evaluate the trustworthiness of the input they receive. The Correlation Framework will therefore include a trust management component that aims to establish the trustworthiness of input based on both direct experiences with the individual input provider and reputation ratings exchanged between the different Correlators in the Correlation Framework.

If the Correlators, distribution analysis entities or code analysis entities detect signs of malicious software, they pass this information to a sub-system which generates Warnings for distribution to Subscribers of the anti-botnet service. This allows the subscribers to initiate various counter measures, e.g. walled-gardens. In addition to warning messages, information (indicated by the dashed arrows) is architecture of-passed back through the system, so that the analysis can be adjusted to focus more accurately on recognisable malicious activity. Both the network sniffers and client analysis entities have access to a (possibly distributed) storage system, to facilitate recording and subsequent in-depth analysis of detected threats.

5.1   Network Traffic Sniffing and Pre-analysis

The network sniffers that monitor and pre-analyse the traffic are entities operating in core networks, e.g. in an ISP backbone, and must therefore be capable of handling traffic at high data rates. For the realization of these sniffers FPGA (Field-programmable gate array) based network interface cards will be used. Such cards can guarantee high-speed packet capture with no packet loss, and they can also be configured to pre-filter/pre-process the packets according to some predefined parameters.

Detection of malicious traffic in core networks is not a new concept. Many approaches, ranging from signature based methods to more sophisticated methods based on machine learning, have been proposed and can be reused to a large extent. However, as described above, we plan to make the pre-analysis adaptive in the sense that it will receive information from the Correlator about threats observed elsewhere. Hence a substantial part of the research and performance optimisation regarding the network sniffers will focus on how existing principles can be used in an adaptive setup. In addition, we will investigate if further performance and/or precision can be achieved by utilising the available FPGAs.

5.2   Client Activity Monitoring

Client activity will be monitored by recording features related to changes in the file system, registry (or similar configuration database) and use of network connections in the individual hosts. This type of monitoring is comparable to what many client IDS systems already do. The collected features will be used as the basis for clustering analysis, and the results of this local analysis will be sent to the Correlators for further investigation of possible correlated activities in separate hosts. Research into performance optimisation of this process will be needed in order to reduce the computational load and storage requirements on the clients as far as possible, while retaining sufficient information for our analysis.

5.3   Client Distribution Analysis

A significant problem in many of the newest botnets is that malware may be distributed by non-traditional routes which will not be detected by traditional on-access AV scanning of mail and web access. Within the last few years, for example, distribution via Facebook spam, YouTube and on-line markets providing apps for smartphones has been observed, and there is every reason to believe that this trend will continue, expanding to cover other platforms. In addition, designers of malware now have access to almost unlimited computing power via cloud computing. This enables them to produce huge numbers of variants of each item of malware, so as to avoid malware collection and analysis by ensuring that each variant only appears very rarely and thus avoids rousing suspicion. We believe that correlation analysis, combined with in-depth post-analysis of harvested code, can mitigate this problem significantly, as we expect to be able to detect behavioural similarities among code items which appear not to be significantly related.

5.4   Correlation Framework

The Correlation Framework is one of the most important elements of our framework, as it should realize correlation of observation generated by various sensors. The Correlation Framework will be realized as two components: A Behavioural Analysis Component and a Trust Management Component.

The behavioural analysis component will analyse the filtered and pre-processed feature data provided by the client and network sensors, in order to search both for network-network and client-network correlations. It will further develop ideas proposed by a variety of research groups, as reported in Oliner et al. [17], Wang et al. [31,32], and Flaglien et al. [4], amongst others. We intend to extend this previous work to cover more scenarios and platforms.

The trust management component has a task of assessing the trustworthiness of data and alerts from the different sensors within the system. Proposals for assessing the information received from the different sensors have been based on trust evaluation of the individual data sources [14], collaborative filtering techniques employing robust statistics [23] or extended with trust metrics [34], or filtering to eliminate outliers in the received data [37]. None of these techniques, however, have been developed for the environment envisaged in the ContraBot infrastructure, where sensor data and alerts are shared among separate collaborating organisations. We therefore need to investigate hybrid techniques, where the results of the different filtering techniques are incorporated with different weights, e.g. the weight of the trust evaluation of the data provider is higher when evaluating input from end-users, because less can be assumed about their motives and competence levels.

The trust management component will assess the trustworthiness of the different sensors using both direct experience and indirect experience through a reputation system. Direct experience will be based on both content based filtering using data contained in the observations, such as the make, model and version of the sensor, and collaborative filtering where the output from one sensor is compared with output from other sensors in order to determine whether the sensor agrees with the majority. The trust management component will monitor the results of this trustworthiness assessment over time and apply the results to a trust evolution function, such as the one proposed for the Wikipedia Recommender System [11]. Moreover, the trust management component will build indirect trust in sensors by exchanging direct trust assessments (reputation scores) with the other trust management components in the Correlation Framework. This will significantly reduce the "cold start" problem and accelerate trust formation among components in the framework.

5.5 Testing

To facilitate tests of algorithms and architectural design, a closed and controlled Internet-like test network, in which experiments can be repeated, is needed. Based on the sniffing equipment, a testbed emulating a subset of the Internet will be designed and implemented. The testbed will facilitate botnet life cycle analysis with real and artificial bots, where spread patterns, infection times, etc. can be studied, both from a client and a network perspective. Furthermore, the testbed will facilitate the development of the client and network entities, as it will facilitate tests in realistic (emulated) conditions. It will also be used to test the scalability of given system architecture proposals. It may here prove possible to reuse substantial parts of the already existing emulab testbed system (http://www.emulab.com) with modifications. We believe that having a testbed on which the framework can be implemented and tested will allow us to achieve a precise, reliable and performance optimised product. Furthermore, as the threats evolve continually, it is important to have a test setup where updated mechanisms and parameters can be tested and evaluated.

6   Discussions and Future Work

In this paper we have presented an overview of existing botnet detection techniques and we have analysed their ability to cope with challenges of detecting modern botnets. Furthermore, we have shown that there is a need for new and more comprehensive detection approaches in order to provide efficient and effective neutralisation of botnets. Finally we introduced ContraBot a novel collaborative botnet detection approach.

To our best knowledge the ContraBot framework could possibly be the first extensive attempt to take counter botnet research to a systematic level, providing the basis for a more comprehensive botnet defence system. The botnet defence system envision by the ContraBot framework will aggregate simultaneous observations from different types of sensors, such as network sniffers and client monitors to identify suspect activities and possibly initiate appropriate counter measures.

The Contrabot framework is partly based on principles similar to existing collaborative botnet detection approaches such as [27,17,4,31,32], but it has a number of advantages: First, the ContraBot will employ traffic analysis in the core network, providing protection for a broader set of end-users. Secondly, our proposed set-up will combine information not only from network and client levels but also from in depth analysis of harvested code in order to improve the detection accuracy even further. Third, the proposed system will provide flexibility of including diverse end-user platforms through development of appropriate client-based analysis entities. Fourth, our system will also introduce the feed-back mechanism. This will provide adaptivity of network- and client-based pre-analysis entities to the bot-related information generated by correlating findings from other sources. This information allows the system to dynamically adapt to changes in behaviour of bots and botnets.

An important future step for testing and evaluating the framework is the development of a prototype system to demonstrate the technical approaches for reliable detection and elimination of botnets. Such a prototype system needs to be systematically evaluated using a suitable testbed. We believe a testbed should be developed specifically for this purpose, capturing salient features of large-scale networks. The prototype could be a first step twoards the development of a full-scale botnet defence platform.

References

1. Antonakakis, M., Perdisci, R., Dagon, D., Lee, W., Feamster, N.: Building a dynamic reputation system for DNS. In: Proceedings of the 19th USENIX Security Symposium (Security 2010). USENIX Association (August 2010)
2. Choi, H., Lee, H.: Identifying botnets by capturing group activities in DNS traffic. Journal of Computer Networks 56, 20–33 (2011)
3. Cuppens, F., Miège, A.: Alert correlation in a cooperative intrusion detection framework. In: Proceedings of IEEE Symposium on Security and Privacy, pp. 202–215 (May 2002)

4. Flaglien, A., Franke, K., Årnes, A.: Identifying malware using cross-evidence correlation. In: Peterson, G., Shenoi, S. (eds.) Advances in Digital Forensics VII. IFIP ACIT, ch.13, vol. 361, pp. 169–182. Springer, Boston (2011)

5. Goebel, J., Holz, T.: Rishi: Identifying bot-contaminated hosts by IRC nickname evaluation. In: HotBots 2007: Proceedings of the First USENIX Workshop on Hot Topics in Understanding Botnets, Cambridge, Mass. USENIX Association (June 2007)

6. Grizzard, J.B., Sharma, V., Nunnery, C., Kang, B.B., Dagon, D.: Peer-to-peer botnets; Overview and case study. In: HotBots 2007: Proceedings of the First USENIX Workshop on Hot Topics in Understanding Botnets, Cambridge, Mass. USENIX Association (June 2007)

7. Gu, G., Zhang, J., Lee, W.: BotSniffer: Detecting botnet command and control channels in network traffic. In: NDSS 2008: Proceedings of the 15th Annual Network and Distributed System Security Symposium, San Diego. Internet Society (February 2008)

8. Gu, G., Perdisci, R., Zhang, J., Lee, W.: Botminer: Clustering analysis of network traffic for protocol- and structure-independent botnet detection. In: Proceedings of the 17th Conference on Security Symposium, pp. 139–154 (2008)

9. Gu, G., Porras, P., Yegneswaran, V., Fong, M., Lee, W.: BotHunter: Detecting malware infection through IDS-driven dialog correlation. In: Proceedings of the 16th USENIX Security Symposium, San Jose, California, pp. 167–182. USENIX Association (July 2007)

10. Hogben, G. (ed.): Botnets: Detection, measurement, disinfection and defence. Tech. rep., ENISA (2011)

11. Jensen, C., Korsgaard, T.: Dynamics of trust evolution: Auto-configuration of disposiional trust dynamics. In: Proceedings of the International Conference on Security and Cryptography (SECRYPT 2008), Porto, Portugal, pp. 509–517 (July 2008)

12. Karasaridis, A., Rexroad, B., Hoeflin, D.: Wide-scale botnet detection and characterization. In: HotBots 2007: Proceedings of the First USENIX Workshop on Hot Topics in Understanding Botnets, Cambridge, Mass. USENIX Association (June 2007)

13. Lu, W., Rammidi, G., Ghorbani, A.A.: Clustering botnet communication traffic based on n-gram feature selection. Computer Communications 34, 502–514 (2011)

14. Marsh, S.: Formalizing Trust as a Computational Concept, PhD thesis, University of Stirling, Dept. of Computer Science and Mathematics (1994)

15. Masud, M.M., Al-Khateeb, T., Khan, L., Turaisingham, B., Hamlen, K.W.: Flow-based identification of botnet traffic by mining multiple log file. In: Proceedings of the International Conference on Distributed Frameworks and Applications (DFMA), Penang, Malaysia (2008)

16. Ning, P., Cui, Y., Reeves, D.S.: Constructing attack scenarios through correlation of intrusion alerts. In: Proceedings of CCS 2002, pp. 245–254. ACM (November 2002)

17. Oliner, A.J., Kulkarni, A.V., Aiken, A.: Community Epidemic Detection Using Time-Correlated Anomalies. In: Jha, S., Sommer, R., Kreibich, C. (eds.) RAID 2010. LNCS, vol. 6307, pp. 360–381. Springer, Heidelberg (2010)

18. Porras, P., Saidi, H., Yegneswaran, V.: A multi-perspective analysis of the Storm (peacomm) worm. Tech. rep., SRI International (2007),
    http://www.cyber-ta.org/pubs/StormWorm/report

19. Porras, P., Saidi, H., Yegneswaran, V.: Conficker C analysis. Tech. rep., SRI International (2009), http://mtc.sri.com/Conficker/addendumC/index.html

20. Ramachandran, A., Feamster, N., Dagon, D.: Revealing botnet membership using DNSBL counter-intelligence. In: SRUTI 2006: Proceedings of the 2nd Workshop on Steps to Reducing Unwanted Traffic on the Internet, San Jose, California, pp. 49–54. USENIX Association (June 2006)

21. Roesch, M.: Snort – lightweight intrusion detection for networks. In: Proceedings of Usenix LISA 1999. USENIX Association (1999)

22. Saad, S., Traore, I., Ghorbani, A., Sayed, B., Zhao, D., Lu, W., Felix, J., Hakimian, P.: Detecting P2P botnets through network behavior analysis and machine learning. In: 2011 Ninth Annual International Conference on Privacy, Security and Trust, Montreal. IEEE (July 2011)

23. Setia, S., Roy, S., Jajodia, S.: Secure data aggregation in wireless sensor networks. In: Lopez, Zhou (eds.) Wireless Sensor Networks Security (2008)

24. Shin, S., Xu, Z., Gu, G.: EFFORT: Efficient and effective bot malware detection. In: Proceedings of 31st Annual IEEE Conference on Computer Communications (INFOCOM 2012), Orlando, Florida. IEEE (March 2012)

25. Sinclair, G., Nunnery, C., Kang, B.B.: The Waledac protocol: The how and why. In: Proceedings of International Conference on Malicious and Unwanted Software, MALWARE (2009)

26. Stinson, E., Mitchell, J.C.: Characterizing bots' remote control behavior. In: Lee, W., Wang, C., Dagon, D. (eds.) Botnet Detection, Advances in Information Security, vol. 36, pp. 45–64. Springer (2008)

27. Strayer, W.T., Lapsely, D., Walsh, R., Livadas, C.: Botnet detection based on network behaviour. In: Lee, W., Wang, C., Dagon, D. (eds.) Botnet Detection, Advances in Information Security, vol. 36, pp. 1–24. Springer (2008)

28. Symantec Inc.: Symantec global internet security threat report, trends for 2010. Security Report XVI, Symantec Inc. (April 2011)

29. Symantec Inc.: Counterclank bot. Tech. rep., Symantec Inc. (2012),
    http://www.symantec.com/security_response/writeup.jsp?docid=
    2012-012709-4046-99

30. Villamarin-Salomon, R., Brustoloni, J.C.: Identifying botnets using anomaly detection techniques applied to DNS traffic. In: Proceedings of 5th IEEE Consumer Communications and Networking Conference (CCNC 2008), pp. 476–481 (2008)

31. Wang, H., Gong, Z.: Collaboration-based botnet detection architecture. In: Proceedings of 2nd International Conference on Intelligent Computational Technology and Automation, Zhangjiajie, China (2009)

32. Wang, H., Hou, J., Gong, Z.: Botnet detection architecture based on heterogeneous multi-sensor information fusion. Journal of Networks 6(12), 1655–1661 (2011)

33. Wang, P., Sparks, S., Zou, C.C.: An advanced hybrid peer-to-peer botnet. In: HotBots 2007: Proceedings of the First USENIX Workshop on Hot Topics in Understanding Botnets, Cambridge, Mass. USENIX Association (June 2007)

34. Weng, J., Miao, C., Goh, A.: Improving collaborative filtering with trust-based metrics. In: Proceedings of ACM Symposium on Applied Computing (SAC), pp. 1860–1864. ACM, New York (2006)

35. Zeng, Y., Hu, X., Shin, K.G.: Detection of botnets using combined host- and network-level information. In: Proceedings of 40th International Conference on Dependable Systems and Networks, DSN (2010)

36. Zhang, J., Perdisci, R., Lee, W., Sarfraz, U., Luo, X.: Detecting stealthy P2P botnets using statistical traffic fingerprints. In: 2011 IEEE/IFIP 41st International Conference on Dependable Systems and Networks (DSN), Hong Kong, pp. 121–132. IEEE/IFIP (June 2011)

37. Zhang, Y., Meratnia, N., Havinga, P.: Outlier detection techniques for wireless sensor networks: A survey. In: IEEE Communications Surveys and Tutorials (2010)

Consensus Building and In-operation Assurance for Service Dependability*

Yutaka Matsuno** and Shuichiro Yamamoto

Strategy Office, Information and Communication Headquarters, Nagoya University

Abstract. Recent information systems have become large and complex by interacting with each other via networks. This makes assuring dependability of systems much more difficult than ever before. For this problem, we observe that requirement elicitation and risk analysis methods should be tightly connected with assurance methods. Furthermore, requirements should be ensured also in operation in such open environment where several interdependency may exist. This paper describes our initial research result and preliminary implementation toward consensus building and in-operation assurance for service dependability. We propose a process cycle for consensus building among stakeholders with assurance cases. We extend conventional assurance cases for ensuring that stakeholders' requirements are satisfied during operation. The extended assurance case is called D-Case[16]. We also describe how D-Case is used for in-operation assurance.

1 Introduction

Recent information systems have become large and complex by interacting each other via networks. This makes assuring dependability of systems much more difficult than ever before.

For assuring dependability of such systems, we observe that stakeholders should reach consensus on dependability requirements, and there should be a mechanism to ensure that dependability requirements are satisfied during in operation in such open environment where several interdependency may exist. We extend conventional assurance cases for ensuring that stakeholders' requirements are satisfied during operation. The extended assurance case is called D-Case[16].

Based on above observation, this paper proposes a consensus building cycle which consists of the following three phases: 1) requirements elicitation and risk analysis, 2) stakeholders' agreement on requirements, and 3) In-operation assurance using D-Case. In the course of consensus building, elicited requirements may possibly be revised. Requirements are also changing when stakeholder's agreements are updated (Fig.1).

Assume that a system is newly developed for some service objectives given by stakeholders. In the first phase, requirements are elicited from each of the

---

* This work was done while the first author was in Information Technology Center, the University of Tokyo.

** matsu@icts.nagoya-u.ac.jp

G. Quirchmayr et al. (Eds.): CD-ARES 2012, LNCS 7465, pp. 639–653, 2012.

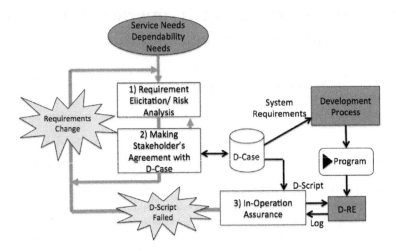

Fig. 1. Consensus Building and In-operation Assurance Cycle

stakeholders who have their needs described in an informal way, and then risks for their requirements are analyzed from various viewpoints. In the second phase, these elicited requirements are argued among the stakeholders using D-Case in order to reach agreement. In case the stakeholders cannot reach agreement on the requirements, some of the requirements will be returned to the first phase to revise. Once the agreement is made, programs are developed according to the D-Case description and other documents such as functional specifications. At the same time, *D-Scripts*, scripting codes for failure mitigation actions, are extracted from the D-Case description, which will be used to monitor the system, to collect logs, and to respond to failures quickly. When the system needs to be revised due to objectives/environment changes, this cycle is restarted with new requirements being elicited and old requirements being modified. This corresponds to the Change Accommodation Cycle.

The third phase provides the means to assure the agreement in the program execution by monitoring and instructing the system and managing requirements online for accountability achievement. A runtime environment called *D-RE*, monitors the system and collects logs of the system as designated by D-Scripts. If some logs show a deviation of some parameters from their in-operation ranges, the corresponding failure responsive actions designated as D-Script codes are activated. D-RE and D-Scripts have been developed in DEOS (Dependable Embedded Operating System) Project[21]. In case a need for a requirements change occurs as a result of the failure responsive actions, the above mentioned cycle is restarted with some requirements being modified. There may be a case that a failure responsive action fails to respond to the failure. Such a case may happen due to some unexpected environment changes, inadequate risk analysis, bugs of the D-Script itself, and so forth. In such a situation, the above mentioned cycle must also be restarted.

The structure of this paper is as follows. In Section 2, we introduce our requirement elicitation and risk analysis methods. Section 3 introduces D-Cases for making agreement among stakeholders and in-operation assurance. Requirements management is described in Section 4. In Section 5, we show current implementation status. Section 6 concludes this paper.

2 Requirements Elicitation and Risk Analysis

The requirements elicitation starts with the service objectives. Stakeholders can be defined according to their service objectives. Requirements are generated from each stakeholder's objectives and needs. Here, requirements include service requirements and dependability requirements. Regulations made by regulatory agencies can be considered as a kind of requirements. The activities for requirements elicitation must include identification of various levels of requirements in order for this task to be manageable.

In requirements engineering, various requirements elicitation methods have been proposed: Ethno-Methodology, Trolling, Business Modeling, Goal Oriented Analysis, Use Case Analysis, Misuse Case Analysis, Triage, etc.[7,24,5,13]

We focuses on dependability in its requirements elicitation and requirements analysis. First, needs are extracted from stakeholders who describe them informally and verbally, and from these, dependability needs are obtained. Second, "dependability requirements" are identified through the analysis of dependability needs. Next, "service continuity scenarios" are created based on risk analysis and service requirements. More precisely, service continuity scenarios are developed by considering and determining countermeasures for each factor causing deviations. Finally, D-Case and D-Script are created through consensus building among stakeholders based on the service continuity scenarios.

Table 1 shows management techniques used to elicit requirements and analyze risks. Service consensus building card (SCBC) is used to define service requirements and to agree on the requirements among stakeholders. Dependability Control Board (DCB) manages consensus building process with SCBC. DCB members are representatives of stakeholders. Dependability Control Map (DCMap) describes relationships among dependability goals as well as roles of stakeholders. D-Cases are stored in D-Case DB and used to achieve dependability goals for dependability requirements of services. Service Risk Brake-down Structure (SRBS) hierarchically decomposes risks into categories. Service Fault Tree (SFT) describes the logical conditions for failures. Service Continuity Scenario (SCS) are designed to mitigate risks for dependability requirements. SCS are implemented by D-Scripts. Service Risk Management Table (SRMT) defines service risks based on probabilities and impacts of failures according to service event scenarios. Service Requirements State Management (SRSM) manages service requirements state not only during online but also offline. Fig.2 shows relationships among techniques given in Table 1. Dependability requirements in DCMap are precisely defined and agreed on using SCBC. SRBS is then used to analyze risk category. SRMT is used to identify and mitigate risks of services

Table 1. Requirement Management Table

Techniques		Explanation
SCBC	Service consensus building card	SCBC is used to define service requirements and agree on among stakeholders
DCB	Dependability Control Board	DCB manages consensus building process with SCBC. DCB members are representatives of stakeholders.
DCMap	Dependability Control Map	DC Map describes relationships among dependability goals as well as roles of stakeholders.
D-Case DB	D-Case data base	D-Cases are stored to achieve dependability requirements of services.
SRBS	Service Risk Braek-down Structure	SRBS hierarchically decomposes risks into categories.
SFT	Service Fault Tree	SFT describes the logical conditions for failures.
SCS	Service Continuity Scenario	SCS are designed to mitigate risks to dependability requirements. SCS are implemented by D-Scripts.
SRMT	Service Risk Management Table	SRMT defines service risks based on probabilities and impacts for service event scenarios.
SRSM	Service Requirements State Management	SRSM manages service requirements state not only online but also offline.

elicited using SCBC. SFT is developed for each scenario in SRMT to show conditions of fault occurences. D-case is developed to confirm the dependability for services against risks based on the information of DCMap and SRMT. identify and mitigate risks of services elicited by SCBC. SFT is developed for each scenario in SRMT to show its occurrence condition. D-case is developed to confirm the dependability for services against risks based on the information of DCMap and SRMT.

An example of Dependability Control Map is shown in Fig. 3. DCMap contains three columns that are stakeholder, roles, and dependability goals. Stakeholders and roles columns constitute RACI matrix [11]. In the role column, RACI identify roles of stakeholders such that Responsible, Accountable, Consulted, and Informed.

The dependability goals column describes goals of stakeholders and their relationships. DCMap can be used to analyze goals as follows. Users want to reach consensus on service dependability. This is accomplished by accountability achievement goal of system providers. The accountability achievement goal is supported by goals of developer and maintainer. Dependability goal of developer is also supported by hardware dependability and valid software authorization.

Table 2 shows an example of service consensus building card. SCBC consists of requirements name, event, response, input, output, functional requirements steps, initiation condition, completion condition, and roles of stakeholders. This figure omits the identification of SCBC for simplicity. Fig. 4 shows an example of Service Risk Breakdown Structure. Service risks are broken down into internal, goal, external, organizational, and technical risks. A service has a goal that is the intention and result that an actor, who wants to use the service, expects to get from the system. By getting an event from actors, services will act on objects and generate a result to achieve the goal. Services will also make responses to actors. Services work on an environment including hardware and network. Deviations

SCBC
DCMap
D-Case
SRBS
SRMT
SFT

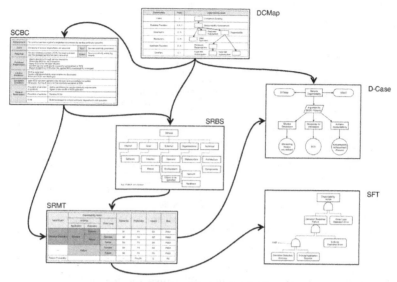

Fig. 4-2 Relationships of RM Techniques

Fig. 2. Relationship of RM Techniques

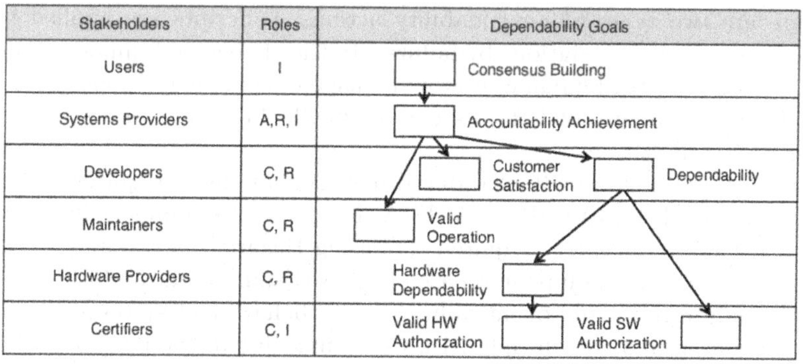

Stakeholders
Roles
Dependability Goals
Users
I
Consensus Building
Systems Providers
A,R, I
Accountability Achievement
Developers
C, R
Customer Satisfaction
Dependability
Maintainers
C, R
Valid Operation
Hardware Providers
C, R
Hardware Dependability
Certifiers
C, I
Valid HW Authorization
Valid SW Authorization

R: Responsible, A: Accountable, C: Consulted, I: Informed

Fig. 3. An Example Dependability Control Map

Table 2. An Example Service Consensus Building Card

Requirements	To keep services running after unexpected occurrences by using service continuity scenarios		
Event	Deviations from service requirements occur	Input	Service continuity parameters
Response	Service continuity scenario(SCS) is activated and the impaired service is repaired	Output	Service continuity activity log records
Functional requirements	•Identify deviations through service execution •Determine SCS for each deviation •Apply SCS to the problem situation •Confirm service continuity by successful achievement of SCS •Report incidents to DCB when the applied SCS unsuccessfully is unsuccessful		
Initiation conditions	DCB is organized Service and dependability requirements are developed Risks and SCSs are developed		
Completion conditions	Valid SCS has been applied to the deviation and successfully completed Otherwise, the result has to be hierarchically is passed on to DCB		
Roles of stakeholders	Providers of services or products	Define parameters for service continuity requirements Agree on the results of SCS application	
	Providers of systems	Develop SCSs	
	DCB	Build consensus on service continuity requirements and operations	

of these ordinal service constituents will cause service risks. Service continuity scenarios can be constructed to mitigate these risks by considering deviations of service constituents. This risk breakdown structure is based on those of PMBOK.

Table 3 shows an example of Service Risk Management Table. SRMT describes initial events, dependability actions, scenarios, probabilities, severity of impacts, and risks. The structure of SRMT is decomposed into two parts. The left part of SRMT describes scenarios using a binary tree of success and failure. The right part of SRMT describes the risk of each scenario.

There are two types of dependability actions. D-Scripts are applied to responsive recovery for deviations by failures. In the change accommodation cycle of DEOS process [21], human operators manage deviations in cooperation with DCB. Logical structure of failure scenarios in SRMT can be described in the similar way of fault trees.

Leveson[15] and Ericson[9] introduced methods for safety requirements analysis, such as FMEA, HAZOP, FTA, ETA. Kotonya and Sommerville showed a method for analyzing safety requirements using Hazard analysis and FTA [13]. Troubitsyna proposed Component based FMEA (Failure Mode and Effects Analysis) to analyze how component failures affect behavior of systems [22]. Sask. and Taniyama proposed Multiple Risk Communicator to the personal information leakage problem [18,20].

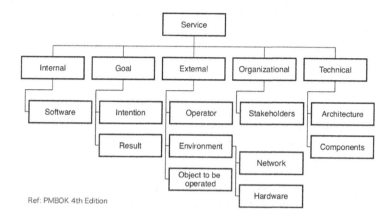

Fig. 4. An Example of Service Risk Breakdown Structure

Table 3. An Example of Service Risk Management Table

| Initial event | Dependability action | | | Scenarios | Probability | Impact | Risk |
| | D-script | | Outer loop | | | | |
	application	execution					
Deviation detection	Success	Success	--	S_1	P_1	S_1	P_1S_1
		Failure	Success	S_2	P_2	S_2	P_2S_2
			Failure	S_3	P_3	S_3	P_3S_3
--	Failure		Success	S_4	P_4	S_4	P_4S_4
			Failure	S_5	P_5	S_5	P_5S_5
Failure probability			--	--	P_3+P_5	S	PS

3 D-Case: Assurance Case for Stakeholders Agreement and In-operation Assurance

It has become almost impossible to sustain dependability of the systems only by conventional methods such as formal methods and testing. We observe that the best way is stakeholders argue dependability of the system with evidences supported by experts, and try to reach agreement that the system is dependable through the whole system lifecycle. For the objectives, first, we need a method to describe and evaluate dependability requirements. Dependability requirements need to be understood by diverse stakeholders involved in the whole system life-cycle. Second, a mechanism should be in place that ensures traceability between dependability agreement and actual system behaviors. The mechanism not only keeps track of the development phases of a system, but also its run-time op-erations by constantly checking whether dependability requirements are being satisfied or not. In particular, we must update dependability agreement when changes occur. To achieve these two goals, we have started our study with sys-tem assurance. The notion of assurance is to convince a person (usually to a certification body) that something is definitely true. We aim to extend assurance to agreement among stakeholders. Risk communication is used in similar contexts, but risk is only a part of dependability. We decided to exploit assurance case [4] to describe and evaluate dependability requirements. Assurance cases are structured documents for assuring dependability/safety/reliability/etc. of systems based on evidences. This simple framework has recently been widely used for safety critical domain. This is because as systems become large and complex, only following some safety checklists does not satisfy safety requirements, but assuring safety of systems becomes crucial. Assurance case is one of promising approach to dependability achievement. Current assurance cases, however, are mostly written in weakly-structured natural languages, and it is difficult to ensure traceability between assurance cases (and associated documents) and system's actual states during the whole lifecycle. Based on the above observations, we propose D-Case [16] to achieve these two goals. The two goals are re-stated as follows:

- Develop a method to evaluate and describe dependability of the system, and reach agreement among stakeholders on the dependability.
- Develop a mechanism to ensure traceability between the dependability description and the systems actual behaviors. We call this mechanism as "In-Operation Assurance".

Due to space limit, in this paper we only show our initial ideas and implementation for "In-Operation Assurance."

3.1   D-Case

Background. System assurance has become very important in many industrial sectors. Safety cases (assurance cases for safety of systems) are required to be submitted to certification bodies for developing and operating safety critical systems, e. g., automotive, railway, defense, nuclear plants and sea oils. There are several standards, e.g., EUROCONTROL [10] and MoD Defence Standard 00-56, which mandate the use of safety cases. There are several definitions for assurance cases. We give one such definition as follows [1].

> a documented body of evidence that provides a convincing and valid argument that a system is adequately dependable for a given application in a given environment.

Assurance cases are often written in a graphical notation. Goal Structuring Notation (GSN) is one of such notations [12]. Writing assurance cases and reusing them in a cost effective way is a critical issue for organizations. Patterns and their supporting constructs are proposed in GSN to enable the reuse of existing assurance cases, which includes parameterized expressions. Another widely used notation is Claims, Arguments and Evidence (CAE), which was developed by Adelard and City University London [2].

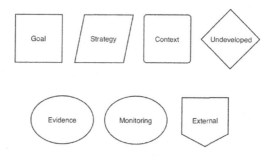

Fig. 5. D-Case Nodes

D-Case Nodes and Example. Based on the assurance cases, we define D-Case. We show D-Case nodes (Fig.5) and an example (Fig.6). Current D-Case syntax is based on GSN with extensions for our needs: monitoring node and external node.

We briefly explain constructs and their meanings in D-Case. Arguments in D-Case are structured as trees with a few kinds of nodes, including: Goal nodes for claims to be argued for, Strategy nodes for reasoning steps that decompose a goal into sub-goals, and Evidence nodes for references to direct evidences that respective goals hold. Undeveloped nodes are attached to goals if there are no supporting arguments for the goals at that time. In D-Case, monitoring nodes are a sub-class of evidence nodes. They are intended to represent evidences available at runtime, corresponding to the target values of in-operation ranges. An external node is a link to the D-Case of other system. External node will be used in cases where part of the dependability of a system is supported by another system. Previously it was called "system component" node [16]. Fig. 6 is a simple example of D-Case. The root of the tree must be a goal node, called top goal, which is the claim to be argued (G1). A context node C1 is attached to complement G1. Context nodes are used to describe the context (environment) of the goal to which the context is attached. A goal node is decomposed through a strategy node S1 into sub goal nodes (G2, G3, and G4). The strategy node contains an explanation, or reason, for why the goal is achieved when the sub goals are achieved. S1 explains the way of arguing (argue over each possible fault: A and B). When successive decompositions reach a sub goal (G2) that has a direct evidence of success, an evidence node (E1) referring to the evidence is added. Here we use a result of fault tree analysis (FTA) as the evidence. The sub goal (G3) is supported by monitoring node M1. In this D-Case, G3 is supported by runtime log results. The sub goal (G4) is supported by external node (Ext1). This indicates that the dependability requirement 3 (security) in C1 would be supported by another system.

3.2   In-operation Assurance

This section shows our initial idea of in-operation assurance by describing a reference implementation. A demo of our idea was presented in Embedded

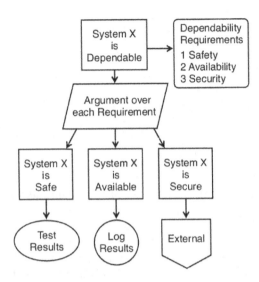

Fig. 6. D-Case Example

Technology 2011, one of the largest exhibitions for embedded systems in Japan. Fig.7 shows a reference system for In-Operation Assurance.

D-Case DB contains D-Case patterns for failure response. D-Case Pattern ⇔ Module Mapping Table contains mappings between variables used in D-Case pattern and corresponding system modules. Using the table, D-Case pattern is translated to D-Script. The right-hand side of Fig.7 is a simplified D-RE, in which the Monitoring Unit and Action Unit have monitoring and failure response action modules, respectively for system components. The key concept of the reference system is that only system behaviors, which are agreed upon and stored as D-Cases, can be executed. Operators of the system would choose appropriate action as a failure response action based on D-Case from agreed upon D-Cases. Fig. 7 shows an example of D-Case pattern, which is an argument for over usage of CPU resources. The D-Case pattern argues that if CPU usage rate becomes over 50% (this can be detected by monitoring), the failure recover control unit invokes CPU resource usage module to restrict CPU usage under 50%. In Fig.8, a monitoring node is exploited. Task "A", "CPU resource usage rate", and "under 50%" in those monitoring nodes are value of parameters which operators and other stakeholders agreed. For example, we can specify the name of some other CPU task instead of "A", "Memory resource usage rate" instead of "CPU usage rate", etc. Setting the values of parameters automatically generates executable codes.

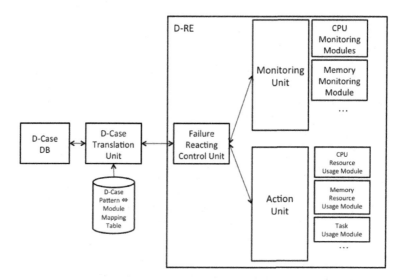

Fig. 7. A Reference System for In-Operation Assurance

4   Requirements Management

In requirements management, as mentioned above, states of requirements are managed. There are four kinds of the states; elicited, agreed, ordinarily operated, and deviated (Fig. 9). First, requirements are elicited from stakeholders. These elicited requirements may conflict with each other. By consensus-building, requirements are agreed upon among the stakeholders. Agreed-upon requirements are then implemented in ordinary operations. When objectives and environments change, some ordinarily operated requirements may become obsolete and new requirements must be elicited again. This is referred to as the change accommodation cycle.

If a requirement is not fulfilled, i.e., there is deviation from the corresponding in-operation range, it moves to the deviated state. When a responsive action is possible, it moves back to the ordinarily operated state. This is referred to as the failure reaction cycle. If the service continuity scenarios cannot work for some requirements in the deviated state, these requirements should be modified and move to the elicited state. If deviations came from the implementation problems, the corresponding elicited requirements do not need any change. But it is necessary to agree on other requirements to revise the faulty implementation. This is done by consensus-building. The elicited and agreed states of requirements are managed at offline, whereas ordinarily operated and deviated states are managed online. The state of the system is represented by a set of these requirements states. Fig.10 shows how this set of requirements are managed by requirements management table as the system evolves.

Traditional requirements management (TRM) methods only consider states of requirements at offline [13,7,19,14,23,17,6]. These requirements engineering text

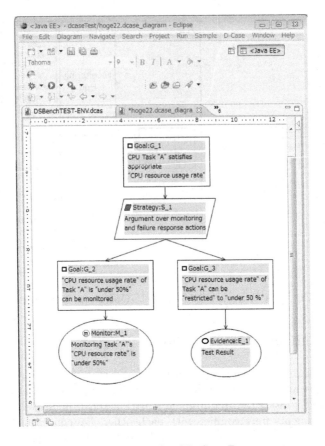

Fig. 8. An Example of D-Case Pattern

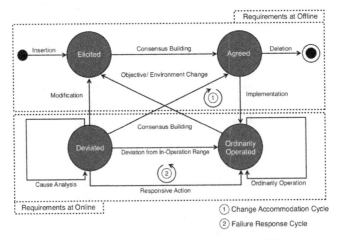

Fig. 9. Requirements State Management Model

Requirements Evolution ➝

Time	R1	R2	R3	R4	R5
T1	E	E	–	–	–
T2	A	A	E	–	–
T3	O	O	A	E	E
T4	O	D	A	A	A
T5	O	O	O	O	O
T6	O	O	O	O	D
T7	O	D	O	O	O
T8	O	A	O	D	D
T9	O	O	O	A	E
T10	O	O	O	–	A

Temporal Progress

E: Elicited, A: Agreed-upon, O:Operated, D:Deviated

■ Offline
□ Online

Fig. 10. System Requirement State Management Table

books describes requirements management process by Change Control Board (CCB) with requirements change requests. TRM does not consider requirements deviations at runtime. Requirements management state model can take into account deviations of requirements at runtime. To detect and manage deviation, it is necessary to record the deviation situations on requirements with identifications, events, inputs, outputs, and responses. Otherwise, there is no evidence on deviations and it is impossible to analyze failures.

5   Implementation Status

Currently the requirement elicitation and risk analysis methods have been designed. Also, we have been developing "D-Case Editor" [3], which is a tool to support stakeholders' agreements, and "D-Case Viewer", which is a tool to monitor whether stakeholders' agreements are satisfied or not. Current D-Case Editor is a graphical editor as an Eclipse plug-in. Fig.8 is also a snapshot of D-Case Editor.

D-Case Editor has several basic functions and experimental functions including the followings.

1. Checks on the graph structure of D-Case (e.g. no-cycle, no-evidence directly below a strategy, etc.)
2. External documents via URL can be attached to a node.
3. "Patterns" with typed parameters can be registered and recalled with parameter instantiations.
4. Graphical diff to compare two D-Cases.
5. A "ticket" in Redmine, a project management web application, can be attached to a goal; the ticket's status can be reflected graphically in D-Case.

The main function of D-Case Viewer is monitoring: a URL to be polled by Viewer can be attached to a node; the answer is dynamically reflected in D-Case.

Fig.11 is a snapshot of web server system demo shown at ET2011, Yokohama, Japan (D-Case Viewer has been currently under development, and D-Case Editor

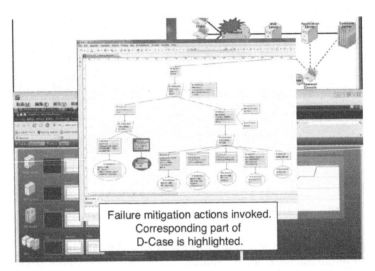

Fig. 11. A Snapshot of Web Server Demo

is instead used for monitoring.) In D-Case Viewer, the monitoring node about access number of the web server and the goal are highlighted as red to indicate that access number of the web server system exceeded over 2500 times/minutes (this is an in-operation range). Nodes highlighted as yellow are about failure response actions invoked at just that time. Using D-Case Viewer, operators of the system can always see that all in-operation ranges are within as required or not, and which failure response actions are invoked, as agreed or not. This correspondence between D-Case description and systems actual behaviors is an important source for achieving accountability[1].

6   Concluding Remarks

This paper has reported our initial ideas and implementation for consensus building and in-operation assurance for service dependability. We have presented several methods for requirement elicitation and risk analysis. Also we have presented D-Case, which is an extension of assurance case for in-operation assurance. One clear challenge is to develop a method to describe D-Case from those requirement elicitation and risk analysis as inputs. Methods for developing assurance cases have been developed in some works such as [8]. We would like to report our progress, and compare with such works in near future.

References

1. http://www.csr.city.ac.uk/research.html
2. http://www.adelard.com/web/hnav/ASCE/choosing-asce/cae.html

---

[1] Interested reader may check a demo video:
http://dl.dropbox.com/u/13455869/demo.mp4

3. http://www.il.is.s.u-tokyo.ac.jp/deos/dcase
4. Workshop on Assurance Cases: Best Practices,Possible Obstacles, and Future Opportunities, DSN 2004 (2004)
5. Aurum, A., Wohlin, C. (eds.): Engineering and Managing Software Requirements Engineering and Managing Software Requirements. Springer (2010)
6. Berenbach, B., Paulish, D., Kazmeier, J., Dudorfeer, A.: Software and Systems Requirements Engineering In Practice. McGraw-Hill (2009)
7. Davis, A.M.: Just Enough Requiremtns Management- Where Software Development Meets Marketing. Dorset House Publishing (2005)
8. Despotou, G.: Managing the Evolution of Dependability Cases for Systems of Systems. PhD thesis, Department of Computer Science, University of York (2007)
9. Ericson, C.A.: Hazard Analysis Techniques for System Safety. John Wiley and Sons, Inc. (2005)
10. European Organisation for the Safety of Air Navigation. Safety case development manual. European Air Traffic Management, 2006.
11. IIBA. BABOK 2.0 (2009)
12. Kelly, T., Weaver, R.: The goal structuring notation - a safety argument notation. In: Proc. of the Dependable Systems and Networks 2004, Workshop on Assurance Cases (2004)
13. Kotonya, G., Sommerville, I.: Requirements Engineering-Process and Techniqeus. John Wiley and Sons (2002)
14. Leffingwel, D., Widrig, D.: Managing Software Requirements A Unified Approach. Addison-Wesley Professional (2000)
15. Leveson, N.G.: Safeware: System Safety and Computers. Addison-Wesley (1995)
16. Matsuno, Y., Nakazawa, J., Takeyama, M., Sugaya, M., Ishikawa, Y.: Toward a language for communication among stakeholders. In: Proc. of the 16th IEEE Pacific Rim International Symposium on Dependable Computing, PRDC 2010 (2010)
17. Pohl, K.: Requirements Enginerring Fundamentals, Principles, and Techniques. Springer (2010)
18. Sasaki, R., Ishii, S., Hidaka, Y., Yajima, H., Yoshiura, H., Murayama, Y.: Development Concept for and Trial Application of a "Multiple Risk Communicator". In: Funabashi, M., Grzech, A. (eds.) Challenges of Expanding e-Commerce, e-Business, and e-Government. IFIP, vol. 189, pp. 203–217. Springer, Boston (2005)
19. Sommerville, I., Sawyer, P.: Requirements Engineering: A Good Practice Guide. John Wiley and Sons (1997)
20. Taniyama, M., Hidaka, Y., Arai, M., Kai, S., Igawa, H., Yajima, H., Sasaki, R.: Application of Multiple Risk Communicator to the Personal Information Leakage Problem, pp. 284–289. World Academy of Science (2008)
21. Tokoro, M.: White paper: Dependable embedded operating system for practical use (DEOS) project, version 3 (2011)
22. Troubitsyna, E.: Elicitation and specification of safety requirements. In: ICONS 2008, pp. 202–207 (2008)
23. Wiegers, K.: Software Requirements- Practical techniques for gathering and managing requirements through the product development cycle. Microsoft Corporation (2003)
24. Zowghi, D., Couling, C.: Requirements Elicitation: A survey of Techniques, Approaches, and Tools. Springer (2010)

Design and Analysis of a Fragile Watermarking Scheme Based on Block-Mapping*

Munkhbaatar Doyoddorj and Kyung-Hyune Rhee**

Department of IT Convergence and Application Engineering,
Pukyong National University,
599-1, Daeyeon3-Dong, Nam-Gu, Busan 608-737, Republic of Korea
{d_mbtr,khrhee}@pknu.ac.kr

Abstract. Due to the wide variety of attacks and the difficulties of developing an accurate statistical model of host features, the structure of the watermark detector is derived by considering a simplified channel model. In this paper, we present a fragile watermarking based on block-mapping mechanism which can perfectly recover the host image from its tampered version by generating a reference data. By investigating characteristics of watermark detector, we make an effective analysis such as fragility against robustness measure and distinguish its property. In particular, we derive a watermark detector structure with simplified channel model which focuses on the error probability versus watermark-to-noise-ratio curve and describes a design by calculating the performance of technique, where attacks are either absent or as noise addition.

Keywords : Fragile Watermarking, Characterization, Block-Mapping, Tamper Localization

1 Introduction

In the past decades, the advent of versatile digital multimedia processing tools has made multimedia duplication and manipulations much easier. The availability of such powerful tools, however, has also provided opportunities for theft and misuse of intellectual properties. As a result, multimedia authentication and integrity verification have become a popular research area in recent years. To address both the authentication and integrity issues, a wide variety of schemes have been proposed for different applications. The authentication schemes can be divided into two categories: digital signature based [13] and digital watermark based [14] schemes. A digital signature can be either an encrypted or a signed hash value of image contents and image characteristics. The major drawback of signature based scheme has limitation to identify the modified regions, that is, it can detect whether the image has been modified or not, however, it cannot

---

* This research was supported by Basic Science Research Program through the National Research Foundation of Korea (NRF) funded by the Ministry of Education, Science and Technology (Grant No. 2012-0001331).
** Corresponding author.

G. Quirchmayr et al. (Eds.): CD-ARES 2012, LNCS 7465, pp. 654–668, 2012.

locate the regions where the image has been modified. To solve this problem, many researchers have proposed digital watermarking based schemes for image authentication.

Watermarking schemes are an alternatives to the concept of cryptographic signatures, specially designed to embed authentication and integrity data within media objects, thus eliminate the need for separate storage. They occur in different security scenarios:

- *Robust* watermarking [10] may be employed if for instance the origin of a media object needs to be determined to trace illicit reproduction. Robust watermarks withstand most digital processing operations in video clips and digital images and can be recognized even after several alterations. However, in order to provide such a tamper resistant method, straightforward usage of cryptographic signatures is all but impossible.
- *Fragile* watermarking [9] may be employed if the integrity of a media object needs to be proven to deem its content authentic. They designed to be instantly destroyed when the media object is tampered with. These schemes are commonly used for tamper detection (integrity proof). Modifications to an original work are clearly noticeable.

Generally, the digital watermarking for integrity verification is called fragile watermarking as compared to robust watermarking for copyright protection [1]. The fragile watermark can serve as an embedded signature to guarantee the authenticity of the data. Ideally, a fragile watermark might even reveal, through how it has been distorted, what processing the original data has undergone. To localize the tampered area, the fragile watermarking techniques for image authentication usually partition the image into blocks with the same size. For each block, watermark data are generated based on the secret key and then inserted into the least significant bits (LSBs) of the same block [5-8]. This way, the tampered block can be easily located by checking the consistency of the content and the embedded watermark in itself.

In watermarking techniques, there have many aspects and problems to be considered, such as embedding domains, characteristics, human perception system (auditory or visual), attacks, security and specific application requirements, so on. We consider the characteristics of watermark detector such that robustness and fragility are intimately connected to, respectively, the copyright protection and the integrity of the host data. Therefore, the investigation of these characteristics is of great interest in order to support a design of techniques for a wide application scenario. To understand the possible functions of watermark detector and in order to reduce complexity of measure, we utilize a simplified channel model with noise addition that is based on information theoretic considerations [4]. The creator develops a piece of watermarked variable content and sends it through a simplified channel and then analyze how the distortions during the processing are affected when simplified channel model is used to simulate distortions.

Our Contribution. The aim of this paper is to demonstrate the characteristics of fragile watermarking scheme through an analysis of watermark detector and to design a scheme for tampering detection and recovery on the spatial domain. We derive the watermark detector structure a simple case, dealing with simplified channel model, where attacks are either absent or modeled as noise addition. Then we evaluate the detection error probability and watermark-to-noise-ratio of our scheme for the simplified channel, being aware that a more accurate experimental analysis is needed to assess the performance of schemes in realistic situations. Hence, the fragility is measured by two types of authentication error probabilities. The result of analysis show that a fragile watermarking scheme is most appropriate to achieve the best trade-off between both error probabilities.

On the other hand, our scheme is based on the block-mapping mechanism which identifies the blocks containing tampered pixels whereas the authentication data allows individual localization of the tampered pixels [18]. Also, how the block-mapping can be used as the scheme to address fragile requirements and embedding distortions in a practical watermarking scheme. The regular structure of such mapping provides efficiency for encryption and verification algorithms that are straightforward to analyze.

The rest of this paper is organized as follows: Section 2 introduces some basic notations and definitions of watermarking schemes and concepts of block division and mapping strategy used in this paper. We formulate the fragile watermark scheme based on block-mapping and derive the embedding and detection (verification) structures in Section 3. In Section 4, we introduce the analysis of proposed scheme, and experimental results are shown in Section 5. Conclusion is drawn in Section 6.

2   Preliminaries

2.1   Notations and Definitions

In this section, we present basic notations and formal abstracted definitions used in the paper. Basically, we follow the terminology in [15]. We write $Y \leftarrow \texttt{Alg}(X)$ to denote running algorithm $\texttt{Alg}$ on input X and assigning the output to variable Y. Optional inputs and outputs are set in squared brackets in $\texttt{Alg}(X_1, [X_2])$, the input of X_2 is optional.

To specify the probability, we use the notation $\textbf{Prob}[\texttt{assign}(v_1, ..., v_n) :: \texttt{pred}(v_1, ..., v_n)]$. This denotes the probability that the predicate $\texttt{pred}$ holds when the probability is taken over a probability space defined by the formula $\texttt{assign}$ on the n variables v_i of the predicate $\texttt{pred}$.

A negligible function $\epsilon(x)$ is a function where the inverse of any polynomial is asymptotically an upper bound, $\forall d > 0, \exists x_0, \forall x > x_0 : \epsilon(x) < 1/x^d$. We denote this by $\epsilon(x) < 1/poly(x)$. If $\epsilon(x)$ cannot be upper bounded in such a way, we say $\epsilon(x)$ is not negligible.

We define 1^n to denote the bit string consisting of n 1's. Finally, we define Boolean values $ind \in \{1, 0\}$, which the presence and absence of the watermark, respectively.

A suitable similarity function or predicate is a key aspect in definition of water-marking schemes. We assume a suitable polynomial time computable *similarity* function as follows:

Definition 1 (Similarity Function). *The polynomial time computable ideal similarity function $sim(Y^\star, Y^\circ)$ for given two items $Y^\star$ and Y°, outputs 1 iff $Y^\star$ can be considered sufficiently similar to Y° (as a manner of usual, agreed semantics), and has been derived from Y°. Note that $sim()$ does not need to be symmetric.*

Definition 2 (Detecting Watermarking Scheme). *A detecting watermarking scheme $W = (GenKey, Emb, Det)$ consists of three probabilistic polynomial time algorithms. We define the intactness or imperceptibility property as formally:*

- **Key generation algorithm:** On input of the security parameter 1^n, the key generation algorithm $GenKey(1^n)$ generates the matching keys (K_E, K_D) required for watermark embedding and detection, respectively.
- **Embedding algorithm:** On input of the host data (cover-data) X, the watermark W_R to be embedded with the key K_E, the probabilistic embedding algorithm $Emb(X, W_R, K_E)$ outputs the watermarked data (stego-data) Y, which is required to be perceptibly similar to the host data X.

$$Y \leftarrow Emb(X, W_R, K_E) \text{ then } sim(X, Y) = 1$$

- **Detection algorithm:** On input of (possibly modified) watermarked data Y', the watermark W_R, the *optional* data (sometimes also referred to as reference data in this context), detection key K_D, the probabilistic detection algorithm $Det(Y', W_R, [optional], K_D)$ outputs a Boolean value $\{0, 1\}$, it is commonly referred to effectiveness of the watermarking scheme.

$$Y' \leftarrow Emb(X, W_R, K_E) \wedge Det(Y', W_R, [optional], K_D) = 1$$

Remark 1. We refer to a watermarking scheme as being symmetric iff $K_E = K_D$ and in this case, we usually denote both keys as K_W. But otherwise, the scheme with $K_E \neq K_D$ is called asymmetric.

Definition 3 (Extracting Watermark Scheme). *An extracting watermark scheme is similarly defined, where a probabilistic extraction algorithm $Ext()$ instead of the detection algorithm that on input of watermarked data Y and the extraction key K_{EX} outputs the watermark contained in this data or the Boolean value 0 if it cannot extract any watermark.*

- **Extraction algorithm:** On input of (modified) watermarked data Y', the optional data (sometimes also referred to as reference data), and the extraction key K_{EX}, the probabilistic extraction algorithm $Ext(Y', [optional], K_{EX})$ either outputs the watermark W_R contained in Y' or fails with output 0.

$$Y' \leftarrow Emb(X, W_R, K_E) \wedge W'_R \leftarrow Ext(Y', [optional], K_{EX}) \text{ then } W'_R = W_R$$

When employing fragile watermarking schemes, the embedding process induces distortions into the original media object, thus inevitably altering the original. Although sophisticated embedding algorithms induce a barely visible distortion into the media object, a lossless reconstruction may be desirable. A fragile watermarking scheme can detect alterations even if the underlying digital work has been (maliciously) modified, as long as the scheme is very sensitive to the slight changes, more formally:

Definition 4 (Fragile watermarking). *A watermarking scheme is called fragile, iff it is computationally infeasible for a probabilistic polynomial-bounded adversary $\mathcal{A}$, given watermarked data Y and the watermark W_R, to produce perceptibly different and altered data Y'.*

$$\mathbf{Prob}[K_W \leftarrow GenKey(1^n); Y \leftarrow Emb(X, W_R, K_W); Y' \leftarrow \mathcal{A}(Y, 1^n);$$
$$:: Det(Y', W_R, [optional], K_W) = 1 \wedge sim(Y', Y) = 1] < \epsilon(x).$$

The main application of fragile watermarking is data authentication, where watermark loss or alteration is taken as an evidence that data has been tampered with, whereas the recovery of the information contained within the data is used to demonstrate origin.

2.2 The Block Division and Mapping Strategy

We will introduce two concepts of block mapping algorithm in this section. These strategies effectively break block-wise independency, and makes the self-recovery watermarking scheme invulnerable against the counterfeiting attacks [11]. An object X is partitioned into non-overlapping blocks $B_i (i = 1, ..., N)$ of 2×2 pixels by the block division as follows:

Definition 5 (Block Division). *A block division scheme is as a tuple of two probabilistic polynomial algorithms $\langle SEPARATE, JOIN \rangle$. On input X and a size of the block $S(m \times m)$, the algorithm $SEPARATE$ produces a tuple of blocks $B_1 \| \cdots \| B_N$. The algorithm $JOIN$ inverts the algorithm $SEPARATE$, on input $B_1 \| \cdots \| B_N$ with S, it outputs X.*

Except with negligible probability, we require that

$$JOIN(S, SEPARATE(X, S)) = X,$$

for object X and size S with $SEPARATE(X, S) \neq FAIL$.

Using secret key K_S, a pseudo-random sequence $ps = (ps_1, ps_2, ..., ps_N)$ is firstly produced, and then an ordered index sequence $(a_1, a_2, ..., a_N)$ such that $(ps_{a_1}, ps_{a_2}, ..., ps_{a_N})$ is obtained by sorting out the pseudo-random sequence ps. For each block, assign the index of block B_i to be $B_i = B_{a_i}$ such that $i = a_i$. Here, the watermark information of the block B_1 is embedded in the block B_2, the watermark of block B_2 is embedded in the block B_3, and the watermark of block B_3 is embedded in the block B_4, and so on.

A random indexed block sequence (RIBS) algorithm generates a pairs of randomly distributed block sequences, such that on input $(\{B_i\}, K_S)$, where block sequence $(\{B_i\}|i = 1, ..., N)$ and a key K_S is generated by key generation function. It outputs a generated pairs of random indexed block sequence, as follows:

$$B_{pair} = \{(B_i, B_{i+1})|i = 1, ..., N\}.$$

The B_{pair} is the block pairs of random indexed block sequence, B_{i+1} is the next block of B_i. According to the security and tamper localization [12], the next block B_{i+1} of each block B_i should be randomly distributed in the whole image.

3   The Proposed Scheme

In this section, we introduce a formal definition of proposed fragile watermark scheme. This scheme provides the block-mapping strategy on the image content. Essentially, we apply the formal definition of watermarking scheme described in the previous section on each block B_i in X, with the exception that the there is some linkage (computed by a reference data extraction function) between the blocks. Technically, we rely on the concept of block-mapping sequence. In particular, our scheme embeds a watermark consisting of authentication and reference data for each block B_i of the host image into the generated block pair B_{i+1} by using the block-mapping construction. On the watermark detector, one can identify the tampered blocks by comparing the extracted authentication data in B_{i+1} with the calculated authentication one in B_i. The reliable reference data, which extracted from block pair B_{i+1} is used to exactly reconstruct the host image, if the block B_i is tampered. Furthermore, our scheme is sensitive to any tiny changes in images so that it provides an ability of optimized tampering localization while it keeps robustness against incidental distortions.

In short, we consider the following requirements for fragile watermarking scheme.

- Robustness and fragility objectives should be simultaneously addressed. When both cannot be completely achieved, one must have a quantitative mechanism to tradeoff between these two objectives.
- The fragile authentication system must be secure against an intentional tampering. For security, it must be computationally infeasible for the opponent to devise a fraudulent message.
- If the watermark is an authenticator, then embedding must be imperceptible.
- The authentication embedding and verification algorithms must be computationally efficient, especially for real time applications.

3.1   General Descriptions

We incorporate a random indexed block sequence mechanism into a fragile watermarking scheme for constructing a fragile watermarking based on block-mapping scheme [18]. The proposed scheme is specified as follows:

Definition 6 (FWBM). *We say that a four triple of probabilistic polynomial time algorithms* $FWBM = (GenKey, Emb, Det, Rec)$ *is a fragile watermarking scheme based on block-mapping iff*

- **Key generation algorithm:** Algorithm $GenKey$ generates the necessary keys for the application. $GenKey$ runs (1^n) to generate a triple tuple of keys $\langle K_S, K_E, K_D \rangle$.
- **Embedding algorithm:** Algorithm Emb takes K_E, a size of block S and an object X. The reference data $(R_{i,j} | i = 1, ..., N$ and $j = 1, ..., 8)$ is extracted from each pixel of block B_i and then embedded into LSB_3 of corresponding pixel in pair B_{i+1}. The output of the algorithm consists of an embedded object Y.
- **Detection algorithm:** Embedded objects can be detected (verified) by the algorithm Det with a public key. Algorithm Det takes the verification key K_D, a size of block S and an embedded object Y. The authentication data is extracted from each pixel of block B_i, while compared with calculated authentication data in pair of block B_{i+1} and outputs a boolean variable.
- **Reconstruction algorithm:** Finally, the algorithm Rec reverses the embedding mechanism and losslessly reconstructs X out of modified object Y'. Rec extracts the reference data $R_{i,j}$ from a pair of tampered block B_{i+1} in modified object Y' and reconstruct the tampered block B_i by using extracted reference data that takes the keys K_S, a modified object Y' and output a recovered object X'.

Note that we have defined all algorithms as probabilistic, which implies that they can fail on certain instances (for example it may not be possible to embed a watermark in an invertible manner); in this case, the algorithms output a special symbol fail. We require that the scheme works for almost all objects that can be authenticated. In particular,

$$Det(Emb(X, K_E, [R]), K_D) = 1 \wedge Rec(Emb(X, K_E), [R]) = X$$

must hold except for a negligible fraction of all objects X with $Emb(X, K_E) \neq FAIL$.

3.2   Construction

The detailed description of the scheme are given as follows:

- **Key generation algorithm:** On input (1^n) the key generation algorithm $GenKey$ outputs a triple of keys $\langle K_S, K_E, K_D \rangle = KeyGen(1^n)$, respectively. The key K_S will be used in to generate the block-mapping step, whereas K_E, K_D are used for embedding and detection(verification). The detection key K_D is a public, whereas keys K_S and K_E are private keys.

- **Embedding algorithm:** On input of Emb takes an object X, a size of block S and keys K_S, K_E. The algorithm produces the following steps:

1. Divide an object X into blocks: $B_1\|\cdots\|B_N \leftarrow SEPARATE(X,S)$.
2. Generate a random indexed block sequence by using K_S:
$B_{pair} \leftarrow RIBS(B_1\|\cdots\|B_N, K_S)$, where $B_{pair} \in \{(B_i, B_{i+1})\}$.
for $i = 1, ..., N$ **do**
3. Extract the reference data $R_{i,j}$ and authentication bits (parity $p_{i,j}$ and check $c_{i,j}$ bits) from each pixel of B_i :
$B_i \in \langle R_{i,j}, p_{i,j}, c_{i,j}\rangle$, where $R_{i,j} = (MSB_3 \oplus LSB_3)$.
4. Embed into $B_{i+1} \leftarrow B_{i+1} \in \langle LSB_3, p_{i+1,j}, c_{i+1,j}\rangle \oplus B_i \in \langle R_{i,j}, p_{i,j}, c_{i,j}\rangle \oplus K_E$.
end for
5. Each embedded blocks are joined to output: $Y \leftarrow JOIN(B_1\|\cdots\|B_N)$.
output Watermarked object Y

– **Detection algorithm:** On input of Det takes an embedded object Y, a size of block S and keys K_S, K_D, as follows:

1. Divide an object Y into blocks: $B_1\|\cdots\|B_N \leftarrow SEPARATE(Y,S)$.
2. Generate a random indexed block sequence by using key K_S:
$B_{pair} \leftarrow RIBS(B_1\|\cdots\|B_N, K_S)$, where $B_{pair} \in \{(B_i, B_{i+1})\}$.
for $i = 1, ..., N$ **do**
3. In order to separate the reference data $R_{i,j}$ and authentication bits (parity $p_{i,j}$ and check $c_{i,j}$ bits) of each pixel in B_i from B_{i+1} :
$B_{i+1} \in (R_{i,j}) \leftarrow B_{i+1} \in (LSB_3) \oplus K_D$,
and $B_i \leftarrow B_{i+1} \in (LSB_3) \oplus B_{i+1} \in (R_{i,j}) \oplus K_D$.
4. Calculate the authentication bits $p_{i,j}$ and $c_{i,j}$ of block B_i.
5. Check the authentication bits between the blocks B_i and B_{i+1}:
if $(p_{i,j} == p_{i+1,j}$ and $c_{i,j} == c_{i+1,j})$ **exit with 1**
return Locations of tampered block l.
exit with 0
end for
6. $Y \leftarrow JOIN(B_1\|\cdots\|B_N)$.
output Boolean value (1 or 0)

– **Reconstruction algorithm:** On input of Rec takes a modified object Y', a size of block S and a locations of tampered block l as follows:

1. Divide an object Y' into blocks: $B_1\|\cdots\|B_N \leftarrow SEPARATE(Y',S)$.
2. Generate a random indexed block sequence by using key K_S:
$B_{pair} \leftarrow RIBS(B_1\|\cdots\|B_N, K_S)$, where $B_{pair} \in \{(B_i, B_{i+1})\}$.
for $i = 1, ..., N$ **do**
3. Get the location of tampered block l.
4. Extract the reference data's of block $B_{l+1,j} : B_{l+1} \in R_{l+1,j} \leftarrow REF(B_{l+1})$.
5. Recover the modified blocks: $B_{l,j} = (B_{l,j}\|R_{l+1,j})$
end for
5. $X' \leftarrow JOIN(B_1\|\cdots\|B_N)$.
output Recovered object X' and $sim(X', X) = 1$

Remark 2. A construction of pixels in a block is denoted as follows: $\langle MSB_3\|LSB_3\|p\|c\rangle_8$, where MSB_3 are three most significant bits, LSB_3 are three least significant bits and authentication bits p and c, which represent a parity and check bits.

4   Analysis of Proposed Scheme

A common way of modeling for watermarking schemes is to treat them as communication systems with appropriate transmission channels. A modeling for watermarking schemes as communication system has advantages for designing and analysing of concrete schemes, because it allows to draw from the established results in the field of communications and signal processing of certain data types. In this section, we only deal with a single aspect of the problem, that is, the analysis of the *robustness* and *fragility* characteristics of the embedded watermark. Two key concepts are central to our discussion. The robustness refers to the ability to reliably extract the watermark information (keeping the watermark detection error probability low) even when the amount of noise introduced by the attacker is large. This robustness condition is mostly desirable for host copyright protection applications. On the other hand, a fragility refers to the ability to prevent the digital watermark from being detected even when the intensity of the attack is low. This fragility condition is mostly desirable for host authenticity and integrity verification applications.

4.1   Problem Formulation

We consider the watermarking as a communication model, where watermark communication channel is characterized by possible attacks against the embedded watermark. In other words, which is called a simplified channel model [19].

One specifically interesting attack is the addition of white Gaussian noise, which can be applied easily so that each watermarking scheme should show good robustness at least against this type of attacks. Since Gaussian noise is the most harmful power-limited additive noise with respect to mutual information, and many derivations can be performed analytically when a Gaussian distribution is employed. Figure 1 depicts the described simplified channel model of watermarking as communication scenario, where an attack by an Gaussian noise is assumed.

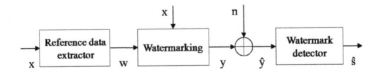

Fig. 1. Problem model for digital watermarking

The problem of simplified channel model is described as follows: The reference data extractor derives from the *host data* $\mathbf{x}$ and to generate the *watermark* $\mathbf{w}$, which is added to the host data to produce the *watermarked data* $\mathbf{y}$. An *embedding distortion* D_w in the watermarked data $\mathbf{y}$ in relation to $\mathbf{x}$ due to the modulation with the watermark $\mathbf{w}$. The $\mathbf{w}$ must be chosen such that the distortion between $\mathbf{x}$ and $\mathbf{y}$ is negligible, which is defined as:

$$D_w = \left[\frac{1}{N} \sum_{i=1}^{n} E\{(y_i - x_i)^2\} \right] < \epsilon(x),$$

where $E\{\cdot\}$ denotes expectation and N is the number of samples. Note that D_w also represents the watermark power ϕ_{wm}^2.

Next, the watermarked data $\mathbf{y}$ might be processed by Gaussian noise $\mathbf{n} \in \mathbb{R}^N$. Such processing potentially impairs watermark communication and thus is denoted as an attacks against the embedded watermark. In general, attacks against watermark are only constrained with respect to the distortion between $\mathbf{x}$ and $\hat{\mathbf{y}}$. The watermark detector input $\hat{\mathbf{y}} = \mathbf{y} + \mathbf{n}$ is presented, which represents the attacked watermarked data. Now, we can express the distortion of watermarked data $\hat{\mathbf{y}}$ in relation to $\mathbf{x}$ as:

$$D_{\hat{y}} = D_w + n = \phi_{wm}^2 + \phi_n^2.$$

The objective of the watermark detector is to produce the best estimate of the watermark from the attacked watermarked data. So that, the receiver must be able to detect the watermark $\hat{\mathbf{s}}$ from the received data $\hat{\mathbf{y}}$.

In following, we introduce some parameters for future analysis. The robustness and fragility behavior analysis will be focused on their dependency to the performance of the watermarking technique. The performance of technique is taken here as the detection error probability p_e. In practice, p_e is estimated by the bit error rate (BER) measurement, corresponding to the number of wrongly

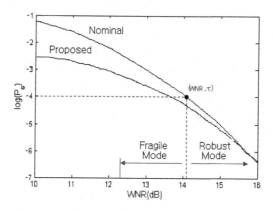

Fig. 2. The characterization curve for a nominal and our scheme

estimated bits, from the attacked signal, over the total number of embedded bits. The strength of attacks is also measured by the watermark to noise ratio (WNR), giving the ratio between the power of $\hat{\mathbf{y}}$ and that of the noise $\mathbf{n} = \hat{\mathbf{y}} - \mathbf{y}$, as follows:

$$WNR = \frac{\sum_{i=1}^{n} E\{\hat{y}^2\}}{\sum_{i=1}^{n} E\{(D_{\hat{y}} - D_w)^2\}} = \frac{\sum_{i=1}^{n} E\{\hat{y}^2\}}{\sum_{i=1}^{n} E\{n^2\}} = \frac{E\{\hat{y}^2\}}{E\{n^2\}} = \frac{\phi_{\hat{y}}^2}{\phi_n^2}$$

4.2   Characterization for Watermarking Schemes

We introduce some design parameters that take into account the robustness and fragility. The first parameter establishes an upper bound to the maximum allowed host distortion D_{max}. Above this distortion, for many copyright protection verification applications, the received signal is considered *useless*. In a covert communication application scenario, if this distortion is exceeded to some extent, the user will easily notice that a third part tried to jam the secret communication. A second parameter establishes a threshold τ for the detection error probability p_e. Above this threshold, the recovered watermark is no longer considered as a reliable one.

A characterization of fragile watermarking scheme in operation modes is classified as the following conditions:

$$OperationModes = \begin{cases} Robust \\ mode & \text{if } (p_e < \tau) \text{ and } (D_{\hat{y}} > D_{max}); \\ Fragile \\ mode & \text{if } (p_e > \tau) \text{ and } (D_{\hat{y}} < D_{max}). \end{cases}$$

We emphasize that inequalities of above described conditions in a definition are represent the robustness and fragility analysis. In the absence of an attack (no noise), the WNR is infinite and the detection error probability is negligible or zero. As the attack intensity increases, the WNR decreases, which is describing on the WNR versus p_e characterization curve of nominal value as shown in Figure 2. If the WNR decreases, the p_e is reached, the scheme is said to be a fragile, otherwise the scheme is said to be a robust.

The performance of our scheme was used to plot in Figure 2. The parameter p_e was chosen to be 10^{-4}, yielding to $WNR = 14.1$dB. The design can now be pursued by selecting appropriate values for the parameter τ and D_{max}. Our scheme is stated in fragile operation mode according to above definition, which is guaranteed by parameters $p_e = 10^{-3.9}$ and $WNR = 13.5$dB.

5   Experimental Results

In this section, we describe our experiments and discuss the results. We simulated our scheme under a PC with 1.8G Hz Dual CPU, 6G RAM, and Windows Vista platform. The simulation was carried out using Matlab version R2008a. In order

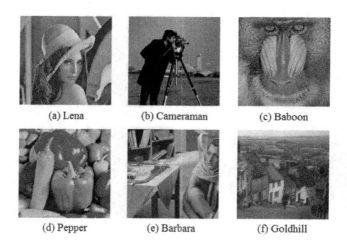

(a) Lena   (b) Cameraman   (c) Baboon

(d) Pepper   (e) Barbara   (f) Goldhill

Fig. 3. Grayscale test images (512×512)

to evaluate the performance of our proposed scheme, we considered six commonly used grayscale images with the size of 512×512 as shown in Fig. 3.

With respect to objective evaluation, the peak signal to noise ratio (PSNR) was used to measure the visual quality of fidelity for the host image and the watermarked image. Among the watermarked images, the image qualities measured by PSNR value were greater than 44dB, where an attack by a Gaussian noise signal $v \sim N(0, \sigma_v^2)$ is assumed. The PSNR value highly depends on the size of tampered regions and the accuracy of tampered block identification. The greater the PSNR, the better the performance of image recovery technique.

Table 1. The performance comparison

.	Proposed		Zhang et. al [16]		Zhu et. al [17]	
Test	Watermarked	Recovered	Wat.d	Rec.d	Wat.d	Rec.d
Images	PSNR (dB)		PSNR (dB)		PSNR (dB)	
Lena	45.63	32.23				
Cameraman	44.95	32.81				
Baboon	45.32	30.65	Average	Average	Average	Average
Pepper	45.53	29.37	39.90	27.79	36.70	22.80
Barbara	44.06	30.62				
Goldhill	45.49	31.86				

Table 1 shows the performance of proposed scheme for all test images by comparing with related methods. From these comparisons, it is observed that our scheme has achieved the higher PSNR values of watermarked and recovered images.

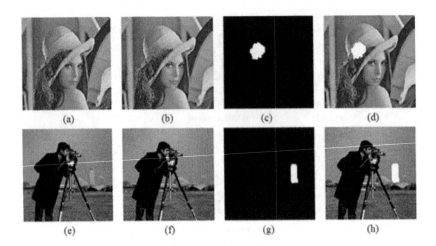

Fig. 4. Example of ordinary tampering detection. (a),(e) The host images, (b),(f) Watermarked images, (c),(g) Tampered block detection and (d),(h) Tamper localization.

We consider ordinary tampering. Two test images Lena and Cameraman sized 512×512 are used as the host image, in Fig. 4(a),(e). The PSNR values due to watermark embedding are 45.63dB and 44.95dB, respectively. We modify the watermarked images by extensively replacing the original content with fake information as shown in Fig. 4(b),(f), and the tampering rates are 8.15% and 6.36%. Fig. 4(c),(g) gives the result of tampered block detection, in which the blocks judged as valid and invalid are indicated by black and white areas. Here, all tampered blocks were correctly located in Fig. 4 (d),(h). Finally, we calculated the PSNR values of recovered images, which are 43.26dB and 41.09dB, respectively. These results indicate that after identifying the tampered blocks, our scheme exactly locate the tampered pixels and perfectly restore the watermarked version. The computational complexity of our scheme is light since it does not need to apply any transform such as discrete cosine transform (DCT) and Fourier transform (FFT). The required processing mainly lies on generating the RIBS, scanning pixels, and embedding and decryption using XOR operation in spatial domain. Hence, the execution time is rather short.

6   Conclusion

In this paper, we introduced design and analysis of a fragile watermarking scheme with tampering localization and recovery mechanism. The focus of our analysis is on characteristics of watermark detector and distinguish its property such as fragility against robustness measure. In order to design effective watermarking scheme, we analyzed the characteristics of our scheme by defining the characterization mode. The proposed scheme utilizes the block-mapping strategy to identify the tampered region by generating the random indexing block sequence.

By using this technique, we can detect any modifications made to the image and indicate the specific locations where the modification was made. As compared with some previous works, the proposed scheme based on block-mapping on spatial domain not only is as simple and as effective in tamper detection and localization, but also provides the capability of tamper recovery by trading off the quality of the watermarked images about 44dB. This implies that the proposed scheme can offer high embedding quality and low image degradation. The experimental results confirm the effectiveness of our scheme by demonstrating that the watermarked image with acceptable visual quality can be recovered as well as tampering detection and localization.

References

1. Rey, C., Dugelay, J.L.: A survey of watermarking algorithms for image authentication. EURASTP Appl. Signal Process. (6), 613–621 (2002)
2. Suthaharan, S.: Fragile image watermarking using a gradient image for improved localization and security. Pattern Recogn. Lett. 25(16), 1893–1903 (2004)
3. Lin, P.-L., Hsieh, C.-K., Huang, P.-W.: A hierarchical digital watermarking method for image tamper detection and recovery. Pattern Recogn. 38(12), 2519–2529 (2005)
4. Merhav, N., Sabbag, E.: Optimal Watermark Embedding and Detection Strategies Under Limited Detection Resources. IEEE Transactions on Information Theory 54(1) (2008)
5. Celik, M., Sharma, G., Saber, E., Tekalp, A.M.: Hierarchical watermarking for secure image authentication with localization. IEEE Transaction on Image Processessing 11(6), 585–595 (2002)
6. Suthaharan, S.: Fragile image watermarking using a gradient image for improved localization and security. Pattern Recognition Letters 25, 1893–1903 (2004)
7. Liu, S., Yao, H., Gao, W., Liu, Y.: An image fragile watermark scheme based on chaotic image pattern and pixel-pairs. Applied Mathematics Computation 185(2), 869–882 (2007)
8. Wang, M.S., Chen, W.C.: A majority-voting based watermarking scheme for color image tamper detection and recovery. Computer Standards and Interfaces (29), 561–570 (2007)
9. Yeung, M., Mintzer, F.: Invisible watermarking for image verification. Journal of Electronic Imaging (7), 578–591 (1998)
10. Swanson, M.D., Bin, Z., Tewfik, A.H.: Transparent robust image watermarking. In: IEEE International Conference on Image Processing, vol. (3), pp. 211–214. IEEE Computer Society Press (1996)
11. Holliman, M., Melon, N.: Counterfeiting attacks on oblivious block-wise independent invisible watermarking schemes. IEEE Trans. Image Processing 9(3), 432–441 (2000)
12. He, H.J., Zhang, J.S., Wang, H.X.: Synchronous counterfeiting attacks on self-embedding watermarking schemes. Internetional Journal Computer Science and Network Security 6(1), 251–257 (2006)
13. Tagliasacchi, M., Valenzise, G., Tubaro, S.: Hash-Based Identification of Sparse Image Tampering. IEEE Transactions on Image Processing 18(11), 2491–2504 (2009)
14. Lai, C.-C., Tsai, C.-C.: Digital Image Watermarking Using Discrete Wavelet Transform and Singular Value Decomposition. IEEE Transactions on Instrumentation and Measurement 59(11), 3060–3063 (2010)

15. Adelsbach, A., Katzenbeisser, S., Sadeghi, A.-R.: A Computational Model for Watermark Robustness. In: Camenisch, J.L., Collberg, C.S., Johnson, N.F., Sallee, P. (eds.) IH 2006. LNCS, vol. 4437, pp. 145–160. Springer, Heidelberg (2007)
16. Zhang, X., Wang, S.: Fragile watermarking scheme using a hierarchical mechanism. Signal Processing (89) 675–679 (2009)
17. Zhu, X., Ho, A., Marziliano, P.: A new semi-fragile image watermarking with robust tampering restoration using irregular sampling. Signal Processing and Image Communication (22), 515–528 (2009)
18. He, H.J., Chen, F., Tai, H.-M.: Performance Analysis of a Block-Neighborhood-Based Self-Recovery Fragile Watermarking Scheme. IEEE Transactions on Information Forensics and Security 7(1), 185–196 (2012)
19. Baeuml, R., Eggers, J.J., Tzschoppe, R., Huber, J.: Channel model for watermarks subject to desynchronization attacks. In: Proc. SPIE, Security and Watermarking of Multimedia Contents IV, vol. 4675, pp. 281–292 (2002)

Author Index